SURVEY OF COMMUNICATION DISORDERS

A Social and Behavioral Perspective

SURVEY OF COMMUNICATION DISORDERS

A Social and Behavioral Perspective

Marylou Pausewang Gelfer

University of Wisconsin—Milwaukee

THE McGRAW-HILL COMPANIES, INC.

New York   St. Louis   San Francisco   Auckland   Bogotá   Caracas   Lisbon
London   Madrid   Mexico City   Milan   Montreal   New Delhi
San Juan   Singapore   Sydney   Tokyo   Toronto

McGraw-Hill

A Division of The McGraw·Hill Companies

SURVEY OF COMMUNICATION DISORDERS
A Social and Behavioral Perspective

This book is printed on acid-free paper.

1 2 3 4 5 6 7 8 9 0   FGR FGR   9 0 9 8 7 6 5

ISBN 0-07-023453-1

This book was set in Bembo by ComCom, Inc.
The editors were Judith R. Cornwell, David Dunham, and Ty McConnell;
the production supervisor was Denise Puryear.
The cover was designed by Karen K. Quigley.
Quebecor Printing/Fairfield was printer and binder.

Cover photo: Comstock

Library of Congress Cataloging-in-Publication Data

Gelfer, Marylou Pausewang, (date).
    Survey of communication disorders: a social and behavioral
  perspective / Marylou Pausewang Gelfer.
        p.   cm.
    Includes bibliographical references and index.
    ISBN 0-07-023453-1
    1. Communicative disorders.   2. Communicative disorders—Social
  aspects.   I. Title.
    [DNLM: 1. Communicative Disorders.   WL 340.2 G316s   1996]
  RC423.G43   1996
  616.85'5—dc20
  DNLM/DLC
                                                95-11270

MARYLOU PAUSEWANG GELFER is an associate professor in the Department of Communication Sciences and Disorders at the University of Wisconsin-Milwaukee. She began her professional career with an M.A. in Speech Pathology from Northwestern University in 1976, and worked as a speech-language pathologist in a variety of school and health care settings. Her experiences with clients of diverse ages and disorder types led to an increasing interest in the underlying physical and acoustic characteristics of speech and voice. In 1984, she received her Ph.D. in experimental phonetics from the University of Florida, and spent a year as a postdoctoral fellow at the Institute for Advanced Study of the Communication Processes, also at the University of Florida.

Prior to her present appointment, Dr. Gelfer taught at Indiana University for five years. During that time, she began teaching an introductory course in communication sciences and disorders, and became interested in how such courses were taught and structured nationwide. This interest led to a survey of practices in introductory communction sciences and disorders classes, and an article published in *Asha* in 1989.

Since moving to the University of Wisconsin-Milwaukee, Dr. Gelfer has continued to teach the department's introductory course, in addition to courses in research methods and voice disorders, her specialty area. She has done research and published a number of articles relating to the perception and measurement of voice in such journals as *Journal of Speech and Hearing Research, Journal of Voice, Phonetica, Journal of Communication Disorders, Folia Phoniatrica,* and *Journal of Phonetics.* She currently lives in Milwaukee, Wisconsin, with her husband and two children.

Just before I began writing this book, my daughter suffered severe brain damage and lost the ability to speak. I dedicate this book to the students who go on to study communication sciences and disorders, with the hope that they or the discoveries they make will someday help my daughter, and children like her, to communicate

CONTENTS

CHAPTER 10 *Introduction to Voice and Voice Disorders* 165

CHAPTER 11 *Special Populations: Cleft Palate* 187

This text is a tour de force. It is written with the deft touch of a professional writer. It is explanatory rather than didactic; it captures the reader's interest. Even when I tried to skim the introductory terminology, thinking it would be dull as dishwater, I was still drawn into close reading. Yet, it is written with the mastery of a professional steeped in competence with her subject matter.

Therein lies my profound admiration. For a single author to undertake an authoritative introduction to the almost explosive expansion of knowledge of science as well as disorders of communication is a herculean task. I know that from experience. I attempted it a quarter century ago, and within a decade the field had expanded so rapidly that I found it too daunting to try again. I find it remarkable that the presentation is so even-handed across all topics that if one did not know Dr. Gelfer, her major area of interest would be difficult to discern.

This is an extraordinarily well thought out text. For one thing, it is user friendly; in addition to chapter summaries, it includes review questions. It has been field tested in the classroom for what works and doesn't work. Experts and instructors have reviewed each chapter.

What is most impressive, however, is that Dr. Gelfer leaped the boundaries of parochial interests. This is a text for nonmajors as well as potential majors. It was developed to fit her university's demands that required general-studies courses to have broad appeal. The result has been increased enrollment from seventeen to eighty students per semester. Not surprising, this text is a potentially powerful recruitment tool for our profession.

WILLIAM H. PERKINS
Distinguished Professor Emeritus
University of Southern California

This book, which is intended for students new to the field of communication sciences and disorders, has grown out of my own experiences teaching a basic introductory course at several universities. My experience has led me to believe that *all* students, regardless of their intended major, come to an introductory course with similar needs. They need to learn the basic concepts and vocabulary of the discipline, and they need to know where this new body of knowledge fits in with respect to other courses they might have taken in other departments.

In this book, I have tried to present many of the important terms and concepts in the first few chapters. I have also tried to define new terms as they arise. Disorders in each content area immediately follow the presentation of background material on normal development and function so that students can clearly see the relationship between the study of basic sciences and disorders. While the depth of coverage in each area is limited, I have attempted to present the full breadth of the field of communication sciences and disorders in order to give students an appreciation of its scope.

Most of all, I hope I have been successful in portraying communication disorders as problems which affect people's lives. Communication disorders do not occur in a vacuum—they touch individuals' self-concepts, goals, and ambitions, their family relationships, and even the society in which we all live. Practitioners in communication sciences and disorders can become so involved in analyzing and describing disorders that we forget the human element—our clients and their daily struggles. This book is intended to introduce students to the content areas and research methods of communication sciences and disorders; but I hope it will also increase their empathy for the speech and hearing handicapped.

McGraw-Hill and I would like to thank the following reviewers for their many helpful comments and suggestions: Betty Carver, University of Alabama; Ronald Chambers, Wichita State University; Paul N. Deputy, Idaho State University; Judith Farmer, New Mexico State University; Mary D. Gospel, Indiana University; Samuel K. Haroldson, University of Minnesota; Kathleen Hoffer, San Diego State University; Stephen B. Hood, University of South Alabama; Ray Hull, University of Northern Colorado; Judith Iacarino, Towson State University; Carolyn Leshyn, Governors State University; Carol Lott, University of Montevallo; Harold Luper, University of Tennessee, Knoxville; Donald Mowrer, Arizona State University; Donna Oas, Western Michigan University; Nancy O'Hare, James Madison University; Elizabeth Ohler, University of North Texas; Nan Ratner, University of Maryland; Joan Roddy Regnell, The George Washington University; Denise LaPrade Rini, Southern Connecticut State University; Stuart Ritterman, University of South Florida; Rosiland R. Scudder, Wichita State University; Jeffrey Stromer, Queensborough Community College; Norma C. Travis, Louisiana State University; Betty Vinson, University of Florida; and Charles Wilhelm, Fort Hays State University.

MARYLOU PAUSEWANG GELFER

SURVEY OF COMMUNICATION DISORDERS
A Social and Behavioral Perspective

An Introduction to Communication Sciences and Disorders

W hat does the term "communication disorders" mean to you? Perhaps in your mind's eye you see someone like Helen Keller, unable to hear, unable to see, unable to speak without difficulty, locked in a silent world. Or perhaps your vision is less dramatic, and you think of hoards of elementary school children who have trouble producing "s" or "r" sounds. You may at one point have known someone who stutters and remember their difficulty in expressing ideas as a communication disorder. Or perhaps an older relative or friend has a hearing loss, or has had a stroke, and is unable to participate in everyday conversation.

All of these individuals indeed have a communication disorder. Communication disorders can refer to any condition that limits an individual's ability to "1) receive and/or process a symbol system, 2) represent concepts or symbol systems, and/or 3) transmit and use symbol systems" (*ASHA*, November 1983, 949). Symbols? What do symbols have to do with communication? It is clear that we must establish some basic concepts in order to understand the underlying commonality of the varied disorders mentioned above.

In this chapter, we will explore some of the vocabulary used in the field of communication sciences and disorders as well as some of its major areas. We will briefly examine the history and current status of the field and the structure and purpose of this book. Review questions at the end of the chapter should help you isolate the most important information.

TERMS AND DEFINITIONS

The academic discipline in which communication disorders are studied is known as *communication sciences and disorders*. As in any area of study, the field of communication sciences and disorders defines its terms in very precise ways. In everyday conversation, words like *communication* and *language* or *voice* and *speech* are sometimes used interchangeably. However, within the field of communication sciences and disorders, each of these terms has a meaning all its own. Figure 1-1 gives you an idea of how these different concepts are related.

COMMUNICATION

Communication is the most basic of the terms we use. Communication requires three elements: a sender, a message, and a receiver. There are no restrictions on the nature of any of these elements—the message can be a very general or simple one, and the sender and receiver do not necessarily have to be human. The medium of the message can be sounds, gestures, postures, positions, or a variety of other means. For example, bees use elaborate flight patterns to communicate danger or the location of flowers. Many animals have unique mating calls that signal their availability to others of their species. Human beings may communicate with each other via a shake of the head for yes or no or by a wave of the hand. In short, communication is a very basic function, not limited to human beings or abstract ideas.

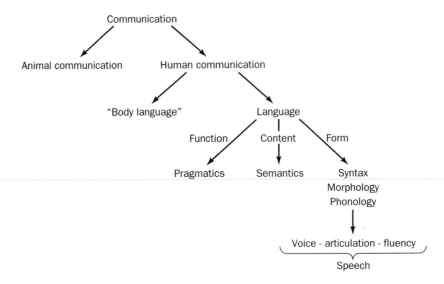

FIGURE 1-1 Terms used in communication sciences and disorders, structured hierarchically. *Communication,* the most basic term, is at the top of this figure. Succeeding terms relate to more and more specific aspects of communication.

LANGUAGE

Language is a uniquely human invention. A language is composed of a set of *symbols* that represent objects, actions, and ideas and a system of rules by which to combine these symbols. The cardinal feature of language is that it allows a communicator to generate novel utterances by using combinations of symbols not previously heard.

The latter is what sets human language apart from the types of communication that animals engage in. It could be argued that many species symbolically represent elements of their environment or internal states, using vocalizations or movements. However, what animals lack is a rule system that would allow them to combine these symbols in such a way as to express unique features in a situation. For example, bees are capable of communicating the distance to nectar to others of their species. However, if a person with insecticide were spraying those flowers, a bee would not be able to include that unique (and dangerous) element of the situation in his message. The communication of bees, and of animals in general, is not flexible. Only certain and very basic information can be represented, and communication segments cannot be combined in more complex ways.

A good example of the flexibility of human language can be seen in the language acquisition of young children. A child's early vocabulary is probably learned by imitation, simply repeated from what is heard in the child's language environment. However, once a child begins to combine words, his possible utterances are endless. If a child can say "Me want juice," then "Me want cookie" or "Me want cake" will not be far behind. The child may never have heard anyone in his environment say these particular sentences, but if he has abstracted (however imperfectly) the rules governing subject + verb + object construction from the adult speech around him, such sentences will easily be produced. Children's early language is not limited to the specific word combinations they have heard in their environment. Once they have mastered the rules for combining symbols, they are capable of generating novel utterances.

Language is composed of five basic elements: semantics, morphology, syntax, phonology and pragmatics. Definitions of each of these elements are presented below.

1. **Semantics.** *Semantics* is the symbol-concept relationship of a language whereby words acquire their meaning. In our definition of language above, semantics would be the set of symbols that represent objects, actions, and ideas. Semantics constitutes the content of a language.

2. **Morphology.** *Morphology* refers to the surface changes made to the structure of a word that alter its meaning. For example, adding an "s" to the end of the word *cat* changes the meaning of the word slightly by increasing the number of the animals in question. The addition of "ed" to the end of *play* changes the time frame of reference. A possessive " 's" changes a noun to an adjective (mother to mother's). These slight modifications result in meaning changes to the word. Morphology is part of the form of language.

3. **Syntax.** *Syntax* refers to the set of rules governing the order of words in word combinations for a particular language. For example, English syntax dictates that an adjective precede a noun, such as in the phrase "a red house." French syntax, in contrast, requires that the noun occur first, followed by the adjective, with a literal translation of "a house red." In the definition of language given above, syntax is part of the system of rules by which symbols are combined. Syntax, like morphology, is part of the form of language.

4. **Phonology.** *Phonology* refers to a set of rules governing the occurrence and order of the speech sounds that form the words of a language. Each language of the world has a distinct phonological system that speakers of that language recognize unconsciously. For example, if you saw the word *mbasso,* you would probably realize that it is not an American English word. In English phonology, the "mb" combination cannot occur at the begin-

ning of a word (although it may occur at the end of a word, such as in *comb*). Similarly, you would recognize *tlet* and *sro* as being non-English combinations because they violate your unconscious knowledge of the phonological rules of English. Like a child learning how to combine words, you might not *know* that you are applying a set of *linguistic* (language-based) rules to the task. However, the phonological rules of your native language are part of you, a filter through which you process all incoming and outgoing spoken stimuli. Should you try to learn a foreign language, the phonological rules of your native language may interfere (more about this in Chapter 6). Like morphology and syntax, phonology is part of the form of language.

5. **Pragmatics.** *Pragmatics* refers to the functional use of language in context. In analyzing language in terms of pragmatics, utterances are classified on the basis of purposes or reasons for communication. For example, the purpose of a specific utterance may be to initiate communication, to change the topic, or to terminate a conversation. A speaker may make requests, assertions, denials, or statements in addition to other types of messages. A pragmatic analysis would detail these aspects of language use. Pragmatics describes the function of language.

"BODY LANGUAGE"

Set in opposition to *Language* in Figure 1-1 is *Body Language*. While language, as described above, is a unique means of human communication, language is not the only way in which humans communicate with each other. The way an individual sits or stands, the distance between speaker and listener, and facial expressions or gestures supplement (or sometimes contradict) the speaker's linguistic message. Thus, what is popularly known as *body language* is an important part of human communication, but it should not be confused with formal language as we have defined it.

ARTICULATION

In Figure 1-1, articulation proceeds from phonology, and indeed the two are closely related. Whereas phonology refers to the rules governing the occurrence and combination of specific speech sounds, *articulation* refers to their physical production. Phonology is a *cognitive* (thought-based) phenomenon, while articulation involves movement of the muscles of the speech mechanism. Articulation is one of the components of speech.

FLUENCY

Fluency refers to the smoothness of transitions between speech sounds and words. It is an automatic by-product of cognitive processes (such as selecting and sequencing the speech sounds one will use) and their physical execution. Fluent speech has a rate and rhythm that is nondistracting to the listener. Most people are unaware of fluency unless the smooth flow of speech is interrupted by repetitions, sound prolongations, or hesitations. In such a case, we might refer to the speaker as a *stutterer*. Like articulation, fluency is one of the components of speech.

VOICE

Voice refers to the tone produced by vibrations of the vocal folds. Since this tone reverberates, or resonates, in the throat, mouth, and nasal cavities, resonance is also part of the total sound of a voice. We use adjectives like *high, low, loud, soft, nasal, clear,* and *hoarse,* among others, to describe the quality of a speaker's voice.

Voice is the third component of speech. To get an idea of what speech would be like without voice, try whispering your name. You used both articulation and fluency in the task, but your vocal folds were not vibrating. You could be understood, but only by someone standing very close to you. Vocal pitch, loudness, and quality are important in carrying the speaker's message.

In conversation, speakers use various attributes of voice not only to be heard but to help convey the meaning of their words. When we want to emphasize an important word in a sentence, we increase the pitch and loudness of the voice. Raising the voice at the end of a sentence denotes a question; lowering it indicates a statement. The rising and falling of pitch during speech is known as *intonation;* without it, the meaning of many utterances would be unclear. For example, a speaker might say "Great!" with an intonation pattern that indicated pleasure and happiness. The same word "Great!" could be said sarcastically to signal displeasure. In both cases, the speaker's use of voice, specifically intonation, clarifies the meaning of the utterance.

SPEECH

Speech is the physical transmission of the sender's message, representing the culmination of a complex chain of events. Prior to producing speech, a human communicator must first select language as the appropriate medium for the message he wants to communicate (*pragmatics*), decide upon the content of the message (*semantics*), and structure it mentally in terms of the morphological, syntactic, and phonological rules of his native language. At that point, speech is needed to transmit the message to the listener. As described above, this physical transmission involves producing speech sounds (*articulation*), stringing them together smoothly (*fluency*), and projecting them so that they can be heard (*voice*). Speech, then, is made up of articulation, fluency, and voice and reflects the end product of the mental activity we call *language*.

It should be noted that speech is not the only way of transmitting a linguistic message. For example, writing could be used. Somewhat further removed from the visual variants of oral language are formal gestural languages, such as American Sign Language. These, too, involve nonspeech forms of transmission. We will discuss transmission systems other than speech in later chapters. However, speech enjoys a central role in the field of communication sciences and disorders and thus will be more fully considered in this text.

HEARING

The pillar of support for language and speech processes does not even appear in Figure 1-1. Yet without this crucial element, human communication could easily be limited to body language. We take hearing very much for granted in our discussions of speech and language, but it is through the *auditory* (hearing) channel that we acquire the various rule systems of our native language. In everyday conversation, we assume that our listeners can hear the sounds around them and that they can mentally *process,* or make sense of, what they hear. *Reception* (hearing) and *perception* (processing) of auditory stimuli are important prerequisites for language and speech. Thus, hearing is an integral part of the human communication process.

Again, there are mediums for reception of the linguistic code other than hearing. Reading is one of the better-known visual forms of language input. But just as speech is more central than writing to the concerns of communication sciences and disorders, so are hearing and its disorders more established as areas of interest than are reading and reading disorders. Reading disorders are most often of primary interest to researchers and teachers in the fields of special education and learning disabilities.

REVIEW

Now let us go back to the definition of communication disorders and to the examples given at the beginning of the chapter. Communication disorders can refer to any condition that limits an individual's ability to "receive and/or process a symbol system." This would include deafness like Helen Keller's as well as the less severe hearing losses often experienced by older people. The "process" part of the definition might relate to the individual who has had a stroke. Although his reception of speech and language may be intact, his ability to mentally process them may be impaired due to neurological damage.

The second part of the definition of communication disorders referred to an individual's limited ability to "represent concepts or symbol systems." This means that the individual could have a problem with *semantics* (coming up with the right word to express a concept), *syntax* (putting words together), *morphology* (modifying words appropriately), or even phonology. Individuals who have had strokes frequently have difficulty mentally manipulating symbol and rule systems—that is, formulating language.

The third part of the definition of communication disorders referred to problems "transmitting and using symbol systems." Transmission, as we have learned, is the primary function of speech. Thus, individuals who have trouble with the physical aspect of speech production, such as children with "s" or "r" problems or the stutterer mentioned above, come under this part of the definition.

The field of communication sciences and disorders is an academic discipline in which deficits in hearing, language, and speech are studied. Because disorders cannot be studied in a vacuum, researchers in communication disorders frequently study normal development and processes. However, the goal of such study is to improve our understanding of the nature and treatment of disorders of communication. Because of its emphasis on the utilization of knowledge to help individuals, communication sciences and disorders is considered an applied science, and it is one of the branches of the social and behavioral sciences.

A BRIEF HISTORY OF THE FIELD

THE ORIGIN OF THE STUDY OF COMMUNICATION DISORDERS

In order to understand the origins of the field of communication sciences and disorders, it is necessary to go back in time to the mid- to late

1800s, when philosophy was the main branch of study of human thought and action. Philosophy during this time period was what is known as a *rationalistic discipline;* that is, philosophers based their theories on logical deduction rather than on systematic observation and experimentation. But new ideas were germinating in Europe, and some scholars decided the time had come to put the study of human behavior on a more empirical footing. What came into being was a new laboratory-centered discipline, which borrowed its principles from the experimental orientation of the physical sciences. This discipline, called *psychology,* was dedicated to the study of human beings through observation and the manipulation of behavior.

By 1887, European-trained psychologists were beginning to offer courses and to set up laboratories for this new discipline in the United States. Even at this early date, some of these psychologists had a strong interest in the process of human communication and its disorders. Carl Seashore, a professor of psychology and later dean of the graduate school of the University of Iowa, was one of these. He was able to use his position as dean to provide leadership and support for research into mental hygiene, child development, and speech. In addition, he and his colleagues developed the first widely marketed instrument for testing hearing (the audiometer) in 1900. It is significant to note that Seashore intended the audiometer to be "suitable for use both in the laboratory and in the schools" (Moeller, 1976, 5). Thus, even in its earliest beginnings, the emerging field of communication sciences and disorders had a dual purpose—to generate scientific information and to provide clinical service.

In addition to psychology, the field of public speaking was also a forerunner of communication sciences and disorders. In the early 1900s, public speaking was considered a subspecialty in departments of English, where elocution and the artistic and persuasive uses of the speaking voice were taught. Because these were the days before microphones, loudspeakers, and modern amplification systems, clear, correct, and forceful speech

was an important part of professional training for many fields. In the years between 1910 and 1920, however, many changes occurred in the study and academic organization of public speaking. Departments of speech became independent of English departments at many universities. The development of instruments that recorded sound on waxed discs or etched acoustic waves on smoked glass enabled scholars for the first time to analyze speech objectively. Of course, these were the days before tape recorders, computers, or any modern electronic instruments. But despite the severe technological limitations of the day, pitch, loudness, and the harmonic structure of voice were examined for the first time during this decade.

In addition to the new fields of psychology and speech, scholars from many disciplines contributed knowledge, questions, approaches, and techniques that would later become integrated into communication sciences and disorders. In medicine, some *otologists* (physicians specializing in the care of the ear) were early pioneers in hearing measurement. Today's audiologists have carried on that work. *Laryngologists* (physicians specializing in the care of the throat and voice production mechanism) wondered how various types of vocal-cord movements caused different voice qualities. The invention of the laryngoscope by Emmanuel Garcia in 1854 permitted these specialists to view the vocal folds for the first time. Much more complex versions of Garcia's laryngoscope are now used by modern speech-language pathologists and laryngologists in hospital settings when treating clients with voice disorders. *Neurologists* (specialists in brain function) questioned the relationship between neurological integrity and various speech and language disorders. The study of individuals with head injuries and strokes and their resulting communication disorders attracted much interest, among both neurologists and psychologists of the day, and contributed to the theoretical foundations of present-day communication sciences and disorders.

In the social sciences, linguists, concerned with the study of normal language, brought with them various analysis techniques for describing an individual's use of phonology, pragmatics, syntax, and semantics. These techniques were adapted over the years for the study of the speech and language patterns of individuals with disorders. Finally, the new field of psychiatry, introduced to the United States in 1909 during a lecture tour by Sigmund Freud, was particularly concerned with stuttering and its possible emotional basis. Although strict Freudian psychiatry is not generally applied to speech disorders today, speech-language pathologists retain an awareness of the importance of emotional variables when treating clients with communication disorders.

In short, communication sciences and disorders became an interdisciplinary field, and this inclusive orientation has continued to the present time. For example, modern researchers in cognitive psychology illuminate the relationship between language and thought, while physiologists provide new ways of measuring the strength and coordination of the speech muscles. Contributions by individuals in computer science, biomedical engineering, genetics, and many other areas continue to enrich our discipline.

The History of Treatment of Communication Disorders

In the early twentieth century, as interest in the study of speech and human behavior grew, so did concern about individuals whose speech was "defective." Educational reformers of the early 1900s, such as Thomas Dewey, encouraged the broadening of what was then the traditional scope of teaching to include a responsibility to atypical children (Moore and Kester, 1953). Parents added their voices to the call for change, demanding that children with speech disorders be given special training to help them succeed in school. In response to such pressures, the Chicago Public Schools instituted a program for "stammerers" in 1910, including both children who stuttered and children with other speech problems. Since there were no teachers trained to work with such children, the superintendent of schools requested that

ten specially selected members of the graduating class of the Chicago Teachers' College be "empowered" to provide speech correction services. These individuals went from school to school in order to work with their charges. Detroit, Boston, New York, San Francisco, and several cities in Wisconsin set up similar programs between 1913 and 1916.

With demand growing for individuals who could work with speech-disordered children, colleges and universities began to institute programs to train professionals for such service. In 1915, the University of Wisconsin established the first university-based speech clinic, where students could be exposed to this new field. By 1916, the University of Iowa had a new speech course that, according to the catalog description, was devoted to "the anatomical and physiological basis of voice, voice analysis, [and the] study of voice defects and their removal (Moeller, 1976, 10). The first graduate program for the clinical study of speech disorders was established at the University of Wisconsin (Moeller, 1976).

In the period from the early 1920s to the 1940s, speech-correction services continued to be provided, mostly to children in the public schools, in small but growing numbers. However, in the years immediately following World War II, interest in studying and treating adults with communication disorders gained momentum. Of particular concern were military personnel who had lost the ability to speak, hear, or formulate language as a result of injuries received in the course of their service during the war. Rehabilitation for these individuals was initially provided in military hospitals and later in Veterans' Administration Hospitals (Flower, 1994). Once interest was sparked in adult disorders, similar rehabilitative services were gradually established in civilian hospitals over the years. Concern for injured veterans of World War II, therefore, was responsible in no small part for the expansion of the field of communication sciences and disorders into treatment for adults.

In the decades following World War II, additional growth in the field has occurred with an increasing commitment in society to children with disabilities. In the 1960s and 1970s, federal legislation at first facilitated, and then mandated, the inclusion of handicapped children in the public schools. Federal laws established their right to a free and appropriate education in the least restrictive environment and charged that special services be provided from birth to 21 years of age. Speech-language pathologists have been increasingly employed to serve not only school-aged children with special needs, but also children of preschool age.

THE FORMATION OF ASHA

A professional association for researchers and clinicians interested in communication disorders came into being in 1925. First called the American Academy of Speech Correction and later the American Society for the Study of Disorders of Speech, it is now known as the American Speech-Language-Hearing Association (ASHA). This organization has responsibility for certifying training programs for students in communication sciences and disorders and setting standards for clinical service in speech and hearing treatment centers. In addition, ASHA provides leadership in identifying research needs in the areas of language, speech, and hearing; publishes and disseminates scholarly journals in the field; and lobbies for legislation in the interest of the handicapped.

Practitioners in communication sciences and disorders are known as *speech-language pathologists* or *audiologists*. According to ASHA standards, these professionals must graduate from an approved master's program, accrue 350 clock hours of supervised clinical practice, pass a national examination, and work professionally for one year under supervision. If they meet these criteria, they are eligible for the Certificate of Clinical Competence, which allows them to work in a variety of health-care and educational settings. As their names imply, a speech-language pathologist is primarily concerned with diagnosing and rehabilitating speech and language

disorders, while an audiologist specializes in the diagnosis and remediation of disorders of hearing.

Another important function of ASHA is to define and monitor ethical professional behavior in speech-language pathologists and audiologists. ASHA's 1994 Code of Ethics outlines the general principles that professionals should follow as well as specific rules of ethics under each principle (see Box 1.1). ASHA also maintains an Ethical Practices Board that specifies procedures for investigating alleged violations of the Code of Conduct and assigns sanctions against professionals found to be in violation.

STRUCTURE AND PURPOSE OF THIS BOOK

Like the field of communication sciences and disorders, this book treats a wide variety of handicapping conditions that include deficits in speech, language, or hearing. In order to organize such diverse information, a structure incorporating both content areas and themes within each area has been adhered to, as seen in Figure 1-2.

The book is divided into six sections, or content areas: (1) language, (2) articulation and phonology, (3) fluency, (4) voice, (5) adult neurological disorders of speech and language, and (6) hearing disorders. These headings can be seen on the left side of Figure 1-2. Each section may have one or more chapters, depending on the complexity of the content area and the availability of information suitable for an introductory text.

Within each content area, the following themes will be developed: (a) normal development; (b) causes and characteristics of disorders; (c) consequences of the communication disorder to the individual; (d) societal reactions and accommodations to those with disorders; (e) the role of various professionals and family members in helping individuals with communication disorders; and (f) moral, ethical, or technological controversies surrounding some approaches to treatment of the communicatively handicapped. These themes can be seen along the top of

Box 1.1 *The Code of Ethics of the American Speech-Language-Hearing Association, revised January 1, 1994**

Principle of Ethics I: Individuals shall honor their responsibility to hold paramount the welfare of the persons they serve professionally.

Rules of Ethics

A. Individuals shall provide all services competently.
B. Individuals shall use every resource, including referral when appropriate, to ensure that high-quality service is provided.
C. Individuals shall not discriminate in the delivery of professional services on the basis of race or ethnicity, gender, age, religion, national origin, sexual orientation, or disability.
D. Individuals shall fully inform the persons they serve of the nature and possible effects of services rendered and products dispensed.
E. Individuals shall evaluate the effectiveness of services rendered and of products dispensed and shall provide services or dispense products only when benefit can reasonably be expected.
F. Individuals shall not guarantee the results of any treatment or procedure, directly or by implication; however, they may make a reasonable statement of prognosis.
G. Individuals shall not evaluate or treat speech, language, or hearing disorders solely by correspondence.
H. Individuals shall maintain adequate records of professional services rendered and products dispensed and shall allow access to these records when appropriately authorized.
I. Individuals shall not reveal, without authorization, any professional or personal information about the person served professionally, unless required by law to do so, or unless doing so is necessary to protect the welfare of the person or of the community.
J. Individuals shall not charge for services not rendered, nor shall they misrepresent, in any fashion, services rendered or products dispensed.
K. Individuals shall use persons in research or as subjects of teaching demonstrations only with their informed consent.
L. Individuals whose professional services are adversely affected by substance abuse or other health-related conditions shall seek professional assistance and, where appropriate, withdraw from the affected areas of practice.

Principle of Ethics II: Individuals shall honor their responsibility to achieve and maintain the highest level of professional competence.

Rules of Ethics

A. Individuals shall engage in the provision of clinical services only when they hold the appropriate Certificate of Clinical Competence or when they are in the certification process and are supervised by an individual who holds the appropriate Certificate of Clinical Competence.
B. Individuals shall engage in only those aspects of the professions that are within the scope of their competence, considering their level of education, training, and experience.

(continued)

C. Individuals shall continue their professional development throughout their careers.

D. Individuals shall delegate the provision of clinical services only to persons who are certified or to persons in the education or certification process who are appropriately supervised. The provision of support services may be delegated to persons who are neither certified nor in the certification process only when a certificate holder provides appropriate supervision.

E. Individuals shall prohibit any of their professional staff from providing services that exceed the staff member's competence, considering the staff member's level of education, training, and experience.

F. Individuals shall ensure that all equipment used in the provision of services is in proper working order and is properly calibrated.

Principle of Ethics III: Individuals shall honor their responsibility to the public understanding of the professions, by supporting the development of services designed to fulfill the unmet needs of the public, and by providing accurate information in all communications involving any aspect of the professions.

Rules of Ethics

A. Individuals shall not misrepresent their credentials, competence, education, training, or experience.

B. Individuals shall not participate in professional activities that constitute a conflict of interest.

C. Individuals shall not misrepresent diagnostic information, services rendered, or products dispensed or engage in any scheme or artifice to defraud in connection with obtaining payment or reim-

bursement for such services or products.

D. Individuals' statements to the public shall provide accurate information about the nature and management of communication disorders, about the professions, and about professional services.

E. Individuals' statements to the public—advertising, announcing, and marketing their professional services, reporting research results, and promoting product—shall adhere to prevailing professional standards and shall not contain misrepresentations.

Principle of Ethics IV: Individuals shall honor their responsibilities to the professions and their relationships with colleagues, students, and members of allied professions. Individuals shall uphold the dignity and autonomy of the professions, maintain harmonious interprofessional and intraprofessional relationships, and accept the professions' self-imposed standards.

Rules of Ethics

A. Individuals shall prohibit anyone under their supervision from engaging in any practice that violates the Code of Ethics.

B. Individuals shall not engage in dishonesty, fraud, deceit, misrepresentation, or any form of conduct that adversely reflects on the professions or on the individual's fitness to serve persons professionally.

C. Individuals shall assign credit only to those who have contributed to a publication, presentation, or product. Credit shall be assigned in proportion to the contribution and only with the contributor's consent.

D. Individuals' statements to colleagues about professional services, research

(continued)

results, and products shall adhere to prevailing professional standards and shall contain no misrepresentations.

E. Individuals shall not provide professional services without exercising independent professional judgment, regardless of the referral source or prescription.

F. Individuals shall not discriminate in their relationship with colleagues, students, and members of allied professions on the basis of race or ethnicity, gender, age, religion, national origin, sexual orientation, or disability.

G. Individuals who have reason to believe that the Code of Ethics has been violated shall inform the Ethical Practice Board.

H. Individuals shall cooperate fully with the Ethical Practice Board in its investigation and adjudication of matters related to this Code of Ethics.

★ASHA—American Speech-Language-Hearing Association. (1993a). Code of Ethics. In American Speech-Language-Hearing Association Council on Professional Ethics (Eds.), *Ethics: Resources for professional preparation and practice* (pp. 1.5–1.9). Rockville, MD: Author.

Figure 1-2. The resulting grid will be filled in by you, the reader, as you progress through the information presented in this text.

The role of this book is to provide a broad overview of the field of communication sciences and disorders within the context of the individual and society. In an increasingly expensive and technologically complex health-care system, it is

FIGURE 1-2 Structure of this text. Content areas are displayed on the vertical axis. The themes that will be developed in each content area are displayed on the horizontal axis.

		Themes					
		Normal development	Causes and characteristics of disorders	Consequences to the individual	Society's reactions	Role of professionals in rehab	Controversies
Content areas	1. Language						
	2. Articulation/ phonology						
	3. Fluency						
	4. Voice						
	5. Adult neurological disorders						
	6. Hearing						

important that all educated people have some knowledge of the costs, benefits, and controversies involved in rehabilitation for the communicatively impaired. It is the purpose of this book to provide such a basic background as well as to establish a foundation for future learning for those who elect to pursue this field.

EPILOGUE

In the six decades since the formalization of the field of communication sciences and disorders, many changes have taken place. Accredited departments of communication sciences and disorders now exist at many universities, and there are literally thousands of qualified practitioners,

researchers, and teachers in the field. An ever-growing body of research underlies much of the therapy done with the speech and hearing handicapped. New technology has improved our ability to measure clients' speech and hearing abilities, to implement therapy, and to circumvent permanent handicaps.

However, over the past decades, some things have not changed. As a field, communication sciences and disorders remains firmly rooted both in the scientific study of speech, language, and hearing and in aiding those with communication disorders. This presents a challenge because there is much to know and much to learn in these areas. But the rewards of participating in a field of study committed both to scientific rigor and to service are great, indeed.

R E V I E W   Q U E S T I O N S

1. What is meant by *communication?* How would you differentiate between *communication, language,* and *speech?*
2. Define *semantics, morphology, syntax,* and *pragmatics.* What are these components of?
3. What is *phonology?* How does it differ from *articulation?*
4. What are the components of speech? Describe each.

5. Which fields contributed to the formation of communication sciences and disorders as a discipline?
6. What are the goals of communication sciences and disorders? What do we call practitioners in this field?
7. What is ASHA? What are its functions?

F O R   F U R T H E R   I N F O R M A T I O N

Ethics: Resources for professional preparation (1993). Rockville, MD: ASHA.

Paden, E. (1970). *A history of the American Speech and Hearing Association, 1925–1958.* Washington, DC: ASHA.

Language Development

W hat does a newborn know about language? Most of us would guess that newborns know very little about anything, including the language spoken in the environment they have so recently joined. However, others would contend that newborns come equipped with an impressive array of perceptual abilities that facilitate their acquisition of a native language and perhaps even with an innate knowledge of some grammatical structures.

The perceptual skills of neonates, even those born prematurely, have been documented in an ever-growing body of research. Newborns are able to discriminate one speech sound from another (such as "b" from "d") and are aware of small differences in pitch, loudness, and duration. By 8 weeks of age, babies are able to recognize the intonation patterns of their native language. Prior to 1 year, they display a preference for meaningful human speech over music or repetitive noise. Thus, babies appear to be born with skills and interests that will enable them to learn language.

If you have ever tried to learn a foreign language, you have some idea of the challenge confronting a newborn. In your first exposure to a foreign language, it was probably difficult for you to tell where one word ended and the next began. As you learned more about the language, you probably became better able to recognize specific words here and there during a conversation. But keep in mind that unlike a newborn,

you had many years of experience with language and communication. You could draw parallels between the new language and your native language, which made your learning task easier. A newborn is learning about the interpersonal aspects of communication, developing concepts about the surrounding world, and learning a new language all at the same time. Yet, despite the complexity of the task, most children are relatively competent communicators by the age of 4.

But the learning process is not equally easy for everyone. Some children experience great difficulty in learning language. These children are of particular interest to those in communication sciences and disorders. Why do a small percentage of children have difficulty learning language? Is it because they are unable to discriminate the building blocks of language, such as letter sounds, pitches, loudness levels, and durations? Are they not interested in human speech? Is it too difficult to learn both new concepts *and* words to represent them? And most important, what can speech-language pathologists do to help such children?

This chapter will examine the ways in which language development has been conceptualized and the developmental sequence of language behaviors observed in children from birth to the age of 6. The five theories of language development described below are based on a review by McCormick (1990d) of perspectives on language acquisition.

THEORIES OF LANGUAGE DEVELOPMENT

BEHAVIORAL THEORY

If children are not born speaking a particular language, they obviously must learn it. And if one is *learning* something, that implies that one is being *taught*. Thus, one way of looking at how children learn language is to examine what parents and other adults do, consciously or unconsciously, to teach them language. The relationship between a child's efforts at expression and the effects of adults' responses is the basis of the behavioral theory of language development.

Behaviorism was popularized by psychologists such as B. F. Skinner in the 1950s, but its roots go back to the experiments of Pavlov in the early 1900s. The basic vocabulary of behaviorism is stimulus, response, and consequence. A *stimulus* is any object or event that causes an individual to react in some way. A *response* is what an individual does (smile, frown, speak, or cheer, for example) when confronted with a stimulus. Finally, *consequence* is the reaction the individual's response elicits from someone (or something) in the environment. A consequence can be positive (reinforcement) or negative (no reinforcement, or punishment).

In its most basic form, behaviorism begins with a certain stimulus evoking a response from an individual. If the response has a positive consequence, or is reinforced, the chances increase that the original stimulus will continue to elicit that response. If, on the other hand, the response has a negative consequence, there is less likelihood that the original stimulus will continue to elicit that response.

In terms of language development, the theory works like this: A child sees her teddy bear across the room and spontaneously says "beah!" Father also sees the teddy bear, recognizes that "beah" probably means *bear,* and gets it for the child. The child is thus positively reinforced by obtaining the desired object. This increases the likelihood that she will say "beah" the next time she wants her teddy bear. After several experiences like this, the child will come to associate particular words with particular objects.

If, on the other hand, the child had said "moo" instead of "beah," the father might not have recognized what she wanted. In all probability, a positive consequence would *not* have occurred, and the child would then have tried to come up with a better approximation of the word. Thus, the behavioral theory of language development stresses the importance of the adult's reinforcement (or lack or reinforcement) in the child's formation of associations between words, objects, and actions.

This theory has a certain intuitive appeal to anyone who has played out scenes like the one described above with a young child. It sometimes seems as if children learn words just so they can ask for things. However, the behavioral theory has a number of weaknesses as a comprehensive theory of language development.

First, the behavioral theory fails to account for the acquisition of receptive language. *Receptive language* is the ability to comprehend the language spoken in one's environment. In contrast, *expressive language* is the ability to produce linguistic units (words, phrases, sentences) according to the semantic, morphological, and syntactic rules of one's language. Behaviorism deals with the observable phenomenon of expressive language, or what the child is capable of expressing. However, most researchers would agree that the ability to understand language precedes the ability to produce it. How does the child acquire word-object relationships prior to his ability to produce them if reinforcement of his spoken attempts is necessary to establish the connection?

The behavioral theory has even more difficulty explaining the acquisition of morphology and syntax. If all possible sentence structures had to be specifically reinforced, language learning would be a very long and tedious process. Further, there is evidence that parents do not respond to the grammar of a child's utterances so much as to the correctness of the child's response. Thus, a parent would probably accept the sentence "I seed a dog" from a young child if, indeed, the child had seen a dog. A parent would not be likely to correct the child unless the animal was a cat, and the statement was thus factually false. If parents are not continually correcting a child and reinforcing accurate morphology and syntax (which they do not appear to be), it is difficult to use the behavioral theory to explain how young children acquire language.

Finally, the behavioral theory relies to a great extent on the assumption of imitation. It is assumed that the child initiates the language-learning process by imitating the words and sentence structures around him, with errors due, perhaps, to insufficient memory. If this were true, the errors young children make in semantics and syntax would be random and very different from child to child. This is not the case. Although imitation may be important in the learning of an initial vocabulary and in speech-sound production, children produce many syntactic structures that they have never heard before. Further, the errors young children make are often quite predictable. For example, most children go through a phase of saying *goed* and *seed,* although the adult models around them use *went* and *saw.* Thus, imitation cannot explain the child's acquisition of morphology and syntax, nor the regularity of the errors observed in young children.

PSYCHOLINGUISTIC THEORY

The psycholinguistic theory addresses some, although not all, of the weaknesses of the behavioral theory. The psycholinguistic theory is associated with Noam Chomsky, who articulated a very influential theory of language structure and its underlying representations in the late 1950s and early 1960s. Although his original theory was not intended to explain language acquisition, he and others have applied it toward that end.

According to the psycholinguistic theory, language is a unique and universal human endeavor with a biological base. Chomsky noted the relative speed of language acquisition, the similarity of acquisition patterns among languages, and the commonalities among linguistic structures in var-

ious languages (such as the occurrence of subject-verb phrases, negatives, and temporal, or time, distinctions in all languages). From these observations, he concluded that there were certain universal grammatical rules of language and that human beings were born with a sense of these rules as well as with the capacity to use them to generate novel utterances. This emphasis on the rules governing word order means that the psycholinguistic theory can be classified as a *syntactic* approach to the study of language.

Chomsky hypothesized that two types of rules governed language use. First, "phrase structure" rules referred to basic relationships or constituent elements underlying all sentences in all languages. For example, if a speaker wants to say that a girl is throwing a ball to a boy, the constituents of the sentence are the same regardless of what language the speaker is going to use. Reference must be made to the girl, the boy, the ball, and the fact that the ball is traveling from one to the other. These basic relationships, or constituents, are universal to communication. It is the ability to discern these relationships that Chomsky considers the "inborn" part of language.

The second type of rules involved in language processing are hypothesized to be "transformational rules." These rules allow an individual to transform the basic sentences generated by phrase-structure rules into complex, grammatically correct sentences. This "transformation" involves reordering constituents according to the syntactic rules of a particular language and linking them together to provide a more complex surface structure. The meaning of the message does not change, only its form, or *surface.* Transformational rules must be learned and are language-specific.

In applying these concepts to language acquisition, Chomsky hypothesized the existence of a "Language-Acquisition Device" (LAD). The LAD was believed to contain phrase structure rules, the basis for linguistic analysis. Although the LAD was assumed to be inborn, it was acknowledged that language input from speakers in the environment was important in order to activate it. According to Chomsky's theory, a child with an intact LAD should be able to hear a sentence, assess the situation the speaker is describing, and make guesses about how the spoken sentence (*surface structure*) relates to the speaker's meaning (*deep structure*). Subsequent adult speech will either confirm or refute the child's predictions. This is the way, it was hypothesized, that the child learns how underlying meanings are translated into grammatical sentences.

Central to Chomsky's theory of language acquisition is the idea that the child is learning rules rather than individual language units. The child's innate knowledge of noun and verb phrases (*phrase structure*) is supplemented by the transformational rules he abstracts from the speech of others in his environment. Thus, as the child learns the various grammatical structures of his native language, he can use those basic structures to come up with an endless variety of utterances simply by substituting different words. The child in Chapter 1 who could say "Me want cookie!" was abstracting, if somewhat imperfectly, the Subject + verb + direct object construction. We would expect that child to also produce utterances such as "Me want cake," "Me want juice," or even "Me see car."

Another prediction that could be made on the basis of Chomsky's theory is the interesting phenomenon of overgeneralization. Many children produce irregular plural nouns and past tense verbs correctly in their early language-learning period but later produce incorrect forms, such as "foots," "doed" or "comed," despite the fact that their language models do not use these words. Why? Someone from the psycholinguistic perspective might argue that the early "correct" use of irregulars reflects the child's rote or imitative use of such forms. As the child learns the rules for regular plural (add "s") and regular past tense (add "ed") forms, she starts applying these rules to *all* nouns and verbs, even in cases where such endings are inappropriate. Of course, as the child matures as a speaker of her native language, she will figure out which words are irregular and again use them correctly. But the occurrence of overgeneralization does show that the child is

learning rules, not just words that are thoughtlessly repeated.

In summary, the psycholinguistic theory has been successful in addressing some of the weaknesses noted in the behavioral theory. It does not rely heavily on imitation or direct parental reinforcement of correct syntax because grammatical structure is seen as the organizing principle of the child's language learning. The psycholinguistic theory is also better able to account for common error patterns seen in the developing language of young children. However, certain problems remain. Many theorists have criticized the notion of the LAD. The lack of specificity, either in terms of neurological location or developmental function, makes the LAD theory appear somewhat simplistic. In addition, it does not explain the acquisition of early language, particularly receptive language, very well. It is not clear from this theory how the child learns his first few words and two-word combinations. Finally, the psycholinguistic theory assumes a great deal of cognitive sophistication on the part of the child. The ability to size up a situation, figure out what is happening, and relate those observations to language in the environment no doubt grows with the child's attention, memory, and understanding of the world. What is missing from the psycholinguistic theory is any reference to the child's cognitive development and how cognition and language relate.

SEMANTIC-COGNITIVE THEORY

In contrast to the psycholinguistic theory, the semantic-cognitive theory is particularly concerned with the early acquisition of language. Researchers such as Bloom (1970, 1973), Brown (1973), and Schlesinger (1977) examined children's two-word utterances and concluded that children are not really applying grammatical rules in the adult sense and that syntax is not a good measure of early language development. Young children appear more likely to use a few rules of word order, such as "Agent precedes action," which are later replaced by a true understanding of syntactic rules and longer grammatical sentences. Early utterances, however, were hypothesized to occur based on word meanings, or *semantics*. And in order to understand the child's meaning, semantic-cognitive theorists became concerned with the *context* in which the communication took place; i.e. the situation, the adult's preceding remarks, and, finally, the child's response.

To illustrate the difference between a syntactic approach and a semantic approach to language acquisition, consider the early sentence "Get on bus." A proponent of the psycholinguistic theory, a syntactic point of view, might conclude that the child who produced this utterance was using the imperative sentence form, commanding someone to get on a bus. Psycholinguists assess a child's level of language development according to the complexity and correctness of such syntactic forms. However, when looked at from the semantic-cognitive point of view, the the context in which the utterance was produced would have to be taken into account. The child might use "Get on bus" to mean "My doll is getting on the bus" while engaged in a play situation. The same utterance might be used to tell the examiner that she gets on a bus to ride to school every morning. The important determinant of language development from the semantic-cognitive point of view is not the structure of the child's utterance but the meaning it is intended to convey.

And why is meaning important? Because the meaning of a child's utterance reflects her attention, memory, and understanding of the world. Language development is seen to occur within the context of cognitive development. Only when the child has learned the basic relationships between objects and actions in the environment (*cognitive development*) can she begin to talk about them (*language development*). In the example above, the child who said "Get on bus" to mean "My doll is getting on the bus" would be assessed at a lower level of language development than the child who said it to mean "I get on the bus and go to school every day." The latter implies a knowledge of time and repetition that is more

sophisticated than the here-and-now observation of the first interpretation.

It is important to note that the dependence on cognitive development in the semantic-cognitive theory refutes the notion of the LAD proposed by the psycholinguistic theory. The LAD, as you will recall, was hypothesized as an innate sense of phrase structure, or the constituent parts (primarily nouns and verbs) of the message to be communicated. In contrast, the semantic-cognitive theory proposes that the basis of early language acquisition is the child's experience with and knowledge of the environment. As the child comes to understand more about the properties of the people and things in his environment and the actions and events that take place in that environment, more and more sophisticated expression becomes possible. Early single-word statements are replaced by two-word sentences in which the order of words is semantically determined. Only later, at three words and beyond, do syntactic rules come into play.

While not as comprehensive as the psycholinguistic theory, the semantic-cognitive theory has been useful in conceptualizing early language development. It emphasizes both the child's experiences as a basis for language-learning and the importance of meaning in interpreting the child's level of language development. However, the semantic-cognitive theory cannot explain a population that is of great interest in communication sciences and disorders: children who fail to learn language despite normal cognitive development. If cognition is seen as the driving force behind early language development, how can there be children with normal cognitive abilities but delayed language? Further, it is not always the case that cognitive development precedes language development. After the age of acquisition, language development may, in fact, stimulate cognitive development. The semantic-cognitive theory also fails to account for the child's syntactic development beyond the level of two- and three-word utterances. Finally, the semantic-cognitive theory does not address the child's underlying motivation for learning language or the relationship of language to the broader phenomenon of communication.

SOCIOLINGUISTIC THEORY

The sociolinguistic theory begins with the individual's intentions. A person can communicate his or her intentions in many ways. Sometimes a nod of the head or a certain facial expression is all that is required. For babies, crying often serves a communicative purpose. However, in many cases, what we want to get across is too complex to be communicated with nods, facial expressions, or cries. According to the sociolinguistic theory, language develops out of a need to communicate our intentions more precisely.

The sociolinguistic theory hypothesizes that language development begins with the earliest interactions between child and parent. Through these interactions, the child learns how to get his parents' attention and initiate communication, how to specify what he wants, and how to influence his parents' behavior. In the earliest months of life, most of this communication is nonverbal. The child may cry for attention, use her eyes to indicate a desired object, and then look at her mother to indicate she should get it for her. Later, gestures such as reaching or pointing are also used. The idea of turn taking in communication is established through simple games such as "build-bash," where the parent builds a block tower and the child knocks it down, or peeka-boo, where child and parent take turns peeking. All these early experiences lay a foundation for later language-based communication.

Proponents of the sociolinguistic theory would begin their assessment of a child's language development prior to even the child's first word. Very young children use eye contact, vocalizations, and gestures to express their communicative intentions, and the sociolinguistic approach provides a framework for their study. Dore (1974) calls these early communications *primitive speech acts* (PSAs). A PSA is defined as an utterance that consists "formally of a single act or a single prosodic (intonation) pattern which functions to convey the child's intention before he acquires sentences" (Dore, 1974, 345). For example, a child may point at a candy bar, look at her mother, and say "dae?" The rising intonation contour denotes a question, the pointing a request. This utterance would be categorized, according to Dore, as a requesting PSA. Other categories of PSAs include labeling, repeating, answering, calling, greeting, protesting, and practicing. By the time the child begins using recognizable words, according to the sociolinguistic theory, he or she is already an experienced communicator. The learning of language merely extends and improves the communication patterns the child has already learned.

Central to the sociolinguistic theory is the idea of interaction. Early communication between the infant and the care giver is established during interactions in which routines are followed, relationships are developed, and the child learns to predict certain events based on his own and the care giver's behavior. Nonverbal patterns of communication gradually give way to verbal ones as parents help children refine the expression of their intentions.

The emphasis on interaction in the sociolinguistic theory is reminiscent of the interactional focus of the behavioral theory. Indeed, both theories put the care giver at the center of the language-learning process. And to some degree, reinforcement is an important component of both theories (indirectly in the sociolinguistic theory). However, a marked difference can be seen in the content of learning according to the two theories. In the behavioral theory, it is assumed that semantics, morphology, and syntax are being reinforced. In the sociolinguistic theory, it is assumed that the communication process (*pragmatics*) is the focus of learning. Thus, although there are similarities between the two theories, they target very different aspects of language.

At this point, there are not enough data on the sociolinguistic theory to make a full assessment of its strengths and weaknesses. Are the "primitive speech acts" hypothesized by Dore and others really seen in large numbers of young children? And if they are, is the proposed classification scheme valid? Further research is needed to answer these questions. In addition, one theoretical weakness evident in the sociolinguistic theory is that it does not explain how children acquire syntax. Although this theory can be credited with bringing the idea of communication into the language-learning process, it best explains only the earliest part of the language acquisition period.

INTERACTIONIST THEORY

One of the most recent perspectives to emerge on language acquisition is the interactionist theory. In essence, this theory states that the infant is predisposed to learn language and that he or she does so because of interaction with language users and the environment. The specifics of *what* the infant is born with and *how* all the complexities of language are acquired is not spelled out. Because of its lack of insistence on specifics, this theory can be used to assess individual learning styles, where children rely differentially on inner resources or various aspects of the learning situation in order to acquire language.

The interactionist model presented by Bloom and Lahey (1978) described three aspects of language: content, form, and use. In Chapter 1, we discussed semantics as the content component of language; morphology, syntax, and phonology as the form component; and pragmatics as the use component. Children gradually develop competence in all three areas during the process of developing language. According to McCormick (1990d), the interactionist model incorporates elements from all the theories we have discussed. The description *interactionist* is appropriate because it is acknowledged that both the child's internal abilities and resources (for content and form) and the social opportunities of the surrounding environment (use) are important in the acquisition of language.

SUMMARY

Although none of the theories described above provides a complete description of language development, there are no doubt elements of truth in each. The sociolinguistic theory is important in that it places language within the broader context of communication. It reminds us that children communicate even before they are able to use language; and we might surmise from the sociolinguistic theory that language might not even develop if no interpersonal interaction patterns are established. The semantic-cognitive theory contributes the idea that actual language development, in terms of semantics, morphology, and syntax, depends, at least in the early stages, on the child's growing knowledge of the world. As a child becomes able to comprehend the properties of the objects and people around him and the actions they engage in, he becomes capable of expressing these relationships verbally. The psycholinguistic theory contributes the notion that as the child begins to use sentences, he is learning syntactic rules, not merely repeating or imitating. Thus, even very young children are able to generate novel utterances they have never before heard. The concept of reinforcement from the behavioral theory is important in explaining why some words, morphological forms, and syntactic structures are heard over and over again—because their use brings about a desired end. And finally, the interactionist perspective attempts to integrate elements from earlier theories into a flexible framework in which both innate capabilities and environmental influences are acknowledged.

SEQUENCE OF LANGUAGE DEVELOPMENT

Regardless of what language they are learning, all young humans go through a similar sequence of language development. As you read earlier in this chapter, some theorists say this invariant sequence is due to some inborn capability for language; others say it is merely the result of an invariant sequence of cognitive development. In either case, researchers and clinicians in communication sciences and disorders must be familiar with the sequence in order to determine which children significantly deviate from it.

It is important to note that not all children progress through the developmental stages outlined below at the same ages. Early development

FIGURE **2-1** By 4 to 5 months, most infants have developed enough control of the head, neck, and upper trunk to prop themselves up on their forearms.

is very idiosyncratic: Some children acquire skills sooner and some later than the "average" ages presented here. However, the sequence of development is the same regardless of the specific age of the child at each stage.

BIRTH TO 6 MONTHS

As indicated in the introduction to this chapter, the tiny, seemingly helpless newborn comes into the world with emerging sensory and perceptual abilities, ready to learn. She is able to discriminate differences in visual, auditory, and *olfactory* (smell) stimuli. Of course, these sensory abilities are limited by the infant's poor motor control of the head and eyes and short attention span and memory. However, during the first six months of life, many developments take place in these areas.

Initially, the infant's movements are limited to primitive reflexes. *Reflexes* are obligatory movements made in response to some stimulus. For

example, when the infant's cheek is stroked, she reflexively turns her head toward the side of the touch (the *rooting reflex*). When something is placed on her lips, she begins automatic sucking movements (the *sucking reflex*). When her head is turned to one side, she extends the arm and leg on the same side (the *asymmetric tonic neck reflex*) as if to reach for what she is looking at. Initially, these reflexes are not under voluntary control.

As the infant matures, however, she gradually learns how to control her movements. Head turning, sucking, and reaching for something become voluntary activities. In general, control proceeds from the head to the feet: Head and neck control are attained first, followed by control of the upper torso and then control of the lower torso. In practical terms, this means that first, the infant is able to lift his head to look around, usually by 3 to 4 months; then he is able to lie on his stomach propped on his forearms, by 4 to 5 months; and finally, by the age of 6 months, he is able to roll into a sitting position. In later months, motor-control abilities extend from the center of the body (head, neck, and trunk) to the limbs and digits (arms and legs, fingers and toes).

Although we do not typically think of these activities as language development, the voluntary control the infant develops in the first six months of life is absolutely essential for the future ability to speak. Speech, as we have learned, is a physical act and requires a great deal of motor control. Breathing must be coordinated with *vocalization* (voice production), and later vocalization must be coordinated with the actions of the tongue and lips. At least the first of these tasks is accomplished during the first six months of life. The infant begins to gain some voluntary control over the breath stream and learns to coordinate vocalizing with breathing.

Initially, the crying an infant does is reflexive, like rooting or sucking. But by the second month of life, the infant has begun to make pleasure sounds, such as cooing, in addition to crying. These noncry vocalizations are voluntary in nature and evidence of the growing control an infant has over her respiratory and phonatory systems. Much development will be needed before the child is ready to make mature speech sounds, but the rudimentary control described above is an important first step.

The infant's earliest noncry vocalizations are prolonged vowels and single syllables of the consonant-vowel (CV) type, although it may be difficult to recognize the exact consonant and vowel. However, as the child moves through the first six months, more complicated vocalizations emerge. Between the ages of 4 and 6 months, babies begin to string CV or VC (vowel-consonant) syllables together in a form of speech called *babbling*. These strings may be short (two or three syllables long), and the consonants and vowels may sound very imprecise or nasal, but their presence indicates growing control over the speech-production mechanism. All babies produce this early type of babbling, even deaf babies who are unable to hear either themselves or the sounds around them.

Thus far we have concentrated on the infant's growing control over the respiratory and phonatory systems and the articulators. But what of comprehension of and memory for objects and actions, which, according to the semantic-cognitive theory, must precede true language development? What cognitive advances are taking place in the birth to 6-month period which lay the foundations for language development?

In the earliest months of life, infants begin to explore their environment, both visually and physically. Movement and exploration enable young children to begin to understand certain things about the objects and actions around them. For example, they begin to realize that objects will reappear though they are momentarily out of sight, and they become increasingly interested in exploring things through mouthing, looking, touching, and even dropping. These early experiences provide information about the size, shape, and texture of objects and the fact that these properties stay constant over time. Attention improves, and visual memory increases to about three hours. Although, again, it is difficult to view these activities and abilities as "language development," children from birth to 6 months of age are, indeed, learning about the world around them in a way that will facilitate their later learning of concepts and words. Without this early exploration and experience, a child's foundation for symbolic representation would be very limited.

7 TO 12 MONTHS

Between 7 and 12 months of age, the child goes through a period of rapid change, in terms of both physical skills and cognitive abilities. During this period, the child changes from a primarily horizontal orientation to a vertical orientation. Improved trunk control permits the child to sit upright for longer and longer periods; and by the end of this period, most children are standing unsupported. Some are even walking.

Prespeech production abilities also rapidly change between 7 and 12 months of age. By 7 months, most children are producing longer and more complex strings of syllables in their bab-

FIGURE 2-2 In the 7- to 12-month period, children are able to search for and find objects that are out of sight. (Elizabeth Crews)

bling. This stage, known as *reduplicative babbling,* is characterized by repetitions within the syllable string. For example, a baby may produce something like "ma-ma-ma-ma-ma" or two-syllable repetitions, such as "ba-doo ba-doo." The quality as well as the quantity of babbling changes too—consonants become more recognizable and begin to sound more like the speech sounds adults use. Because 7-month-olds often produce utterances that sound like "ma-ma" and "da-da," many parents believe that their children say their first words at this age. However, at least in the initial part of this period, it is more likely that the child is simply playing with sounds and does not have a specific referent in mind for the utterances he produces.

As the child moves toward 12 months of age, additional capabilities are noted. *Variegated babbling* is seen—babbling in which syllables are produced in rapid succession without a repetition pattern. Somewhat later, the child's syllable strings take on recognizable intonational patterns similar to those heard in adult speech. This prespeech form is known as *jargon.* At this stage, many babies sound as if they are speaking a foreign language. And the facial expressions and gestures that accompany jargon signal an increased communicative intent. The young child may make eye contact with a listener and inquire "Ba bee bo na ta di?" with such earnestness that the listener almost feels compelled to respond. By 12 months of age, most children seem to be able to produce the *form* of communication, such as pragmatic gestures and intonation patterns, if not the *content.*

In terms of cognitive development, memory and knowledge of the world are also increasing. Children in the 8- to 12-month period become able to anticipate events and the outcomes of certain actions, such as the crash a sugar bowl in midair will make when it hits the floor. They are also able to search persistently for hidden objects and recognize them when they reappear. This indicates increasing development of the concept of *object permanence,* the fact that objects have an independent existence even when out of sight. Development of this concept reflects the child's improved attention and memory. Although the concept of object permanence (along with attention and memory capabilities) will undergo further refinement during the next year and a half, the level achieved by an 8- to 12-month-old child is probably sufficient to allow true language development to begin.

In addition to object permanence, other cognitive abilities that facilitate language development also reach a functional level during the 8- to 12-month period. During this developmental phase, children realize that others in their environment besides themselves can be a source of action. In earlier months, the child realized that *he* could reach for something, but not until the age of 8 to 12 months does he realize that if he reaches for something and can't get it, *someone else can.* This is known as the concept of *causality,* the idea that an action can be caused by others besides the self. A child who places his parent's hands on a windup toy to reactivate its motion is demonstrating knowledge of causality. This concept is seen as an important precursor to language.

A second important prelanguage skill that matures during this period is *means-end behavior.* This is the notion that one object can be used to act upon another. The child who grabs a place mat on the table in order to get an out-of-reach cup of juice placed upon it is exhibiting means-end behavior. The fact that both the juice and the placemat hit the floor more often than not is incidental (except to the parent who must clean it up). The important aspect of the action is that the child used one object (the place mat) as a tool in order to obtain a desired object (the cup of juice). Since language can also be seen as a tool (or a means) to acquire a desired object (an end), this concept can be considered a precursor to language development.

Given all that has come before, it is not surprising that receptive language begins to emerge during the 7- to 12-month period. As described earlier in this chapter, receptive language refers to the linguistic forms—nouns, verbs, sentences, and so on—that a child can understand. Receptive language is a function of both cognitive understanding of an object and its properties and the specific labels, or words, used in the child's environment. When the child begins to associate specific words with concepts, receptive language development has begun. By 12 months of age, most children can recognize their own names, and point to or hand objects to an adult on request.

THE FIRST WORD

The first spoken word marks the onset of expressive language. Expressive language, as described earlier, is the ability to produce linguistic units such as words, phrases, and sentences according to the semantic, morphological, and syntactic rules of one's language. Receptive language is generally acknowledged to precede expressive language. In the model we are developing, the child became capable of understanding some specific words in the 7- to 12-month period, thus evidencing the beginnings of receptive language. Some time at the end of the first year—or perhaps even as late as 18 months of age—the child at last begins to produce words, or to initiate expressive language. This is an important landmark for child-development specialists, as well as for parents.

Many parents consider almost any utterance their child produces during babbling to be a *word.* Yet linguists have a number of fairly specific criteria for what constitutes a child's first word. Three of these requirements are as follows: (1) the word must stand for a category of objects, not just an isolated item or person; (2) the word must be used in novel instances; and (3) the word should be used to name objects both in the immediate environment and out of sight. For example, if *doggie* is truly a word in the child's vocabulary, it should not refer only to the family dog when present but to a whole category of animals, including those the child has never seen. In this regard, much information can be gleaned from children's labeling errors. If a 12-month-old points to a horse and says "doggie," a linguist is not disappointed. This incorrect label reveals that the child is using the word *doggie* to refer to a category; unfortunately, the category is too broad. As the child gains more experience with animals, he will learn that not all four-legged creatures are dogs. Meanwhile, it is clear that the child is learning a concept, not just an isolated label. It is also clear that the child can use the word (or misuse it, as the case may be) in a novel instance. If the child pointed to the family dog's bed when the dog was not in it and said "doggie," we would acknowledge that the child had, indeed, attained his first word.

13 TO 18 MONTHS: THE PERIOD OF RECEPTIVE-VOCABULARY GROWTH

Following production of the first word, most of us assume that the child will go on to produce word after word after word, rapidly growing in expressive-language ability. This is generally not

FIGURE 2-3 In the 13- to 18-month period, children develop locomotion skills and begin to follow simple commands. (Elizabeth Crews)

the case. After producing his first word, the child acquires perhaps ten or twenty more and then appears to plateau. For many children, much of their attention and energy during this period is devoted to perfecting gross motor and locomotion skills. Language development, however, is not dormant. The months after the emergence of the first word are usually considered to be a period of great receptive-language growth.

By 18 months of age, most children can follow a variety of commands, such as pointing to body parts or to pictures of objects. Expressively, most children can produce at least twenty words, or as many as fifty. The difference between conceptual development and expressive-language abilities can be seen in the child's use of *holophrases* (one-word sentences). A child may pick up her father's belt off the bed and say "Daddy!" Of course, she is not confusing the belt with her father. Rather, she is indicating her knowledge of the ownership of the belt, a concept she understands but is not yet able to express in a clear way. Finally, by 18 months of age, many children are beginning to combine two words.

It should be noted that the jargon developed earlier in the child's life has not disappeared just because the child is able to produce some true words. Although there is great variation from child to child, children who frequently engaged in babbling prior to saying their first words will continue to do so for a good many months. In some cases, actual words will be inserted right into a stream of jargon. "Ma ti no cookie?" a child may ask. Other children produce very little babbling and seem to use only true words once they begin to talk. We expect a child of 18 months to understand a variety of words and commands and to be able to produce a number of meaningful words. However, the overall pattern of a child's communication style at any given age is likely to be very individualistic.

18 TO 24 MONTHS: THE PERIOD OF EXPRESSIVE VOCABULARY GROWTH

The phase just prior to the second birthday has often been called the *naming stage*. During this

FIGURE 2-4 Between 18 and 24 months, children learn many new words associated with household routines and play. (Elizabeth Crews)

period, a child goes from having only a handful of words in his expressive vocabulary to having from 250 to 300. The jargon observed in the earlier stages may persist during the early part of this period, although an increasing number of true words are interspersed throughout the syllable stream. In addition, occasional *echolalia* may be observed—the child may repeat what he has heard adults say.

As the child moves through the 18- to 24-month period, jargon gradually decreases, and most of the child's utterances become actual words or two-word phrases. It may seem to parents that the child is learning a new word every day. Word combinations include noun + verb constructions, such as "Dog go," verb + object constructions, such as "Get book," or adjective + noun constructions, such as "Big car." The child may use some pronouns (often incorrectly, such as "Him run"), prepositions such as *in* and *on,* the

plural marker *-s,* and *-ing* verb endings. However, much is omitted from the child's speech. The auxiliary verbs *is* and *are* are rarely used, nor are articles (*a, the*) and many prepositions. "Me go school," a child might announce. The word order is correct, and a pronoun has been used; but clearly the child has a long way to go. The speech used in this developmental period, with its reduced grammar, has been labeled *telegraphic speech,* referring to the child's tendency to include only content words in his sentences.

2 TO 3 YEARS: THE PERIOD OF SYNTACTIC ELABORATION

Between the ages of 2 and 3, the child switches from simple word combinations to more recognizable sentence forms. Telegraphic speech is still seen, but more and more refinements emerge in the child's expressive language. Improved use of

FIGURE 2-5 In what has been called the *terrible two's*, children often test their limits. They are also able to use simple sentences to express demands and intentions. (Michael Weisbrot)

pronouns can be observed, as well as use of negatives, auxiliaries, and "wh-" questions. *Overgeneralization,* the tendency of the child to regularize all verbs and plural noun forms, is frequently seen during this time period. Although a child in this stage usually restricts his conversation to the here and now, the past tense is occasionally used, indicating an ability to sequence events.

By approximately 2½ years, the child's intonation patterns during sentence production have become more adultlike. The child has begun to put emphasis on the important words in his sentences. Proper use of emphatic stress, plus the inclusion of many previously eliminated function words improve the child's *intelligibility,* or the extent to which a listener can understand him.

If you have spent time with a taciturn 2- to 3-year-old child and failed to notice these burgeoning language abilities, take heart. There is a wide range of normal behavior at this age. Some children speak very little, preferring to rely on nonverbal forms of communication. Even if the child speaks, you may not be able to understand her unless you have spent considerable time with her. At 2 years of age, most children are only about 50 percent intelligible to individuals outside the family. This means that even if the child is talkative, you will only understand what she says about half the time. Further, a 2-year-old's pragmatic skills are limited. A child of this age is unable to take into account the listener's point of view. The child may begin, with no introduction, to talk about a friend or pet you have no knowledge of in a sentence that you don't quite "catch." Intelligibility should improve to 75 percent, however, by the age of 3. A parent, alert teacher, or speech-language pathologist should be able to tell the difference between a child who is simply not performing at this age and one whose capabilities are truly below age expectation.

Despite the 2- to 3-year-old's linguistic limitations, his achievements thus far have been impressive. He has an understanding of the objects and people in his world and a *label* (word) for almost all of them. He is aware of the daily routines in his life and is able to predict what will happen in certain situations based on his memory of past experiences. He has become an expert communicator, using a combination of nonverbal and verbal mechanisms (including intonation patterns). He has acquired enough morphological and syntactic rules to enable him to use sentences to express a wide variety of thoughts and intentions. These accomplishments may not always be evident to a stranger, but the child between 2 and 3 years of age has established the foundations of all future learning and language use.

3 TO 4 YEARS: THE SWITCH TO ADULT STRUCTURES

Between the ages of 3 and 4, the child's expressive language continues to undergo refinement.

FIGURE 2-6 In the 3- to 4-year-old period, children begin to converse and ask questions. (Elizabeth Crews)

Sentence length increases to an average of five words. Sentences may be combined, using conjunctions such as *and* and *but* and may include embedded clauses. An example of a sentence using a conjunction is "We went to the park *and* played on the swings." An example of an embedded clause is "Here's the toy *my mommy bought me.*" By the age of 3, most children have a spoken vocabulary of 900 to 1000 words. By the age of 4, this has grown to 1500 to 1600 words.

During this stage, language takes on a more important communicative function. Up to the age of 3, many children use language more as a supplement to communication than as their primary communication medium. By the age of 4, however, the child is able to converse, ask questions, and gain new information about the world around him by verbal means. Language in this period is more flexible, less tied to the here and now, as the child begins to use the past tense as well as the future tense more frequently. The child also begins to learn to take the listener's perspective into consideration in a conversation. The child's social skills and cognitive understanding of time and events, combined with his linguistic abilities, result in a fairly sophisticated level of communication.

4 TO 5 YEARS: LANGUAGE AS A MEANS OF SOCIALIZATION

Between the ages of 4 and 5, a new focus is brought into the communication process. Up to this point, many children's language and communication attempts were aimed primarily at adults. But between the ages of 4 and 5, most children become interested in playing and communicating with their peers. If development has proceeded on schedule, the child's social and linguistic abilities should be up to the task. Children in this age range are able to converse with a wide variety of people, acquire information through language,

FIGURE 2-7 Between the ages of 4 and 5 years, language takes on a more communicative function. Children use language to pretend, guess, and argue.

argue, guess, and pretend. By 5, a child should be able to play organized games with simple rules.

During this period, children improve upon their use of language in social situations. They must refine their skills in taking turns during conversation and initiating and changing topics. They also must become better able to modify their communication style to facilitate their listeners' comprehension. The latter is especially important because children of this age are now beginning to communicate with younger, less capable communication partners. We have not discussed language disorders up to this point, but it is clear that a child whose language development is delayed will be at a distinct disadvantage at this stage. Opportunities for play and socialization will be limited if the child cannot keep up verbally with his peers and conform to adult expectations. Beyond the age of 4 or 5, language takes on a social significance that goes beyond the confines of communication within the child's home and family. We

can look at language-delayed children in terms of their linguistic deficits, but we must not forget that language delays and disorders also have social consequences.

5 TO 6 YEARS: KINDERGARTEN

Entrance into the formal educational system is a major milestone for most children. It is expected that by this age, a child will be able to speak in grammatically correct and intelligible sentences, understand all that is said to him, interact appropriately with adults and peers, and conform to the demands of the school situation. With form taken for granted, emphasis shifts to the information content of the child's speech. Formal activities involving concepts such as color, numbers, spatial relations, time and sequencing, to name a few, will be presented for the first time. The child will be expected to know, learn, remember, and express many things.

FIGURE 2-8 Between 5 and 6 years of age, children are expected to be able to participate verbally in a formal educational setting. (Elizabeth Crews)

At some point in kindergarten, sound-letter relationships will be introduced as a precursor to reading. Children will be asked to segment words into sounds, to identify beginning and ending sounds of words, and to associate sounds with printed letters. In addition to these phonological analysis skills, children need to be familiar enough with the linguistic rules of their language to predict the next word in a partial sentence if they are to learn to read successfully (Kahmi & Catts, 1989).

Success in school depends upon the successful attainment of a sequence of language skills during the preschool years. A child with a language delay or disorder will have difficulty meeting the expectations of the school situation. Such a child is at risk for academic difficulty and could probably benefit from a preschool language-stimulation program.

Language development does not end with the onset of formal education. A child's grasp of semantics, morphology, syntax, and pragmatics continues to develop into adulthood. Although language development in childhood and adolescence is beyond the scope of this text, it is an area of increasing interest in communication sciences and disorders.

SUMMARY

Language development is a long, complex, but orderly process. At the very earliest ages, from birth to 6 months, infants gain rudimentary control over their respiration and voicing and begin to learn about their environment through vision and voluntary movement. Between the ages of 7 and 12 months, their ability to produce speech sounds improves as they practice more and more complex patterns of babbling. The concepts of object permanence, causality, and means-end behavior are also established at a basic level at this age, and receptive language development begins. Some time after the age of 12 months, infants say their first true words, and expressive language development is also initiated.

In the period following production of the first words, at approximately 13 to 18 months of age, only a few new words are gained expressively, but receptive language develops rapidly. The gap between children's conceptual and receptive development and their expressive abilities can be seen in their use of holophrases. In contrast, the period from 18 to 24 months of age is one of rapid expressive vocabulary development, a time when children appear to learn a new word every day. During this period, children also begin to combine words into two-word phrases.

The period from 2 to 3 years of age is characterized by rapid development of syntactic elaboration. Children progress from jargon and occasional single words and two-word combinations to primitive sentences known as *telegraphic speech*. Between 3 and 4 years of age, a switch to adult structures is seen. Sentence length and complexity increase, although errors still occur. More important, language becomes the primary means of communication for children, replacing their earlier reliance on nonverbal communication—crying and simple vocalizations.

Between 4 and 5 years of age, language takes on an important social function. Children use language to play, argue, guess, and pretend with their peers. Children with delayed language are at a distinct disadvantage. Finally, the kindergarten years, ages 5 and 6, require an excellent command of language and communication skills as children enter the formal school situation and begin learning to read.

EPILOGUE

This chapter has provided a very brief overview of five major theories of language development and the sequence of language development from birth to the age of 6. Language development, however, is a major area of inquiry that has involved a number of disciplines over the years. If you are in communication sciences and disorders, you will probably go on to take one or two more courses devoted exclusively to language development in order to prepare yourself for the study of language disorders and their remediation. If you are in psychology, you will study language development more extensively in your courses in developmental and cognitive psychology. If you are in linguistics, you will learn about language acquisition from the point of view of the major linguistic theorists. Students in education, especially early childhood education, will study language development as it relates to appropriate educational activities for young children. The information presented in this text provides only a brief glimpse of this very complex area.

If you look back at Figure 1-2 on page 11, you will see that we have completed the first theme (normal development) for our first content area (language). Because language development is such a major area, we have spent a great deal of time here. The next chapter in this book will continue in the content area of language, developing the themes of causes and characteristics of disorders, consequences to the individual, society's reactions, the role of professionals, and controversies in the field.

R E V I E W   Q U E S T I O N S

1. What is the behavioral theory of language development? What are its weaknesses?
2. In the psycholinguistic theory, why did Chomsky propose that language had a biological base?
3. Differentiate between phrase structure rules and transformational rules.
4. What is meant by the phrase "generate novel utterances?" Why is this important in the psycholinguistic theory?
5. How does the semantic-cognitive theory differ from the psycholinguistic theory?
6. What is the importance of interaction in the sociolinguistic theory?

7. What is interactionist theory? Why do most theorists today consider themselves interactionists?

8. What is meant by *babbling? Reduplicative babbling? Variegated babbling? Jargon?* At what ages are these phenomena seen?

9. What are the criteria for the first word?

10. What is meant by *receptive language? Expressive language?*

11. Describe language development between the time the child acquires her first word and the age of 3.

12. What is *overgeneralization?* Why is it a positive sign?

13. What characterizes language learning in the 3- to 4-year-old period? The 4- to 5-year-old period?

14. What language abilities is a child expected to have by the time he enters kindergarten?

FOR FURTHER INFORMATION

Bloom, L. (1970). *Language development: Form and function of emerging grammars.* Cambridge, MA: MIT Press.

Bloom, L., and Lahey, M. (1978). *Language development and disorders.* New York, NY: Wiley.

Chomsky, N. (1972). *Language and the mind.* New York, NY: Harcourt Brace Jovanovich.

Owens, R. (1992). *Language development: An introduction* (3rd ed.). Columbus, OH: Merrill Publishing.

Skinner, B. (1957) *Verbal behavior.* New York: Appleton-Century-Crofts.

Childhood Language Disorders: An Overview

I n the first two chapters, we learned that language consists of (1) symbols representing objects, actions, and ideas and (2) a set of rules governing symbol combinations. We explored some theories of why and how children acquire language. We also examined the sequence of language development, from a child's first exposure to his native language at birth to his relatively competent receptive and expressive abilities by the age of 5 or 6 years.

Language development appears to take place so universally in children of various linguistic backgrounds, and so efficiently within a given child, that some researchers have hypothesized that the ability to process and learn language must be genetically predetermined (see the discussion of the psycholinguistic theory in Chapter 2). Yet not all children learn language so readily. In spite of the general efficiency of the process, marked individual variations do occur. For reasons both known and unknown, a certain percentage of children fail to demonstrate age-appropriate understanding and use of the semantic, morphological, and syntactic elements of their native language. It is this population, children with language disorders, that will be discussed in this chapter.

WHAT IS A LANGUAGE DISORDER?

A *language disorder* is a deficit in the comprehension or production of the semantic, morphological, or syntactic forms appropriate for the chrono-logical age of the child. For example, a 4-year-old child with a language disorder might have an expressive vocabulary of 200 words and communicate in two- to three-word phrases, in a manner similar to that of a 2-year old. Because this 4-year old is below age-expected performance in his spoken vocabulary (*semantics*) and use of sentences (*morphology* and *syntax*), he fits the criteria for a language disorder. It is important to note that a language disorder can involve either receptive or expressive language or both. A child may have difficulty understanding language appropriate for his chronological age; or a child's primary difficulty may be in producing appropriate language forms. Many different patterns of deficits are possible.

Pragmatic difficulties may also be a component of a language disorder. As described in Chapter 1, *pragmatics* refers to the functional use of language in social contexts, or the communicative function of language. After all, one must know more than words and word-combination rules to communicate. In order to be able to converse with others in one's culture, one must know the accepted ways of getting a listener's attention, initiating a conversation, changing from one topic to another, or making assertions or denials. These are known as *pragmatic skills*. Difficulty with such communicative activities is sometimes (although not always) present in children who evidence semantic, morphological, or syntactic deficits.

So far, we have discussed all of the major components of language we learned about in Chapter 1 with the exception of phonology. For the purposes of this text, we will consider phonology and its disorders separately from language. This is because phonology involves rules governing the production, occurrence, and sequencing of speech sounds. Language disorders, as we have defined them, involve difficulties with larger units of meaning—words and sentences and their organization—in the communication of novel thoughts and ideas. Problems with the knowledge and use of phonological rules and the correct production of sounds with the tongue, the lips, and the teeth will be considered in a later chapter on phonological and articulation disorders. However, it is frequently the case that the child with a language disorder as defined above also has a phonological or articulation disorder. An important part of a speech-language pathologist's job is to analyze the communications of a child who is difficult to understand in order to determine the degree to which the disorder is caused by immature vocabulary and sentence patterns as opposed to improperly formed speech sounds.

CAUSES OF LANGUAGE DISORDERS

Every parent of a child with a language disorder has the same question, Why? Unfortunately, the causes of language disorders are not well understood. In some cases, there is an obvious physical, genetic, or neurologic cause for the disorder. In the majority of cases, however, the *etiology* (cause) of the disorder remains a mystery.

The prevailing view today in the field of communication sciences and disorders is that the etiology of a language disorder is not as important as it was once believed to be. According to McCormick (1990a), "Children with different disability labels have many similarities in language characteristics, and there are often differences among children with the same label" (p. 163). In other words, the children we will discuss below, whether labeled cognitively disordered, neurlogically disordered, or specific-language impaired, may have similar language abilities and deficits regardless of the nature of the underlying disorder. McCormick (1990a) argues that it is more

important to focus on the individual child's characteristics, in terms of her sensory abilities, learning potential, output capabilities, and interests than it is to base language assessment and therapy on some etiological label.

There are, however, legitimate reasons for seeking the cause of a language disorder rather than just describing its characteristics. First, the cause of the disorder, if known, may affect the type of language intervention a child needs. As Aram (1991) recounts, we would not treat a child with a language disorder due to severe hearing loss with an exclusively auditory approach. Second, the cause of the disorder may affect the child's *prognosis,* or the likelihood that he or she will ultimately achieve normal communication abilities. Some causes of language disorders affect many areas of functioning and achievement, and a speech-language pathologist should set goals with those long-term implications in mind. Finally, if the underlying physical or psychological cause of a language disorder is known, it may be possible to eliminate the cause and thus "cure" the language impairment. For example, Aram (1991) mentions a specific form of epileptic disorder that causes auditory perception problems. It is possible that the child's language disorder might be minimized or even eliminated if this seizure activity could be controlled early on. Because of the potential benefits of recognizing etiology, this text will present childhood language disorders in terms of causative factors. However, the student should be aware that for goal setting and intervention planning, the cause of a language disorder may not be especially important.

Language disorders are frequently grouped into organic disorders and functional disorders. This text adds a middle category, environmental disorders. *Organic language disorders* are those due to known physical, genetic, or neurological problems that interfere with the child's ability to use age-appropriate language forms. *Environmental language disorders* have a probable cause—extreme environmental deprivation and abuse—but the link between the etiology and the disorder is weaker. *Functional language disorders,* on the other hand, have no apparent cause. A list of potential

---

TABLE 3-1 Causes of Language Disorders

A. Organic Causes
 1. Hearing impairment
 2. Cognitive disorders
 3. Specific genetic syndromes
 4. Neurological disorders
    a. Acquired disorders (aphasia)
    b. Developmental disorders
       1) Spina bifida
       2) Pervasive developmental
          disorder (PDD)
B. Environmental Causes
 1. Severe neglect
 2. Severe abuse
C. Functional Categories
 1. Mild developmental delay
 2. Specific language impairment (SLI)

---

causes of language disorders is presented in Table 3-1.

ORGANIC LANGUAGE DISORDERS

1. Hearing Loss. In Table 3-1, we see that hearing loss, a physical problem, is associated with language disorders of the organic type. A hearing loss may prevent a child from receiving the linguistic input necessary for normal language development. Such a child might be below age expectations in both receptive and expressive language. We will more fully examine the effects of hearing loss on language ability in later chapters in this book.

2. Cognitive Disorders. Development cognitive disorders, also known as *mental retardation,* are another cause of organically based language impairment. Cognitive disorders themselves have a variety of causes, including genetic syndromes, prenatal exposure to harmful substances, and severe childhood illnesses. These factors presum-

ably interfere with the growth and development of the brain, resulting in limited intellectual potential. Language is thus just one of many areas in which a child with cognitive disorders will be delayed. These children typically have receptive and expressive language capabilities that are roughly commensurate with their mental ages (as opposed to their chronological ages), but as we will learn in the next chapter, language capabilities may vary considerably in different subgroups of this population.

3. Specific Genetic Syndromes. A frequently overlooked organic cause of language disorders is language- or speech-specific genetic syndromes. Such syndromes may be characterized by only mild physical malformations or cognitive involvement. Speech and language deficits, by contrast, might be the most prominent symptoms. For example, anomalies involving the sex chromosomes (X and Y) may cause language disorders of various types. Girls with 47,XXX syndrome (three X chromosomes instead of two) have been noted to have delayed language development, auditory perceptual problems, and problems with verbal expression, as well as social difficulties (Nielsen et al., 1979). Boys with an extra Y chromosome (47,XYY syndrome) have been reported to have mild cognitive disorders and learning disabilities (Batshaw and Perret, 1992b). Such syndromes are frequently unrecognized in children, even today. However, with the advances in genetic research that have occurred over the past few years, it is likely that this area will receive more clinical interest than it has in the past. Many children who at present have an unknown etiology for their language disorder may be found in the future to have a language-specific genetic syndrome.

4. Neurological Disorders. Neurological disorders, both acquired and developmental, can also cause language impairment. An example of a neurologically based language disorder of the acquired type is aphasia. Acquired aphasia is not common in children but may occur in a normally developing child if damage is localized in the language centers of the brain, such as may occur after a stroke or following surgery to remove a tumor. The child's subsequent use of language may be impaired (although, fortunately, many children eventually regain their language abilities if the injury is not extensive). What distinguishes an acquired from a developmental disorder is that it is preceded by normal development and a period of normal functioning.

An example of a developmental neurological disorder associated with language impairment is spina bifida, a condition in which the child's spinal cord and sometimes the brain fail to develop properly prior to birth. These children may exhibit language abnormalities characterized by fluent and grammatical social language (e.g., Hello, how are you, I'm a big girl), but difficulty understanding and responding to specific questions (Charney, 1992). This disorder would be considered developmental because it is present from birth and prevents normal development.

Another developmental neurological disorder associated with language impairment is pervasive developmental disorder (PDD). According to the American Psychiatric Association (1994), PDD is actually a group of serious childhood disorders, one of which is autism. Children with PDD typically have severe language impairment as well as severe social-interaction problems and cognitive delays. Many develop no oral language at all, and some only echo what they have heard. These children almost always have poor pragmatic skills and often have limited nonverbal communication behaviors. In the past, autism in particular was believed to be caused by cold, rejecting mothers who subconsciously failed to respond appropriately to their children and, thus, drove their children further and further into isolation from the environment. According to current authorities, however, research (much of it dating back to the 1970s) has failed to support this *psychogenic,* or psychologically based, etiology (Tiegerman, 1993). It is commonly accepted today that all forms of PDD are caused by diseases affecting the brain or by neurological abnormalities. We will discuss this disorder in more detail in the next chapter.

ENVIRONMENTAL LANGUAGE DISORDERS

Although many people assume that language disorders are caused somehow by parents or the home environment, this is generally not the case. Children with language disorders come from all social, educational, and economic levels and usually have adequate language models from their parents as well as opportunities for interaction. The fact that the siblings of children with language disorders usually have normal language development supports the idea that parental ineptitude is not a primary causative factor.

There are some cases, unfortunately, where the general rule of exonerating parents from blame may not apply. For severely neglected or abused children, the environment in general and parental behavior in particular might cause language disorders. We will refer to these as *environmental language disorders,* or language disorders caused by the child's environment. However, as we shall see, in even these severe cases, the connection between maltreatment in the social environment and language ability is not entirely clear.

1. Severe Neglect. *Neglected children,* by definition, are those whose minimal physical needs are not provided for in an ongoing or continuous manner. This would include abandoned children, children left alone for long periods during the day, or children incarcerated in the home among other examples. It may be hypothesized that neglected children are not exposed to adequate language models, don't have adequate opportunities for interaction with a care giver, and thus are more likely than are children from nonneglecting homes to experience language disorders. A study by Allen and Oliver (1982) did, indeed, find that neglected children scored lower on a test of language comprehension and expression than did either abused children or children from nonmaltreating homes. Allen and Oliver interpreted their findings to support the idea that lack of stimulation significantly hinders language development.

There is another possible explanation for Allen and Oliver's findings, however. It may be that the neglected children were neglected, at least in part, *because* they had language disorders and difficulty communicating. A child who does not respond adequately to his parents is likely to be ignored in future communications. It is also possible that neglect and communication disorders form a vicious circle. A child with a communication disorder might be more likely to be neglected by his parents because they are frustrated by the child's lack of responsiveness. The neglect, in turn, might worsen the language disorder (and the resulting behavior problems), prompting even more parent frustration and more severe neglect. Thus, although it is tempting to draw a conclusion of causality between neglect and deficient language, it is not clear whether the language delay observed in the neglected group was the *result* of neglect or the *cause* of neglect.

2. Severe Abuse. The effects of child abuse on language development are even more equivocal. Child abuse includes physical damage sustained by a child in the form of cuts, bruises, concussions, broken bones, and so on. The abuse can occur at infrequent intervals or can be ongoing in nature. Clearly, extreme child abuse can and often does result in neurological damage, with subsequent deficits in the child's motoric, perceptual, speech, and language abilities. However, when these children with known neurological damage are removed from the subject population, a clear correlation between abuse and language disorders is not always found.

It is interesting to note, however, that even investigators who reported no significant differences between abused and nonabused children on specific language tests did note other differences between the two groups. For example, Blager and Martin (1976) found it extremely difficult to test their abused subjects at all because of their poor cooperation and little interest in the task. It may be that abuse affects a child's desire to communicate and interact, thus affecting primarily the pragmatic aspect of language. Again, however, the relationship between abuse and language abilities may be complicated by a vicious-circle effect, as well as by psychological problems, and may therefore not be simple to ascertain.

FUNCTIONAL LANGUAGE DISORDERS

It should be noted that children whose language disorders have known organic or environmental causes are in the minority in the typical speech-language pathologist's caseload, unless he or she is in a specialized setting. By far the majority of children diagnosed as having a language disorder have no known cause for their problem. For lack of a better term, we will identify these children as having *functional language disorders.* That is, the child functions below age expectations in terms of linguistic abilities, but no definitive statement can be made about the cause of the disorder.

1. Mild Developmental Delay. Children who show a mild delay in many areas of early development constitute one category of functionally language-disordered children; that is, children who are delayed in their acquisition of language and have difficulties in other areas as well. Intellectual performance may be somewhat below age expectations, or behavioral problems may be apparent. These children could be considered mildly developmentally delayed because their development in a variety of cognitive and social areas is somewhat behind schedule. Some of these children may eventually catch up with their peers, with or without special help. Others may remain in the low-normal category throughout their educational careers. Since the exact cause of this delay cannot be specified, we would consider the associated language disorder to be functional.

2. Specific Language Impairment. One especially interesting population of language-disordered children has been labeled as having *specific language impairment,* or SLI (Lahey, 1988). In 1981, Stark and Tallal defined this disorder as a language deficit characterized by performance at least twelve months below chronological age, based on a battery of tests, despite normal hearing, normal intelligence, no symptoms or history of a neurological disorder, no severe behavior or adjustment problems, and no obvious abnormalities of the speech mechanism. In other words, the child with specific language impairment (SLI) has no obvious reason for his problems in acquiring language. Stark and Tallal's (1981) definition continues to be used by current researchers, according to Craig and Evans (1993).

It was once common to see the terms "childhood aphasia," "developmental aphasia," and "minimal brain dysfunction" used to describe isolated language disorders in the presence of normal development in all other areas. Currently, the terms "specific language impairment," "specific language disorders," and "specific language deficits" are used. As one might guess from some of the earlier terms, it was originally hypothesized that children with SLI had some subtle neurological deficit underlying their disorder. However, no definitive nervous system lesion has yet been identified, so this disorder remains in the functional category.

Despite the unresolved questions about the cause of specific language impairment, SLI children have been and continue to be the focus of much behavioral research in the field of communication sciences and disorders. Their very existence challenges most theories of language acquisition and the relationship between language and cognition. For example, the semantic-cognitive theory described in Chapter 2 postulates that language development is a direct reflection of a child's increasing cognitive abilities, or intelligence. How, then, can you have a child who is cognitively normal in terms of development (i.e., scores in the normal range on intelligence tests) but deficient in language? Further, it was noted in the previous chapter that after the age of 3, language development may stimulate cognitive development. Again, how can there be a child who is slow in language development but intellectually normal?

In recent years, there has been some question regarding the existence of an SLI disorder (Leonard, 1991) and whether the concept of specific language impairment is a useful one for clinical and research activities (Aram et al., 1993). However, research on SLI children and their abilities continues to appear in the best-known journals in communication sciences and disorders, and interest in the disorder shows no sign of abating.

For this reason, we will look more closely at the SLI population in this chapter.

SPECIFIC LANGUAGE IMPAIRMENT

As described above, SLI children have been the focus of continuing interest and research in the field of communication sciences and disorders because of their unusual pattern of symptoms. Questions about the "normalcy" of the SLI child's cognitive functioning have been raised, as well as questions regarding the prognosis for SLI children and the long-term consequences of specific language impairment. In the following section, we will explore these topics.

COGNITIVE FUNCTIONING OF SLI CHILDREN

1. Theories of Intelligence. If cognitive development drives language development, as the semantic-cognitive theory holds, or if cognitive development and language development proceed together, as most other theories imply, then how could a child who scores in the normal range on an intelligence test be delayed in his or her acquisition of language? Isn't normal intelligence incompatible with learning difficulties? The answer to these questions depends on how *intelligence* is defined.

Since the development of the first intelligence test by Binet in the early 1900s, psychologists have been questioning the nature of intelligence. Originally considered a unitary quantity, theorists in the early and middle 1900s began to hypothesize that intelligence was actually composed of a variety of unrelated specific abilities or intellectual skills. At the dawn of this debate, Spearman (1904) articulated a theory of intelligence that combined the ideas of intelligence as a unitary entity and also as an aggregate of specific skills. Although more complex models of intelligence have been developed since the time of Spearman, his ideas are particularly useful in attempting to explain the SLI child.

According to Spearman, intelligence is made

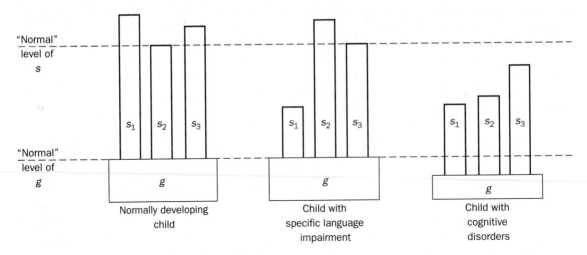

FIGURE **3-1** Spearman's theory of intelligence. Specific abilities "s¹" and "s²" presumably underlie the ability to learn language.

up of two components. The first, a "general" component or factor, usually labeled "g," is comprised of an individual's ability to comprehend, evaluate, and react appropriately to situations. Spearman conceived of this as "mental energy."

This general intelligence, or "g," does not necessarily involve spoken language. For example, a young child who sees her parents standing by the door with their coats on, following the arrival of an adult she recognizes as a babysitter, needs no verbal explanation of what is about to happen. Obviously, her parents are going out, and she is being left behind. The child is able to draw on her previous experience and knowledge of people, objects, and functions to comprehend and evaluate the situation without a word being spoken. Thus, the "g" factor of intelligence relies on memory, knowledge of the environment, and an ability to draw conclusions on the basis of these raw materials. It does not necessarily require understanding or production of language.

In addition to this general factor of intelligence, Spearman also hypothesized that performance on intelligence tests was determined by a number of factors specific to the given task. These specific factors were denoted by the letter "s" and a subscript. Thus, performance on a math-reasoning subtest would be determined by $g + s_1$, performance on a vocabulary test would be determined by $g + s_2$, and so on.

The division of intelligence into a general factor and various superimposed specific abilities is useful in explaining how SLI children can evidence normal intelligence and still have difficulty mastering language. We would infer that SLI children have a normal quantity of "g," as shown in Figure 3-1, but a deficiency in whatever specific ability or abilities are necessary for language learning. Thus they would perform appropriately on nonverbal tests of intelligence, which presumably test "g," but below their age level on specific tests involving the "s" required for language learning. We can also differentiate SLI children from children with cognitive disorders, who, according to this theory, have a deficient quantity of "g" and thus perform below their age level in *all* types of tests. Figure 3-1 demonstrates these relationships in graph form.

2. Specific Cognitive Deficits. If SLI children are deficient in some specific cognitive skills, what are those skills? What abilities are necessary for the successful learning of language? Arriving at appropriate areas for study has been a difficult process because both language and cognition are extremely complex and multifaceted functions. According to Masterson (1993), research to date has focused in three ability areas: symbolic representation, drawing inferences, and reasoning.

Interest in SLI children's ability to use and manipulate symbols (*symbolic representation*) has led to numerous investigations. Language, after all, is a symbol system and requires mental manipulation of symbols; one could hypothesize that SLI children might have difficulty with symbolic representation in general. This line of thinking led some researchers to investigate SLI children's use of representational thinking as evidenced in their play. For example, Roth and Clark (1987) found that SLI children between the ages 5 and 7½ showed significant deficits in symbolic play, in adapting play materials to the situation, and in social interaction when compared with normally developing (although somewhat younger) children of similar linguistic abilities. Other researchers have examined the abilities of SLI children to use mental imagery in performing various tasks (Kamhi, 1981; Savich, 1984), such as identifying shapes perceived through the sense of touch and predicting the appearance of rotated figures. In most research of this type, children with SLI did not do as well as their nonlanguage-impaired peers.

Drawing inferences is another area where children with SLI appear to have difficulty. *Drawing inferences* refers to the ability to answer questions correctly regarding a presented situation even when the necessary information has not been directly stated. Consider, for example, the following statement: "I called home at three and told Dad to meet me at the dentist's." Where was Dad at three? Although it is not directly stated, most of us would surmise that Dad was at home, because the speaker gave him a message. The process of answering such a question is known as drawing inferences. Ellis Weismer (1985), Crais and Chapman (1987), and Bishop and Adams (1992) have found that SLI children have more difficulty drawing inferences than their peers.

Finally, the most recent investigations into the cognitive abilities of SLI children have focused on reasoning skills, the ability to derive and apply rules from a series of examples. In this area, most researchers (Nippold et al., 1988, Kamhi et al., 1990) found no differences in the reasoning abilities of SLI children compared with normally developing children. Masterson et al. (1993) did find some differences but concluded that those differences were due to verbal complexity. In a later, single-author study, Masterson (1993) provided still more information in this area by testing SLI children in two different ways: first, children were asked to select the appropriate rule governing the order of a progression of geometric shapes from five possibilities; and second, they were required to derive the rule for themselves in predicting the next shape in a sequence. Subjects performed at the same level as controls for the first task; but more poorly than controls for the second. Masterson concluded that SLI children are not necessarily deficient in their reasoning ability but, rather, in their ability to abstract rules, which she compared to inference drawing.

In summary, the research to date indicates that SLI children are not *completely* normal in their cognitive abilities, despite normal scores on nonverbal intelligence tests. When one probes deeper with specific tests that involve complex symbolic behavior, inference drawing, and rule abstraction, SLI children do not perform at age-expected levels. Recently, there has been speculation that specific language impairment can be explained on the basis of slower processing speeds for auditory and visual information (Kail, 1994). However, none of these observations or theories can definitively answer the question posed at the beginning of this section: What cognitive abilities are necessary for the successful learning of language? We do not yet know whether the cognitive deficits seen in SLI children cause their language disorder, if such deficits are a result of their language disorder, or even if the deficits merely coexist with the disorder and there is no cause-effect relationship at all. Until that question can be answered, our treatment of children with SLI is likely to target only the symptoms of their language disorder and not its underlying cause.

Given the growing body of evidence of cognitive involvement in SLI children, would it be more accurate to categorize SLI children within the category of cognitive disorders, or mental retardation? In fact, it would not. First, it should be emphasized that unlike cognitively disordered children, SLI children *appear* to be normal in terms of their developmental skills. Aside from the obvious difference in language ability, the cognitive deficits they do evidence are revealed only through careful testing of specific abilities. They tend not to show the broader and more significant, across-the-board delays of the cognitively disordered. Thus, classifying SLI children within the category of cognitive disorders does not appear to be warranted.

PROGNOSIS FOR SLI CHILDREN

How do SLI children fare as they grow older? Do they tend to outgrow their language disorder, or does the disorder persist? Apparently, the child's age at the time of diagnosis is important. According to Silva (1980), only half of the 3-year-old children identified as having language disorders continued to have those disorders when tested two years later.

However, disorders that are present beyond the age of 3 might have more long-term consequences. Aram and colleagues (1984) studied twenty children (ages 3½ to 7 years) with language disorders over a ten-year period. They found that fourteen of the twenty still had subtle problems with the production and comprehension of language ten years later, mostly with abstract word usage and discourse abilities. In addition, fifteen of the twenty children experienced academic difficulties, as evidenced by placement in special classes, repeating a grade, or ongoing tutoring. An older study by Cooper and Griffiths (1978) reported that out of forty-nine "severely-language-impaired" children, aged 5 to 9, all had difficulty with reading and writing when tested two years later.

These studies suggest that young children diagnosed as having specific language impairments have a fifty-fifty chance of catching up with their normally developing peers by the time they enter kindergarten. However, children whose language deficits persist beyond the age of 3 appear to be at risk for academic difficulty during their school years.

Which children are most likely to improve in their language abilities? Some information relevant to this question comes from a study done by Schery (1985), who collected extensive data over an eight-year period on 718 children with language disorders. These children were enrolled in special day-class programs for the severely language-disordered in the Los Angeles county schools. Data on every imaginable aspect of each child's life were collected, including socioeconomic factors, physical and health-related characteristics, intelligence-test results, family variables, and social-emotional adjustment. These factors were then correlated with each child's improvement in scores on language tests over the years to see which factors could be used to predict language gain.

Interestingly, no factor other than age was strongly correlated with improvement in language performance. That is, the younger children tended to make greater gains. There were slight correlations between nonverbal intelligence-test results and language improvement and between social-emotional factors and higher language scores. In other words, for some children, the higher the child's measured IQ, the more progress he or she made in language development; and the more positive the family felt about the child's behavior and personality, the greater the improvement. However, these relationships were neither strong nor consistent. Some children with low intelligence scores from unsupportive families made as great or greater gains in their language abilities as did children from supportive homes with high intelligence-test scores.

In summary, the prognosis for children with specific language impairments must be considered guarded. Many of these children, perhaps the majority, will go on to experience school learning problems in addition to continuing, if subtle, problems with the spoken language. And we have no reliable way to predict which SLI children will make rapid gains in their language abilities over the years. Speech-language pathologists must continue to explore the nature of specific language impairment, and they must try to find more effective remediation techniques to ensure that these children will have the best chance possible for school success and personal fulfillment.

CONSEQUENCES OF SPECIFIC LANGUAGE IMPAIRMENT

The consequences to the individual of specific language impairment are many. As discussed above, one important consequence may be school learning problems. In many cases, children with specific language impairment in their preschool years are diagnosed as learning disabled when they reach elementary school. According to the National Joint Committee on Learning Disabilities (1991), "learning disabilities" is a broad term referring to a heterogeneous population of children with difficulties in oral language, written language, mathematics, or reasoning abilities that are not due to physical or cognitive handicaps. This term has been applied primarily to children aged 6 and up with academic difficulties. In order to be considered learning disabled, students in most school districts must present an uneven profile of abilities—i.e., some test scores are in the normal range for the child's chronological age while others are below age level. A discrepancy between intelligence scores and reading scores is also sometimes specified, but the validity of this identification method has been questioned (Lahey, 1988).

It should be noted that not every child diagnosed as having a learning disability has an oral-language disorder contributing to the academic problem. For example, some learning disabilities appear to be based on visual and spatial perceptual difficulties (Wiig and Secord, 1994). Such children may reverse letters when reading and writing, or they may see letters upside down.

However, a large percentage of learning-disabled children *do* have functional language deficits at the base of their learning problems. Specific language impairment and learning disabilities are closely related because a problem in the learning and use of oral language often results in a similar problem with written language. In fact, it has been estimated that 40 to 60 percent of all children identified as language-disordered in their preschool years continue to have difficulty with language and academic subjects in the school years (Lahey, 1988). Thus, difficulties with the language may be a precursor of learning disabilities that can restrict the individual's educational and vocational opportunities throughout adolescence and adulthood.

A more subtle consequence of language disorders and learning disabilities may be socialization problems. These problems may start as early as the age of 4, when children normally extend language into their play and begin to play cooperatively. The SLI child who cannot keep up with his peers' use of language in social contexts such as role playing, pretending, and arguing may often be left out of the game. In addition to missing out on the opportunity to practice and enhance his language abilities through play, the SLI child also misses learning how to cooperate and give-and-take with others. Social problems may be especially acute during the teenage years, when verbal exchanges in activities like phone conversations and dating take on even more importance. As a result of these less-than-optimal educational and social experiences, the SLI individual may have a low self-concept and expectations of failure.

It should be noted that not all SLI individuals will experience these consequences to the same degree. There is a wide range of abilities among SLI individuals, and those with more intellectual resources to draw on are likely to be better able to compensate for their disabilities. According to Johnston (personal communication), we might visualize SLI children in terms of their overall abilities with respect to some arbitrary standard for "normal" performance. Figure 3-2 illustrates this idea. On the vertical axis is ability level, with a "normal" ability level in the center of the axis. We will define *normal* as the ability to succeed in traditional school programs.

Obviously, above-average ability level and below-average ability level will fall above and below the normal level on this axis. On the hor-

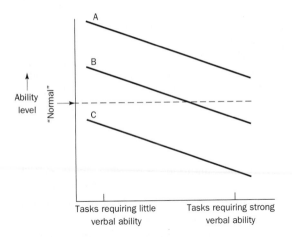

FIGURE 3-2 Ability ranges among individuals with specific language impairment.

izontal axis, a continuum of tasks is represented, beginning with those that require few, if any, verbal or language skills and progressing to those that require excellent verbal-language skills. For example, the left (low) side of the axis might include tasks such as drawing or playing video games. The right (high) side of the axis might include tasks like writing poetry.

By definition, SLI children would demonstrate better ability in tasks with a low language component than in tasks with a high language component, resulting in an uneven overall ability level. Despite this uneven performance, some SLI children are at or above the level required for school success. These children are represented by the line labeled "A" on Figure 3-2. Such children do well in tasks requiring limited language use (high ability level on the left side of the graph) and considerably worse in tasks requiring extensive language involvement (lower level on the right side of the graph). However, despite the relative difficulty with language, their overall ability level is still adequate to permit success in traditional education programs.

An example of an individual represented by "A" is Albert Einstein. Hailed as a genius who revolutionized the field of physics, Einstein was reportedly delayed in his acquisition of language

and had difficulty in his early school years (Kirk, 1972). His remarkable abilities in limited-language-use areas (physics and mathematics) were far superior to his linguistic skills, although even there his faculties were at least in the normal range or above by adulthood. Did he suffer the social and psychological consequences (limited educational and vocational opportunities) that we described as resulting from early language impairment? Probably not to a great degree. Despite a relative deficiency in language-related skills, he was able to draw on other strengths and skills to live a life of remarkable achievement. Although most SLI children do not reach these heights, those with high overall ability levels are not likely to suffer severe consequences from their language deficit.

The child represented by "B" on Figure 3-2 is in a considerably weaker position than the child represented by "A." Child B has numerous abilities at or above the level needed for success in school but below-average language-related abilities. Since the early years in school focus heavily on language-related skills, this child may rarely experience school success. She may come to believe she is not intelligent or capable and may lose interest in the educational process long before she is exposed to subjects that she would do well in. This child, usually identified as being learning disabled, has a language-learning disorder at the base of her academic deficiencies.

The child represented by "C" is below normal ability level in all areas, even his areas of strength. Such a child is most often found in a class for the *cognitively disordered,* or mentally retarded. As we shall discuss in the next chapter, the term cognitive disorders covers a very heterogeneous population. Like child C, some children with cognitive disorders have particular difficulty in language-related skills; others have strengths in the language area; still others present a more even profile of across-the-board delays. The child labeled cognitively disordered will have many social and psychological consequences to overcome, but they are not necessarily the same as those described above for the SLI child.

In considering the consequences of specific

language impairment, we see that academic, psychological, and social problems are more likely to occur when the child is at or somewhat above normal in skills requiring only limited language but below normal in language-related skills. Since the early years of school concentrate heavily on the learning of reading, such a child is at risk for developing a negative self-image and low motivation in addition to experiencing learning problems. Children who function nearer to the normal level in language skills and who can draw on their strong low-language abilities as a source of pride and feelings of competence are less likely to suffer the negative consequences of early language impairment.

SUMMARY OF SLI

In the previous sections, we dealt with only one type of language disorder—specific language impairment. Superficially, SLI children appear normal in all other abilities except for language, and this has puzzled psychologists and speech-language pathologists. Research over the past decade has revealed that despite the appearance of normal performance in all areas, SLI children do seem to have subtle cognitive deficits, particularly in the areas of symbolic representation and inference-drawing. Whether these deficits are the reason for the language disorder or merely coexist with the language disorder is not known. It has also been found that SLI children are at risk for academic learning problems, particularly in the areas of reading, writing, and spelling. Because of their academic and language difficulties, SLI children may suffer various social and psychological consequences.

THE ROLE OF THE FAMILY IN REMEDIATING LANGUAGE DISORDERS

At this point, let us turn our attention from specific language impairment to language disorders in the general sense. One of the goals of this text is to examine the role of the family in remediating communicatively handicapped individuals. In this section, we will consider the family's involvement in the intervention process for the child with a language disorder. After all, a child has more contact with his or her family than with any professional. If family members provide an environment that fosters language development, the potential for helping the language-disordered child is greatly enhanced.

There are three levels of involvement in the remediation of a language disorder that a family might choose. At the most basic level, family members can simply take the child's attempts at communication seriously. This means paying attention to the child's utterances and gestures, no matter how difficult to understand, and attempting to respond to them. Although this may sound like an extremely easy thing to do, and one that any "good" parent *should* do, the reality of a busy, noisy, multichild family can make this seemingly simple task quite difficult. The demands of a job, maintaining a household, and responding to the needs of several children can leave parents short of time and patience. It is not always easy to stop what one is doing and focus attention on a child whose vocabulary and sentence structure are inadequate to convey a message that may be totally irrelevant to the task at hand. Thus, although we consider this the most basic level of involvement, the difficulty for the family should not be discounted.

The next level of family involvement is for family members to modify their own speech when addressing the child. There are two ways of doing this: (1) reduce the length and complexity of the language used with the child, and (2) expand the child's utterances. By reducing the length and complexity of their utterances, family members can facilitate the child's understanding and ability to abstract rules. This does not mean talking "baby-talk" to language-disordered children (using deliberate sound errors like "wittle" for *little*) or using incorrect grammar. The goal is to keep sentences short and simple, particularly when giving instructions, and avoid stream-of-consciousness speech. For example, a parent who says, "Tommy, I want you to go and get your shoes and socks—I think they're in the bedroom—

because we need to go out in a few minutes, and I want you to be ready" may be furnishing too much information for a language-disordered child to cope with. A more helpful way of talking to Tommy would be to say, "Tommy, get your shoes and socks." Once this task is completed, other information can be presented.

Expanding the child's own spontaneously produced utterances is another way family members can modify their own speech to help the child with a language disorder. For example, if Tommy says "Dog run!" as he watches a dog go down the street, the mother or brother can respond, "Yes, the dog is running!" Note that the listener did not correct the child by pointing out errors in the child's language use. The listener simply repeated what the child said in a more advanced and grammatically correct form. This is reinforcing to the child because he knows his message has been understood; at the same time, it furnishes a linguistic model that the child can incorporate into future utterances.

The last level of involvement for family members is to carry out structured, therapy-type activities at home under the direction of a speech-language pathologist. A speech-language pathologist can provide parents with the materials and instructions they need to work on some of the skills or language structures taught during a therapy session. Many speech-language pathologists call this a "home program" and consider it an important way to move language skills learned in therapy into the home environment. It should be noted that not all parents are temperamentally suited to this role. In many families, the parent-child relationship is one of unconditional acceptance and emotional support from the parent, and any attempt to impose performance demands will be met by resistance on the part of the child and feelings of discomfort on the part of the parent. On the other hand, some parents are able to elicit better behavior and more structured language from the child than is the child's speech-language pathologist. If families are willing to take on this role, they should be encouraged; however, parents who are unable or unwilling to carry out a home program should not be considered unloving and uninterested.

THE ROLE OF THE SPEECH-LANGUAGE PATHOLOGIST IN ASSESSING AND REMEDIATING LANGUAGE DISORDERS

The primary responsibilities of a speech-language pathologist for any child with a communication disorder are:

1. To assess the problem and determine its nature, characteristics, maintaining factors, and, if possible, its cause.
2. To formulate long-term and short-term goals (based on assessment results) aimed at improving the individual's communicative function.
3. To implement a program of treatment appropriate to the established goals.
4. To monitor the child's progress toward each goal in an ongoing way.

Let us examine how these responsibilities are carried out in the case of a child with a suspected language disorder.

ASSESSMENT

A language assessment is usually initiated by the parents, teacher, or other adults concerned about a child's language development. Or perhaps the child has failed a language *screening,* a brief test designed to separate those whose development is well within normal limits from those who may need help. When a child fails a speech and language screening, a more extensive language evaluation is indicated.

During a language evaluation, the speech-language clinician interviews the parent for a thorough description of the problem and carefully observes and tests the child. During these activities, the goals of the speech-language pathologist are to: (1) determine whether or not a language disorder is actually present; (2) identify, if possible, causative and contributing factors to the problem; and (3) identify, as specifically as possible, the child's language deficits and level of development (Reed, 1994). Finally, the speech-language pathologist is charged with making recommendations for interventions such as therapy, treatment at home, or educational programming, if necessary. A wide range of interview scales, formal language tests, and spontaneous language analysis methods may be used.

THERAPY

Following a language assessment, an individualized therapy plan for the child is devised. Despite the diversity of needs from child to child, some general goals and treatment methods are commonly employed. According to McCormick (1990b), current language therapy procedures can be divided into two major categories: direct teaching approaches and naturalistic teaching approaches. We discuss these below.

1. Direct Teaching Approaches. Direct, or *directive*, instruction generally refers to a structured type of program where the speech-language pathologist selects measurable objectives for the child, provides modified language input to emphasize those language objectives, gives specific instructions to the child regarding the responses expected, and differentially reinforces the child's responses according to their correctness. Many of the instructional techniques in the direct approach derive from a behavioral orientation. As you will recall from Chapter 2, the important concepts in the behavioral philosophy are stimulus, response, and consequence. However, the direct approach is not the equivalent of the behavioral approach to language therapy once espoused by some speech-language pathologists. Although behavioral principles are used, other theoretical perspectives have been incorporated into the current direct approach. As we shall see,

FIGURE 3-3 An example of the direct therapy approach, in which the speech-language pathologist works with a child or small group of children outside the child's normal environment and elicits various language forms in response to modified language input. (Elizabeth Crews)

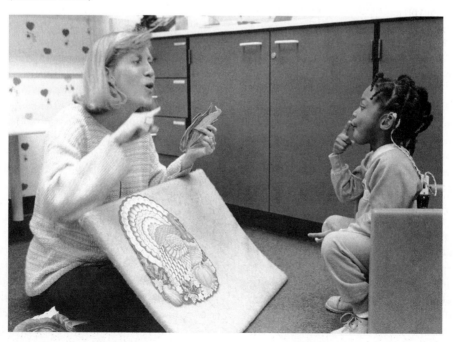

behavioral principles are also incorporated into the naturalistic approach.

The focus of direct instruction, according to McCormick (1990b), is on developmentally appropriate language forms and structures. In other words, the goals for the child are selected according to the normal sequence of development for specific semantic, syntactic, or morphological structures. Most of the exchanges during therapy are adult-initiated, with the child expected to respond. Children working on receptive language are expected to point to appropriate pictures or objects or follow commands, while children working on expressive language are expected to repeat or generate words, phrases, or sentences. Correct responses to questions and stimulus materials (such as pictures or toys) are rewarded. In most cases, this type of therapy is conducted in special rooms removed from the normal events and routines of the child's environment.

The isolation of therapy from the child's environment is one of the major limitations of the direct approach. The child is placed in a situation where he or she has little to talk *about* and little motivation to talk at all (McCormick, 1990b). Not surprisingly, there is a problem with *generalization,* or using the targeted language structures in the child's natural environment. The comprehension and expression skills developed in the therapy room may not be used much in real life.

Direct teaching does have its advantages, however. According to McCormick (1990b), direct instruction is "more likely to be used with students with severe and/or multiple disabilities than with children whose impairments are less pervasive" (p. 191). Children with disabilities such as cognitive disorders or pervasive developmental disorders typically require large numbers of trials to learn a desired behavior, and the direct approach provides that opportunity. The direct approach is also useful for very young children in eliciting motor and vocal imitation, developing an initial object-label repertoire, and in the initial training of linguistic rules, such as plurals (Kaiser and Warren, 1988).

2. Naturalistic Teaching Approaches. As suggested by its label, naturalistic teaching approaches take place in the child's natural environment. The speech-language pathologist's goal in this type of therapy is to arrange opportunities for the child to talk about objects and events of interest in his life. Adult-child interactions are more often child-initiated, and the clinician tries to follow the child's lead in terms of the topic. The child's verbalizations are expanded by the speech-language pathologist into more advanced models, and the child is requested to produce more sophisticated utterances (McCormick, 1990b). Often, naturalistic instruction takes place in a group setting, and child-child interactions are also a part of the therapy.

Despite its de-emphasis on the stimulus-response-consequence paradigm, the naturalistic approach still contains some elements of behaviorism. The speech pathologist provides models (a type of stimulus) for example, and prompts the child for responses. However, responses to the clinician's prompts and models are not demanded to the degree seen in the direct approach. Similarly, the reinforcement of correct or more advanced speech productions is also less structured. The child is rewarded by natural consequences, such as getting the object she is requesting, eliciting the attention of the teacher, or continuing an interaction. It is believed that the more meaningful stimuli, the less rigid response requirements, and the more natural consequences and reinforcement incorporated in the naturalistic approach facilitate generalization of language skills learned in therapy into real life.

To a novice, the naturalistic approach often sounds like merely playing with a child or group of children and letting language just happen. In fact, it is often more difficult to structure meaningful naturalistic language experiences than it is to use a direct approach. The speech-language pathologist using the naturalistic approach needs to be able to think on his or her feet and respond to unexpected opportunities that arise. Sometimes the conversation takes an unanticipated turn, such as when a 5-year-old on the author's caseload began discussing with her classmates the relative

FIGURE 3-4 In the naturalistic approach to therapy, the speech-language pathologist plans and carries out activities in the regular classroom that provide opportunities for a language-disordered child to use and improve his or her language skills. (Elizabeth Crews)

merits of having children before or after one is married, as her older sisters were doing.

Like the direct approach, the naturalistic approach has its weaknesses. Its effectiveness has not been extensively studied, particularly in reference to individuals with specific disabilities, such as cognitive disorders and pervasive developmental disorders. In fact, it has been suggested that the naturalistic method is not appropriate for these groups (McCormick, 1990b). Second, as alluded to above, it is difficult to structure and carry out naturalistic therapy sessions, and the sessions may be unduly disruptive to classroom and home activities. As with any type of therapy, the needs of the child and the constraints of the child's situation must always be kept in mind.

SUMMARY

The role of the speech-language pathologist with a language-disordered child is to (1) assess the child's level of language functioning, (2) formulate a set of goals based on the results of testing, (3) implement a therapy program to carry out the goals, and (4) monitor the child's progress. In carrying out these goals, a speech-language pathologist may plan a therapy program based on the direct teaching approach or may use a naturalistic teaching approach. The latter is most appropriate for children with mild and moderate language disorders who appear to be functioning normally in other ability areas; the former appears to be most appropriate for special populations with more severe disorders.

SOCIETY'S RESPONSE TO LANGUAGE DISORDERS

How has United States society in the 1990s responded to the needs of individuals with language disorders of various types? There appears to be a growing consensus that all individuals with disabilities should be helped to reach their full potential so as to become productive members of society rather than members who will need a lifetime of support and special services. There also appears to be a consensus that early intervention holds the most promise if this goal is to be achieved, and early intervention for language-disordered children requires that we identify those individuals in need of special services.

Early identification is one of the educational objectives covered by Pub. L. No. 94-142, the Education for All Handicapped Children Act of 1975. This federal law has had a profound effect on children with disabilities of all types. According to this law, public schools must provide free and appropriate education to all children aged 3 to 21 regardless of handicap. A 1986 amendment to this act, Pub. L. No. 99-457, extended the law to cover handicapped children from birth to the age of 3. The responsibilities of the school include the identification, evaluation, and placement of the student. Thus, identification of children with disabilities, including language disorders, has become a federally mandated priority.

The success of Pub. L. No. 94-142 and 99-457 in ensuring early identification and the provision of services to children with language disorders has been mixed. Although these laws were passed at the national level, they are implemented at the state and local levels by state boards of education and individual school districts. Thus, there is wide variability from one part of the country to another in how zealously handicapped children are sought out and how extensively services are provided to them. By this time, most school districts have Child Find organizations, which, as the name implies, try to find children in the community who need special services. Child Find personnel educate professionals and the public regarding different handicapping conditions and elicit referrals. In some cases, they also conduct preschool screenings. Again, the success of such programs, particularly for the child with a functional language disorder, is dependent on the resources of the school district and its commitment to identifying *all* children in need of services.

The programs available to the language-disordered child also vary tremendously in terms of quality and effectiveness. Many school districts provide half-day programs for preschoolers with language and speech disorders, combining specific therapy with a regular preschool curriculum. These programs serve preschoolers with organic, functional, and environmental language disorders. During the school-age years, these children may be seen several times a week by the school speech-language pathologist, usually in groups of children of similar cognitive abilities and with comparable disorders. This is the direct, or traditional, therapy model. Or the speech-language pathologist might serve as a consultant to the classroom teacher, helping him or her provide appropriate language stimulation in the context of the regular curriculum. The latter is an example of the naturalistic approach. Some states have self-contained classrooms for children with specific language impairment (SLI) where they can receive special instruction in their academic subjects as well as training in language and communication. Finally, for the child who has a diagnosed learning disability, resource-room programs staffed by teachers trained in special education are generally provided. Depending on the child's level of disability, the amount of time spent in the resource room may vary from a few hours per week to nearly full-time.

Colleges and universities have also begun to respond to the needs of the individual with a specific language impairment or learning disability. These institutions have recognized that some individuals with these problems may be capable of doing college-level work in business courses or the sciences even though they are incapable of meeting certain requirements such as a foreign language or writing. Thus, a number of universities accept SLI or learning-disabled individuals with modified requirements. For example, students may have to take several additional courses *about* language rather than passing four semesters of a foreign language.

In summary, society within the past decades has taken some steps to respond to the needs of individuals with language disorders by providing legislation mandating identification and appropriate treatment and by improving access to higher education. However, the implementation of these programs is usually done on a local level and thus limited by local expertise, interest, and budgetary constraints. Special programs for those with language disorders (and other handicaps) must compete with the needs of the law enforcement community, public works, environmental cleanup, and so on. These are not easy choices for a society to make, and taxpayers of the future will no doubt be faced with many difficult decisions regarding the level of services offered to those with language disorders.

EPILOGUE

In this chapter, we defined the term *language disorder* and examined the causes, categories, and characteristics of language disorders. We discussed in detail a particular type of language disorder, specific language impairment, in terms of its cognitive characteristics, prognosis, and consequences to the individual. Returning to the topic of language disorders in general, we looked at society's response to individuals with language deficits of various types and the role of the family in helping language-disordered children. Finally, we reviewed the speech-language pathologist's role in remediating language disorders.

If you look back at Figure 1-2, you will see that in the content area of language we have developed the themes of causes and characteristics of the disorder, consequences to the individual, society's reactions, and the role of professionals and parents in rehabilitation. These themes will become more and more familiar to you as we develop additional content area. If you are a student in communication sciences and disorders, you will go on to take at least one or two more courses in this area.

Despite the enormous amount of research on language disorders that has been generated over the past decades, some of the most important discoveries have yet to be made. Why do some children have specific language impairments? How can learning disabilities be prevented? What educational strategies work best for language-disordered children? How can we ensure that all individuals with language-learning problems get the best possible remediation and education? The answers to these questions will require the combined efforts of speech-language pathologists, linguists, cognitive psychologists, developmental psychologists, educators, and neurologists. With the involvement of researchers and specialists in these and other fields, perhaps the next decades will see the answers to our most important questions.

R E V I E W   Q U E S T I O N S

1. What do we mean by the term *language disorders?*
2. What are some of the organic, functional, and environmental causes of language disorders in children?
3. What do we mean by the terms *acquired* and *developmental?*
4. How do we define specific language impairment?
5. Explain Spearman's theory of intelligence. How can this theory be used to explain the existence of specific-language impaired children with normal intelligence?
6. According to recent research, are children with specific language impairment completely normal in terms of their cognitive abilities? How does this alter our definition of specific language impairment and our ideas about how to deal with this disorder?
7. What are the consequences of a specific language impairment for the individual? Do all individuals with a specific language impair-

ment experience the same consequences? Why, or why not?

8. What, if any, is the relationship between specific language impairment and later learning problems? Explain.

9. How can the family become involved with helping a child with a language disorder? Describe the three types of involvement discussed in this chapter.

10. What are two different approaches a speech-

language pathologist might use to work with young language-disordered children? What are the advantages and disadvantages of each approach?

11. What is Pub. L. No. 94-142? Pub. L. No. 99-457? How have they affected education for children with language disorders or learning disabilities? How else has our society attempted to accommodate individuals with these disorders?

FOR FURTHER INFORMATION

Bernstein, D., and **Tiegerman, E.** (1993). *Language and communication disorders in children* (3rd ed.). Columbus, OH: Merrill.

Lahey, M. (1988). *Language disorders and language development.* New York, NY: Macmillan.

McCormick, L., and **Schiefelbusch, R.** (1990). *Early language intervention: An introduction* (2nd ed.). Columbus, OH: Merrill.

Nelson, N. (1993). *Childhood language disorders in context: Infancy through adolescence.* New York, NY: Macmillan.

Reed, V. (1994). *An introduction to children with language disorders* (2nd ed.). New York, NY: Macmillan.

Special Populations: Cognitive Disorders and Pervasive Developmental Disorders

I n the last chapter, we discussed cognitive disorders and pervasive developmental disorders (PDD) as causes of language disorders. In almost all cases, children with these diagnoses are below age expectations in their semantic, morphologic, syntactic, and (especially in the case of PDD children) pragmatic abilities. Although their language characteristics do not always differ substantially from those of children with functional language disorders, individuals with cognitive disorders or PDD have much more than a language disorder challenging them. Both conditions affect every facet of the individual's life. Family and social relationships, educational and vocational potential, and ultimate place in society may all be limited for these individuals. And in both cases, the primary responsibility for improving the quality of life for the affected individual rests with education and rehabilitation personnel. Regular and special education teachers, speech-language pathologists, occupational therapists, physical therapists, and other professionals must work closely together in order to obtain the best eventual level of functioning and lifestyle for a given individual. Because of the complexity of these disorders and their far-reaching consequences for the affected person, the family, and society, we will examine these two populations in greater detail in this chapter.

DEFINITIONS

COGNITIVE DISORDERS

A cognitive disorder (or *mental retardation,* as it is also called) has three primary characteristics, according to the American Psychiatric Association (1994). The first characteristic is significantly subaverage intellectual functioning, as evidenced by a score of 70 or below on an individually administered IQ test. The second is deficits or impairments in adaptive functioning. *Adaptive functioning* refers to a person's effectiveness in areas such as "communication, self-care, home living, social/interpersonal skills, use of community resources, self-direction, functional academic skills, work, leisure, health and safety" (American Psychiatric Association, 1994, 39). Thus, our definition so far specifies deficits in both formal testing performance and practical living skills. The third characteristic is that the disorder must have its onset prior to the age of 18. Because of this age distinction, cognitive disorders are considered developmental rather than acquired. The impairment is considered to have originated during the developmental years, thus preventing the assumption of the normal adult role.

Cognitive disorders are usually classified as mild, moderate, severe, or profound. *Mild cognitive disorders* are associated with IQ scores of between 50 and 70; about 85 percent of the cognitively disordered fall into this category. *Moderate cognitive disorders,* which are associated with IQ scores of 35–40 on the lower extreme and 50–55 on the upper extreme, encompass about 10 percent of the cognitively disordered population. *Severe cognitive disorders* are associated with IQ scores of 20–25 on the lower end and 35–40 on the upper end; only 3 to 4 percent of the cognitively disordered fall into this category. Finally, the profound level, which is characterized by IQ scores below 20 or 25, includes 1 to 2 percent of those with cognitive disorders (American Psychiatric Association, 1994). Individuals with mild cognitive disorders are usually able to live either independently or with some supervision in a group home and to engage in competitive employment. Individuals with profound cognitive disorders, at the other end of the spectrum, may also live in group homes, but many are found in nursing homes, institutions, or intermediate-care facilities. They may be able to perform simple tasks in sheltered workshops, but they need close supervision. In addition, individuals with severe or profound cognitive disorders often have associated physical or neurological problems that restrict their ability to function independently.

Although not explicitly stated in the definition, a child with a cognitive disorder generally exhibits developmental delays in many areas. Early gross motor skills—such as lifting the head for the first time, sitting alone, pulling to a standing position, and walking—are likely to be achieved later than the expected ages. Self-care skills, such as eating and toileting, are also delayed, as well as fine-motor, speech, language, and social abilities. These lags occur because overall cognitive development is delayed, although, in general, cognitively disordered individuals go through the same developmental stages that nonimpaired individuals go through. The overall picture is usually one of slowness or delay in all areas of development.

Cognitive disorders, or mental retardation, is a very broad category, defined only by intellectual and adaptive functioning. According to the American Psychiatric Association (1994), there are no specific personality or behavioral features unique to those with cognitive disorders. Individuals with these disorders may be passive, affectionate, aggressive, or impulsive. Furthermore, individuals with cognitive disorders may have other, co-existing disorders, such as attention-deficit/hyperactivity disorder (ADHD), pervasive developmental disorder (PDD), mood disorders, stereotypic-movement disorder, or dementia. In general, we can say that those with simple cognitive disorders develop in the same way as non-handicapped individuals, only slower; however, those with co-existing disorders may be "different" in terms of their learning and abilities rather than just "delayed."

PERVASIVE DEVELOPMENTAL DISORDERS

A *pervasive developmental disorder* (PDD) is characterized by three classes of behavior that are distinctly deviant even when the child's intellectual level is taken into account. First, the child displays a severe and pervasive impairment in reciprocal social interaction. Second, a similar severe disorder is observed in the child's communication skills, especially in the area of pragmatics. Third, the individual demonstrates stereotyped behaviors, or unusual activities and interests that can be obsessive (American Psychiatric Association, 1994).

Pervasive developmental disorders often occur along with cognitive disorders, although some individuals with PDD score in the normal range or above on tests of intelligence. According to the American Psychiatric Association (1994), approximately 75 to 80 percent of all PDD children also have cognitive disorders, while 20 to 25 percent do not.

The American Psychiatric Association (1994) lists five types of pervasive developmental disorder (PDD): autism, Rett's disorder, childhood disintegrative disorder, Asperger's disorder, and pervasive developmental disorder not otherwise specified. Of these, autism is the best known and best documented in terms of its associated behavioral characteristics.

The child with autism displays his impairment in reciprocal social interactions in a variety of ways. These may include a seeming lack of awareness of the existence of others, no concept of the needs of others, a failure to seek comfort when in pain or distress, an inability to imitate gestures or actions, and an inability to form friendships with peers. Although these characteristics may be seen to a limited extent in the general population (perhaps you know someone who fits this description), the autistic child frequently displays these behaviors to an extreme degree.

In terms of communication, some autistic children have no means of communicating at all; others simply echo what is said to them or repeat phrases, sentences, or songs they have heard in the past. Autistic children who are able to speak often have extreme difficulty with the pragmatic aspects of language, such as initiating and sustaining a conversation. Eye gaze, facial expression, body posture, and gestures are not used appropriately in nonverbal communication. In addition, these children generally do not demonstrate symbolic play, such as mothering a baby doll, and show little interest in stories or imaginative events.

Instead, the autistic child may spend a large part of his or her day performing odd body movements over and over *(stereotyped movements),* such as rocking back and forth or flapping the hands. These activities are referred to as *self-stimulatory.* It is hypothesized that some of the self-abusive behaviors that autistic and other PDD children engage in (rubbing, biting, pinching, or scratching themselves) may also be self-stimulatory in nature. In addition, there is often preoccupation with repetitive actions—spinning the wheels of a toy car, for example—to the exclusion of using the toys or objects in their intended manner. In keeping with the desire for repetitive activities, the autistic child may demand sameness in all aspects of his environment. Such children have been known to respond with violence or self-abuse to new care givers, new household routines, or even new furniture. Some high-functioning autistic children become obsessed with a particular idea, book, activity, or field of science and focus all of their energies around that.

In general, the symptoms of autism are usually observed early in life, although in some children there may be a period of apparently normal development up to the age of 1 or 2. However, in order to be diagnosed "autistic," the disorder must present itself prior to the age of 3 (American Psychiatric Association, 1994).

Children with other types of PDD may show some or all of the symptoms above to various degrees. Age of onset also varies from one type of PDD to another. Children who have difficulty in reciprocal social interactions and display abnormal obsessive interests, but who have only mild language deficits involving pragmatics, are now diagnosed as having Asperger's disorder. Asperger's disorder typically has its onset during the school years and, unlike most cases of autism, does not include intellectual impairment. In the past, such an individual might have been labeled *high-functioning autistic.*

Some forms of PDD, on the other hand, are characterized by very severe behavioral symptoms and intellectual impairment. Girls who appear normal at birth, develop normally for the first 5 months of life, and then begin to regress in terms of social and language functions are now diagnosed as having Rett's disorder. A distinguishing characteristic of this disorder is constant hand rubbing and movement, with a loss of functional hand skills. These individuals demonstrate severe social-interactional deficits, stereotyped and repetitive behavior, and profound intellectual impairment. Children of both genders who appear to develop normally and then lose social and communication skills later in childhood are diagnosed as having childhood disintegrative disorder. All of these children fall under the general category of PDD.

The terms *childhood schizophrenia* and *childhood psychosis* were once used to describe autistic and other PDD children, but these terms have become more differentiated as well. They are now applied only to children with delusions or hallucinations.

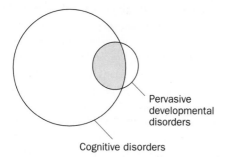

Pervasive developmental disorders

Cognitive disorders

FIGURE 4-1 The relationship between cognitive disorders and pervasive developmental disorders.

THE RELATIONSHIP BETWEEN COGNITIVE DISORDERS AND PERVASIVE DEVELOPMENTAL DISORDERS

The relationship between cognitive disorders and PDD is summarized in Figure 4-1. In this figure, the larger circle represents cognitive disorders, indicating that these are more common than PDD, represented by the smaller circle. Indeed, according to the American Psychiatric Association (1994), an estimated 1 percent of the population suffers from some form of cognitive disorder, compared to the 0.05 percent estimated to have PDD. Most PDD individuals (75 to 80 percent) are also cognitively disordered; but most individuals diagnosed as having a cognitive disorder do *not* have the constellation of behavioral symptoms (severe impairment in social interaction and communication relative to intellectual functioning and stereotyped behavior, interests, and activities) that are characteristic of PDD.

CAUSES OF COGNITIVE DISORDERS AND PERVASIVE DEVELOPMENTAL DISORDERS

COGNITIVE DISORDERS

According to the American Psychiatric Association (1994), about 50 percent of cognitive disorders can be traced back to a genetic, medical, or physical problem. In another 15 to 20 percent of cases (mostly those who are mildly impaired),

TABLE 4-1 Causes of Cognitive Disorders, and Examples

1. Genetic and chromosomal abnormalities
   a. Down syndrome (trisomy 21)
   b. Fragile-X syndrome
   c. Metabolic disorders (e.g., Tay-Sachs disease, phenylketonuria)
2. Prenatal exposure to diseases, toxins, and other harmful conditions
   a. Rubella
   b. Cytomegalovirus
   c. Fetal alcohol syndrome
   d. Fetal malnutrition
   e. Oxygen deprivation
3. Problems occurring at birth
   a. Oxygen deprivation
   b. Head trauma
   c. Prematurity
4. Diseases and conditions acquired in childhood
   a. Encephalitis
   b. Meningitis
   c. Lead poisoning
   d. Head trauma
5. Environmental influences
   a. Deprivation of nurturance
   b. Prolonged isolation, impoverished environment
   c. Mental illness (childhood psychosis or scizophrenia)

environmental influences or mental illness can be identified as the cause. The remaining 30 percent of cases have no identifiable cause. A list of some of the major causes of cognitive disorders is presented in Table 4-1. We will not discuss all of these syndromes or conditions in detail. However, in order to illustrate the diversity of the cognitively disordered population, some of the more common causes and their characteristic behavioral patterns will be discussed.

1. Down Syndrome. When most of us picture a cognitively disordered individual, a Down-syndrome child often comes to mind. Down syndrome, formerly called *Mongolism,* is characterized by short stature; round, upward-slanting, wide-spaced eyes; a flat face; and a broad nose. Down syndrome is fairly common, with an incidence of 1 in every 700 live births (Shapiro et al., 1992). It occurs because a particular chromosome, the twenty-first, fails to separate properly from its counterpart during formation of the egg or sperm cell, resulting in an egg or sperm cell with an extra chromosome. If this defective gamete is fertilized, the resulting individual has too much genetic material.

For reasons not completely understood, this extra twenty-first chromosome interferes with normal growth and development, producing the characteristic appearance, cognitive delay, and behavioral pattern of Down-syndrome individuals. Down-syndrome children usually fall into the mild or moderate classification of cognitive disorders and appear to be "delayed" rather than "deviant" in their cognitive abilities (Shapiro et al., 1992). Language, social and interpersonal skills are generally commensurate with mental age.

2. Fragile-X Syndrome. Unlike Down syndrome, fragile-X syndrome does not bring to mind any easily recognizable physical features. In fact, due to the mildness of physical manifestations (large ears, large testes in males, prominent chin) fragile-X syndrome was only identified as a syndrome in 1969 (Lubs, 1969). The basis of this disorder is an unusually thin, often fragile stalk of genetic material near the end of the X chromosome, which often breaks off. The X chromosome is a sex-linked chromosome. Females have two X chromosomes, while males have one X plus one Y. Given this information, one might speculate that fragile-X syndrome is more common in males than females, since it is unlikely that a female would have *two* fragile-X chromosomes, and the good X chromosome might protect her

from the deleterious effects of the defective chromosome. This, in fact, is true. The incidence of fragile-X syndrome in males is estimated to be about 1 per 1,350 live births, while the incidence in females is 1 per 2,033 live births (Wolf-Schein et al., 1987).

The cognitive disorder caused by fragile-X syndrome is often in the severe range, in contrast to Down syndrome, where the cognitive disorder is usually mild or moderate. Initial estimates of IQ in fragile-X individuals may be more positive, but these scores tend to decrease over time (Shapiro et al., 1992). When individuals with fragile-X syndrome and Down syndrome are compared, they tend to differ most markedly in language and social characteristics. In a study comparing Down-syndrome males to fragile-X males of the same mental ages, Wolf-Schein et al. (1987) found that fragile-X males were significantly poorer in their use of nonverbal communication (e.g., gestures, nodding, facial expressions). Fragile-X males were also more likely to engage in aberrant communication behaviors, such as talking to themselves, echoing statements directed to them, introducing tangential or inappropriate information into conversations, and talking in *jargon* (meaningless sound combinations). In fact, fragile-X syndrome is sometimes considered a cause of pervasive developmental disorders as well as cognitive disorders (Brown et al., 1986). In summary, the comparatively severe communication disorders, social deficits, and abnormal interests and activities of the fragile-X population set them apart from the Down-syndrome population.

3. Fetal Alcohol Syndrome (FAS). Unlike Down syndrome or fragile-X syndrome, fetal alcohol syndrome is not part of a person's genetic makeup. Fetal alcohol syndrome occurs when an otherwise healthy developing fetus is exposed in utero to the toxic effects of alcohol due to maternal alcohol abuse. The incidence of this disorder has been extremely difficult to estimate, since few mothers of handicapped children are willing to admit to drinking during pregnancy, but it is considered to be the single greatest cause of cognitive disorders (Conlon, 1992). Current estimates are that 2 children out every 1000 born are affected by the full fetal alcohol syndrome (both physical and cognitive symptoms), while 4 to 6 children per 1000 show fetal alcohol effect (cognitive symptoms only) (Abel and Sokol, 1987).

Fetal alcohol syndrome is associated with growth retardation, small eyes, flattened facial contours, microcephaly, and poor coordination. Severity of cognitive disorder appears to range from severe to borderline normal, with an average IQ of between 60 and 70 (Streissguth et al., 1986). However, in addition to cognitive disorders, fetal-alcohol-syndrome children appear to be prone to behavior problems such as hyperactivity, impulsiveness, and poor attention span. Language delays and speech production problems also appear to occur in this population with a frequency greater than one would expect on the basis of mental age alone (Sparks, 1984).

4. Environmental Influences. The role of social environmental influences in causing cognitive disorders is not clear. The American Psychiatric Association (1994) states that "deprivation of nurturance and of social, linguistic and other stimulation" can cause cognitive disorders, but the authors do not elucidate further on this idea. Ratokalau and Robb (1993), in their review of the literature, found that low socioeconomic status, maternal anxiety and depression, exposure to lead, and poor nutrition and diet are all associated with lower mental-development scores and poor cognitive abilities. Lead exposure and poor nutrition are physical hazards to development, besides being part of the environment, and as such can cause abnormalities in brain growth and functioning. However, can neglect and deprivation of social and linguistic stimuli cause permanent limitations in cognitive functioning?

Research in this area is obviously difficult to do. One cannot ethically expose normally developing children to deprived environments just to see what will happen. So early researchers in this area approached the question from a somewhat different angle. They took institutionalized preschool children known to have low IQ scores and provided early stimulation programs or improved environments for them. After a period of from 1½ to 3 years, the IQ levels of these stimulated children (originally in the 60–70 range) were compared with children who had not received treatment (originally in the 80 IQ range). Studies of this nature revealed that the stimulated groups gained from 10 to 20 IQ points, while the nonstimulated, institutionalized group lost from 10 to 20 points (Skeels and Dye, 1939; Kirk, 1958, 1965). One researcher did a follow-up study of his subjects twenty-one years later (Skeels, 1966) and found that the school achievement level of the stimulated group averaged twelfth grade while the nonstimulated group averaged a third-grade education. Thus the gains appeared to be maintained over time (Kirk, 1972).

Although somewhat tangential to the initial question, these studies did point to a relationship between environmental stimulation and intellectual performance. The question of permanent cognitive deficit due to a deprived environment has still not been answered, but at least it appears that a stimulating social environment can raise a low-functioning child's ability level.

5. Fetal Cocaine Exposure. A new and growing threat in our society is that of the exposure of children prenatally to a variety of illegal drugs. This threat is extremely difficult to study for a number of reasons. First, many women who abuse drugs during pregnancy ingest multiple drugs as well as alcohol. Thus, the effects of any particular drug on the infant are difficult to determine. Second, the amount and timing of the substance abuse is an important determinant of the child's degree of handicap, which complicates comparisons between one drug-exposed child and another or to a nonexposed child. Finally, the drug-exposed child's postnatal environment may be one of neglect or even child abuse, especially if the mother's addiction continues after the child's birth and her attention is focused primarily on securing drugs. Lack of prenatal care and the mother's lack of role models in parenting round out an unfortunate picture of both organic and environmental hazards to normal cognitive development (Feig, 1990).

A recent government report (Feig, 1990) mentions that "crack" cocaine is a special problem because of its popularity among young women. Like alcohol use, cocaine use cuts across all races and socioeconomic levels, although it may not be suspected in middle- and upper-class women. Feig cites reports of urinary-tract deformities and prenatal strokes, as well as developmental and behavioral deficits, in infants born to cocaine-addicted mothers. In the newborn period, cocaine-exposed children have been observed to be irritable and hypersensitive to stimulation. It has been reported that they have difficulty bonding with their mothers. As they grow older, Feig reports they appear to continue to be hyperactive and have attention deficits. They may also be withdrawn, disorganized, and unable to structure their play or relationships (Howard et al., 1989).

The severity of the long-term effects of fetal cocaine exposure is not currently known. According to Chasnoff (1990), by the age of 2, the intelligence of these children appears to be in the normal range. However, 30 to 40 percent of these children display some neurodevelopmental abnormalities, most commonly in language acquisition. In addition, cocaine-exposed children have been found to be at risk for a variety of behavioral problems, such as hyperactivity, short attention span, distractibility, impulsivity, and poor frustration tolerance. In the school years, learning disabilities and poor organizational skills have been reported (Chasnoff, 1990). As these children mature and continue to move into the public schools, the long-term effects of their early drug exposure and environmental deficiencies will no doubt become more apparent.

6. Comparisons among Causes. Although children with Down syndrome, fragile-X syndrome, and fetal alcohol syndrome all have cognitive disorders, their specific patterns of ability and disability are different. Down-syndrome children show an overall pattern of delayed development but generally have social and language skills commensurate with their mental ages; fragile-X children exhibit aberrant nonverbal and verbal communication behaviors that are more characteristic of pervasive developmental disorders; and fetal alcohol syndrome children and cocaine-exposed children are likely to have behavior problems stemming from hyperactivity and poor attention spans, even though the latter group may show intelligence in the normal range. Some children, particularly those in the mild range of cognitive disorders, may have an environmental cause for their disorders. Such children may improve markedly with an adequate environment and stimulation. There is obviously a considerable amount of diversity in the cognitively disordered population, and knowledge of the cause of the child's cognitive disorder can help the education or rehabilitation professional plan more appropriately for a particular child.

PERVASIVE DEVELOPMENTAL DISORDERS

While the causes of cognitive disorders are usually identifiable genetic or health-related problems, the causes of pervasive developmental disorders are less well known. Some cases of autism have been associated with *encephalitis* (a disease of the brain), fragile-X syndrome, anoxia during birth, maternal rubella, *phenylketonuria* (a genetic metabolic disorder that causes toxic substances to build up in the brain), and *tuberous sclerosis* (a rare genetic disorder that causes brain malformations). Some scientists have found evidence to indicate that specific parts of the brains of autistic children (e.g., sections of the cerebellum and basal ganglia) do not develop properly, thus inhibiting the normal processes of sensory input and perception (Courchesne et al., 1988). However, in the vast majority of cases, the cause of the autism remains a mystery.

At one time, autism was assumed to be an emotional disturbance stemming from maternal rejection and indifference. This theory, known as the *psychogenic theory,* was popularized by Bettleheim (1967). How subtle maternal attitudes could cause so severe a disorder as autism, while overt and life-threatening neglect and abuse resulted in much milder and more transient problems, was never adequately explained. Although it is generally recognized that psychological factors can exacerbate autistic symptoms, a psychogenic etiology for autism is no longer accepted among scientists, psychologists, or educators.

The other types of PDD described previously in this chapter have even less well specified causative agents. The etiologies of Rett's disorder, childhood disintegrative disorder, Asperger's disorder, and PDD not otherwise specified are not even alluded to by the American Psychiatric Association (1994). However, some of these disorders are noted to be characterized by abnormal brain waves, small head circumference, seizure disorders, and other problems suggesting neurological abnormality. In the future, specific genetic and biochemical agents will undoubtedly be found to underlie these disorders.

SUMMARY

At present, cognitive disorders are generally acknowledged to have physical, medically related causes. These include genetic syndromes, prenatal exposure to toxins or disease, perinatal problems, or severe childhood illnesses that have affected brain development. Environmental deprivation may also be a factor in cognitive delay, although its exact role in causing permanent disability is not known. Pervasive developmental disorders, on the other hand, are less likely to have identifiable causes. In some cases, genetic and biochemical disorders have been associated with autism, but the exact cause of the social and communication abnormalities and the repetitive, obsessive activities is not yet known. For the less common types of PDD (Rett's disorder, Asperger's disorder, childhood disintegrative disorder, and PDD not otherwise specified), even less is known about etiology.

LANGUAGE CHARACTERISTICS

COGNITIVE DISORDERS

Given the variability in cognitive disorders—in terms of severity and cause—general statements about language development and language behav-

ior are difficult to make. Certainly no pattern is characteristic of *all* individuals with cognitive disorders. Still, through the use of careful subject-selection procedure, we shall see that researchers have been able to draw some conclusions about language development in the cognitively disordered.

In observing the language development of cognitively disordered children, we first note a marked delay in the acquisition of linguistic skills. Depending on the rate of cognitive development and the severity of the cognitive disorder, an affected child may not say his first words until the age of 6; and word combinations would be delayed as well. After that, according to Owens (1993), cognitively disordered children appear to go through the expected sequence of sentence development, in terms of the emergence of various syntactic and morphological forms, although at a slower rate than nonaffected children and with less complete mastery. For example, these children tend to use shorter and less complex sentences than expected, even when compared to their normally developing peers of the same mental age. In terms of semantics, they are more concrete in their use of words. A cognitively disordered child may use the word *blue* in reference to a color but may not be aware that the word also means "sad." Finally, in the area of pragmatics, children with cognitive disorders exhibit similar developmental patterns to normally developing children but, again, are delayed in many cases beyond what would be expected based on their mental ages. In summary, *delayed* is probably the best descriptor for the language of children with cognitive disorders, but *different* can also be applied. Children with cognitive disorders have language that is often less complex, less flexible, and less functional that the language of normal children, even when mental age is taken into account.

It is important to note that not all children with cognitive disorders develop oral language at all. Some cognitively disordered children have motor handicaps that involve the speech production mechanism. These children may have receptive language skills at the expected level for their mental age but poor coordination of the lips, tongue, and jaw that prevents them from expressing their knowledge. We will talk more about this problem in our chapter on cerebral palsy.

In addition, children in the severe and profound categories may fail to develop oral language even if no motor handicaps are present. This may be due to a lack of stimulation in the environment, especially if the child is institutionalized. Or it may be that the child's cognitive development is proceeding so slowly that she has not yet reached a level where language is possible. Lenneberg (1967) hypothesized that language must be established before brain maturation is complete at puberty. According to this theory, if a child reaches puberty before acquiring language, whether because of slow cognitive development or insufficient language stimulation, his language-learning capabilities will fade. Although this theory is not universally accepted, it provides a strong argument for early education and speech-language therapy for cognitively disordered children.

In summary, the pattern of language development seen in children with cognitive disorders appears to be similar to that observed in nondisordered children, only slower. However, children with cognitive disorders may not master advanced sentence forms and flexible word use as effectively as their normally developing mental-age peers. And some severely and profoundly involved children with cognitive disorders may not develop oral language at all.

PERVASIVE DEVELOPMENTAL DISORDERS

As with cognitive disorders, it is difficult to make generalizations about the language patterns characteristic of individuals with pervasive developmental disorders. PDD encompasses various subtypes of disorders with a wide range of severity levels and behavioral deficits and probably different etiologies. However, since communication and language impairments are such a prominent part of PDD, we will explore some of the language characteristics that have been noted in this population, although not *all* PDD children will show *all* of these features.

The majority of PDD children are delayed in producing their first words, if they say any words at all. Some children are totally silent *(mute),* except for crying. Others produce babbling sounds or jargon and progress no further in oral language production. Still others appear to develop relatively normally for a period of time before losing all language abilities. According to Tiegerman (1993), researchers have estimated that from 28 to 61 percent of all PDD children with autism never develop speech or language at all.

One puzzling subgroup of PDD children, usually diagnosed as autistic, is initially mute but suddenly begins to use very intelligible words, phrases, and sentences, usually between the ages of 3 and 5. The normal developmental progression of babbling to protowords to words to word combinations is not evident in these children. Instead, their language production is echolalic in nature. *Echolalia* has been defined as "the meaningless repetition of someone else's words" (Tiegerman, 1993, 441). Autistic children, in particular, may directly echo or repeat what is said to them, or they may echo nursery rhymes or TV commercials they have previously heard. In any case, the echoed speech is rarely appropriate for the situation, and the child appears unable to produce novel utterances.

In addition to mutism and echolalia, several pragmatic deficits also characterize the language behavior of individuals with various types of PDD. At the most basic level of communication, there may be difficulty or unwillingness to establish eye contact during the interactional process. Children with PDD do not orient themselves toward their communication partners and may actually turn away when they are being spoken to. Prelanguage forms of communication, such as the primitive speech acts (PSAs) described in Chapter 2, are characteristically absent from the PDD child's behavioral repertoire. Nonverbal initiation of contact through gaze or vocalization, and making requests through pointing, may not be seen.

The mildest forms of PDD may be characterized by delayed language development and only occasional echolalia. These children may have relatively normal ability in the areas of semantics, syntax, and morphology. However, pragmatic skills remain problematic in even the highest-functioning PDD individuals. The ability to initiate and sustain a conversation is deficient, and the speaker with PDD may not use the correct intonation patterns or facial expressions to express communicative intent. In short, individuals with PDD at every level of functioning have trouble with the interpersonal aspects of communication, regardless of their other deficits.

The patterns of language functioning in the PDD population are extremely varied. Mutism, echolalia, delayed language, and pragmatic deficits are all seen, although to different degrees in different individuals. In contrast to the cognitively disordered population, where language development is slow but follows a normal progression, the PDD population shows an aberrant pattern of language development that is not characteristic of any developmental level. In general, the pragmatic or interpersonal aspects of language are the most impaired in PDD individuals, regardless of functional level.

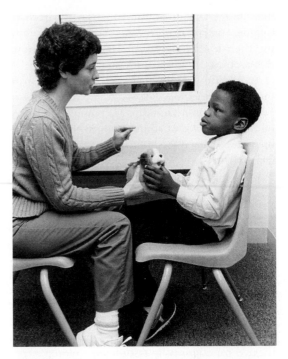

FIGURE 4-2 In the direct model, language therapy is carried out in a nondistracting and controlled environment. It may be necessary to teach basic skills in this type of environment before a more naturalistic setting can be used. (Alan Carey/The Image Works)

LANGUAGE THERAPY MODELS

As described in Chapter 3, approaches to language remediation can be roughly divided into two types: the direct approach and the naturalistic approach. Direct-approach language therapy is generally conducted in a separate room away from the child's natural environment and includes mostly adult-initiated activities and topics. Pictures and objects of the speech-language pathologist's choosing serve as the stimuli for language learning. The child is expected to respond promptly to all models and is reinforced by the speech-language pathologist for correct productions or responses. According to McCormick (1990b), the direct approach appears to be most appropriate for children who require numerous repetitions in order to master a concept or language structure and those who may require a nondistracting and controlled environment in

order to learn new language forms and behaviors. Many children with cognitive disorders and PDD would have such needs. However, in order to ensure that these language behaviors are carried over into real life, a switch to a naturalistic setting may be important after some basic skills are acquired (Nelson, 1993).

In recent years, speech-language pathologists have, indeed, attempted to use more a naturalistic approach in providing language therapy to children with cognitive disorders and pervasive developmental disorders. As you will recall, the naturalistic approach to language therapy involves a more natural therapy setting, such as the child's home or classroom. The stimulus for communication comes from the people, objects, and events in the child's own environment. Ideally, most utterances are child-initiated, with the speech-language pathologist, teacher, or parent following the child's lead on the topics to be discussed. Reinforcement occurs as a natural consequence of the situation; i.e., the child gets what he wants by asking for it, or a communication exchange is begun and maintained. We will discuss two examples of naturalistic approaches that have been used with the special populations under consideration here: (1) integrated therapy and (2) peer modeling.

THE INTEGRATIVE MODEL

Integrated therapy, according to McCormick (1990c), is "provided in the natural environment in the context of ongoing routines" (p. 271). For handicapped children under the age of 3 under Pub. L. No. 99–457, this has primarily meant "in the home." For these very young children with cognitive disorders and PDD, the speech-language pathologist frequently goes into the home and trains the child's parents in language-facilitation techniques. In this model, parents become the primary agents of behavioral change. The role of the speech-language pathologist is to help the family adapt particular therapy techniques to the home routine, to provide information and feedback to the parents about language development and their performance as facilitators, and to monitor the child's progress (Haynes et al., 1990).

In school settings, the integrative model has meant that children with disabilities, even severe disabilities, are based in the regular classroom. The speech-language pathologist and the classroom teacher then work together to provide the handicapped child with the necessary language training in the context of class activities. It should be noted that direct therapy may be used initially, with the speech-language pathologist taking the cognitively disordered or PDD child out of the classroom several times a week to the "speech room," where new skills in behavior and attention can be established. However, if the integrative model is adhered to, the child is ultimately returned to the classroom for both general education and language therapy.

PEER MODELING

Parents have long known that the behavior of one child can influence the behavior of another. This phenomenon is known as *peer modeling*—the actions of one child serve as a model for his or her peers. In classrooms, where the more easily led students follow the example of a troublemaker, peer modeling is often considered a negative phenomenon. However, interest in the positive uses of peer modeling was stirred in the late 1970s, when a number of researchers demonstrated that the behavior of severely handicapped children could be altered by specially trained, normally developing peers (Odom et al., 1985). Although far from a widespread practice, some speech-language pathologists and special educators have begun to incorporate peer models into educational programs for young children with PDD and severe cognitive disorders. Since these programs are usually conducted in the child's classroom, and since the stimulus and reinforcement for communication comes from ongoing activities in the environment, peer modeling is considered here to be a naturalistic approach.

The use of peer models has received particular attention in the case of PDD or autistic children because these individuals were previously believed to have little or no interest in other children or in the environment. In these programs, the peer models are generally normally developing children who attend half-day early educational programs with children who have PDD. These peer models are usually trained in methods of engaging their unresponsive classmates in activities and communication, and in some cases are reinforced for doing so (Handleman et al., 1991; Harris et al., 1991; Odom et al., 1985).

The peer-model programs reported on by Harris and her colleagues and by Odom and his colleagues have experienced some success in improving IQ scores and social-interaction frequency in autistic preschoolers. Most of the

FIGURE 4-3 In peer-modeling programs, children with PDD have an opportunity to interact with their normally developing peers.

research done to date appears to concentrate on autistic children who were relatively high-functioning to begin with, so the efficacy of this technique for the more severely involved cannot be determined. In any case, these programs are extremely expensive to implement because of the low student-teacher ratio (3:1) required. Most peer-modeling programs have been instituted by universities, using grant funds. Whether peer modeling will find its way into the public educational system, especially during times of economic difficulty, is uncertain.

SPECIAL INTERVENTION STRATEGIES

As we have seen, children with cognitive or pervasive developmental disorders are treated using either direct or adapted naturalistic therapy models, similar to their counterparts with functional language disorders. However, these special populations often have mental, behavioral, and physical limitations that require intervention strategies beyond those used for children with functional language disorders. In recent years, the cognitive and social approach, augmentative and alternative communication, and facilitated communication have all been used to address these exceptional needs.

THE COGNITIVE AND SOCIAL APPROACH

Traditionally, the goals of language therapy have emphasized the comprehension and production of words and sentences. However, in the late 1970s and early 1980s, a new focus on the cognitive and social underpinnings of language changed the goals and objectives of language therapy for many young, nonverbal, handicapped children. As the semantic-cognitive theory of language acquisition gained recognition, speech clinicians became increasingly concerned with the prelinguistic child's level of cognitive development and whether or not low-functioning children were *ready* to learn a symbolic system like language. Therapy for nonverbal children with cognitive disorders and PDD began to include the exploration of objects and structured play with common toys as precursors to concept formation and language acquisition. For example, speech-language pathologists may target means-end behavior for the prelingual child in order to stimulate cognitive development to a level sufficient to permit language learning (Owens, 1993).

The sociolinguistic theory has also been influential in speech-language pathologists' conceptualization of appropriate goals for low-functioning children. As the importance of various prelinguistic communication behaviors became recognized, behaviors such as eye contact, gaze, pointing, and gesturing while vocalizing were also seen as targets for language therapy. Thus, over the years, the focus of intervention has changed for young children with cognitive disorders and PDD. Although word comprehension and production remain important eventual goals, prelinguistic cognitive and pragmatic development have been incorporated into the beginning of the therapy hierarchy.

ALTERNATIVE AND AUGMENTATIVE COMMUNICATION

But what about the child (or adult) for whom oral language appears to be, even temporarily, an unrealistic goal? Many individuals with cognitive disorders and PDD have extreme difficulty with conventional forms of expressive language because of their mental or physical limitations. They still have a need to communicate their basic personal needs and preferences, however. Even for the most severely impaired, communication exchanges with caregivers may facilitate cognitive development and cooperative behavior. In these and many other cases, alternative and augmentative communication systems may be introduced.

Alternative communication refers to the use of some nonvocal medium for communicating basic wants and needs. *Augmentative communication* also involves a nonvocal medium but is used to *supplement* rather than *replace* the individual's natural speech. The distinction between these two is often blurred in the developmentally disabled population: What was once an alternative system may become augmentative as speech is gradually learned. For convenience, we will refer to both uses of nonvocal media as *alternative,* with the understanding that any particular system could serve both functions.

There are numerous types of alternative communication systems to choose from. One especially helpful alternative strategy is teaching the cognitively disordered individual sign language (Silverman, 1989). Sign language, primarily used by the deaf, is a system of hand gestures representing objects and actions. American Sign Language (ASL) is one sign-language system. It has its own semantics (hand gestures), morphology, and syntax (conventions for combining signs into sentences). In order to use a sign language, the cognitively disordered individual has to have relatively good control of his hands and arms (not always possible with those who are physically handicapped). Children and adults with severe or profound cognitive disorders are often able to use isolated signs such as those for *eat* or *toilet* to indicate their basic needs. However, these individuals do not always learn how to combine signs into longer units. One drawback of this method is that the individual's communication partner must know the same signs.

Another alternative system is the communication board or book. In this system, the cognitively disordered individual points to what he wants to say. The vocabulary elements on the communication board may be simple line drawings, photographs, symbolic representations of objects and actions, or even printed words. A number of symbol systems, such as rebus or Blissymbols, have been used successfully with the cognitively disordered. The word depicted by the drawing or symbol is generally printed underneath to facilitate communication with others who do not know the particular symbol system being used. As with sign language, nonspeaking individuals are often able to point successfully to pictures or symbols representing basic needs. However, this form of communication relies on the presence of the board. What happens if the child forgets it at home? In addition, combining words to form phrases and sentences may be difficult for the individual because of the abstractness of the linking words or symbols.

For some nonspeaking individuals with cognitive disorders, an electronic version of the communication board may be tried. This device is actually a small and specialized computer that can be programmed for a given child's needs. Such a system is generally portable, like the communication board, and displays pictures, symbols, or words for the individual to point to. It shares many of the same drawbacks as the traditional communication board. However, an electronic device may include some type of output mechanism to facilitate combining symbols. The output device may be a display of words or sentences on a small screen, or a printer that prints the child's message on a paper tape. The more sophisticated systems even include speech synthesizers so that the child's message is actually "spoken." This type of feedback, especially synthesized speech, may encourage the child to form longer word combinations and, ultimately, to communicate more effectively. We will discuss alternative and augmentative forms of communication for nonspeaking individuals in Chapter 8.

It should be noted that a child's use of alternative communication does not preclude him from participating in a regular classroom. Nor does it change the speech-language pathologist's responsibility to consult with the classroom or special education teacher and participate in an integrative treatment model. Children who use alternative methods of communication may be seen as a challenge in the classroom, but they can provide an excellent educational experience for the nondisabled children in the class (Taylor, 1992). In addition, success in communicating with peers using alternative means of communication can motivate some cognitively disordered children to work harder at developing oral language (Silverman, 1989). Regardless of how the child communicates, speech-language pathologists and other education personnel have the responsibility of providing as stimulating and integrated an environment as possible so that each child can develop to her full potential.

FACILITATED COMMUNICATION

Facilitated communication, a recently proposed strategy for establishing communication with the autistic, has become very controversial. It was introduced to the educational community by an Australian educator named Rosemary Crossley in the 1980s. The technique consists of holding the hand, wrist, or arm of the nonverbal individual as they point to pictures, words, or letters. A typewriter or computer keyboard is commonly used so the communicating individual can spell out messages.

Facilitated communication differs from the alternative communication method described above in that with facilitated communication, the communicating individual is aided by a facilitator in selecting vocabulary units. Theoretically, the facilitator steadies the hand or arm of the communicating individual, helps him point accurately, and pulls his hand back after a selection has been made. It is important to note that autistic users of this technique are *not* able to point to letters and spell words *without* assistance; but with facilitation, they appear able to respond correctly to questions.

Crossley and an American educator, Douglas Biklen, claim some startling results using this technique. "I'M NOT RETARDED," typed one 24-year-old man previously considered severely retarded (Biklen, 1990). One kindergarten student typed "YELL T KIDS THAT I CAN TALK. I NOT RETRDED" (Biklen and Schubert, 1991). "I BELIEVE ANITA HILL," typed one young man profiled on a TV news show, commenting on the scandal-ridden confirmation of a Supreme Court judge. Although numerous spelling errors could be seen, children and adults previously thought to be at a prelinguistic level of intelligence were typing grammatically correct and comprehensible sentences. They were expressing anger, frustration, and even interest in current events. But they could only do it with facilitation—hand support, or perhaps only a touch on the forearm or shoulder, but contact nonetheless.

Why? Why should individuals previously unable to communicate be able to do so simply because they are being touched? Were these responses the facilitator's and not the autistic individual's? That is the conclusion many speech-language pathologists, special educators, and researchers have drawn. The idea of a severely retarded, aggressive, self-abusive teenager expressing interest in the latest Supreme Court nomination is too much for many to believe. And where did these individuals learn how to read and write? Most of the students who have been exposed to facilitated communication have spent their entire lives learning self-care and simple vocational skills, not reading and writing. Why did these individuals never demonstrate any reading or writing knowledge prior to facilitation? The marked difference between skills and abilities with and without facilitation has made many professionals skeptical (Prior and Cummins, 1992).

Facilitated communication raises many more questions than it answers, and it is likely to be a point of controversy for many years to come. The technique has been seized upon by many parents and teachers of autistic children and currently enjoys wide use. The abilities shown by autistic individuals during facilitated communication challenge everything we know about pervasive developmental disorders. Many professionals dismiss facilitated communication as a fad or a fake, while others hail it as a revolutionary advance in the treatment of the autistic. More research on this controversial technique is needed in order to determine if it does, indeed, permit handicapped individuals to express what they know, who the best candidate is for this type of therapy, and under what circumstances it works best.

COGNITIVE DISORDERS, PERVASIVE DEVELOPMENTAL DISORDERS, AND SOCIETY

The concept that society has a responsibility to care for those with limited functional and intellectual abilities had its origins in the mid-1800s. Prior to that time, such individuals either lived with their families or were incarcerated in prisons or institutions. The treatment they typically received can best be described as inhumane. They were chained to walls, beaten, and otherwise abused. However, in 1843, a retired American teacher named Dorothea Lynde Dix became concerned with the plight of the mentally handicapped and lobbied for reform. She is credited with inspiring the legislation that set up thirty state-supported hospitals in the United States (Cartwright et al., 1989). By the early 1900s, there were separate state-run facilities in almost every state for those considered *mentally ill,* or out of contact with reality, and those who were *mentally retarded,* or intellectually limited. The original purpose of these hospitals was to rehabilitate their residents or train them in simple vocational skills, and return them to the community (Kirk, 1972).

Unfortunately, as these institutions became entrenched, many problems arose. First, those with cognitive disorders and pervasive developmental disorders were being isolated from their families and communities (Cashdan, 1972). Although some families attempted to keep contact through periodic visits, many institutionalized individuals were essentially abandoned. Moreover, local communities lost the feeling of responsibility for their mentally handicapped members. Since the state furnished institutional care, there was no pressure at the local level to provide programs or services that might allow a family to keep its handicapped child at home.

In addition, overcrowding became a problem almost from the beginning. Although the original intention of the state hospitals was to train individuals and then return them to the community, they soon became inundated with "totally dependent" children whom they could not turn away

FIGURE 4-4 Adolescents and adults with cognitive disorders are now integrated into the community work force as much as possible. (Greenlar/The Image Works)

(Kirk, 1972). During the depression and World War II years, overcrowding and understaffing at state mental hospitals became especially critical because of the shortage of both materials and manpower (Kirk, 1972). As a result, able-bodied adult residents were given physically demanding jobs as part of their "rehabilitation" and "vocational training," although they were not paid or otherwise compensated for the work. Children and less able adults were often left to sit in crowded dayrooms, day in and day out, with little supervision. Many were given large doses of psychoactive drugs to keep them compliant. Although some therapists and teachers were hired to provide rehabilitative and educational services, they were far too few in number to reach more than a small percentage of the residents.

Since the 1940s and 1950s, many changes have occurred in the treatment of those with cognitive and pervasive developmental disorders. Attitudes toward those with mental handicaps did not change overnight, and new ideas about treatment for such individuals have taken a long time to

evolve. However, over the years, parents have become more concerned with finding appropriate educational opportunities and living arrangements for their handicapped children outside of the institutional system. The idea arose that handicapped children should live and be treated as normally as possible in order to minimize their differences (Cartwright et al., 1989). A greater focus on integrating the handicapped back into school, family, and community activities gradually developed.

By the mid-1970s, most states were reducing the population of their state mental hospitals through a process known as *deinstitutionalization.* Able adult residents of institutions were being sent to live out in the community, usually in small, private nursing homes. Children were not being admitted to institutions in great numbers, being left, instead, in the care of their families. Pressure from parents, educators and concerned citizens eventually resulted in the passage of landmark legislation, Pub. L. No. 94–142 and Pub. L. No. 99–457, which mandated appropriate educational services be provided to all children regardless of handicapping condition.

At present, most cognitively disordered and PDD children live at home and receive educational and rehabilitative services in their local schools in accordance with Pub. L. No. 94–142 and Pub. L. No. 99–457. As they approach maturity, these individuals are usually placed in group homes rather than nursing homes, although those with ongoing medical needs may still be placed in the latter. Group homes are generally located in local communities throughout the state, and an effort is made to place individuals close to their home communities. Varying degrees of supervision are provided in these homes, depending on the functional level of the residents. Many residents are employed by local sheltered workshops or spend their days in community education and recreation programs. Some work in local businesses under the supervision of mental health personnel. Most are taught self-care skills and encouraged to perform household chores.

Society's treatment of the cognitively disordered and pervasively developmentally disordered has obviously changed over the past several decades, but what does this mean for professionals in communication sciences and disorders? Today, the focus of language intervention is likely to be functional rather than strictly developmental. The goal is to prepare the handicapped individual to perform and communicate appropriately within the family, the community, and in some type of employment. A speech-language pathologist working with this population must be goal-oriented, yet flexible, and able to work with other members of the rehabilitation team.

CONSEQUENCES TO THE INDIVIDUAL

What are the consequences of a cognitive disorder or pervasive developmental disorder to the individual? As is clear from the foregoing discussion, such an individual loses much of his or her independence, in keeping with a reduced capacity to assume the role of a self-sufficient adult. Even with improved treatment and better educational

opportunities, the mentally handicapped are among the most vulnerable citizens of our society. They are easy targets for those who would cheat, abuse, or otherwise take advantage of them. In addition, many of these individuals will be dependent upon publicly funded programs for educational opportunities, vocational training and placement, or living arrangements. The quality and availability of such programs cannot always be assured when times are hard and budget cuts must be made.

Much progress has been made in the past several decades to assure as normal a life as possible for those with cognitive and pervasive developmental disorders. Attitudes toward handicaps in general are changing, and recent legislation, such as the 1992 Americans with Disabilities Act, has done much to sensitize citizens to the needs of the disabled. However, individuals with cognitive and pervasive developmental disorders remain dependent to a large extent on the commitment of the general public to securing their rights and welfare.

THE ROLE OF THE FAMILY

Few disabilities require more of a family than cognitive and pervasive developmental disorders. As soon as the condition is diagnosed, parents are expected to be partners in various medical, therapeutic, and educational endeavors. Regardless of their prior knowledge or experience, and regardless of their emotional ability to cope with their child's disorder, they must learn the jargon of a variety of professionals and how to act in their child's best interest.

Since many children with cognitive and pervasive developmental disorders have physical handicaps or abnormalities, one of the first roles of the parents is to seek out and decide upon appropriate medical treatment. For example, children with Down syndrome may be born with heart or digestive system defects that require immediate surgery. If the child was premature or oxygen-deprived at birth, extended hospitalization may be necessary. Children with metabolic disorders may require special diets. If the child has seizures, various seizure-control medications may have to be tried before the condition can be brought under control. At first, coping with these crises may seem overwhelming for the whole family.

As the child grows and develops, behavioral problems may become more prominent than health-related concerns. The child with cognitive or pervasive developmental disorders may require constant parental attention to keep him or her out of danger. It is often a slow and frustrating process to try to teach such a child basic self-care skills. Tantrums and aggressive behavior may be difficult to control, especially in public places. Finding help for behavioral and educational problems, and learning the limits of what is possible for one's child, can be an exhausting task. Parents may feel that they have to restrict their own activities and interests to accommodate the limitations of their child and that they will never be free of the caregiving role.

Against this backdrop of daily demands, parents are also important teachers of their special-needs child. They must provide love and nurturance, good models, firm and consistent discipline, and reasonable expectations for their child's performance. In addition, they may be expected to carry out specific therapy-type activities for cognitive, motor, or language development. Although most parents want very much to be part of their child's education and development, the demands that are placed on them by early-education personnel may be too stressful considering the multiple demands of caring for a child with special needs (McCormick, 1990c).

Given time, most parents eventually adjust to their handicapped child's need for endless repetition and the realization that acquisition of skills will be delayed. As the child develops new abilities and interests, slow though they may be, most parents also gain an appreciation of their child as an individual with desires, talents, and strengths as well as limitations. The role of the parents gradually changes from crisis manager, to seeker of information, to mediator of a new definition of *normal* for the family (Miller, 1994). There may continue to be feelings of anger, sadness, depression, and loss, however, and the sense of an overwhelming burden.

In short, the birth of a child with a developmental disorder has a profound effect on the life of the family; and the role of the family in teaching such a child is extensive and long-ranging. Teachers and therapists need to have an appreciation for the difficulties that a special-needs child brings to a family and adjust their demands on the parents accordingly.

CONTROVERSIES

In the area of language therapy for the cognitively and pervasively developmentally disordered, controversy centers around integrated therapy and facilitated communication. In the case of the former, the integrative model has sometimes met with resistance from both professionals and parents. Special education teachers and speech-language pathologists have expressed some discomfort at being cast into the consultant role instead of having frequent direct contact with special-needs children (McCormick, 1990c). Classroom teachers may be concerned about their ability to provide the necessary language stimulation and enrichment in the regular classroom, especially for the severely handicapped (McCormick, 1990c). Some parents have been concerned that their children would no longer receive the level of therapy or counseling they received with the direct approach. And all worry that the school district might reduce funding for programs for the handicapped if such children are placed in regular classrooms (Taylor, 1992). Yet full integration has many strong proponents among parents and professionals, and their voices are increasingly being heard.

In the case of facilitated communication, the often incredible claims made for this therapy strategy has alarmed some parents and professionals as well. Because there is so little known about the type of child most likely to benefit from facilitated communication, expectations in any particular case may far exceed outcome. As some opponents of the procedure have noted, this could be emotionally devastating for parents (Prior and Cummins, 1992). However, facilitated communication has many strong proponents and, though a topic of controversy, may be around for some time.

In addition to these language therapy–related controversies, broader controversies also exist in the areas of cognitive disorders and PDD. For example, the appropriate level of treatment for individuals with cognitive disorders and PDD is not completely agreed upon in terms of funding priority. Programs for cognitively disordered and PDD individuals are expensive in the short term. The special services provided for handicapped children by the public schools are partly funded through the federal government, but they are also supported by local property taxes. And group homes, sheltered workshops, and community day centers are usually supported by taxes at the state level. As many government agencies consider ways to cut costs, programs for special-needs children and adults may be seriously considered for reductions.

Looked at from another point of view, however, programs that keep mentally handicapped individuals in their homes and communities are extremely cost-effective in the long term. Compared to the cost of institutionalization and wasted human potential, these programs represent an exceptionally constructive use of public funds. Certainly no one wants to return to the days of ignoring or incarcerating handicapped individuals. But as states and communities face growing deficits and demands for services by more and more groups, difficult decisions will have to be made.

EPILOGUE

In this chapter, we have defined *cognitive disorders* and *pervasive developmental disorders* and outlined the causes and language characteristics of each. We have discussed various approaches to language therapy, as well as general education, and reviewed society's treatment, consequences to the individual, the role of parents, and controversies. If you look back at Figure 1-2 you will see that in the content area of language, we have developed the themes of causes and characteristics of the disorder, consequences to the individual, the role of professionals and parents in rehabilitation, and society's reactions, for the special populations of cognitive disorders and pervasive developmental disorders.

Cognitive disorders and pervasive developmental disorders are not one-dimensional problems: These conditions affect every facet of an individual's life. A professional in communication sciences and disorders may be most concerned with language training for these individuals, but larger questions of societal treatment, rights, and responsibilities cannot be ignored. A broad understanding of these disorders is necessary for rehabilitation professionals, educators, and informed citizens, whose decisions will affect so many lives.

R E V I E W   Q U E S T I O N S

1. What is meant by the term *cognitive disorder?* Give both a qualitative and a quantitative definition.
2. What is meant by *pervasive developmental disorder (PDD)?* What is *autism?* Describe their associated characteristics.
3. What are some causes of cognitive disorders? Is the cause always apparent?
4. What are some possible causes of PDD? How has the notion of the cause of PDD changed over the years?
5. What are some of the general language char-

acteristics of individuals with cognitive disorders? Does their language appear delayed or different?

6. What are some language characteristics associated with PDD?

7. What are the language therapy approaches and strategies used for individuals with cognitive disorders and PDD?

8. Up until the 1950s, what was the most common lifestyle for individuals with moderate cognitive disorders and PDD? How has this changed in recent times?

FOR FURTHER INFORMATION

Bernstein, D., and Tiegerman, E. (1993). *Language and communication disorders in children* (3rd ed.). Columbus, OH: Merrill.

Cartwright, G., Cartwright, C., and Ward, M. (1989). *Educating special learners* (3rd ed.). Belmont, CA: Wadsworth.

Haring, N., and McCormick, L. (1994). *Exceptional children and youth* (6th ed.). Columbus, OH: Merrill.

Miller, N. (1994). *Nobody's perfect*. Baltimore, MD: Paul H. Brookes.

Silverman, F. (1989). *Communication for the speechless* (2nd ed.). Englewood Cliffs, NJ: Prentice-Hall.

Cultural Differences in Language Form and Use

T he previous two chapters dealt with language disorders. In Chapter 3, we examined basic concepts in language disorders and explored in some detail one type of language disorder—specific language impairment. In Chapter 4, we reviewed and expanded upon two subgroups within the language-disordered population, those with cognitive disorders and those with pervasive developmental disorders.

In Chapter 5, we will change our focus from language disorders to language differences. The United States is a country of many different geographic regions, ethnic groups, and cultures. Although the common written language is English, our geographic origins, ethnic backgrounds, races, and cultures tend to influence our style of speaking English. As a result, there is a considerable amount of diversity in the normal language and speech patterns one hears from one part of the country to another and from one ethnic group to another. Speech-language pathologists and educators must have an appreciation for the many variants of English used across the country if they are to differentiate true language disorders from regional language differences. It is this diversity in language and speech patterns to which we now turn.

DIFFERENCES IN LANGUAGE FORM

STANDARD AMERICAN ENGLISH

Before we can talk about variability and diversity, we must first know what is meant by the "stan-

dard" language form in a country. In the United States, Standard American English is what we aspire to. According to Naremore (1980), Standard American English is an idealized form of the language, used in writing and in formal situations. Standard American English is what we learned in our grammar classes in school and is what we probably think of as "proper" English. It is not associated with the speech patterns of any geographic location or with any particular ethnic or racial group. It exists mainly in the written form and is spoken only with great vigilance.

Do you speak Standard American English? You may *think* that your speech adheres to the grammatical correctness you learned in school, but consider the following exchange:

Speaker 1: You gonna go to the dance tonight?
Speaker 2: Nah, I gotta finish my paper.

If you listen carefully to your own spoken language, or to the spoken language of your friends, you will hear many sentences that are less than perfect according to the Standard American-English rules. Yet you and your friends understand one another with no difficulty and could provide more standard translations of the above sentences if asked.

Speaker 1: Are you going to go to the dance tonight?
Speaker 2: No, I must finish my paper.

It is clear that Standard American English is something all of us *know* (to varying degrees), but it is a form we are most comfortable with when writing. Few, if any, of us speak Standard American English without feeling that our language is stilted and pretentious.

DIALECT

If we don't speak Standard American English, what *do* we speak? Most of us speak one or more of the many dialects used in the United States. A *dialect* is defined as a systematic variation of the standard produced by a large group of people. These variations can be phonological, semantic, morphological, or syntactic; but, it is important to note that they are *rule-governed*. That is, the changes from the standard are not random errors. They represent a different underlying linguistic rule structure.

1. Phonological Variations. Most of us are probably familiar with phonological variations from one region of the country to another, also called *accents*. For example, natives of Brooklyn, a borough of New York City, often replace the voiced "th" sound with "d." Thus, *them* becomes "dem," *these* becomes "dese," and *those* becomes "dose." The "r" sound can also be added or deleted in various dialects, particularly at the ends of words. Natives of Boston often add an "r" to the end of words ending in the vowel "a," such as *idea* ("idear"), or *formula* ("formular"). Yet words ending in "er" often have an "ah" substituted instead, so that a word like *winter* becomes "win-tah." This particular substitution of "ah" for "r" at the ends of words is also common among natives of the southeastern section of the United States. Midwesterners, on the other hand, tend to simplify consonant blends that occur in the middle of words. So for a native of the midwest, *winter* becomes "winner."

Would we say that New Yorkers, Bostonians, southerners, and midwesterners have phonological disorders? If their speech patterns are different from yours, you might be tempted to say yes! But keep in mind our definition of *dialect:* a systematic variation of the standard produced by a large group of people. If a particular consonant or vowel is consistently produced a certain way in a specific context, and if a considerable number of people in some city or state share that particular variation, it is considered part of a regional dialect and not indicative of a disorder.

2. Semantic Variations. What do you call the sweet carbonated beverage that comes in cans or bottles? Depending on where you live, you might call it *soda,* or *pop*. Still others might argue that regardless of its brand or flavor, it is referred to as *coke*. It is clear that there is some variation from one part of the country to another regarding the meaning of words, as well as the variation in their pronunciation previously discussed.

Perhaps more notable, there is also variation among people of different ages in word usage. Chances are that you and your parents do not always share the same meanings for some words. Your parents may refer to your nonstandard use of words as *slang,* but if those word meanings are shared by a large number of your peers, they may be considered part of a dialect based on age.

3. Morphological Variations. *Morphology,* as you will recall, refers to word suffixes and prefixes—linguistic units that have limited meaning in and of themselves but which change the meanings of the words to which they are appended. For example, "s" by itself has no meaning, but if added to the word *dog,* it changes the meaning of that word from one to more than one dog. Or used in another way *(dog's),* it may indicate that the dog has changed from the subject of the sentence to a possessor of the subject of the sentence (The dog's bone).

A morphological change that occurs in various dialects in English is the modification of the *-ing* suffix to "-in" so that present participles like *fighting* become "fightin." As noted by Wardhaugh (1976), this morphological change is more characteristic of the speech of men than women. Does this mean that dialect can stem from gender differences as well as geographic and age differences? Many would argue that there are, indeed, salient dissimilarities between the language of men and of women and that these systematic differences between groups represent different dialects.

4. Syntactic Variations. As seen in the conversation between speaker 1 and speaker 2 above, the syntax used in everyday conversation is often far from standard. White, middle-class individuals who generally consider themselves speakers of a fairly standard form of English actually use numerous word orderings and contracted forms that are not standard at all. For example, Standard American English requires that interrogative statements, or questions, involve a reversal of the subject and the auxiliary verb of the sentence, so that the verb occurs in the first position. In the question "Are you going to work today?" the words *you* and *are* have been correctly reversed from their conventional ordering in a declarative sentence. Yet questions like "You going to work today?" abound in the spoken form. Clearly, the standard rules governing the ordering of words in sentences are often modified in the speech of middle-class individuals. A study of upper- and lower-class individuals would reveal that they too have their own variations in syntax (and in the other components of language as well). If we listen carefully to our own language and the language of others around us, we will find that dialectal differences in syntax are extremely common and that social class can be a determinant of dialect.

5. Dimensions of Dialectal Differences. We have alluded to the existence of many dialects in the United States. We also stated that dialects can differ from Standard American English along the dimensions of phonology, semantics, morphology, and syntax. However, it is important to keep in mind that not all dialects vary from the standard to an equal extent along every dimension. Some dialects based on geographic origin vary primarily in terms of phonological features from Standard American English; they vary little from standard forms of morphology or syntax. On the other hand, dialects based on age may vary primarily along the semantic dimension, with no recognized phonological dissimilarities from the

standard. And dialects based on ethnic group or race tend to incorporate many morphological and syntactic modifications. Clearly, it is possible for an individual to use language variations characteristic of several dialects simultaneously.

It is also important to note that some dialects vary from Standard American English more than do others when all differentiating features are totaled. An individual who uses the language patterns of one of these highly differentiated dialects is more likely to be recognized (and perhaps stigmatized) as a member of a particular group than is an individual whose dialectal patterns involve less marked variations from the standard.

Finally, we must realize that just because an individual is a speaker of a highly differentiated dialect, he or she might not use *all* the nonstandard features of that dialect at all times. In other words, even though a particular dialect has 100 differences in phonology, semantics, morphology, and syntax from Standard American English, a speaker of that dialect may use only 20 of those differences in their speech.

If the above discussion has led you to the conclusion that the effect of dialect on an individual's spoken language pattern is complex, you are correct. Dialects are multidimensional in nature in that they involve phonology, semantics, morphology, and syntax to different extents; and some dialects have fewer features in common with Standard American English than others. Regardless of the number of differentiating features, some speakers of various dialects will incorporate more nonstandard forms into their language than will other speakers. The speech pathologist or teacher who wants to discriminate language disorders from dialectal forms of language must be prepared to examine the influence of numerous factors on a child's speech and to become aware of the dialects used in the child's language community.

6. Difference or Deficit? The position taken so far in this chapter is that the various dialects of English are different from Standard American English, but they are not linguistically inferior to it. This position represents the difference theory.

It has been stated that the variations between different dialects and the standard form are due to rule-governed changes, and they do not represent a failure on the part of the speaker to abstract linguistic rules. We would say that a speaker of a highly differentiated dialect has learned different rules than speakers of a more standard form of English but that both are consistently applying the semantic, morphological, and syntactic rules they originally learned from the speakers in their environment.

It is also the position in this chapter that all dialects are equal in terms of the complexity and richness of ideas they can express. There is no dialect that reflects or restricts one to concrete thought or cognitive simplicity. There are no "illogical" dialects in which it is impossible to convey the logical relationships between things. In the words of Perkins (1978, 72), "The logic of one language or dialect is no better or worse than that of another."

In the past, however, the deficit theory was far more commonly held. The *deficit theory* stated that dialects were inferior versions of the standard, "spoken by people who were attempting to use Standard English, but could not" (Haynes et al., 1990, 157). The failure to use Standard American English was seen as a deficit in language-learning ability. Some authorities went so far as to suggest that since language reflects thought, speakers of dialect must be intellectually incapable of rational thinking.

Although most linguists accept the difference theory, the deficit theory remains unchallenged in the minds of many ordinary citizens. But interestingly, even those who accept the deficit theory do not apply the assumption of deficient language skills to *all* dialect speakers. Most people recognize that native speakers of foreign languages may use unusual pronunciations and sentence structure based on their native language and may even find these dialectal variations "charming" (Haynes et al., 1990). On the other hand, Americans of African descent are often thought of as having deficient linguistic abilities because of *their* dialectal variations. Later in this chapter, we will discuss

the association of dialects with various negative stereotypes that permit the preservation of the notion that some dialects (and the people who speak them) are inferior. However, the more commonly held position today is that all dialects are equal and that the selection of one dialect as more desirable or proper than another is done on sociopolitical, not linguistic, grounds.

7. Summary. *Dialect* is a systematic variation of the standard language of a country that is spoken by a large group of people. Dialect can involve phonological changes, semantic differences, morphological variations, or syntactic modifications. Again, however, we must emphasize that the variations seen in phonology, semantics, morphology, and syntax do not occur as random errors; they occur as the result of linguistic rules. These variations sound right to a large group of people, and thus, they can be differentiated from true errors, which are not characteristic of the language community.

As we have seen in the examples presented in this section, dialect can reflect an individual's geographic origin, age, gender, and social class. Ethnic group and race must also be added to the list of determinants of dialect. Since we all come from somewhere and are all members of some social class, age group, ethnic group, and race, it can be expected that all of us incorporate some elements of various dialects into our language patterns (unless we try very hard not to). Although dialects vary in their dimensions of difference from the standard, and in the number of nonstandard or differentiating features they include, dialectical forms of language are widely used by all segments of society. No one dialect can claim superiority over the others on linguistic grounds, and no one group can claim to use only Standard American English.

REGISTER

Another important concept in our discussion of Standard American English and its variations is register. *Register* refers to situational differences in the speech and language patterns of a given individual. For example, when speaking to a very young child, most adults raise the pitch of their voices, increase the variability of their intonation patterns, and use short, simple phrases and sentences (Taylor and Payne, 1994). When speaking to an authority figure, the same adults might use a lower speaking pitch, more monotonous or less variable intonation patterns, and standard language forms. Variations of this nature can be observed in all speakers, regardless of their dialectal background. All normal speakers use more than one register. In general, speakers rely on their knowledge of listener characteristics, topic of conversation, place, and purpose of the conversation to guide their language style (Naremore, 1980).

When you are with a group of friends, in a very relaxed and casual atmosphere, what are your language patterns like? You probably use a very different vocabulary than you do when talking to your parents, and your morphology and syntax reflect frequent modifications of Standard American English. You may even rely on intonation patterns, facial expressions, gestures, and knowledge of shared events more than on actual words and sentences. A stranger overhearing your conversation, in fact, might have no idea at all what you were talking about.

Such communication represents a very informal register. Trudgill (1974) calls this informal style *restricted code*. In order to understand a restricted code, a listener must rely on extra-linguistic variables, such as gestures, and must be familiar with the repertoire of topics and experiences that are likely to be conveyed by the speaker. Restricted-code communication is the most informal of an individual's registers.

When, on the other hand, you are in the office of a potential employer for a job interview, your use of language most likely represents a very formal register. You consciously try to use more complex words and longer sentences than you would in less formal situations. In attempting to communicate your qualifications clearly, you may strive to find the right word or phrase, rather than relying on facial expressions or gestures to express your meaning.

Trudgill (1974) refers to this as *elaborated code*. Elaborated code is used in formal situations when the speaker wants to convey his or her message independent of context. When using an elaborated code, it is especially important to select standardized vocabulary and grammatical structures, in order to communicate meaning clearly in the absence of nonverbal or extraverbal cues. Elaborated code is usually the most formal of an individual's registers.

The concept of register is useful in explaining the variability of language forms used by a single individual. In the most informal situations, a person uses an informal register or a restricted code. Selected topics, shared experiences, and nonverbal cues become an important basis for communication in such circumstances. The more informal the situation, the more likely it is that the speaker will use nonstandard or dialectal forms in his or her language. As the situation becomes more formal, the language patterns used by speakers become less restricted and more elaborated, or less dependent on contextual cues and shared knowledge. In the most formal of situations, formal register is used. Speakers attempt to use standard semantic, morphological, and syntactic forms to the best of their ability, as they depend on language alone to convey their meaning.

The relationship between code, register, dialect, and situation is presented in Figure 5-1. We can see that, ideally, as the formality of the situation increases, use of dialectal forms progressively decreases while use of standard forms increases. However, not all speakers are able to accomplish this with equal ease. A speaker who is not sensitive to the need to change register may have difficulty speaking in an appropriate and socially acceptable manner as the needs of the situation vary. A speaker who is unfamiliar with Standard American English will have problems in situations where more formal language is required. Further, using a more elaborated code (i.e., speaking in a formal register, or using a more standard form of English) may be uncomfortable

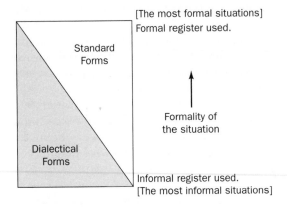

FIGURE 5-1 The relationship between code, register, dialect, and situation. As the formality of the situation increases, fewer dialectal forms and increasingly more standard forms are used.

for some speakers because it requires abandoning one's cultural identity. Thus, Figure 5-1 presents an ideal that is not always achieved.

THE ORIGIN OF DIALECTS

If we have a common written language in the United States—English—why do different spoken dialects exist? Why do people from different geographic regions, ethnic groups, age groups, socioeconomic groups, or genders have recognizably different language forms? The answer appears to be a combination of three factors: language background, language evolution, and isolation.

One important reason why different parts of the United States have different dialects is that the various immigrant groups who settled this country brought their native language patterns with them. For example, the English who colonized Massachusetts in the 1700s were from a different part of England than those who came to Virginia. Even though both groups spoke British English, their dialects were somewhat dissimilar, and those dissimilarities were perpetuated in the geographic areas in the new world in which each group settled. As we noted in our discussion of phonological variations, there are many similarities between the Boston dialect and the southeastern dialect—not surprising since both dialects reflect the original British English of the two groups of colonists. Yet differences also exist, reflecting the fact that the two groups came from two different parts of England.

In the 1800s and early 1900s, the European immigrants who populated the United States brought with them the phonological systems, vocabularies, and morphological and syntactic rules of numerous foreign languages. In many cases, this language background affected their learning of American English. Some of the phonological and semantic variations today seen in different parts of the country can be traced back to the native languages of the original immigrants who settled there.

In addition to language background, language evolution most likely played a role in the origin of dialects as well. Languages, like all other dynamic systems, are in a constant state of development. Only *dead languages,* languages which are no longer spoken and exist only in written form, remain unchanged over the centuries. Linguists have specified a number of predictable changes that spoken languages go through. According to Wolfram (1986), the linguistic rules of any language or dialect tend to become more general with time, so that they apply to a greater number of cases, and there is a tendency to regularize irregular forms. Wolfram describes other changes as well, but the important point to be noted is that language changes. We can speculate that the emergence of dialects in the United States was caused, to some degree, by predictable changes that occur in spoken language over time.

The ideas of differences in language background and language evolution would not explain dialect well without adding the concept of isolation. To return to our historical perspective, travel was difficult and dangerous in the early days of this country, and there was limited contact between different regions. This geographic isolation permitted the speech and language differences of local populations to evolve over the years. The more isolated the area, the more pronounced the difference between its dialect and Standard American English.

But other types of isolation can also occur. The social isolation of socioeconomic groups has perpetuated dialects associated with lower, middle, and upper classes. Segregation of Americans of European descent from those of African descent, often legally imposed in our country's troubled past, has helped to maintain and evolve the dialect known as Black English. Individuals of different educational levels are also often socially separate, and thus a dialect based on education can be seen. And finally, the social separation of men from women, as well as their differences in social stature, gave rise to some dissimilarities in the speech and language patterns of males and females. Clearly, isolation does not have to be physical to have an effect on communication style. If groups of people do not interact frequently with each other, or if they interact only in roles of unequal stature, they will not develop or maintain a shared linguistic style.

According to Naremore (1980), regional dialects today are not as distinct as they once were because of increased mobility and the influence of radio and television. However, even with a transient society and the homogenizing influence of the mass media, dialects remain a part of the social reality of life in the United States. With less and less geographic isolation in the United States of today, and with the increased emphasis on breaking down the barriers between different racial, ethnic, and gender groups, it may be surprising to some that dialects still exist at all. The fact that they do indicates that they continue to serve an important function.

THE FUNCTION OF DIALECTS

In many ways, dialect functions as a restricted code, as described above. It signals an individual's membership in and the exclusion of others from a particular in-group. Dialect can serve as a means of identification, not only with a particular cultural, ethnic, or racial faction, but also with the values and aspirations of those who share that background. For some individuals, use of a dialect is an important part of their self-definition, and a sign of pride in their origins.

Unfortunately, dialect can also be used for less positive purposes. Although all dialects are linguistically equal in that they are all rule-governed, some dialects have been stigmatized because of the stereotypes associated with the people who speak them. For example, some Americans consider it an insult to be told they have a New York accent. If asked *why* they are insulted, they may respond that the dialect "sounds terrible" or give some other aesthetic justification for their disdain. If probed further, however, they might admit to believing New Yorkers have a reputation for being impolite, overly concerned with money, and somewhat dishonest, and they would not like to be associated with those qualities. In other words, the speech and language patterns of New Yorkers have come to be associated with negative stereotypes for some people, and speakers of that dialect may be stigmatized in some areas. Additional negative stereotypes could be explored for the speech and language patterns of individuals from the Appalachian mountain region, from the southeastern United States, or from various ethnic groups.

Dialects are all too often perceived in a prejudicial way. Regardless of the content of the message, a listener may form a negative opinion of the speaker's intelligence, honesty, and capabilities simply based on his use of language. The words of G. B. Shaw's character Henry Higgins are no less true in twenty-first-century America than they were in nineteenth-century England: "An Englishman's way of speaking absolutely classifies him, The moment he talks, he makes some other Englishman despise him." (Loewe and Lerner, 1956).

Without the association of negative qualities with various language patterns, dialects would simply be another interesting phenomenon, studied by linguists and ignored by everyone else. However, value judgments regarding the speakers of different dialects have important implications for those individuals' social, educational, and vocational opportunities. Thus, the issue of dialect has become a highly charged one, especially in the context of the struggle for racial equality in the United States.

"BLACK ENGLISH"

1. Definition. One of the prominent dialects spoken in American society today is Black English, also known as African-American Language, Ebonics, Black Dialect, or Black English Vernacular. Black English, according to Taylor and Payne (1994, 155) is loosely defined as "a linguistic code used by working-class African Americans, especially for communication in informal situations within working-class African American speech communities."

The term *Black English* is somewhat misleading because Black English is not spoken by *all* individuals of African-American descent. Nor is it a single language entity: Its features vary some-

---

TABLE 5-1 Some Linguistic Features of Black English*

Phonological Features

1. The use of "d" for voiced "th" in the initial position of words. (Ex: "dese" for *these.*)
2. The use of "f" for voiceless "th" in the medial position of words. (Ex: "nofin" for *nothing.*)
3. The deletion of "r" when it occurs between two vowels. (Ex: "ca'at" for *carrot.*)
4. The deletion of the final consonant in consonant clusters. (Ex: "mus" for *must,* "des" for *desk;* See related morphological rules below.)
5. The use of "skr" instead of "str" in the initial position of words. (Ex: "skreet" for *street.*)

Syntactic Features

1. The deletion of copula *is.* (Ex: *It red.*)
2. The deletion of auxiliary verbs. (Ex: *He swimmin.*)
3. The use of double subjects. (Ex: *John he goin swimmin.*)
4. The use of double modals. (Ex: *John might could go.*)

Morphological Features

1. The deletion of the possessive " 's" when the possessor precedes the possessed object, but the inclusion of " 's" when the possessed object is deleted. (Ex: *It John book. It John's.*)
2. The deletion of the plural "s." Instead, plurals are denoted by articles and descriptors. (Ex: *ten cent.*)
3. The deletion of "ed" past-tense endings for verbs ending in a consonant. (Ex: *Yesterday he walk there.*)
4. The use of "es" plural endings for nouns in which the final consonant of a consonant blend has been dropped. (Ex: "des" instead of *desk;* the plural form is then "*desses.*")
5. The deletion of final "g" in "ing" endings. (Ex: "goin" for *going.*)

---

*After Naremore (1980), Language variation in a multicultural society. In T. Hixon, L. Shriberg, and J. Saxman, *Introduction to communication disorders.* Englewood Cliffs, NJ: Prentice-Hall.

what from one part of the country to another (north, south, rural, urban). Finally, Black English and Standard American English are so similar that speakers of Black English and speakers of white and middle-class dialects have little difficulty understanding one another. In fact, the overwhelming majority of the utterances of Black English speakers conform to Standard American English rules (Loman, 1967).

In summary, we can consider Black English to be a dialect of Standard American English, with which it shares a great many features. While speakers of Black English are almost always individuals of African-American ancestry who live and socialize in predominantly segregated urban or rural communities, it is also true that many African Americans do not routinely use Black English. As with most speakers of dialects, speakers of Black English are most likely to use dialectal forms when speaking in an informal register.

2. Features. According to Williams and Wolfram (1977), approximately twenty-nine linguistic rules of Black English differ from the rules of Standard American English. Some of these variant rules are listed in Table 5-1. For example, in terms of the phonological component of language, Standard American English phonology accepts the occurrence of consonant clusters in the final position of words such as *test* and *desk.* In contrast, Black English phonology does *not* permit consonant clusters in the final position of words. Thus, speakers of Black English reduce final consonant clusters, saying "tes" rather than *test* and "des" rather than *desk,* in keeping with their phonological rules.

But even a minor change in phonology can have implications for other components of language. The change in the final letters of the words *test* and *desk* result in additional differences between Standard American English and Black English when the morphological rules for plural formations are applied. In Standard American English, plurals are formed by adding an "s" to the end of most words ending in consonants. Thus, *desk* becomes *desks,* and *test* becomes *tests.* However, both Standard American and Black

English make a special exception for words ending with the letters "s," "sh," or "ch." In words like *dress, brush,* or *watch,* plurals are formed by adding the "es" morpheme *(dresses, brushes, watches).* Applying this rule, the Black English "tes" becomes the plural "tesses," and "des" becomes "desses." Rather than being a random error or speech problem, the Black English use of "tesses" instead of *tests* reflects predictable, rule-governed variations from the standard plural form.

Another prominent feature of Black English involves subject-verb agreement. In Standard American English, singular subjects *(he, she, it)* require *marked verbs,* verbs with the morpheme "s" at the end. Plural subjects *(we, they)* require *unmarked verbs,* verbs without an "s" morpheme. Thus, according to the morphological rules of Standard American English, it is correct to say *He sits* and *They sit.* In Black English, on the other hand, the opposite rule applies. Singular subjects require unmarked verbs, and plural subjects require marked verbs. So according to the morphological rules of Black English, it would be correct to say *He sit* and *They sits.*

Other phonological, morphological, and syntactic variations in Black English are contained in Table 5-1. It is important to recall that these variations do not represent faulty language learning, impaired language capabilities, cognitive deficits, or language disorders. The differences between the two language forms are the result of different phonological, morphological, and syntactic rules, generated by the same factors that caused regional dialects—differences in language background, language evolution, and isolation. The linguistic rules that govern some of the variant forms of Black English can be traced to the native African languages of the ancestors of the present African-American population and several European languages as well.

3. Origins. How did Black English originate? According to Taylor and Payne (1994), the "creolist" theory is currently the most popular. This theory maintains that when groups of people who speak different languages come together, there is an immediate need for a common form of communication. In response, the nondominant group or groups develop an informal pidgin language. According to Trudgill (1974), a pidgin language has no native speakers. It is a simplified language, with a reduced vocabulary and grammar, in which complexities have been eliminated. It is based on the language of the dominant group, usually consisting of single words, few morphological endings, and many gestures. The nondominant group continues to speak its native language with other group members and uses the pidgin language primarily in trading or in limited-contact situations with the dominant group.

The creolist theory also maintains that this pidgin language eventually evolves into a *creole* language. That is, the common language originated by the nondominant group becomes more formal. It comes to include many vocabulary items imported from the language of the dominant group, combined with the phonological and grammatical systems of the nondominant group's native language. As it acquires the complexity of a true language, this creole language becomes accepted as the native language of the nondominant group and the earlier native language dies. Finally, a process of *decreolization* takes place, as the nondominant group becomes assimilated into the dominant culture. The creole language acquires more and more of the standard forms of the dominant language and becomes less and less differentiated (Taylor and Payne, 1994).

It is hypothesized that this process of linguistic evolution began in Africa, when contact with Europeans was initiated, and continued on plantations in the West Indies and North America. Elements of various African languages, British English, Dutch, French, and Portuguese gave rise to a hybrid pidgin language (Taylor and Payne, 1994). As this pidgin evolved into a creole language, the African languages generally fell out of use. After the Civil War, the creole of African Americans began to incorporate more features of the English spoken in the south, as interaction with the dominant white class increased. African-American creole was further influenced by the written forms of English as former slaves obtained

more formal education. (Prior to the Civil War, it was illegal in many states to teach African Americans how to read and write.) At this time, according to Perkins (1978), "The older field-hand creole English began to take on more of the features of southern white dialects. Conversely, many of the creole characteristics also crept into white English" (p. 77).

From the above history, we can see that the evolution of creole into Black English has not only been affected by the language of the dominant class but has affected it as well. Various words, expressions, and grammatical forms of earlier African-American creole have influenced the English spoken by the white middle class today. At the same time, the speech of African Americans has become more and more similar to Standard American English. However, despite the verifiable linguistic roots of Black English, and its present close similarity to the standard form, speakers of Black English are often singled out as speaking an impoverished form of language and as being "ignorant" or otherwise incapable of producing "proper" English. According to the difference theory previously discussed, this is simply not true. We will discuss the consequences of these attitudes toward Black English later in this chapter.

SPANISH-INFLUENCED ENGLISH

1. Definition. *Spanish-influenced English* refers to a dialect of Standard American English spoken by individuals whose native language is Spanish. Speakers of Spanish-influenced English are usually from Puerto Rico, Mexico, Cuba, or other Central-American and South-American countries. The children of these immigrants, if they are brought up speaking Spanish or brought up in communities where Spanish is the primary language spoken, may also evidence features of this dialect.

Spanish-influenced English results from the interference of the speaker's native Spanish on the learning of English. However, it is difficult to specify the nature of that interference or the exact features any Hispanic-American may use. First, various Hispanic groups speak somewhat different dialects of Spanish. Depending on the features of the speaker's dialect, its effect on English may be different. Second, the dialect of English being learned must be considered. An individual from Mexico living in Boston will be exposed to a very different dialect of English than a similar individual living in a small town in Texas. Thus, the features of Spanish-influenced English discussed below must be viewed as broad generalizations at best, and they may not characterize the dialect of *all* Hispanic-Americans.

2. Features. Table 5-2 lists some of the phonological, morphological, and syntactic features that may be observed in the English of native Spanish speakers. First, it can be seen that since English and Spanish phonology differ, native speakers of Spanish may have difficulty with some English sounds. For example, there are no "th," "z," "zh" (such as in *beige*), "sh," "h," or "j" (such as in *jump*) sounds in Spanish, and "b" is not distin-

TABLE 5-2 Some Features of Spanish-Influenced English Speech*

Phonological Features

1. The use of "s" for "z." (Ex: "soo" for *zoo*.) This is because there is no "z" sound in Spanish.
2. The use of "ch" for "sh." (Ex: "choe" for *shoe*.) Again, Spanish phonology does not have "sh," although it does have "ch."
3. The use of "b" and "v" for one another. (Ex: "base" for *vase*.) In Spanish no distinction is made between these sounds.
4. The use of alternative articulations for "r" and "l". These sounds are produced differently in Spanish, such as in the word *Maria*.
5. Substitutions for the vowels short "i" (as in *hit*), short "a" (as in *hat*), and short "u" (as in *sun*). In Spanish, these vowels do not exist. These words are likely to be pronounced "heet," "heht" and "sahn."

Syntactic Features

1. The elimination of pronoun subjects. (Ex: Maria is my sister. Is here now.)
2. The use of negatives preceding verbs. (Ex: Juan no is here.)
3. The elimination of obligatory *do* in questions. (Ex: You go there?)

Morphological Features

1. The omission of plural "s." (Ex: many dog.)
2. The omission of past tense "ed" (Ex: They walk there yesterday.)
3. The use of *more* and *most* instead of the comparative "er" and the superlative "est" English morphemes. (Ex: She is more pretty. He is the most big.)
4. The omission of "ing" endings. (Ex: He is play.)

*After Naremore (1980), Language variation in a multicultural society. In T. Hixon, L. Shriberg, and J. Saxman, *Introduction to communication disorders*. Englewood Cliffs, NJ: Prentice-Hall.

guished from "v." This means that a native Spanish speaker can be expected to substitute familiar Spanish sounds for these unfamiliar English ones as he learns English words. Thus, *sheep* may be pronounced "cheep" because the Spanish speaker has "ch" in his phonological repertoire but not "sh."

The influence of Spanish syntax may also be detected in a native Spanish speaker's use of English. Such speakers may literally translate Spanish sentence structure into English. For example, a Cuban American might say "This is the house of my brother" in the correct word ordering for Spanish rather than "This is my brother's house," the correct English syntax.

3. Origins. The origins of Spanish-influenced English are, obviously, in the Spanish language. Its influence is clear and unambiguous in the English of individuals of Hispanic origin learning English as a second language. Because of the clear roots of this dialect, Hispanic speakers are less likely to be thought of as intellectually and linguistically incapable compared to speakers of other English dialects with less clear origins. This does not mean, however, that speakers of Spanish-influenced English find significantly more acceptance of their language patterns than speakers of Black English, only that the reasons for rejection and stigmatization are different.

THE EFFECTS OF ASIAN LANGUAGES ON THE LEARNING OF ENGLISH

1. Asian Languages in the United States.
Many recent immigrants to the United States come from a variety of Asian countries: China, Vietnam, Laos, Cambodia, the Philippines, Korea, Japan, and others. Unlike Central and South America, where Spanish-based languages are used throughout the region, a wide variety of languages are used on the Asian continent. For example, in China, Mandarin and Cantonese are the most commonly spoken forms of Chinese, but an additional eighty-six dialects are used in various regions. In the Philippines, eighty-seven

different dialects are spoken. Even in Vietnam, three distinct dialects are used (Cheng, 1987). Because of the linguistic diversity among Asian Americans, depending on their country of origin and language background, there is no identifiable Asian-influenced English dialect.

It should be noted, however, that all of the native languages spoken by Asian-American immigrants are very different from European languages in general, and English in particular. The influence of Mandarin, for example, or Khmer (the language spoken in Cambodia) may be difficult for a native speaker to ignore in attempting to learn English. In this section, we will look specifically at two Asian languages, each used by over half a million people in the United States—Chinese (Mandarin and Cantonese) and Vietnamese—to see how they affect the learning of English.

2. Differences between Chinese and Vietnamese versus English.
Chinese and Vietnamese (as well as Laotian) are *monosyllabic languages,* meaning each written character stands for a single syllable. Most English words, by contrast, are polysyllabic. Native speakers of Chinese and Vietnamese often have difficulty in correctly producing and accenting polysyllabic words. For example, they might pronounce *television* "tel-EH-vision," with the accent on the second syllable (Cheng, 1987).

In addition, Chinese and Vietnamese are *tonal languages,* meaning that the pitch of the voice when saying a word—high, low, middle, rising, or falling—can change the meaning of the word. For example, in the Cantonese dialect, the syllable "yi," when said with a high pitch, means *clothes.* It can also mean *chair* if said with a high but rising pitch; *meaning* if said with a steady mid level pitch; *child* if said with a low to falling pitch; *ear* if said with a low to rising pitch; and *two* if said with a steady, low pitch. In short, speakers of Chinese and Vietnamese learn to use vocal pitch to give a single syllable many meanings.

By contrast, in English, vocal pitch is used to signal emphasis. Speakers of English tend to raise the pitch of the most important word in a sentence. For example, if an English-speaking child was asked, "Who knocked over the lamp?" the child's response might be "The dog did it," with the word *dog* said in a higher pitch than the other words in the sentence. We also use rising intonation to denote a question ("Are you going to school?") and falling intonation to denote a statement ("Yes, I am going.") Needless to say, the very different functions of vocal pitch in Chinese and Vietnamese compared with English can make the learning of English difficult for native speakers of those languages. Speakers of these languages are often said to have a "singsong" quality to their speech that is a direct result of their difficulty in learning to use vocal pitch for emphasis.

3. Features of Chinese- or Vietnamese-Influenced English. Some of the phonological, morphological, and syntactic features of the English of native speakers of Chinese and Vietnamese can be seen in Table 5-3. We can see that final consonants in English words are a problem for such speakers, as well as the "l" and "r" sounds and "th." In terms of morphology and syntax, omission of plural markers, past-tense endings, and auxiliary verbs can be noted (Cheng, 1987). These specific difficulties arise as the native speaker of one language attempts to learn a new language with very different phonological, morphological, and syntactic rules.

Despite the linguistic difficulties of learning a

TABLE 5-3 Some Features of Chinese- and Vietnamese-Influenced English Speech*

Phonological Features

1. The use of "s" for "th."
2. The omission of final consonants.
3. For speakers of Mandarin and Cantonese, the use of "f" for "v"; and an "uh" added to blends ("buh-lue") or to the ends of words ("good-uh").
4. For speakers of Vietnamese, the use of "sh" for "ch," "b" for "p," and "th-d" for "j."
5. For speakers of Mandarin and Cantonese, difficulty with discrimination of "l" and "r". Mandarin speakers are likely to use "r" and "l" interchangeably, while Cantonese speakers are likely to substitute "l" for "r."

Morphological Features

1. The omission of plural "s." (Ex: many dog.)
2. The omission of *is* and *are* or use of an incorrect form. (Ex.: I going; I is walking.)
3. The omission of *do* or use of an incorrect form. (Ex.: He not want to eat; he do not go to school there.)

Syntactic Features

1. The incorrect ordering of words in interrogative sentences. (Ex.: You are there?)
2. The omission of articles, such as *the* and *a*.
4. The omission of "ed" in past tense. (Ex.: He walk yesterday.)
5. The misordering of subject-object-verb relationship. (Ex.: I wrote out it.)

*After Cheng, L. (1987). Cross-cultural and linguistic considerations in working with Asian populations. *Asha*, June, 33–38.

second language, the pragmatic aspects of communicating in middle-class American culture may be even more problematic for an individual from a traditional Asian culture. Such speakers, particularly if they are from non-Western or non-middle-class cultural groups, tend to have different rules and expectations for behavior in communication situations. Who is permitted to speak to whom, under what circumstances, and about which topics are issues that vary from culture to culture. Perhaps more than differences in language *form*, differences in language *use* between one group and another interfere with communication in a multicultural society.

CULTURAL DIFFERENCES IN LANGUAGE USE

If you were to go over to an adult friend's house to watch a basketball game and your friend's 3-year-old child was present, what kind of behavior might you expect from that child? If you are from a middle-class background, chances are that you would expect the child to talk to you. He or she might ask you your name, show you some toys, and try to engage you in play. You, in turn, might ask the child questions such as, "What do you do with these?" when shown various toys, even though you knew the answers quite well. By your questions, you would provide the child with an opportunity to show off, and the child would expect your attention and interaction. In fact, if there were no other caretaker for the child once the basketball game started, you and your friend might have difficulty watching because of the child's demands for continued conversation.

This is typical language use in middle-class households. Language is used by adults to provide models for children, to instruct, to maintain contact, and to discipline (Naremore, 1980). Children come to expect that they will interact with adults, answer whatever questions are asked, and initiate new topics. However, children in other cultural groups are not always exposed to this type

of language use. For example, in lower socioeconomic households of rural black individuals, Ward (1971) found very different interaction patterns between adults and children. In this cultural milieu, children were expected to speak to adults only when they had something relevant or important to say that the adult did not already know. A child who asked questions with obvious answers, such as "What's that?" when he saw a dog, was likely to be considered rude or badly behaved. Ward observed that these children were not expected to "perform" linguistically or to talk for the sake of talking. In fact, in collecting her language samples, she had difficulty getting them to talk into her tape recorder.

In considering Ward's dilemma, Naremore (1980) hypothesizes the following rules governing the communication behavior of lower-class children:

1. *Adults do not ask questions to which they already know the answers.*
2. *If they do, it is some kind of trick, and the obvious answer must not be right.*
3. *If you can't figure out the right answer, keep quiet* (p. 206).

The adult interviewer, on the other hand, was operating under a set of rules appropriate to the middle class.

1. *Children must answer whatever questions you ask.*
2. *If you want quick answers, ask easy questions.*
3. *A child who does not answer easy questions is of low intelligence or rude or both* (p. 206).

It is clear that two groups of people can share the same phonology, semantics, morphology, and syntax and still have trouble communicating because of different expectations about the communication situation.

In contrast to the relatively constrained adult-child interactions observed by Ward (1971), very active child-child interactions are described by Perkins (1978) among lower-class urban black children. According to Perkins, young children in this cultural group are often cared for by older children and form strong and early attachments to their peer groups. Peer-group language is characterized by intense verbal competition, dynamic and demonstrative public behavior, and verbal strategies and games aimed at controlling both peers and authority figures. It is not difficult to imagine that these communication behaviors, both acceptable and status-enhancing in the child's home environment, are not looked upon favorably in middle-class schools.

In another example of cultural differences in language use, Saville-Troike (1986) reports on an interchange between a white, middle-class teacher on a Navaho reservation and the father of one of her Navaho pupils. As the man came into the classroom, he did not speak. Nor did he respond when the teacher introduced herself by name. When the teacher asked if he was there to pick up his son, the man replied yes. The teacher continued talking about the child, partly to cover her confusion and embarrassment about the man's silence. As the man and boy turned to leave, she said "Bye-bye." Again, there was no response (Saville-Troike, 1986).

From the teacher's point of view, this was a very unsatisfactory communication event. According to her rules of behavior, it is polite to introduce yourself to a stranger, to state your business, and to engage in small talk while waiting for someone. The man's failure to respond to her efforts to smooth over the situation seemed, to her, to indicate that he was critical or unfriendly.

The Navaho father had a different interpretation of the situation. From his point of view, he had maintained a respectful silence, which the teacher did not return. Since there is a Navaho taboo about saying one's own name, her stating her own name with the anticipation that he would do the same was very disquieting to him. Furthermore, her continued talking when no talk seemed required seemed, to him, to indicate that she was rude and presumptuous.

In summary, we can see that despite a common language, differences in the rules governing the use of language can result in misunderstandings between individuals of different cultures. In fact, differences in language *use* may create more barriers to communication than do differences in language *form*. We can usually "read through" the semantic, morphological, and syntactic variations of another speaker, no matter how different his dialect. However, if the speaker behaves in a way that seems to us rude, uninterested, or even overly friendly, that message will almost certainly override the speaker's actual words. Only knowledge of other cultures and their behavior patterns can help keep the lines of communication open and free of negative stereotypes.

THE CONSEQUENCES OF DIFFERENCES

As we have discussed above, an individual who uses dialectal forms of language often experiences negative consequences, particularly if he or she is from a non-middle-class cultural group. The phonological, semantic, morphological, and syntactic variations that occur in the individual's dialect may be seen by the majority as a language disorder or speech disorder. If the dialect is a stigmatized one, these linguistic differences may be interpreted as indicative of low intelligence or a reduced capacity for language acquisition. Also, the individual who does not conform to the behavioral expectations of the majority in a communication situation is likely to be labeled socially inept.

In the late 1960s and early 1970s, the consequences of using Black English in the educational setting was investigated by a number of researchers. The question was of particular importance at that time because school integration in the nation's major cities was finally occurring as a result of court-sanctioned busing. Many white urban teachers who had never been exposed to the speech and language patterns of inner-city African-American children suddenly found these children in their classrooms. Researchers became interested in the teachers' attitudes toward Black English and the students who spoke it.

Early studies in this area showed that when teachers or prospective teachers heard tapes of children speaking Black English, negative ratings of the child's language ability, effectiveness, and even intelligence ensued (see, for example, Guskin, 1970, and Hewitt, 1971). Tapes of African-American children who spoke a more middle-class dialect did not produce this result. More recently, Taylor (1983) has provided a summation of research findings on teacher attitudes toward nonstandard dialects. He reported that major research in this area revealed a wide range of teacher (and student) attitudes, ranging from very positive to very negative. However, he goes on to question the validity of the research. He notes that it may be impossible to distinguish between the attitudes the subjects *professed* to hold and what they truly believed and felt, especially after the issue of dialect had become politicized.

In addition to research on teacher attitudes, Williams (1976) reported on some research designed to investigate the attitudes of employers toward speakers of various dialects. Employers were asked to rate the speech samples of potential employees and to evalute their fitness for certain positions (executive, public relations, skilled technician, sales, clerical, and manual labor). The samples employers were given to listen to included a speaker of relatively Standard American English, a speaker of Black English, a white speaker with a southern dialect, and a speaker of Spanish-influenced English. Results of this study indicated, to the surprise of the researchers, that language usage and dialect did not have a major effect on the ratings of potential employers. There was one exception to this finding, however: The employer's perception of the interviewee's language had "greater predictive value when the decision is being made relative to a white-collar or supervisory type of position than when it is relative to a clerical or technical position" (p.118). In other words, the speaker of Standard American English was seen as being more qualified for a managerial position than the other applicants.

What do these research results mean to the speaker of a dialect? For speakers of Black English, there is an indication that at least some teachers will react negatively to dialect use. This could result in limited expectations for the child and perhaps fewer educational opportunities. In the job market, dialect does not appear to be a major obstacle at the lower end of the career ladder, but it could be a hindrance in achieving a supervisory or managerial position.

Given their differences in language form and use, compounded by negative attitudes toward them, it is not surprising that speakers of dialect sometimes have difficulty benefiting from the traditional instructional methods and strategies of the public schools. The public schools are geared toward white, American middle-class children, steeped in middle-class values and culture, who already speak an accepted variant of Standard English. Familiarity with primarily dialectal forms may make reading and spelling in Standard American English more difficult. Further, cultural differences in language use can cause difficulty for children from nonmainstream groups. For example, middle-class children who regularly converse with adults and use language to "show off" for them are better able to interact with the teacher and conform to her expectations than are lower-class children who are silent around their elders, speak only when spoken to, and converse primarily with their peers. Finally, children who are given subtle messages that their manner of speech and behavior is somehow "wrong" are not likely to develop the self-confidence needed to master unfamiliar linguistic and communication rules, let alone academic subjects. Far from being simply "interesting" and inconsequential, dialect can have important implications for an individual's social acceptance, academic achievement, and later vocational achievement as well.

TO CHANGE OR NOT TO CHANGE?

What should the position of educators be when faced with students' dialectal differences? What should the position of the speech-language pathologist be when asked to provide language therapy for speakers of dialect? These questions, faced by education professionals daily in the public schools of the United States, have been answered in a number of ways.

LANGUAGE DIFFERENCES IN THE PUBLIC SCHOOLS

In the 1970s and 1980s, a number of judicial and legislative precedents provided a conceptual framework for language and dialect issues in the public schools. In the landmark decision *Lau v. Nichols* (1974), the U.S. Supreme Court ruled that the exclusive use of English in the San Francisco public schools violated the civil rights of Chinese students who could not speak English. The court agreed with the plaintiffs, who argued that the students were being deprived of an "equal education" (Taylor, 1986). According to Taylor, *Lau v. Nichols* led to the passage in 1976 of the Bilingual Education Act, in which schools were obligated to provide transitional educational programs in the student's native language.

In 1978, a U.S. district judge in Michigan extended *Lau v. Nichols* by ruling that a school district had the legal obligation to provide information to teachers on the dialect spoken by minority students in the district and that teachers had the obligation to take dialect use into account in order to teach the reading and writing of Standard English more effectively (Chambers, 1983). The case, formally titled *Martin Luther King Junior Elementary School Children v. Ann Arbor School District Board,* has since become known simply as the Ann Arbor decision.

The suit was brought against the school district by the families of fifteen African-American children. The parents complained that their children were being inappropriately referred for special education programs (learning disabilities, emotional impairment) when their academic difficulties, in fact, stemmed from cultural, social, and economic differences that the teachers were not aware of. As a result of this decision, teachers in Ann Arbor, Michigan, were provided with twenty hours of instruction in Black English and

how to use it to facilitate the teaching of reading to their African-American students.

Since the Ann Arbor decision was never appealed and thus never came before the U.S. Supreme Court, its effect was somewhat limited. Many states and school districts continued to ignore the issue of dialect. However, this decision did raise national awareness of the legitimacy of dialects as language forms, the need for teachers to take language differences into account in their instructional strategies, and the problems speakers of dialects might have in achieving academic success.

At this time, there is tremendous variability in the extent to which school districts acknowledge language differences and dialect issues and the extent to which such awareness affects classroom instruction. Part of this variability is due to the ambivalence of both parents and teachers on the extent to which instructional programs should incorporate dialect. Although some extension of trends that began in the 1970s has been attempted (for example, writing textbooks in Black English to teach lower-class African-American children using a more bilingual strategy), the effort has generally met with strong parental disapproval. Covington (1976) reported that the minority parents in her study did not want specific language-intervention programs, bilingual education strategies, or textbooks written in Black English because they did not want their children to be singled out as disadvantaged. They were, in fact, adamant that their children learn Standard English. They wanted their children's teachers to speak Standard English at all times and to apply the same standards for written work to all students.

The judicial precedents of the 1970s, plus the attitudes of minority parents, provide a clear mandate to teach speakers of all language and dialect backgrounds to read and write Standard American English. However, the mandate to teach students to speak Standard English is far less clear. In fact, the parents in Covington's (1976) study requested that their children not be reprimanded for speaking Black English in school. This presents an interesting dilemma because children tend to write the way they speak. That is, if they use dialectal phonological, morphological, and syntactic forms in their oral language, they tend to do so in their written language (Haynes et al., 1990). So the lack of emphasis on oral Standard English may actually inhibit the student's mastery of written Standard English.

In the best of all possible worlds, all students and teachers would see Standard American English simply as the most formal register of any English dialect, to be used for infrequent but important formal speaking situations. Dialectal variations would be viewed as appropriate, and indeed desirable, in informal speaking situations. In an ideal world, there would be no competition between dialectal and standard forms. Instead, there would be the complementary relationship pictured in Figure 5-1. All students would naturally become "bidialectal," or able to "code-switch" as the situation demanded.

Unfortunately, in the world as it is, Standard American English is usually presented as the only correct form of language, regardless of the situation. Although teachers themselves may use their own class-based or regional dialects, they often convey the impression that their students' dialects are nothing more than erroneous versions of Standard English, which should be corrected if possible. In response, students become resistant to using standard forms because it would appear to repudiate their background and culture. The stage is thus set for a struggle in which both students and teachers emerge as losers.

Haynes et al. (1990) specifically suggested that classroom teachers accept the fact that dialects are not "disorders," that they are, in fact, important parts of a student's cultural identity, and that "a greater understanding of social dialects will benefit all the people involved in this thorny issue" (p. 170). They further suggested that teachers provide good models of spoken Standard English, that they specify their grading requirements for written work, that they allow students to speak at least some of the time in their native dialect, and that they try to incorporate examples of a variety of social dialects when teaching in appropriate areas (such as drama or music).

The educational system in a multicultural society has the important responsibility of educating *all* children, and preparing them to compete in a larger society. At present, mastery of Standard American English is an important prerequisite for entrance into this larger society, and there is no indication that its importance will diminish in the near future. Many questions remain to be answered regarding the best methods to teach Standard English and how to encourage bidialectalism in culturally diverse populations. As minority populations in the United States continue to grow in number and economic importance, these questions will become more critical.

LANGUAGE DIFFERENCES AND THE SPEECH-LANGUAGE PATHOLOGIST

What should a speech–language pathologist do when confronted with a dialect-speaking child in a white middle-class school? Should this child be seen for therapy to learn standard language forms, or should the child not be considered for services? In 1983, the American Speech-Language-Hearing Association (ASHA) issued a position statement to help guide speech–language pathologists in making such judgments (Battles et al., 1983). According to this document, the speech–language pathologist must be familiar enough with the child's dialect to be able to distinguish a dialectal language pattern from an actual language or speech disorder. The primary responsibility of the speech–language pathologist should be to provide services to children with language delays in *both* their dialect *and* in Standard English and to children with articulation, fluency, voice, and hearing disorders. However, services may be provided to speakers of dialect on an elective basis, as long as the integrity of the individual's first dialect or language is not compromised, and as long as it is clear that Standard English is being taught as a situation-specific language form.

The ASHA position attempts to find the delicate middle ground between acknowledging that speaking a variant dialect of English is not a language disorder, while at the same time acknowledging that speakers of dialects might have a legitimate interest in acquiring standard language forms to enhance their educational and vocational opportunities. Respect for other cultures and language forms, however, will not universally occur simply because a position paper recommended it. It is up to teachers and speech-language pathologists to educate themselves on dialect issues and to treat such situations objectively and without prejudice.

SUMMARY

The issue of dialect and cultural language differences is one that touches a broad segment of American society. All of us can find examples in our own speech of variations in phonology, semantics, morphology, or syntax that do not conform to the correct form of English we learned in our grammar classes. We are more likely to use these variations in informal rather than formal situations, but in most cases, our variations are well tolerated by others. However, some dialects have become associated with negative stereotypes, and this has created problems in many areas of society. Speakers of various dialects, especially if they are from culturally different populations, run the risk of limited educational and vocational opportunities. The public schools have not been completely successful in ensuring that all students acquire a basic competency in Standard American English, and there is even some dispute as to whether or not they can or should enforce such a standard, particularly in spoken language. Speech-language pathologists have taken on the responsibility of working with speakers of dialect who want to learn more standard forms of English, but only on an elective basis after those with true communication disorders have been served. With growing multiculturalism in our society, the issue of dialect, especially in the educational setting, is likely to be one of controversy for the foreseeable future.

R E V I E W   Q U E S T I O N S

1. What do we mean by *Standard American English?*
2. What do we mean by *dialect?* Why do different dialects exist?
3. What is meant by *register?*
4. What is *Black English?* Describe some of its features.
5. What are the linguistic origins of Black English?
6. Describe some of the features of Spanish-influenced English.
7. Why do native speakers of Chinese or Vietnamese often have difficulty in using the correct vocal pitch to signal emphasis or to denote a question in English?
8. What is meant by "cultural differences in language use?" Why did we say that these differences may interfere with communication to a greater degree than dialects?
9. What are some of the consequences of speaking a dialect in the United States? Do all dialects carry the same consequences? Explain.
10. What judicial precedents were set in the 1970s with regard to dialect and Standard American English in the public schools? What are the concerns of parents? Differentiate between reading, writing, and speaking the language.
11. What is *code-switching,* or *bidialectalism?* Why might it be difficult to achieve?
12. What might a classroom teacher do to promote the learning of Standard American English?
13. What are the responsibilities of the speech-language pathologist toward speakers of nonstandard dialects?

FOR FURTHER INFORMATION

Chambers, J. (1983). *Black English: Educational equity and the law.* Ann Arbor, MI: Karoma.

Taylor, O. (1986a). *Nature of communication disorders in culturally and linguistically diverse populations.* San Diego, CA: College-Hill Press.

Taylor, O. (1986b). *Treatment of communication disor-ders in culturally and linguistically diverse populations.* San Diego, CA: College-Hill Press.

Trudgill, P. (1974). *Sociolinguistics: An introduction.* Baltimore, MD: Penguin Books.

Wolfram, W. (1990). *Dialects and American English.* Englewood Cliffs, NJ: Prentice-Hall.

Basic Concepts and Development in Articulation and Phonology

U p to this point, we have been dealing with the content area of language. If you look back to Figure 1-2, you will see that we have covered the normal-development theme for the area of language, as well as causes and characteristics of disorders, consequences to the individual, the role of professionals and parents, society's reaction, and controversies. We have looked at language disorders in childhood and at the language disorders of special populations (those with cognitive disorders and pervasive developmental disorders). In addition, we also considered language differences associated with various regional, cultural, and ethnic groups.

In the next chapters, we will change our focus to the content areas of articulation and phonology. *Articulation,* one of the components of speech, refers to the movements of the structures of the speech mechanism that produce speech sounds. *Phonology* (which is actually a component of language) is the study of the cognitive-linguistic rules governing the production, occurrence, and distribution of speech sounds. Together, these two concepts can be used to explain why the physical movements that produce speech occur as they do and, more important, what can go wrong with speech sound production.

THE SPEECH PRODUCTION MECHANISM

In order to consider disorders of articulation and phonology, we must first have a basic under-standing of the speech production mechanism. Figure 6-1 illustrates the most important structures used to generate speech.

At the bottom of the speech production mechanism, we can see the vocal folds located within the neck. The vocal folds are encased in a protective cartilaginous framework called the *larynx* (pronounced laer' inks). For speech purposes, the function of the vocal folds is to vibrate when air passes through them. The vibration of the vocal folds generates the tone we call *voice.* We will discuss the vocal folds and voice production in more detail in the chapter on voice disorders. For now, it is most important to know that the vocal folds vibrate during the production of all vowel sounds and some consonants but not others. For example, put your hand against your throat as you prolong the sounds "m" or "l." Do you feel a buzzing sensation on your throat? This means that vocal-fold vibration is part of the production of these sounds. For contrast, prolong the sounds "s" or "sh," again with your hand against your throat. No similar buzzing sensation should be felt. This means that the "s" and "sh" consonants do not involve vocal-fold vibration.

Above the vocal folds is a somewhat irregularly shaped tube that extends from the vocal folds, past the back of the mouth, and right up to the nasal cavities. This tube is known as the throat, or *pharynx* (faer' inks). During speech, the pharynx transmits sound generated by the vocal folds to the *oral cavity* (or mouth) and nasal cavities. In addition, some consonant sounds are made by pressing the back of the tongue against the pharynx.

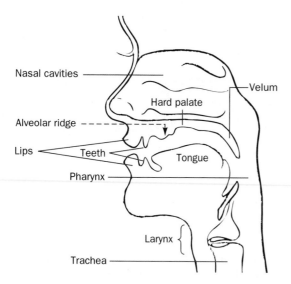

Nasal cavities

Velum

Hard palate

Alveolar ridge

Lips

Teeth

Tongue

Pharynx

Larynx

Trachea

FIGURE 6-1 The speech production mechanism.

When most of us think about the speech production mechanism, the oral cavity and the structures it contains immediately come to mind. The lips, tongue, teeth, hard palate, and *velum* (or soft palate) are the primary articulators used to form speech sounds. The lips can be brought together, puckered, or pulled back to form different sounds. Say the vowels "oh" and "oo" and the consonants "m" and "p," and notice the contribution your lips make.

The tongue is another important articulator associated with the oral cavity. As we can see from Figure 6-1, however, only the surface of the tongue is visible from the oral cavity. The back (or *posterior*) part of the tongue extends down into the pharynx. The tongue is such an important articulator that it is divided into sections: The tip is the front part of the tongue, the blade is immediately behind the tip, and the mid and back portions are behind the blade.

Immediately above the tongue is a bony shelf that separates the nasal cavities from the oral cavity. This bony shelf is the *hard palate*. The front (or *anterior*) part of the hard palate contains the teeth. Like the hard palate, the teeth are part of the speech mechanism. Several consonant sounds can be produced by bringing the tongue

or bottom lip into contact with the upper teeth.

Immediately behind the teeth is a rounded bump known as the *alveolar ridge*. Behind the alveolar ridge, the hard palate arches upward to form the *palatal vault*. The alveolar ridge and hard palate serve as contact points for the tongue during the production of various consonants.

If you run your tongue from your front teeth over the alveolar ridge and the palatal vault, and keep on going backward, you will feel the bony portion of the hard palate come to an end. Beyond this point, you will feel only soft tissue. This soft-tissue extension of the hard palate, the soft palate (or velum) continues the hard palate's function of separating the oral and nasal cavities. Unlike the hard palate, however, the velum is a movable structure.

Normally during speech, the velum is in a raised position, forming a tight seal between the oral and nasal cavities. Only for the sounds "m," "n," and "ng" does the velum lower temporarily. When the velum is in its relaxed position, hanging down in back of the pharynx, air and voice energy can pass into the nasal cavities. Obviously, for breathing through the nose, the soft palate must be lowered. However, during speech, a consistently lowered velum can result in undesirable nasal air emission from the nose, weak consonant production, and a hypernasal voice quality. We will discuss the function of the velum and its effects on speech and voice quality in greater detail in the chapters on voice disorders and cleft palate. In terms of articulation, however, it is important to remember that the velum is an active part of the speech-production mechanism, in a raised position for the production of all vowels and most consonants, and in a lowered position for the nasal consonants "m," "n," and "ng."

SYSTEMS FOR CLASSIFYING SPEECH SOUNDS

The speech mechanism is capable of producing hundreds of different sounds. You would have difficulty, however, if you tried to describe all of those sounds using the letters of the alphabet. For example, put your lips together as if you were preparing to say the letter "p," but blow the air gently through your lips instead of compressing them. The sound you produce should sound something like the "f" sound, although it is not an "f." How would you classify the sound you produced? There is no letter of the English alphabet to which it corresponds. If you were a linguist trying to describe an unfamiliar language, or a speech-language pathologist working with a child with that error in his speech, you would need an unambiguous way to label the sound.

THE TRADITIONAL APPROACH—VOWELS

Numerous methods have been used to categorize or describe speech sounds independent of alphabetic representation. Vowels, for example, can be described in terms of tongue height (high, middle, or low), point of maximum constriction (front, mid, or back), amount of tongue tension (tense or lax), and amount of lip rounding (rounded or unrounded). Using this traditional phonetic description scheme (Kent, 1993), the vowel "ee" would be classified as high, front, tense, and unrounded. That is, the tongue is high in the mouth, and its highest point is just under the hard palate. The tongue is tense, and the lips are slightly retracted. The vowel "oo," by contrast, would be classified as high, back, tense, and rounded. In this vowel, the tongue at its highest point is under the soft palate, and the lips are slightly protruded.

THE TRADITIONAL APPROACH—CONSONANTS

Place, manner, and voicing are the characteristics used to classify consonant sounds in traditional phonetic description (Kent, 1993). These characteristics are discussed below.

1. Place of Articulation.

In the traditional approach, place of articulation reflects the parts of the speech mechanism used to produce speech sounds. The most common places of articulation are:

Bilabial: made with the two lips. The English sounds "p," "b," "m," and "w" are bilabial sounds.

Labiodental: made with the lower lip against the top teeth. The English sounds "f" and "v" are labiodental sounds.

Linguadental: made with the tip of the tongue on the top teeth. The "th" sounds (as in *them* and *thin*) are linguadental sounds.

Lingua-alveolar: made with the tip or blade of the tongue against the alveolar ridge. Many sounds in English are lingua-alveolar, including "t," "d," "s," "z," "l," and "n."

Linguapalatal: made with the blade or mid portion of the tongue against the hard palate, including the English sounds "sh," "zh" (as in *vision),* "ch," "j," and "r."

Linguavelar: made with the back of the tongue against the velum, including "k," "g" and "ng" (as in *swimming*) in English.

Glottal: made by constricting the vocal folds. In English, there is only one glottal sound, "h."

In our example above, the "not an 'f'" sound would be considered bilabial, since it was made by putting the lips together.

2. Manner of Articulation.

While a useful concept, place of articulation is not completely adequate to differentiate one consonant from another. The "p" and "m" sounds are both bilabial, as is our "not an 'f'" sound, yet each is recognizably different from the others. To describe the differences among consonants that have a similar place of articulation, it is necessary to specify how the sounds are made. This is referred to as *manner of articulation.* The following are common manners of articulation in English:

Stop: produced by completely occluding the breath stream behind firmly closed articulators and then suddenly releasing it. This manner is sometimes also called "plosive" instead of *stop.* English stops include "p," "b," "d," "t," "k," and "g." As you make these sounds, feel how air pressure builds up behind the articulatory contact and is then suddenly released.

Fricative: produced by narrowly occluding the breath stream so that air is forced through closely approximated articulators. As the air rushes through this narrow constriction, such as between the tip of the tongue and the alveolar ridge, it creates a "hissing" sound that characterizes fricatives. English fricatives include "f," "v," voiced "th" (as in *them*), voiceless "th" (as in *thin*), "s," "z," "sh," "zh" (as in *vision*), and "h." Again, note the amount of pressure built up behind the articulatory contact as you produce these sounds.

Affricate: produced by first completely occluding the breath stream and then releasing it through closely approximated articulators. This manner can best be described as a combination of a stop followed by a fricative. That is, the breath stream is completely stopped behind closed articulators as is characteristic of stop consonant production; then it is released in a narrow constriction so that the sound ends in a "hissing" noise like a fricative. English affricates are "ch" and "j" (as in *jury*).

Nasal: produced by lowering the velum so that acoustic energy will travel through the pharynx and into the nasal cavities. In English, only three nasals exist, "m," "n," and "ng."

Glide: produced by moving from one articulatory position to another within the sound. In English, the "w" and "y" sounds are considered glides. The "w" starts as the vowel "oo," and the "y" starts as the vowel "ee." Both are characterized by movement of the tongue and lips into the following vowel. Neither sound can be prolonged by itself.

Lateral: produced by lowering the sides of the tongue while simultaneously making full contact between the tip or blade of the tongue and the alveolar ridge or hard palate. In English, the only lateral consonant is "l."

Rhotic: produced by pointing the tip of the tongue toward the back of the mouth (retroflex), or "bunching up" the tongue in the middle of the mouth (Kent, 1993). In English, "r" is a rhotic.

We can now be more specific in describing the "not an 'f' " sound from the example above. Earlier, we decided that the place of articulation was bilabial, because the sound was made with the lips together. The air was blown gently through the lips, according to our instructions. Since the lips formed a narrow constriction that air was forced through, we can conclude that the manner of sound production was fricative. Thus the "not an 'f' " sound appears to be a bilabial fricative.

3. Voicing. One more component is necessary in order to differentiate speech sounds from one another. Consider the following example: "s" and "z" are both *lingua-alveolar fricatives,* meaning they have the same place and the same manner of articulation. However, the "z" sound is produced with vibration of the vocal folds, in addition to the hissing or frication noise made as air is forced between the tongue and the alveolar ridge. The "s" sound is generated by air turbulence alone. As you did earlier, put your hand on your throat. You will feel a buzzing during "z" production that is absent during "s" production. This means that "z" is a voiced lingua-alveolar fricative while "s" is a voiceless lingua-alveolar fricative.

It is now possible to completely specify the "not an 'f' " sound as a voiceless bilabial fricative. We do not use this sound in English and have no letter to which it corresponds. It could easily be confused with "f" because "f" is a voiceless *labiodental* fricative—i.e., it is made by passing air through a constriction formed by the lower lip and the upper teeth—and "f" is a familiar English sound. You can produce a voiced bilabial fricative instead of the voiceless one you were instructed to produce by making your bilabial fricative more similar to a "v" than to an "f."

By using the components of place, manner, and voicing, a linguist or speech-language pathologist can describe many sounds for which no

	Stop		Fricative		Affricate		Nasal		Glide		Lateral		Rhotic	
	ⱴ	v	ⱴ	v	ⱴ	v	ⱴ	v	ⱴ	v	ⱴ	v	ⱴ	v
Bilabial	p	b						m		w				
Labio-dental			f	v										
Lingua-dental			θ	ð										
Lingua-alveolar	t	d	s	z				n				l		
Lingua-palatal			ʃ	ʒ	tʃ	dʒ				j				r
Back velar	k	g						ŋ						
Glottal			h											

FIGURE 6-2 IPA symbols classified according to place, manner, and voicing for the phonemes of English.

English alphabet letter exists. Most linguists and speech-language pathologists, however, also learn the International Phonetic Alphabet (IPA), which provides a set of symbols for a wide variety of place-manner-voicing descriptions. These symbols serve as a kind of shorthand for the more complicated three-component descriptions. For example, instead of saying that a sound is a "voiceless bilabial fricative," as we did above, we could use the phonetic symbol [Φ]. Figure 6-2 shows some of the IPA symbols as a function of their features.

THE DISTINCTIVE-FEATURE APPROACH

Linguists often use more complicated systems for classifying the speech sounds symbolized by the IPA. While the traditional approach includes three components (place, manner, and voicing), the distinctive-feature approach includes many more features as possible descriptors for sounds (for example, grave, acute, vocalic, continuant, diffuse, compact, and so on, as described in Jakobson et al., 1963). Each of the features in most distinctive-feature systems is rated according to a *binary system* (present + or absent −). Thus the "p" sound could be described as +consonantal, −vocalic, −sonorant, +interrupted, −lateral, −voiced, +anterior, −coronal, −rounded, and −nasal (Kent, 1993). Some of the better-known distinctive-feature systems have been proposed by Jakobson et al. (1963) and Chomsky and Halle (1968).

Distinctive-feature analysis is used primarily by

linguists, who study the sound systems of various languages, the rules governing speech-sound changes (for example, why the "k" sound used in *electric* becomes an "s" sound in *electricity*) and how speech-sound differences affect word meaning. For the speech-language pathologist, however, the traditional place-manner-voicing system is used most widely.

PHONES, PHONEMES, AND ALLOPHONES

So far, we have been talking about speech sounds as purely physical phenomena, produced in a particular place and manner using the speech mechanism. This very physical way of conceptualizing speech sounds is the basis of a branch of linguistics called *phonetics*. The concerns of phonetics include the way speech sounds are produced by the speech mechanism and the acoustic properties of the sounds that are generated (Lowe, 1994). There is, however, a broader context that can be considered. Speech sounds are, after all, the building blocks of words, part of a complex relationship between language and meaning. What is missing from the phonetics approach is how sounds function as part of a language. The study of the occurrence and distribution of speech sounds in a language is *phonology*. But in order to look at speech sounds from a phonological orientation, we need some additional vocabulary.

Beginning with the most general term, a *phone* is any sound that can be produced by the human speech mechanism. There are literally hundreds of phones that anyone with normal oral-motor control and a normal speech mechanism can produce. In contrast, a *phoneme* is a phone that denotes a change in meaning in a particular language. That is, if changing one sound to a second alters the meaning of a word, those two sounds would be classified as different phonemes. Phonemes are most easily identified in *minimal pairs;* i.e., two words that differ with respect to only one sound.

Let us consider the minimal pair *cap-cab*. The two words that make up this pair are identical except for the final sounds ("p" and "b"). Since the two words do not mean the same thing, we can conclude that the change from "p" to "b" caused a change in meaning; thus we would say that in English, "p" and "b" are *phonemes*. You can demonstrate many other phonemes to yourself through the use of minimal pairs: *cat-cap,* for example, shows that "t" and "p" are different phonemes; *pat-fat* shows that "p" and "f" are different phonemes.

But what about sounds that do *not* signal a change in meaning? These are somewhat harder to demonstrate, but consider the following minimal pair: Pronounce the word *cup* with a strong and explosive "p" on the end; then say it with a very *gentle* "p" that is not even released. The first is an example of an aspirated "p," while the second is an example of an unaspirated "p." Do the two words mean the same thing? You probably recognize that although the two words *sound* somewhat different, they both refer to a drinking vessel. We would consider the different final sounds for the two words to be essentially the same "p" phoneme, despite their obvious differences. In this case, it is clear that the aspirated and unaspirated "p" sounds in English are *not* phonemes because they do not signal a change in meaning. They are *allophones,* or contextual variants of a single phoneme.

Allophones are speech sounds within a particular *phonological system* (all the sounds included in a language) that can be used alternatively for each other because their use does not cause a change in meaning. It is interesting to note that allophones in English may be phonemes in another language. In our example above, aspirated and unaspirated "p" sounds are allophones in English—both are variants of the "p" phoneme, and can be used interchangeably—but aspirated and unaspirated "p" sounds are phonemes in the Thai language. In Thai, [pʰaa] with an aspirated "p" means "forest," while [paa] with an *unaspirated* "p" means "to split" (Hyman, 1975). Use of one sound as opposed to the other causes a change in word meaning.

It is also true that phonemes in English may be allophones in other languages. For example, the "r" and "l" phonemes in English are allophonic variants of one another in many Asian languages. Chinese, Japanese, and Korean speakers often have great difficulty in producing these two phonemes and discriminating one from the other as they learn English because in their native languages, such a distinction does not exist. After a lifetime of learning that two sounds are *not* different—because they do not affect meaning—it is difficult to learn a new phonological system in which the two sounds are, indeed, distinctive with respect to word meaning.

From these examples, it is clear that the labels *phoneme* and *allophone* are language-specific. While phones exist as physical entities, the classification of a phone as a phoneme or an allophone can only be made in the context of a particular language. The crucial element in their classification is meaning. As we shall see in the next section, a child's learning of the phonological system of his native language is intimately connected with his learning of words and their meanings.

THE DEVELOPMENT OF PHONOLOGICAL-PERCEPTUAL ABILITIES

The phonological systems of all spoken languages are comprised of a set of *phonemes,* or sounds important in conveying meaning, and *allophones,* or acceptable variants of each phoneme that do *not* alter word meanings. An individual learning to understand a new language must learn to distinguish its phonemes from its allophones. That is, he or she must learn to listen for sound contrasts that are important in determining meaning and to ignore sound contrasts that do *not* signal a change in meaning.

How does an infant learning a first language accomplish this difficult task? How do infants born in the United States, for example, learn that aspirated versus *un*aspirated "p" is not important but "r" versus "l" is? Their Thai counterparts are learning just the opposite: that aspiration is an important perceptual difference to cue into while "r" and "l" are unimportant variants of one another and can be used interchangeably.

Some research by Janet Werker (1989) attempted to answer just this question. Werker studied the ability of both babies and adults to discriminate between sounds that are allophones in their native language, English. For this research, she selected two (English) allophonic variants of the phoneme "t": "t" made with the tip of the tongue on the alveolar ridge and "t" produced with the tip of the tongue bent back toward the palatal vault. The latter is referred to as a *retroflexed "t."* The tip-alveolar "t" and the retroflexed "t" are allophones of the "t" phoneme in English, but they are two different phonemes in Hindi.

To check the perceivability of the difference between tip-alveolar "t" and retroflexed "t," Werker first asked adult native speakers of Hindi to listen to tapes containing different "t" + vowel syllables and to indicate whether they heard the tip-alveolar or the retroflexed "t." Adult Hindi speakers were able to discriminate between the two forms with 98 percent accuracy. American English-speaking adults, however, achieved only 8 percent accuracy in their discriminations. As dramatic as this difference was, it was not surprising. Hindi speakers have learned over a lifetime that it is important to be able to distinguish between the two forms of "t" in order to understand words correctly. Speakers of English, on the other hand, have no reason to cue in to the tip-alveolar versus retroflex distinction and thus have learned *not* to hear it.

The surprising aspect of this study was in the performance of a group of 6- to 8-month-old American babies. Using a careful behavioral conditioning procedure, Werker found that these infants were able to discriminate between the two types of "t" with 90 percent accuracy, almost as well as the adult native speakers of Hindi. Thus, American babies appear to be able to hear non-phonemic differences among speech sounds better than do their adult counterparts. According to Werker's terminology, the babies were not yet "native listeners," influenced by the phonological rules of their soon-to-be native language.

If 6- to 8-month-old babies can easily perceive allophonic differences in English that adults have difficulty with, it is obvious that sometime during the years of maturation, babies' perceptual abilities decline. Werker's next question was, *when* do babies become native listeners? When does the ability to perceive subtle nonphonemic contrasts in one's native language fade? In order to answer this question, she tested three groups of babies: one group 6 to 8 months of age, one group 8 to 10 months of age, and one group 10 to 12 months of age.

In this study, Werker again found unexpected results. The 6- to 8-month-old babies perform-ed even better than their earlier counterparts, discriminating the tip-alveolar "t" from the retroflexed "t" with 95 percent accuracy, but the 8- to 10-month-old group got only 70 percent of its discriminations correct, and the 10- to 12-month-old group achieved only 20 percent accu-racy. This research showed that at around the age of 10 months, there is a sharp reduction in the ability to perceive subtle nonphonemic differ-ences among speech sounds in one's native lan-guage. In other words, at around 10 months of age, babies appear to become native listeners.

Concerned that perhaps one group of babies was smarter than another, Werker repeated her research again, this time using the same group of children for all three measurements in a *longitudi-nal study*. That is, she tested a group of babies at the age of 6 to 8 months, waited two months and tested them again at 8 to 10 months of age, and, after a second two-month interval, tested them a third time at 10 to 12 months of age. A design such as this reduces the possibility that different levels of intelligence or alertness among groups will cause differences in perceptual accuracy.

The results of this study were even more clear-cut. At 6 to 8 months, babies were able to dis-criminate the two forms of "t" with 98 percent accuracy. Two months later, their accuracy was still good, at 95 percent. However, when tested at 10 to 12 months of age, their average score was 0 percent correct. Clearly, something had hap-pened at about 10 months of age that changed the infants' way of perceiving speech sounds.

According to Werker, that "something" was the emergence of receptive language. In Chapter 2, we discussed the idea that during the 7- to 12-month-old period, children begin to associate specific words with concepts. They are able to recognize their own names, hand objects to an adult on request, and follow simple commands involving going or getting. As children learn words and their meanings, they must simultane-ously learn the sounds that carry meaning.

Somewhere around the age of 10 months, the undifferentiated sea of sound that surrounds a child must start to take shape. Some sounds and sound combinations emerge as important, key cues for various words, while others fade as unim-portant. A child in an English-speaking environ-ment who was once as attentive to the difference between aspirated and unaspirated "p" as he was to the difference between "p" and "t" now finds himself ignoring aspiration. After all, what differ-ence does it make? The child gradually learns to tune his perceptions toward phonemic differences and loses the ability to perceive nonphonemic or allophonic contrasts. As the child's perceptual abilities are shaped by his native language and phonological system, he becomes a native listener. And all this occurs before he speaks a single true word!

THE DEVELOPMENT OF ARTICULATORY AND PHONOLOGICAL PRODUCTION ABILITIES

In the preceding section, we saw that children are not born with knowledge of phonemes and allo-phones in their native language, just as they are not born with the ability to understand their native language. Both abilities develop over the first year of life. Very young babies appear to be universal perceivers in that they are able to hear subtle allophonic differences among speech sounds in their native language that adult native speakers are not. However, as receptive language develops at the age of approximately 10 months, perceptual orientation changes. Babies appear to become attuned to the differences among speech sounds that affect semantic meaning in their native language (i.e., *phonemes*) and begin to ignore the differences among speech sounds that do *not* signal a change in meaning (i.e., *allophones*).

This development of perceptual and receptive language capabilities sets the stage for the later development of spoken words and phoneme production. Babies babble for six to eight months before producing true words, a valuable step in learning to control the articulators and imitate syllable and intonation patterns. But these babbled sounds cannot truly be considered phoneme productions because they do not yet carry meaning. Once a child begins to produce meaningful words, at the age of approximately 1 year, it is clear that he has isolated at least some phonemes in his native language. Now his speech mechanism, honed by months of practice, must be commanded to reproduce the sounds that he has heard and understood.

THE DEVELOPMENT OF INTELLIGIBILITY

There are many ways of looking at the development of children's speech-production abilities. One global measure of a child's ability to articulate clearly is intelligibility. *Intelligibility* is defined as "the degree of clarity with which one's utterances are understood by the average listener" (Nicolosi et al., 1989). Articulation is certainly a major determinant of intelligibility, but as Nicolosi and colleagues go on to state in their definition, intelligibility is also influenced by rate, fluency, vocal quality, and intensity. Thus, intelligibility is perhaps more accurately thought of as a measure of speech proficiency, not just of articulation. However, since articulation proficiency must ultimately be judged in the context of conversational speech (as opposed to single syllables or isolated words), intelligibility is important to measure.

As in all other areas of communication behavior, intelligibility develops gradually over the first few years of life. It is difficult to assess intelligibility at the time the child says her first words because in the 12- to 18-month-old period, variegated babbling and jargon may still be present. However, by the age of 18 to 24 months, or 1½ to 2 years, most children have enough language to be able to assess their understandability. According to Weiss et al. (1987), children in this age range are approximately 25 percent intelligible. That is, it is possible for the average listener to understand the child about one-quarter of the time, although familiar listeners, such as parents and baby sitters, may considerably better. In the 2- to 2½-year-old period, intelligibility improves to about 60 percent. Between the ages of 2½ and 3, a child should be 75 percent intelligible; and between the ages of 3 and 4, most children will be 90 percent intelligible. Weiss et al. (1987) state that by the age of 4, most children are intelligible almost 100 percent of the time, although intelligibility may diminish during periods of excitement or stress.

This high level of intelligibility, however, does not mean the child's speech is perfect. Most 4-year-olds misarticulate at least *some* consonants, such as "r" and "s." A child's speech may be comprehensible despite errors on specific sounds. In fact, speech errors are a normal part of almost all children's development. Some consonants, for a variety of reasons, are not produced correctly until later in childhood, while others are present at the time of the child's first words. At this point, we turn our attention to the sequence of development in the production of speech sounds.

ARTICULATION DEVELOPMENT

Which speech sounds is a child likely to *first* produce correctly in words? Many researchers and clinicians argue from a phonetic point of view that the speech sounds which are the easiest to produce physically are the ones first used correctly in words and phrases. It has also been suggested that the most frequently used sounds, those the child hears most often and which most frequently signal important meaning changes in a word, are the ones learned first. Finally, the ease with which speech sounds are *perceived,* both auditorily and visually, may be factors in determining which sounds emerge first.

According to Owens (1994), the first sounds to be produced correctly in words are those that are both easiest to produce and easiest to perceive. This is because the child's neuromuscular development is still incomplete during the early phases of speech and language development, thus control over the speech mechanism is somewhat limited. Owens further states that children simplify their speech-sound production in predictable ways because of this reduced control and, in addition, may have a simplified phonological rule system.

Several researchers over the past decades have investigated the question of *when* children are able to produce the various phonemes of English correctly (Wellman et al., 1931; Poole, 1934; Templin, 1957; Prather et al., 1975; Smit et al., 1990). This information has traditionally been important to speech-language pathologists, who must answer the question of what is normal or abnormal in terms of speech abilities for each age range. However, results of these "age-of-acquisition" studies are difficult to summarize because different researchers have adopted different standards for "mastery" of a sound. For example, Poole (1934) did not consider a sound "mastered" unless *all* subjects at a given age were able to produce it correctly in all positions of words, while Templin (1957) considered a sound "mastered" when 75 percent of the subjects could produce it accurately. Not surprisingly, Poole reports the mastery of sounds at later ages, in general, than does Templin.

This variability in mastery criteria makes it very difficult to specify a particular age at which we can expect a child to produce a given sound consistently. It is also clear from the age-of-acquisition variability among studies that some children are able to produce various speech sounds earlier than others, although all of them may be developing normally.

To reflect the wide variety of ages of acquisition for different phonemes, Sander (1972) argued for looking at an age *range* for the normal acquisition of speech sounds. He reanalyzed the data of Wellman, Poole, and Templin into age ranges for each sound, where the lower extreme of the range represented the age at which 50 percent of the subjects produced the sound correctly and the upper extreme represented the age at which 90 percent of them produced the sound correctly. Presumably, even at the highest age in the age range, approximately 10 percent of all children

would still be unable to produce the sound correctly.

In Figure 6-3, the ranges calculated by Sander have been combined with data reported by Panther et al. (1975) and Smit et al. (1990). The results of the studies on speech-sound acquisition and the information presented in Figure 6-3 can be summarized as follows:

1. Between the ages of 1 and 3, all of the English vowels are mastered.
2. Between about 1½ and 3 years of age, the "m," "p," "h," "n," and "w" sounds are gradually mastered in words. Half of the children are able to say these sounds by the age of 1½, while, by the age of 3, 90 percent of the children can produce these sounds correctly.
3. Between about 2 and 4 years of age, the "d," "b," "g," "t," "k," "f," and "y" sounds are mastered. Again, 50 percent of all children can say them at the age of 2, or at the low end of the age range. There is more disagreement about the age of acquisition for these sounds, but, in general, it appears that 90 percent of all children develop these sounds by the age of 4. The exception is "t," which often is not produced correctly even by adults in words like *butter*.
4. Between about 3 and 7 years of age, the "l," "sh," "ch," "j," voiceless "th," and "ng" sounds are mastered (50 percent at the lower age of the age range and 90 percent at the upper age). Again, there is some dispute about "ng" because this sound is often produced as simply "n" at the ends of words—by both children and adults.
5. By the age of 8, the "r," "v," voiced "th," and "zh" sounds are produced correctly by 90 percent of *all* children.
6. The "s" and "z" sounds may not be correctly produced by 90 percent of all children until the age of 9, although 50 percent of all children are producing these sounds correctly by about 3 years of age.

Thus, we can see that all children do not learn the various phonemes of English on an invariant

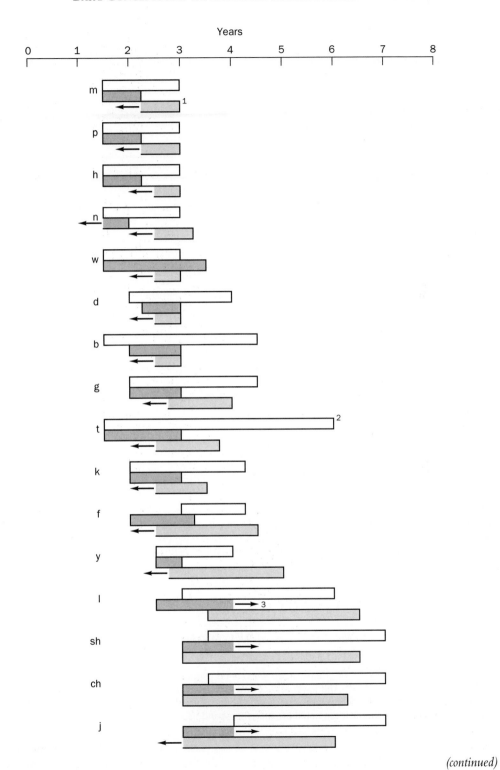

(continued)

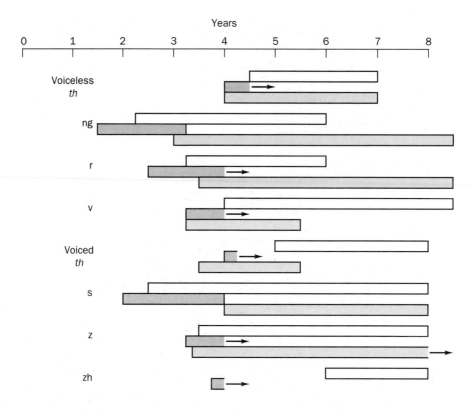

[1] Smit et al. (1990) did not study children younger than three years of age, thus the limit of 50 percent mastery cannot be specified for some early-developing sounds.

[2] In one of the studies summarized by Sander (1972), the "t" sound was not considered correct until it was produced in the initial, final, and *medial* positions. Few children (or adults) precisely articulate medial "t," such as in the word *butter*; therefore, the age of 90 percent acquisition is artificially high.

[3] Prather et al. (1975) only studied children up to 4 years of age. If 90 percent of those children did not show mastery of a sound, an arrow to the right (→) indicates that 90 percent mastery would occur at a later age for that particular sound.

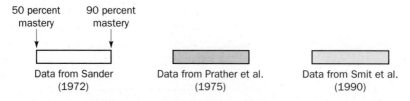

FIGURE 6-3 Combined results of studies of speech-sound acquisition from Sander (1972), Prather et al. (1975), and Smit et al. (1990). The lower end of each bar represents the age at which 50 percent of the children in the study could consistently produce the sound. The upper end of each bar represents the age at which 90 percent of the children could produce the sound.

timetable. Some children may master their sounds at the early end of each age range, while other children may not be able to produce various speech sounds correctly until some years later. There are great individual differences in the development of articulatory competence, just as there are in the acquisition of language.

With our knowledge of speech-sound classification in mind, we can now make some generalizations about the development of speech-production abilities. In terms of manner, it appears that nasals are among the earliest speech sounds to be acquired, with "n" and "m" coming in by the age of 3. The glides "w" and "j" are also early developing sounds. Plosives are used early and are generally produced consistently by the age of 4. On the other hand, fricatives and affricates (with a few exceptions), along with the lateral "l" and rhotic "r" appear to be the most difficult manners to produce correctly. These sounds are among the last to be developed.

Up to this point, we have been referring to "errors" in speech-sound production as if all errors were the same. Our discussion thus far has centered on whether a particular speech sound is "right" or "wrong" at a given age. However, as we shall see in the next section, there are many different ways of producing a speech sound incorrectly. The particular type of error that a child is making can be a factor in his intelligibility, the response of others to his speech, and the developmental level to which we would assign him.

Development Through Single-Phoneme Error Types

In addition to intelligibility and articulation development, we can also assess children's speech-production abilities in terms of the types of errors they make as they learn to produce various sounds. One type of error that we often see in the speech of very young children is an *omission,* where a speech sound is left out of a word altogether. For example, the child who says "I ee coo-ee" has omitted the final "t" from *eat* and the medial "k" from *cookie.* In older children, omis-

sions may occur in consonant blends, such as the "sk" in *sky* or the "tr" in *truck.* Saying "pay" instead of *play,* for instance, is an omission of the "l" from the "pl" consonant blend.

In general, omissions have an extremely negative impact on intelligibility. If many consonants are missing from a child's phrases or sentences, the adult listener has few cues upon which to draw in determining meaning. When we hear such a speech sample, we are likely to judge the speaker to be a very young child or, perhaps, someone with a physical problem restricting her speech.

A second type of error pattern is a substitution. A *substitution* occurs when one phoneme in English is used in place of another. A common substitution in the speech of very young children is the use of "t" in place of the "k" sound in words, such as "tat" for *cat* or "tey" for *key.* Other common substitutions are "th" for "s" ("think" for *sink*) and "w" for "r" ("wed" for *red*).

Substitutions do not impact intelligibility as negatively as do omissions because substitutions are usually quite similar to the sounds they replace. A child who says "I thee the wed thoo" would be somewhat difficult to understand, but an adult could probably figure out that "thee" should be *see,* "wed" should be *red,* and "thoo" should be *shoe.* Like omissions, but to a lesser degree, substitutions in a child's speech give the impression of immaturity.

A third type of error pattern is a distortion. *Distortions* occur when the target phoneme is almost correct, but production differs from the standard in some important respect. We might consider a distortion to be an unacceptable allophonic variant of the target sound rather than the substitution of one phoneme for another. It is difficult to present distortions in writing, but some images can be called to mind. The "s" sound used by Sylvester the Cat, for example, is not a recognizable English phoneme and thus would not be considered a substitution. Instead, Sylvester's "s" is a distortion, created by passing air over the sides of the tongue, resulting in a "wet" sound. Speech-language pathologists call this a *lateral "s."*

Some "r" errors are also distortions. Normal "r" production requires a certain amount of tension in the tongue. If the tongue is too relaxed, the "r" produced is incorrect, but it is not the same as a "w." This lax "r" would also be considered a distortion.

Distortions have the least impact on intelligibility of all the error patterns we have discussed so far. When we hear distortions in a person's speech, we are almost sure to understand them, but we are likely to form unfavorable impressions about that person's intelligence and capability.

In terms of a developmental sequence, omissions of various phonemes are almost always seen in a child's earliest word attempts. As the child becomes older and more proficient at phoneme production, omissions may be replaced by substitutions. Greenlee (1974) gives the following example of a child learning to say the word *play:* initially, the child may pronounce the word as simply "ay," deleting both the "p" and the "l." In a second stage, weeks or months later, the child may say "pay" instead of *play,* omitting only one of the initial consonants. In a third stage, the child may improve her production to "pway," substituting a "w" sound for "l." The fourth stage would be correct articulation of the word *play.* Not every child will go through the four distinct phases outlined in this example, but it is a common pattern to go from omissions of particular phonemes to substitutions prior to correct production.

The error patterns we discussed above are useful in describing *single-phoneme errors,* or the child's specific type of error on a single phoneme. But for very young children in the early stages of learning their phonological system, this type of analysis can be cumbersome. For example, many children use the *stop phonemes* ("p," "t," "k," "b," "d," and "g") successfully at the beginnings of words but omit them at the ends of words. In order to describe the child's error pattern, therefore, all the stop phonemes would have to be recorded individually, with a note that the omissions were in the final position only. If the second phoneme of a two-consonant blend was con-

sistently omitted, again each individual phoneme and blend would have to be specified. Children's early errors in sound learning often appear to have a pattern or regularity to them, and this information is lost when we describe errors on a phoneme-by-phoneme basis. For this reason, we need another way of analyzing children's speech-production abilities, a way that incorporates the idea of developmental trends in overall error patterns.

PHONOLOGICAL PROCESSES DEVELOPMENT

In the early 1970s, a new way of looking at children's phonological development—phonological-process analysis (Stampe, 1973)—gained popularity. According to this theory, young children's early speech-sound errors, and changes in error patterns over time, are rule-governed and predictable rather than random and individualistic.

The original phonological-process theory postulated that children "knew" the correct form for each speech sound—in other words, on a cognitive level, they had an accurate *phonological representation* of the sounds adults use—but because of limitations in their neuromuscular control, experience, and mental development, children's *surface form,* or actual articulatory production, was simplified in a predictable way. These simplifications were referred to as *phonological processes,* defined as "systematic sound change(s) affecting an entire class of sounds or sound sequence(s)" (Edwards and Shriberg, 1983). It was further hypothesized that as children mature, they learn to suppress these simplifications, and so adult forms are eventually achieved (Lowe, 1994).

At present, the idea that normally developing children "know" how speech sounds should be produced is not universally accepted. Some researchers, such as Elbert (1985) and Stoel-Gammon and Dunn (1985), propose that the child's phonological representations may also start out in a simplified form and that over time, knowledge of phonological correctness changes. Regardless of what the child "knows" about phonology, phonological-process analysis is currently used to describe children's speech-production abilities by both researchers and speech-language pathologists.

There is also some dispute regarding the exact nature and number of phonological processes employed by normally developing children. The classification scheme proposed by Ingram (1976) is often used (Stoel-Gammon and Dunn, 1985; Weiss et al., 1987; Creaghead, 1989). It includes various types of syllable structure processes, assimilation processes, and substitution processes. These are reviewed briefly below.

1. Syllable Structure Processes. It has been hypothesized that the simplest, most basic, and most natural type of syllable is the CV (consonant-vowel) model (Stampe, 1969, 1973). For example, the word *to* conforms to the CV configuration. Most English words, however, are more complex in form. Words like *bib* and *cup* have a CVC structure, *blue* is a CCV pattern, and *spoon* is CCVC. (In the latter two examples, we see that a single-vowel sound, like "oo" may have different spellings, or *graphemic representations*. We do not consider the "ue" in *blue* to be two different vowels, merely the graphemic representation of a single vowel.)

According to the theory of natural phonological processes, children in early language-learning stages try to fit all words into the easiest syllable structure possible—the CV configuration. In order to do this, they must (1) delete final consonants, (2) reduce consonant clusters to a single phoneme, and (3) delete unstressed syllables. In the examples above, a very young child might say "bi" instead of *bib,* and "cu" instead of *cup.* These modifications reflect the syllable-structure process of final consonant deletion. Consonant cluster reduction would be indicated in the child's use of "bu" for *blue* or "poo" for *spoon.* An example of unstressed syllable deletion might be the child's use of "way" for *away,* as in the phrase "Go 'way!" often directed at younger siblings. (Again, *way* is considered a CV form because the "y" is part of the long "a" vowel and does not represent an actual consonant.)

If you think back over your own experiences

with young children, you will probably be able to recall at least a few examples similar to the simplifications we have been discussing above. We accept these simplifications and production "errors" in the speech of very young children, perhaps unconsciously, because of their age and lack of experience with speech. But when do we *stop* accepting syllable structure simplifications? At what ages do children move on to adult word forms?

Grunwell (1987) presented a developmental chronology of phonological processes that is based on her own research and the research of others. According to Grunwell, final consonant deletion is evident in the speech of children up to the age of 2½, with a gradual reduction around the age of 3 and complete disappearance by the age of 3½. Consonant cluster reduction for blends involving "r" and "l" follows a similar pattern. Consonant cluster reduction for blends involving "s," however, occurs through the age of 3, diminishing by 3½ and disappearing by 4. Finally, deletion of the unstressed, or "weak," syllable continues as late as the age of 3½, diminishing around the age of 4. We can conclude that by 4 years of age, syllable structure processes have been replaced with more adult phonological patterns in the speech of normally developing children.

2. Assimilation Processes. To return to the theory of natural phonological processes, it is hypothesized that we can predict the speech-sound error patterns of young children based on ease and naturalness of production. It appears to be easier for a child to produce a sequence of sounds (such as a word) using a single place of articulation rather than several places of articulation. In other words, children might be prone to repeating the same consonant several times in a word, even if that consonant is not the correct one, simply because it is physically easier than changing from one sound to another. This is indeed the case, and the process is known as *assimilation.*

Assimilation has been defined as occurring "when a sound is changed to become more similar to another sound in the word, or when a syllable in a word is changed to become more like another syllable in the word" (Weiss et al. 1987, 69). An example of a sound change within a word would be a child's production of the word "goggie" instead of *doggie.* Here we see that the "g" sound in the middle of the word influenced the production of the initial "d," causing it to change to "g." Similarly, *tiger* might be produced as "kiger." According to Grunwell (1987), it is most common for lingua-alveolar sounds in the initial position to become velarized under the influence of later velar sounds. It is interesting to note that a child who says "goggie," substituting a "g" for a "d," will most likely use the "d" sound correctly in a word like *door* where there is no velar consonant to influence the production of the "d" sound.

Besides assimilation to a velar sound, other types of assimilation also occur. Although less common, assimilation may be toward the alveolar place of articulation, so that *cat* becomes "tat." In addition, the first sound in the word may affect subsequent sounds, so that *coat* becomes "coak." Grunwell (1987) states that the process of assimilation does not occur in the speech of *all* young children and, if present, usually diminishes fairly early. She reports that by the age of 2½ assimilation has begun to diminish in normal children and that it does not persist beyond the age of about 3.

3. Substitution Processes. In contrast to assimilation processes, substitution processes involve the substitution of one type of speech sound for another *without* the influence of surrounding phonemes (Weiss et al., 1987). According to the natural phonological-processes theory, some sounds are simply easier to produce than others. In general, a more easily produced class of phonemes is substituted for a less easily produced class in the developing speech of young children. And predictably, as the child's neuromotor system matures and she gains experience with the rapid and precise movements needed to produce speech, these substitution processes will fade and the adult target sounds will be used correctly.

One very common substitution process is *stop-*

ping, or substituting stops as a class for fricatives, especially in the initial position of words. The substituted stops usually share place of articulation and voicing characteristics with the fricatives they replace. Thus "p" replaces "f," "b" replaces "v," "t" or "d" replace "th" (depending on whether it is unvoiced or voiced), "t" replaces "s" or "sh," and so on. A child using the substitution process may say "pate" instead of *face,* "ban" instead of *van,* and "dood" instead of *shoes.*

Another substitution process is *fronting,* or substituting a front consonant for a back consonant. This could involve the replacement of back velar sounds like "k," "g," and "ng" with the alveolar sounds "t," "d," and "n." Fronting can also involve affricates, so that "ch" is produced "ts." Finally, the use of "t" for "sh" represents both stopping *and* fronting because "sh" is normally made in the linguapalatal position and "t" is produced in the more fronted lingua-alveolar position.

According to Grunwell (1987), these substitution processes persist longer than all the other phonological processes in the speech of normally developing children. In terms of stopping, the "f" and "s" phonemes are the earliest to be corrected. The "p" for "f" and "t" for "s" substitutions usually disappear by the age of 3½. The "b" for "v" and "d" for "z" substitutions are resolved by the age of 4. However the "sh," "ch," and "j" sounds are likely to be produced as stops until the age of 4½, to be followed by the substitution of fronted fricatives and affricates. The use of stop consonants in place of both voiced and unvoiced "th" is likely to persist until after the age of 5.

4. Summary. So far in our unit on the development of articulatory and phonological production abilities, we have looked at speech-sound production in terms of overall measures of intelligibility, articulation development on a phoneme-by-phoneme basis, single-phoneme error types, and phonological-processes development. What advantage is gained from the phonological-processes approach? What can it tell us about speech-sound development that the other methods cannot?

The most important contribution of phonological-processes analysis is that it summarizes and explains error patterns that would otherwise be difficult to discern. Very young children make numerous errors in their speech-sound productions, and to try to describe each error on a phoneme-by-phoneme basis is often impossible. Take, for example, the child who says "goggie" for *doggie* and "doat" for *goat* but produces the word *door* correctly. Would we say that the child has mastered "d" in the initial position? When a phoneme is produced correctly in one context and incorrectly in another, our notion of mastery breaks down. Using the phonological-processes approach, however, we can hypothesize that the child was using the assimilation process in the word *doggie* and the substitution process of fronting in *goat*. We could also predict that the "d" in *door* would be produced correctly because "d" is not usually the target of substitution processes and because there is no place-contrasting final consonant to cause it to assimilate.

Phonological-processes analysis can help reveal the rule-governed nature of children's early attempts at speech production. Just as we saw that many early language errors are common and predictable (such as saying "foots" instead of *feet*), it appears that many early articulation error patterns are also predictable. In short, phonological-processes analysis gives us a theoretical framework for predicting and understanding the errors that occur in children's emerging attempts at articulate speech.

EPILOGUE

This chapter has provided an overview of many basic concepts in the areas of articulation and phonology. We discussed the speech production mechanism and the physical aspects of speech, ways of classifying speech sounds, the development of speech perception, and the development of speech production abilities. We discussed speech production development in terms of intelligibility, mastery of individual phonemes, single-phoneme error types, and phonological-processes analysis.

The purpose of this chapter was to acquaint you with the information you need to understand articulation and phonological disorders. If you look back to Figure 1-2, you will see that we have completed the first theme, normal development, for our second content area—articulation and phonology. In our next chapter, we will continue to explore this major content area in communication sciences and disorders.

R E V I E W   Q U E S T I O N S

1. Draw and label the important parts of the speech production mechanism. Include in your diagram the following: lips, teeth, alveolar ridge, hard palate, velum, pharynx, nasal cavities, larynx, and tongue (tip, blade, middle, back).
2. What do we mean by *place of articulation*? *Manner*? *Voicing*? Why are these useful concepts?
3. Define and give examples of the following manner features of articulation: *stop, fricative, affricate, nasal, glide, lateral, rhotic.*
4. What is a *phone?* A *phoneme?* An *allophone?* Give examples of each (specify language for the latter two).
5. Do all languages use the same phonological system? How could you tell which speech sounds were phonemes and which were allophones in a language you have never heard before?
6. According to Werker's research, when do babies appear to lose the ability to perceive differences between nonphonemic (or *allophonic*) contrasts in their native language? Why might this happen?
7. What is meant by *intelligibility?* How does intelligibility develop in young children?
8. In terms of the acquisition of individual phonemes, which *classes* of speech sounds

seem to be the easiest to produce? The hardest?

9. What are four phoneme-specific types of errors seen in the production of speech sounds? Which interferes with intelligibility the most? What is the developmental sequence of these errors?

10. What is meant by the term *phonological process*? Give some examples of phonological processes that can be seen in the speech of young children.

11. How does analyzing a child's speech for single-phoneme errors differ from analyzing a child's speech for phonological processes? In which situations would each type of analysis be more useful?

F O R   F U R T H E R   I N F O R M A T I O N

Bernthal, J., and **Bankson, N.** (1993). *Articulation and phonological disorders* (3rd ed.). Englewood Cliffs, NJ: Prentice-Hall.

Creaghead, N., Newman, P., and **Secord, W.** (1989). *Assessment and remediation of articulatory and phonological disorders* (2nd ed.). Columbus, OH: Merrill.

Grunwell, P. (1987). *Clinical phonology* (2nd ed.). Baltimore, MD: Williams and Wilkins.

Hulit, L., and **Howard, M.** (1993). *Born to talk*. New York, NY: Macmillan.

Weiss, C., Gordon, M., and **Lillywhite, H.** (1987). *Clinical management of articulatory and phonologic disorders* (2nd ed.). Baltimore, MD: Williams and Wilkins.

Articulation and Phonological Disorders: An Overview

I n our last chapter, we looked at the physical mechanism for speech production and the development of speech-production abilities. We considered a number of ways of evaluating speech proficiency in young children, including ratings of intelligibility, mastery of individual speech sounds, single-phoneme-error analysis, and phonological-processes analysis. Not surprisingly, these same strategies can be used to evaluate the speech of an individual with a phonological disorder.

Although most children move from a simplified phonological system to correct speech-sound formation in a normal, fairly rapid manner, others have difficulty in this area. Some children are slow in developing intelligible speech. At the age of 5 or 6, when we would expect close to 100 percent intelligibility, such children may be understood less than half of the time. Other children are intelligible but continue to misarticulate one or two phonemes even in late childhood, giving their speech a "babyish" sound.

Persistent unintelligible speech or persistent phoneme errors are of concern to parents and teachers; children who exhibit these behaviors are frequently referred to speech-language pathologists for evaluation and treatment. In this chapter, we will discuss the causes and characteristics of these phonological disorders, their effects on children, the roles of parents, teachers, and speech-language pathologists in remediating such disorders, and controversies in treatment.

DEFINITIONS

As noted in the title of this chapter, two terms are used to describe the problems a child might have with speech-sound production: articulation disorders and phonological disorders. In the past, all speech-sound production problems were referred to as articulation disorders. It was assumed that children who did not produce certain speech sounds correctly at the expected ages had a disorder primarily of physical production, due to a structural or neuromotor problem, an incorrectly learned motor pattern, a "bad habit," or a subtle perceptual deficit. Speech-language pathologists used remediation methods such as tongue exercises, speech-sound-production drills, and auditory training that were consistent with this philosophy.

However, within the last two decades, the term and philosophy of phonological disorders has gained popularity. A *phonological disorder* is a speech-production problem based upon an immature or even deviant set of phonological rules governing the occurrence, sequencing, or production of speech sounds in a language, different from the rules used by competent speakers. Thus, labeling a disorder as phonological introduces a linguistic-cognitive component—a rule system—that was not acknowledged in the articulation-disorder label.

The appeal of the phonological perspective is based on the descriptive power of developmental phonological processes, discussed in the preceding chapter. Like very young children just learning speech-sound production, children with speech-sound disorders often evidence predictable error patterns that are difficult to describe on a phoneme-by-phoneme basis. This difficulty stems from the fact that a single phonological process— the substitution process of stopping, for example—affects more than one phoneme. When a child makes multiple and seemingly inconsistent errors, a phonological-process analysis can reveal and clearly describe the rules used to generate these errors.

On the other hand, the term articulation disorder appears to be appropriate for children whose errors are restricted to a few consistently mispronounced phonemes. For example, a child's production errors may involve only a lateral "s" or a distorted "r." In such a case, use of the term *articulation disorder* may be valid because the problem appears related only to the physical formation of a specific sound.

In keeping with recent trends in the field of communication sciences and disorders, this text will use the term phonological disorders to refer to speech-sound-production problems in general, both articulatory and phonological in nature. It should be noted that it is often possible to differentiate between the two types of disorders. However, at this point in time, articulation is generally acknowledged to be a subcategory of phonology because phonological rules govern speech-sound production. Since the term phonological disorders is accepted as being more general and inclusive, it will be used for the remainder of this chapter.

CAUSES OF PHONOLOGICAL DISORDERS

The causes of phonological disorders are roughly grouped into two categories: organic and functional. *Organic disorders* are those due to known physical, genetic, or neurological problems. In contrast, *functional disorders* have no apparent physical origin. Currently, it is acknowledged that the vast majority of phonological disorders have no identifiable cause (Bernthal and Bankson, 1993). It is also important to remember that the causes of some phonological disorders may not be easily

classifiable as purely organic or functional; and some disorders may have multiple etiologies (Weiss et al., 1987).

ORGANIC PHONOLOGICAL DISORDERS

1. Structural Deviations of the Speech Mechanism. When a child has a phonological disorder, parents may worry that it is caused by some unnoticed malformation of their child's mouth, tongue, or throat. In fact, minor structural deviations of the speech mechanism are rarely the sole cause of phonological disorders, although they can act as contributing factors. Dental problems, missing teeth, enlarged tonsils, tongue-tie, and too large or too small a tongue are examples of minor anomalies that do not usually have a major impact on articulation abilities (Bernthal and Bankson, 1993).

A much more severe structural abnormality that can affect speech production is cleft palate. A *cleft palate* occurs when the three shelves of embryonic tissue that ultimately form the palate fail to join together during the eighth to twelfth weeks of gestation. A cleft palate can occur alone or with a cleft lip. This disorder can range in severity from very mild (only a small cleft in the back of the velum) to very severe (a complete opening through both the velum and the hard palate, extending forward through the alveolar ridge, lip, and nostril).

Although cleft palates are generally repaired surgically during infancy or early childhood, the repaired palate may not be large enough or mobile enough to completely close off the nasal from the oral cavity. Further, a very slight palatal cleft may not be noticed and therefore not repaired. In either case, acoustic energy and air turbulence that would normally be released in the oral cavity are channeled into the nasal cavities as well. This results in excessive nasal resonance during speech production and nasal air emission on pressure consonants such as "s" and "ch." We will discuss cleft palate and its resulting voice and phonological disorders in Chapter 11.

2. Neuromotor Disorders. Articulation is a very rapid process. Normal conversational speech requires the formulation and production of four to five phonemes per second. It might be hypothesized that individuals with *neuromotor disorders,* or disorders of muscle control, would have speech-production difficulties. And indeed, brain and nervous system damage and disease are strongly associated with various patterns of speech disorders, especially in adults. We discuss here two types of neuromotor disorders that can affect speech: dysarthria and apraxia.

Dysarthria is a speech disorder caused by damage to the motor control centers or pathways in the brain and nervous system. It is characterized by paralysis, weakness, incoordination, involuntary movement, or disturbed muscle tone in the speech muscles. In adults, dysarthria is usually an acquired disorder, resulting from head injury, stroke, or illnesses such as Parkinson's disease. As you will recall, an *acquired disorder* means the individual has experienced normal development and normal communication abilities up to the time of injury or disease. Although the symptoms vary depending on the cause and the location of the damage, adults with dysarthria usually have slurred and imprecise speech, often with excessive nasality and a monotone pitch. Intelligibility is severely impaired in some cases. We will talk more about dysarthria in our chapter on adult disorders of speech and language.

In children, the most common cause of dysarthria is cerebral palsy. *Cerebral palsy* is a *developmental disorder* rather than an acquired disorder. This means that the brain injury that causes it occurs prior to, during, or shortly after birth, so that the individual has never experienced normal motoric development or normal communication. The articulation patterns of children with cerebral palsy are extremely varied—as with acquired adult dysarthria—and depend on the location and extent of the cerebral injury. Some mildly involved children have normal speech-production abilities; at the other extreme, severely involved children may not be capable of articulate speech at all. We will discuss cerebral palsy at greater length in the next chapter. In both adult and childhood dysarthria, the paralysis, weakness, incoordination, involuntary movement, and disturbed muscle

tone that affect speech also affect nonspeech functions, such as eating and swallowing.

Apraxia of speech, in contrast, is caused by damage to the speech motor programming centers of the brain. This part of the brain is believed to store the commands for voluntary movement and to direct the motor control centers, which then send information out to individual muscle groups. Unlike the individual with dysarthria, people with apraxia of speech do not experience paralysis, weakness, abnormal muscle tone, and so on. However, they may have to articulate several different sounds or syllables before finding the right one. Their speech is generally slow and halting, with many sound substitutions and word revisions. However, reflexive or vegetative functions, such as eating and swallowing, are unaffected.

Developmental verbal apraxia, or verbal apraxia with its onset in childhood in the absence of stroke, brain injury, or disease, is somewhat more controversial (Air et al., 1989). Some children have difficulty in voluntarily forming speech sounds— and sometimes nonspeech oral movements— despite normal comprehension abilities. However, the brain lesion–speech disorder relationship is not as clear as it is in the acquired verbal apraxia seen in adults, prompting some to speculate that these disorders in children and adults are fundamentally different. At present, some researchers and clinicians in communication sciences and disorders accept the terms developmental verbal apraxia or "developmental verbal dyspraxia" in children as a legitimate diagnosis while others do not (Bernthal and Bankson, 1993).

3. Cognitive Disorders. As discussed in Chapter 4, cognitive disorders usually cause an across-the-board delay in almost all aspects of a child's development, including articulatory abilities and phonological knowledge. In general, a child with cognitive disorders will produce speech sounds at a level commensurate with his or her mental age. However, it is difficult to predict how any given child will function.

According to Owens (1993), children with cognitive delays exhibit phonological processes similar to those of normally developing children, although these processes may persist far longer. It is common to see syllable simplification processes such as reduction of consonant clusters and final consonant deletions, even though the child is capable of producing the deleted or modified sound. Children with cognitive disorders are also more likely to exhibit deviant articulation and phonological patterns that are unlike those we expect in normally developing children. And finally, cognitively disordered children are more likely than are normally developing children to have difficulty with the physical production of individual phonemes because many of them also have neurological damage. Thus, in the intellectually impaired population, we are likely to see phonological disorders due to both delays in overall development and neuromuscular dysfunction.

4. Hearing Impairment. If a child cannot hear speech sounds clearly, it is not difficult to imagine that his production of those sounds will be incorrect. Speech-language pathologists and audiologists routinely test the hearing of all their clients with speech disorders to rule out this causative factor.

Those with hearing loss are generally divided into two groups according to the severity of their hearing problem: the deaf and the hard of hearing. The *deaf,* as we shall discuss later on in this book, are those whose hearing abilities are so limited that they must use manual or visual means, (such as sign language and lip reading) for communication. The *hard of hearing* have less severe hearing loss and retain their speaking and listening skills, usually through the use of hearing aids. In general, the deaf have more severe phonological disorders because their ability to perceive sound is so diminished. Indeed, many deaf individuals cannot speak intelligibly. The more impaired the individual's hearing, the more impaired we would expect his speech to be (Ling, 1976).

The phonological disorders seen in the hard-of-hearing population vary greatly depending on the type of hearing loss, its severity, and the age of onset. For example, a child who acquires a hearing loss after developing language is likely to have fewer speech errors than is a child who is hard of

hearing from birth. A child with a hearing loss primarily in the high frequencies is likely to have difficulty both perceiving and producing voiceless fricatives and affricates because the hissing noise that characterizes these sounds is also high-frequency in nature. In both cases, the hearing loss generally relates strongly to the characteristics of the child's phonological disorder.

5. Summary. The organic causes of phonological disorders can be categorized as structural deviations of the speech mechanism, neuromotor disorders, cognitive disorders, and hearing impairment. Of the structural deviations discussed, cleft palate has the most negative effect on speech-sound production. Speech in cleft-palate individuals may be excessively nasal or may be distorted by air that escapes through the nose during consonant production. Neuromotor impairment may cause *dysarthria,* a speech disorder that can include slow speech, imprecise consonants, excessive nasality, and a monotone voice quality. *Apraxia* of speech, also caused by neuromotor impairment, results in numerous and inconsistent speech-sound errors and difficulty in programming voluntary speech movements.

Individuals with cognitive disorders display articulatory and phonological delays commensurate with their delayed development in other areas. And finally, individuals with hearing loss exhibit phonological disorders that reflect the severity of their hearing impairment, its nature, and its time of onset.

FUNCTIONAL PHONOLOGICAL DISORDERS

Despite the fairly lengthy list of possible organic causes, no known cause can be found for the majority of phonological disorders, even with the best diagnostic techniques available. These disorders thus fall into the *functional* category. Some children with functional phonological disorders misarticulate only a few sounds; others are quite unintelligible. Scientists and clinicians in communication sciences and disorders have long sought causative factors or correlates for these functional disorders, but so far they have had limited success.

Causative agents for functional phonological disorders have been hypothesized to include subtle abnormalities in structure and function of the speech mechanism, hearing and auditory perception, cognitive-linguistic abilities, and psychosocial factors (Bernthal and Bankson, 1993). Findings in each area are presented below.

1. Structure and Function of the Speech Mechanism.

Since it is well known that a cleft palate can cause articulatory deficits, perhaps it is the case that less obvious structural abnormalities might be the hidden cause of functional disorders. But so far, research has not supported such a hypothesis. Most individuals appear able to compensate quite successfully for anomalies of the teeth, tongue, and jaw, particularly if they are few in number; however, occasionally some speakers cannot. At present, it appears that minor structural abnormalities such as a large tongue or dental deviations might contribute to a phonological disorder in *some* individuals, but not for the majority (Weiss et al., 1987).

Another possible hidden cause of functional phonological disorders is a subtle motor disorder—a slight degree of weakness, abnormal muscle tone, or incoordination—that is not immediately apparent. When oral motor skills have been tested, however, the results have been inconclusive. Oral motor skills are frequently assessed through rapid repetition of nonsense syllables such as "puh," "tuh," and "kuh." In one study of syllable repetition rates, Dworkin (1978) found that children with speech-sound deficits performed syllable repetitions more slowly than did their normally developing peers. However, later, in 1985, Dworkin and Culatta found no difference between the groups in a similar study. Thus, the relationship between slight oral motor deficits and functional phonological disorders appears to be neither strong nor consistent.

Besides structure and motor abilities, some researchers have examined the relationship between oral, sensory, and perceptual abilities and phonological disorders. In producing speech sounds, it might be hypothesized that it is important to be able to feel tongue position and rate and direction of movement. Sensory feedback might arguably be important in adjusting movements so that clear speech is produced. In this area, however, again a consistent pattern has not been found. In some studies, slight decrements in oral sensitivity and discrimination were observed in individuals with "r" misarticulation (McNutt, 1977). However, it has also been found that some individuals with very poor sensory feedback have normal articulation (McDonald and Aungst, 1970).

Do individuals with functional phonological disorders have subtle abnormalities in oral structure, deficits in oral motor skills, or oral sensation and perception disorders? The answer may be yes for some individuals but no for most others. Variables related to structure and function of the speech mechanism do not appear to account for the presence of functional disorders.

2. Hearing and Auditory Perception.

If output variables cannot account for functional phonological disorders, perhaps input variables can. It is well-known that a permanent hearing loss has a negative impact on articulatory abilities. Would a mild or transient hearing loss have a similar effect?

The question of mild and transient hearing loss and its relationship to functional phonological disorders has been studied primarily in the context of otitis media. *Otitis media* is an inflammation of the middle ear. The middle ear is an extension of the upper respiratory system, and when a child has a cold, allergy, or infection, the middle ear may become filled with fluid. This fluid acts as a damper to sound transmission; and when it is present, the child generally has a slight or mild hearing loss. However, when the condition is resolved and the child is healthy, hearing may return to normal. Can periods of mild hearing loss affect phonological development?

Again, the research has been equivocal. Some investigators have found that children with a history of otitis media have identifiable phonological deficits different from those of otitis-free children, and these children may be more likely to develop phonological disorders in the moderate-to-severe range (Shriberg and Smith, 1983; Churchill et al., 1985; Shriberg and Kwiatkowski, 1982). Other researchers have found that there do not appear to be any distinguishing patterns of phonological errors between children with a history of otitis media and those without and that there is wide variability (ranging from normal to severely disordered) in the phonological skills of the former group (Paden et al., 1987; Paden et al., 1989). In summary, a history of otitis media *may* be a related factor for *some* individuals with functional phonological disorders. However, such a relationship is not always present.

Another possible factor related to phonological disorders is auditory discrimination. *Auditory discrimination* refers to a child's ability to differentiate one phoneme from another. Some children, despite normal hearing, have trouble with this task. We might hypothesize that if a child has difficulty attending to and perceiving subtle differences between speech sounds, he or she might also have difficulty in producing those sounds. For example, a child who substitutes "w" for "r" might be expected to have trouble hearing the difference between "w" and "r" when the examiner produces them. In fact, such a correspondence between discrimination difficulties and production difficulties has been inconsistent in the research (Bernthal and Bankson, 1993). Even when the child's own error productions were imitated by the examiner, up to 70 percent of the children were able to perceive correct versus incorrect productions (Locke, 1980). However, children with phonological disorders have somewhat poorer *overall* scores on auditory-discrimination tests than do their normally developing peers (Winitz, 1984). Thus, auditory-discrimination abilities may be another factor in phonological delay, but the exact causal relationship between the two is not clear.

3. Cognitive-Linguistic Abilities.

Cognitive and linguistic variables include such attributes as intelligence and language development (Bernthal and Bankson, 1993). In the area of intelligence, it is known that those with cognitive disorders, as a group, have a higher incidence of phonological

disorders. However, research targeting children whose intelligence test scores were in the normal range failed to find a relationship between intelligence and articulatory abilities (Weiss et al., 1987).

Studies of the relationship between language disorders and phonological disorders have been more revealing. According to a review by Bernthal and Bankson (1993), young children with severe phonological disorders are more likely to have a language delay or disorder than their peers with mild or moderate phonological disorders. Stoel-Gammon and Dunn (1985) concluded that although language and phonological disorders coexist in many children, receptive language is not often affected. In terms of expressive language skills, use of syntax appears to correlate most closely with phonological disorders. It is not clear what the causative relationship of these two disorders is, however. Do phonological disorders cause language disorder? Do language disorders cause phonological disorders? Are the two types of disorders caused by the same underlying cognitive deficit, such as difficulty with rule abstraction? Or is there some other factor that can account for the relationship? At this point, we do not know.

4. Psychosocial Factors.

A number of social and personal factors have also been investigated to determine their relationship, if any, to the incidence of phonological disorders. These factors have included (1) socioeconomic level, (2) gender, (3) sibling status, (4) speech stimulation and reinforcement in the environment, (5) the child's motivation, and (6) personality and adjustment. Of these factors, research results on socioeconomic status and on personality and adjustment showed no consistent relationship to the prevalence of phonological disorders (Bernthal and Bankson, 1993). Studies on gender have shown that more boys than girls have phonological disorders, but tests of articulatory competence were seldom statistically significant between the two groups (Weiss et al., 1987).

Sibling status, in contrast, showed some surprising relationships to phonological development. Two reviews, one by Bernthal and Bankson (1993) and one by Weiss et al. (1987) concluded that first-born children, children without siblings, and children who were widely spaced in age were likely to have better articulation skills than were second-born children; and the youngest child in the family is most at risk for a phonological disorder (Beckey, 1942). Furthermore, twins are more likely to have phonological delays than are singletons. The authors of both these reviews speculated that children who spent more time with their parents, and thus had more opportunity for adult modeling and interaction, had fewer phonological disorders than did children who had to compete with closely spaced age mates and additional brothers and sisters for parental attention.

Little research has been carried out regarding the relationship between a child's motivation to communicate and his phonological development. Weiss et al. (1987) hypothesize that when a child's wants are anticipated so that he does not *have* to speak, or when a child's unintelligible utterances are so well understood by his parents that he does not have to improve his speech to get what he wants, speech development may be slowed. In both cases, the child's motivation to improve his articulatory competence is low. Unfortunately, there are few studies directly studying motivation that could be cited to confirm or refute such a clinical observation. More research is needed to determine whether or not a relationship between motivation to improve one's speech and progress in phonological development is indeed strong and consistent.

5. Summary. In summary, what can we say about potential causes and correlates of functional phonological disorders? In some children, minor structural and functional abnormalities in the speech mechanism may contribute to a phonological disorder; a history of otitis media or poor auditory discrimination abilities may also be a factor. Gender and position in the family are also loosely associated with phonological status. Other variables, such as motivation to communicate, are more speculative. At this point, there is an "absence of any one-to-one correspondence between the presence of a particular etiological factor and the nature of an individual's phonological status" (Bernthal and Bankson, 1993, 215). For now, at least, the reason why a particular child has a functional phonological disorder cannot be specified.

RANGES OF SEVERITY

Phonological disorders have a tremendous range of severity, from the almost unnoticeably mild to the severe and unintelligible. Consider the following examples[1]:

EXAMPLE 1

Examiner: Now—baseball. What about baseball?
 Child 1: The batheball playerth almotht went on thtrike, ath we all know. A thrike altho meanth that you thwing and mith the ball.

Child 1 is a 10-year old boy. He consistently uses a somewhat fronted "s" that is almost (but not quite) the "th" written above. His disorder is so mild that many students who listen to a tape recording of his speech feel that his articulation is normal. However, despite the sophisticated message he is conveying, most students who hear this sample estimate that he is 6 or 7 years old. Thus, even a slight phonological disorder can give the impression that a child is younger than he actually is.

EXAMPLE 2

Examiner: (giving a standardized speech test) What is Uncle Fred doing?
 Child 2: In bed.
Examiner: (turning to the next picture in the test) How about this one?

---

[1]From the Speech Development and Disorders Laboratory at Indiana University, under the direction of Mary Elbert, Ph.D.

Child 2: Him dau on hih ha—hey, how—hey
how bau him ta tay a new day-dih.

Examiner: A new David?

Child 2: A *newd* day-dih. How bau him lai
da—

Examiner: A news station? OK—

Child 2: —and the name of ih wo-wo-wo.
Hey—do you lai ta lih da wo-wo-wo?

Examiner: (long pause) Sometimes.

Child 2 is a 6-year-old boy. Most students who
listen to a tape recording of his speech are unable
to understand what he is saying except for his
direct answers to the examiner's questions, like "in
bed." His spontaneous speech is at least 75 percent
unintelligible. From this sample, it also appears that
child 2 has some degree of language disorder in
addition to his phonological disorder. At the age of
6, we would not expect a child to begin a sentence
with "him" as the subject. However, a complete
evaluation of child 2's expressive language would
be difficult due to his low intelligibility.

It is interesting to note that both child 1 and
child 2 have functional phonological disorders.
Neither child has any obvious structural deviations,
neuromuscular disorders, cognitive disorders, or
hearing impairment. We often think that organic
disorders must be somehow much more severe
than "mere" functional disorders, but, in fact, functional disorders can also cause unintelligibility.

PROGNOSIS FOR INDIVIDUALS WITH PHONOLOGICAL DISORDERS

What happens to children with phonological disorders? Will they ever achieve normal-sounding
speech? Will they need therapy to overcome their
disorder? These are questions that parents and
teachers frequently ask regarding phonologically
disordered children. Unfortunately, the answers
are not always clear.

There is evidence that *some* children with
phonological disorders that are functional in nature
do correct their own errors. Much of the research
in this area was done in the 1960s and early 1970s,
when speech services were not always available in

the public schools, and there was no legal mandate
to treat children with handicaps (as there is today).
For example, Sax (1972) reports on a five-year
study in which 396 third-grade and 223 fourth-
grade students were identified as having one to
four speech sounds in error. Since remediation
services could not be provided, these children
were placed on a "waiting list." One year later,
23.7 percent of the third graders and 20 percent
of the fourth graders had achieved normal-sounding speech with no clinical intervention. In a separate study of 399 kindergarten children, 35 students produced lateralized distortions of fricatives
and affricates, but 18 of them produced the sounds
correctly by the end of third grade.

Bralley and Stoudt (1977) found 60 children
with at least one "articulation error" (as the term
was used then) entering first grade. The average
number of errors was 6.63 per child. Over the
next four years, the majority of these children
corrected their errors without intervention. By
the beginning of fifth grade, only 13 children
remained in the study, with an average of 1.32
errors each. Again, these children had not
received any therapeutic services.

Based on these studies, it appears that many
children correct their own speech-sound errors
eventually, if their disorders are functional and
relatively mild. The key words in this statement
are *many* and *eventually*. Unfortunately, we still do
not have a proven and reliable method of predicting who will and who will not self-correct;
and it may take a child the duration of his or her
elementary school years to achieve this.

What about child 1 in our example? His distortion of "s" appears to be a mild disorder. If left
alone, is he likely to self-correct? When we ask
such a question about a specific child, it is clear
that our ability to predict who will and who will
not need therapy is limited. It is true that child 1
has a mild disorder, which is a positive prognostic
sign. However, he is also 10 years old. Most
authorities believe that phonological development
is essentially complete by the age of 8 or 9, and
beyond that age, a child is less likely to self-
correct (Bernthal and Bankson, 1993). Thus,
we might conclude that child 1 will need therapy

in order to overcome his phonological disorders.

Children with severe phonological disorders (especially if coupled with language disorders) may also self-correct to some degree, but there is a higher probability that the child will need continuing therapy for multiple articulation errors and language (Shriberg and Kwiatkowski, 1988). Child 2 is an example of a child with both a severe phonological disorder and a language disorder. Without therapy, his speech may improve to the point of being relatively intelligible by the end of his elementary school years, but this outcome is not certain. Bralley and Stoudt (1977) noted that two of the subjects in their study who had had early speech-production problems continued to show numerous errors in the fifth grade. Thus, prognosis without therapy is somewhat guarded. With therapy, however, the prognosis for children with functional phonological disorders of any severity level is almost always good. Although therapy cannot be successful in every case, most individuals with functional disorders can be helped to achieve normal speech.

The prognosis for children with organic phonological disorders depends to a large degree on the nature of the underlying physical disorder and how well it can be corrected (Air et al., 1989). If the problem is a slight one and can be resolved at an early age through medical treatment, the child might achieve normal speech even without therapy. However, children with organic disorders are less likely to correct their own errors than are children with functional disorders. When the speech mechanism is compromised, it is often necessary to provide some specific training for children in order to maximize their potential for normal-sounding speech. In the case of mild organic disorders, the prognosis varies, but it is almost always better with therapy than without. Again, some of these disorders may persist into the adult years.

Children with severe organic disorders may not be capable of achieving intelligible speech at all, with or without therapy. In these cases, however, therapy *can* help the child *communicate,* if not to speak (Air et al., 1989). The speech-language pathologist can teach the child to point to pictures, words, or letters, to use sign language, or to use a number of other augmentative or alternative forms of communication. Without therapy, the potential of the child to develop communication skills and participate in society is limited. Even with therapy, the prognosis for speech may be poor, but the prognosis for communication and for the ability to function socially is vastly improved.

CONSEQUENCES OF A PHONOLOGICAL DISORDER

Does a child with a phonological disorder—or an adult, for that matter—experience any educational, social, or vocational consequences as a result of the disorder? The answer appears to depend somewhat on the severity of the problem. We will examine the areas mentioned above one by one in order to explore potential consequences and controversies.

EDUCATIONAL CONSEQUENCES

The general consensus emerging from over two decades of research is that children with *only* problems of speech-sound production generally *do not* appear to be at risk for reading, educational, or continued communication disorders (Flynn and Byrne, 1970; Hall and Tomblin, 1978; Catts et al., 1989; Shriberg and Kwiatkowski, 1988). It is important to note that this applies only to individuals who have articulation errors, as defined in the first section of this chapter—disorders based on faulty motor patterns rather than deficient rule systems.

Those whose phonological disorders involve a deficient rule system, or who have difficulties with syntax and morphology as well as phonology, *are* at risk for continuing communication disorders, reading problems, and special education placement (Shriberg and Kwiatkowski, 1988; Catts, 1986; Katz, 1986; Catts et al., 1989; Felsenfeld et al., 1992). Thus, the educational significance of a phonological disorder appears to depend on its subtype: production-based or rule-based. Children with isolated misarticulations of a few speech sounds, such as "s," "z," "r," or "l"—like child 1 in our example—are not likely to encounter academic difficulties. However, children who demonstrate multiple and inconsistent substitutions and perhaps sentence formulation difficulties, too—like child 2—may experience long-range educational consequences.

SOCIAL CONSEQUENCES

Recent research on the social consequences of phonological disorders provides support for the idea that negative social consequences are attached to even mild speech errors. For example, Hall (1991) looked at the attitudes of fourth graders and sixth graders toward peers with and without mild articulation errors involving "r," "s," and "z." She found significantly more negative attitudes toward peers who exhibited articulatory errors. Silverman and Paulus (1989) got similar results for high school sophomores.

Studies examining attitudes toward adults with minor articulatory errors (such as an "s" distortion) show the same results. Mowrer et al. (1978) found that the presence of a fronted "s" in a male speaker resulted in lowered ratings of the speaker's intelligence, speaking ability, education, masculinity, and social appeal compared to a speaker with no articulation errors. Silverman (1976) found the same attitudes toward female speakers.

The results of these studies suggest that the presence of a phonological disorder—even a mild one—negatively affects a speaker's social standing, regardless of age. Although there are cases of movie and television stars with phonological disorders (Barbara Walters comes to mind) who have obviously done very well, we should not ignore the potential negative impact of such a disorder on the individual's social adjustment.

VOCATIONAL CONSEQUENCES

Do phonological disorders affect one's career aspirations and achievement? This question is more difficult to answer. A severe disorder in adulthood that causes reduced intelligibility would be most likely to have a negative impact on employment success. Even if intelligibility is not compromised, however, negative consequences may still occur.

For example, if an applicant's mild speech disorder causes potential employers to stereotype him or her as less intelligent, less educated, and less appealing than average, then the applicant's chance of being hired and promoted would seem to be reduced. We might therefore infer negative vocational consequences from a phonological disorder. On the other hand, as discussed above, some individuals in highly visible fields have achieved outstanding success despite speech-sound errors. The effect of a phonological disorder on an individual's vocational success is most likely highly dependent on the individual's abilities, personality, attitudes, and desire to overcome obstacles, as well as the particular requirements of the field they have chosen to pursue.

THE ROLE OF PARENTS AND TEACHERS

Parents and teachers have three primary roles to play with regard to phonological disorders: (1) they can help prevent such disorders from occurring in the first place by providing good models for their children; (2) they can refer any child with a suspected phonological disorder for a speech evaluation; and (3) they can work with the speech-language pathologist to help the child with a disorder to generalize his new sound to the home and school environment.

PREVENTION

The most important role of parents and teachers may be in preventing phonological disorders, according to Weiss et al. (1987). Although parents and teachers may not be able to prevent a specific child from developing a phonological disorder, their use of good models for effective communication can enhance overall speech and language development. Adults who interact with the child daily serve as role models in many areas of behavior, including speech. If parents and teachers speak clearly and correctly to children and provide a positive and reinforcing atmosphere, it is likely that the children (if they are able) will try to produce such language forms themselves. However, it should be

FIGURE 7-1 Reading and other language activities can help provide children with the stimulation and reinforcement they need to learn good phonological skills. (Elizabeth Crews)

noted that some children—for organic, developmental, or unknown reasons—may not be able to produce clear speech despite their parents' efforts.

REFERRAL

What about the child who doesn't sound like everyone else his age? The child who is difficult to understand? The child who has one, two, or more speech-sound errors? For parents, teachers, and other professionals who work with children, the line between normal errors that are part of the learning process and a possible phonological disorder may be difficult to discern.

In deciding whether or not to refer a child for a speech evaluation, four general guidelines for referral appear to be warranted, regardless of the age of the child. First, if the parents are concerned about

the child's speech and feel it is interfering with family, school, or social communication, the child should be referred for further evaluation (Newman and Creaghead, 1989; Weiss et al., 1987). Second, any child who is being teased by peers and classmates, feels self-conscious about his speech, or restricts his classroom participation because of concerns about his speech should be referred for a speech-language evaluation (Bernthal and Bankson, 1993). Third, any child suspected of having a hearing loss should be referred for further evaluation even if the phonological disorder seems mild. A child with an input deficit is not likely to be able to correct his or her own speech without specialized help. Frequent ear infections often cause periods of hearing loss, so such children should be carefully monitored. And fourth, any child with a known physical handicap should be referred to a speech-language pathologist for a phonological evaluation (Weiss et al., 1987). As previously discussed, some structural and neuromuscular disorders cause known speech impairments, and children with these disorders may need professional intervention in order to improve their speech.

For children who appear phonologically delayed but do not evidence any hearing loss, physical disability, or emotional reaction, the guidelines for referral are less clear. This author would recommend the criteria listed in Table 7-1. Preschool children who have limited intelligibility or multiple phoneme errors should be referred for an evaluation, especially if their language development also appears to be delayed. Children of kindergarten age should also be referred for intelligibility problems or if their speech-sound-production errors are interfering with their acquisition of prereading skills. In many schools, kindergartners learn to recognize all the letters of the alphabet, to associate a sound with each letter, and to identify beginning and ending sounds in words. A child with a phonological disorder may have difficulty with these activities if he or she cannot produce certain sounds. In such cases, professional help with speech may improve the child's educational experience.

Children in second and third grade can be referred for less serious errors involving specific phonemes. Children who are 9 years old or older

---

TABLE 7-1 Indications for Referral for Speech Evaluation

Children of Any Age Who:

---

1. Have parents who are concerned about their speech.
2. Are being teased because of their speech patterns, feel self-conscious about their speech, or restrict their class participation because of it.
3. Are suspected of having a hearing loss or have a history of middle-ear infection.
4. Have physical impairments.

Children of Preschool Age Who:

---

1. Cannot be readily understood (at least 75 percent of the time for a 3- to 4-year-old and 90 percent of the time for a 4-to-5-year-old).
2. Have multiple speech-sound substitutions (for example, "t" for "k," "d" for "g," "t" for "s," "t" for "sh," and so on) or omissions of speech sounds and syllables.
3. Appear to be delayed in their language development in addition to their difficulties in producing speech sounds.

Children of Kindergarten and First-Grade Age Who:

---

1. Have any of the problems described above.
2. Have speech-sound-production errors that are interfering with their success in their academic activities, such as prereading, reading, and spelling skills.

Children in Second Grade Who:

---

1. Have any of the problems described above.
2. Have isolated misarticulations of "sh," "ch," "j," or "l."

Children in Third Grade Who:

---

1. Have any of the problems described above.
2. Have isolated misarticulations of "s," "z," "r," "v," "th," or any other speech sound.

(the typical age of children at the end of the third or the beginning of the fourth grade) are unlikely to self-correct and thus should be referred for any consistently produced distortion (Bernthal and Bankson, 1993). However, it should be noted that speech–language pathologists in the public schools may not necessarily enroll a child with only one or two phonemes in error for therapy. In responding to the requirements of Pub. L. No. 94-142 to provide educational services for all handicapped students, school districts continue to wrestle with the issue of eligibility. Depending on the district's criteria for speech and language handicaps, children with milder disorders may no longer qualify for therapy. We will discuss this controversy in service provision later in this chapter.

Clearly, parents and teachers are in an excellent position to note the speaking skills of the children around them and to identify the children who seem to be functioning at a lower level than their peers. Referring such children for evaluation and possible therapy is an important role for these adults.

WORKING WITH THE
SPEECH-LANGUAGE PATHOLOGIST

If a child is receiving speech therapy for a phonological disorder, the speech-language pathologist, the classroom teacher, and the parents can work together to ensure that correct sound production is generalized into conversational and classroom speech. As the child's production becomes better-established and more automatic in therapy, the speech-language pathologist may provide activities that the parents can do with the child at home or that the teacher can incorporate into the classroom. The key to successful generalization is often a concerned adult in the daily environment who can furnish support and reinforcement for the child as she stabilizes her new speech pattern.

EVALUATION OF
PHONOLOGICAL DISORDERS

The primary purpose of a phonological evaluation is to determine whether an individual has a problem that needs intervention. In addition, the speech-language pathologist (1) tries to identify the factors that may have caused or contributed to the disorder, (2) decides on the appropriate intervention targets and strategies, and (3) gives a prognosis for success in therapy (Bernthal and Bankson, 1993). The first step in the entire process is usually to obtain a case history. If it is a child who is being evaluated, case-history information can be obtained from the child's parents and teachers and from school records, prior to the evaluation itself. A case history can provide important information on the background, course, and consequences of the problem.

A hearing (or *audiological*) test is another important part of the speech evaluation. This test is performed by either the speech-language pathologist or by an audiologist, in order to determine whether hearing loss is a causative factor in

the phonological disorder. An oral-peripheral examination is also administered. In an *oral-peripheral examination,* the speech-language pathologist does a thorough inspection of the individual's speech mechanism to rule out structural defects. He or she also assesses the client's ability to perform voluntary movements with the tongue, lips, and velum in order to determine if neuromuscular involvement is a factor in the disorder.

The speech-language pathologist might also do an auditory-discrimination test, as described previously in this chapter. Although the relationship between auditory discrimination and articulation ability is not always clear, the client's performance on this test may indicate weaknesses that should be addressed in therapy. And since many children with phonological disorders have language disorders as well, the speech-language pathologist may also do language testing to see if this area, too, should be addressed in therapy.

The heart of a phonological evaluation, however, is the articulation and phonological assessment. During this assessment, the speech-language pathologist obtains samples of the client's spontaneous connected speech in conversation, while describing pictures, or while playing with toys. A sample of articulation in single words during picture-naming and imitation activities is also elicited. It is important to examine different types of speech samples, because the client's error productions may be so inconsistent that isolated words do not accurately represent his error patterns. This is particularly true for clients with multiple phoneme errors and limited intelligibility. A phonological-processes analysis is often done on spontaneous or elicited connected-speech samples.

Sometimes a client is not able to use phonemes correctly in connected speech but can produce them in isolated syllables or words when the speech-language pathologist models them. This is known as *stimulability*. A speech-language pathologist generally does stimulability testing to see how easily a client can correct faulty production. Stimulability has been found to be an important prognostic factor: If a child is stimulable for a particular phoneme, he is likely to correct that phoneme even if it is not directly addressed in

 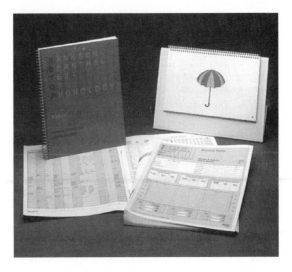

FIGURE 7-2 These are some of the articulation tests used by speech-language pathologists. (Left: Goldman-Fristoe Test of Articulation by Ronald Goldman & Macalyne Fristoe © 1969, 1972, 1986 American Guidance Service, Inc., 4201 Woodland Road, Circle Pines, Minnesota 55014-1796. Reproduced with permission of the Publisher. All rights reserved. Right: Bankson-Bernthal Test of Phonology © 1995 Reproduced with permission of The Riverside Publishing Company, Chicago.)

therapy (Powell et al., 1991; Sommers et al., 1967).

Once all the tests have been administered and the analyses performed, the speech-language pathologist has the responsibility of synthesizing and interpreting the results to determine whether the client being tested requires remediation. He or she must also decide whether and when to enroll the client for therapy and must suggest the initial goals.

THERAPY FOR PHONOLOGICAL DISORDERS

Therapy for phonological disorders can be divided into three general phases: establishment, generalization, and maintenance (Bernthal and Bankson, 1993). The content of therapy varies according to whether the individual has a rule-based true phonological disorder or a more physically based articulation disorder. In either case, therapy is guided by learning or behavioral principles. That is, specific (and measurable) goals for speech or perceptual behaviors are set, teaching

begins with and builds on what the client *can* do, and new skills are introduced while positive reinforcement for successful attempts is provided (Weiss et al., 1987).

ESTABLISHMENT

If you have ever tried to correct a child who pronounced a word incorrectly, you have some appreciation for why the establishment phase of therapy is so important:

> *Adult:* "Say rabbit instead of wabbit."
>
> *Child with an*
> *"r" distortion:* "I *said* wabbit, not wabbit."
>
> *Adult:* "No, try again: r-r-rabbit."
>
> *Child (somewhat*
> *frustrated by*
> *this point):* "I *did* say wabbit! W-w-wabbit! You're not listening!"

Just *telling* a child his sound production is incorrect, and providing a correct model, is not always adequate to cause a child to correct his error. First, the child may not be aware that his production is *really* incorrect, as in the above example. This is especially true when the sound in error is a distortion. The child may be able to hear the differences in *your* contrasting productions, but may simply accept his own distortion as an acceptable allophonic variant of your correct model. Second, even if the child *does* recognize the deficiency in his own production, he might not know what to do with his tongue, lips, and jaw to make the sound correctly. Parents' and teachers' corrections of children with phonological disorders, and endless requests for repetitions, can result in frustration for all parties involved.

Speech-language pathologists use a number of different techniques to help a child recognize his own errors and correct them. Regardless of whether the problem is primarily one of rules knowledge or of physical difficulty, therapy may include a period of auditory training. This process is usually initiated by having the child listen to the correct and incorrect productions of others on tape. Eventually, the child learns how to incorporate these phonemic patterns into his own speech and to monitor his own sound production during ongoing speech.

Another technique used during the establishment phase is phonetic placement. In this technique, dating from the 1920s, the speech-language pathologist instructs the child regarding the appropriate placement of the tongue, lips, and so on. The child is taught to produce the sound slowly and deliberately at first, concentrating on how it *feels* to form the phoneme correctly while listening to how it *sounds*. The goal is to help the child associate specific motor patterns with "good-sounding" phonemes. The phonetic-placement technique is associated with traditional articulation therapy.

Newer techniques for sound acquisition based on the phonological-processes model stress the elimination of phonological processes. Phonological processes, as you recall from Chapter 6, involve simplifications to word structure made by very young children who are just learning speech. Some of the phonological processes we discussed were: syllable simplifications, such as deleting final consonants, deleting at least one consonant from a consonant blend, and deleting unstressed syllables; assimilation; and substituting one class of sounds for another, such as substituting stop consonants for fricatives.

Speech errors due to persistent phonological processes are often seen in children with phonological disorders. An important goal for such children is the elimination of these persistent error patterns. The minimal-contrast procedure is one technique that can aid in this elimination. This procedure involves the use of paired words that are the same except for a phoneme that is part of the child's error pattern. For example, if the speech-language pathologist wanted to eliminate the process of final consonant deletion, she might contrast meaningful words, such as "bow" and "boat," or "row" and "rose" (Weiner, 1981). In order to make a distinction between the words and correctly label pictures of a bow, a boat, a row, and a rose, the child would be forced to attend to the final sounds. Research with this technique has shown good results (Gierut, 1992; Powell et al., 1991).

GENERALIZATION

As the child gets better at producing his "error sound" correctly at one particular level (such as in isolation or in syllables), the sound must then be incorporated into successively longer units of speech (words, phrases, sentences). Similarly, if the child has learned to produce his error sound correctly only at the *beginnings* of words, the sound must next be corrected in the middle and at the end of words. The process of expanding correct production into new contexts is known as *generalization*.

Ideally, generalization should occur naturally, as an outgrowth of the child's growing proficiency with speech. We would hope that if the child has mastered the "s" sound in the word *silly*, he would be able to go on to use a correct "s" in the words *missing, cats,* and *slide*. In reality, however, not all children are able to successfully generalize from one context to another, thus goals for facilitating generalization are always a part of therapy. The speech-language pathologist may specifically teach the sound in several word positions, especially if one context (such as blends) is particularly difficult for the child. The amount of generalization that occurs without training is highly variable from individual to individual (Bernthal and Bankson, 1993). Obviously, children who generalize easily from one context to another, and from one length of utterance to another, will make faster progress in therapy.

Once a child is able to produce his target sounds correctly and with some degree of proficiency, it is important to extend this production into longer units of speech and more natural situations. This is yet another aspect of generalization. Many children produce excellent speech in the therapy room but go back to their old faulty productions when they leave. New correct patterns require conscious effort for quite a while after they are learned, until they can be used rapidly and effortlessly in conversation. The transition from structured situations monitored by the speech-language pathologist to complete self-monitoring can be difficult.

Boone and Plante (1993) suggest several techniques to help generalize new speech patterns to everyday speech. In order to strengthen new motor patterns and increase their automaticity, they suggest using the new sound in *carrier phrases,* phrases that are said over and over again in the course of an activity. Sentences and tongue twisters could also be used.

To monitor generalization of target sounds and phonological processes to situations outside the therapy room, the speech-language pathologist may observe the client in more natural settings. In a public school, the speech-language pathologist may arrange with the child's classroom teacher to be present during a class discussion or reading group, to see if the child is transferring his or her new phonological patterns into such situations.

MAINTENANCE

The final phase of therapy involves periodic monitoring of the individual to ensure that correct production is maintained and that backsliding into old, incorrect patterns has not occurred. The client may see the speech-language pathologist on a reduced schedule (monthly, for example, instead of weekly) as the primary responsibility for monitoring and sustaining correct speech-sound production is shifted to the client. The ultimate goal of therapy will hopefully be realized in this phase: automatic usage of standard phonological and articulation patterns in all conversational and spontaneous speech, both in and out of the clinic, without deliberate or conscious effort (Weiss et al., 1987).

Therapy for phonological disorders requires an organized and systematic approach to behavior change. It also requires creativity, because each client is an individual and responds to different cues and instructional strategies. A well-trained speech-language pathologist generally has excellent results with therapy for phonological disorders.

SERVICE PROVISION: A CONTROVERSY

Speech therapy for individuals with phonological disorders is provided in a number of settings. Adults and children can be seen as private clients in hospital-based clinics, in independent clinics, or in a private practice. In some cases, insurance will cover the cost of therapy for phonological disorders in these settings, but, more frequently, it becomes an out-of-pocket expense for the client or family. Another treatment option is a university-based training clinic. In this setting, student clinicians provide therapy services under the supervision of certified staff and faculty, usually at greatly reduced prices.

By far the most common setting for the treatment of children with phonological disorders is the public school. The remediation of such disorders has traditionally been considered part of the student's education. However, as the scope of the public school speech-language pathologist's responsibilities has increased, these traditional assumptions are being questioned.

As you will recall from previous chapters, handicapped individuals from birth to the age of 21 are now eligible for special education services such as speech therapy, based on the mandate of

Pub. L. No. 94-142 and Pub. L. No. 99-457. The inclusion of many formerly excluded children in the public schools is an important step in assuring the rights of the handicapped to an education, but it also provides a challenge for administrators. As Pub. L. No. 94-142 and Pub. L. No. 99-457 have been implemented in school districts around the country, special education personnel have had to grapple with the definition of "handicapped" and decide who is eligible for services.

In a previous section, it was noted that a child with only one or two phonemes in error may not be seen by the public school speech-language pathologist. Hall (1991, 338) states, "Although numbers are not available, there are some school districts that do not provide speech-language pathology services to children who present only one or two articulatory errors because their articulation is not believed to adversely affect academic performance." In other words, children with mild phonological disorders might not be considered handicapped and thus might be deemed ineligible for speech-therapy services under current regulations.

The denial of services to children with mild phonological disorders is not currently widespread, but it is a controversial development in the field of communication sciences and disorders (Shriberg, 1980). On one hand, the research we have reviewed suggests that many children with mild phonological disorders self-correct by the fifth grade. On the other hand, we have no reliable way of separating those who will self-correct from those who won't. Further, the social consequences of even a mild disorder may be detrimental to the child's socialization (Hall, 1991). In view of the latter, some school districts have broadened their criteria for eligibility beyond "academic performance" so that the effect of the disorder on the child's social interactions can be considered, too.

In attempting to provide speech and language therapy services for the maximum number of children, some school districts have hired *communication aides,* individuals with district-determined qualifications who theoretically work under the direction of a certified speech-language patholo-

gist. According to ASHA's Ethical Practices Board, a speech-language pathologist may legitimately supervise communication aides but remains responsible for the services received by the client (ASHA, 1994). Unfortunately, no guidelines regarding the educational and training qualifications of these communication aides have been issued, and there is no assurance that schools and hospitals will provide adequate supervision for these individuals.

As we move into the twenty-first century, new challenges in the area of service provision will have to be met, and new ways of meeting the needs of clients may have to be devised. Students going into communication sciences and disorders are likely to see many changes in the field in the course of their professional lifetimes. Taxpayers will also have to make decisions regarding which children should qualify for services and what training the individuals who provide these services need. Today, these questions apply primarily to children in the public schools. But provision of health-related services to adults in need is a topic of growing urgency in view of the aging of the American population. We will discuss this subject further in Chapter 13.

SUMMARY

In this chapter, we defined *articulation* and *phonological disorders* and explored their causes. The prognosis for individuals with phonological disorders was considered, both with and without therapy; and the consequences of a phonological disorder to the individual was examined. The role of parents and teachers was also discussed. Finally, we looked at what the speech-language pathologist might do during an evaluation of and therapy for an individual with a phonological disorder, and at some of the controversies in service provision.

If you look back at Figure 1-2, you will see that in the content area of phonology, we have developed all the major theme headings. As we did in the language unit, we will now look at a special population of phonologically disordered individuals.

R E V I E W   Q U E S T I O N S

1. What is meant by the term *phonological disorder*? How can phonological disorders be differentiated from articulation disorders? Why is *phonological disorders* considered the more general term?
2. What are some organic causes of phonological disorders?
3. What are some of the factors that appear to be related to functional phonological disorders?
4. What is the prognosis, with and without therapy, for children with phonological disorders? Include age, cause of the disorder, and severity as factors in your answer.
5. What are some of the consequences of a phonological disorder in terms of educational limitations, social difficulties, and vocational considerations?
6. What can parents, teachers, and other concerned adults do to foster good phonological development and to help a child with a suspected phonological disorder?
7. What criteria might be used in deciding whether to refer a child to a speech-language pathologist for a phonological evaluation?
8. What are some components of an evaluation for phonological disorders?
9. What are the stages of therapy for phonological disorders? What techniques might be used at each step?
10. What are some of the arguments for and against providing therapy for phonological disorders in the public schools to children who have only one or two sounds in error?
11. What do you think about the use of communication aides in schools and clinics? What kind of regulations (if any) would you recommend for this job category?

F O R   F U R T H E R   I N F O R M A T I O N

Bernthal, J., and **Bankson, N.** (1993). *Articulation and phonological disorders* (3rd ed.). Englewood Cliffs, NJ: Prentice-Hall.

Creaghead, N., Newman, P., and **Secord, W.** (1989). *Assessment and remediation of articulatory and phonological disorders* (2nd ed.). Columbus, OH: Merrill.

Hodson, B., and **Paden, E.** (1991). *Targeting intelligible speech* (2nd ed.). Austin, TX: Pro-Ed.

Stoel-Gammon, C., and **Dunn, C.** (1985). *Normal and disordered phonology in children.* Baltimore, MD: University Park Press.

Weiss, C., Gordon, M., and **Lillywhite, H.** (1987). *Clinical management of articulatory and phonologic disorders* (2nd ed.). Baltimore, MD: Williams and Wilkins.

Special Populations: Cerebral Palsy

We conclude our discussion of phonological disorders by examining a special population that displays the disorder in question as well as other handicapping conditions. One group that frequently manifests phonological disorders, sometimes to a severe degree, is the population of children and adults with cerebral palsy. Cerebral palsy is primarily a motor disorder—that is, it affects an individual's ability to perform voluntary movements in a controlled way. Since speech requires rapid and precise voluntary movements, it is not surprising that many children and adults with cerebral palsy have phonological disorders. However, individuals with cerebral palsy often experience additional problems—in cognition, perception, sensation, and physical and psychological health—that complicate the process of learning to communicate. The speech-language pathologist who works with these individuals must be prepared to function as a member of an interdisciplinary team that addresses a broad range of handicapping conditions and rehabilitation strategies. Because there is no medical cure for cerebral palsy, it is up to education and rehabilitation personnel—teachers, speech-language pathologists, occupational therapists, physical therapists, recreation specialists, social workers, and so on—to help these individuals maximize their abilities and find a place in society.

WHAT IS CEREBRAL PALSY?

Cerebral palsy is a constellation of disorders that has at its base motor dysfunction. It is caused by damage to specific parts of the brain, sustained prior to birth, during birth, or shortly after birth. This means that cerebral palsy is a developmental disorder—that is, the brain damage, or *lesion,* occurs before the child has had a chance to develop mature motor skills.

This early onset means that children with cerebral palsy have a different set of problems from those experienced by adults who sustain similar damage from a stroke or head trauma later in life. An adult has had a lifetime of normal motor functioning, time during which joints and muscles have developed normally. Adults have memories of normal physical sensations and movement patterns that they can draw on as they attempt to regain lost skills. A child with cerebral palsy, on the other hand, has not had the chance to experience normal movement. Motor skills such as sitting, walking, reaching, and so on must be acquired through a dysfunctional system and are sometimes acquired in maladaptive ways. For example, in an attempt to gain head control, a child with cerebral palsy may arch his back and extend his head backward in what is called an *extensor position.* In addition, because of imbalances in muscle tone and abnormal movement patterns and postures, children with cerebral palsy may have decreased muscle mass, restricted joint motion, shallow joint sockets and spinal deformities (McDonald, 1987a). The latter structural problems further complicate the acquisition of motor skills. Thus, despite the similarity of brain lesions in cerebral palsy and acquired neuromotor disorders suffered by adults, the two are not directly comparable (Hardy, 1994).

The symptoms of cerebral palsy and its resulting deficits vary greatly from one individual to the next. One individual may demonstrate abnormally tense muscle tone while another demonstrates abnormally relaxed muscle tone, involuntary movements, incoordination, or problems with balance. Some may walk with little difficulty while other, more severely involved, individuals have to rely on wheelchairs. As a result of their brain lesions, cerebral-palsied individuals may also experience cognitive disorders of varying degrees of severity, seizures, perceptual-sensory problems, and communication disorders. Because of limited opportunities for interpersonal interaction and independent experience, they may have social-emotional or educational problems. Cerebral palsy is clearly a complex disorder, not limited to an easily defined set of motor symptoms.

Our definition of cerebral palsy included the idea that it is caused by damage to "specific parts" of the brain. Not surprisingly, these "parts" are those that play an important role in generating or regulating motor movement. To help us understand the relationship between damage to the brain and the symptoms of cerebral palsy, let us review some basic neurophysiology.

THE NEUROMOTOR SYSTEM

For the purposes of this text, we will define *neuromotor system* as those parts of the brain and nervous system that are necessary for planning and carrying out voluntary motor movement. Since voluntary movement almost always begins with an idea or a desire to carry out a certain activity, we will begin our review at the highest level of neurological functioning, the cerebral cortex of the brain.

The cerebral cortex is what most of us visualize when we think about the "brain." It consists of a wrinkled-looking surface that upon closer inspection, is an arrangement of gray "hills" and "valleys," known to neurologists as *gyri* and *sulci*. Some of the more distinguishable gyri and sulci have been named in order to provide landmarks

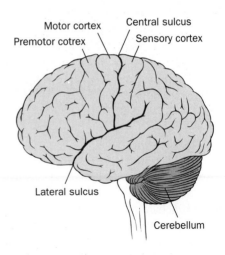

FIGURE 8-1 Lateral view of the cerebral cortex. The front (anterior aspect) of the brain is on the left, and the back (posterior aspect) of the brain is on the right.

for those studying the brain. In Figure 8-1, note the central sulcus and the lateral sulcus.

Immediately in front of the central sulcus is the precentral gyrus, or motor cortex, as shown in Figure 8-1. And directly in front of the motor cortex is the premotor cortex. It is at these specific locations in the brain, scientists believe, that motor movements are planned and initiated. According to Larson (1989), the premotor cortex (and a contiguous area, the supplementary motor cortex) plays an important role in the conceptual and general aspects of movement. These areas are involved in making the decision to perform a certain action and appear to be active in preparing the body in a global way to initiate the action by regulating muscle tone (Larson, 1989). Thus when a forceful movement—such as picking up something heavy—has been planned, the premotor cortex also initiates increased tension in the body's supporting and postural muscles. Against this stable "base," or background, the primary lifting muscles—the arms and hands—can function with greater accuracy and coordination.

The consciously planned movements of the arms and hands, in this example, are usually associated with the motor cortex. From this area of the brain, messages for muscle contraction are sent through long neural pathways that extend from the cortex down to connections in the spinal cord and then out to the *peripheral,* or local, nerves that innervate individual muscles. Thus, the motor cortex is associated with the specific aspects of a particular movement, such as the muscle contraction that occurs in the hand and fingers when an individual picks up a small object.

It is also hypothesized that the motor cortex plays a role in the relaxation of *antagonistic,* or opposing, muscles (Larson, 1989). For example, in order to reach for an object by extending the arm, the triceps muscle must be contracted. At the same time, the *biceps* (a muscle that bends or contracts the arm at the elbow) must be relaxed to some degree. If the biceps is not relaxed, the triceps and biceps (extending and contracting muscles) would effectively fight against each other, resulting in an arm that could not be fully extended and that might not be able to complete the desired reaching movement.

In summary, the highest levels of the neuromotor system are located in the cortex, or the highly developed external part of the brain. The premotor cortex is active in planning for a movement and preparing the body in a general way to carry it out. The motor cortex receives information from the premotor cortex and then activates the specific muscles necessary to perform the activity. As important as these functions are, however, many other parts of the neuromotor system must play their respective roles before the desire to perform a voluntary movement becomes a reality.

Looking at the cerebral cortex, one would imagine that the brain resembled a plate of spaghetti. This is not the case, however. The sulci and gyri of the cortex exist only on the surface. The cortex itself is only approximately ⅜ in (1.5 mm) to 1¾ in (4.5 mm) thick. Beneath the outer layer of cortex, the brain looks very different. A large part of the inner mass of the brain is white in color. Although it appears solid, it is actually composed of vast numbers of tightly compacted nerve fibers that link the cortex with lower neurological centers. Embedded within this white matter are

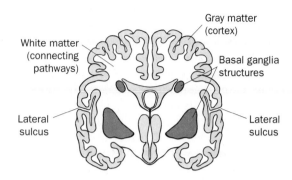

FIGURE 8-2 Subcortical structures associated with movement. In this figure, we are looking at the brain from the front (coronal view).

numerous islands of gray matter, processing centers for incoming sensory stimulation or outgoing motor commands (see Figure 8-2). It is to these gray islands that we will next turn our attention.

A group of *subcortical* (below the level of the cortex) structures associated with movement are the basal ganglia. Collectively, the basal ganglia appear to be important in the subconscious aspects of motor movement. According to Zemlin (1988, 339), they are active "in the regulation of complex motor functions such as posture, locomotion, balance, and such activities as arm-swinging during walking." Most readers would probably agree that they seldom directly plan their balance or arm swinging when engaged in voluntary movement. Although we can certainly swing our arms voluntarily (planning and initiating with the premotor and motor cortex) or attend to our body's position in space, most of the time we just let these things "happen" automatically. Zemlin also cites the role of the basal ganglia in inhibiting unwanted movements. Again, we rarely think about inhibiting the movement of one arm when we reach with the other. Although the functions of the basal ganglia are acknowledged to be poorly understood (Larson, 1989; Barr, 1979), it is most likely that they generate unconscious and automatic movements that accompany and perhaps facilitate voluntary movement.

At the base of the brain is another structure with important functions in motor movement: the cerebellum. According to Larson (1989, 79), the "cerebellum appears to be more directly related to motor *coordination* [italics the author's] than perhaps any other area of the brain." Researchers have discovered a network of feedback loops between the cerebellum, the basal ganglia, sensory parts of the brain, and the cortical motor centers, so that voluntary movement is constantly being refined and guided by input from the cerebellum. Automatic movements are also smoothed and coordinated. It is important to note that the cerebellum does not *generate* movement, as the cortical areas and basal ganglia do. Rather it serves to *regulate* motoric impulses coming from other neural centers. The more primitive parts of the cerebellum directly influence equilibrium and *gait* (walking pattern). Other areas of the cerebellum affect rapid sequential movements—such as piano playing—helping maintain the speed, direction, and timing of each movement. When too much alcohol is ingested, the cerebellum is noticeably affected. A wide-based gait, tilting posture, inability to walk a straight line, and slurred speech are all symptoms of temporary cerebellar dysfunction due to alcohol.

Cerebral palsy occurs when the parts of the neuromotor system described so far—the premotor cortex, motor cortex, basal ganglia, or cerebellum—are damaged early in life. The location and extent of the damage determines, to some degree, the motor symptoms that will characterize an individual's disorder. We will now examine the major types of cerebral palsy and the associated neurological damage that causes them.

TYPES OF CEREBRAL PALSY

Because of its variation in motor symptoms, cerebral palsy historically has been divided into different classifications. Although there has been some dispute regarding specific nomenclature, the labels *spasticity, dyskinesia, ataxia,* and *mixed type* appear to be used most frequently (Healy, 1990).

SPASTICITY

Those with *spasticity,* or the spastic form of cerebral palsy, have a primary disorder of muscle tone. The damage that causes this form of cerebral palsy is usually acknowledged to be in the premotor cortex, motor cortex, or in the nerve fibers immediately under these areas that transmit their commands to lower neurological centers (Batshaw et al., 1992). Individuals with spastic cerebral palsy generally have increased muscle tone during voluntary movement, because the primary muscles involved in any voluntary activity are abnormally opposed by their antagonists. This results in slow and strained voluntary movements, with a limited range of motion, and compensatory movements that appear contorted and bizarre. In addition, the abnormal tension between the muscle groups often results in aberrant postures and contractures; e.g., a bent wrist and elbow that the individual is unable to straighten out. In the upper extremities, the flexor muscles may be constantly tense. In the lower limbs, extended knees and pointed toes are likely to be seen; the extensor muscles of the legs abnormally predominate. Of 2004 individuals with cerebral palsy studied in St. Louis, about 63 percent were found to be spastic (O'Reilly and Walentynowicz, 1981).

Patterns of spasticity in the body can vary greatly from individual to individual. Depending on the precise location of the damage within the cortical motor centers, one might see involvement of the legs only (called *paraplegia*), involvement primarily in the legs with only slight effect on the arms *(diplegia),* spasticity in all four limbs with equal severity *(quadriplegia),* or even involvement of only one side of the body *(hemiplegia).* Thus a diagnosis of spasticity is usually specified further by indicating the *topography* of the disorder, or what part of the body is most affected.

DYSKINESIA

Those with *dyskinesia* have a primary disorder of involuntary or excessive movement. This disorder is generally thought to be due to damage to parts of the basal ganglia and their connecting pathways (Batshaw et al., 1992). Dyskinesia can take several forms, including athetosis and rigidity.

Individuals with *athetosis* generally experience varying degrees of arrhythmic, involuntary movement. These involuntary movements may be small in amplitude, such as writhing movements in the fingers, or larger in amplitude, such as involuntary chopping motions of the arms (the latter is sometimes referred to a *choreoathetosis*). The involuntary movements seen in athetosis are uncontrollable, and they often interfere with the execution of voluntary movements. For example, when trying to speak, an individual with this disorder may find his mouth opening or his tongue protruding involuntarily, interrupting his production of a word or sentence. In addition to involuntary movements, those with athetosis may have trouble maintaining a stable posture and problems with fluctuating muscle tone. These normally automatic functions, mediated by the basal ganglia, are disrupted when damage to those structures occurs.

Those with *rigidity* experience continuous and simultaneous contraction of various opposing muscle groups. This disorder is sometimes referred to as "lead-pipe rigidity" because it is difficult for these people to flex or extend any part of their bodies (McDonald, 1987a). The consistency of excessive muscle tone is what differentiates this disorder from spastic cerebral palsy. Those with spastic cerebral palsy most frequently experience excessive muscle tone in the limbs during voluntary movement. At other times, their muscle tone may actually be somewhat relaxed. In rigidity, the trunk and postural muscles are involved and have excessive contraction even at rest. Persons with rigid cerebral palsy are capable of only slow movement in a limited range.

The muscle contraction seen in rigidity is both excessive and involuntary, and thus the disorder can be considered a dyskinesia, although athetoid and choreoathetoid-type movements are not seen. According to O'Reilly and Walentynowicz, 19 percent of their subjects were diagnosed with dyskinesia: 12 percent with athetosis and 7 percent with rigidity.

ATAXIA

The primary problem of those with the ataxic form of cerebral palsy is with maintaining balance and coordinating movement. It is generally acknowledged that this form of cerebral palsy is due to damage to the cerebellum. Unlike the types so far discussed, the muscle tone of those with ataxia is hypothesized to be excessively relaxed rather than fluctuating or excessively tense. Although cerebral-palsied children of all types are at risk for walking difficulties, the child with ataxic cerebral palsy has an unusual wide-based gait, with the feet placed far apart and slapped down while taking steps (McDonald, 1987a). While sitting or standing, the child with ataxic cerebral palsy, if not prevented, may lean farther and farther to one side until he topples over. He is also likely to have trouble connecting with a target object. For example, in attempting to reach for an object, the individual may grasp beyond it, then in front of it, several times before he is able to make contact. Finally, ataxia is characterized by an inability to maintain serial repetitive movements, such as tapping a finger on the table over and over. This type of disorder accounts for 5 percent of the cerebral-palsied population, according to O'Reilly and Walentynowicz (1981), although Healy (1990) estimates that it is only 1 percent.

MIXED TYPE

Various researchers over the years have acknowledged that an individual can show symptoms of more than one type of cerebral palsy at any given time (Crothers and Paine, 1959; Denhoff and Robinault, 1960; Schleichkorn, 1983; Healy, 1990). Estimates of how many cerebral-palsied individuals fall into the "mixed" category differ widely, but all of the researchers listed above agree that the most common combination seen is spasticity plus dyskinesia. According to the classification scheme devised by O'Reilly and Walentynowicz (1981), 12 percent of their cerebral-palsied population was diagnosed as mixed.

It is clear that if we consider motor symptoms

only, cerebral palsy is an extremely varied condition. In terms of muscle tone, an individual with cerebral palsy may show excessive tone, fluctuating tone, or low muscle tone. Involuntary movements may be present or absent. Voluntary movements may be slow and limited in range, interrupted by involuntary movements, or normally executed but inaccurate. These symptoms may be seen only in particular locations in the body (in the case of spasticity), or generalized throughout the body. And although severity has not previously been discussed, the severity of all forms of cerebral palsy can range from so mild as to be unnoticeable to extremely severe.

CAUSES OF CEREBRAL PALSY

We now know that cerebral palsy is caused by damage to the motor cortex, premotor cortex, motor pathways leading from the cortical motor areas, the basal ganglia, or the cerebellum. But what can cause this kind of damage?

The causes of cerebral palsy can be grouped roughly into four categories: (1) infections, (2) toxins, (3) oxygen deprivation, or (4) traumatic injuries (see Table 8-1). Infections are primarily a factor in the prenatal period. During this period, bacterial or viral infections that the mother experiences may also infect the fetus and cause chemical changes that interrupt the development of the fetus's brain and nervous system. Some examples of these illnesses are maternal *rubella* (German measles), maternal cytomegalovirus, toxoplasmosis, and herpes. Less frequently, in the postnatal period, meningitis, encephalitis, or brain abscesses can harm the child's developing motor system.

Toxins can affect both the developing fetus in the prenatal period and the child in the postnatal period. The toxins that a mother might ingest during pregnancy include alcohol, cocaine or other illegal drugs, or even prescription drugs. Like bacteria and viruses, these agents may cause chemical changes in and interfere with development in the fetal brain. Toxic substances that the young child might ingest include lead, arsenic,

and coal-tar derivatives. These toxins can cause damage leading to cerebral palsy.

The brain requires a constant supply of oxygen in order to develop and function properly, and any interruption in oxygen supply can have devastating effects on an individual at any stage of life. During the prenatal period, the fetus's oxygen supply may be mildly reduced if the mother is anemic or has high blood pressure *(hypertension)*. More serious interruptions may occur if the placenta, through which the fetus is nourished, prematurely separates from the uterine wall (*placenta abruptio*) causing blood flow to the fetus to stop. Kinks or knots in the umbilical cord can also reduce blood supply, and hence oxygen, to the fetus. In the *perinatal period,* during birth, oxygen supply can temporarily be cut off during a long and difficult delivery, a breech delivery, or one where the placenta is delivered first (*placenta previa*). Finally, if mucus or other bodily fluids fill the lungs, the infant, in the newborn or immediately postnatal period, may experience oxygen deprivation until the lungs can be cleared.

Traumatic injury is most common during the birth process, although it can occur in the postnatal period as well. Particularly during a cesarean section, the newborn experiences rapid pressure changes as he is taken from the intrauterine environment and into the atmosphere. This rapid pressure change, the equivalent of going from the bottom to the top of Mt. Everest in a few minutes, can cause stroke or rupture of cerebral blood vessels. This is especially a hazard for premature infants whose blood vessels are fragile and underdeveloped. If forceps are used to pull the baby's head through the birth canal, there is also a risk that the pressure of the instrument on the baby's relatively soft skull will cause injury. However, most modern obstetricians are aware of this possibility and position the forceps on the newborn's jaw if an instrumental delivery is necessary. Finally, in the postnatal period, any injury to the head due to falls, auto accidents, beatings, and so on can result in cerebral palsy.

In summary, cerebral palsy is caused by a variety of injuries, oxygen-depriving conditions, tox-

---

TABLE 8-1 Potential Causes of Neurologic Dysfunction, Including Cerebral Palsy

---

I. Infections

  A. Prenatal Period

    1. Maternal rubella

    2. Maternal cytomegalovirus

    3. Maternal toxoplasmosis

    4. Maternal herpes

  B. Postnatal Period

    1. Meningitis

    2. Encephalitis

    3. Brain abscesses

II. Toxins

  A. Prenatal Period

    1. Maternal alcohol ingestion

    2. Maternal ingestion of cocaine, other illegal drugs, or even prescription drugs

    3. Maternal diabetes

  B. Postnatal Period

    1. Rh incompatibility between fetus and mother, causing excessive bilirubin to build up in the newborn's blood in the early postnatal period, with toxic effects to the brain

    2. Metabolic disorders (e.g., urea cycle disorders, where a child's inability to break down protein leads to a buildup of toxic ammonia in the body and brain)

    3. Ingestion of or exposure to toxic substances such as lead, arsenic, coal-tar derivatives, carbon monoxide, and so on

III. Conditions Causing Oxygen Deprivation

  A. Prenatal Period

    1. Maternal anemia or hypertension

    2. Defects in the placenta or umbilical cord

    3. Rh incompatibility between fetus and mother, resulting in the mother's immune system attacking the fetus's blood supply and consequent anemia of the fetus

    4. Premature separation of a normal placenta (*placenta abruptio*)

  B. Perinatal Period

    1. An abnormally placed placental attachment (*placenta previa*), resulting in delivery of the placenta prior to delivery of the infant, and subsequent anoxia to the infant

    2. Long and difficult delivery due to factors such as *cephalopelvic disproportion,* a condition in which the infant's head is too large to pass through the mother's pelvis

(continued)

TABLE 8-1 Potential Causes of Neurologic Dysfunction, Including Cerebral Palsy

---

    3. Breech delivery, where the shoulder, buttocks, or legs present first

    4. Prolapsed umbilical cord, where the umbilical cord precedes the fetus down the birth canal. When oxygen comes into contact with the umbilical cord, the transmission of blood and oxygen to the fetus is cut off.

    5. Respiratory difficulties in the newborn due to prematurity, collapsed lungs, depressed function resulting from maternal anesthesia, aspiration, and so on

  C. Postnatal Period

    1. Drowning

    2. Asphyxiation due to obstruction in the respiratory tract, strangulation, and so on

    3. Smoke inhalation

IV. *Traumatic Injuries*

  A. Prenatal Period: maternal injury resulting from car accidents, violence, and so on

  B. Perinatal Period

    1. Injury to the head during forceps delivery

    2. Intracranial hemorrhage due to cesarean section, precipitate delivery, or prolonged labor

  C. Postnatal Period

    1. Fractures of the skull as a result of car accidents

    2. Penetrating head wounds

    3. Falls

    4. Violence and abuse

---

ins, and diseases at several stages of early development. But it is important to note that these ailments often affect more that just the child's neuromotor system. Other areas of development may be compromised as well, creating associated problems that often (although not always) accompany cerebral palsy. Some of these problems are *primary,* meaning that the insult to the brain that caused the cerebral palsy also damaged adjacent areas. Other problems may be *secondary,* meaning they resulted from the reaction of the individual, the family, or society to the disorder. In either case, the occurrence and severity of associated problems will greatly affect the education, goals, and eventual level of functioning of the cerebral-palsied individual.

ASSOCIATED PROBLEMS

COGNITIVE DISORDERS

If a prenatal or birth injury damages the motor or premotor cortex, it is not difficult to imagine that the injury might also damage contiguous parts of the brain. Immediately in front of the premotor cortex are the intelligence centers of the brain, associated with such skills as learning, rational thought, logic, and planning. Damage to the intelligence centers interrupts the development of these skills. Thus, a child with cerebral palsy who has sustained damage to the premotor or motor cortex is at risk for cognitive disorders as well.

    The severity and frequency of the occurrence

of cognitive disorders in the cerebral-palsied population is difficult to estimate. According to Batshaw et al. (1992), those with spastic quadriplegia, dyskinesia, and mixed cerebral palsy are most at risk. McDonald (1987a) states that the greater the degree of damage to the cortical motor areas, the higher the likelihood that the damage will have spread to the intelligence centers. But it is certainly *not* the case that all spastic quadriplegics are severely cognitively disordered or, conversely, that all individuals with limited lesions have normal intellectual functioning. In fact, it is impossible to predict the level of cognitive ability of any individual based on motor symptoms.

The overall incidence of cognitive disorders in the cerebral-palsied population has been estimated to be anywhere from 50 percent to 70 percent (Lord, 1984; Hardy, 1994; Healy, 1990). A recent study of cerebral palsy in Atlanta, Georgia, found an incidence of cognitive disorders of 65 percent (Murphy et al., 1993). However, it may be difficult to measure the intelligence of the individual with cerebral palsy accurately, especially in cases of severe physical involvement. Children who are unable to speak clearly and who have only limited ability to make voluntary arm or finger movements may be greatly underestimated in terms of their intellectual potential. Individualized materials and techniques may be needed, and not all testing psychologists have the training needed to examine the physically challenged. For this reason, any estimate of the incidence of cognitive disorders in the cerebral-palsied population must be interpreted with caution.

SENSORY AND PERCEPTUAL PROBLEMS

1. Bodily Sensory Problems. We have just discussed the likelihood that damage to cortical motor areas may extend forward into the intelligence centers of the brain. We also must acknowledge the possibility that the damage may extend backward. Immediately behind the motor cortex is the sensory cortex, the part of the brain that receives and interprets information coming from the skin, muscles, and joints. Sensations such as temperature, light touch, pain, bodily movement, and awareness of body position in space are all mediated here. Damage to this part of the brain affects an individual's ability to receive and interpret this type of information, making it difficult, if not impossible, for him to use sensory feedback to guide his movements or protect himself. As with cognitive disorders, bodily sensory disorders are more likely to occur in cases of spasticity. Murphy et al. (1993) found an incidence of sensory problems of 15 percent in the cerebral-palsied population they studied.

2. Visual Problems. In addition to bodily sensory problems, visual problems are also common in individuals with cerebral palsy. Movement of the eyes requires precise motor coordination of numerous ocular muscles. Individuals with cerebral palsy often have difficulty with such coordination because of abnormal muscle tone in the eye muscles, muscle-tone imbalances, or involuntary movement or incoordination of the eye muscles. Thus, they may have difficulty focusing their eyes on objects in the distance or on printed matter close at hand. In the words of Geri Jewell, a comedienne with cerebral palsy, "I wasn't the world's fastest reader, because my eye muscles lacked fine motor control, a condition common among those with CP. My eyes changed lines often, making even the most mundane sentence a moving experience" (Jewell and Weiner, 1984, 131). All teachers and rehabilitation personnel should be aware of the potential for visual problems in the cerebral-palsied population because this disorder can have an important impact on their success in educational or vocational endeavors. Healy (1990) estimated that 50 percent of all cerebral-palsied children have an eye-muscle-imbalance problem.

3. Auditory Problems. As we discussed previously, lack of oxygen and chemical changes in the brain are major causes of cerebral palsy. Just as oxygen deprivation and biochemical disruptions can affect the brain and the developing neuromotor system, they can also affect the developing nerves and processing centers of the *auditory* (hearing) system. Thus, individuals with cerebral palsy, especially of the athetoid type, are at risk for sensorineural hearing loss and difficulty interpreting what they hear.

In addition to possible hearing losses due to oxygen deprivation, ear infections and *conductive* hearing losses are also prevalent in the cerebral palsied population. This is because the jaw muscles and the lower portion of the face of individuals with cerebral palsy tend to be underdeveloped. A combination of weakness, abnormal muscle tone, and incoordination frequently result in poor chewing and reduced use of the masticatory muscles, and a subsequent failure of the jaw to reach its full size and mass. An underdeveloped face causes an underdeveloped middle ear (the part of the ear behind the eardrum, which is encased by the bones of the skull) and sets up favorable conditions for infection to develop. Again, an undiagnosed hearing problem can severely reduce a child's chances of success in an educational program. It is important for all who interact with persons with cerebral palsy to be aware of this potential problem. According to Hardy (1994), there are no good estimates of the incidence of hearing impairment in children with cerebral palsy.

SEIZURES

Seizures can be likened to electrical storms in the brain. They usually occur because some part of the brain has been damaged, and abnormal electrical impulses develop around the damaged area. These electrical impulses discharge periodically, causing changes in consciousness and physical movements that we call *seizures* or *convulsions*. Seizures can be very dramatic, involving alternating periods of rigidity and shaking *(tonic-clonic seizures),* or as anticlimactic as brief but frequent lapses of consciousness *(absence seizures).* Due to the brain damage sustained before, during, or shortly after birth, about half of all children with cerebral palsy develop seizures (Aksu, 1990).

While the seizures themselves are disruptive to concentration and learning, the medications given to control them can also cause attention problems and hyperactivity. Children with cerebral palsy must be monitored carefully for the presence of seizures and may require numerous medication trials to control them. All of this has a negative impact upon a child's ability to function in an educational setting or in a vocational setting.

SOCIAL AND EMOTIONAL PROBLEMS

Consider for a moment the life of the child with cerebral palsy. From the time her disorder becomes apparent, her parents hover over her. She needs more help with feeding, dressing, and grooming than do her brothers and sisters, so she does not have a chance to experience the satisfaction of independent self-care. Because of her physical limitations, she can not readily explore her world—get into the cabinets, bang on pots with spoons, pull a wagon, or push a swing. In fact, depending on the severity of her disability, she may never have had an opportunity to see how her own actions can *cause* things to happen. If her communication is limited, she may be unable to express her preferences as to food or clothing or defend herself in arguments with siblings. Life is most likely "a series of things done for her and to her" (Perkins, 1978, 184), despite the best intentions of her parents.

It is no wonder that many individuals with cerebral palsy develop a passive attitude and fail to function at their full potential. They are also likely to develop a negative self-concept and low self-esteem. Again, to quote Geri Jewel, on her first day of high school, she described herself in the following terms: "I walked like a drunk, I was deaf as a haddock, and I had all the personality and the maturity of an eleven-year-old. It was going to be difficult to make friends here. Heck, it was going to be difficult to make acquaintances" (Jewell and Weiner, 1984, 127). Such feelings will affect not only the individuals' ability to interact and socialize with others but also their ability to learn and achieve.

COMMUNICATION PROBLEMS

Because of the motor disorders that characterize cerebral palsy, and all the associated problems mentioned above, children with cerebral palsy are especially at risk for communication disorders. The production of speech sounds in a smooth and rapid way is dependent upon an intact neuromotor system. Abnormal and fluctuating muscle tone, involuntary movements, unreliable automatic movements, and problems with achieving movement targets all interfere with the unconscious and automatic production of intelligible speech. In terms of associated disorders, cognitive deficits negatively affect the child's ability to develop clear speech at the expected ages as well as to learn language. Sensory and perceptual problems may make motor control of the speech musculature more difficult because the child does not receive adequate feedback to guide his efforts, and hearing problems reduce the speech and language input to which the child is exposed. Finally, social and emotional problems and feelings of hopelessness may diminish the child's desire to try to communicate intelligibly. In short, the culmination of the neuromotor aspects of cerebral palsy and all the problems associated with it is frequently speech disorders of various types, as well as possible disorders of language.

SPEECH CHARACTERISTICS OF CEREBRAL PALSY

As described in Chapter 7, the primary cause of the speech disorders experienced by those with cerebral palsy is dysarthria. *Dysarthria* is a general term applied to a wide variety of speech disorders caused by damage to the neuromotor system. These disorders are characterized by abnormal or fluctuating muscle tone, involuntary movements, incoordination, and weakness or paralysis in the speech muscles. Dysarthria can be developmental, as is the case with cerebral palsy, or acquired, as is the case with disorders originating in adulthood. As we shall see, the speech characteristics

of dysarthria are extremely varied even when we limit our discussion to the developmental dysarthria that accompanies cerebral palsy.

ARTICULATION-PHONOLOGICAL DISORDERS

Children and adults with cerebral palsy often have difficulty producing specific phonemes—especially the more difficult sounds such as fricatives and affricates—because of problems controlling the tongue. Phonemes that require continuous tension in the tongue, prolonged tongue postures, or rapid movement from one articulatory position to another tend to be simplified in some way. McDonald (1987b) reports that lingua-alveolar fricatives and linguapalatal glides are the most frequently misarticulated.

Besides difficulty with the more difficult speech sounds, an individual with cerebral palsy may have trouble articulating even those sounds that are considered easy, such as "t" and "d." Speech intelligibility may be further compromised by the individual's difficulty controlling the soft palate *(velum)*. Most speech sounds are produced with firm palatal closure, which permits air pressure to be built up in the oral cavity for controlled release during stops, affricates, and fricatives. A cerebral-palsied person who lacks good velar control might sound as if they are producing "m"s and "n"s rather than the intended sounds.

FLUENCY DISORDERS

In addition to specific phoneme errors and phonological patterns of nasalization and simplification, individuals with cerebral palsy typically have difficulty combining sounds. Longer units of speech—such as words, phrases, and sentences—require greater coordination and the ability to move rapidly from one phoneme to the next. Coordination and rapid movement are frequently problematic for individuals with cerebral palsy. Because of their motor disorders, the speech of those with cerebral palsy is often slow or slurred. These characteristics may be a direct result of the cerebral palsy or may occur as the speaker tries to compensate for his or her disorder by deliberately speaking in a slower and more connected way.

Although a listener is not likely to consider this slow, slurred, and occasionally interrupted speech as stuttering, it is certainly a disorder of *fluency* (the smooth and rapid transition from one sound to another or from one word to another). Thus, the speech disorders of the individual with cerebral palsy may involve problems with fluency as well as articulation.

VOICE DISORDERS

Voice disorders are also often a part of the dysarthric speech pattern of those with cerebral palsy. Voice disorders occur because of abnormal or fluctuating muscle tone, involuntary movements, or incoordination of the *vocal folds,* the muscles of voice production. These control difficulties with the muscles of voice production are reflected in a hoarse voice quality, monotone voice, *inappropriate pitch variations* (raising or lowering the voice at improper points in a sentence), or explosive voice onsets with tension. In addition, the voice may be consistently *hypernasal,* or overly nasal, because of difficulty controlling the soft palate.

RESPIRATION PROBLEMS

The severely involved child with cerebral palsy may even have difficulty with one of the most basic prerequisites for speech—controlled breathing. Breathing for life is an automatic reflex that is mediated by the *medulla,* one of the lower centers of the brain just above the spinal cord. But breathing for speech demands overriding this reflex so that inhalation can be very quick, relatively speaking, and exhalation long and controlled. After all, we speak on exhalation; and if we cannot keep the breath stream going out to the end of a sentence, our speech will be limited to single words and short phrases. Because of muscle-tone abnormalities and fluctuation and involuntary movements, even the simple act of prolonging an exhalation for speech may be difficult for the child with cerebral palsy. Thus,

speech may be compromised because of neuro-motor involvement in the muscles of respiration as well as the muscles of speech production.

SEVERITY OF INVOLVEMENT AND CONSEQUENCES TO THE INDIVIDUAL

A tremendous range of severity levels exists within the cerebral-palsied population, depending on the type and extent of motoric involvement as well as the number and severity of associated problems, such as cognitive disorders. The problems facing the mildly involved child with cerebral palsy are quite different from those facing the severely involved child.

The mildly involved child is usually *ambulatory* (able to walk), sometimes with the aid of braces, a walker, or other assistive devices. However, the child's *gait* (walking pattern) may include toe walking, turned-in toes and knees, shuffling, or other abnormalities that tend to make the child look "different." Intelligence is likely to be in the normal range, although visual, hearing, and learning disorders may again serve to separate the child from his or her nonhandicapped peers. Speech may be slurred or unusual-sounding but is nonetheless functional.

The challenge for the mildly involved child is to develop intellectually, emotionally, and socially to the point where full integration into society is possible. Of all those with cerebral palsy, these are the children with the best chance of succeeding in competitive employment in their adult years and in becoming completely independent. According to O'Grady et al. (1985), only about 10 percent of those with cerebral palsy are entirely self-supporting as adults, despite the fact that (according to the estimate of O'Grady et al., 1985) 40 percent have normal intelligence. Thus, the challenge is clear for educational and rehabilitation personnel, for parents, and for the mildly involved children themselves.

The individual with severe cerebral palsy has a greater number of challenges to overcome. He or she is usually limited in terms of ambulation and must rely on a wheelchair for mobility. Both the legs and the arms are typically involved. Even reliable head movements may be problematic. Finally, many individuals with severe cerebral palsy have associated cognitive disorders of varying degree.

In the severely involved population, intelligible oral speech is not usually a realistic goal. The individual may be able to use his or her voice to get attention and may be able to produce some word approximations, but control is usually inadequate for clear articulation. In order to communicate and participate as fully as possible in society, these individuals generally need augmentative or alternative communication devices, which will be discussed later in this chapter.

Even without intellectual limitations, the severely involved individual faces formidable challenges to independent living. Wheelchair-accessible living and transportation facilities and personal attendants can help maintain these individuals in the community. However, many, especially those with cognitive disorders, require more sheltered living arrangements, such as group homes or (in some cases) residential institutions.

EARLY INTERVENTION: AN INTERDISCIPLINARY APPROACH

The child with cerebral palsy has the best chance to achieve both controlled voluntary movement and intelligible speech if intervention begins within the first few months of life (Jenkins et al., 1982; Kanda et al., 1984). Early intervention, however, is more challenging to provide than one might think, because it is often difficult to even *recognize* cerebral palsy at this stage. Healy (1990) claims that most cases of cerebral palsy can be detected by the age of 12 months, and nearly all can be identified by the age of 18 months. However, Piper et al. (1988) report that over half of the infants suspected of having cerebral palsy at the age of 12 months "outgrow" their symptoms by the age of 2. This indicates a continued possibility of a missed or erroneous diagnosis of cerebral palsy.

The purpose of early diagnosis is to provide early intervention programs and a variety of services to young children and their families, so that as many problems as possible can be ameliorated or prevented before the child reaches school age. Ideally, young children suspected of having cerebral palsy should receive programming in physical therapy, occupational therapy, speech-language pathology, and early childhood education. Frequent medical evaluation should also be made. If possible, a social worker should be available to coordinate services. However, outside of major metropolitan areas with specialized children's hospitals and outreach services, coordination of the interdisciplinary team often becomes the responsibility of the parents.

The common goal of all members of the interdisciplinary team is to ensure the best possible physical development for the child. Especially in the early years, this is accomplished through exercises and activities to facilitate normal motor experiences. For example, the child might be "motored through" rolling, reaching, and sitting movements, even if he is not independently capable of performing these activities. This is known as *handling*. Handling is based on the belief that the use of normal movement patterns is inhibiting to maladaptive movements such as the backward thrust of the head and the back arching that cerebral-palsied children use in compensatory ways. Although the lesion that causes cerebral palsy is not *progressive* (i.e., it does not get worse over time), the motoric disorder itself may worsen as maladaptive movement patterns become established. Early intervention can help reduce these abnormal responses and encourage more normal development.

During the early intervention period, the speech-language pathologist is likely to become involved in establishing more normal oral–motor patterns during the process of feeding (Alexander, 1987). As in the gross motor area, maladaptive oral-motor patterns may become habituated early on, and they may later interfere with voluntary use of the speech mechanism. Oral reflexes such as rooting, sucking, and biting must be brought under voluntary control so that the child can integrate them into more mature lip, jaw, and tongue movements. In addition, the child may not be receiving good sensory feedback from the oral area. Without sensory feedback, the voluntary movements of chewing and of speech cannot be performed skillfully. Thus, the speech-language pathologist may also work on a program of providing oral-motor stimulation to encourage the child to attend to and enjoy such sensations. Oral-motor control for feeding may not guarantee adequate control for intelligible speech but it certainly increases the chances (Alexander, 1987).

The speech-language pathologist may also work with the occupational therapist and physical therapist in positioning the child with cerebral palsy so that optimal control is facilitated in a wide variety of activities. *Positioning* usually involves seating or propping the child with good hip flexion, pressure on forearms, or other postures that increase stability of the trunk and shoulder girdle. Work on feeding, for example, is most productive if the child is in a stable position. The speech-language pathologist may also try to elicit

FIGURE 8-3 Speech-language pathologists must be able to position children with cerebral palsy to enhance control for voluntary movement. (Courtesy Rifton)

vocalizations and babbling when the child is positioned.

In addition, the speech-language pathologist may become involved with other professionals in stimulating the child's cognitive development. Much early learning is accomplished through physical exploration. The child with cerebral palsy is at a disadvantage because he or she may have difficulty stretching, reaching, grasping, and releasing in order to explore the environment. Early cognitive skills, such as cause-effect and means-ends behavior may be delayed. The professionals on the team, in conjunction with the parents, must make sure the child experiences as much as possible to foster cognitive development (Carlson, 1987).

Finally, the speech-language pathologist must work with the parents to make sure that the infant with cerebral palsy is exposed to plenty of language stimulation. Because most children with cerebral palsy are delayed in their speech development and not always able to respond to their parents' attempts to communicate, parents often talk little to them, assuming the child will not understand. However, it is extremely important to provide rich and varied language models to the child with developmental delays. It is also important to set up situations where the child is required to communicate in some way and to encourage and reward all attempts at communication (Carlson, 1987). These strategies will help ensure these children have the best possible chance to acquire both receptive and expressive language.

THE ROLE OF THE SPEECH-LANGUAGE PATHOLOGIST

THE MILDLY INVOLVED CHILD

The most difficult aspect of speech for the mildly involved child is likely to be *articulation*—the physical production of speech sounds. The speech-language pathologist may need to work with these children on individual phonemes, such as "t" or "k," and then on combining these phonemes with vowels. As it becomes easier for the child to produce these CV (consonant-vowel) syllables, the speech pathologist moves on to words that contain the target sounds. Through drill and practice, more and more sounds and words are added. As they are mastered, words are combined into phrases and sentences.

In order to obtain maximum intelligibility, the child with cerebral palsy will probably need to speak somewhat slowly and carefully, paying conscious attention to his tongue, lip, and jaw movements. During periods of excitement and emotional stress, intelligibility is likely to be lost. It is clear that the speech-language pathologist is not *curing* the child's cerebral palsy, or the dysarthria underlying the speech disorder. Even with intensive therapy, the mildly impaired child will probably not attain the thoughtless speed and precision of speech of the nonhandicapped child. However, improved and intelligible speech can often be achieved, despite the need to be conscious and deliberate (McDonald, 1987b).

THE SEVERELY INVOLVED CHILD

The role of the speech-language pathologist with severely involved children is one of crucial importance. As discussed in Chapter 3, augmentative and alternative methods of communication can be used at any time when an individual's oral speech needs to be supplemented or even replaced. The speech-language pathologist, with a broad commitment to communication rather than just speech, is usually the professional who assists the handicapped individual and family in selecting and using this type of device, if the goal of articulate speech is not in the immediate future.

Augmentative communication refers to aids that supplement the individual's speech. *Alternative communication* refers to a nonspeech method of communication that replaces the individual's speech. The distinction between these two may not always be clear, however. In many cases, a young child with cerebral palsy may start out with an alternative-communication device that may later be considered augmentative as his speech intelligibility improves. We will refer to both types as *alternative* for convenience, with the understanding that any device may serve both functions.

For those with severe cerebral palsy, an alternative-communication device can become a lifeline through which wants, needs, and ideas are expressed. The simplest device used with the cerebral-palsied population is the *communication board,* literally a board (or folder or booklet) containing a number of words, symbols, pictures, or letters that the individual can point to. It is usually attached to the individual's wheelchair so that it will be readily accessible. If arm and hand coordination are not adequate for pointing, a long pointer mounted on a headband can be used instead. The individual then selects vocabulary items with head movements instead of hand movements.

For those with limited head control as well as limited arm and hand control, an eye-gaze board can be used. This alternative device consists of a large plexiglass board mounted vertically between the individual with cerebral palsy and the communication partner. Pictures with the same thing on both sides are put in the four corners of the board so they can be seen by both parties. The handicapped individual then uses her eyes to point to her selection: upper right, upper left, lower right, lower left. The first stage is usually to select a category (the pictures or words in each of the four corners may represent categories such as "foods," "people," "activities," and so on). Once a category is selected, the communication partner replaces the four initial pictures with additional pictures of specific items in that category (banana, candy, sandwich, or apple in the "food" category, for example). The handicapped individual then uses her eyes to point to her next selection. Although this method of communication is extremely slow, it has the important advantage of permitting a severely involved individual with no other means of expression to communicate.

Looked at from an engineering perspective, one could say that individuals with severe cerebral palsy are in need of more effective transmission systems to convey their communicative intents to listeners—a challenge to technology. And since the late 1970s, technology has played an increasingly active role in finding accessible means of communication for the severely handicapped. With improvements in computers and electronic miniaturization, a new generation of high-tech devices has recently become available to individuals with cerebral palsy. These devices are often similar to their "low-tech" counterparts, although sometimes they provide functions that simple pointing boards cannot.

For example, the electronic counterpart of a communication board may store the selections a speaker makes and then "say" the word or sentence in synthetic speech generated by computer circuits within the device. Less costly communicators display the message on an LCD display or on paper tape. For those with poor hand–arm control, the conventional head pointer can be replaced with an infrared scanning device that mounts on a headband near the eye. As the individual moves his head, he can make direct selections of letters, pictures, symbols, or words from an electronic communication board.

For the most severely involved, a function known as *scanning* can be helpful. In scanning, a cursor or light stops briefly at each element (word, letter, symbol) on the electronic communication board. When the cursor gets to the desired element, the individual must depress a

FIGURE 8-4 For nonverbal individuals with cerebral palsy, an electronic alternative communication device can provide a means for communicating in educational and vocational situations. (Reproduced with permission of the Prentke Romich Co.)

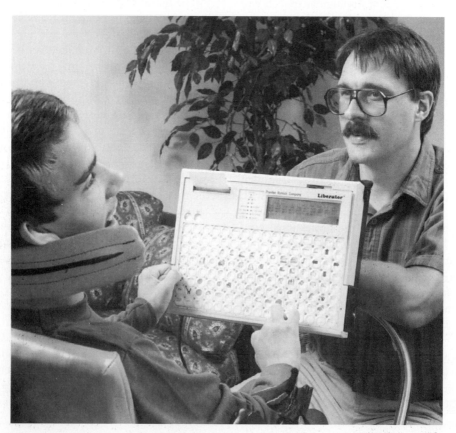

FIGURE 8-5 Technology has provided a wide array of assistive devices for individuals who cannot produce intelligible speech. Some of these devices include speech synthesizers that "speak" the individual's message; others provide LED or paper-tape display.

simple switch to stop it. A second touch to the switch enters the element into the device's memory, and a third touch confirms it. The cursor then begins moving again. The selected symbols, letters, or words are displayed on a screen or paper tape as they are selected. The switch in scanning can be actuated by pressure from the foot, the knee, or any other part of the body over which the individual has some control. Switches can be mounted to the footrests of a wheelchair, the armrests, or any other location accessible to the individual.

The use of pressure switches to operate electronic equipment has been an important development in creating products for the physically handicapped. Motorized wheelchairs, which can be operated by simple switches and joysticks, are increasingly available. Electronic toys for young children with physical handicaps are also available. By activating the toy with a switch, the child with cerebral palsy can experience cause-effect behavior and thus exert some control over his environment.

As mentioned above, the individual with severe cerebral palsy is more likely to experience cognitive disorders than are those with milder forms. In the past, the extent and severity of these disorders could be easily exaggerated because response modalities for handicapped individuals were so limited. Today, as more and more communication options are available for those with severe motoric limitations, their true abilities have a greater chance of being realized. Even with cognitive disorders, those with severe cerebral palsy have more potential to communicate, socialize, and participate in meaningful activities than has been acknowledged in the past. Technology cannot yet provide a cure for cerebral palsy; nor can it negate the effects of cognitive and educational limitations. But it can be used to facilitate the possible.

THE ROLE OF PARENTS

As with cognitive disorders and pervasive developmental disorders, the role of the family in cases of cerebral palsy can seem overwhelming. Since the condition may not be diagnosed until the child is 12 to 18 months of age, parents must often go through the difficult process of learning to accept their child, once believed or hoped to be normal, as handicapped. At the same time that this emotional upheaval is occurring, the family may also be inundated with therapy suggestions, home programs, and other activities designed for them to help their child. While some families find comfort and a sense of purpose in this flurry of activity, others find that it only adds to their feelings of guilt and self-doubt (Miller, 1994).

As time goes by, most parents gain more confidence in their role as "in-home therapists" and are better able to make decisions regarding which activities and therapies would be most helpful to their child (Miller, 1994). In many cases, highly specific home programs are abandoned. Hinojosa and Anderson (1991) found that mothers of handicapped children selected "activities that were doable and that they could integrate into their daily routines and interactions. Some important characteristics of these activities were that they were enjoyable for the child and not stressful for the child, the mother, or the family" (p. 273).

Hardy (1994) notes that as the child with cerebral palsy matures, the need for professionals may diminish. However, parents continue to play a critical role as members of the interdisciplinary team, ensuring that their children continue to receive needed rehabilitative services, optimal vocation counseling, and an acceptable living arrangement.

THE HANDICAPPED AND SOCIETY

Pub. L. No. 94-142, Pub. L. No. 99-457, and the Americans with Disabilities Act of 1991 (ADA) are evidence of the growing commitment of society to the integration of those with handicaps into schools and the workplace. Individuals with multiple handicaps—which those with cerebral palsy often have—are legally entitled to an appropriate education in the least restrictive environment and are eligible for services from birth to the age of 21. In the workplace, they must be provided with access to buildings, restrooms, and any equipment necessary for job performance.

Yet despite advances in their legal rights and in laws against discrimination, children with cerebral palsy are still frequently stigmatized by their handicap. They may not be fully accepted by their peers or by teachers because of their physical appearance, and they may not be afforded the opportunities for learning and achievement that nonhandicapped children enjoy. Fostering acceptance and integration of the handicapped into society is a complex challenge. Both activism and personal assertion on the part of individuals with cerebral palsy and their families are needed if more accepting attitudes are to become a reality.

If the physically handicapped are to become full participants in society, technology will almost certainly play a role. Modern technology—especially advances in communication and mobility devices—has had an undeniably positive impact on the lives of those with severe physical handicaps. Those with physical limitations now have more opportunities than ever before. However, those with physical handicaps have *affected* modern technology as well as being affected *by* it. For example, both the typewriter and the telephone were initially invented as aids to the disabled— the typewriter for the blind, the telephone for the deaf. Devices and strategies developed with the handicapped in mind have often found their way into wider use. In addition, companies that design products for those with physical disabilities are now hiring disabled individuals to act as consultants and product-development specialists. Thus, those with physical limitations are becoming more actively involved in designing and marketing the products that will help them and others lead more independent lives.

SUMMARY

Cerebral palsy is a constellation of disorders that has as its base motor dysfunction. It is developmental in nature, having its onset in the prenatal, perinatal, or early postnatal period. Although not a part of cerebral palsy per se, associated disorders of cognition, sensation and perception, emotional and social adjustment, and communication often affect those with cerebral palsy.

Early intervention is extremely important in maximizing the potential of children with cerebral palsy. Various professionals must work closely with parents so that improvement of motor function, inhibition of maladaptive motor patterns and behaviors, cognitive stimulation, and speech-language development can be promoted.

In later years, those with mild involvement can be encouraged to live independently and work in competitive situations. Those with more severe involvement of physical and mental functions have had few options for independence in the past. Today, these individuals may gain increased access to social and vocational activities through assistive devices for communication and ambulation.

The greater use of technology with the physically and mentally disabled provides a challenge to rehabilitation personnel to stay informed of new developments. Speech-language pathologists in particular must seek information and training in the area of alternative communication devices in order to best serve those with cerebral palsy.

R E V I E W   Q U E S T I O N S

1. What is *cerebral palsy*?
2. What are the major parts of the central nervous system that control motor movement? What is the function of each part in motor movement?
3. What are *spasticity, athetosis, rigidity,* and *ataxia*? Where is the cerebral damage that causes each of these disorders?
4. What are some causes of cerebral palsy?
5. What are some associated problems an individual with cerebral palsy might have? Why are these likely to occur?
6. What is *dysarthria*? What symptoms may be seen in those with cerebral palsy?
7. What early intervention strategies are used by various professionals in working with children with cerebral palsy?
8. How has *mild cerebral palsy* been defined in this text? What strategies might a speech-language pathologist use in working with children with mild cerebral palsy?
9. How has *severe cerebral palsy* been defined in this text? What strategies might a speech-language pathologist use in working with individuals with severe cerebral palsy?
10. What are some forms of alternative communication that may be used by those with physical handicaps? What are their advantages and disadvantages?
11. What is *scanning*? What population might find it useful?
12. How have individuals with cerebral palsy been affected by modern technology? How have they affected modern technology?

F O R   F U R T H E R   I N F O R M A T I O N

Batshaw, M., and **Perret, Y.** (1992). *Children with handicaps: A medical primer* (3rd ed.). Baltimore: Paul H. Brookes.

Hardy, J. (1983). *Cerebral palsy.* Englewood Cliffs, NJ: Prentice-Hall.

McDonald, E. (Ed.) (1987). *Treating cerebral palsy: By clinicians for clinicians.* Austin, TX: Pro-Ed.

Schleichkorn, J. (1983). *Coping with cerebral palsy.* Austin, TX: Pro-Ed.

Fluency, Disfluency, and Stuttering

Consider the following individuals: Clara Barton, founder of the American Red Cross; Sir Issac Newton, physicist and mathematician; Marilyn Monroe, actress and entertainer; Charles Darwin, naturalist and originator of the theory of evolution; Winston Churchill, prime minister of England during World War II. What do these individuals have in common? As you might guess from the title of this chapter, it has to do with fluency. All of these individuals are known, or believed, to have stuttered at some time in their lives.

Like articulation, fluency is a component of speech. Where *articulation* refers to the physical production of speech sounds, *fluency* refers to the smooth and rapid flow of one sound into another, one word into another, one phrase into another. If *speech* (the physical transmission of the sender's message) is to be intelligible, phonemes must be appropriately blended as well as precisely articulated as individual units. In our chapters on articulation, phonology, and phonological disorders, primary emphasis was put on phonemes as discrete elements and the difficulty some individuals have in producing them. When we discussed speech production in cerebral palsy, however, we saw both imprecise production of individual speech sounds and difficulty in making rapid transitions from one phoneme to the next. Both types of speech disorder resulted from damage to the neuromotor system.

In this chapter, we will look at a speech disorder that primarily involves difficulty in making smooth, rapid transitions despite the absence of diagnosed lesions of the neuromotor system. This disorder, which we know as *stuttering,* has been recognized as far back as the ancient Greek civilizations. It has afflicted brilliant and accomplished individuals who changed the course of history as well as those of less stellar abilities. Yet despite its long history and the research it has engendered, we are still unsure of the exact cause of stuttering in most individuals and, more important, how to cure it.

DISFLUENCY VERSUS STUTTERING

If fluency refers to the smooth flow of speech, *disfluency* is anything that disrupts the smooth flow of speech. Disfluency is characterized by repetitions, interjections, revisions, dysrhythmic phonations, or tense pauses (Johnson, 1961). These behaviors are listed in Table 9-1.

As we can see from Table 9-1, repetitions may involve sound repetitions, such as in "b-b-b-ball," or syllable repetitions, such as in "muh-muh-muh-mother." These are sometimes called *part-word repetitions.* In addition, speakers may repeat whole words or even phrases. A repetition of any type is a disruption in the smooth flow of speech.

A second (and very common) type of disfluency is the interjection. *Interjections* are "fillers" such as "um," "uh," and "er." All of us have experienced speakers who interject "um" or "uh" into every phrase or sentence, and it is often difficult to attend to their disjointed speaking style.

The tendency to stop and revise what one is

TABLE 9-1 Types of Dysfluency (based on Johnson, 1961)

A. Repetitions
    1. Part-Word Repetitions
        a. Sound repetitions (Ex.: "It's a *b-b-ball.*")
        b. Syllable repetitions (Ex.: "*un-un-under* the chair")
    2. Whole-Word Repetitions (Ex.: "*my—my—my* book")
    3. Phrase Repetitions, (Ex.: "*It's in the . . . it's in the* mail.")
B. Interjections (Ex.: um, er, ah)
C. Revisions/Incomplete Phrases
    1. Word Revisions (Ex.: "Our *pet,* our *dog* is white.")
    2. Phrase Revisions (Ex.: "We *went to* the, we *visited* the shop.")
    3. Incomplete Phrases (Ex.: "They stopped at . . . and then I saw it.")
D. Dysrhythmic Phonations
    1. Prolongations (Ex.: "*mmmmmmmm*month")
    2. Broken Words (Ex.: "pur . . . ple")
E. Tense Pauses (Ex.: "I [explosively produced] do, too.")

saying is also a disruption in the smooth flow of speech. The most common types of revision are word and phrase revisions. For example, a speaker might say, "The *huge,* the *enormous* number of immigrants peaked in the early 1900s." In this example, the word *huge* was revised. Similarly, a speaker might say, "They *set out for,* they *came to* the United States to find a better life." In this case, a whole phrase was revised. Incomplete phrases are also sometimes grouped with word and phrase revisions. *Incomplete phrases* are those in which the original phrase is interrupted and the thought never completed, such as in "They wanted to . . . and here they were."

Dysrhythmic phonations result when the timing or rhythm within a word is abnormal. Prolongations are one type of dysrhythmic phonation. They involve extended vowels or consonants at the beginnings of words, such as the initial vowel in "oooonly," or the "s" in "sssssssee." A second example of a dysrhythmic phonation would be *broken words,* or words with pauses between the syllables, such as "pa- (pause) -per."

Tense pauses, in contrast to disrhythmic phonations, occur between words. For example, a speaker might have difficulty releasing the "p" sound in the word *pie.* In the sentence "I like pie," a listener would perceive this difficulty as a pause after the word *like* and before the word *pie* was uttered. Tense pauses, also called *blocks,* usually are accompanied by muscular tension in the lips or face and barely audible breathing (Silverman, 1992).

Are these disfluencies the same as stuttering? Not exactly. Many speakers show disfluencies in their speech—such as revisions, interjections, and word and phrase repetitions—and we do not consider them stutters. Think of some of the college instructors you have had. During a lecture, these individuals may grope for just the right word, break up their sentences with "um"s and "uh"s, or go back and revise the wording of a point they just made. Chances are you do not regard these disfluencies as stuttering, although you might find them annoying. Similarly, a speaker with cerebral palsy may speak slowly and with many hesitations and prolongations, but we would probably not consider that person a stutterer either. How, then, does stuttering differ from disfluency?

Interestingly, despite the thousands of years that stuttering has been recognized, it is still difficult for the experts to agree on an exact definition. To paraphrase a Supreme Court judge who was asked to define pornography, we can't define it, but we know it when we hear it. In fact, Bloodstein (1987) suggests that one definition of *stuttering* is what reliable listeners who agree with one another perceive to be stuttering.

According to Silverman (1992), what is considered the "standard definition" of stuttering was proposed by Wingate (1964). Wingate's definition states that stuttering is a disruption in fluency, or in the smooth transition between sounds, syllables, words, or ideas. These disruptions are characterized as involuntary repetitions and prolongations, either audible or silent, seen during the production of sounds, syllables, and single-syllable words. They occur frequently during speech, but not on every word, and they are not controllable by the speaker. Wingate also specifies that the speech behaviors above may be accompanied by physical mannerisms—such as eye blinks or head jerks—that appear to be related to the struggle to produce speech. The individual who is stuttering is aware of his or her speech difficulties and experiences emotional reactions such as fear, embarrassment, or frustration when speaking.

This rather complex definition contains a number of key points. First, it states that stuttering is a phenomenon involving repetitions and prolongations of the smallest units of speech—sounds, syllables, and single-syllable words. Repetitions of longer units of speech—such as words or phrases—are less likely to be considered stuttering. Second, the repetitions are involuntary. This distinguishes stuttering from intentional disfluencies, such as the "um"s and "er"s that signal that a speaker is trying to assemble his or her thoughts but still wants to "hold the floor." Third, stuttering does not occur on every word. Even the most disfluent speakers produce some words without struggle. Thus, stuttering is an intermittent disorder. Finally, stuttering results in emotional and sometimes physical reactions in the individual. This gives stuttering a psychological component not always seen in other disorders of speech and language.

In summary, *stuttering* may be defined as involuntary repetitions and prolongations of sounds and syllables that occur with varying frequency during speech and to which the individual reacts in a negative way. Stuttering can, at least theoretically, be distinguished from normal disfluency because of the greater tendency in stuttering for multiple repetitions of the smallest units of language (sounds and syllables), the tension and struggle that accompany speech attempts, and the sense that the person's fluency disruption is involuntary. *Disfluency,* in the broad sense, refers to anything that interrupts the smooth flow of speech. Stuttering may thus be seen as a special subcategory under the broader heading of "disfluency."

ACCESSORY BEHAVIORS

Repetitions, prolongations, and tense pauses (or blocks) are called *core behaviors* (Van Riper, 1982), or those speech characteristics that are at the heart of stuttering. However, in addition to these core behaviors, stuttering in any given individual may also be characterized by accessory, or secondary, behaviors, used in an attempt to "postpone, interrupt, escape from, avoid or disguise the core behaviors" (Starkweather, 1987, 118–119). Although the distinction between core behaviors and accessory behaviors is somewhat artificial, it is still useful to note that an individual's reaction to his own disfluency can be an important component of the problem.

For example, some stutters adopt rhythmic movements—tapping their feet or fingers or nodding their heads—to help themselves initiate and proceed through a sentence despite their fear of disfluent interruptions. Others use abrupt movements—the sudden blink of the eyes, slap on the leg, or stamp of the foot—to "snap" themselves out of a long block. While these mannerisms may work initially, they tend to lose their fluency-enhancing effect as the individual gets used to them. This usually results in an escalation of the accessory behavior—two eye blinks instead of one, and with more tension—as the stutterer struggles to maintain fluency. Besides physical movements, stutters often use a wide variety of postponement, or avoidance, techniques when they sense they are about to become disfluent. They may look up at the ceiling and pretend to be lost in thought, shuffle their feet, or say "you know" or "OK." These are behaviors a nonstutterer might use when trying to gather his thoughts, and so they are accepted by listeners as relatively normal in conversation (Starkweather, 1987). Unfortunately, postponement techniques for the stutterer are likely to postpone only the inevitable episode of stuttering.

A potentially more dangerous type of accessory behavior is circumlocution. Many stutters believe that particular sounds or words act as triggers for disfluency. Some stutterers anticipate trouble producing labial sounds, such as "p," "b," "m," and "w." Others have primary difficulty with fricatives, such as "s," or lingua-alveolar sounds, such as "t" or "l." Still others have difficulty with words that evoke an emotional response. In an attempt to remain fluent, a stutterer may try to avoid saying a word beginning with a "feared" sound by saying a different word instead or by rephrasing the sentence. This attempt to "get around" feared sounds and words is known as *circumlocution* (Silverman, 1992). In some cases, circumlocution is merely inconvenient for the stutterer, who must function as a walking thesaurus in order to avoid certain types of words. This would be the case for the young boy described by Fraser (1987), who had to think quickly enough to say "I'll have to check with my folks" instead of "I'll have to ask my mother" in order to avoid stuttering on *mother,* a particularly difficult word for him to say. But in other cases, stutterers may provide false or irrelevant information in their effort to avoid feared words, and this can get them into serious trouble. Perkins (1980, 458) describes a young man who overdid his use of circumlocutions during his employment in a bro-

kerage firm. According to Perkins, "he was so much in terror of stuttering that he quoted fictitious prices on which he did not expect to stutter rather than risk blockage on the actual prices that should have been given. His tenure in this position was brief."

In addition to physical movements, postponements, and circumlocutions, many other accessory behaviors are possible. According to Starkweather (1987), some stutterers pretend not to know the answer, not to have heard the question, or, indeed, to be deaf. Regardless of the form they take, most accessory behaviors ultimately make the stuttering worse. Postponements can become unending, circumlocutions more complex and incorrect, and physical movements more violent. Avoidance of a speaking situation by pretending not to be able to respond is damaging to the ego. In the end, the stutterer will, in most cases, still be confronted with the task of getting through repetitions or a block on a particular word.

THE DEVELOPMENT OF FLUENCY

Just as children must learn the pragmatics, semantics, syntax, morphology, and phonology of their native language, and gain articulatory competence, so must they learn how to produce fluent speech. Fluency, like other aspects of communication, develops with maturity and experience. However, as we shall see, its course may be somewhat less linear.

Numerous researchers have investigated the development of fluency in normally developing children. For example, Yairi (1981; 1982) studied the number of sound and syllable repetitions, word repetitions, phrase repetitions, interjections, revisions, prolongations, and tense pauses present in young children's speech. He found that for a group of nonstuttering children who averaged 25 months of age, the number of disfluencies was fairly low. But disfluency appeared to increase when these children were tested four months later at the age of 29 months. For a second group of children, aged 33 months, Yairi (1981) reported the number of disfluencies was even greater than the number seen in the younger group. Again, a second test was done four months later, when these children were 37 months of age, and it was found that here, too, the number of disfluencies had increased.

In fact, the number of disfluencies in these children's speech appeared to peak around their third birthday. Between the ages of 37 and 40 months, the number of disfluencies Yairi observed in the second group decreased nearly to the level of the first group when they were 25 months old. What was seen in the preschool years, then, was a gradual increase in the number of disfluencies in children's speech, beginning around the age of 2 and peaking around the third birthday. After that, disfluency appeared to decrease up to the age of 40 months (or 3½ years).

After the age of 3½, the total number of disfluencies in a speech sample appears to decrease only slightly as the child matures, according to other investigators. Research by Wexler and Mysak (1982) indicates that between the ages of 4 and 6, there is little change in the total percentage of disfluencies. And according to a comprehensive study by Kowal et al. (1975), there is a decrease of only about 2 percent in the number of disfluencies in the speech of high school students as compared with the speech of kindergartners. From these data, one might conclude that the total amount of disfluency in a nonstuttering individual's speech stays fairly constant after approximately the age of 3½.

But more important than the actual *number* of disfluencies may be the *types* of disfluencies characteristic of different ages. As children's linguistic capabilities develop, their style of disfluency appears to become more complex as well. Two-year-old children use primarily interjections, word repetitions, and single-unit sound and syllable repetitions, such as "b-ball," or "un-under" (Yairi, 1981; 1982). By the age of 3 however, revisions have come to predominate—a longer, more complex, and less disruptive type of disfluency (Yairi, 1982). Thus, although disfluency in the normally developing child appears to reach its peak at the age of 3, the net effect of this increase

on the listener may be small because of the nature of the disfluencies.

In the school-age years, Kowal et al. (1975) found a new category of disfluency—parenthetical remarks. According to Andrews and Summers (1991), *parenthetical remarks* are inserted clauses that contain information not relevant to the main idea of a sentence. An example that they give is "Bill, *he's my brother,* is a very good football player" (p. 172). Such remarks have the effect of interrupting the sentence but in a much less obvious way than word repetitions or even revisions. Thus, parenthetical remarks might be considered disfluencies in the broad sense, but they represent a relatively sophisticated way of keeping an audience while gathering one's thoughts to finish the sentence. Kowal et al. (1975) found that this form of disfluency increased proportionally with age, while revisions and interjections *decreased* proportionally.

In summary, the research on fluency development suggests that early disfluencies of normally speaking children are characterized by behavior that fragments words and sentences: interjections; whole-word repetitions; and single-unit, part-word repetitions. These behaviors decrease as the child matures, however, and, by the age of 3, revisions are seen more frequently. Revisions continue to be the most predominant type of disfluency in children's speech up to kindergarten age. Between kindergarten and the high school years, revisions and interjections begin to diminish, while parenthetical remarks increase. Thus, although the absolute number of disfluencies may decrease only slightly during the school years, the type of disfluency continues to evolve.

It appears that individuals of all ages need to rethink what they are saying as they speak and to change direction during an ongoing conversation. But it also appears that these shifts and breaks are done by most people in linguistically integrated ways that become less disruptive to the flow of speech as the individual matures. In fact, Starkweather (1987, 87) suggests that parenthetical remarks can be considered conversational devices to help maintain listener interest and, as such, should perhaps "be considered as a legitimate aspect of language pragmatics" rather than a type of disfluency.

THE ONSET OF STUTTERING

Given this pattern of fluency development from the age of 2 to high school age, when and how does stuttering develop? The "when" part of this question is easier to answer than the "how."

Most experts agree that in the majority of cases, stuttering begins between the ages of 2 and 5 (Yairi, 1983; Andrews et al., 1983). Yairi and Ambrose (1992b) found that 75 percent of the risk of stuttering is over by the age of 3½. In most cases, onset is gradual (Van Riper, 1982), although it *can* be sudden (Yairi, 1983); and there is usually no obvious cause for the stuttering. Stuttering may be acquired by a previously fluent child or adult as a result of neurological injury or stroke. However, *idiopathic stuttering* (stuttering with no known cause, the primary focus of this chapter) is far more common, and it very rarely begins after puberty (Andrews et al., 1983).

There is considerable dispute regarding how stuttering develops. According to an extensive review of the literature by Hamre (1992a), one widespread and often-accepted theory is that stuttering is simply an outgrowth of normal disfluency. This "continuity" theory, articulated by Bloodstein (1987), postulates that stuttering is "a relatively severe degree of normal disfluency or of those specific types of normal disfluency from which it [can] not be readily demarcated" (p. 352). Thus, some researchers see stuttering as similar to normal disfluency except in terms of quantity, with a considerable amount of overlap between normal disfluency and stuttering.

It is also possible that stuttering is categorically different from what we call *normal disfluency*. One study supporting this point of view was conducted by Yairi and Lewis (1984). These researchers found that children who were considered stutterers tended to show multiple units of sound and syllable repetitions (e.g., "ba-ba-ba-ba-ball") and prolongations, while normally disfluent children used primarily interjections, revisions, and word repetitions. Another study supporting the categorical point of view was done by Hamre (1992b), who concluded that parents rarely mistake normally disfluent children for stuttering children. If the types of disfluencies seen in a "normally" disfluent child and a stutterer are different, then perhaps the development of stuttering is not related to normal disfluency.

Regardless of whether stuttering is an outgrowth of normal disfluency or fundamentally different from normal disfluency, most experts agree that early stuttering is characterized by multiple units of sound and syllable repetitions and sound prolongations, with a higher-than-expected percentage of disfluencies overall in connected speech (Silverman, 1992). These multiple repetitions are rare in normally developing children, who typically repeat initial sounds or syllables only once or twice. There also appears to be agreement that stuttering fluctuates in severity, although the direction can be variable: According to Andrews et al. (1983), some young stutterers recover spontaneously while others get worse. However, based on the severity of the disfluency, it is difficult to tell which children will change in which direction (Yairi and Ambrose, 1992a).

PREVALENCE, INCIDENCE, AND RECOVERY

The frequency of stuttering in the general population can be studied in terms of both prevalence and incidence. *Prevalence,* according to Andrews (1984), refers to the number of individuals experiencing the disorder at any one time divided by the total population. Studies of the prevalence of stuttering indicate that 0.9 percent of all prepubertal school-age children stutter at any given time (Andrews et al., 1983). There are no studies, according to Andrews et al. (1983), of the prevalence of stuttering in adulthood. However, some researchers have studied the number of adults who report that they stuttered at some time in their lives. This is referred to as *incidence,* or the percentage of the population who have experienced a disorder over some time period (in this case, during the individual's life). Looked at in this way, it appears that approximately 4.9 percent of the adult population has stuttered at one time or another (Andrews, 1984).

If 4.9 percent of the population stuttered at one time or another in their lives, but only 0.9 percent currently stutter, then a large percentage of those who stutter must recover. Indeed, according to Andrew's et al.'s (1983) review of six studies, 78 percent of all children who stutter will recover by the age of 16. These data need to be interpreted with some caution, however, because the 78 percent recovery rate does not apply equally to all children who stutter. In fact, that figure may apply only to very young children who have just begun to stutter. For example, Yairi and Ambrose (1992a) found that in a group of 27 preschool children identified as stutterers, the greatest decrease in disfluencies occurred in the twelve to fourteen months immediately following the onset of the disorder. By two years post-onset, 67 percent (18 out of 27 children) were judged to be recovered by their parents and the investigators. Of the 33 percent (9 children) who continued to stutter, 6 recovered during the early elementary school years. The remaining 3 continued to stutter beyond elementary school. It appears that the longer a child stutters, the more likely it is that the stuttering will become chronic.

Finally, we should note that in terms of both prevalence and incidence, the vast majority of stutterers are male. The ratio of males to females who stutter is approximately 3 to 1 in early childhood (Andrews et al., 1983). And as age increases, the difference becomes even larger. Wingate (1983, 256) states that the ratio is closer to 4 males to 1 female in later childhood, and in adulthood, the "female stutterer is rather rare."

CAUSES OF STUTTERING: A REVIEW OF PAST AND PRESENT THEORIES

Why do some children stutter? This question has been of interest to parents and researchers alike for generations. Various theories have been put forward to explain the development of stuttering in individuals, but, to date, none has been conclusively proved. Let us briefly consider some of these theories and the evidence for and against them.

BEHAVIORAL THEORIES

In theories based on learning principles, or *behaviorism,* stuttering is believed to originate as a learned response to external consequences. It is hypothesized to be, at the outset, an externally driven behavior rather than one which arises in response to internal factors. Behavioral theories of stuttering were most popular in the period from the late 1930s to the middle 1970s, when the behavioral branch of psychology was flourishing.

One of the most influential behavioral theories of the cause of stuttering was articulated by Johnson (1955; 1959). Johnson was not able to find any differences, biological or physiological, between stutterers and nonstutterers in his early research; so he concluded that stuttering was a learned behavior. Specifically, he hypothesized that stuttering originated in the normal disfluencies children produce in their preschool years. According to Johnson's *diagnosogenic* theory, the problem begins when the parents of stutterers-to-be become overly concerned about their child's normal disfluencies. This concern is relayed to the child through negative reactions: admonitions to speak better, clearer, or without stuttering or through actual punishment for disfluent behavior. Such parental concern, according to Johnson, makes the child anxious about speaking. Feelings of anxiety cause further disruptions in the child's fluency. Again, the child's parents react with admonitions and punishment, and the child becomes even more anxious and more disfluent. A vicious cycle is set up, with the parents' concerns gradually escalating, and the child's anxiety level and disfluency increasing, until a true stuttering problem develops.

According to Johnson, stuttering is caused by both a speaker *and* a listener. The speaker is not inherently a stutterer but rather is made one by an intolerant listener. A quote that has been attributed to Johnson regarding the origins of stuttering is that "stuttering is in the ear of the mother, not the mouth of the child." Thus, behavioral theories of the origin of stuttering direct a certain amount of blame toward the parents of stutterers (especially mothers). However, these theories have an optimistic aspect: If stuttering is a learned behavior, then surely it can be *un*learned, especially if anxiety and other negative emotions are kept under control.

Criticism aimed at behavioral theories center around three primary assumptions behind these theories: (1) that normally developing children demonstrate sufficient disfluencies of a stutterlike nature to concern their parents; (2) that the parents of stutterers have higher expectations for fluency and are more critical of their children's speech than are the parents of nonstutterers; and (3) that stuttering can be "unlearned."

The first assumption has become a point of contention, as described earlier in this chapter. The idea that stuttering is merely an extension of normal disfluency has been challenged, in particular by Hamre (1992a and b). Hamre (1992b) concluded, based on his review of the literature, that parents are often unaware of normal disfluencies in their children and rarely become concerned about them. He cites a report by Starkweather and others in 1990 in which they describe their experience over a decade with fifty-five families of stuttering children. Of the fifty-five families who sought help at Starkweather's clinic, only one set of parents was overly concerned about normal disfluency. Further, Starkweather himself noted that with respect to normal disfluency versus stuttering: "Parental concern seems hardly ever misplaced (Starkweather et al., 1990, 34).

The second assumption is that the parents of stutterers-to-be treat their children differently than do the parents of nonstutterers. According to a review of the literature by Wingate (1983), parents of stutterers and nonstutterers have not been found to differ substantially in terms of bonding with their children. Overt punishment of disfluency has not been observed. However,

Healey (1991), in his own review of the literature, noted research results suggesting that mothers of stutterers speak more quickly, both to stuttering and to nonstuttering children, than do mothers of nonstutterers. This rapid speech rate is somewhat removed from the pattern of concern, admonition, and punishment hypothesized by Johnson. Can a behavior as subtle as a rapid speech rate on the part of mothers cause stuttering in children? Again, we do not know. But given the research findings, one can certainly question the behavioral theory's central premise that parental overreaction to normal disfluency causes stuttering.

The third assumption of behavioral theories is that stuttering can be unlearned, or that it is amenable to behavioral therapy and conditioning. Again, the evidence is equivocal. Andrews et al. (1983) cite a number of studies which demonstrate a reduction in both stuttering and accessory behaviors through behavioral conditioning. However, if learning theories are accurate in their portrayal of the origins of stuttering, changing a speaker's deviant attitudes toward speech and reducing his anxiety level should also eliminate stuttering. According to Andrews et al. (1983), such programs provide modest gains in speech fluency, but they are less effective than speech retraining programs that do not directly address attitudes.

In summary, what does the research tell us about behavioral theories of the origin of stuttering? First, such theories do not appear to believably explain the true source of stuttering. The idea that stuttering grows out of normal disfluency because of the parents' reactions to the child's speech does not appear to be supported. However, behavioral theories may give us valuable insights into the maintenance of stuttering and why stuttering changes (and often worsens) over the years. As stutterers develop fears and anxieties about speech as a result of their stuttering, more severe stuttering and accessory behaviors may become learned responses to external consequences. Finally, behavioral theories appear to generate relatively effective models of therapy for stuttering.

PSYCHODYNAMIC THEORIES

In theories of stuttering based on psychodynamic or psychoanalytic principles, stuttering is seen as the manifestation of inner conflicts or repressed needs. Unlike behavioral theories, psychodynamic theories do not emphasize the specific shaping of normal disfluency into stuttering. The individual is believed to stutter primarily because of unresolved internal conflicts, although listener reactions to both the child himself and his speech are acknowledged to play a role.

Psychodynamic theories of stuttering were heavily influence by Freud. According to Freudian theory, each individual has a primitive part of the psyche, the *id,* that demands fulfillment of desires for comfort, dependence, aggression, sex, and other impulses. The *superego,* hypothesized to be the internalization of society's rules, represses the id. The *ego,* or the individual's capacity for rational thought, tries to mediate between the id and the superego, so that personal wants can be satisfied in socially acceptable ways. Psychodynamic theories of stuttering generally postulate that stuttering occurs because of an unusually strong conflict between the id and the superego. From the middle 1930s to the early 1970s, such constructs enjoyed relative popularity.

Travis (1971) summarized his own views of the psychodynamic origins of stuttering in a report entitled "The Unspeakable Feelings of People with Special Reference to Stuttering." According to Travis, people who stutter were not given adequate care and comfort as infants. He suggests that parents' rigidity in dealing with their crying, feeding, toileting, sexual feelings, and aggression resulted in the child's internal drives being frustrated. These frustrations were repressed by the superego but continued to simmer in the id. The child needed to speak about these "unspeakable" needs and desires but feared that he would lose the love of those around him if he did so. Therefore, anxiety about speaking was high, and this high anxiety led to stuttering. In this point of view, stuttering is seen as the ego's way of keeping the child socially acceptable, by obstructing what he really wants to say.

According to these theories, stutterers would be expected to demonstrate more neurotic symptoms in general than nonstutterers (since the basis of their disorder is repression), and psychoanalytic or psychiatric counseling would be expected to resolve the stuttering problem. Neither of these predictions has survived the scrutiny of research. According to Andrews et al. (1983), stuttering does not appear to be part of a general syndrome of psychological disorder, and neither stutterers nor their parents show neurotic symptoms to a greater degree than nonstuttering children and *their* parents. For example, a bonding study published by Parker in 1979 revealed no significant differences in the parenting behaviors of the parents of stutterers versus the parents of nonstutterers.

The results regarding the efficacy of psychoanalytic therapy for stuttering are also generally more negative than positive. Travis (1971, 1032) reported that after over 150 hours of therapy, six out of eleven adult stutterers were "cured" while the remaining five were "helped greatly." Yet most researchers in the field of fluency do not agree that psychotherapy alone is beneficial (Shames, 1990; Andrews et al., 1983; Wingate, 1983; Perkins, 1980). As Perkins notes, "Although stutterers are likely to feel better about themselves and their speech after psychotherapy, most will continue to stutter" (p. 464).

ORGANIC THEORIES

Like psychodynamic theories, organic theories assume that the origins of stuttering are internal. But where psychodynamic theories consider stuttering to be induced by repressed feelings and needs, organic theories are based on the hypothesis that stuttering is caused by some physical deficit, most likely in the neuromotor system or the language-processing areas of the brain.

1. Stuttering as a Neuromotor Disorder. As you will recall from our discussion of neurophysiology in Chapter 8, the neuromotor system has many levels that play various roles in executing voluntary movement. In the cortical motor centers (the premotor area and the motor area), voluntary movement is planned and generated, and appropriate muscle tone is set. The sensory area of the cortex, directly behind the motor areas, provides information about ongoing movement so that moment-to-moment adjustments and refinements can occur. Among the subcortical motor centers (the basal ganglia and the cerebellum), the basal ganglia appear important in generating unconscious movements that accompany or facilitate the primary movement. The cerebellum, with its connecting pathways to cortical movement centers, sensory centers, and the basal ganglia, coordinates both the voluntary and unconscious aspects of movement, so that actions can be executed in a smooth, integrated, and accurate way. For decades, some researchers have believed that stuttering is due to a disruption in this system but, unlike cerebral palsy and other neuromotor disorders, a disruption that affects only the muscles of speech to a noticeable degree.

Some of the earliest speech research in the 1920s and the 1930s was based on the belief that stuttering had a physical cause. For example, it was known even at that time that the left hemisphere of the brain controlled speech and language functions, and that in most individuals, it was the "dominant" hemisphere. Travis (1931) (yes, the same Travis of psychodynamic fame) hypothesized that a failure to establish strong dominance of the left hemisphere over the right was the root cause of stuttering. A "mixed dominance" condition, he believed, resulted in the two hemispheres of the brain sending competing signals to the speech musculature, disrupting the smooth sequencing of speech movements.

As it happened, research during this time period did not support either Travis's specific theory of cerebral dominance or the more general organic theories of other researchers. Such theories would predict the presence of some additional physical symptoms of neuromotor dysfunction—besides stuttering—if a true organic disorder existed. However, no evidence of a more generalized motor deficit was ever found in stutterers. In addition, therapy based on cerebral-dominance principles proved ineffective. For example, Travis tried to cure stuttering by putting a cast on the

right arm and hand of his stutterer subjects, forcing them to use their left hands and presumably to reestablish their original dominance patterns. After a year of this treatment, stuttering in his subjects had not improved (Travis, 1978). Failing either to find convincing evidence that stutterers actually were different in terms of their neuromotor functioning from nonstutterers *or* to get a positive response to his cerebral-dominance therapy, Travis then turned his attention to psychodynamic theories. Other researchers underwent similar changes in their orientation. Interest in organic theories of stuttering languished for the next few decades.

Theories on a neuromotor basis for stuttering again began to emerge in the 1970s. New research techniques and instruments, new interpretations of older data, and disillusionment with the behavioral and psychodynamic approaches provided impetus for this change. For example, Wingate (1969; 1970) concluded that stuttering appeared to improve under conditions where vocal-fold behavior was either absent or controlled. It had been known for some time that whispering, singing, chanting, altering rhythms, and controlling intonation patterns enhanced fluency. Wingate proposed that the reason for this enhancement was reduced demand on the vocal folds for the rapid, moment-to-moment changes spontaneous speech requires. He hypothesized that stuttering might be caused by a "discoordination" between the muscles of voice production in the throat and the oral muscles of speech. Although a neurological source was not directly postulated, it was implicit that this discoordination had a physical base.

More recent investigations into the neuromotor bases of stuttering have focused on comparing stutterers' fluent speech samples with the fluent speech samples of nonstutterers. According to the neuromotor perspective, if some discoordination does underlie the stutterer's disfluencies, one might reason that the same discoordination would be seen in the stutterer's fluent speech, although to a lesser degree, and that the stutterer's fluent speech would thus be somehow different from the nonstutterer's speech. A review of the literature by Healey (1991) revealed findings of height-ened levels of activity in the stutterer's vocal folds during perceptibly fluent responses. Increases in voice onset time, voice reaction time, and initia-tion and termination of voicing have also been observed in the fluent speech of stutterers (Healey, 1991). These findings suggest the pres-ence of generalized motor involvement in the speech mechanisms of stutterers even when their speech is not perceptually abnormal. However, any organic theory must be considered tentative until an actual lesion causing the disorder is found.

2. Stuttering as a Neurolinguistic Disorder. In the previous section we looked at stuttering as a *dysarthria;* that is, as a speech disorder caused by abnormalities in the neuromotor system. How-ever, the research of some investigators has indi-cated that stutterers differ from nonstutterers in the way they process and formulate language. For example, Hubbard and Prins (1994) found that stutterers (and even nonstutterers) were more dis-fluent when reading sentences that contained unfamiliar words than they were when reading sentences containing familiar words. They con-cluded that phonological *encoding,* or the cogni-tive process of phoneme selection, is a source fac-tor in instances of stuttering. A focus on linguistic encoding is quite different from our previous concern with the coordination between the vari-ous parts of the speech mechanism during the production of speech.

If stuttering is caused by difficulties with lan-guage decoding, encoding, or formulation, this argues for a higher level of neurological involve-ment than the neuromotor system. As we shall learn in Chapter 13, specific areas of the *cerebral cortex,* the most advanced part of the brain, are associated with decoding the words that we hear, associating words with concepts and meanings, encoding ideas into words, phrases, and sentences, and selecting the proper sequence of phonemes to express them. Abnormalities in the function of these cortical areas might lead to difficulties in learning and using language—and, perhaps, to stuttering.

In fact, the connection between language abil-ities and stuttering has been of interest for some time. As previously discussed, the onset of stut-tering usually occurs during the language-learn-ing years, and children who are experiencing delays in language acquisition may also have diffi-culty with fluency (Wall and Myers, 1984). It is not hard to imagine that the young child strug-gling with new speech sounds, vocabulary words, and the rules of syntax could experience disfluent interruptions in ongoing speech.

The idea of a language deficit contributing to stuttering is supported by Andrews et al. (1983). In their review of the literature, these authors reported that six current studies have found that stutterers are late in passing developmental mile-stones related to speech and language. Further, eight current studies "have shown that stutterers perform more poorly than non-stutterers on some tests of language" (Andrews et al., 1983, 230). The same authors also report that stutterers are much more likely to have phonological disorders than are nonstutterers, although that finding was not supported by Throneburg et al. (1994).

Nelson (1986) expresses a point of view that combines, to some degree, the idea that neuro-motor limitations contribute to stuttering with the idea that language encoding and formulation may play a part. According to Nelson (1986, 33),

We believe that some children may be disfluent because motorically they are attempting to coordinate respiratory, phonatory and articulatory systems at a level above their physical capability. We also believe that the greater the uncertainty about information, the longer and more com-plex the sentence formulation, and the greater the num-ber of linguistic decisions to be made, the more likely it is that coordination will be disrupted and disfluency occur.

Thus, Nelson appears to acknowledge a "pre-disposition" toward stuttering based on immature control of the speech-production mechanism. However, stuttering is also hypothesized to be influenced by the length and complexity of the child's utterances. Stuttering, Nelson and others would argue, is most likely to occur when linguistic demands (i.e., formulating long and complicated sentences) outstrip the child's capabilities for coordinated execution. Perkins et al. (1991) present a more recent and complex version of this theory that stuttering is caused by both neurolinguistic and neuromotor components. However, again we must note that physical evidence of abnormal structure or function in the language centers of the brain (or the motor centers) has not been found in stutterers. Unless some physical differences between stutterers and nonstutterers can be documented, this theory remains tenuous.

3. Genetic Factors in Stuttering. Perhaps the most powerful argument for an organic basis for stuttering is the strong genetic component that appears to be present in this disorder. In examining the evidence for an environmental versus an organic cause of stuttering, Andrews et al. (1983, 229) note that "stutterers appear to come from the same environment as do nonstutterers, with one exception: they come from families with an excess of stuttering relatives." By pooling data from 725 families covered in two separate studies, Andrews et al. estimate that for men who have ever stuttered, the expected incidence of stuttering in their daughters is 9 percent and in their sons 22 percent. The same researchers concluded that for women who have ever stuttered, 17 percent of the daughters and 36 percent of their sons will stutter. Keep in mind that the incidence of stuttering in the general population is about 4.9 percent. Thus, a greatly increased risk of stuttering is clearly present in the children of stutterers.

Could this increased risk possibly be related to child-rearing practices and not to genetic factors? Studies examining patterns of stuttering in twins tend to refute the environmental theory. If one twin of a *monozygotic,* or identical, pair stutters, the chances are 77 percent that the other twin will also stutter (Howie, 1984). For *dizygotic,* or fraternal, twins, there is only a 32 percent chance (Howie, 1984), and for nontwin siblings, the risk is 18 percent (Andrews et al., 1983). Presumably all these twins (and siblings) were exposed to the same child-rearing practices, so environmental factors could not explain the differences in concordance between monozygotic twins, with identical genetic material, and the other groups.

The research on stuttering patterns in families strongly indicates that there is a genetic component to stuttering—what Starkweather (1987) calls a "genetic predisposition to stutter." However, it is also clear that genetic factors alone are not sufficient to produce stuttering, and that the environment must also play some role (Howie, 1984). There *are* discordant pairs of monozygotic twins, instances where one twin stutters and the other does not. Environmental variables might explain the discrepancy. Environmental variables might also explain why dizygotic twins are more concordant than nontwin siblings, despite the fact that both groups have similar genetic relationships. In addition, genetic variables do not appear to explain the severity of stuttering or the recovery patterns (Starkweather, 1987). That is, severe stuttering in a parent does not necessarily correlate with severe stuttering in the child; and conversely, early recovery in a parent does not ensure early recovery of the stuttering child. Thus, environmental variables such as the parents' reactions to the child's speech patterns and the parents' speech models, among others factors, may determine the course of the disorder despite a genetic predisposition.

THEORIES ON THE CAUSES OF STUTTERING: A SUMMARY

The acknowledgement of a genetic predisposition and possible organic basis for stuttering does not satisfactorily answer the question of why stuttering occurs. We still do not know whether the problem is primarily one of speech control or language formulation—or both—or neither. The nature and location of the neurological "abnormality" that some believe is the root cause of the disorder has never been specified. We cannot explain, if this is an organic-physical problem, why the spontaneous recovery rate is so high. We hypothesize that environmental and psychological variables determine the progression and severity of the disorder, but we are uncertain as to *which* variables. In short, many questions about the origin, nature, and course of stuttering remain to be answered.

TREATMENT OF FLUENCY DISORDERS: THE YOUNG STUTTERER

What are the roles of parents and speech-language pathologists in the case of a young child who is just beginning to stutter? Given the strong possibility of spontaneous recovery (78 percent by the age of 16, according to Andrews et al., 1983), especially within the first year after the onset of the disorder (67 percent, according to Yairi and Ambrose, 1992a), some might contend that there is no need for concern or action. However, we have no way of knowing which children will experience recovery and which will not.

There is also the possibility that the parents' behavior toward the child and his speech difficulties will influence the outcome. For example, Martin and Lindamood (1986) pointed out that "spontaneously"-recovered stutterers and their parents often report using a variety of formal and informal treatment techniques, such as slowing the speaking rate and stopping or repeating a stuttered word. As we shall see, these two techniques are often incorporated into speech-therapy programs. Given the impossibility of predicting recovery, and the possible importance of the parents' behavior, conscious or unconscious, most speech-language pathologists would agree that if the parents are concerned about their child's speech, help should be sought.

What happens when parents contact a speech-language pathologist because of concern about stuttering in their child? According to Gregory (1984), it is the responsibility of the speech-language pathologist to determine if there should, indeed, be concern about the child's speech, and if so, what should be done about it. The parents are asked to provide a brief description of the problem and are observed interacting with their child in a play situation. The speech pathologist should also interact with the child and observe the child's speech. To gain a more complete picture of the child's communication abilities, his language, phonological, and hearing abilities should also be tested.

If the speech-language pathologist determines that the child's disfluencies are essentially normal (single-unit sound, syllable and word repetitions, interjections, and revisions with no strain or tension), or even slightly atypical, the primary intervention may be counseling for the parents (Gregory, 1984). This counseling is done by the speech-language pathologist and is designed to give parents information about speech and ways to help their child communicate more easily. Descriptions of normal fluency development are often provided to reassure parents that a certain amount of disfluency is to be expected. Perkins (1980; 1992) provides numerous suggestions for parents of children who stutter. Among them are the following:

1. Parents and, indeed, the entire family, should provide models of slow, easy, relaxed speech. Rather than simply telling the child to "slow down," "calm down," or "relax," family members should demonstrate these mannerisms. Parents should slow their own rate of speech by prolonging their vowels somewhat, pausing frequently, and using a relaxed tone. In addition to slowed speech, Perkins recommends making a game of slowing everything down, both speech and physical movements, during certain times of the day.

   It is important that all members of the family demonstrate this speech pattern rather than adopt a "do as I say, not as I do" attitude (Perkins, 1992). Why? First, the child should not feel "singled out." This could cause self-consciousness and a consequent increase in disfluency. Second, modeling has a powerful effect on the speech of young children. Especially in the preschool years, when language and phonological patterns are being formed, children are easily able to modify their productions based on what they hear around them. In later childhood and adulthood, when speech and language patterns have become well-established and automatic, others' models are not as effective in changing behavior. Third, we must keep in mind that the child's cortical language centers and neuromotor system are still maturing. As described previously, the child might not be physically capable of producing speech (and perhaps of formulating language) as rapidly as necessary for the smooth and fluent expression of ideas. When the pressure to communicate is high, as it would be when competing with a rapidly speaking adult, the child's motor production of speech may break down (Kent, 1983). If a slower and more relaxed communicative context is set up, such breakdowns in fluency are less likely to occur.

As discussed above, research has shown that mothers of stuttering children tend to speak more rapidly than do mothers of nonstuttering children (Meyers and Freeman, 1985). In a related study, Starkweather and Gottwald (1984) found that reductions in both parents' and children's speech rates were predictive of recovery from stuttering. Thus, adults' rate of speech may, indeed, affect a child's fluency.

2. Reduce the pressure to communicate. While easy and relaxed speech can reduce some of the pressure on the child to "compete for the floor," other steps should also be taken. If at all possible, parents should try to spend some time alone with the child each day in a one-to-one situation. This gives the child a chance to communicate without interruptions from other siblings and adults. The fluency experienced in such situations is highly reinforcing. In addition, parents can decrease the number of questions they ask the child, relying instead on comments about what the parent is feeling or what the child is doing. With this strategy, children can "chime in" if they want but are under no pressure to do so (Nelson, 1986).

Perkins (1992) also recommends paying attention to the child when he is fluent rather than waiting until he is frustrated and disfluent. For example, if a child asks for assistance in a fluent manner, it is better to attend to the request than to wait until the child has made

several requests, each progressively more disfluent. In the latter instance, parents may unintentionally be reinforcing disfluency as a way to get attention.

The child can be expected to be most disfluent in emotionally charged situations, such as defending himself when accused of misbehavior. In such situations, parents should refrain from demanding a full account of the bad behavior until tempers have cooled and the subject can be discussed more rationally.

3. Keep the child well-rested and healthy. The pace of life in our society has quickened tremendously in the past several decades. With both parents working outside the home in many families, evenings often become the only time that families have to spend together. This can result in children getting to bed later than they should, only to be awakened early the next morning and rushed off to the baby sitter or to the daycare center.

Fatigue is detrimental to performance in individuals of any age. However, young children who are struggling with their developing motor capabilities and heavy demands for rapid, fluent speech can be more seriously affected. A motor system that can just barely keep up with the demand for speech production under the best of circumstances may break down when fatigued. Keeping the child well-rested and healthy can enhance the chances for coordinated and fluent speech.

If the stuttering problem appears to the speech-language pathologist to involve more than easy and effortless repetitions, interjections, and revisions, then a more direct approach may be required. The speech-language pathologist may work directly with the child in individual therapy, usually twice per week. In therapy, the speech-language pathologist models the easy, relaxed speech patterns described above and attempts to achieve a basal level of fluency with the child. If the child cannot produce fluent sentences, he is required only to produce words. When single words can be produced fluently and easily, multiword phrases are introduced. The child must then respond to therapy activities using fluent phrases. As the child becomes better able to produce fluent speech, sentences and, finally, spontaneous connected speech are required. The therapist may also introduce some impediments to fluency as the child's fluency patterns become more stable. For example, she may speed up her own rate of speech, or interrupt the child period-ically. According to Gregory (1984, 350), "These procedures . . . should be done only by the clini-cian, not the parents."

The aim of this type of therapy is to establish spontaneous fluency in the child. According to Peters and Guitar (1991), *spontaneous fluency* is a normal speech flow with only occasional repeti-tions or prolongations. Most important, in spon-taneous fluency, "fluency is not maintained by paying attention to speech; *rather, the person just talks and pays attention to his ideas*" (Peters and Guitar, 1991, 119, italics the author's). We would hope that with therapy, all stutterers would be able to achieve spontaneous fluency. However, as we shall see shortly, this goal may be most attain-able with the young stutterer.

TREATMENT OF FLUENCY DISORDERS: THE CHRONIC STUTTERER

If stuttering persists throughout childhood and into adulthood, the chances of spontaneous recovery are sharply reduced. In addition, as the individual's stuttering receives increasingly more negative reactions, attitudes of fear and avoidance toward speaking situations can easily develop. Accessory behaviors may also be adopted as the stutterer struggles to remain fluent. The stutter-ing may begin to affect the individual's social life and vocational goals, resulting in reduced feelings of competence and self-worth. The chronic stut-terer brings a complexity of attitudes, experiences, and coping attempts to the therapeutic process, and these must be dealt with directly or indirectly.

Approaches to therapy for the chronic stutterer fall into three major categories: (1) psychother-

apy, (2) stuttering modification therapy, and (3) fluency shaping.

PSYCHOTHERAPY

Psychotherapy involves treatment by a psycholo-gist or psychiatrist to help an individual determine and resolve problematic emotions or maladaptive behaviors. In the context of stuttering, this means a focus on the individual's personality, experi-ences, and overall behavior patterns rather than on his speech. For example, a stutterer might be asked to recall early interactions with his parents and his emotional response to these interactions. Such therapy would have the goal of helping the stutterer gain a better understanding of himself and why he feels and behaves the way he does.

As discussed earlier, most investigators in the area of fluency have agreed that psychotherapy is not an effective "cure" for stuttering. Stuttering does not appear to be caused by neuroses (Andrews et al., 1983) and does not appear to resolve in most cases with psychodynamic thera-pies. However, a stutterer may still benefit from some form of psychological intervention and counseling. Many stutterers have interpersonal difficulties as a result of their stuttering, even if psychological problems did not cause the stutter-ing. Thus, a depressed stutterer with low self-esteem and difficulties with family members or extreme anxiety about speaking situations may be helped to cope with these life stresses by psy-chotherapy.

STUTTERING-MODIFICATION THERAPY

The stuttering-modification approach to therapy was originally based on the idea that "the root of stuttering is in the struggle to be fluent" (Perkins, 1980, 476). Specific therapy procedures have been detailed by Bloodstein (1975), Conture (1990), Prins (1984), and Van Riper (1982). In general, the goals of stuttering-modification ther-apy are (1) to decrease the speaker's fears and apprehensions about speaking and (2) to help the stutterer stop trying to avoid stuttering and, in fact, to stutter more easily and openly. The theory is that if the stutterer's anxieties about speech subside, and if he stops trying so hard *not* to stutter, his stuttering behavior will gradually disappear to reveal only "normal" types and amounts of disfluency.

While researchers of the 1990s might not agree completely with the premise upon which this therapy is based, many would agree that stuttering, regardless of its roots, is worsened dramatically by the stutterer's fears about speaking and attempts to avoid it by using accessory behaviors. Thus, the basic principles of stuttering-modification therapy may be useful even if a strict behavioral theory of origin is not accepted.

Stuttering-modification therapy generally begins by confronting, sometimes very directly, the speaker's fears and anxieties related to speech and stuttering. The individual may be encouraged to observe himself in a mirror as he stutters and then to repeat his mannerisms voluntarily. He may be asked to stutter on purpose, even on words he is normally able to say fluently (Peters and Guitar, 1991). He may be asked to observe the reactions of those around him carefully as he speaks and later to discuss those reactions, as well as his own feelings, with the speech pathologist.

This phase of therapy is designed to "desensitize" the stutterer to his stuttering. Its purpose is to take what the stutterer believes to be a shameful and uncontrollable event and cast it in a more objective, unemotional light. By stuttering voluntarily, the stutterer learns that he *can* control many aspects of his speech. By watching the reactions of others, the speaker comes to realize that those reactions are not as negative as he believed. Proponents of this theory argue that the activities and experiences of this first phase of therapy should reduce the individual's fear and anxiety about speech and decrease his need to use avoidance or postponement behaviors on feared words or in feared situations.

The second phase of stuttering-modification therapy is designed to provide the stutterer with alternative behaviors to stuttering. He may be encouraged to stutter using easy, regular repeti-

tions instead of tense blocks and prolongations. For example, the stutterer anticipating difficulty with an "m" word may learn to say "ma-ma-machine" in a relaxed manner instead of struggling for fluency and producing, instead, tense blocks and head jerks. This use of easy repetition is known as *bouncing.*

If the stutterer *does* encounter prolonged tension and disfluency on a particular word, he is encouraged to stop and repeat the word immediately with a less disruptive type of disfluency—again, a few easy repetitions or a relaxed prolongation. This is known as *cancellation,* repeating an unacceptable disfluency in a less intrusive way. *Pullouts,* or easy prolongations to get out of a block, and *preparatory sets,* preparing mentally to ease into speaking, are also taught to the stutterer.

The problem with stuttering modification is that it appears to focus on how to stutter *better* rather than how to achieve spontaneous fluency. According to Peters and Guitar (1991), the result of this type of therapy may be "controlled fluency," or even "acceptable stuttering," rather than spontaneous fluency. Peters and Guitar define *controlled fluency* as fluent-*sounding* speech, although the individual must attend to and modify his speech patterns in order to maintain fluency (rather than just attending to his ideas, as a normal speaker would). They define *acceptable stuttering* as occurring when "the speaker exhibits noticeable but not severe disfluency and feels comfortable speaking despite his disfluency" (Peters and Guitar, 1991, 119). Inherent in the stuttering-modification approach is an acceptance of the idea that "you may be a stutterer all of your life, so learn to stutter effortlessly and openly, and try to live with it gracefully" (Perkins, 1980, 476).

FLUENCY-SHAPING THERAPY

The fluency-shaping approach to therapy is based on the idea that if stuttering is a learned behavior, it can be *un*learned, and fluent speech can be systematically introduced to replace it. Fluency-shaping programs have been proposed by Ryan (1974), Perkins (1984), Webster (1980), Shames and Florance (1985) and Boberg (1984), among others.

In the fluency-shaping approach, speech patterns are rebuilt "from the ground up," beginning with techniques to enhance fluency. First, the stutterer learns to say words in a monotone, prolonging each vowel and producing each syllable with equal stress and timing. In addition, an early component of some fluency-shaping programs is the use of *delayed auditory feedback,* or DAF, in which the client's speech is played back to him through headphones with a 150 to 250 millisecond delay (Peters and Guitar, 1991). Talking under conditions of DAF causes an individual to speak more slowly. In stutterers, this procedure facilitates fluency.

Once fluency is established using this unusual speaking style, the pitch, rhythm, and rate of speech are varied. Gradually, more normal stress and intonation patterns are demanded, although rate is kept slow. DAF, if used initially, is slowly reduced. In the final stages of therapy, speech rate is increased until it approximates normal speed.

Establishing this abnormal-sounding fluent speech usually occurs quickly during the therapy process. The greater challenge for the speech-language pathologist is to help the client retain this newfound fluency while moving toward appropriate intonation patterns, stress, and rate. The importance of achieving normal-sounding speech cannot be overemphasized. As Perkins (1980, 478) puts it, "when fluent speech sounds unnatural, many stutterers view this 'cure' as worse than their 'disease.' They would rather stutter expressively than be fluent monotonously."

In the fluency-shaping approach, avoidance behaviors (accessory behaviors) and attitudes toward speech are not directly addressed. It is assumed that as the speaker becomes more and more fluent, negative feelings and attitudes will be replaced with confidence as a consequence, and avoidance behaviors will therefore be reduced. However, this assumption may not always be justified. If avoidance behaviors and negative attitudes continue to interfere with establishing and maintaining fluency, then more

direct therapy is indicated. It may be beneficial to use a combined approach to therapy, so that feelings, attitudes, and behaviors are worked on using the stuttering-modification approach, while speech improvement is achieved using the fluency-shaping approach (Peters and Guitar, 1991).

The ultimate goal of fluency-shaping therapy is spontaneous fluency in conversational speech. If spontaneous fluency is not achievable, *controlled fluency* would still be considered adequate; that is, the individual may occasionally (or even frequently) have to attend to his speech and reduce his rate and modify his rhythm in order to maintain fluency. However, *acceptable stuttering,* as defined above, would not be considered a successful outcome (Peters and Guitar, 1991).

TREATMENT OUTCOMES

How successfully can stuttering be treated in children and adults? Is there any justification for the idea, discussed in our section on stuttering modification, that chronic stuttering is likely to be lifelong? Guitar and Peters (1980, 45) observed that "Adult stutterers are notorious for relapsing. Most speech-language pathologists have had the opportunity of watching one of their successful clients slip back to the pre-therapy level of disfluency." Yet Andrews et al. (1983, 234) state that "For 10 years there has been good evidence that a planned and disciplined approach to therapy is effective." Which point of view is more accurate?

A review of the literature by Andrews et al. (1980) sheds some light on this question. These authors studied the effects of stuttering therapy reported in forty-two studies in which a total of 756 stutterers were treated. Components of both the stuttering-modification approach (easy onsets) and the fluency-shaping approach (prolonged vowels, rhythm alterations) were used in these studies. Based on the compiled results, Andrews et al. concluded that stuttering therapy *is* effective in that frequency of stuttering decreases measurably after approximately eighty hours of treatment. Further, these improvements appear to be maintained for some time. Andrews et al. (1983, 234), in a similar review, estimated that "The average subject, who originally stuttered on some 14 percent of his or her syllables, stutters on only 1 to 2 percent 18 months to 2 years after treatment." However, the gains achieved during stuttering therapy may not be permanent. According to Howie et al. (1981), *some* subjects will have relapsed two or more years after treatment and may, at that point, be in need of additional intervention.

The data on treatment outcome indicate that speech therapy can be very beneficial for stutterers even if, years after the treatment, a relapse occurs. Thus both of the points of view presented above appear to be valid to some degree. Speech-language pathologists may not be able to *cure* stuttering, but they can help stuttering clients *manage* their disorder and continue to communicate despite occasional difficulties.

THE CONSEQUENCES OF STUTTERING TO THE INDIVIDUAL

One might imagine that a disorder as disruptive to communication as stuttering would have many negative psychological effects on an individual. It could be hypothesized that all stutterers would tend to be withdrawn underachievers who have difficulty socializing and who are very limited in their vocational choices.

In fact, stutterers can be found in all walks of life and appear to be no more troubled or neurotic than nonstutterers (Andrews et al., 1983). As in the general population, some individuals who stutter are better adjusted than others. Although some undoubtedly choose less challenging career paths because of their speech disorder, many become teachers, attorneys, politicians, actors, and so on. As stated in the introduction to this chapter, some of the men and women who have changed the course of history have been stutterers. Stuttering can certainly be viewed as a challenge to the individual in achieving his social and vocational goals. However, with determination

on the part of the stutterer—aided by appropriate speech therapy—the speech disorder need not become a limiting factor in the individual's life.

SUMMARY

Stuttering is a special type of *disfluency,* or disruption of the smooth flow of speech, characterized by repetitions and prolongations of sounds and syllables, which are involuntary in nature, and which the individual struggles to end. Accessory features, such as physical mannerisms, postponements, or circumlocutions, may also be part of the stuttering syndrome. There is some dispute as to whether stuttering is simply an outgrowth of the normal disfluencies seen in all speakers (interjections, revisions, parenthetical remarks) or if it is fundamentally different from normal disfluency. In either case, children in the prime speech- and language-development years, ages 2 through 7, appear to be more disfluent than adult speakers. These are also the years when stuttering is most likely to have its onset.

There are numerous schools of thought regarding the origin of stuttering. Behavioral theorists stress the importance of the environment, in particular the responses of parents and others to the child's normally disfluent speech. Psychodynamic theorists stress the importance of the child's early experiences and the persistence of unresolved inner conflicts. Organic theorists postulate the existence of some neurological or physical abnormality, possibly inherited, that predisposes the individual to stuttering. While none of these theories has been conclusively proved, there appears to be a growing acceptance of the idea that both an organic predisposition and environmental factors combine to precipitate stuttering.

Therapy for the adolescent and adult stutterer today generally involves the stuttering-modification approach, the fluency-shaping approach, psychotherapy, or some combination of the three. A carefully planned program of therapy has been found to result in a reduction of disfluencies in the speaker's spontaneous speech. However, in some cases therapy gains may not last more than two years, after which the stutterer may need additional intervention to reestablish fluent speech.

The research indicates that stuttering may, indeed, be an extremely difficult disorder to eradicate. However, with therapy and determination, stutterers can expect to successfully meet the communication challenges confronting them and to achieve their goals in life.

REVIEW QUESTIONS

1. What do we mean by the terms *fluency, disfluency,* and *stuttering*?

2. What are the five major types of disfluency? Which are more likely to be considered "normal," and which are more likely to be considered stuttering?

3. What accessory or secondary behaviors are associated with stuttering? Why do stutterers adopt these behaviors? Do these behaviors generally help the problem or make it worse?

4. How does fluency develop as the child is learning language and phonology? What types of disfluencies are typically seen in young children's speech? How do these change over time?

5. When does stuttering usually have its onset? What behaviors mark the onset of stuttering? How similar is early stuttering to "normal" disfluency?

6. What is the prevalence of stuttering in the general population? What is the ratio of male to female stutterers? What percentage of stutterers appear to recover spontaneously?

7. Briefly describe the three schools of thought on the cause of stuttering. What view appears to be gaining consensus at this point in time?

8. What are some suggestions to parents for helping young children who stutter?

9. What approaches might a speech pathologist take when working with children who stutter?

10. What are three therapy approaches that might be used in working with chronic stutterers?

11. What is the difference between stuttering-modification therapy and fluency-shaping therapy?

12. How successful has speech therapy been in "curing" stuttering?

13. What are the consequences of stuttering in adulthood?

FOR FURTHER INFORMATION

Any publication of the Stuttering Foundation of America, P.O. Box 11749, Memphis, TN 38111. Books are available upon written request.

Bloodstein, O. (1987). *A handbook on stuttering.* Chicago, IL: National Easter Seal Society for Crippled Children and Adults.

Healey, E. (Ed.) (1991). *Readings on research in stuttering.* New York, NY: Longman.

Perkins, W. (1992). *Stuttering prevented.* San Diego, CA: Singular Publishing Group.

Peters, T., and Guitar, B. (1991). *Stuttering: An integrated approach to its nature and treatment.* Baltimore, MD: Williams and Wilkins.

Silverman, F. (1992). *Stuttering and other fluency disorders.* Englewood Cliffs, NJ: Prentice-Hall.

Starkweather, C. (1987). *Fluency and stuttering.* Englewood Cliffs, NJ: Prentice-Hall.

Wall, M., and Myers, F. (1984). *Clinical management of childhood stuttering.* Austin, TX: Pro-Ed.

Introduction to Voice and Voice Disorders

I n our definition of *speech* in Chapter 1, we included the elements of articulation, fluency, and voice. So far, we have discussed articulation, the phonological rules that guide it, and disorders involving the production of phonemes. We have also explored the concepts of fluency, disfluency, and stuttering. By now, it should be clear that the sounds of speech must be rapidly and precisely produced and smoothly connected if speech is to be considered "normal."

The last, and somewhat more elusive, component of speech is voice. As we previously defined it, *voice* refers to the tone generated by the vibration of the vocal folds. Although not *all* speech sounds are produced with vocal-fold vibration, most are; thus the voice component is consistently present during speech. A speaker's voice is important both in projecting a spoken message and in expressing the emotional content of the message.

To get an idea of what speech would be like without the component of voice, try whispering your full name very, very softly. (If you whisper too forcefully, you will unintentionally generate some voicing.) When you whisper very softly, you will notice that your lips, tongue, and jaw move in the patterns necessary to form speech sounds and that one articulatory position flows smoothly into another in a fluent way. However, your message will not be heard, even if a listener is relatively close to you. Similarly, if you try to whisper your name very softly but in an angry or questioning manner, the emotional intent of your message will probably not be understood either (except as conveyed by your facial expressions). If you kept up your efforts at voiceless speech long

enough, you would become fatigued and frustrated from trying to make yourself heard and understood.

Individuals with voice disorders often have much the same problems as those just described. If something is wrong with the vocal folds, an individual may not be able to speak loudly enough, or may have feelings of tension and discomfort in the throat. It may be difficult to express intended emotions vocally. On an aesthetic level, the individual's voice may have such an unpleasant quality to it—despite normal articulation and fluency—that their speech is difficult to listen to. Voice disorders can vary tremendously in terms of their causes, symptoms, severity, and consequences.

In this chapter, we will first explore some of the basic concepts related to normal voice production and the evaluation of vocal adequacy. The structure and function of the voice production mechanism will be described in some detail in order to provide a context in which vocal pathologies can be considered. Finally, we will take a closer look at some of the disorders of voice that prompt individuals to seek the help of a speech-language pathologist.

THE VOICE PRODUCTION MECHANISM

ANATOMY

In order to understand voice disorders, we must first be familiar with the voice production mechanism. The components of the voice production

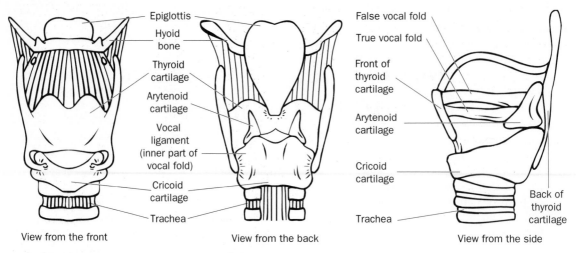

FIGURE 10-1 The larynx from a front, back, and side view.

mechanism are illustrated in Figures 10-1 and 10-2. Note that the *larynx* is really a collection of structures located between the hyoid bone at the top and the trachea at the bottom. It includes the thyroid, cricoid, and arytenoid cartilages; the epiglottis; and the vocal folds (Zemlin, 1988). The *vocal folds* are small bands of muscle and connective tissue that protrude into the airway just above the trachea. They are connected in front to the inside of the thyroid cartilage and in back to the two arytenoid cartilages. In their open position, they form a "V" configuration. In their closed position, they totally *occlude,* or close off, the airway. Also note that there are really two sets of vocal folds, the true vocal folds that we use to produce voice with and the false vocal folds just above them.

BASIC PHYSIOLOGY

Most traditional anatomy texts consider the larynx to be part of the respiratory system (Pernkopf, 1963), and with good reason. The cartilages that are part of the larynx can be seen as an upward extension of the *trachea,* the passage to the lungs. As air is inhaled and exhaled, it must pass between the vocal folds through an opening known as the *glottis.*

FIGURE 10-2 The vocal folds as viewed from above during laryngoscopic examination.

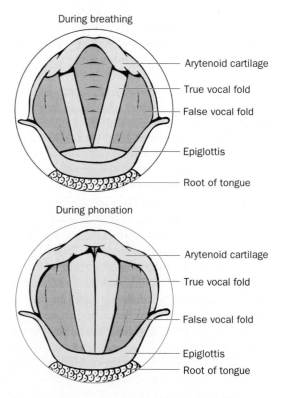

In addition, the true vocal folds, false vocal folds, and epiglottis function to protect the trachea and lungs. These structures close tightly during swallowing so that food and liquids will not enter the lower respiratory tract, where they could cause infection. When they have failed in this primary protective function, the true vocal folds, false vocal folds, and epiglottis are active in *coughing* (alternating forceful closures and openings) to expel foreign substances (Zemlin, 1988). In summary, the vocal folds act as part of a "gatekeeping" system for the respiratory tract, allowing air to be taken in and released and food and liquids to be kept out.

THE VOICE PRODUCTION PROCESS

In addition to their valving functions, the vocal folds are also used to produce voice—in concert with the actions of the respiratory system. Indeed, it is impossible to achieve *phonation* (the production of voice) without respiration.

Prior to initiating phonation, the vocal folds are in their normal open position to permit breathing. In order to prepare for speech, an individual usually inhales very quickly and somewhat more deeply than during unconscious or rest breathing. Exhalation, by contrast, is steadier and more prolonged for speech, as shown in Figure 10-3 (Perkins and Kent, 1986). It is this controlled exhalation that drives the vocal folds in the production of voice.

Phonation is initiated by bringing the vocal folds together, using various "closing" muscles in the larynx *(adductors),* and maintaining the vocal folds in a closed, yet relaxed, position. Exhaled air coming up from the lungs is then forced through these lightly closed vocal folds. The effect is similar to what happens if you hold two pieces of

FIGURE 10-3 Rest breathing and breathing for speech.

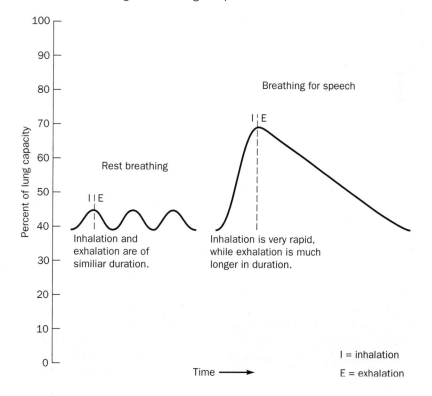

paper loosely together and blow through them. In response to the aerodynamic forces imposing upon them, the two pieces of paper begin to flutter, or *vibrate,* causing a sound.

This is similar to what happens in the larynx. But let us examine this fluttering, or *vibration,* in more detail. First, exhaled air builds up under the closed vocal folds. When the subglottic pressure is sufficient, it blows them apart. Very quickly, however, the natural elasticity of the vocal folds stops their outward movement and begins to draw them back toward their original, closed position. As the *glottis* (the space between the vocal folds) narrows, exhaled air is forced to move faster. This rapid rushing of air creates a partial vacuum (the Bernoulli effect), and the vocal folds are sucked together. Back in a closed position, the continuing exhaled air stream again begins to build up under the vocal folds, and when the pressure is sufficient, it again blows them apart (Colton, 1994).

This cycle of fluttering, or *vibration,* is repeated hundreds of times per second for as long as the exhalation continues and the muscles of adduction keep the vocal folds at midline. When the individual runs out of air, he or she opens the vocal folds, takes a quick inhalation, closes the vocal folds, and begins to exhale while initiating phonation again. Obviously, it is important to coordinate respiration and phonation in order to keep reinitiating voice during prolonged speaking.

SOME PERCEPTUAL FEATURES OF VOICE AND THEIR LARYNGEAL CORRELATES

VOCAL PITCH OR FREQUENCY

When we hear someone speak, one of the first things we notice about the voice is whether it is high or low. The perceived highness or lowness of a person's voice is what we call *pitch,* a perceptual phenomenon. The pitch we perceive in a voice depends on the speed of the vocal-fold vibration. If we measure how fast the vocal folds vibrate, or the frequency of their vibration, we can quantify our subjective impressions of pitch. Specifically defined, *frequency* is the number of times per second that the vocal folds are blown apart and come back together, or the number of vibratory cycles per second (Ladefoged, 1962). Frequency is measured in cycles per second, or *hertz* (Hz).

In general, the larger and more massive an individual's vocal folds, the slower they vibrate (Zemlin, 1988). Since slow vibration is perceived by listeners as a low pitch, we can say that low-pitched voices are due to large, slowly vibrating vocal folds. Men's vocal frequencies are typically lower than women's, in keeping with their generally larger size and more massive muscles. In fact, the average speaking frequency for young adult to middle-aged men is about 120 Hz, while the average speaking frequency for young adult to middle-aged women is approximately 200 Hz (calculated from information presented in Baken, 1987).

Although a speaker might be characterized as having an "average" speaking frequency, in reality all speakers use many different frequencies, from low to high. For example, a speaker typically drops his or her vocal frequency below average levels at the end of a declarative sentence and raises it at the end of a question. In fact, speakers require a range of nine to twenty semitones to convey their emotional meaning (Baken, 1987). Singers may use almost three octaves, or thirty-six semitones.

An individual speaker changes the frequency of his or her voice by using various laryngeal muscles to either stretch or shorten the vocal folds. When the vocal folds are stretched, they appear longer and thinner. Because thinner vocal folds have a smaller cross-sectional area and are less massive per unit of length, they vibrate faster and produce higher frequencies. When the vocal folds are shortened, they appear compressed and fatter. This configuration results in a relatively larger cross-sectional area, more mass per unit of length, slower vibration, and relatively lower frequencies (Colton, 1994).

In normal speech, a speaker is constantly stretching and shortening the vocal folds, causing frequency to rise and fall repeatedly. Rising and falling frequencies are important in signaling the speaker's emotional intent, indicating the end of a sentence, stressing words for emphasis, or asking a question. Poor control over the laryngeal muscles that stretch and compress the vocal folds results in a monotone voice.

VOCAL LOUDNESS OR INTENSITY

A second perceptual characteristic of voice is its loudness. If we wanted to quantify the loudness we perceive in a person's voice, we could measure vocal intensity. *Vocal intensity* refers to the force with which the vocal folds come together as they vibrate (Zemlin, 1988) and the corresponding force of the sound waves they generate. The intensity of a person's voice is usually measured in decibels (dB) at some specified distance (usually 6 or 12 inches) from the lips. In general, the greater the intensity, the louder we perceive a voice to be (Ladefoged, 1962).

The intensity, or loudness, of a voice is determined to a great extent by the force of the air coming up from the lungs. This is referred to as *subglottic pressure,* or air pressure that builds up below the vocal folds. The greater the subglottic pressure, the louder the voice. However, the vocal folds themselves also play a role in determining loudness. Subglottic pressure cannot be built up under the vocal folds unless the vocal folds are tense and provide substantial resistance to the upcoming air. Thus, vocal-fold tension is also a determinant of loudness (Colton, 1994).

The human vocal mechanism is capable of producing a wide range of intensities. The average speaker can speak at intensity levels as low as 50 to 60 dB (without whispering) and as high as 100 to 110 dB (Ryan, 1993). In general, most speakers habitually use the lower end of their total intensity range, about 70 dB, in conversational speech, but they are capable of much softer or much louder levels, depending on the demands of the situation (Ryan, 1993). However, speakers with respiratory disorders, for example, or an inability to maintain tension in the vocal folds, may not be able to generate adequate levels of intensity in demanding situations. Such individuals may become quite fatigued in their attempts to be heard.

LARYNGEAL QUALITY

Laryngeal quality is not as easy to define or measure as *frequency* or *intensity*. For the purposes of this text, *laryngeal quality* will refer to the perceived roughness or smoothness of a voice. Poor laryngeal quality is characterized by harshness, hoarseness, or breathiness. Good laryngeal quality is characterized by a clear, bell-like sound.

Where does roughness come from in a voice? One source is irregular vocal-fold vibration. In order for a voice to have a smooth and clear quality, the vocal folds must vibrate in a relatively regular and even manner, opening and closing symmetrically during the vibratory cycle (Horii, 1979). If, for some reason, the vocal folds do *not* vibrate symmetrically—if one vocal fold vibrates somewhat faster or slower than the other or if several aberrant short cycles interrupt a pattern of long and regular vibratory cycles—then the listener is likely to perceive bursts of noise in the speaker's voice (Lieberman, 1963; Koike, 1967). These noise elements can be distracting to the listener, can weaken the intensity of a voice, and, if severe enough, may even interfere with intelligibility.

In the past, laryngeal quality was evaluated primarily in terms of the speech-language pathologist's perceptual judgment. However, with the advances in computer technology and availability over the past two decades, instrumental methods of assessing the regularity of vocal-fold vibration (and, by implication, laryngeal quality) have proliferated. Analysis programs for measures such as relative average perturbation, percent jitter, amplitude perturbation quotient, percent shimmer, signal-to-noise ratio, and harmonic-to-noise ratio, among others, are commercially available and used in schools, hospitals, and university clinics around the country (Baken, 1987). At this point, there are no measures of voice quality that all speech-language pathologists can agree upon. However, objective measures of voice quality are gaining acceptance as a component of voice evaluations and voice-therapy programs, and normative data are slowly being established.

RESONANCE

It is important to realize that vocal-fold vibration is not the *only* physiological determinant of voice quality. Resonance also contributes to the sound of a person's voice. What is *resonance,* and how is it created?

According to Ladefoged (1962), the phenomenon of resonance occurs when the vibrations of one body set another body in motion. In our consideration of voice, the initial vibrating body is the vocal folds. As the vocal folds vibrate, however, they set a second body into vibration—the air in the vocal tract. The air in the vocal tract vibrates in a much more complex way than the vocal folds appear to. While the vocal folds open and close a certain number of times per second, at the fundamental frequency of the voice, the air molecules in the vocal tract vibrate at a variety

of higher speeds. Vocal-fold vibration thus generates an entire spectrum of frequencies in the vocal tract. This spectrum consists of the fundamental frequency and a series of overtones, or *harmonics,* which are multiples of the fundamental frequency and which become increasingly less intense in the higher frequencies (Borden and Harris, 1994). Figure 10-4 shows a typical laryngeal spectrum.

We must also realize that the size and shape of the vocal tract will affect the laryngeal spectrum. The *vocal tract* (pharynx, oral cavity, and nasal cavities) can be likened to a series of caves, or echo chambers. The fundamental frequency *reverberates* (or causes air to vibrate) in these chambers, generating an individual's laryngeal spectrum. Depending on the physical dimensions of the vocal tract, some frequencies in the laryngeal spectrum will be amplified while others will be reduced, or *damped.* This pattern of amplification and damping gives each individual's voice its characteristic sound, based on his or her unique anatomical configuration.

The clearest perceptual example of resonance

FIGURE 10-4 The laryngeal spectrum. Note that the fundamental frequency is the lowest and most intense of the frequencies in the laryngeal spectrum. Each harmonic of the fundamental is increasingly less intense as frequency increases.

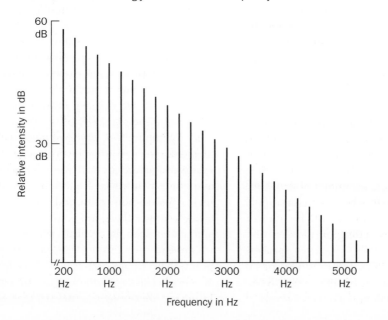

occurs when voice is produced with either excessive or insufficient nasality. Normally, the velum is in a closed position during speech, effectively separating the nasal cavities from the rest of the vocal tract. The nasal cavities are only added to the vocal tract when certain sounds are produced—"m," "n," and "ng" in English—during which time the velum is briefly lowered. However, if the velum *remains* in a lowered position, the resonance characteristics of a voice will change. Instead of being reverberated primarily in the pharynx and oral cavity, elements of the laryngeal spectrum will be created in the nasal cavities as well. Since the nasal cavities have a very small exit (the nostrils), many frequencies will be "trapped" inside them. Those frequencies, then, will not be transmitted well to the listener's ear; that is, they will be damped. This trapping and damping of frequencies gives the voice a muffled, humming quality and decreased intensity that we call *hypernasality*.

In contrast, if the velum fails to lower for "m," "n," and "ng," a speaker will have a dull voice and give the impression of having a stuffed-up nose. We would notice this unusual voice quality primarily when the speaker tried to produce nasal sounds. Words such as *mommy* and *nanna* would come out "bobby" and "dadda." This voice quality, called *denasality,* reflects an inadequate amount of nasal resonance in the speech signal. It is most common to hear denasality when a speaker has a head cold.

It should be noted that both hypernasality and denasality can be present in a voice that has the appropriate laryngeally determined features of frequency, intensity, and laryngeal quality. This is because the laryngeal components of voice are essentially independent of the resonance components. The features of a voice that are determined by vocal-fold vibration can be quite normal in an individual who, nonetheless, has trouble keeping his velum firmly elevated and who thus produces a hypernasal voice. Conversely, an individual with a low-pitched, soft, and rough voice may have no difficulty at all with velar movement and will therefore produce a normal nasal-resonance balance in his voice despite his laryngeal problems.

THE NORMAL VOICE

Before we can consider voice disorders, we need to define what we mean by a *normal voice.* According to Wilson (1987, 2), a normal voice should have the following characteristics: "(1) pleasing vocal quality, (2) proper balance of oral and nasal resonance, (3) appropriate loudness, (4) a speaking fundamental frequency (habitual or modal pitch level) suitable for age, size and sex, and (5) appropriate voice inflections involving pitch and loudness." This definition is particularly useful in that it separates voice into five distinct dimensions: laryngeal quality, nasality, intensity, frequency, and variability. These dimensions correlate well with the properties of vocal fold vibration previously discussed (the laryngeal component), and the contribution of the resonance component.

However, this definition also has some weaknesses. According to Wilson, a normal voice has "proper" resonance, "appropriate" loudness and variability, "suitable" frequency—in other words, a normal voice is normal! Such a definition leaves open the possibility that what is judged "suitable" and "appropriate" by one person (or one speech-language pathologist) may not be so judged by another, and the delineation of "normal" versus "disordered" voices may be quite subjective.

Indeed, in the past, aesthetic judgments regarding voice were more the province of singing teachers and drama coaches than of speech-language pathologists. According to Stemple (1984, 9), it was not until the late 1930s that "speech correctionists," as they were then called, began to work with patients with medical conditions involving the vocal folds. As Stemple notes, "Using drills and exercises borrowed from training manuals designed for the normal voice, these specialists attempted to modify the production of the disordered voice." Clearly, aesthetic judgments regarding "normality" were being made by these new professionals, and given the limited technology of the time, they were making them on a very subjective basis.

Many changes have occurred in the evaluation and treatment of voice-disordered clients in the years since the 1930s. Speech-language pathologists are now able to apply not only the aesthetic standards and exercise techniques of the voice coach but also the knowledge of anatomy, physiology, and instrumentation of the scientist. After decades of research, much is now known about characteristics of the normal voice. A large body of data exists, for example, on normal ranges for speaking fundamental frequencies and the intensity capabilities of the human voice. (See Baken, 1987, for a summary of these studies.) The modern speech-language pathologist can measure various dimensions of a client's voice, compare these measures to normative data gathered from large groups of speakers, and determine whether or not any of the client's vocal measures are "abnormal" compared to the general population.

Modern technology has made it possible for the speech-language pathologist to determine if a voice is "normal" in a more objective way than was previously possible. However, objective measures cannot always help establish whether a disorder exists. Despite our computers, instruments, and data, if a client feels that her voice does not meet her daily needs, then she does, indeed, have a voice disorder no matter what the numbers say (Vaughan, 1982). A subjective element continues to be present both in establishing the disorder and in determining the success of remediation. In the following section, we will examine the concept of a voice disorder in more detail.

WHAT IS A VOICE DISORDER?

The definition of a *voice disorder* is similar to the definition of a *normal voice*. According to Wilson (1987), voice disorders include (1) a disturbed laryngeal quality, characterized by hoarseness, harshness, or breathiness; (2) hypernasality, denasality, or other disorders of oral-nasal resonance balance; (3) too soft or too loud a habitual intensity; (4) a speaking fundamental frequency too high or too low for an individual's age, size, or gender; and (5) inappropriate stress and intonation patterns. To this we add the disorders of having no voice at all and having pain or fatigue

in the laryngeal area. Any of these conditions, singly or in combination, could be considered a voice disorder.

The most important determinant of a voice disorder, however, is whether the individual feels handicapped by his condition (Vaughan, 1982). Our culture is very tolerant of aberrant vocal qualities and resonance characteristics, and most individuals do not pay much attention to the quality of their voice. Indeed, some individuals have made unusual vocal qualities their trademark in the music and entertainment industries (Vaughan, 1982). If an individual with a clinician-judged "abnormal" voice feels that his voice is adequate for his social and vocational needs, the label *disorder* may not be completely appropriate.

On the other hand, some classical singers or actors with only minor vocal aberrations, as judged by a speech-language pathologist, may consider themselves to have career-threatening voice disorders. Such individuals may suffer a reduction in their speaking or singing ranges, feel fatigue by the end of the day, or experience periods of mild vocal roughness. To an individual whose livelihood depends on a consistently performing vocal instrument, these slight difficulties can be a cause for concern. Because such individuals consider themselves to have voice disorders, they often seek the treatment of a speech-language pathologist and are added to the voice-disorders caseload.

The identification of voice disorders in children is a somewhat more complex issue. Certainly, children whose aberrant vocal qualities interfere with intelligibility or those who lose their voices for long periods of time would be considered to have voice disorders. An excessively loud or hypernasal voice that attracts attention and the comments of other children might also be considered a handicap. And if the child himself is concerned and wants to change the sound of his voice, that child, too, would be identified as having a voice disorder.

For all practical purposes, however, the prime determinant of whether a child has a voice disorder is the concern of the parents. If the parents feel the child has a problem, their concern should be taken seriously by the speech-language pathologist. The child's perception of the problem and the degree of handicap he experiences in daily life should also be taken into account. If these concerns are absent, however, the speech-language pathologist is likely to be fighting an uphill battle in trying to convince families and the child's teachers that a disorder exists.

CAUSES AND CHARACTERISTICS OF VOICE DISORDERS

Voice disorders have traditionally been categorized according to their location and cause (Aronson, 1990; Boone and McFarlane, 1994; Case, 1991; Wilson, 1987). One basic distinction is between voice disorders involving the larynx and disorders of the hard and soft palates that affect resonance. In addition, all of the authors cited above recognize that some voice disorders are caused by the individual's use (or misuse) of the vocal mechanism, while other voice disorders are due to diseases and other conditions over which the individual has no control. For purposes of this text, voice disorders and their causes will be divided into four categories: (1) laryngeal voice disorders with functional etiologies, (2) laryngeal voice disorders with organic etiologies, (3) voice disorders with psychogenic causes, and (4) resonance disorders (both functional and organic).

FUNCTIONAL CAUSES OF LARYNGEAL VOICE DISORDERS

We are familiar with the term *functional* from other disorder areas in this book as a term meaning "no known cause." However, in the area of voice disorders, *functional* is defined somewhat differently. A *functional voice disorder* is one that is caused primarily by the individual's vocal abuse or bad habits. Functional voice disorders involving the larynx typically result in abnormal laryngeal quality and, possibly, a low speaking frequency. Functional causes of laryngeal disorders include vocal nodules, vocal polyps, contact ulcers, and chronic laryngitis.

1. Vocal Nodules. *Vocal nodules* are small, whitish bumps, or calluses, located slightly forward of the middle of each vocal fold, as seen in Figure 10-5a. Nodules tend to occur *bilaterally,* one on each side, and are believed to be the result of continued and excessive use of the vocal mechanism, causing the vocal folds to become swollen and irritated (Colton and Casper, 1990). Just as a blister (and later, a callus) will form on the palm of an individual who uses her hands excessively, vocal nodules will form on vocal folds that are used too often and too forcefully for too long.

The voice of someone who has vocal nodules is usually hoarse and breathy, with frequent voice breaks. The breathiness occurs because the nodules prevent the vocal folds from closing completely, with the result that air is escaping even when the vocal folds are in the closed phase of their cycle (DeWeese and Saunders, 1982). The

FIGURE 10-5 Vocal nodules and vocal polyps.

(a) Vocal nodules

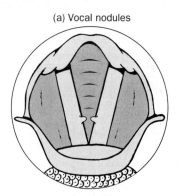

(b) Vocal polyp (pedunculated)

hoarseness occurs because the added mass of the nodules disturbs the normal, regular vibratory pattern of the vocal folds (Case, 1991). Voice breaks occur because on occasion, vocal-fold vibration cannot be sustained, and the voice turns into a whisper. *Voice breaks* have been described as "the voice cutting in and out."

Because vocal nodules are the result of certain behaviors, they should usually be treated behaviorally. Newly formed nodules can often be eliminated by simply resting the voice and consulting a speech-language pathologist. Long-standing nodules may require more intensive therapy but can often be eliminated in three to six months. If nodules are removed surgically with no attempt at changing vocal behavior, they can redevelop (Case, 1991). Nodules in childhood are more common in boys than in girls (Green, 1989); but in adolescence and adulthood, nodules are more common in women than in men (Toohill, 1975; Aronson, 1990).

2. Vocal Polyps. *Polyps* are white, fluid-filled lesions that occur in a similar location to nodules, as shown in Figure 10-5b. They are usually *unilateral,* occurring on only one vocal fold, and tend to be larger and more organized in their internal structure than nodules (Colton and Casper, 1990). Like vocal nodules, vocal polyps are thought to be caused by overuse and abuse of the voice; however, unlike nodules, it is believed that a polyp can result from a single abusive incident (Boone and McFarlane, 1994; Colton and Casper, 1990). It has been hypothesized that small areas of broken blood vessels, or *hemorrhagic irritations,* can swell and develop into polyps (Boone and McFarlane, 1994).

The voice of an individual with a vocal polyp is likely to be hoarse, rough, and breathy. Often, the client reports the sensation of something in the throat (Colton and Casper, 1990). A *sessile,* or broad-based, polyp adds mass to the vocal fold it is attached to, causing disruptions in the vibratory pattern of that vocal fold that listeners perceive as a "rough" quality. If the polyp is *pedunculated,* or attached to the vocal fold by means of a slender stalk, the laryngeal-quality disorder may be inter-

mittent. Roughness may be perceived when the polyp rests *on* the vocal fold. However, when the polyp drops beneath the vocal fold, its vibration may be quite normal (DeWeese and Saunders, 1982). When listening to the voice of a client with a vocal polyp, students report the desire to tell the individual to "clear your throat."

Behavior therapy is usually the first course in treating polyps. However, because polyps are generally more massive and developed than nodules, it may not be possible to eliminate a polyp with voice therapy alone. Surgery to remove the extra tissue from the surface of the vocal fold may be necessary.

3. Contact Ulcers. *Contact ulcers* are reddened and irritated areas of tissue at the posterior part of the vocal folds. Like nodules, they are usually bilateral as shown in Figure 10-6a. Unlike nodules and polyps, they can be painful. Moreover,

FIGURE 10-6 Contact ulcers and chronic laryngitis.

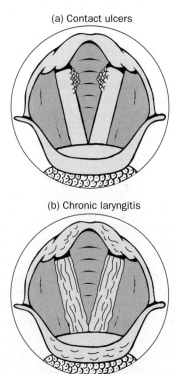

(a) Contact ulcers

(b) Chronic laryngitis

the pain may be difficult to localize: some clients report a persistent earache or pain in the temporomandibular joint (TMJ pain) before the contact ulcers are discovered.

There is some dispute over the cause of contact ulcers. It was once believed that these lesions were due to the use of an excessively low speaking frequency along with excessive loudness and a hard glottal attack (an abnormal voice-initiation pattern) (Aronson, 1990; Boone and McFarlane, 1994; Colton and Casper, 1990; and others). However, it is now believed that *gastric reflux,* or regurgitation of the contents of the stomach into the esophagus and throat during sleep, may be a predisposing factor (Colton and Casper, 1990; Boone and McFarlane, 1994). In either case, these lesions are considered to be rare. When seen, they typically occur in men over 40 (Aronson, 1990).

The voice of an individual with a contact ulcer is "low-pitched, hoarse and grating," according to Aronson (1990, 128). Throat clearing and vocal fatigue may also accompany this disorder. Contact ulcers are often treated with voice therapy, but reports of success are mixed. According to Boone and McFarlane (1994), this disorder responds fairly well to systematic voice therapy. However, Colton and Casper (1990) state that the success of such intervention has not been documented. Further, they note that even after surgical removal, the lesions tend to recur.

4. Chronic Laryngitis. Most of us associate laryngitis with a bacterial or viral infection of the upper respiratory tract. However, the hoarse, rough, breathy quality and reduced loudness we associate with infectious laryngitis can become chronic, persisting even after the precipitating illness has been resolved (Colton and Casper, 1990). This condition, known as *chronic laryngitis,* is most likely to occur if the individual abuses his or her voice during the period of acute infection. Under such circumstances, the vocal folds may not return to their normal, healthy condition even after the infection is over. Additional overuse and abuse of the voice can cause further physical deterioration of the vocal folds. Thus, this disorder may *begin* as a disease, but the chronic and persis-

tent nature of the problem is due to continuous vocal abuse (DeWeese and Saunders, 1982).

The vocal folds of someone with chronic laryngitis are usually inflamed to some degree, as shown in Figure 10-6b. They may be somewhat thickened, swollen, or reddened (Colton and Casper, 1990). The swelling is usually due to excessive fluid retention in the mucous membranes and connective tissue covering the muscular mass of the vocal folds. The reddened appearance is due to dilated blood vessels. In severe cases, a condition called *polypoid degeneration* may occur, in which the surface of the vocal folds has been swollen and stretched so often that excessive tissue is present (Boone and McFarlane, 1994).

The voice symptoms in chronic laryngitis vary from mild hoarseness to severe difficulty with voice production. Colton and Casper (1990) specify marked hoarseness or roughness, a somewhat higher than normal speaking frequency, and an inability to speak loudly as symptoms of laryngitis. They also note that the individual may feel dryness or even discomfort in the throat. DeWeese and Saunders (1982) report that the client may complain of a nonproductive cough and a throat that aches and feels tired. In order to eliminate chronic laryngitis, behavioral treatment is necessary, although surgical stripping to remove excess tissue from the vocal folds is also common (Boone and McFarlane, 1994).

5. Precipitating and Maintaining Factors in Functional Laryngeal Disorders. Functional voice disorders of the larynx are primarily attributed to excessive and abusive vocal practices. However, it may also be the case that various health-related conditions, drugs, and toxic substances increase an individual's susceptibility to the laryngeal and pharyngeal conditions described above. Andrews (1986) lists frequent upper respiratory tract infections, allergies, and asthma as health-related conditions that predispose an individual to laryngeal pathologies of a functional nature. These conditions increase fluid retention *(edema)* and the production of secretions (mucus) in the upper respiratory tract, thereby increasing irritation and the probability of tissue damage.

Colton and Casper (1990, 174) cite over-the-counter drug preparations as affecting "the laryngeal mucosa and laryngeal motor control" in ways that can increase susceptibility to vocal abuse. For example, decongestants and diuretics dry the laryngeal mucosa, causing feelings of irritation, frequent throat clearing, and the possibility of vocal-fold lesions. Bronchodilators and antihistamines affect the nervous system, including the nerves that supply the larynx. Finally, tobacco and alcohol have been identified as predisposing and maintaining factors in numerous functional voice disorders, such as chronic laryngitis (DeWeese and Saunders, 1982).

It is important to note that these substances and conditions in and of themselves are not believed to cause nodules, polyps, and so on. Instead, they are thought to irritate the laryngeal mucosa, making it more likely that vocal abuse (or even normal voice use) will cause tissue damage.

ORGANIC CAUSES OF LARYNGEAL VOICE DISORDERS

A second major group of voice disorders is caused by diseases, agents, and conditions that affect the larynx and over which the individual has no control. Organic voice disorders are extremely varied, depending on their specific cause, and are thus hard to summarize. However, they can affect any or all of the aspects of voice we have discussed: laryngeal quality, speaking frequency, loudness, variability, and resonance. Organic causes of voice disorders include infectious laryngitis, paralysis of one or both vocal folds, dysarthria, papillomas, and laryngeal cancer.

1. Infectious Laryngitis. *Infectious laryngitis* is an upper respiratory tract condition caused by a bacteria or virus. The vocal-fold abnormalities that are part of this condition are due to an infectious agent and not to the client's behavior. The larynx is typically inflamed, with reddened and swollen vocal folds, as shown in Figure 10-7a. An increase in secretions, especially mucus, may add further discomfort and irritation to the laryngeal area.

(a) Infectious laryngitis, with subglottic swelling and secretions

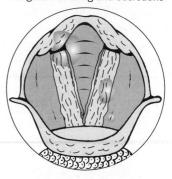

(b) Unilateral vocal fold paralysis of the (patient's) left vocal fold

FIGURE 10-7 Infectious laryngitis and vocal-fold paralysis (unilateral).

The individual with infectious laryngitis has a hoarse, rough, breathy voice and may, in fact, even be *aphonic* (unable to produce voice at all). Unlike chronic laryngitis, infectious laryngitis is an acute condition that can be expected to resolve as the body heals. However, as discussed above, it is important for the individual to refrain from excessive vocal use during laryngeal infection. The vocal folds can be easily damaged in this condition, setting the scene for a more chronic problem.

2. Paralysis of One or Both Vocal Folds. In order to produce voice, the vocal folds must be brought to midline and held there with enough tension to provide resistance to the upcoming air stream. If the muscles controlling one or both vocal folds (or the muscles of the vocal folds themselves) are paralyzed, voice production will be affected.

Paralysis generally occurs because the nerves that cause a particular muscle to contract become damaged or cut. In the case of the larynx, most of the muscles important to voice production are innervated by the *recurrent laryngeal nerve,* a meandering nerve that comes out of the base of the skull, goes down into the chest cavity, and then turns upward to go into the larynx from underneath. This nerve can be damaged by injuries to the head, neck, and chest, or by viral infections, and is even sometimes severed inadvertently during chest surgery. If the recurrent laryngeal nerve is damaged on only one side, unilateral vocal-fold paralysis occurs on that side, as shown in Figure 10-7b. If the recurrent laryngeal nerves on *both* sides are damaged, bilateral vocal-fold paralysis occurs.

Unilateral vocal-fold paralysis generally results in a hoarse, breathy, and weak voice. Since the unparalyzed vocal fold has normal tension while the paralyzed fold is lax and flaccid, the two vocal folds vibrate at different speeds. This results in the perception of *diplophonia,* or two frequencies at once.

In bilateral vocal-fold paralysis, the voice is extremely weak and breathy. Depending on the position of the paralyzed folds, the individual may not be able to generate much voice at all. The danger in bilateral vocal-fold paralysis is that the inability to fully *abduct,* or open the folds, might result in airway blockage and respiratory difficulty. If this condition occurs, the vocal folds can be surgically fixed in a more open position.

Medical-surgical treatment for vocal-fold paralysis is limited. Medical science cannot yet reestablish damaged neural pathways, although that day may be coming. The primary treatment for paralysis is compensatory therapy, in which the speech-language pathologist helps the client manage his vocal limitations and avoid further damage due to vocal abuse.

3. Dysarthria.

We previously defined *dysarthria* as a speech disorder characterized by weakness, paralysis, incoordination, involuntary movement, or abnormal or fluctuating muscle tone in the speech muscles due to damage to the neuromotor system. According to this definition, vocal-fold paralysis would be considered a dysarthria, albeit a very limited and localized one. Most forms of dysarthria, however, involve more generalized neuromotor damage and a more complex pattern of speech and voice symptoms (Aronson, 1990).

In the adult population, dysarthria is often seen in various neurological diseases. For example, Parkinson's disease can cause muscle rigidity, tremor, and weakness. In the vocal mechanism, these symptoms result in a weak, monotone voice, possibly with tremor and hoarseness (Case, 1991). The individual often has difficulty coordinating respiration and phonation because of the rigidity of the muscles of both systems. Coordination problems also affect articulation, which becomes rapid but imprecise.

Dysarthria can also occur as a result of a stroke or head trauma (Colton and Casper, 1990). If the motor centers of the brain sustain injury, the individual will suffer from a variety of physical symptoms, including weakness and fluctuating muscle tone. Such deficits, if they affect the speech and respiratory muscles, can cause slow, slurred, and hypernasal speech. The voice may sound strained, hoarse, or weak, or it may even be absent.

We will discuss adult neurological disorders and their treatment further in Chapter 13. For purposes of this chapter, however, it is important to recognize that injuries to and diseases of the neuromotor system can cause dysarthria and that both laryngeal voice disorders and resonance disorders are often a part of the dysarthric speech pattern (Aronson, 1990).

4. Papillomas.

Laryngeal papillomas, sometimes called *juvenile papillomas,* are small, wartlike growths that can cover the entire interior of the larynx. Papillomas are pictured in Figure 10-8a. They are most common in children under 6 years of age (Boone and McFarlane, 1994) and are caused by the papova-virus (Colton and Casper, 1990). Although the lesions themselves are *benign* (noncancerous), they are dangerous nonetheless

(a) Laryngeal papillomas

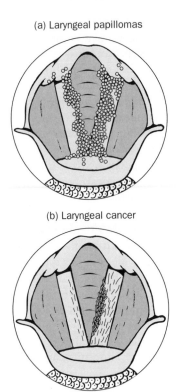

(b) Laryngeal cancer

FIGURE 10-8 Laryngeal papillomas and laryngeal cancer.

because of their tendency to proliferate and obstruct the airway. Papillomas tend to disappear at puberty, although in approximately 20 percent of cases, the condition persists beyond puberty (Kleinsasser, 1979). Persistent papillomas are extremely difficult to eradicate.

The child with papillomas will probably have a hoarse voice. In addition, he or she may be short of breath, have difficulty breathing *(dyspnea),* produce voice during inhalation *(stridor),* or have no voice at all *(aphonia),* according to Wilson (1987). Children with hoarse voices should always be evaluated by an ear, nose, and throat (ENT) specialist or *otolaryngologist* as they are also called, to insure that this disorder (or some other organic pathology) is not present.

Numerous medical and surgical treatments are used for papillomas. When the airway is threat-ened, surgery must be performed to clear the vocal folds and glottic area. Unfortunately, like warts elsewhere on the body, papillomas have a tendency to recur, often necessitating multiple operations. This can cause scarring of the vocal folds and poor voice quality even after the papillomas have resolved (DeWeese and Saunders, 1982). In addition to traditional surgery, CO_2 laser surgery, *microcautery* (burning off the lesions), and *cryosurgery* (freezing off the lesions) have been used (Wilson, 1987). The role of the speech-language pathologist is primarily a supportive one during this process, working with the child when possible to try to establish a usable voice.

5. Laryngeal Cancer. Of all the organic voice disorders, laryngeal cancer is the most serious. Laryngeal cancer, like all cancers, occurs when groups of cells *mutate,* or become malignant, and begin to proliferate wildly (Stemple, 1984). If the lesion remains localized to a single structure, it can often be treated successfully. For example, the lesion in Figure 10-8b is confined to the patient's left vocal fold. Over time, however, malignant cells have a tendency to migrate, or *metastasize,* to other sites, causing secondary cancers to form (Case, 1991).

One of the early signs of laryngeal cancer is persistent hoarseness, and, for that reason, every individual with hoarseness lasting for more than two weeks should be evaluated by an otolaryngologist (DeWeese and Saunders, 1982; Ogura and Thawley, 1980). The severity of the hoarseness depends upon the location of the lesion. Cancers that begin on the vocal fold itself and cause immediate hoarseness are likely to be detected and treated much earlier than are cancers that begin on the pharyngeal wall or the false vocal folds. In addition to hoarseness, other symptoms of laryngeal cancer are the sensation of a lump in the throat or in the neck or, in advanced cases, swallowing and respiratory problems and soreness (Stemple, 1984).

Treatment of laryngeal cancer depends on the stage at which it is detected. In the early stages, radiation and chemotherapy might be used, either alone or in combination with surgery. In later stages, surgery might involve excision of a single vocal fold or of the entire larynx (Colton and Casper, 1990). The latter procedure, known as *laryngectomy,* has many life-altering consequences for the individual. We will consider this special population in Chapter 12.

PSYCHOGENIC CAUSES OF VOICE DISORDERS

If you have ever tried to talk during a period of strong emotion, you probably noticed that your voice was not completely under your control. An individual in a highly emotional state often experiences feelings of tightness in the throat, and there is a corresponding strained sound to the voice. There may be a *tremor,* or shaking, in the voice, and a speaking frequency that is unusually high or low. Strong emotion can also produce the sensation of tightness in the chest and constricted breathing. These changes are automatic and involuntary in nature. Even if the individual tries to control them, the symptoms generally persist for as long as the emotion does.

Given the involuntary response of the voice production mechanism to emotions, it has been hypothesized that strong emotions, particularly when suppressed, could cause psychogenic voice disorders (Aronson, 1990). Strong emotions, even if they are not consciously acknowledged, may arouse the unconscious parts of the neuromotor system in such a way that normal phonation is interfered with. The vocal folds may look and function normally for nonspeech functions, such as coughing, but may not "cooperate" when the individual tries to speak. Aronson refers to these as *conversion disorders,* because the individual is converting an emotional conflict into a physical symptom.

Individuals with conversion aphonia do not produce voice but communicate through whispering. These individuals are able to cough sharply and clear their throats, indicating good vocal-fold closure and adequate function for speech. However, they steadfastly maintain that they are unable to produce voice, or normal-sounding speech, and resist all suggestions that they "could speak if they wanted to." These individuals honestly believe that some medical or physical problem prevents them from communicating normally.

What kind of situation might precipitate a psychogenic voice disorder? DeWeese and Saunders (1982, 105) believe that such a disorder occurs when an individual hopes "to be relieved of some unpleasant duty." It may also follow an upper respiratory infection (Boone and McFarlane, 1994). If an individual is protected in some way by not being able to speak loudly, a case of laryngitis might be unconsciously prolonged. For example, if an accountant is unhappy and frustrated in her job but afraid to leave it, her aphonia may be very useful. She is unable to confront her supervisor, or boss, unable to make her unhappiness known, and thus unlikely to experience the negative consequences of confronting her supervisor. If she fears interviewing for a new position, her aphonia protects her from having to face that, too. Until such an individual is willing to confront her frustrations and fears, the aphonia will probably persist (Aronson, 1990).

Psychogenic voice disorders are not common, but they do occur. They are often misdiagnosed initially as organic or functional laryngeal problems until the client does not respond to therapy in the expected ways. In order to deal with such cases, speech-language pathologists must develop their interviewing and counseling skills as well as their knowledge of the technical aspects of voice disorders.

RESONANCE DISORDERS

Up to this point, our discussion of voice disorders has centered on disorders of the larynx. However, abnormalities of the hard and soft palates can also affect the sound of a voice. If these structures do not completely separate the oral from the nasal cavities, the individual's voice will be perceived as *hypernasal,* or excessively nasal. If there are obstructions in the nasal cavities, the expected nasal resonance on "m," "n," and "ng" will be absent, and the individual's voice will be perceived as *denasal.* As with laryngeal disorders, resonance disorders can be *organic,* due to some physical condition or disease, or *functional,* due to faulty use of the velum.

1. Cleft Palate. Cleft palate is one organic cause of hypernasality. As we shall learn in Chapter 11, this condition occurs when parts of the hard palate, soft palate, or lip do not form correctly during fetal development. Although clefts of the palate are usually corrected surgically within the first few years of life, the resulting structures sometimes cannot adequately close off the nasal cavities from the rest of the vocal tract. In some cases, the surgically repaired palate is too small; in others, the nerves and muscles are damaged during surgery so that the palate does not elevate completely.

The child with a repaired cleft may have articulatory distortions as well as a hypernasal voice. If the child cannot build up sufficient pressure in the oral cavity, phonemes like "s," "sh," "p," "t," and "k" will be imprecise or weak. To compensate for a hypernasal and weak voice, some children with cleft palate speak with excessive effort and thus increase their risk for vocal nodules and polyps.

Not all children with repaired clefts have voice and articulation disorders, but it is estimated that approximately 25 percent continue to have difficulty with velar function for speech (McWilliams et al., 1990). For these children, additional medical and surgical intervention is necessary before acceptable speech and voice quality can be obtained.

2. Functional Hypernasality. Hypernasality can have an organic cause even in the absence of cleft palate. For example, the *velum* (soft palate) may simply be too short to close off the nasal cavities from the rest of the vocal tract. Neurological damage can result in a partially paralyzed velum that cannot move adequately. Deformities of the facial bones, hard palate, and jaw might affect the soft palate and its movement.

However, there are individuals with excessively hypernasal voices who are completely normal in terms of their velar structure and function.

There is no apparent physical cause for their hypernasality. These cases are referred to as *functional hypernasality*.

Like chronic laryngitis, functional hypernasality may have had its roots in an upper respiratory tract infection. If the back of the throat were extremely sore and inflamed, an individual might have "learned" to leave the velum in a lowered position in order to avoid the pain of contact. A child with frequent bouts of tonsillitis might have had this experience repeatedly. Even when the infection subsided, the child might have continued to raise his velum only partially during speech, resulting in a hypernasal voice. As long as the hypernasality did not interfere with intelligibility, the child might persist in this habit and come to accept the resulting voice as his own.

Individuals with functional hypernasality often do not realize that their voice quality is different from others. Some are surprised when their unusual resonance patterns are pointed out to them in drama or public speaking classes or when they fail a speech screening test for entrance into education, law, or business careers. However, if these individuals decide to change the resonance aspect of their voices, they are generally very successful in doing so. Functional hypernasality, like functional dysphonia, is amenable to behavioral treatment.

3. Enlarged Adenoids. The *adenoids* are pads of tissue located on the back wall of the throat (or the nasopharynx) just opposite the nasal cavities. In young children, the soft palate makes contact with the adenoid pad during closure, as shown in Figure 10-9. By adulthood, the adenoid pad has generally shrunk and is no longer a contact point for closure of the velum (Zemlin, 1988).

If the adenoids become enlarged due to inflammation or infection, they can block entrance to the nasal cavities, causing the child's voice to sound denasal. Thus, enlarged adenoids are an organic cause of denasality. If the condition persists, the adenoids can be surgically removed. However, following surgical removal,

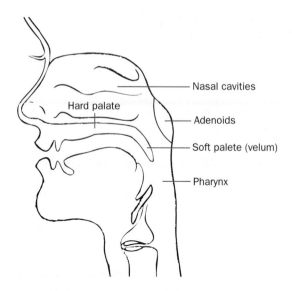

FIGURE 10-9 Location of the adenoids in the posterior nasopharynx. The adenoids may provide a point of contact for palatal closure in children.

the child may sound *hyper*nasal for a period of time. This is because the velum may not be long enough to make contact with the back wall of the nasopharynx and thus may not effectively separate the oral and nasal cavities. In time, as the child's oral structures grow and develop, this condition generally resolves.

THE INTERVENTION PROCESS

EVALUATION

1. The Otolaryngological Evaluation. The initial step in evaluating any voice disorder should be an examination by a qualified otolaryngologist. Only an otolaryngologist can rule out the presence of life-threatening conditions such as laryngeal cancer or papillomas. This determination often requires a biopsy or other laboratory procedures that speech-language pathologists are not trained to do. It is also important to determine

FIGURE 10-10 The endoscopic/stroboscopic examination permits the otolaryngologist or speech-language pathologist to assess the condition of the vocal folds and their movement during voice production. (Courtesy Kay Elemtrics Corp.)

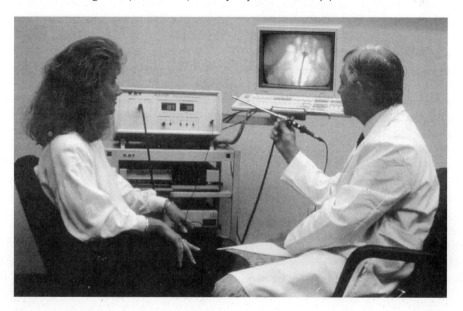

whether there is some other organic basis for the disorder, and only a physician can make such a diagnosis. Finally, the effect of the disorder (if any) on the status of the vocal folds should be assessed.

Part of the physical examination of the vocal folds includes visualization with a fiberoptic endoscope. One type of endoscope is inserted into the client's mouth; a smaller and more flexible type might be inserted into the nostril. If the endoscope is coupled with a stroboscope, the movements of the vocal folds during phonation can be observed. In hospital settings, the speech-language pathologist is often the professional who performs the endoscopic-stroboscopic examination and records the results on videotape. The otolaryngologist then views the examination for signs of laryngeal disease, while the speech-language pathologist uses such recordings to assess the client's response to voice-therapy techniques (Boone and McFarlane, 1994). Speech-language pathologists must be trained in this procedure in order to comply with the guidelines of the American Speech-Language-Hearing Association (ASHA, 1992a).

2. The Speech and Voice Evaluation. The speech-language pathologist typically begins a voice evaluation by taking a case history (Case, 1991). The goal of this activity is to uncover predisposing and maintaining factors contributing to the disorder, including the client's medical history, daily use of voice, and psychological state (Boone and McFarlane, 1994). In addition, the speech-language pathologist performs specific tests to determine the frequency, intensity, and respiratory capabilities of the individual. Both perceptual judgment and instrumental measures are typically used. Laryngeal quality and resonance are also assessed, optimally with the appropriate instruments (Case, 1991). These data are compared to normative data to see how similar to or different from the general population the client really is. They can also serve as a baseline against which improvement during therapy can be documented.

THERAPY FOR FUNCTIONAL VOICE DISORDERS INVOLVING THE LARYNX

Because functional disorders have their origin in poor vocal habits and behaviors, the way to eliminate these disorders is through behavioral treatment. Once the disorder has been diagnosed, the speech-language pathologist has the primary responsibility for planning and implementing therapy. Boone and McFarlane (1994) have outlined a program of treatment for functional voice disorders that includes identifying the vocal abuse, reducing its occurrence, searching for the "best" voice the client can produce using facilitating techniques, and generalizing new skills into conversational speech.

The vocal abuse is usually identified when the case history is taken, as the speech-language pathologist questions clients about their voice use and observes their habitual intensity and frequency levels. Frequent cheering at sporting events may be an important maintaining factor for some clients; while simply talking at too high an intensity and too low a frequency may be the primary factor for others.

Once the vocal abuses have been identified, reducing their occurrence is often more difficult than it sounds. While the second client in the example above may have little difficulty reducing the intensity of his voice and raising its frequency slightly, it may be difficult for the first client to eliminate cheering at games. Sometimes, reducing the occurrence of vocal abuse requires lifestyle changes that the client resists. Here, too, the speech-language pathologist must function in the role of counselor, helping the client discover less abusive substitutes for harmful vocal behaviors and helping them find the courage for change.

In addition to vocal abuses, the client may have other faulty voice production habits: excessive tension in the neck and shoulders, poor breath support, an explosive style of speaking, and so on. In order to teach a more natural and relaxed speaking style, the speech-language pathologist may use any or several of a variety of "facilitating approaches," such as relaxation exercises, breathing exercises, whisper attacks, and humming, among others. Ideally, these facilitating approaches will improve the sound of the client's voice as they improve his mode of voice production.

When the client is able to produce a better sounding voice during vocal exercises, the next step is to generalize his new skills into words, phrases, and sentences. It is often difficult for a client to transfer relaxation, for example, or better breathing directly from exercises into everyday conversation. New habits must be built up gradually. Within the therapy setting, the speech-language pathologist introduces easy and then harder contexts for practice. When the client can consistently use the new behavior in conversational speech, he is ready for dismissal.

THERAPY FOR ORGANIC VOICE DISORDERS INVOLVING THE LARYNX

If the voice disorder is caused by some disease process or physical condition, the first question the speech-language pathologist must ask is whether and to what extent the client will recover. If the condition will clear up with little or no intervention, or if it can be relieved through medical or surgical treatment, the speech-language pathologist's role will be limited.

If the condition will not resolve itself, and if medical or surgical treatment is not effective, the speech-language pathologist must then ask what can be done to help the client compensate for a damaged voice production mechanism. The focus of therapy will not be on eliminating the disorder but, rather, on helping the client preserve his voice production mechanism as effectively as possible. A team approach with the client's otolaryngologist or neurologist is the most effective way to plan treatment. Such an arrangement facilitates coordination of any medical or surgical treatments and behavioral therapy, both of which may be necessary for the rehabilitation of individuals with organic voice disorders.

Therapy for organic disorders is similar to therapy for functional disorders except that there is less emphasis on identifying and reducing vocal abuse. The first step is usually to discuss with the client their voice needs for their career and social life. This will give the speech-language pathologist some idea of how best to help the client. For example, if a client with vocal-fold paralysis needs to lecture to large groups and therefore wants to increase her vocal loudness, the clinician might decide to (1) work on improved breath support, (2) experiment with a personal amplification system for the client, or (3) check into the possibility that surgical intervention might increase her loudness capabilities. It may not always be possible for the client to return to old vocal use patterns, however. In addition to voice therapy, the speech-language pathologist may have to help the client adjust to new limitations.

The second stage of therapy is to institute a program of vocal hygiene and compensatory rest. Many individuals with organic voice disorders will need to exercise care in order to prevent further damage to their vocal mechanism. The speech-language pathologist can instruct the client on avoiding excessive voice use and on the importance of rest prior to and following periods of heavy vocal demands.

In searching for the best voice possible through facilitating approaches, the same techniques discussed for use with functional disorders can be used with those who have organic disorders. The goal is to help the client produce the best-sounding, most useful voice in the least stressful manner. Finally, generalization of new skills into words, phrases, sentences, and everyday conversation is introduced. When the client has achieved satisfactory voice production in conversational speech or has progressed as much as possible in the opinion of the speech-language pathologist, the client is dismissed from therapy.

THERAPY FOR PSYCHOGENIC VOICE DISORDERS

A psychogenic voice disorder can be treated successfully by a speech-language pathologist who is able to convince the client that nothing is wrong with the speech production mechanism and that all that is needed is some reeducation to retrain the muscles to produce speech and voice (Boone and McFarlane, 1994; Aronson, 1990). This approach is most successful with clients who have reduced or at least acknowledged the source of the emotional conflict that precipitated the disorder. Initiating voice on a prolonged cough or during throat clearing is usually the first step in therapy, followed by vocalizations of "a-hem," vowels, syllables, words, sentences, and so on (Boone and McFarlane, 1994). If the client is ready to get his or her voice back, this procedure may take anywhere from a few minutes to an hour.

If this approach doesn't work, the speech-language pathologist should encourage the client to seek psychological counseling and should then form a "team" with the psychologist. Combined psychological counseling and voice therapy has the best chance of success in cases where the individual has not yet confronted his or her emotional conflicts. Unfortunately, some clients with psychogenic voice disorders are extremely resistant to the suggestion of counseling. The speech-language pathologist must then decide whether to continue the client's therapy, despite its lack of success, or to dismiss the client.

THERAPY FOR RESONANCE DISORDERS

Because resonance disorders are so often organic in nature, it is important for the speech-language pathologist to work closely with various medical specialists in order to obtain the best outcome for the client. Behavioral treatment may include (1) perceptual training to teach the individual to attend to and discriminate between acceptable and unacceptable resonance quality and (2) biofeedback devices to help the child change his speech patterns. However, if the voice or speech problems are organic in nature, medical intervention will be needed. After the medical intervention, a period of trial therapy might be initiated to see if any gains can be made on a behavioral basis. If the voice remains unsatisfactory, further surgical treatment might be considered. Medical, surgical, and speech-language treatment of children with cleft palate and resonance disorders will be discussed further in Chapter 11.

OUTCOMES OF INTERVENTION

In general, clients with functional disorders who are motivated to change their voices make excellent progress. This is true for both clients with functional laryngeal disorders and functional resonance disorders. Because the new methods of voice production they learn in therapy both feel and sound better than their former abusive habits, carryover from the therapy room to everyday life is more likely. Individuals should make noticeable progress within three months of starting therapy (Case, 1991). Vocal nodules should be eliminated in this time period as well, although in this author's experience, sometimes as much as six months of therapy is required for the elimination of long-standing fibrotic nodules.

Outcome of therapy for organic disorders is more variable. It often depends on the following factors: (1) the source of the problem and whether it will recur; (2) how successfully the disorder can be resolved by medical or surgical means; (3) the amount of damage to the vocal mechanism or velum that has occurred; and (4) the demands the individual has for his or her voice. Therapy can usually improve the voice of a client with an organic voice disorder, but the voice may not sound normal and may not be adequate for the client's social and vocational needs.

Outcome of therapy for psychogenic disorders is also variable and depends on the client's willingness to address the underlying emotional conflicts that precipitated the voice disorder. According to Aronson (1990), most clients in this category respond to voice therapy fairly quickly, usually within a session or two. However, clients who are unwilling to give up the protection their aphonia affords them may be difficult to treat and may remain aphonic for years.

CONSEQUENCES OF A VOICE DISORDER

The consequences of a voice disorder to an individual are extremely varied. At one end of the continuum, there may be no negative consequences at all, especially if the disorder is a mild one. Deterioration in voice quality, periodic feelings of fatigue, or even loss of voice does not interfere with everyone's vocational or social activities. Unless they are stigmatized by coworkers and friends, such individuals suffer very few repercussions.

As the voice disorder increases in severity, however, it becomes more difficult to escape limitations in the workplace or with friends. For example, communication in noisy environments may be inefficient, if not impossible. When we consider that cars are noisy environments, as well as bars, restaurants, parties, sporting events, rock concerts, and just about everywhere else people congregate, it is clear that not being able to communicate in a noisy environment could cause serious problems in an individual's lifestyle.

Aberrant-sounding voices can also cause people to feel self-conscious and thus to limit their communications with others. This can be a problem in the workplace as well as socially. Further, the disordered voice may make a negative impression on others. An individual who cannot be heard, or whose voice is unpleasantly distracting, may be considered "rude" for not accommodating better to the listener. They may not advance in their jobs or careers because of subtle prejudices on the part of others.

In summary, the consequences of a voice disorder could range from none at all to social isolation, lack of self-confidence, and vocational limitations. With therapy, many of these negative consequences can be reduced or eliminated.

SUMMARY

Voice disorders are characterized by disturbed laryngeal quality, hypernasality or denasality,

too soft or too loud an intensity, a speaking fundamental frequency that is inappropriate for the client's age and gender, or inappropriate stress and intonation patterns. Voice disorders are often a direct result of a vocal-fold lesion, neurological damage, or the abnormal structure or function of the soft and hard palates. Some vocal-fold lesions, such as nodules and polyps, are a result of vocal abuse. A voice disorder or laryngeal pathology caused by abusive or bad habits is said to be functional, and generally it responds well to behavioral treatment. In contrast, some voice disorders and abnormalities of the speech and voice production mechanisms are due to diseases, conditions, or injuries outside of the client's control. Such disorders are called organic, and they usually require medical or surgical treatment. The success of voice therapy in organic cases depends upon whether the underlying condition can be eliminated or corrected and how badly damaged the voice mechanism has become as a result of the condition.

The responsibility of the speech-language pathologist is to help clients analyze their vocal demands, adjust their vocal use and behavior where possible, and adopt a more relaxed and less stressful speaking style. A working knowledge of anatomy and physiology, as well as acoustics, may be necessary in order to pinpoint the cause of an individual's disorder and to prescribe the appropriate treatment. In addition, because of the behavioral and emotional aspects of voice disorders, the voice clinician needs to develop counseling skills. Working with clients with voice disorders can be challenging but also very rewarding in that clients often attain improved or even completely normal vocal function as a result of therapy.

R E V I E W   Q U E S T I O N S

1. What do we mean in communication sciences and disorders by the term *voice*? What is the difference between voice and speech?

2. Where, in general, are the vocal folds? What is their normal position during breathing? During phonation?

3. How, in general, is voice produced?

4. What perceptual features of voice are determined laryngeally? What aspects of vocal-fold behavior or movement cause each feature?

5. What is *resonance*? What parts of the vocal tract contribute to the sound of a voice? What primary perceptual attribute of voice is determined by the resonance characteristics of the vocal tract?

6. What is the definition of a *voice disorder*? Why is a voice disorder more subjective in nature than a phonological or language disorder?

7. What is meant by a *functional voice disorder*? An *organic voice disorder*? Give examples of each.

8. What is a *psychogenic voice disorder*?

9. Why is it important for voice clients to be evaluated by an otolaryngologist prior to beginning voice therapy?

10. Once a medical evaluation has been completed, what are the steps a speech-language pathologist should go through in the intervention process for functional voice disorders?

11. How does intervention in organic voice disorders differ from intervention in functional voice disorders?

12. How are psychogenic voice disorders treated by the speech-language pathologist? What factors determine a client's response to this therapy?

13. What is the prognosis for recovery of a normal-sounding voice and normal laryngeal-palatal function for individuals with functional voice disorders? Organic voice disorders?

14. What are some possible consequences of a voice disorder for an individual? Which groups are most likely to have and be concerned about voice disorders?

FOR FURTHER INFORMATION

Aronson, A. (1990). *Clinical voice disorders: An interdisciplinary approach* (3rd ed.). New York, NY: Thieme.

Baken, R. (1987). *Clinical measurement of speech and voice*. Boston, MA: College-Hill Press.

Boone, D., and **McFarlane, S.** (1994). *The voice and voice therapy* (5th ed.). Englewood Cliffs, NJ: Prentice-Hall.

Case, J. (1991). *Clinical management of voice disorders* (2nd ed.). Austin, TX: Pro-Ed.

Colton, R., and **Casper, J.** (1990). *Understanding voice problems: A physiological perspective for diagnosis and treatment*. Baltimore, MD: Williams and Wilkins.

Wilson, D. (1987). *Voice problems of children* (3rd ed.). Baltimore, MD: Williams and Wilkins.

Special Populations: Cleft Palate

I n our chapter on voice disorders, we touched briefly on the condition known as *cleft palate*. A cleft palate, with or without a cleft lip, occurs because of an interruption in the normal formation of the face and oral area during embryonic development. Cleft lips and palates are not uncommon—they occur about as frequently as Down syndrome, one of the causes of cognitive disorders we discussed in Chapter 4. The occurrence of cleft lip and palate has been estimated at approximately 1 in 1000 live births for those of European ancestry, 1.7 per 1000 births for those of Asian ancestry, and 1 per 2500 for those of African ancestry (Gorlin, 1993).

Before the advent of cosmetic surgery, an individual with a cleft lip or palate was shunned and stigmatized. Victims were often erroneously considered mentally defective and excluded from the normal activities of their time. Fortunately, since the early 1900s, surgical repair of cleft lip and cleft palate has steadily improved, reducing the extent of the physical deformity and hence the ostracism once suffered by these individuals. Even with modern methods of treatment, however, a cleft lip or palate can still have a profound effect on an individual. Despite early surgical intervention, voice and articulation disorders are common in this population. Children with this condition look and sound "different" and may be stereotyped in ways that limit their social, educational, and vocational opportunities. Frequent hospitalizations and painful reconstruction procedures may have to be endured periodically from infancy to adulthood.

In addition, some individuals with cleft lip and palate have these impairments as part of a genetic syndrome and a larger constellation of handicaps.

In this chapter, we will explore the causes, characteristics, and consequences of cleft lip and palate. We will also review the medical and surgical treatment of this population and the involvement of the speech-language pathologist.

EMBRYONIC DEVELOPMENT

In order to understand the types of clefts typically observed and why they occur, we must first understand something about embryonic development. As mentioned previously, cleft lip and palate occur because of abnormal development in the face and oral area during fetal life. The face and palate are formed very early in the gestational period and are subject to disruptions due to both genetic factors and environmental hazards.

FORMATION OF THE FACE AND LIP

Figure 11-1a illustrates the "face" of a 4-week-old fetus. At this developmental stage, the nasal placodes, which will ultimately become the nasal cavities, are on the lateral aspects of the face (Zemlin, 1988). Between the nasal placodes is an area known as the *frontal prominence*. Below the frontal prominence is the primitive mouth, or *stomodeum*. At the lower border of the stomodeum is the mandibular arch. Two upper projections on

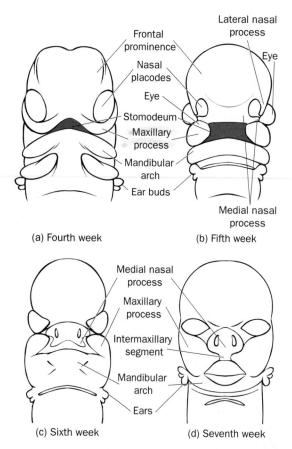

FIGURE 11-1 Embryonic development of the face during the fourth through seventh weeks of gestation.

either side of the mandibular arch, known as the *maxillary processes,* are growing toward midline. The mandibular arch will ultimately develop into the lower lip and jaw, while the maxillary processes will contribute to the upper lip, upper jaw, and palate (Gorlin, 1993).

In the 5-week-old embryo (Figure 11-1b), we can see that the nasal placodes are being surrounded by ridges of tissue. The swellings, or *prominences,* on the outer edges of the nasal placodes are called the *lateral nasal processes.* The ridges on the inner sides of each nasal placode are called the *medial nasal processes.* During the sixth week of embryonic development, the medial and lateral nasal prominences on either side fuse,

enclosing each nasal pit and forming what will become the nostrils.

Between the sixth and eighth weeks of embryonic life, several important developments occur in the face and oral area (see Figures 11-1c and 11-1d). As the maxillary processes continue to grow toward midline, they push the developing nostrils on either side closer to one another. The two medial nasal processes, one on each side, fuse at this time, forming a single midline division between the nostrils and the mid-most portion of the upper lip (Gorlin, 1993). In addition, this single, fused medial nasal process (called the *intermaxillary segment*) is approached on either side by the ingrowing maxillary processes. These three structures also fuse, completing the upper lip. The upper lip is thus derived from the intermaxillary segment in the center and the two maxillary processes on each side. By the end of the eighth week, the development of the eyes, nose, and mouth have progressed enough to form a recognizable face (Zemlin, 1988).

If there is a disruption in the development of these structures during the sixth to eighth weeks, a cleft lip may result. If, for example, the intermaxillary segment failed to fuse on one side with the maxillary process growing in toward it, as shown in Figure 11-2a, a cleft on that side of the lip would occur. Clefts of the lip are typically located under one nostril or the other, along the line where the maxillary processes should fuse with the intermaxillary segment. If the earlier union between the medial and lateral nasal processes had occurred successfully, the cleft lip would not affect the nostril. This is called an *incomplete cleft* of the lip. However, if the medial and lateral nasal processes did not successfully fuse together, the cleft lip would be *complete,* involving the nostril as well as the lip, as shown in Figure 11-2b (McWilliams et al., 1990).

FORMATION OF THE HARD AND SOFT PALATE

The hard palate and the *velum* (the soft palate) together separate the oral cavity from the nasal cavities. The hard palate is formed by the union of three independent structures: the premaxilla in

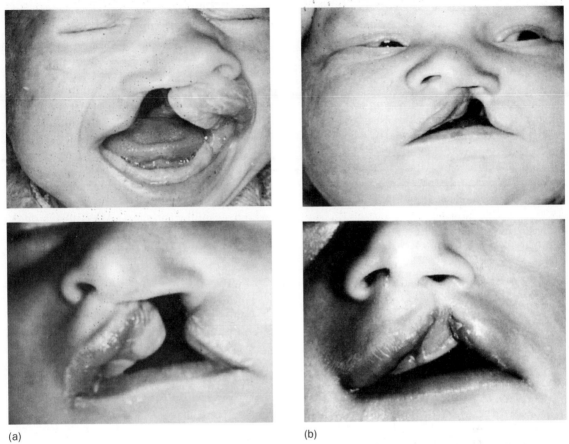

(a) (b)

FIGURE 11-2 (a) A cleft of the lip occurring because of failure of the intermaxillary segment to fuse with the maxillary process on one side *and* a failure of the lateral and medial nasal processes to close off the nostril. This is known as a *complete cleft* of the lip. (b) A cleft lip occurring because of failure of the intermaxillary segment to fuse with the maxillary process on one side. This is also known as an *incomplete cleft* of the lip. Note that the nostril for each child in column B is complete on the side with the cleft. (Standard APA)

the front and center position and the two palatal shelves coming in from either side. Where do these structures come from?

The premaxilla arises from the fused medial nasal process, or the *intermaxillary segment.* Recall that during the sixth week of embryonic development, the medial nasal processes unite and that this new structure is called the *intermaxillary segment.* The intermaxillary segment includes a labial portion, which forms the division between the nostrils and the mid-most area of the upper lip, as we have already discussed. However, there is also a palatal portion, directly behind the labial por-

tion, that is called the *premaxilla.* The premaxilla develops into a triangular-shaped bone in the center of the oral area that will ultimately comprise the front of the alveolar ridge and hold the top four incisors (Gorlin, 1993).

The palatal shelves arise from the maxillary processes. We have already described the contribution of the maxillary processes to the formation of the upper lip. In addition, inward growth of the maxillary processes forms the palatine processes, or *palatal shelves,* which will ultimately join with the premaxilla and each other to form the hard and soft palates.

Around the eighth week of fetal development, the inward-growing edges of the palatal shelves make contact on either side with the premaxilla and fuse with it. As shown in Figure 11-3, fusion proceeds to the tip of the premaxilla; and then the palatal shelves begin to fuse with each other at midline. This fusion proceeds from the front of the oral cavity toward the back. When the joining of the hard palate is complete, the two sides of the soft palate merge with one another. This process continues until the uvula, the very end of the soft palate, fuses by approximately the twelfth week of embryonic development (McWilliams et al., 1990).

If the fusion process is disrupted—by chemical agents, by trauma, or by genetic factors—various types of cleft palate may result. The mildest type of cleft is a submucous cleft palate, which is not visible upon inspection of the oral cavity. In a *sub-mucous cleft,* the posterior-most parts of the hard palate may fail to join with one another or the muscular bundles that form the soft palate might fail to unite at midline. However, the skin or mucosal covering of the hard and soft palates is intact, and thus the cleft is not visible except through endoscopic examination of the nasal surface of the palate. An individual with a submucous cleft often has a palate that is not completely normal in terms of movement capabilities and which is somewhat short (McWilliams et al., 1990).

Other mild clefts involve only a midline sepa-

FIGURE 11-3 Formation of the hard and soft palate during the eighth through twelfth weeks of embryonic development. The palate and lip are viewed from below looking up.

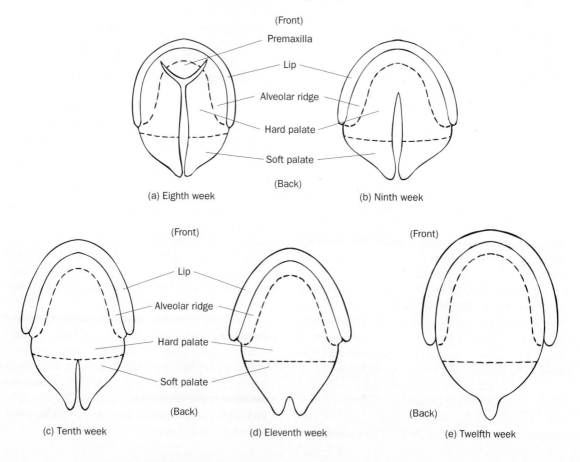

ration of the uvula or the soft palate (see Figure 11-4a). These clefts are generally apparent during careful visual examination of the oral cavity. However, in some cases they might be so slight that they remain unnoticed unless the child has difficulty with his speech.

A more extensive cleft might begin at the point where the palatal shelves should have fused with one another at midline, behind the premax-

FIGURE **11-4** Types of clefts seen in infants with cleft lip and palate. The nose, lip, and palate are viewed from below looking up.

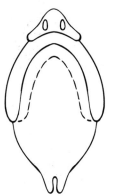

(a) A bifid uvula—a very mild cleft of the soft palate

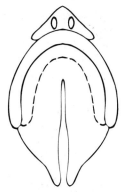

(b) A midline cleft of the hard and soft palates

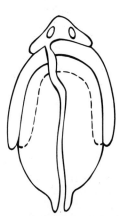

(c) A unilateral cleft of the lip and palate not affecting the nostril

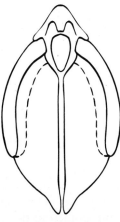

(d) A bilateral cleft of the lip and palate affecting both nostrils

illa, as pictured in Figure 11-4b. This results in a midline opening running from the back part of the alveolar ridge through the remaining length of the hard palate and the entire soft palate. A severe cleft would involve the soft palate, hard palate, and the alveolar ridge and lip, as pictured in Figure 11-4c. Since union between the premaxilla on one side with one maxillary shelf is affected, this is called a *unilateral cleft*. Finally, the most severe clefts extend around the premaxilla on both sides. This type of bilateral cleft often involves the lip and nostril as well (see Figure 11-4c and d).

About 25 percent of all children with some type of cleft have a cleft of the hard or soft palate with no involvement of the lip (Gorlin, 1993). Surprisingly, the cleft condition that occurs most frequently (in 50 percent of all cases of cleft, according to Gorlin) is a cleft of both the palate and the lip. The remaining 25 percent of children with some type of cleft have a cleft of the lip alone.

CAUSES OF CLEFT LIP AND PALATE

The major causes of cleft lip and palate are generally acknowledged to be genetic factors and environmental teratogens (McWilliams et al., 1990). In our next section, we will explore these factors both alone and in combination.

CLEFT LIP OR PALATE DUE TO GENETIC SYNDROMES

Some children with cleft lip or palate are born with a pattern of physical abnormalities that comprise a recognized genetic syndrome. For example, a child may have a cleft palate as part of Crouzon's syndrome, which is characterized by bulging and widely spaced eyes, a large and malformed head, and dental abnormalities.

Genetic syndromes such as Crouzon's are the result of a single faulty gene with a dominant mode of inheritance. This means that if an individual has one "good" (non-Crouzon's) gene from one parent but a defective (Crouzon's) gene from the other, he will have the physical symptoms of the syndrome. Such an individual would have a 50 percent probability of passing the disorder on to his or her children.

It is interesting to note that despite the fact that dominant genetic disorders are passed from parent to child, there may be no family history of the disorder with which the child has been diagnosed. In Crouzon's syndrome, for example, this occurs in about one-fourth of all cases (Jones, 1988). This is because the faulty gene can originate as a mutation in the parent's egg or sperm cell. The otherwise normal parent unknowingly passes this mutant gene on to his or her child. Although the initial occurrence of the dominant genetic disorder in a family may be due to a mutation, however, the affected individual can then pass the disorder along to future generations, with the same 50 percent probability mentioned above. Lynch and Kimberling (1981) have identified forty-seven genetic disorders with dominant inheritance patterns involving cleft lip or palate.

Other syndromes that include cleft palate may be due to a recessive mode of inheritance. Recall that for each trait an individual possesses, there are two genes—one from the mother and one from the father. In the dominant mode of inheritance just discussed, having one gene of that gene pair was sufficient for the trait (or *syndrome*) to be expressed. For a recessive disorder to be expressed, however, the individual must have *two* genes of the gene pair, one from each parent.

In the case of a recessive genetic syndrome, an individual can unknowingly carry one defective gene of the gene pair without having any symptoms of the syndrome himself. We refer to such individuals as *carriers*. The problem occurs when one normal-appearing carrier marries another and both pass their defective gene (instead of their normal gene) on to their child. The statistical probability of two carriers producing a child with the syndrome is 25 percent. The child with two defective genes in the gene pair will show the symptoms of the syndrome. In the next generation, all of the affected individual's children will be carriers of the disorder. If the affected individual marries another carrier, they run a 50 percent

risk of passing along the condition to their offspring. According to Lynch and Kimberling (1981), there are fifty-five recessive genetic disorders that cause cleft lip or cleft palate.

CLEFT LIP OR PALATE DUE TO MULTIFACTORIAL INHERITANCE PATTERNS

In actuality, only a small percentage of children with cleft lip or palate have that anomaly as part of a recognizable syndrome with a known dominant or recessive transmission pattern. Gorlin (1993) estimates that only about 5 percent of clefting is syndromal. In a larger percentage of cases (10 to 15 percent, according to Gorlin), cleft lip or palate runs in the family—that is, several members of the family in different generations have it—but few, if any, additional deformities are present, and the expected patterns of inheritance are not evident (50 percent or 25 percent in successive generations). In such cases, it is difficult to predict which family members are most at risk for producing children with clefts.

It is hypothesized that these nonsyndrome occurrences of cleft lip or palate are due to multifactorial inheritance patterns. This means that instead of a single gene causing the disorder, or two defective genes in a gene pair, multiple genes must be present in order for a cleft lip or palate to be expressed. In addition, certain environmental conditions may also be necessary (Gorlin, 1993). Thus, multifactorial disorders are caused by a combination of genetic and environmental influences.

What types of environmental influences might cause cleft lip and palate in a developing fetus? Surprisingly few agents or substances have been specifically implicated. According to Fraser (1971), the rubella virus can cause clefting in susceptible individuals if the mother has the disease early in her pregnancy. He also cites the formerly prescribed drug thalidomide as a possible cause of cleft palate. (Thalidomide, given to many pregnant women in the 1950s to prevent morning sickness, was found to cause serious malformations, particularly of the arms and legs, in some fetuses. It was withdrawn from the market some time ago.) The Center for Disease Control has also found that Valium, a tranquilizer, increases the risk of cleft lip with or without cleft palate by a factor of four if the drug is taken in the first trimester of pregnancy (Golbus, 1980). McWilliams and her colleagues (1990) cite Dilantin, a seizure-control medication, as being a possible cause of cleft palate. All these drugs would be referred to as *teratogens,* or deformity-causing substances.

According to McWilliams et al., "Infections, diseases, irradiation, environmental chemicals, maternal metabolic and endocrine imbalances, drugs, nutritional deficiencies and excesses have all been implicated" (p. 25). But other than the few agents and substances mentioned above, little is known about specific environmental causes of cleft palate. With controlled studies on pregnant women impossible, and with the limited generalizability of animal models to human populations, this is likely to be an area of speculation for some time.

SPORADIC OCCURRENCES

With only approximately 5 percent of all cases of cleft lip and palate related to genetic syndromes and 10 to 15 percent of a familial nature and due to multifactorial inheritance, a large portion of cleft lip and palate cases (80 to 85 percent) remain unaccounted for in terms of etiology (Gorlin, 1993). These cases may be due to environmental influences acting alone, unrecognized familial trends (such as when an extensive family history is not available), spontaneous genetic mutations, or unrecognized genetic syndromes. The latter possibilities are especially credible if the child has other physical malformations in addition to the cleft. The possibility of a child having more than one independently caused malformation is very small. It is much more likely that if more than one anomaly is found, the two have the same cause—an underlying genetic disorder. Shprintzin and his colleagues (1985) found, through careful study, that as many as 53 percent of their cleft lip or palate clients had either identifiable genetic syndromes or "provisionally unique pat-

tern syndromes." Only 47 percent appeared to have "clefts in isolation," or clefts with no other physical anomalies to suggest a genetic etiology.

In summary, the causes of cleft lip or cleft palate are not easy to identify. In a small percentage of cases, the cleft is part of a more extensive syndrome of physical deformities; in other cases, it may be part of a familial pattern that includes only minor physical anomalies in addition to the cleft. It has been hypothesized that both a genetic predisposition and environmental factors are necessary to produce a cleft lip or palate, although the environmental factors have not been well-specified. Currently, the majority of cases have no known etiology. However, more careful testing methods and new advances in genetics may provide further insights into what are probably the many causes of this disorder.

A BRIEF HISTORY OF SURGICAL TREATMENT FOR CLEFT LIP AND PALATE

SURGICAL PROCEDURES FOR CLEFT LIP

Treatment procedures for cleft lip were known as far back as A.D. 390 in China, according to a review presented by Shons (1993). In Europe, the first known description of cleft-palate repair was published in 1561. Until the use of anesthesia, which began in the middle 1800s, however, the state of the art remained relatively unsophisticated. Indeed, mortality rates during surgery were so high during the early days of medicine that only lifesaving procedures were typically attempted.

Modern methods of cleft-lip treatment had their genesis in the middle 1800s, when surgeons began using flaps of tissue raised on either side of the cleft to fill in the cleft area. It was recognized at that time that simply stretching the existing portions of the lip toward each other and sewing them together gave a poor cosmetic result. Thus, surgeons began experimenting with cutting into the lip on each side of the cleft and freeing a triangle on two sides, with the base still attached at the inner margin of the cleft. These flaps of muscle and connective tissue were then rotated inward across the open area and sewed to one another. Such a technique, reportedly used as early as 1844, was the forerunner of today's flap-closure operation (Shons, 1993).

TREATMENT OF CLEFT PALATE

Treatment procedures for cleft palate have a less extensive history. In his review of this area, Shons notes that surgical closure of the palate did not begin until the early 1800s, although various crude devices for occluding the palatal opening were constructed as early as the middle ages. By the 1860s, surgeons had begun to use flaps, as previously discussed in the repair of cleft lip. To repair a cleft of the hard palate, flaps consisting of the mucosal covering of the palate plus a thin layer of bone were raised at either side of the cleft and moved toward one another to cover the opening. The advent of antibiotics improved the success of the procedure, reducing the probability of infection and the subsequent disunion of the joined tissues (Converse, 1963).

In the 1920s and 1930s, new surgical techniques to reposition existing palatal tissue and lengthen the palate gained popularity (Converse, 1963). However, surgical techniques for preserving the *mobility* of the soft palate—the ability of the palatal muscles to contract and elevate the palate—have remained problematic. Currently, efforts to reposition the muscles in the velum and to preserve blood vessels and the nerve supply via microsurgery "offer hope for more frequent functional reconstructions [of the velum] at an earlier age" (Bzoch, 1989, 89).

DISORDERS ASSOCIATED WITH CLEFT LIP AND CLEFT PALATE

Up to this point, we have been focusing on the lip, the palate, and the cleft—in terms of normal development, causes of disruptions to normal development, and the history of surgical repair for cleft conditions. Let us now broaden our focus to include the infant, child, or adult who has a cleft lip or palate and the associated disorders he or she frequently experiences.

PHYSICAL APPEARANCE

Clefts on one or both sides of the *primary palate* (the lip and alveolar ridge) can have a profound effect on the physical appearance of the newborn. As we have discussed, a cleft of the lip may cause the nose to be asymmetrical, flattened at the tip, and otherwise misshapen. If a cleft of the alveolar ridge is present, and especially if the cleft is bilateral, the segment of the upper jaw containing the upper four incisors (the *embryonic premaxilla*) may extend outside of the mouth and into the nose.

Fortunately, modern methods of surgery are quite successful in restoring a relatively normal facial configuration. In some cases, good cosmetic outcomes occur as early as infancy or early childhood. More frequently, however, cosmetic repairs are done in stages, and some facial abnormalities may persist until a final round of plastic surgery is undertaken in adolescence or young adulthood. Ultimate success of the reconstructive surgery is limited to some degree by the extent of the deformity. Incomplete clefts and clefts in isolation generally have a better cosmetic outcome than do clefts that are part of a more extensive genetic syndrome involving deformities of several facial and *cranial* (skull) features (McWilliams et al., 1990). For example, individuals with Crouzon's syndrome may need surgery to reshape the head, reposition the eyes, and rebuild the chin as well as repair a cleft palate.

Despite the generally good outcome of cosmetic surgery, even minor residual abnormalities can be problematic in our appearance-conscious society. This is especially true at puberty, when body consciousness is at a maximum. We will discuss this issue further in the upcoming section on psychosocial adjustment in individuals with cleft lip and palate.

SPEECH DISORDERS

Perhaps the most common disorders associated with a cleft palate are difficulties with articulation

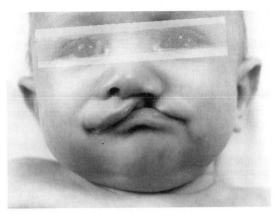

(a)

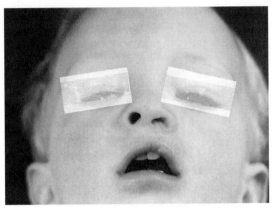

(b)

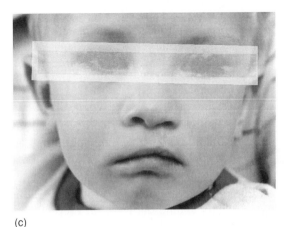

(c)

FIGURE 11-5 (a) An infant with a complete unilateral cleft of both the lip and palate . (b) The same child after surgical repair. (c) The same child two and a half years later.(Courtesy Dr. Janusz Bardach, University of Iowa)

and voice. Even if the cleft is repaired early and relatively successfully, the palate may still not be long enough or mobile enough to seal off the oral cavity from the nasal cavities. In such cases, air and sound energy can escape into the nasal cavities during speech, causing articulation and resonance disorders.

In order to produce sharp, clearly articulated consonants—especially plosives, fricatives, and affricates—a speaker must be able to build up air pressure in the oral cavity. The release of this built-up pressure gives each of these consonants its distinctive sound. If an individual cannot build up *intraoral pressure* (air pressure inside the mouth) due to air leakage through the nose, these consonants will have an indistinct, mushy quality that makes them difficult to understand. In addition,

cleft-palate speakers may produce pressure consonants with *nasal emission,* or audible air escapage from the nose (Trost-Cardamone and Bernthal, 1993).

A variety of substitutions and omission errors is also common in the cleft-palate population. Young children in the preliminary stages of palatal repair often develop unusual sound productions— such as glottal stops or pharyngeal fricatives (made in the back of the throat)—in their speech. These are called *compensatory articulations* and are used in an attempt to build up pressure in the oral or pharyngeal cavity below the level of the cleft. When these children mature and further palatal surgery is done, they frequently retain these unusual substitutions (Broen and Moller, 1993).

Finally, in addition to articulatory distortions and substitutions, the resonance characteristics of the cleft palate speaker's voice are often noticeably different from the general population. This is because even a small opening between the oral and nasal cavities results in listener perceptions of *hypernasality,* or excessive nasal resonance in the voice. Mild hypernasality is not always a problem for a speaker, given today's relatively lax standards for acceptable voice quality. In addition, mild hypernasality rarely interferes with intelligibility. However, moderate and moderately severe degrees of hypernasality may reduce the speaker's intelligibility and may also be socially stigmatizing.

HEARING PROBLEMS

Clefts of the palate (although not clefts of the lip) greatly increase the likelihood that the child will suffer periodic hearing loss due to fluid buildup and infection in the middle-ear cavity behind the eardrum. As we shall learn in our chapters about hearing, fluid behind the eardrum prevents this structure from vibrating freely in response to sound waves. If the eardrum cannot vibrate freely, sound energy is not adequately transmitted to the internal parts of the ear and the perceived loudness of sound is thus reduced.

The condition of fluid behind the eardrum, known as *otitis media,* has been found by some researchers to be almost universal in children with cleft palates. Stool and Randall (1967) found that forty-seven out of fifty babies had this condition at the time of their palatal-repair surgery. Paradise et al. (1969), who also examined fifty cleft-palate children, reported that ninety-six out of the one hundred ears had fluid in them. Although otitis media can be treated, principally with antibiotics if it becomes infectious, children with cleft palate tend to have repeated bouts of this disorder. They sometimes suffer permanent changes to the ear and permanent hearing loss as a result.

Why are cleft-palate children so subject to otitis media and hearing loss? In order to answer this question, we must first understand that the bony structures that form the palate, and the muscles that attach to them, also contribute to the structure and function of the hearing mechanism. If the bones of the palate are malformed, parts of the hearing mechanism internal to the eardrum may also be malformed. The muscles that attach to these undersized or misplaced structures will not be able to act effectively to prevent fluid buildup behind the eardrum. Because of these anatomical and physiological differences, a child with a cleft palate needs to be followed carefully from infancy so that occurrences of otitis media and the result-

ing hearing loss can be minimized (Ulvestad and Carlstrom, 1993).

DENTAL ABNORMALITIES

If normal development of the palate is interrupted during the embryonic period, the developing teeth will almost always be affected as well. The "tooth buds," or precursors to the primary teeth, begin to form during the fifth or sixth week of gestation (Zemlin, 1988). Tooth buds in the primary palate and in the palatal shelves eventually form the upper teeth; those developing in the mandibular arches form the lower teeth.

The upper teeth in the palatal shelves are the most likely to be affected by clefting of the palate. Some segments of the palate may develop without tooth buds at all, meaning that no teeth will erupt in some areas. In other areas, the teeth that do erupt may be tilted, misplaced, or misshapen (Zemlin, 1988).

In addition, early surgery to repair cleft conditions may interfere with the normal growth and development of the palate, resulting in an abnormally small upper jaw. The teeth that do come in may be crowded together. If the palate is underdeveloped, the *mandible,* or lower jaw, may be proportionally too large, so that the lower teeth overlap the upper teeth (normally, the upper teeth partially cover the lower) (McWilliams et al., 1990).

Like problems with physical appearance, dental abnormalities can often be corrected through oral surgery, orthodontics (repositioning existing teeth) and prosthodontics (false teeth, bridges, or caps). Success will again depend on the extent of the abnormality and the presence of additional facial deformities (McWilliams et al., 1990).

PSYCHOLOGICAL ADJUSTMENT DIFFICULTIES

As previously mentioned, our society places an inordinate amount of importance on physical appearance. How do physical differences affect the way a child is treated in our society? Research summarized by Richman and Eliason (1993) indicates that children who are judged to be attractive are rated more positively by teachers, unfamiliar adults, and other children. Specific studies on children with cleft lip and palate indicate that teachers have a tendency to underrate the intellectual ability of cleft-palate children with severe facial disfigurement (Richman, 1978). From their own research, Richman and Eliason (1993) concluded that peers are less likely to choose a child with a cleft lip and palate as a friend than they are to choose children with other handicapping conditions. All this suggests that the child with a cleft lip and palate will be at a social disadvantage, especially if the facial involvement is severe. The negative attitudes of teachers, peers, and perhaps future employers may limit the educational, social, and vocational opportunities of the cleft lip-palate child.

How do these negative attitudes affect the child's self-esteem and psychological health? Research in this area has been equivocal. For example, Kapp (1979) found that elementary school–aged children with clefts had lower self-concepts than their nonhandicapped peers; but Brantley and Clifford (1979) found that high school students with clefts actually had a more positive self-concept than their controls. Surveys of parents and teachers on the personality traits of cleft lip and palate children have revealed no major psychological problems except a tendency to be inhibited and an exacerbation of the typical feelings of self-consciousness in adolescence (Richman and Eliason, 1993). Thus, as a group, individuals with cleft lip and cleft palate have not appeared to demonstrate major problems in psychological adjustment. However, this is not to say that the child with a facial disfigurement will have no negative psychological consequences. Each individual is affected differently and may need different levels of support to develop self-confidence and self-esteem.

CURRENT TREATMENT PROCEDURES IN CLEFT LIP-PALATE: THE INTERDISCIPLINARY TEAM

Modern treatment procedures for individuals with cleft lip and palate rely heavily on an interdisci-plinary team composed of a variety of different specialists (Moller, 1993). These teams, which are typically coordinated within a hospital setting (often where the child was born), provide medical-surgical care and make early efforts at rehabilitation at or very shortly after the child's birth. Ideally, the team continues to follow the child through adolescence and early adulthood—or at least until all the necessary treatments have been completed.

According to the American Cleft Palate–Craniofacial Association, the minimum team consists of a reconstructive surgeon, a dentist, and a speech-language pathologist. This team meets regularly to discuss a particular client or clients (Moller, 1993). Additional team members depend on the needs of the individual child and family.

What other specialists might be on the team? In terms of the medical component, an *otorhinolaryngologist* (ear, nose, and throat, or ENT, specialist—sometimes referred to as simply *otolaryngologist*) is an important member of the reconstruction team. In addition, a pediatrician, nurse, or *radiologist* (x-ray specialist) might participate in group meetings on the care of a particular child. If the child has deformities of the skull or needs repositioning of the eyes, a neurosurgeon and opthalmologist may also be called upon (Moller, 1993).

In terms of the dental component, a key specialist is often the orthodontist, who repositions the child's existing teeth and *dental arches* (the parts of the palate that support the teeth). In addition, a *prosthodontist,* who constructs artificial substitutes for missing or inadequate structures, will often participate. An oral surgeon, family dentist, and dental hygienist complete the dental component of the team.

The speech and hearing component includes a speech-language pathologist, mentioned above, and an *audiologist,* who specializes in hearing evaluation. Finally, the psychosocial component of the team could include a psychologist, social worker, and a *geneticist,* who specializes in identifying genetic disorders and counseling the family regarding the risk of recurrence. Let us look more specifically at the role of each of the primary members of the team and the current treatment practices in each area for cleft lip and palate.

THE ROLE OF THE MEDICAL MEMBERS OF THE TEAM

The medical members of the interdisciplinary team, in particular the reconstructive surgeon, are involved in the earliest stages of the treatment of the cleft lip–cleft palate child. Surgery for a cleft lip may take place as soon as the first two to three days of life, although Shons (1993) states that he prefers to perform this surgery at the age of 4 to 6 weeks. According to Osborn and Kelleher (1983), lip repair most commonly is done at the age of about 3 months and may be put off even longer if the child has other problems (McWilliams et al., 1990).

The timing of the surgery to close a cleft of the hard palate is more controversial. The goals of surgery, according to Shons (1993, 65) are "creation of a mechanism capable of producing normal speech . . . and minimal interference with facial growth." Unfortunately, for many years, these goals were considered mutually exclusive. Based on the work of Graber (1949, 1950, 1954), it was believed that closure of the hard palate prior to the age of 12 months inhibited growth of the midfacial region and resulted in a poor appearance. On the other hand, late closure of the palate (beyond the age of 2) appeared to result in poorer speech development. Most surgeons currently compromise, closing the hard and soft palates between the ages of 12 and 18 months (Shons, 1993).

More recent research, however, indicates that earlier palatal surgery may facilitate both facial growth and development and better speech. Ross (1987) did a comprehensive study of children who had had cleft-palate surgery at thirteen treatment centers and a large control group of non-cleft children. He concluded that the children whose palates had been repaired before their first birthdays had a "slight advantage" in terms of facial growth and development over children whose palates had been repaired later.

Normal speech proficiency also appears to be facilitated by earlier palatal closure. For example, Dorf and Curtain (1982) found that there was only a 10 percent incidence of abnormal articulation in children whose clefts had been repaired prior to their first birthdays. If the cleft repair was delayed until after the age of 1, an 86 percent incidence of the same speech disorder was found. Desai (1983) reported no hypernasality in a group of children whose palates had been repaired at the age of 16 weeks. If the results of these studies are accepted by the medical community, the medical members of the interdisciplinary team may move in the future toward earlier surgical intervention for cleft palate than has been the case until now.

In addition to repair of the lip and the palate, many children with cleft palate currently require additional surgeries as they grow and mature. A secondary closure of the palate may be needed when the child is between 6 and 12 if good palatal function has not been attained and speech is poor (McWilliams et al., 1990). Secondary surgeries of the lip and nose are also common. The goal of these surgeries is to improve the appearance of the lip scar and to make the lip and nose more symmetrical. The age at which these surgeries take place varies greatly (McWilliams et al., 1990) but often occurs in adolescence and early adulthood, when facial growth is complete (Shons, 1993).

Because the nature and timing of the child's surgery will affect the treatment of all the other specialists involved with the child's care, it is especially important for the reconstructive surgeon to maintain good communication with the other members of the interdisciplinary team. In particular, the reconstructive surgeon must maintain a good relationship with the child's parents in order to help them understand the goals and possible outcomes of surgery and to elicit their cooperation. Patients and families who are not well informed tend to be less actively involved in treatment and less compliant with recommendations, resulting in a poorer outcome (Moller, 1993).

THE ROLE OF THE DENTAL MEMBERS OF THE TEAM

1. The Orthodontist. The dental members of the team become involved surprisingly early in the treatment of the cleft lip–cleft palate child. If the cleft involves the primary palate, the frontmost segment of the child's upper jaw may be rotated out of the mouth or may protrude into the nose. In order to permit lip and palatal repair, and to create a continuous dental arch that can support teeth, the orthodontist may be asked immediately after birth to reposition the protrusive primary palate. In extreme cases, a cotton and elastic retainer-type device may be used. This device fits over the protrusive premaxilla and goes around the head. It exerts gentle pressure on the extrusive segment, eventually bringing it into better alignment with the rest of the upper jaw. Such treatment can be expected to have the desired effect in one to three months (Cronin, 1977).

When realigning a protrusive primary palate, the orthodontist must also deal with the possibility of palatal collapse. Following cleft-repair surgery, scar tissue frequently forms on the parts of the palate where the flaps we discussed earlier were raised and repositioned. This scar tissue tends to pull inward on the growing and healing palate, sometimes with such force that one side of the palate simply collapses toward midline. Palatal collapse has a disastrous effect on the shape of the dental arch and subsequent positioning of the teeth. Thus, orthodontists are involved immediately after palatal-repair surgery to construct devices for the child which will prevent or minimize this condition. Such a device is pictured in Figure 11-6.

Once the child's teeth begin to erupt, the orthodontist takes on the more familiar role of constructing braces to reposition the child's teeth. He or she may also be involved in decisions regarding bone grafts for areas where the dental arch is interrupted. Since some of these treatments may interfere with speech therapy, orthodontic and speech treatment need to be carefully coordinated.

2. The Prosthodontist. The role of the prosthodontist is also an important one. A *prosthodontist* constructs bridges, dentures, and various appliances to replace missing teeth, to obstruct openings in the hard palate, and to separate the oral and nasal cavities if good movement of the soft palate cannot be attained.

Missing teeth are usually replaced by constructing a dental bridge and appropriate tooth replacements or dentures. These do not differ from the partial or complete dentures of older adults, although it may be somewhat more challenging to find anchoring teeth to which the denture can be attached in the cleft-palate child. More recently, dental implants have been introduced. Dental implants are "man-made tooth analogues that are surgically implanted into edentulous (toothless) regions of the jaw to replace missing teeth" (Leeper et al., 1993, 154). Although not yet widely used, dental implants may be very helpful in replacing the missing teeth of cleft-palate children.

Hard and soft palate repair are usually managed by surgery in current practice (McWilliams et al.,

FIGURE 11-6 An orthodontic device designed to prevent or reduce palatal collapse. In this illustration, we are looking upward into the upper jaw. The individual has a repaired unilateral (left) cleft with palatal collapse on the repaired side.

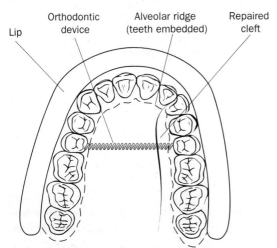

Lip
Orthodontic device
Alveolar ridge (teeth embedded)
Repaired cleft

1990). However, in the case of the hard palate, *fistulas,* or holes, may open up on either side of the repaired cleft due to the pulling of scar tissue. Such defects are often occluded with a prosthetic device, similar in appearance to a bridge that holds dentures, until a second operation can be performed when the child is older (Leeper et al., 1993).

In the case of inadequacy of the soft palate, a prosthetic device is more controversial. Despite the availability of corrective surgical procedures, sometimes an appliance known as a *speech bulb* is recommended (see Figure 11-7a). A speech bulb looks like a partial denture, but it has an extender on the back that attaches to a roughly spheroid structure that fits into the area between the soft palate and the back of the throat. When the speech bulb is in place, it partially occludes the nasal cavities. It can be removed and replaced by the individual as necessary during eating and sleeping. A speech bulb is typically used in hypernasal children with poor speech intelligibility due to a short or insufficient palate, but who are believed to be too young for secondary palatal surgery.

A second type of device constructed by prosthodontists is a palatal lift, pictured in Figure 11-7b. A *palatal lift* is composed of an anterior portion similar to a dental bridge, as was the case with the speech bulb. However, the back portion of the palatal lift is a flat, shoehorn-shaped device designed to elevate an adequately long palate that is weak or paralyzed. Since the palatal lift requires normal palatal length, it is not typically used with cleft-palate children (McWilliams et al., 1990). It is used more often for individuals with movement limitations.

Like the orthodontist, the prosthodontist must coordinate his or her treatment with the speech-language pathologist. For example, if the appliance used to occlude a fistula of the hard palate blocks the alveolar ridge, the child will have difficulty producing a large number of speech sounds. The prosthodontist and speech-language pathologist must work together to ensure that this does not happen. They must also work together in determining the need for a speech bulb. And both must communicate with the reconstructive sur-

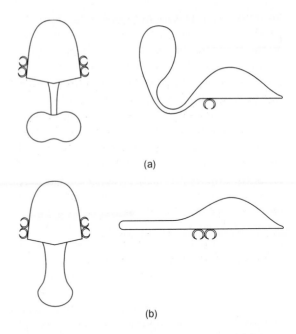

(a)

(b)

FIGURE 11-7 Two prosthodontic appliances. (a) A speech bulb, or obturator, which facilitates complete closure of the velum when it is insufficient in length. (b) A palatal lift, which facilitates complete closure of a velum that is normal in length but of limited mobility.

geon in determining the timing of and necessity for secondary palatal repair.

THE ROLE OF THE SPEECH AND HEARING MEMBERS OF THE TEAM

1. The Speech-Language Pathologist. Like the members of the dental component, the speech-language pathologist's involvement may begin surprisingly early with cleft lip and palate children. Children with clefts of the hard or soft palate frequently have feeding problems before (and even following) surgical repair. This is because liquids taken into the mouth can leak into the nasal cavities and come out of the nose. Coughing, choking, limited food intake, and poor weight gain can all result. The speech-language pathologist, as the "feeding specialist" on the team, often works with the parents to establish feeding techniques and positions, and to introduce simple devices, that can improve the child's ability to channel liquids appropriately (Paradise and McWilliams, 1974).

Another early role of the speech-language pathologist is that of a language development consultant. Children with clefts that are part of a more extensive genetic syndrome are more likely to evidence cognitive disorders than are noncleft children (McWilliams and Witzel, 1994). As described in the previous chapter on cognitive disorders and pervasive developmental disorders, such children need early language stimulation in order to develop to their full potential. In addition, even cleft-palate children of normal intelligence are frequently somewhat language-delayed because of factors such as early hearing loss and poor ability to produce intelligible speech (McWilliams et al., 1990). Early language stimulation programs can be carried out effectively by parents in the home, with supervision and instruction from the speech-language pathologist.

Although the speech-language pathologist's role is initially one of a consultant, a more active role may be appropriate as the child enters the preschool years. Direct group language therapy often helps develop the social and pragmatic aspects of language. Also in the preschool years, the speech-language pathologist's role as diagnostician begins. The speech-language pathologist must be able to assess the child's speech and voice abilities accurately and determine the extent to which the child's physical defects interfere with her speech. Much of the surgical, orthodontic, and prosthodontic treatment planned for the child will have the specific goal of improving the child's speech intelligibility and resonance. The speech-language pathologist needs to continually re-assess the child's abilities, to determine the success of the surgical-dental treatment, and to make suggestions for further interventions.

Finally, in his or her role as therapist, the speech-language pathologist will work with the cleft-lip or cleft-palate child to improve her speech and voice quality. The therapist role may begin as early as the preschool years and will likely last through adolescence. The clinician must be especially sensitive to the child's effort

level in therapy and her subsequent progress over time in order to determine whether any continuing speech difficulties are due to physical limitations or to insufficient motivation. As noted by McWilliams and Witzel (1994, 477), "It is possible to spend an inordinate amount of therapy for only limited gains." If therapy is not effective, every effort should be made to determine the cause of the problem and to secure proper treatment, if possible. Ongoing interaction with other team members is clearly important in this regard.

2. The Audiologist. The *audiologist* is the professional responsible for determining a child's hearing status; he or she also serves as a source of information for the otolaryngologist and the speech-language pathologist. As a result of frequent audiological evaluations, for example, the audiologist might determine the presence of ongoing otitis media and refer the child to an otolaryngologist for medical treatment. Because ongoing hearing disorders have implications for speech and language development, it is important to keep the speech-language pathologist apprised of hearing status. According to McWilliams et al. (1990), hearing should be tested routinely every three to six months as long as any hearing problem is evident. Once the child's hearing has stabilized, audiological testing should continue to be done at least yearly until all other medical and surgical treatments are completed.

THE ROLE OF THE PSYCHOSOCIAL MEMBERS OF THE TEAM

The psychologist or social worker of the interdisciplinary team plays several important roles. The initial role of these professionals is often to help the parents of the cleft-palate child cope with the news of their newborn's handicap. Parents frequently react to the birth of a child with a physical defect with shock, anger, grief, anxiety, confusion, and depression (Clifford, 1973). According to Spriestersbach (1973), the type of information parents are given when they are first told of their child's disorder, and the way that the information is presented, has long-lasting effects on the parents' later feelings and on their success in developing coping mechanisms. The skillful psychologist or social worker can help the family through the initial trauma to an emotional acceptance of the child's condition.

As the child grows and develops, the psychologist may become active in testing the child for any suspected developmental or learning delays. As discussed previously, children who have a cleft lip or palate as part of a more extensive genetic syndrome are at greater risk for cognitive disorders of various degrees. The psychologist can monitor the child's developmental status and help guide the parents into early special education programs if necessary.

Finally, the psychologist or social worker may work directly with the child on feelings, attitudes, and coping strategies, if problems develop in these areas. Although there is no evidence that children with cleft lips or cleft palates are seriously emotionally disturbed, their experiences with nonaccepting teachers and peers can cause them to be withdrawn and inhibited (Williams et al., 1990). The psychologist or social worker may also interface with the child's school because "school adjustment is probably marginal for many children with clefts" (McWilliams et al., 1990, 135). If necessary, the psychologist or social worker can serve as an advocate for the child and provide information to school personnel regarding the child's disorder and its treatment.

CONSEQUENCES OF THE CLEFT LIP OR CLEFT PALATE TO THE INDIVIDUAL

We have already discussed a variety of possible psychological, social, and educational consequences of cleft lip or palate. Now let us examine this topic more systematically, to see what is currently known about the effects of a cleft on the child's development, personality, school adjustment, and future potential.

The parents' initial (and perhaps continuing) negative feelings toward the child with a cleft have been hypothesized to affect the child's early development. Most studies have shown that in the absence of other deformities, development prior to the age of 2 is generally within normal limits for children who have clefts of the lip or the palate (Plotkin et al., 1970; Starr et al., 1977). However, other researchers have noted that after the age of 2, these children tend to be "passive," reduced in imaginative play, less responsive to their mothers, and somewhat delayed in their overall development (Starr et al., 1977; Smith and McWilliams, 1966; Fox et al., 1978).

In terms of personality, most researchers agree that there is no particular "cleft-palate personality" (McWilliams and Witzel, 1994). Both Goodstein (1968) and Wirls (1971) found no evidence of continuing emotional disturbance in cleft lip or palate children although they "may have some problems with social acceptance." Despite these reassuring findings, McWilliams et al. (1990) cite additional studies and persistent clinical impressions of maladjustment, inhibition, and lack of emotionality. For example, Kapp-Simon (1986) found that children with clefts rated themselves less "acceptable" than did their peers, felt that they were more likely to require assistance, and reported more feelings of sadness and anger. Richman (1983) found elevated scores in social introversion, lack of feelings of self-worth, and excessive worry.

In short, there is some evidence that the residual facial deformity associated with postsurgical cleft palate and the possible speech differences do have an effect on the personalities of individuals with cleft lips or palates. These individuals must "cope with stresses that are less common in the lives of their peers" and, in the process, may "sacrifice something of their freedom to express themselves fully" (McWilliams et al., 1990, 135).

Unsurprisingly, fewer cleft lip and palate children than noncleft children liked school, volunteered to speak, liked their schoolmates, or wanted to continue their schooling after high school, according to a study done by Spriestersbach (1973). As previously discussed, the school adjustment of cleft-palate children is often poor, although school achievement is not markedly below average (Richman, 1976). In fact, individuals with cleft palates appear to attend and graduate from college with the same frequency as their noncleft siblings (McWilliams and Paradise, 1973), indicating that family patterns of education are more influential in determining a child's eventual level of education than is the cleft condition (McWilliams et al., 1990).

In terms of occupational status, McWilliams et al. concluded from their review of the literature that adults with cleft lips or cleft palates tended to make less money and derive less satisfaction from their jobs than did randomly selected control subjects. They also tended to aspire to higher-status jobs. It is interesting to note that the siblings of cleft-palate individuals showed some of the same characteristics, but to a lesser degree. McWilliams and her colleagues caution that more research needs to be done to assess the effects of cleft lip or palate, not only on the individual but on the family, and to determine whether the adult with a cleft lip or palate is truly limited in his job outlook.

CONSEQUENCES OF THE CLEFT LIP OR PALATE TO THE FAMILY

It is easy, and tempting, to blame the family for some of the negative psychological and social consequences that befall the individual with a cleft lip or cleft palate. For many years, psychiatrists have been blaming "cold, rejecting mothers" for various severe disabilities in their children (see our discussion in Chapter 4 about the causes of autism). However, we must be aware that the birth of a child with a cleft condition is more than simply an emotional trauma for a family: It is also a tremendous financial and physical burden.

The child with a cleft condition will require numerous surgeries, often within the first two years of life. The costs of hospitalization, doctors, and special supplies can be considerable, even for the well-insured. In addition, the child's parents must take time off from work, sometimes for extended periods, in order to care for the child, both during the hospital stay and in the delicate postsurgical period. This means transportation costs—often to medical centers in distant cities—and baby sitters for siblings. The worry associated

with these surgeries, and having to deal with an infant in pain postsurgically, can be exhausting.

The physical care of a cleft-palate child can also be daunting. Most children with cleft palates have early feeding difficulties due to leakage through their noses. They must be fed in small amounts at regular intervals. They are often hungry because of insufficient food intake and therefore tend to cry frequently. The normal insecurities parents feel in trying to satisfy the needs of any newborn are magnified when the child has a cleft condition. Finally, McWilliams and Paradise (1973) report that parents worry that because of the extra time and effort spent caring for the cleft-palate infant, other children in the family are neglected. It is difficult to determine how realistic this concern is.

Clearly, the emotional consequences of having a cleft-palate child are not the only ones that will affect a family. Parents would no doubt feel less sad, angry, and guilty if some relief from the financial burdens and the routine of care for the cleft-palate infant could be provided. It is important to remember that parents are feeling more than the "loss of the perfect child" (McCollum, 1984) when a child with a cleft condition is born to them. They are also trying to adjust to the new and chaotic lifestyle that the disability has brought them.

On the positive side, it must be realized that the extra care and financial burden will diminish with time. As the surgeries are completed and feeding becomes easier, the family unit can return to its more normal interactional patterns. Although speech and dental treatment may be ongoing, the extreme lifestyle changes experienced during the early years do fade. If the family can find appropriate support initially—from family, friends, agencies, and counselors—the long-term negative consequences may be minor.

SUMMARY

Cleft lip or cleft palate is a malformation of the oral area due to a disruption of normal development early in embryonic life. In some cases, the cleft is part of a more extensive genetic syndrome. In some cases, isolated clefts "run in the family." But in most cases, the cause of the disorder is unknown.

The child with a cleft lip and palate requires early surgical intervention to repair the defects. The lip is typically repaired first, within the first few months of life, while the palate may be repaired at some time within the first two years of life. It was once thought that early palatal closure would prevent the palate and midface region from growing and developing properly, but recent research has challenged this contention. In terms of speech development, early palatal closure actually facilitates the acquisition of normal speech patterns than are attained with closure past the age of 1 or 2.

Children with cleft lips and palates may have an abnormal appearance, speech disorders, hearing problems, dental deviations, and psychological adjustment difficulties. Because of the wide range of problems encountered in this disorder, children with cleft lips and palates are most effectively treated by an interdisciplinary team. Team members typically include a reconstructive surgeon and other medical specialists, an orthodontist and other dental specialists, a speech-language pathologist and audiologist, a psychologist, and a geneticist. These specialists try to address the problems of the child in infancy and in childhood with the goal of reducing the severity of the effects of the disorder on both the child and the parents.

The speech-language pathologist plays many roles with this population. He or she assists with early feeding, provides language programs if necessary, administers various tests and diagnostic procedures, and treats speech and resonance disorders. It is also the responsibility of the speech-language pathologist to consult the other members of the team if progress in speech is being limited by structural and functional constraints.

Most researchers have concluded that cleft-palate children do not suffer severe psychological maladjustment as a result of their disorder. However, the child may have some difficulty with social acceptance, may dislike school more than the average child, and may not achieve the occupational status later in life that noncleft-palate individuals attain. Families of cleft-palate children often have a difficult time adjusting to the child's defect in the early years and coping with the medical and surgical complications of the disorder later. However, once the lip or palate have been successfully repaired, family life becomes more normal, especially if the child has no other associated cognitive or learning problems. Supportive family, friends, and social agencies can help ease the transition for parents.

REVIEW QUESTIONS

1. What structures form the upper lip during the sixth through the eighth weeks of fetal development? Why does a cleft of the lip occur on one side or the other but not in the middle?

2. What structures form the hard and soft palates during the eighth through the twelfth weeks of fetal development? Describe the kinds of cleft conditions one might see if those structures failed to unite.

3. What are some of the causes of cleft lip and palate?

4. What disorders are often associated with cleft lip and palate?

5. Name the members of the interdisciplinary team that treat individuals with cleft lips and palates. Describe the role of each member of the team.

6. At what age is repair of the lip usually done? Repair of the hard and soft palates? What issues are important to consider in the timing of these surgeries?

7. Why do cleft-palate children often have hearing problems?

8. What are the consequences of a cleft lip or palate to the individual?

9. What are the consequences to the family when a child is born with a cleft lip or palate?

FOR FURTHER INFORMATION

Bzoch, K. (1989). *Communicative disorders related to cleft lip and palate* (3rd ed.). Austin, TX: Pro-Ed.

McWilliams, B., Morris, H., and **Shelton, R.** (1990). *Cleft palate speech* (2nd ed.). Philadelphia, PA: B. C. Decker.

Moller, K., and **Starr, C.** (1993). *Cleft palate: Interdisciplinary issues and treatment: For clinicians by clinicians.* Austin, TX: Pro-Ed.

Special Populations: Laryngectomy

The most severe voice disorder we will discuss is the *aphonia,* or loss of voice, that occurs as a result of a total laryngectomy. *Total laryngectomy* is the surgical removal of the entire larynx. As we discussed in Chapter 10, a laryngectomy is performed in response to laryngeal cancer. Its purpose is to save the life of the individual and prevent the further spread of cancerous cells. Although it is generally successful—the five-year survival rate for laryngeal cancer is approaching 90 percent, according to McKenna et al. (1991)—a laryngectomy is a life-altering operation. The individual's breathing and eating are affected, as are many other activities of daily living. Communication, especially, is compromised because the voice production mechanism is removed during the procedure. In the following chapter, we will discuss in greater detail the effects of a laryngectomy on an individual's anatomy and physiology and the consequences of this operation for communication and other activities. We will also examine the role of the speech-language pathologist in the rehabilitation of individuals who have undergone a laryngectomy.

WHO GETS CANCER OF THE LARYNX?

According to Rohe (1994), the typical patient with cancer of the larynx is a man over 50 years of age who is both a heavy smoker and a drinker. Statistics show that males more frequently have cancer of the larynx than females, with a ratio of approximately four men for every woman (Gra-

ham, 1983; Rohe, 1994). In terms of age of onset, Rohe reports that 64 percent of those with laryngeal cancer are diagnosed between the ages of 50 and 70, with a mean age of 59. However, age of onset can be much lower: Newman and Byers (1982) found thirty-three patients with laryngeal cancer in the age range of 5 to 34, with a mean age of 29. The American Cancer Society (1991) estimated that in 1991, approximately 12,500 new cases of laryngeal cancer would be diagnosed, up from 10,000 in 1980. This indicates that laryngeal cancer is a fairly common disease. And unfortunately, according to Lawson et al. (1989), the occurrence of laryngeal cancer appears to be increasing.

In summary, cancer of the larynx appears to be a relatively widespread disorder, albeit affecting males more than females and older individuals more than younger individuals. It is especially common in those who use both tobacco and alcohol. In fact, 50 to 70 percent of all oral and laryngeal cancer deaths are associated with cigarette smoking or a combination of smoking and drinking, although other factors may play a role as well (U.S. Department of Health and Human Services, 1982).

TREATMENT OPTIONS FOR CANCER OF THE LARYNX

As we briefly mentioned in Chapter 10, the type of treatment selected for laryngeal cancer usually depends on the location and extent of the *lesion,* or cancerous mass. Small and localized lesions, those that have not invaded the muscles underlying the vocal folds, may be treated with x-ray irradiation alone (Kowalski et al., 1993). In this type of treatment, patients undergo daily or weekly sessions in which x-rays are focused on the lesion, with the anticipated outcome of the lesion's destruction. Changes to the voice may occur as a result of the irradiation of the larynx (Colton et al., 1978), but these changes are mild compared to the effects of other treatments. If successful, radiation therapy destroys the cancerous mass while leaving the rest of the vocal mechanism relatively intact. According to Case (1991, 230), "the cure rate [for limited lesions] is from 85 to 96% by irradiation." However, other researchers have found a higher rate of cancer recurrence in those treated with radiation compared to those treated with surgery (Kowalski et al., 1993).

Somewhat more extensive lesions may require a combination of surgery and x-ray irradiation. Many levels of surgery are possible. For example, if only one vocal fold is involved and it is still movable (meaning that the tumor has not invaded the underlying muscle, causing the vocal fold to be stiffened and fixed), a *cordectomy* might be considered. This is when the true vocal fold alone is removed. A slightly more extensive procedure requires that the arytenoid cartilage on that side and the false vocal fold be taken as well.

In cases where the tumor is limited to one side of the larynx but has spread, at least superficially, to structures above and below the vocal fold, a procedure known as a *hemilaryngectomy* is performed. This operation involves removing all or most of the structures that comprise the larynx, but on one side only (one true vocal fold, one false vocal fold, half of the cricoid and thyroid cartilages, and so on). However, a hemilaryngectomy can interfere with the protective role of the larynx. Difficulties channeling food and liquid away from the airway and into the digestive tract frequently ensue after this type of surgery, putting the patient at risk for aspiration of foreign substances into the lungs (Flores et al., 1982).

The relatively conservative procedures described

above assume that the cancer (1) has been caught early and (2) is primarily localized on one vocal fold or the other. Unfortunately, neither assumption may be warranted in any given case. Many individuals ignore the early symptom of hoarseness and fail to consult a physician. Furthermore, those who do seek medical attention may be given medication for an upper respiratory infection and not examined thoroughly enough to detect the cancerous lesion. If laryngeal cancer has advanced beyond the early stages, more radical surgery may be required, and in this case, the patient's chances of long-term survival are reduced (Graham, 1983).

Like the first assumption, the second assumption is also frequently untrue. Laryngeal cancer is not always located on the vocal folds themselves. The site of lesion may be on or outside the epiglottis, in the throat below the vocal folds, on or above the false vocal folds, and so on. This is problematic, because a lesion that is not on the vocal folds is not likely to cause the early symptom of hoarseness and thus may not be investigated as soon. In addition, the more external parts of the larynx are rich in lymph glands and vessels (Graham, 1983). The lymph system, like the heart and blood vessels, circulates fluid throughout the body—in this case, lymphatic fluid. If cancer cells from lesions in the external part of the larynx find their way into the lymph system, the individual's cancer could spread to other organs and tissues in distant parts of the body. Thus, cancer of the larynx that is not detected early and that is not limited to the vocal folds can be a life-threatening disorder requiring extensive surgery.

The most extensive type of surgery performed to combat laryngeal cancer is a total laryngectomy. Because of the seriousness of this surgery, some writers call it *laryngeal amputation*. Total laryngectomy is considered when there is major involvement of both vocal folds or when the cancer extends above or below the vocal folds on both sides. It is also recommended when at least one vocal fold is so involved that it is fixed (as opposed to movable) or when the cancer has been detected in a more external part of the larynx, where there is a risk to the lymph system (McKenna et al., 1991).

Total laryngectomy consists of removal of all the structures in the neck, from the hyoid bone to the second or third tracheal cartilages. According to Salmon (1994a), the removed specimen includes the hyoid bone, the thyroid cartilage, the cricoid and arytenoid cartilages, the outer muscles of the neck (known as the *strap muscles*), the true and false vocal folds, the epiglottis, and the upper two or three rings of the trachea.

If the cancer has already spread to the lymph system, one additional surgical intervention may be attempted: radical neck dissection. This procedure, done at the same time as the patient's total laryngectomy, involves the removal of the lymph nodes on one or both sides of the neck, depending on the extent of the cancer. Since the lymph nodes are embedded in the muscle and connective tissue of the neck, numerous muscles of the neck and shoulder may be removed as well. Parts of the thyroid gland, one of the salivary glands, parts of several major blood vessels, and part of the spinal accessory nerve (11th cranial nerve) may also be sacrificed (Salmon, 1994a). The individual who has had radical neck dissection generally has more negative consequences to deal with following surgery than the individual who has had a total laryngectomy only, since the appearance of the neck will be more abnormal, and movement and feeling in the arm and shoulder may be impaired.

ANATOMY AND PHYSIOLOGY OF RESPIRATORY, PHONATORY, AND DIGESTIVE FUNCTIONS FOLLOWING TOTAL LARYNGECTOMY

As discussed in Chapter 10, the larynx serves an important protective function to the lower respiratory system in addition to its function as a sound generator for speech. The *upper respiratory tract*— the mouth and *pharynx* (or throat)—accommodates both the passage of air during breathing and the passage of food and liquids during eating. When we breathe, the epiglottis, false vocal folds, and true vocal folds remain in an open position, permitting air from the atmosphere to flow into the trachea and the lungs. When we eat, how-

ever, these laryngeal structures close to form a protective seal at the top of the trachea. Food and liquids are then shunted behind the trachea, into the esophagus and digestive tract, as pictured in Figure 12-1. The larynx thus acts as a gatekeeper for the respiratory and digestive systems so that they can share the use of the mouth and throat. Should the epiglottis and the true and false vocal folds fail in their protective function, permitting food or liquids to enter the respiratory tract, we cough reflexively to expel the foreign substance. If these substances actually get into the lower trachea and lungs, they can cause infection, pneumonia, and eventually death.

A person who has had a laryngectomy can no longer use his mouth and throat as a common passageway for breathing and eating. With his larynx removed, there is no natural valve to prevent food and liquid from getting into the lungs, a life-threatening situation. Thus, during the surgical removal of the larynx, the trachea and respiratory pathway must be rerouted. The surgeon bends the trachea forward, creates a hole at the base of the neck, and attaches the open trachea at that point. This hole, or *stoma,* is the passage through which the person subsequently breathes. Air from the outside enters the stoma through the shortened trachea on its way to the lungs. The mouth and throat, meanwhile, remain attached to the esophagus and the digestive tract. Thus, food and drink can safely be consumed, because there is a direct connection from the mouth to the stomach but no connection from the mouth to the trachea and respiratory system.

THE PHYSICAL ASPECTS OF LIFE WITHOUT A LARYNX

This new anatomical configuration has several major consequences to the individual. First, the individual can no longer breathe through his nose or mouth, because these structures lead only to the stomach. This diminishes the sense of smell because airborne particles no longer pass over the olfactory sensors in the nasal mucosa. The sense of taste is also reduced to some degree (Damste,

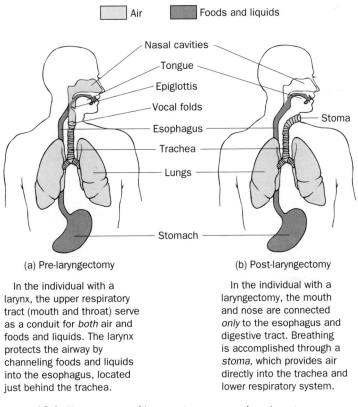

☐ Air   ▨ Foods and liquids

(a) Pre-laryngectomy

In the individual with a larynx, the upper respiratory tract (mouth and throat) serve as a conduit for *both* air and foods and liquids. The larynx protects the airway by channeling foods and liquids into the esophagus, located just behind the trachea.

(b) Post-laryngectomy

In the individual with a laryngectomy, the mouth and nose are connected *only* to the esophagus and digestive tract. Breathing is accomplished through a *stoma*, which provides air directly into the trachea and lower respiratory system.

FIGURE 12-1 The anatomy of laryngectomy pre- and post-surgery.

1994). Second, all air exchange is through the stoma; the warming, moisturizing, and cleansing functions of the upper respiratory tract are bypassed. Cold, dry air passes directly into the trachea and lungs, often irritating them. As a result, the individual with a laryngectomy is more prone to excessive mucus production *(secretions),* coughs, colds, and lower respiratory disorders (Gilmore, 1994). Further, when coughing or sneezing, the individual must remember to cover his stoma rather than his nose and mouth. Since the nose and mouth are no longer connected to the respiratory system, air and secretions are expelled through the stoma. This is initially very disconcerting to a *laryngectomee* (someone who has had a total laryngectomy).

The laryngectomee also faces a life of new hazards due to his altered respiratory anatomy. Bathing, swimming, and boating put the individ-

ual at risk for getting water into the stoma, and from there into the lungs. Even showering without a special protective covering for the stoma could be dangerous. The laryngectomee must also be careful to keep his neck free of any obstruction to breathing. And if the individual ever needs assistance with breathing, such as during a heart attack, mouth-to-mouth resuscitation would not work. Emergency personnel would need to realize that air should be directed into the laryngectomee's stoma instead of his mouth. Some laryngectomees wear medical alert tags saying "I am a neck breather" in case of just such an emergency.

Another complication of the laryngectomee's altered anatomy is a reduction in physical strength, especially if he has had radical neck dissection in addition to a total laryngectomy. During the surgical procedure to remove the larynx, some of the neck muscles are cut away. These muscles help to stabilize the shoulders and provide resistance to arm movement; when they are severed, the arms are less able to bear weight. In addition, the larynx itself helps to "fix" or stabilize the chest by preventing air escapage from the lungs and unnecessary rib movement during heavy lifting and pushing. The lack of ability to "fix" the chest also leads to a reduction in physical strength. These physical limitations may not be significant enough to effect the daily functioning of most laryngectomees, but for some, the limitations add to their feelings of hopelessness and helplessness (Gilmore, 1994).

Because of the extensive reconstruction in the throat and esophagus area during removal of the larynx, some laryngectomees experience difficulty with swallowing following surgery (Maragos, 1994). The thyroid and cricoid cartilages and hyoid bone are important points of attachment for many muscles involved in chewing and swallowing. When these supportive structures are removed, muscles must be rerouted and reconnected; as a result, they sometimes do not function as well. Scarring at the top of the esophagus may also leave a restricted opening, which interferes with normal food and liquid intake.

Finally, the altered anatomy and physiology of the laryngectomee is not conducive to the production of voice. As you recall from Chapter 10, voice production requires a stream of air to set the loosely approximated vocal folds into vibration. As the vocal folds vibrate, they cause sympathetic vibrations in the air in the various cavities of the vocal tract, giving the voice its resonance characteristics. Thus, normal voice production requires an air stream, a vibrating element, and a resonance chamber directly above it.

For the laryngectomee, exhaled air from the respiratory system is diverted outward through the stoma. This change is even more critical to the individual's voice production difficulties than the loss of the vibratory element (the vocal folds) itself. In fact, after the removal of the larynx, some of the muscles that are reattached at the top of the esophagus can actually function as "new" vocal folds. As long as these muscles retain enough mobility to close over the top of the esophagus and provide adequate resistance to upcoming air, they can function as the missing vibratory element. However, with no air stream to set these masses into vibration, voice production is not possible. As we shall learn later in this chapter, a major challenge for otolaryngologists and speech-language pathologists has been to devise a method for diverting exhaled air from the stoma into the esophagus so that muscle remnants at the top of the esophagus can be used to generate voice.

THE PSYCHOSOCIAL ASPECTS OF LIFE WITHOUT A LARYNX

The individual with a total laryngectomy may experience a number of psychological and social consequences in addition to the physical difficulties imposed by amputation of the larynx. Depression following the surgery is well-documented, especially after the laryngectomee is dismissed from the hospital and must suddenly cope with the lifestyle changes enforced by his altered anatomy (Bronheim et al., 1991). Some individuals are extremely self-conscious about the physical disfigurement associated with total laryngectomy and radical neck dissection (Boone and McFarlane, 1994). In fact, the neck scarring and stoma may be covered so well by ties, scarves, and high-necked clothing that the casual observer may not be aware of any disfigurement at all, but with family and marriage partners it may remain a problem. More serious is the worry that there will be a recurrence of the cancer. As mentioned earlier in this chapter, the five-year survival rate for individuals with laryngeal cancer is nearly 90 percent. However, of those survivors, some 32 percent develop additional cancers (American Cancer Society, 1991). Thus, the laryngectomee's tendency to worry about the future and additional bouts with cancer is sadly realistic.

Many laryngectomees have trouble returning to their previous employment and report financial loss as one of their primary problems following surgery. Lehmann and Krebs (1991) found that approximately half of the laryngectomees they studied lost their jobs as a result of their illness. After an extensive review of the literature, Richardson (1983) concluded that laryngectomees had more trouble returning to their preoperative employment or finding new jobs than did victims of any other type of cancer, probably due to their limited communication skills.

The laryngectomee's lack of a voice production mechanism, and subsequent difficulty in communicating, impacts life in many ways. We discussed the lack of ability to produce voice as one of the physical aspects of laryngectomy. However, the severe communication disorder resulting from laryngectomy is likely to produce psychological and social consequences as well. According to a review of the literature by Gilmore (1994), many laryngectomees report continuing acute embarrassment in some situations over their voice and speech, especially women. Since the fundamental frequency of both esophageal and tracheoesophageal voice is more suitable to the male range than the female range, female laryngectomees often feel angry and frustrated at the quality of their new voice. Individuals who have recently undergone laryngectomy have reported feelings of depression and dependency because of their limited communication abilities. Similarly, spouses reported feelings of loneliness and frustration at not being able to communicate with the individual at first, and noted that they had to be careful not to "baby" their laryngectomized spouse (Salmon, 1994b). In short, the loss of communication abilities affects the individual's psychological health and relationships as well as vocational potential. Restoration of audible speech is therefore an important priority for individuals who have undergone laryngectomy.

OPTIONS FOR RESTORING VOICE

Given the unfavorable anatomy for voice production, how can the laryngectomee produce audible speech? There are three primary methods: the artificial larynx, esophageal speech, and tracheoesophageal speech.

THE ARTIFICIAL LARYNX

An *artificial larynx* is a small device, usually battery-powered, that delivers a "buzz," or an artificial laryngeal tone, to the resonating cavities of the vocal tract. This buzz from the artificial larynx sets the air in the vocal tract into vibration, just as the tone generated by the vocal folds would under normal circumstances. The individual with a laryngectomy can then use his *articulators*—his tongue, lips, and so on—to form phonemes and words as he normally would.

If we break speech into its component parts (articulation, fluency, and voice), we see that the individual using an artificial larynx is articulating phonemes precisely, and stringing them together fluently, on his own. The function of the artificial larynx is to replace the voice component of speech, so that the spoken message can be produced audibly. Its externally produced vibrations eliminate the need for air coming up from the lungs to cause some structure in the throat to vibrate.

There are many different types of artificial larynges, but for the purposes of this text, we will divide them into two categories: (1) the neck type and (2) the mouth type. The neck type, as pictured in Figure 12-2, is usually roughly cylindrical, 4 to 6 inches in length, and at one end contains a vibrator that produces a buzz. The rest of the artificial larynx serves as a handle and receptacle for batteries. The laryngectomee holds the buzzing end of the device against his neck, positioning it carefully so that optimum resonance is achieved through the muscles and connective tissues overlaying his throat. If the buzz is resonating properly in his throat and oral cavity, he should be able to simply mouth words and "shape" the buzz into audible speech (Salmon, 1994c).

The mouth type of artificial larynx, also pictured in Figure 12-2, works on a similar principle of delivering a tone into the speaker's vocal tract. The most common units, according to Salmon (1994d, 157), consist of "a battery-powered pulse generator connected by a cord to a handheld tone generator." Sound is delivered into the mouth via a short plastic tube. Again, the laryngectomee

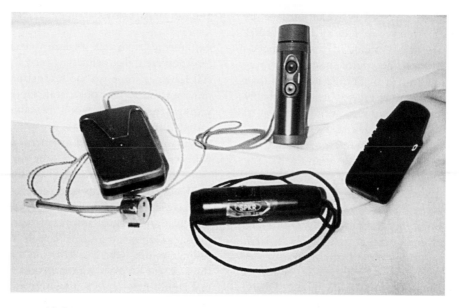

FIGURE 12-2 Four types of artificial larynges. The device on the left is a mouth-type artificial larynx, while the other three devices are of the neck type.

must position the tube so that maximum resonance is obtained. Then he simply articulates phonemes and words (whispering or voice production are not necessary) to form audible speech around the buzz.

Artificial larynges are useful for laryngectomees, but they have disadvantages as well as advantages. On the positive side, an artificial larynx of either type is relatively easy to use (Stemple, 1984). The laryngectomee generally needs to learn to articulate more clearly than usual, and to speak slowly in order to maximize his intelligibility. Sometimes it is also necessary to experiment with placement (Salmon 1994c). However, once these basic skills are mastered, the laryngectomee can speak almost as soon as surgery is over. This is reassuring to the patient as well as to his family, both of whom worry about how he will call for help if a medical emergency arises during the recovery period.

On the negative side, the buzz produced by the artificial larynx sounds, to many, unacceptably mechanical. Even modified by the resonance characteristics of the laryngectomee's throat and mouth, the voice produced by an artificial larynx does not sound natural (Stemple, 1984). In addition, the pitch contours a natural speaker uses to indicate declarative sentences and questions are difficult to achieve with an artificial larynx. Pitch fluctuations during ongoing speech are possible on many newer models, but are often difficult to control (Salmon, 1994c). Further, the neck type of artificial larynx may be difficult for some laryngectomees to use, especially if they have had radical neck dissection and are experiencing pain and swelling during the healing process. The mouth type may also be less than ideal. Placement of the tube can restrict movement of the tongue, and sometimes the collection of saliva in the tube delivering sound to the mouth can be a problem. According to Boone and McFarlane (1994, 218), "There has yet to be invented a totally satisfactory instrument that produces a pseudovoice for the laryngectomy patient . . . ."

Despite its disadvantages, the artificial larynx can be a useful device in restoring communication to the laryngectomee. It is generally introduced immediately after surgery and used in the postoperative period when other methods of voice restoration are being experimented with. For some laryngectomees, it is a transitional device, to be used only until esophageal speech is learned or until the individual can undergo additional surgery for a tracheoesophageal puncture and valve (both to be discussed later in this chapter). For others, it is a long-term solution to a severe communication disorder. The choice is usually up to the individual and his family.

ESOPHAGEAL SPEECH

For years, children have delighted in embarrassing their parents by burping loudly (and quite voluntarily) at inopportune moments. In order to accomplish this feat, the child must learn to relax the top of his or her esophagus so that a small quantity of air can be "pumped" in. This air is then forced back up, where it momentarily sets the top of the esophagus vibrating. A youngster who has perfected this technique is guaranteed parental attention, if only of the negative kind.

Esophageal speech requires exactly the same skill. In some respects, the process of taking air into the esophagus and forcing it back up is even easier for the laryngectomee, because he no longer has the complication of the larynx and the possibility that the air directed toward his esophagus will accidently go into the trachea and lungs, where it belongs.

Under optimal circumstances, the laryngectomee can use his esophagus as an "accessory lung" for the temporary storage of air (admittedly in very small quantities), and the muscles at the top of his esophagus can be used as a "neoglottis," or substitute for vocal folds. Air is taken into the esophagus using a variety of methods, and then the muscles at the top of the esophagus are closed loosely. When the individual forces air out of his esophagus, the loosely approximated muscles are set into vibration. The duration of that vibration, or *phonation,* is not very long because the esophagus is capable of accommodating only about 3 tablespoons of air (in comparison to the 3½ to 5 liters stored in the lungs). However,

for that brief interval, a voice is produced. If a laryngectomee articulates during those short voiced periods, he is using what we call *esophageal speech.*

As was the case with the artificial larynx, there are both advantages and disadvantages to this method of voice restoration. On the positive side, esophageal speech is a relatively natural method for a laryngectomee, requiring no devices or additional surgeries. On the negative side, esophageal speech can be very difficult to learn. Stemple (1984) states that it frequently takes six months or more for someone to develop a modest proficiency, and it may take years of practice, patience, and dedication to become a truly accomplished esophageal speaker. One extremely proficient esophageal speaker, often mistaken for a normal speaker, reported that it took him five years of intensive practice to develop his ability (Perkins, 1978).

It also appears that some laryngectomees cannot master this method. One group of researchers estimated that only about 30 percent of the total laryngectomee population can use esophageal speech well enough to meet their daily communication needs (Gates and Hearne, 1982), although Salmon (1994e) estimates a success rate closer to 64 percent. Failure with this method is often related to the specific anatomical changes that have occurred as a direct or indirect result of the laryngectomy. Esophageal speech requires an unimpaired segment of striated muscle at the top of the esophagus which the individual is capable of voluntarily opening for air intake and closing prior to air release. For some individuals, factors such as spasms in the esophagus, pharyngeal scarring, a narrowing of the top of the esophagus (known as *stenosis*), or damage to nerves supplying the muscles of the throat and esophagus interfere with the acquisition of esophageal speech.

For those who are physically able and sufficiently motivated, esophageal speech can be a good long-term solution to the problem of communication following a laryngectomy. However, it does not appear to be a solution for everyone. The speech-language pathologist needs to be able to help the laryngectomee explore this option without raising undue hopes or, alternatively, being overly discouraging.

TRACHEOESOPHAGEAL SPEECH

Most laryngectomees have a possible substitute sound source for the vocal folds that have been removed: the muscles remaining at the top of the esophagus. A major problem, however, is the air supply to drive this vibratory element. In esophageal speech, as we have just learned, air is taken into the esophagus and then forced back up to set these muscles into vibration. But this is more difficult than it sounds. Simply getting air into the esophagus is problematic for many speakers. In addition, the amount of air taken in is so limited that the generation of voice is difficult. If somehow air from the lungs could be diverted into the esophagus to drive the new sound source, the ease, duration, and quality of the resulting voice would surely be superior.

Ever since the late 1800s, otolaryngologists and, later, speech-language pathologists have been trying to come up with an acceptable way to rechannel air from the stoma into the esophagus. The easiest way would be to create a hole, or *fistula,* through the back of the trachea and into the front of the esophagus, thus creating a "window" between the two structures. This would allow air from the lungs to pass through the fistula and into the esophagus. In order to accomplish this change in airflow direction, a laryngectomee would have to block the stoma so that the air could not take the path of least resistance and escape through the larger stoma to the outside but would be forced to exit through the smaller fistula.

Unfortunately, an open fistula between the esophagus and the trachea would also channel saliva, food, and liquids into the respiratory system, causing infection and pneumonia. Thus, the simple idea of an open fistula between the trachea and the esophagus was not considered practical. Over the years, doctors tried a variety of devices and surgical reconstructive procedures, but none were able to solve the problem of food and liquid leakage successfully. In addition, the surgically created structures between the esophagus and the trachea tended to either break down or close up (Stemple, 1984).

In 1979, Eric Blom, a speech-language pathologist, and Mark Singer, an otolaryngologist, came out with the first device to successfully maintain a passageway between the esophagus and the trachea without leaking. The device, known as the Blom-Singer® Voice Prosthesis, or "duckbill," is pictured in Figure 12-3. The duckbill is inserted into a fistula that has been surgically created at the back of the stoma, and extends into the esophagus. The fistula can be created at the same time as the laryngectomy is performed or, if the patient and surgeon so decide, at a later date, when the initial healing from the laryngectomy is complete.

As described above, the fistula provides a window between the trachea and esophagus so that air in the lungs can ultimately be channeled to the muscles at the top of the esophagus, which will vibrate to produce the laryngectomee's new voice. The design of the duckbill prevents saliva, food, and liquid from flowing backward into the respiratory system. How? A valve slit on the tip of the duckbill opens in response to incoming air pressure but remains closed during eating and swallowing.

In order to force air through the duckbill and into the esophagus, the laryngectomee must firmly close off the stoma. Initially, this was done with the thumb or index finger. When air from the lungs is prevented from escaping through the stoma, it is forced into the duckbill, where it blows the valve slit open. Air then flows into the esophagus, where it can cause the upper esophageal segment to vibrate. The vibratory element is the same for both esophageal speech and tracheoesophageal speech. The difference between these two voice-restoration methods is that with esophageal speech, voice is powered by the limited amount of air taken into the esophagus. With tracheoesophageal speech, voice is powered by the air in the lungs.

Numerous individuals and companies have since come up with designs similar to the original Blom-Singer® Voice Prosthesis. Modifications

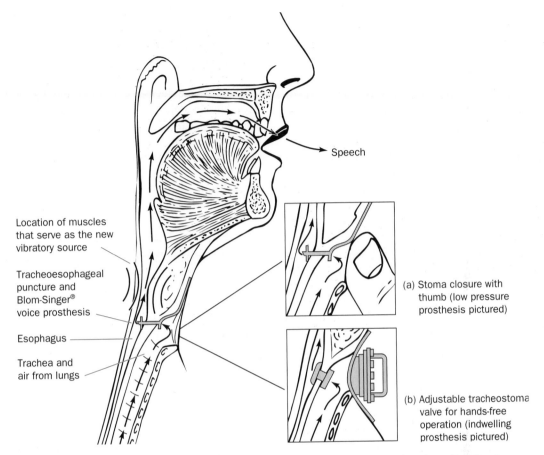

Speech

Location of muscles that serve as the new vibratory source

Tracheoesophageal puncture and Blom-Singer® voice prosthesis

Esophagus

Trachea and air from lungs

(a) Stoma closure with thumb (low pressure prosthesis pictured)

(b) Adjustable tracheostoma valve for hands-free operation (indwelling prosthesis pictured)

FIGURE 12-3 A Blom-Singer® tracheoesophageal voice prothesis in place. Note that the patient has to either (a) occlude the stoma with the thumb or (b) use an automatic valve that permits breathing, but closes when speech is desired. (Courtesy of InHealth Technologies, Inc.)

over the years have made it more effective and easier to use. Currently, most voice prostheses also come with a pressure-sensitive valve that fits into the stoma. The laryngectomee no longer has to occlude the stoma with a finger; the valve closes automatically in response to the rapid outrush of air that occurs prior to phonation. The valve remains open during the lower-pressure inhalations and exhalations associated with breathing.

In terms of advantages, the success rate for achieving good, clear speech with a voice prosthesis is high. Fukutake and Yamashita (1993)

found that 68 percent of their patients were able to produce tracheoesophageal voice immediately after surgery and that about 82 percent eventually used their voice prostheses successfully on a daily basis. Case (1991, 267) calls the device "a remarkable advancement in voice restoration after laryngectomy." Problems with air intake, so prominent in esophageal speech, are eliminated by the use of the lungs to power the individual's phonation. And although some training in the use of the device is necessary, successful voice production occurs almost immediately.

There is some dispute in the literature as to

whether or not tracheoesophageal speech is superior to conventional esophageal speech. In spite of the fact that both esophageal and tracheoesophageal speech rely on the same vibratory mechanism (the upper segment of the esophagus), some claim that tracheoesophageal speech produces better intelligibility and voice quality (Singer et al., 1981; Robbins et al., 1984; Doyle et al., 1988). Other research has indicated that when listeners compare excellent esophageal speakers and tracheoesophageal speakers, there are no preferences for one type of speaker over the other (Sedory et al., 1989). However, when one considers the time required to become an excellent esophageal speaker, and the relative ease of good voice production using a voice prosthesis, the advantages of the latter are clear.

On the negative side, the voice prosthesis cannot be used by everyone. Stemple (1984) cites difficulties with diabetic patients and chronic alcoholics. According to Singer et al. (1989), the stoma must be well healed, of an appropriate size, and the laryngectomee must be capable of the careful personal hygiene that is necessary to maintain the device. Most models must be removed and cleaned frequently, and individuals who are unable or unwilling to do so are not good candidates. This includes patients who have arthritis of the hands, even mild dementia, psychological instability, chronic lung disease, or low motivation to communicate. However, the most recent type of prosthesis, an indwelling model, may eliminate some of these limitations.

There is also the cost to consider. An additional surgical procedure or second surgery may not be covered by the individual's insurance because creation of the fistula may be considered "elective" surgery. For some, the cost may be prohibitive. Finally, as with esophageal speech, the individual's new anatomy may be problematic. If the individual experiences spasms in the upper esophageal segment, neither esophageal nor tracheoesophageal speech will be possible. In such cases, the upper esophagus closes too forcefully to permit vibration. However, new surgical procedures to release such spasms have been used suc-

cessfully (Case, 1991), and this is no longer considered as important an obstacle as it once was.

In short, tracheoesophageal speech and the use of voice prostheses have been a major development in the area of voice restoration for laryngectomees. These devices appear to provide relatively good intelligibility and voice quality at least to the level of superior esophageal speech, but without the months and years of practice. Although not everyone is a good candidate for a voice prosthesis, and the procedure is costly, tracheoesophageal speech is used successfully by many.

THE ROLE OF THE SPEECH-LANGUAGE PATHOLOGIST

The speech-language pathologist plays an important role in the rehabilitation of laryngectomees. Because so many of the laryngectomee's needs revolve around communication, the speech-language pathologist is frequently involved in the individual's care from the presurgical period through months, possibly years, after surgery.

PREOPERATIVE COUNSELING

The speech-language pathologist may be asked to speak to the individual and spouse about the communication options they will have even before the surgery occurs. Preoperative counseling is not done universally, but if the surgeon and patient request it, the clinician becomes involved at this point. It is highly desirable to do so, from the point of view of the speech-language pathologist, because it gives him or her a chance to meet the patient, assess the patient's presurgical communication abilities, and establish a relationship of trust prior to the trauma of surgery. It also gives the clinician a chance to allay any fears the patient has that he may never be able to speak again and give him a more realistic idea of what to expect after surgery. Patients may be given literature from the American Cancer Society or the International Association of Laryngectomees (IAL), an organization of and for laryngectomees that provides support, referrals, and information. In some cases, a laryngectomized speaker from the community also attends a part of this initial session, again to reassure the individual that there is life after laryngectomy (Salmon, 1994b).

POSTOPERATIVE COUNSELING

Immediately after any surgery, the primary concern is that the patient survive the early postsurgical period and begin the healing process. Complete bed rest for a day or two is usually required. As the patient gains strength and begins eating, moving, and walking again, the surgeon may give the go-ahead for speech therapy to begin. Ideally, this is done before the individual is discharged from the hospital (Boone and McFarlane, 1994).

During the initial session, usually about two weeks postsurgery (Case, 1991), the speech-language pathologist may introduce the artificial larynx and instruct the patient on how to use it. Case also recommends that the patient be introduced to esophageal speech during the first session. If the patient has had a *tracheoesophageal puncture* (creation of a fistula) at the time of the laryngectomy and has received a voice prosthesis, the care and use of the device should be explained. The first session may have to be brief so as not to tire the patient, but the speech-language pathologist should leave the patient with positive feelings about his eventual ability to communicate.

OUTPATIENT THERAPY

The final phase of the speech-language pathologist's intervention begins when the laryngectomee leaves the hospital and starts to see the clinician for speech therapy on an outpatient basis. This stage may last for weeks, months, or even years, depending on the type of voice restoration the client has selected and his or her need for continued counseling. If the client has decided to work on esophageal speech, the course of therapy will

be much longer than if an artificial larynx or voice prosthesis is used. Even with the latter two methods, however, the individual might need some instruction in articulation and phrasing to improve intelligibility. Some speech-language pathologists run speech-improvement groups for laryngectomees under the auspices of the American Cancer Society or IAL. Occasionally, they run support groups as well, where laryngectomees meet to discuss their problems and their progress in general.

In this writer's experience, the involvement of the speech-language pathologist often extends beyond speech and communication disorders. As the professional with whom the laryngectomee has the most contact on an ongoing basis, speech-language pathologists are often asked for information regarding wearing apparel, stoma covers, and other devices the laryngectomee has heard of and believes might be helpful. They are also asked numerous questions regarding the laryngectomee's physical state: what to do about excessive secretions, how to suction the stoma, and so on. While speech-language pathologists must necessarily refer many of the health-related questions on to the laryngectomee's physician, they may find themselves becoming a referral source for items and services far beyond the scope of speech.

THE ROLE OF THE FAMILY

The families of laryngectomees face much the same challenges as any family with a handicapped member. On the one hand, they must recognize the limitations of the individual and adjust their demands and expectations to realistic levels. For example, a spouse who believes that successful rehabilitation means the laryngectomee will speak and otherwise function exactly as she did prior to the surgery is doomed to disappointment. Such expectations interfere with healthy adjustment and accommodation to the new situation. On the other hand, the family must be careful not to "baby" the laryngectomee to the point that he or she is not encouraged to take on new challenges and develop new abilities. Such a situation is equally undesirable because it makes the laryngectomee feel dependent and incompetent. The balancing act between accepting the individual's limitations and demanding effort and new-skill development in rehabilitation is not easy for any family (Gilmore, 1994).

The spouses of laryngectomees must also cope with their own feelings of fear and apprehension regarding the possible recurrence of the cancer, the family's ability to meet its financial obligations, and their own abilities to care for their spouses. According to Salmon (1994b), the spouses of laryngectomees whom she interviewed would have appreciated an opportunity to visit with the spouse of another laryngectomee prior to the operation and would have appreciated more information about how to deal with swallowing difficulties, coughing and choking, the need for a humidifier, and other topics. Salmon also mentions their continuing concern with communication, especially in the early days at home.

Amputation of the larynx affects not only the individual who has had the operation but also the family and spouse. Many of the questions and problems that arise are the result of the laryngectomee's altered anatomy and new physical limitations. But the loss of a means of communication, at least initially, is also a very serious problem. The speech-language pathologist who works with this population needs to be (1) aware of the problems her client is facing, (2) knowledgeable about laryngectomy itself, and (3) able to make appropriate referrals when necessary.

SUMMARY

Laryngectomy is a surgical procedure usually performed to treat cancer of the larynx and to prevent (to whatever extent possible) its spread to other parts of the body. In performing a total laryngectomy, the surgeon removes the patient's entire larynx, including the vocal folds. The patient's trachea is then rerouted to a hole at the base of the neck called a *stoma,* through which all breathing will take place for the rest of the patient's life. The mouth, nasal passages, and throat will connect only to the esophagus. Breathing through the mouth and nose after laryngectomy is no longer physically possible.

Having a laryngectomy affects many aspects of an individual's life. Restrictions on certain activities, a reduction in physical strength, swallowing disorders, and communication problems are all common. Psychological and social consequences may occur as well, such as depression, job loss, and marital problems.

The laryngectomee has three major options for postsurgical communication: (1) an artificial larynx, (2) esophageal speech, or (3) tracheoesophageal speech using a voice prothesis. Of these, the tracheoesophageal method, which involves a surgically created connection between the trachea and esophagus, appears to be the most satisfactory in terms of the quality of voice and the ease of learning. Both the speech-language pathologist and the family have an important role in making sure that the survivor of cancer of the larynx reestablish communication skills and develop a positive attitude toward active participation in the rehabilitation process.

R E V I E W   Q U E S T I O N S

1. At what point in the life cycle is cancer of the larynx most common? Is it more likely to be seen in males or females?
2. How is cancer of the larynx treated? In what cases are conservative procedures more likely to be used? Which cases will require extensive surgery? Why?
3. What is *radical neck dissection*?
4. Draw the laryngeal-esophageal relationship before and after laryngectomy.

5. Besides loss of the ability to produce voice, and hence loss of the ability to speak, what other effects might a laryngectomy have on an individual?

6. What are three methods of voice restoration following laryngectomy? What are the advantages and disadvantages of each?

7. Describe the role of the speech-language pathologist during the preoperative period, in the immediate postoperative period, and in terms of rehabilitative care.

8. What challenges must be faced by the family, in particular the spouse, of the individual who has had a laryngectomy?

FOR FURTHER INFORMATION

Edels, Yvonne (1983). *Laryngectomy: Diagnosis to rehabilitation.* London: Croom Helm.

Keith, Robert L. and **Darley, Frederic L.** (Eds.) (1994). *Laryngectomy rehabilitation,* (3rd ed.), Austin, TX: Pro-Ed.

Adult Neurological Disorders

I n the minds of many, communication disorders are associated with childhood. Indeed, a large percentage of language and phonological deficits are *developmental* in nature; i.e., they affect a child's emerging linguistic skills. However, language and phonological disorders can be acquired in adulthood as well, after a lifetime of normal communication abilities. In this chapter, we will focus on such acquired disorders of speech and language.

It is sometimes difficult to believe that an adult who has been a normal communicator all of his or her life could suddenly have trouble with language comprehension, sentence construction, phonological selection and sequencing, or speech production. Yet this type of disability happens to tens of thousands of older adults each year, usually as a result of damage to the brain or the neuromotor system. In this chapter, we will discuss the various types of communication disorders experienced by adults, their specific causes and treatments, and how families and professionals can work with and around these disorders. As usual, we will begin with a summary of normal communication development.

COMMUNICATION AND THE NORMAL AGING PROCESS

How does aging affect communication functions? What constitutes normal communication development as an individual ages? If we look specifically at the broad areas of hearing, speech, and

language, we see that hearing is the most negatively affected by normal aging. According to Alpiner et al. (1993), over 30 percent of all those over the age of 65 have some degree of hearing impairment. In addition to reduced sensitivity of hearing, older individuals may also need more time to process auditory information. This increase in processing time means that rapidly presented auditory information, particularly speech, may be somewhat more difficult to understand for an older individual. However, speech that is both adequately loud and appropriate in terms of rate should permit normal comprehension performance for the aging adult (Peach, 1987).

Speech functions do not appear to be as negatively affected as hearing functions by advancing age. For example, articulation is generally agreed upon as remaining adequate. According to Sonies (1987, 193), "In the normal elderly individual there are few, if any, effects on speech articulation caused by alterations in oral-facial structure or function (as a result of the aging process)."

It should be noted that voice, one of the elements of speech, does appear to be influenced to a somewhat greater degree than articulation. Older individuals tend to have more roughness, tremor, breathiness, and pitch instability in their voices (Kent and Burkard, 1981; Shipp and Hollien, 1969). These changes do not generally interfere with intelligibility, though, and, while noticeable, are usually quite mild. Research by Ramig and Ringel (1983) indicates that an individual's physical health and fitness may have a greater effect on acoustic measures of vocal efficiency than age per se.

The language abilities of normally aging adults can be looked at from a variety of perspectives. As we have already discussed, since auditory processing time is longer for the elderly, language comprehension suffers to some degree if speech is rapid. In a review of the literature, Peach (1987) found that other factors may also reduce language comprehension. For example, older adults may have trouble processing complex sentences and drawing inferences from the speech of others. However, Peach also cited research demonstrating that the elderly are often able to compensate for these deficits by using context cues and grammatical redundancy. Thus, although language comprehension ability declines to some degree with age, it is not markedly imparied in normally aging adults.

In contrast to language comprehension, which is made more difficult by auditory disorders, expressive language does not appear to be affected much by age. Word usage and vocabulary knowledge generally do not decrease until after the age of 70 (Katzman and Terry, 1983). *Syntactic abilities,* or proficiency in generating complex, grammatically correct sentences, also does not appear to deteriorate with age. In fact, older subjects' written productions may contain even more complex sentences than those of younger subjects (Obler and Albert, 1981).

And what about *cognitive abilities,* or the individual's ability to think logically and respond appropriately to the environment? Although cognition is not generally considered an element of communication, it is clearly an important prerequisite to the communication process. One way to assess cognitive abilities is to look at performance on tests of intelligence as the individual matures and ages. Based on an extensive review of the literature, Robertson-Tchabo and Arenberg (1987) concluded that intelligence scores remain relatively stable until the age of 60, at which point some declines are seen, although variability among subjects is large. Performance on non-timed tests tends to be superior to test that include an element of time pressure, and they show less

change over time. Test scores do not appear to decline significantly until the age of 75 (Jarvik and Bank, 1983). Robertson-Tchabo and Arenberg (1987) go on to cite studies revealing deficits in specific cognitive skills, such as the learning and retrieval of new information and memory capacity. Despite these failing abilities, however, normally aging individuals appear to maintain relatively good performance on tasks requiring a variety of cognitive skills.

In summary, the primary deficit in communication among the normally aging is in the area of hearing. Both acuity and speed of processing of auditory information are reduced, thus causing some difficulties in hearing and understanding speech. It should be noted, however, that these deficits can usually be compensated for so that most normally aging individuals are able to understand and respond appropriately in conversational situations. Speech and expressive language functions, by contrast, do not appear to be negatively affected, with the possible exception of voice quality. And in terms of cognitive abilities, little decline in performance is seen until the end of the eighth decade of life. According to Boone and Plante (1993, 146), "Despite some hearing and visual decrements with increasing age, the typical older person communicates quite effectively."

BRAIN FUNCTIONS IN SPEECH, LANGUAGE, AND COGNITION

From the preceding discussion of hearing, speech, language, and cognitive abilities over a life span, it would seem that communication disorders should not be frequent in those who are aging normally, with the exception of disorders directly related to hearing loss. In fact, when an adult acquires a speech or language problem, it is generally due to an injury or disease affecting the brain or the neuromotor system. The location of the damage determines, to a large extent, the symptoms of the disorder. In order to understand the relationship between neurological injuries or diseases and the speech, language, or cognitive disorders that result from them, we must first appreciate how the various parts of the brain function in the communication process.

HEMISPHERES

Since the late 1700s, we have known that the brain is divided into two halves, or *hemispheres*. This division is most apparent when one looks at the surface of the brain, but in fact the hemispheres are internally connected to one another via a large body of fibers known as the *corpus callosum*. The two halves appear very similar to one another, and in fact, each hemisphere contains a full set of neurological processing centers that govern the motor and sensory functions of the body. In general, the left hemisphere controls the activities of the right side of the body, and the right hemisphere controls the left side of the body (Murdoch, 1990).

Despite the similarity between the two cerebral hemispheres, there are some important differences between them. For example, one hemisphere is usually considered dominant, and the other nondominant, for specific functions. In right-handed individuals (93 percent of the population), the dominant hemisphere is almost always the *left* hemisphere. Even in the 7 percent of the population that is left-handed, it is estimated that 70 percent are also left dominant. Of the remaining 30 percent of left-handed individuals, 15 percent are truly right dominant while the other 15 percent may show a pattern of mixed dominance (Davis, 1993).

Since 1861 and the pioneering research of Paul Broca, language functions have been attributed to the left, or *dominant,* hemisphere of the brain. Additional research over the years, particularly by Sperry and his colleagues in the 1970s and 1980s, suggests that the right (or *nondominant*) hemisphere is responsible for spatial, tactile, and constructional tasks. There has been speculation that the left hemisphere is "logical, analytical and verbal" while the right is "intuitive, holistic and perceptual-spatial" (Love and Webb, 1992, 168).

This apparent dichotomy of function between the two hemispheres should be approached with some caution, however, as Love and Webb note. It is highly unlikely that only one hemisphere of the brain functions during some tasks while the opposite hemisphere exclusively controls others. The corpus callosum provides extensive communicating pathways between the two hemispheres, and it is more likely that for any given task, both hemispheres are involved, perhaps in a sequential way (Molfese et al., 1983; Gelfer, 1987). However, it is equally undeniable that injuries and diseases that affect the left (or dominant) hemisphere of the brain result in language disorders, while those affecting only the right (or nondominant) hemisphere do not. For the majority of the population, then, an intact left hemisphere is extremely important to normal language functioning.

CORTICAL LOCALIZATION OF FUNCTION

Although the left hemisphere of the brain is dominant for language in most cases, it is also true that different locations within that hemisphere appear to be specialized for different aspects of language. In addition, other cortical centers also contribute to the communication process through their roles in mediating sensation, perception, cognition, memory, and voluntary movement. Let us now delineate the major divisions of the cortex and the functions that have been attributed to them. We will assess each cortical area for its contribution to communication and examine the effects of damage to each area on the communication process.

Recall from Chapter 8 that we defined the *cerebral cortex* as the wrinkled-looking surface of the brain, arranged into various hills and valleys known as *gyri* and *sulci*. Figure 13-1 is a side view of the cerebral cortex, along with the landmarks described in Chapter 8. The major cortical areas are also labeled.

1. Frontal Lobe. The *frontal lobe* is the part of the brain in front of the central sulcus. Its lower border is the lateral sulcus (see Figure 13-1). The *posterior,* or back part, of the frontal lobe contains the motor areas of the brain, including the pre-

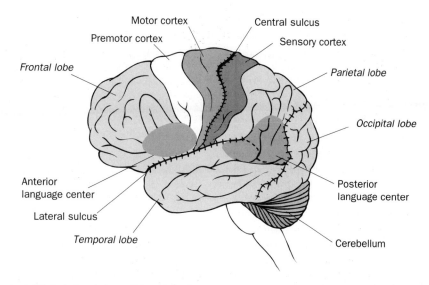

FIGURE 13-1 Lateral view of the cerebral cortex. The front (anterior aspect) of the brain is on the left, and the back (posterior aspect) of the brain is on the right.

motor cortex and motor cortex. These structures are associated with preparation for, planning, and execution of voluntary movement. Injury to these parts of the frontal lobe causes *spasticity* (abnormal muscle tone in response to stretch), weakness, or paralysis. The specific part of the body affected by these motor abnormalities depends on the location of the damage within the motor or premotor areas. If the damage occurs in the areas of the frontal lobes that control the lips, tongue, jaw, or larynx, a speech disorder can result (Love and Webb, 1992).

In addition to its role in motor movement, the frontal lobe appears to serve other functions as well. The *anterior* (front) part of the frontal lobe, known as the *prefrontal region,* is associated with "abstract thinking, foresight, mature judgment, tactfulness, and forbearance" (Gilman and Winans, 1982, 182). Injury to this part of the brain would be expected to result in *cognitive disorders,* or disorders of intellectual ability.

Finally, there is an area at the lower part of the frontal lobe, just above the lateral fissure, called the *anterior language area.* The anterior language area is at the base of the motor cortex, adjacent

to the lower prefrontal region, and may extend into the lateral fissure. Its lower border is the *temporal lobe,* a part of the brain associated with auditory functioning (which we will discuss later). Unlike the motor control areas and prefrontal area, this specific structure is generally seen only in the dominant hemisphere.

The anterior language area appears to be specialized for the motor planning of phoneme production and expressive language—not surprising, given its location near the motor cortex. However, damage to this area does not result in weakness and spasticity. Instead, an individual is likely to have difficulty selecting and sequencing phonemes, and, depending on the extent of the damage, formulating grammatical sentences (Mateer, 1989).

2. Parietal Lobe. Behind the central sulcus is a major division of the cortex known as the *parietal lobe.* It extends from the central sulcus backward, although it does not include the most *posterior* (back) part of the brain. The part of the parietal lobe directly behind the central sulcus is known as the *sensory cortex.* It is associated with a wide variety of sensations from the surface of the body, the muscles, and the joints. Touch, pressure, pain, heat or cold, position of the body in space, and similar sensations are received and interpreted in this part of the brain (Love and Webb, 1992). A parietal-lobe lesion close to the central sulcus results in an inability to interpret such sensations.

The back and lower portion of the parietal lobe, where it borders the occipital and temporal lobes, contributes to the *posterior language area.* In this area of the brain, sensory information from the various senses (touch, vision, hearing) is integrated and associated. This confluence of sensory impressions has been hypothesized to permit the formation of stable concepts and the attachment of symbolic labels to such concepts—the basis of language (Murdoch, 1990). Not surprisingly, the posterior language area is important to the perception and interpretation of spoken and written language. Damage to this part of the parietal lobe could result in a receptive language disorder and difficulty formulating "internal linguistic concepts" (Love and Webb, 1992, 184).

3. Temporal Lobe. The temporal lobe is located below the lateral sulcus, just below the frontal and parietal lobes. This part of the brain is primarily associated with the reception and interpretation of auditory stimuli. Like the parietal lobe, it contributes to the posterior language area and thus is important in the interpretation of spoken language.

Damage to the upper and central portion of the temporal lobe, just below the lateral sulcus, could result in *cortical deafness,* a condition in which the individual is unaware of auditory stimuli despite a normal hearing mechanism. With more diffuse damage, generalized auditory perceptual disorders, where an individual has difficulty interpreting various types of sounds, can also occur. Damage specifically to the posterior language area at the upper back part of the temporal lobe will affect an individual's ability to understand and use language.

4. Occipital Lobe. The posteriormost part of the brain is the occipital lobe. This part of the brain is located behind the parietal and temporal lobes. Its primary functions are visual reception and visual association. Like the parietal and temporal lobes, the occipital lobe contributes to the posterior language area. Damage to the central part of the occipital area can cause *cortical blindness,* a condition where the individual is unable to see despite normal eyes and visual nerves. Damage to more peripheral parts of the occipital area can cause visual field defects, where an individual is unable to see objects to the left, right, above, or below eye level. Other disorders of the occipital lobe can cause difficulty in making visual associations and difficulty in interpreting written language.

SUBCORTICAL FUNCTIONS

As we discussed in Chapter 8, the wrinkled gray surface of the brain, or the *cortex,* is only an inch or so thick. Directly beneath the cortex are a variety of subcortical structures. These include: (1) tightly packed white nerve fiber bundles that carry messages from one part of the brain to the other and transmit information to and from the body's surface, muscles, and organs; (2) the *basal ganglia,* a collection of neural processing centers with numerous connections to the cortex; (3) the various structures of the brainstem; and (4) the cerebellum. These subcortical structures—nerve fiber tracts, basal ganglia, brainstem components, and the cerebellum—are extremely important to an individual's motoric, sensory, and cognitive functioning. They may also play a role in processing language, suppressing neural activity in non-language areas of the cortex during linguistic tasks, and arousing cortical language centers (Mateer, 1989). Clearly, subcortical damage could result in a wide array of disorders involving language, cognition, and speech.

Of all the disorders that could result from subcortical damage, motoric and speech problems *(dysarthria)* have been the most extensively documented. You will recall from Chapter 8 that dysarthria is a speech disorder caused by damage to the neuromotor system. One common subcortical site for damage is the white nerve fiber bundles leading away from the motor and premotor areas. These fiber bundles, called *upper motor neurons,* carry motor commands from the cortical motor areas to lower processing centers in the basal ganglia, cerebellum, brainstem, or spinal cord.

If upper motor neurons are damaged, the individual's speech musculature could be affected by weakness, paralysis, or spasticity. These symptoms are similar to what one would see if the motor or premotor areas themselves were damaged. The individual's speech might be slow, slurred, hypernasal, weak, or strained, depending on which specific pathways were damaged.

Another common subcortical site for damage is the *lower motor neurons,* nerve fibers that originate where the upper motor neurons end in the brainstem or spinal cord, and that carry motor commands out to the muscles. Damage to the lower motor neurons results in weakness or paralysis of a specific muscle or muscle group. If the affected lower motor neurons are those that supply the speech musculature, imprecise, weak, breathy speech might result.

In contrast, lesions of the basal ganglia result in involuntary movements that interrupt and interfere with speech production. The voice may have a tremor to it, and speech may be unusually rapid. Cerebellar damage often causes badly distorted vowels and consonants because the individual has difficulty with coordination of the tongue and lips and tends to overshoot or undershoot articulatory targets (Darley et al., 1975). Speech-language pathologists who specialize in adult neurological disorders must learn to recognize different patterns of articulation, voice, and fluency symptoms and relate them to different levels of motor involvement.

Finally, we must also acknowledge the contribution of subcortical structures to cognitive processing. In order for the prefrontal area to reason, remember, use logic, and so on, it must be able to receive and transmit information from and to all parts of the brain. If the white nerve fiber bundles and processing centers that relay such information are damaged through injury or disease, a cognitive disorder can result.

COMMUNICATION DISORDERS IN ADULTHOOD

In the preceding section, we discussed the functions of various parts of the brain and noted whether speech, language, or cognitive disorders would be likely to result from an injury to that part. In the following section, we will examine the most common types of communication disorders seen in adults in terms of their characteristics, causes, and treatment. Specifically, we will look at (1) aphasia; (2) right-hemisphere damage; (3) dysarthria; (4) dementia; and (5) traumatic brain injury.

APHASIA

When an adult acquires a specific disorder of language comprehension and verbal expression as a result of brain injury, we call that disorder *aphasia* (Wertz, 1984). Aphasia might be compared to the communication disorder you yourself would experience if you were suddenly to find yourself in the middle of Berlin, Tokyo, or Kabul—anywhere where the language was unfamiliar to you. Your thought processes would continue to be normal, and your physical ability to speak would be unimpaired, but you nevertheless would have great difficulty communicating because of your inability to understand or speak the language. Similarly, individuals with aphasia are generally believed to think normally and are physically capable (in most cases) of producing speech. Their difficulty lies in their reduced ability to decode and encode language.

Aphasia is caused by damage to the anterior language area, the posterior language area, or both areas, in the dominant cerebral hemisphere. Typically, the individual's use of both the printed word and the spoken word are affected. The aphasic individual who has trouble understanding speech also has difficulty with reading comprehension, and the person unable to select and sequence phonemes during speech has similar problems when trying to write a word.

1. Characteristics. There are three primary types of aphasia: nonfluent, fluent, and global (adapted from Mateer, 1989). Let us consider the characteristics of these in more detail.

A. Nonfluent aphasia (including the subtypes of Broca's aphasia and transcortical motor aphasia) occurs when the anterior language area of the left hemisphere and its surrounding tissues are damaged. For individuals with such injuries, speech is typically produced slowly and effortfully, with poor articulation and deficient intonation and stress patterns (Brookshire, 1992).

Some individuals with nonfluent aphasia also show various degrees of *apraxia,* an inability to program voluntary motor movements. In *apraxia of speech,* the individual is unable to produce various speech sounds or words on command, even though he or she understands the task and can think of the sound or word. Features of apraxia of speech include numerous speech-sound substitutions (not distortions), groping for words and phonemes, speech initiation problems, and inconsistency of errors (Wertz et al., 1991). Despite these difficulties, such an individual may be able to perform nonverbal oral movements on command, such as puckering the lips or sticking out the tongue.

A more severe apraxic disorder is *oral apraxia,* in which all voluntary oral movements are affected. Such an individual would not be able to pucker the lips or stick out the tongue oncommand. However, it should be noted that this disability extends only to voluntary movements performed in response to commands. Individuals with apraxia can usually use the oral musculature for vegetative functions, such as eating and swallowing, with no problem (Wertz et al., 1991). Not all individuals with nonfluent aphasia are truly apraxic, but the two disorders often coexist.

In addition to slow and effortful speech and problems with speech-sound selection, the utterances of those with nonfluent aphasia are usually very short in length, with frequent morphological and syntactic errors *(agrammatism).* The language of the nonfluent aphasiac may be telegraphic in nature, including only uninflected nouns, verbs, and an occasional preposition. The rate of speech is also reduced, rhythm is abnormal, and the voice lacks emotional expression. Writing may also be affected: many individuals with nonfluent aphasia have difficulty forming letters and organizing words into sentences (Brookshire, 1992).

It should be noted that the articulatory and writing disturbances in nonfluent aphasia are not due to paralysis, weakness, incoordination, involuntary movements, or spasticity. Instead, the difficulty appears to be with higher-level linguistic processes that control the selection and sequencing of phonemes and the planning of phoneme production in accordance with phonological rules. Because the problem with speech-sound production appears to involve linguistic rules rather than physical abilities, and because the difficulty typically occurs in both speaking and writing, nonfluent aphasia is considered a language disorder and not a speech disorder.

It is interesting to note that the individual with nonfluent aphasia is usually relatively unimpaired in terms of comprehension as compared to expressive functions. The nonfluent aphasic typically is able to understand the speech of others, recognize his own errors, and read with comprehension (Davis, 1993).

The following is from a conversation between an individual with nonfluent aphasia and a speech-language pathologist:[1]

> **SLP:** *Do you remember what happened to you? Why are you in the hospital?*
> **Client:** *(Pause) Stroke . . . (gestures toward his head) . . . Hah-pital.*
> **SLP:** *What were you doing before your stroke?*
> **Client:** *(Pause) School.*
> **SLP:** *Where were you going to school?*

---

[1]Courtesy of Richard J. Hodach, M.D., Ph.D., S.C.

Client: (Pause) Maeh . . . maeba . . . I can't say it.
  SLP: The University of Alabama?
Client: Yes.

Like many individuals with nonfluent aphasia, this client appeared to understand the questions the speech-language pathologist asked and supplemented his words with gestures to communicate more effectively. He also demonstrated some interesting inconsistencies in his speaking abilities. He paused prior to answering all questions and appeared to have difficulty selecting his words. Yet he clearly and quickly produced the phrase "I can't say it" when he had difficulty with "University of Alabama." Many individuals with nonfluent aphasia are similarly able to produce phrases such as "I don't know" or "I can't do it" in a fluent manner despite great difficulty formulating answers to specific questions. These fluent and normal-sounding phrases, known as *stereotypic utterances,* frequently mislead the listener about the extent of the aphasic's language impairment.

B. Fluent aphasia (including the subtypes of Wernicke's aphasia and transcortical sensory aphasia) occurs as a result of injury to the posterior language area or to more diffuse damage to the posterior part of the left hemisphere. In contrast to the nonfluent types, individuals with fluent aphasia speak easily and effortlessly. Phrase length, intonation patterns, and emotional expression in the voice are all appropriate. Even syntax is superficially acceptable (Brookshire, 1992).

Unfortunately, the fluent aphasic often fails to make sense. Speech is frequently devoid of content words, filled with references to "it" and "them" and "there" to the point where the listener has no idea who or what is being talked about. To complicate matters further, the fluent aphasic's speech is also often characterized by *literal paraphasias,* in which letters in contiguous words or syllables are transposed, or *verbal paraphasias,* in which an inappropriate word is substituted for the desired word (such as *fork* for *pen*). *Neologisms,* completely made-up words, may also be present. In severe cases, the individual may speak in fluent but meaningless jargon containing no recognizable words at all (Brookshire, 1992).

Unlike the nonfluent aphasic, the fluent aphasic has difficulty understanding language. He typically does not comprehend the printed word well, and recognition of his own speech errors is also poor. Considering the function of the posterior language area, this pattern of deficits is not surprising. If the individual is not able to link sensory impressions to concepts, and concepts to spoken or written words, that individual will have difficulty understanding both what he himself says and what others say. In terms of expressive language, individuals with posterior language area damage can be expected to be deficient in formulating their own communications meaningfully. It is also common for fluent aphasics to be unaware of the extent of their difficulty.

The following is an exchange between a fluent aphasic and a speech-language pathologist:[2]

SLP: Mr. W., do you know why you're in the hospital?
Client: In the hospital, yes, and there's a lot of noise and people up all night and you know, and it bothers me and they're bothered and I want to go home.
SLP: I believe you had a stroke, Mr. W., and that you're in the hospital recovering. What did you do before your stroke?
Client: I was at home and the garden, and working and planting, let me see, some peas, and beans, and tomatoes.
SLP: Were you retired?
Client: Yes.
SLP: What did you do before you retired?
Client: Let me see, the garden and planting, and beans and tomatoes, and the grass, and around the basmin (gestures a square with both index fingers).
SLP: Oh . . . were you a gardener before you retired?
Client: Yes, and the basmin and around the grass and like this.

---

[2]Courtesy of Richard J. Hodach, M.D., Ph.D., S.C.

During this exchange, the client spoke very rapidly and with no hesitation. Despite his rapid and fluent responses, however, it is not clear from his answers that he understood the questions of the speech-language pathologist. He appeared to perseverate on the topic of gardening, using similar responses to several different questions. *Perseveration,* the continuation or return to a response or topic that is no longer appropriate, is characteristic of individuals with fluent aphasia.

C. Global aphasia occurs as a result of large lesions involving both the anterior and the posterior language areas (Mateer, 1989). All language functions are severely depressed. The individual is unable to speak fluently, due to anterior involvement, and has difficulty understanding as well, due to the posterior damage. However, such individuals can often produce stereotypic utterances such as "Hi, darlin', how are you?" even though they have no other speech. Communication typically occurs through facial expression, expressive vocalizations, and gestures (Davis, 1993).

2. Causes. Aphasia is usually the result of a *cerebrovascular accident (CVA),* or stroke, in which only a localized area of the left hemisphere is damaged. A stroke occurs when either blood vessels supplying the brain become occluded so that blood cannot circulate freely (known as *ischemic stroke*), or when the wall of a cerebral blood vessel thins and ruptures *(hemorrhagic stroke).* In either case, parts of the brain are deprived of oxygen and cease functioning. Unless the oxygen supply is quickly restored, the damage is usually permanent. If bleeding occurs in the brain itself during a hemorrhagic stroke, any nervous tissue that comes into contact with the blood is destroyed as well (Murdoch, 1990).

Strokes that affect the anterior or posterior language areas of the dominant hemisphere can cause aphasia. However, strokes can also cause other types of communication disorders. For example, speech disorders can occur if various parts of the neuromotor system are damaged by the loss of oxygen or by bleeding, and cognition can be affected if the prefrontal areas in both hemispheres or their connecting pathways are harmed.

Besides strokes, aphasia can be caused by penetrating head injuries, such as gunshot wounds; localized traumatic injuries; tumors; or a central nervous system infection (Murdoch, 1990). However, the damage must be relatively localized to the cortical language centers of the dominant hemisphere in order to cause the symptoms of aphasia. Subcortical lesions, more extensive brain damage, or specific damage to the nondominant hemisphere cause other symptoms and other disorders.

3. Treatment. Speech-language pathologists have a long history of intervention with aphasic clients (Davis, 1993). Many different treatment philosophies and therapy methods are currently in use, depending on the training and biases of the clinician.

The speech-language pathologist's intervention usually begins with a period of testing to determine the individual's primary areas of strength and weakness. Although aphasics as a population can be divided into fluent, nonfluent, and global, each individual aphasic has a unique pattern of language deficits and severity levels, depending on the exact location and extent of the neurological damage. In addition, *premorbid* (or prestroke) levels of language functioning affect the client's poststroke abilities and expectations. Testing provides the information necessary to begin a treatment program.

Wertz (1984) cites four broad groups into which intervention for aphasics can be divided. First, traditional therapy involves a behavioral approach, similar to what we described for children with language disorders. The emphasis here is on "stimulus-response-reinforcement" and the content of language. This type of therapy, which seeks to minimize the language impairment by reteaching linguistic strategies for semantics, morphology, and syntax, can be used with any type of aphasia.

The second type of therapy, specific therapy, is aimed at a population with a certain pattern of symptoms (Wertz, 1984). Rather than focusing on general language use and linguistic rules, specific therapy may target a particular modality (vision, for example) or only one facet of language (e.g., involuntary utterances). However, like traditional therapy, specific therapy aims to reduce the aphasic's underlying impairments.

The third approach to therapy, called *functional therapy,* emphasizes language context rather than language content (Wertz, 1984). It seeks to improve the aphasic's communication in the broad sense, rather than focusing on linguistic skills such as semantics, morphology, and syntax. The aphasic individual may be taught how to give gestural cues, use an alphabet board to point to the first letter of a word, or cue himself and his listeners in other ways. He may learn to observe his listener closely for evidence that he or she does not understand and develop techniques to "repair" this breakdown in communication. This approach to therapy emphasizes helping the aphasic compensate for his language deficits instead of reteaching language. And in many cases, compensation may be the more realistic goal.

Fourth and last, some speech-language pathologists use *group therapy,* where two or more aphasics are seen together in a more social context. Interaction among group members is encouraged, although structured stimulus-response tasks may be incorporated as well. Due to its social nature and its opportunities for meaningful and spontaneous conversation, the group-therapy approach may have the greatest potential to address members' disabilities and handicaps with regard to functional communication. The group can also provide emotional support for its members and reassurance that they will again be able to communicate.

These therapy approaches are easily combined and can be used sequentially. For example, in the initial phases of therapy, when the aphasic's language skills are the most impaired, the traditional or specific approaches might be used to reestablish some language function. As the aphasic becomes more capable linguistically and socially, functional or group therapy might be introduced.

4. The Effectiveness of Therapy. How effective is speech and language therapy in aphasia? To

what extent can language functions be restored? Prognosis for improvement in aphasia is difficult. While we can say with some confidence that most clients will improve to some degree with therapy, it is impossible to specify a terminal level. Eventual improvement will depend on factors such as the *etiology,* or cause, of the aphasia and the size of the lesion. In general, those whose aphasia is due to ischemic stroke rather than a hemorrhagic stroke will make better gains, and, not surprisingly, those with smaller lesions also have a more favorable prognosis. Location of the lesion is also important, with those having anterior lesions doing better in general. Those in good general health can be expected to recover more completely than those with complicating health problems, and those with mild language symptoms in the initial recovery period usually reach a higher level of competence than do those with severe language symptoms in the initial recovery period.

Finally, time elapsed since the stroke or trauma is important. It is believed that a great deal of "spontaneous recovery" takes place in the initial months after the injury and that therapy during this period can be extremely effective. An individual who is less than six months posttrauma can be expected to make greater gains than an individual who is six years posttrauma.

To return to our question on the effectiveness of therapy and how well we can expect aphasic clients to regain language, research has shown the following: Individuals who have had a single stroke, especially of the ischemic type, who are less than six months poststroke, and who receive treatment for at least three hours a week for six months will make the best improvement in terms of the return of linguistic function (Rosenbek et al., 1989). Other individuals may regain less in terms of language but can still be helped to communicate better in everyday situations. In such cases, the focus may be on compensation rather than on retraining.

5. The Role of the Family. Regardless of the disorder—aphasia, right-hemisphere damage, dysarthria, dementia, or traumatic brain injury— most families initially respond to the individual's communication disorder with shock and disbelief. Communication is a function that most of us take for granted, and one that we do not fully appreciate in ourselves or others until it is impaired. In the absence of normal communication abilities, families may be uncertain about what the impaired individual is aware of or understands and may assume the worst.

It is important for families to receive information from the speech-language pathologist early in the recovery period regarding the nature of their loved one's communication disorder. Families need to know whether the problem involves thinking ability, comprehension, expressive language, speech only, or some combination. They also need to know the extent of the speech, language, or cognitive problems, the prognosis for recovery of communication skills, and strategies for how to cope at home. The family almost always plays an important role in helping the client reestablish or maintain communication, feelings of self-worth, and meaningful activities.

A specific role for the family has not been delineated for all of the disorders we will review in this chapter. However, speech-language pathologists frequently work with the families of those with aphasia and those with dementia. Thus, we will examine the role of the family in the restoration of communication functions in aphasia, and in the preservation of communication functions in dementia, as these disorders are introduced.

For an aphasic individual, it is important for the family to provide as much language stimulation as possible, to help the individual remember and relearn disrupted skills. Hess and Bahr (1981) describe the role of language stimulation in the recovery of actress Patricia Neal from a stroke and subsequent aphasia. Ms. Neal's husband arranged for six friends a day to come in, one after the other, to talk or read to her for an hour each. Not every aphasic who is given language stimulation will recover as well as did Ms. Neal, who was able to resume her acting career after her stroke. However, the emotional support and interpersonal involvement provided by the family's language stimulation can, at the very least, foster a positive attitude and willingness to learn that the aphasic might not otherwise have.

If the aphasic has trouble comprehending, the family must remember to speak slowly and to use shorter, less complex sentences. They should be prepared to repeat their messages, using different words if the individual does not understand it the first time (Hess and Bahr, 1981). It is also important for family members to make sure they have the aphasic's full attention before speaking to him or her and to reduce competing distractions, such as a radio or television, in the background. Finally, gestures should be used to supplement speech.

To help counter expressive difficulties, the family must remember to give the individual adequate time to respond to questions and conversation. It may take time to "find" the desired word, remember the phonemes that comprise it, and form them with the mouth. Hess and Bahr recommend waiting at least thirty seconds for a response and accepting one- and two-word phrases as answers. Finally, Linebaugh (1984) discusses the idea that some of the "communicative burden" needs to be assumed by the listener. That is, when communication breaks down, the listener should probe for additional bits of information, try to rephrase what he understood the aphasic to say and ask for confirmation, or otherwise try to retrace the conversational steps so that understanding can be restored.

RIGHT-HEMISPHERE DAMAGE

As we stressed in the preceding section, the language disorder known as *aphasia* occurs only when damage is sustained in the left, or *dominant,* hemisphere of the brain. Does this mean individuals who have lesions in the right, or *nondominant* hemisphere, have no communication problems as a result of their injury? In fact, such individuals do not evidence language disorders comparable to those with left-hemisphere damage. However, they do experience subtle communication deficits, as well as deficits in specific cognitive skills.

1. Characteristics. Individuals with right-hemisphere damage may evidence problems with attention, spatial perception, and body image. Some have what is known as *unilateral neglect* (Davis, 1993), in which stimuli on one side of the body are not noted or responded to. This is a particular problem when dressing, resulting in a disorder known as *dressing apraxia*. An individual with dressing apraxia may not realize that the left shoe, sock, or other article of clothing has not been appropriately placed (Murdoch, 1990). Right-hemisphere patients may also have difficulties with visual perception, auditory perception, *construction* (the ability to draw or build simple constructions), or in interpreting symbols.

One of the most striking communication deficits of those with right-hemisphere damage, according to Boone and Plante (1993), is poor expression of emotional intent. The voice of right-hemisphere patients tends to be flat and monotonous, lacking in normal word stress and intonation patterns (Ross and Mesulam, 1979). Emotional expression through gesture and facial expression are similarly impaired (Ross, 1981). Further, individuals with right-hemisphere damage may also have trouble interpreting the emotional intent of others. The emotions that a speaker expresses vocally, facially, or through gesture may all be missed by the listener with right-hemisphere damage (Love and Webb, 1992). For example, if someone said in a sarcastic tone of voice, "Bob failed again—great!" the individual with right-hemisphere damage might conclude that the speaker believed Bob's failure was a good thing.

Finally, because of their difficulties with attention and interpretation of speakers' emotions, right-hemisphere patients frequently have pragmatic deficits. According to Murdoch (1990, 150), such individuals are often unable to "appreciate the context and tone of a conversation or the presuppositions entailed. Their discourse often focuses on insignificant and tangential details and includes inappropriate humor and comments, giving their language an excessive and rambling nature." The individual with right-hemisphere damage thus may have difficulty providing a context for the listener, taking turns in a conversation, maintaining a topic of conversation, or other interactional skills.

Spatial and body image problems, difficulty with emotional interpretation and expression, and isolated pragmatic deficits cannot be considered true language disorders despite their negative effect on the individual's ability to participate in conversational interactions. Instead, these difficulties might be considered specific cognitive deficits, nonlinguistic in nature but detrimental to communication.

2. Causes. Right-hemisphere damage can be caused by strokes, penetrating wounds, or traumatic injuries. Whereas aphasic symptoms are seen only if the damage to the left hemisphere is relatively localized to the language areas, the symptoms of right-hemisphere damage may be seen with more *diffuse* (widespread) lesions.

3. Treatment. The speech-language pathologist's role with right-hemisphere patients has been limited up to this time. According to Wertz (1984, 56), "The patient with right hemisphere involvement has been treated as interesting—and seldom treated." Based on his review of the literature, it appears that when speech-language pathologists do work with such individuals, they use a traditional behavioral approach. Goals for therapy include improvement of perceptual and sequencing abilities, auditory comprehension, organizational ability, and problem solving, among others (Adamovich, 1981). Yorkston (1981) suggests teaching right-hemisphere clients to use verbal cues to "talk" themselves through tasks they have difficulty with. In terms of improving comprehension, Tompkins (1991) notes that a speaker's *semantic redundancy,* or repeated use of key words, improves the ability of individuals with right-hemisphere damage to comprehend emotional intent. The use of language-based strategies thus might be the most appropriate for right-hemisphere patients because their language abilities are relatively unimpaired, compared to their more global perceptual, memory, and organizational abilities.

4. The Effectiveness of Therapy. Since speech-language pathologists have such limited involvement with this population, it is not surprising that there are few data available regarding the efficacy of communication treatment. In terms of the recovery of general functions, Gordon et al. (1978) found that right hemisphere patients were more deficient than left-hemisphere patients (aphasics) in self-care skills, even though the former group received more time in rehabilitation. Wertz (1984) is somewhat guarded in his appraisal of the prognosis for those with right-hemisphere lesions. However, specific intervention strategies must first be developed and implemented by speech-language pathologists before an estimation of improvement in communication function can be made.

DYSARTHRIA

The communication disorders we have discussed so far—aphasia and right-hemisphere damage—affect linguistic and cognitive abilities but do not cause physical impairment. Let us look now at a very different group of disorders. If certain parts of the neuromotor system are damaged, the individual's physical ability to control the muscles of respiration, phonation, resonance, and articulation is impaired. The individual has no difficulty with comprehension, of either the spoken or the written word, and is able to write in clear, complex, and complete sentences (unless there is paralysis of the arm or hand). However, because physical control of the speech production mechanism is limited, the individual experiences a speech disorder. This speech disorder, resulting from damage to the neuromotor system, is what we already discussed in Chapter 8 as dysarthria.

1. Characteristics. The particular speech characteristics associated with dysarthria are extremely varied, depending on where in the neuromotor system the damage has occurred. For example, the motor cortex, premotor cortex, or *upper motor neurons* (nerve pathways descending from these cortical motor areas) could be affected. Or there might be damage to the basal ganglia, the brain stem, the cerebellum, the spinal cord, or even the *lower motor neurons* (nerves that originate in the

brain stem or spinal cord and run out to individual muscles). With so many potential locations for damage, it is no wonder that a variety of symptoms are also possible. Depending on which parts of the neuromotor system are damaged by the disease, one might see weakness, paralysis, incoordination, involuntary movements, or abnormal muscle tone.

In this section, we will consider four common neuromotor conditions seen in the elderly population—damage to the motor and premotor areas of the cortex and the upper motor neurons that exit from them; Parkinson's disease; *amyotrophic lateral sclerosis,* or Lou Gehrig's Disease; and tardive dyskinesia. We will combine a discussion of these causes of dysarthria with an exploration of the speech characteristics that typically accompany them.

1. Causes

A. Damage to the motor cortex, premotor cortex, or upper motor neurons. The most common causes of this type of lesion are hemorrhagic and ischemic strokes and injury to the head. As we have learned, if the damage is localized in either the anterior or posterior language area in the dominant hemisphere, aphasia will occur. If there is damage to the motor or premotor areas or their neuronal connections, and it is *unilateral* (or in one hemisphere only), the effects on speech are likely to be mild or transient (Love and Webb, 1992). However, if bilateral damage has been sustained, the individual often experiences weakness and abnormal muscle tone in the speech muscles.

For patients with this type of disorder, articulation tends to be slow and slurred because the tongue and lips are too stiff and slow moving to reach their intended positions for many speech sounds. A hypernasal voice quality is common for the same reason—the velum or soft palate moves too slowly to keep up with the speaker's production of nasal and nonnasal sounds and often fails to reach its target position. Finally, the voice often sounds strained and harsh because of excessive muscle tone or weakness in the muscles of the larynx (Murdoch, 1990).

In addition to articulation and voice disorders, individuals who have suffered damage to the motor and premotor areas may have swallowing disorders, or *dysphagia*. Dysphagia is due to reductions in muscle strength and control in the tongue, pharynx, and upper part of the digestive tract. As a result of these physical limitations, food and liquids are likely to by-pass the protective valving of the epiglottis, false vocal folds, and true vocal folds and enter the respiratory system. This is known as *aspiration*. Individuals who aspirate are at risk for pneumonia and other life-threatening respiratory conditions. In recent years, speech-language pathologists have become involved with diagnosing and treating swallowing disorders.

Individuals who have experienced a stroke or head injury can be expected to improve in terms of speech function and swallowing during the period immediately following the accident. "Spontaneous recovery" will continue for about six months to one year following the trauma (Murdoch, 1990), at which point the rate of improvement usually slows. However, gradual improvement in speech functions may still continue for a period of years, especially with therapy.

B. Parkinson's disease. Parkinson's disease occurs when a specific part of the basal ganglia begins to *atrophy* (shrink due to degeneration) and no longer produces *dopamine,* a neurotransmitter. As dopamine production decreases, the individual has increasing difficulty with movement. He or she experiences weakness, develops a shuffling walk, becomes rigid or stiff, and may develop a tremor of the hands. The face becomes blank and expressionless, even though the individual's emotions are normal.

Speech is often affected as well (Yorkston et al., 1988). The rigidity of Parkinson's disease causes the individual to speak with reduced mouth and tongue movements. It is interesting to note that the Parkinson's patient often speaks very rapidly and can often repeat syllables such as "papapa" faster than the speech-language pathologist. But the reduced range of articulatory movements, combined with rapid rate, greatly reduce the speaker's intelligibility. Further, the normal function of the basal ganglia, which is to program automatic aspects of movement, is diminished, and so the individual's voice has little emotional expression unless he consciously thinks about it. The voice may be tremorous, soft, and hoarse. Finally, as with so many other disorders of the neuromotor system, Parkinson's disease may also cause swallowing disorders, or *dysphagia*.

In the early stages, Parkinson's disease can be treated with a synthetic form of dopamine that replaces the body's natural supply and helps control the physical symptoms. After a period of years, however, drug therapy becomes less and less effective (Lang and Blair, 1984), and the individual becomes weaker, more rigid, and less mobile. The disease is a progressive one, which means that its severity increases with time; but individuals with this disorder typically survive for ten to twenty years after the initial diagnosis.

C. Amyotrophic lateral sclerosis. Amyotrophic lateral sclerosis is known by many as Lou Gehrig's disease, named after the famous baseball player who suffered from this condition. It is also referred to as ALS. ALS is characterized by degeneration of the upper and lower motor neurons. Its cause is unknown, although some forms appear to be hereditary and others may be caused by slow-acting viruses or toxins.

The individual with ALS experiences early symptoms of weakness, paralysis on one side of the body, and clumsiness in a hand or leg. Some have early speech and swallowing difficulties *(dysphagia)*. Speech is initially slow and imprecise, and the voice is strained and hypernasal. The symptoms are similar to those seen when damage to the motor and premotor cortex occurs. As the disease progresses, the individual becomes weaker and weaker and has more and more difficulty in movement, speech, swallowing, and breathing. Weakness and paralysis increase until the individual is immobile and unintelligible. ALS is usually fatal within three years of diagnosis, but some individuals have lived much longer (Murdoch, 1990).

It is important to remember that despite the

impaired appearance of individuals with ALS, only motor functions, including speech, are affected. Language and cognitive abilities are not compromised.

D. Tardive dyskinesia. *Tardive dyskinesia* refers to a syndrome of jerky involuntary movements, or *tics,* primarily involving the face, jaw, lips, and tongue, although the torso and extremities may be affected as well (Foster, 1987). The involuntary movements produced in the tongue and face tend to interfere with speech production, mainly in the form of irregular interruptions of phoneme and word productions. Phonemes may be imprecise if a tic occurs while the individual is trying to speak, and words may be either prolonged or truncated.

Tardive dyskinesia occurs as a result of long-term use of *neuroleptic* drugs such as sedatives, tranquilizers, and antipsychotics, which apparently affect the basal ganglia (Foster, 1987; Murdoch, 1990). Since drugs of this type are taken frequently by older adults and their effects on the neuromotor system are cumulative, tardive dyskinesia is most likely to show up in the elderly. Unfortunately, tardive dyskinesia tends to persist for months or years after the causative drug is discontinued (Murdoch, 1990).

2. Treatment. As in the area of aphasia, speech-language pathologists have a long history of working with those suffering from dysarthria. According to Yorkston et al. (1988), dysarthria is second only to aphasia among the most frequently treated disorders by speech-language pathologists in hospitals and medical centers.

Because there is so much diversity in the underlying causes of dysarthria, and in the symptom patterns and prognoses for recovery, it is difficult to generalize about therapy approaches a speech-language pathologist might use. For those with progressive and fatal diseases of the neuromotor system, the primary job of the speech-language pathologist is to preserve intelligible speech as long as possible. The speech-language pathologist might encourage the patient to do things such as slow her rate of speech, overarticulate conso-

nants, maintain adequate loudness, pause in the appropriate places in a sentence, and take other compensatory actions. The clinician is also likely to introduce alternative means of communication, such as signaling devices or alphabet cards, in the later stages of the disease, when intelligible speech and perhaps voluntary movement as well are no longer possible. Individuals with Parkinson's disease and ALS would both fall into this category. Such cases are both technically and emotionally challenging for the speech-language pathologist.

For those with dysarthria due to a nonprogressive cause, such as stroke or head trauma, the potential for some recovery of function is much better. In addition to the compensatory strategies described above (slowing the speaking rate, over-articulating, and so on), the speech-language pathologist might also try to reduce the client's level of impairment through drills and exercises involving various speech sounds and muscles. Deterioration of function is not expected with these patients, and, with therapy, their intelligibility should improve.

Speech-language pathologists have also recently become involved in treating dysphagia. Prior to the 1970s, patients with swallowing disorders were typically tube-fed (Groher, 1984). Since that time, various medical specialists have become involved in trying to improve or prolong an individual's ability to eat orally. These specialists include radiologists, who provide information via x-ray on the patient's swallowing ability; nurses, who manage the patient's day-to-day care; dieticians, who monitor nutritional status; and occupational therapists, who are concerned with the patient's ability to engage in the activities of daily living. Speech-language pathologists are thus part of a team and must work cooperatively with the team's other members.

The speech-language pathologist's therapy for dysphagia may include altering posture during eating for maximum swallowing efficiency, slowing movements, and coordinating respiration and swallowing with eating, among other things (ASHA, 1993b). Knowledge of anatomy and physiology of swallowing is an important prerequisite for this type of work. The skills and competencies needed for working with patients with dysphagia are highly specialized and have recently been outlined by the American Speech-Language-Hearing Association (ASHA, 1990).

3. The Effectiveness of Therapy.

How effective is speech therapy for those with dysarthria? Again, it depends on what caused the dysarthria in the first place, its severity, and whether or not it is progressive. According to Yorkston et al. (1988), most studies dealing with treatment efficacy at this point have documented the effects of a single technique on a specific type of dysarthria. While these studies usually report some degree of success, it is difficult to generalize their results to the dysarthric population as a whole. More research is needed in this area to guide speech-language pathologists in selecting and evaluating appropriate therapy approaches for their clients.

DEMENTIA

In discussing aphasia, right-hemisphere damage, and dysarthria, we have made the assumption that the individual's problem centers on something other than rational thought. The aphasic may have difficulty understanding or formulating words and sentences, but we assume he or she is still in contact with reality and can interpret events in the environment. The patient with right-hemisphere damage is similarly impaired in specific cognitive abilities, but is also assumed to be rational, despite some subtle difficulties in communicating. The discrepancy between rational thought and communication ability is even clearer in dysarthria. The dysarthric individual can think clearly and formulate language internally. However, the message may be difficult to understand because of uncooperative speech muscles. The failure of communication is due to physical limitations, not limitations of rational thought. The problem in dementia is quite different.

1. Characteristics.

The individual suffering from dementia gradually loses the cognitive functions of memory, attention, orientation, and rational thought. Initially, memory problems pre-

dominate. The person may forget where he put his glasses or parked his car, the names of new acquaintances, or recent events (although memory of events long past is generally unimpaired). He may become disoriented in unfamiliar locations, forgetting where he is and why he came. Language disorders are generally not prominent at this stage, although they can be found if probed for (Murdoch, 1990). The individual may use exceptionally long and complex sentences during verbal discourse (Overman and Geoffrey, 1987), but may also have difficulty with word-finding. The word-finding problems are usually masked by *circumlocution,* in which the client might say a sentence describing the word without actually using it (Obler and Albert, 1981).

As the dementia progresses, more obvious functional declines can be observed. The individual may be unable to travel independently, even to familiar locations; to manage personal finances; or to perform many of the ordinary activities of daily living. A loss of initiative and judgment may be seen. In terms of language, the individual might begin to resemble a fluent aphasic. Difficulties with comprehension become apparent, and *content words* (specific nouns and verbs) may be replaced with *it, them,* and *there.* Paraphasias and neologisms may be seen (Murdoch, 1990). Reading and writing abilities also diminish (Overman and Geoffrey, 1987). The speech-language pathologist who works with the elderly population will need to be able to discriminate between fluent aphasia and dementia, although the individual's level of functional skills will usually aid in differentiating between the two groups.

In the advanced stages of dementia, the individual becomes totally dependent, unable to remember any relevant information about names, places, or events, and unable to complete dressing or other self-care skills. Language may become extremely limited. The individual rarely initiates communication, even to express wants and needs. Attempts at speech may be characterized by nonfluent repetitions and jargon. It is not until the very end of this disorder that phonology and syntax are disturbed (Overman and Geoffrey, 1987; Bayles and Boone, 1982). The advanced dementia patient may have language disabilities similar to those of a global aphasic (Murdoch, 1990).

Clearly, the communication disorders seen in dementia are of a different nature than those seen in aphasia, despite some similarities in symptomatology. The individual with dementia experiences language disorders as a part of a broader spectrum of functional deterioration, terminating in total dependence. The individual with aphasia has a primary difficulty with language functions. Although the communication disorder may limit the aphasic's independence to some degree, severe and progressive decline does not occur.

2. Causes. The most common cause of dementia is Alzheimer's disease. Alzheimer's disease causes from 50 to 75 percent of all dementias, according to the Office of Technology Assessment (1985). This disease afflicts from 5 to 15 percent of all Americans over the age of 65.

Alzheimer's disease is characterized by a loss of *neurons,* or nerve cells, especially in the prefrontal area and the parts of the temporal lobe that communicate with the limbic system. In addition, neurofibrillary tangles are seen when microscopic studies of brain tissue are performed. These convoluted structures interfere with the normal functioning of a nerve cell (Murdoch, 1990). Finally, deposits known as *plaques* are also characteristic of Alzheimer's disease. These, too, interfere with nerve cell function, particularly the transmission of nerve impulses (Murdoch, 1990). Both neurofibrillary tangles and plaques have been noted in the brains of individuals who are aging normally, although to a lesser degree than in Alzheimer's patients (Foster, 1987). Why some aging individuals go on to develop more extensive amounts of both these abnormalities while others do not is unknown at present.

While Alzheimer's disease may be frequently suspected in an older individual who is becoming more forgetful and less functional, its presence is not easy to ascertain. In most cases, a definitive diagnosis cannot be made until an autopsy is performed after the individual's death. Occasionally,

the diagnosis can be made on the basis of *biopsies*—small specimens of tissue taken from living subjects—but this is difficult because of the need to document cellular changes in numerous parts of the brain. Thus, most cases of Alzheimer's disease are identified on the basis of behaviorial criteria alone (Foster, 1987).

The second most common cause of dementia is a series of mild strokes that in and of themselves do not do much damage, but cumulatively destroy the cortex and its connecting pathways. These mild strokes are known as *transient ischemic attacks* (TIAs). They often produce so few symptoms that the individual may not realize that a TIA has occurred. In contrast to a major stroke, during which loss of conscious, voluntary movement, and speech might occur, TIA sufferers may feel only tiredness and confusion. However, the diffuse damage caused by repeated minor strokes can eventually disrupt neuronal function and communication within the intelligence centers of the brain. Dementia due to these mild strokes, known as *multi-infarct dementia,* probably causes 15 to 25 percent of all cases of dementia.

The remainder of dementias are caused by degenerative diseases, brain trauma, toxic metabolic disturbances, oxygen deprivation, Parkinson's disease, and other conditions (Overman and Geoffrey, 1987). Parkinson's disease, discussed earlier in this chapter as a cause of dysarthria, can be a cause of dementia as well. As you recall from our previous discussion, Parkinson's disease is progressive in nature. And in some cases, the lesion in the basal ganglia may spread into the connecting pathways to the prefrontal area, thus affecting the functioning of the intelligence centers of the brain. In such cases, Parkinson's disease can be a cause of cognitive as well as speech disorders.

3. Treatment. According to Miller (1977), dementia is usually diagnosed but not treated—at least, not by speech-language pathologists. The decline in linguistic abilities is typically less rapid and less problematic than the dramatic reduction in functional abilities; thus the focus of treatment is usually on preserving functional skills (Wertz, 1984).

Occasionally, the speech-language pathologist may be called upon during the diagnostic process to help differentiate dementia from fluent aphasia. The speech-language pathologist may also be responsible for helping the family cope with the dementia at home. According to Wertz (1984, 58), "What we have to offer is designed to slow deterioration of behavior or lessen demand as behavior deteriorates." The inexorable decline in cognition and functional skills is not conducive to intensive speech-language therapy efforts.

4. The Role of the Family. Because the dementia an individual experiences can be expected to worsen with time, the primary role of the family is to preserve communication and other functions for as long as possible. The family should try to establish and maintain a fixed schedule so the individual with dementia will have as much stability as possible in his or her daily routine. The home environment should also remain constant and as simple as possible. However, "orienting" materials, such as calendars, clocks, pictures of family members, and so on, should be prominently displayed. It is also important to try to keep the individual with dementia in good health through proper nutrition and adequate rest (Bayles, 1982).

Boone and Plante (1993) suggest that in the early stages of dementia, the family can encourage the client to keep a diary, schedule, or appointment calendar and to carry identifying information to keep them oriented. To facilitate comprehension for as long as possible, the family can try to simplify their verbal instructions to the individual. The individual with dementia may occasionally become confused and try to argue with family members; the family should try to avoid these arguments by changing the subject whenever possible. However, as dementia clients become worse, their bizarre behavior and lack of judgment may put them in danger. For this reason, nursing home or institutional placement is

usually necessary for the final years of the individual's life.

TRAUMATIC BRAIN INJURY

Traumatic brain injury is somewhat different from the disorders we have discussed so far in this chapter in that it is much more common in young adults than in older adults. In fact, traumatic brain injury (TBI), is the leading cause of death and disability in those under 40 years of age (Swiercinsky et al., 1987). It is most common in young adult males as the result of automobile, bicycle, or motorcycle accidents (Boone and Plante, 1993). Like dementia, traumatic brain injury primarily affects cognition and language. However, unlike dementia, the cognitive and linguistic disorders resulting from traumatic brain injury are not progressive, and they improve to some degree with physical recovery.

1. Characteristics. When traumatic brain injury or "closed head injury" occurs, the resulting damage to the brain tends to be diffuse rather than localized, and many symptom patterns are possible. Cognitive deficits are frequently seen, including problems with memory, orientation, and sequencing (Swiercinsky et al., 1987). Personality and emotional disturbances are also common. The individual may laugh and cry easily, have wide mood swings, be insensitive to the feelings of others, and be extremely impulsive. The ability to consider consequences and exercise good judgment is often impaired (Love and Webb, 1992).

Speech, language, and swallowing disorders may also result from TBI. The motor centers of the brain may be damaged, causing dysarthria or dysphagia of varying degrees of severity. Language symptoms may be present as well. There is some dispute regarding the nature of these symptoms, however. According to a review of the literature by Murdoch (1990), some researchers have noted word-finding problems, confused and empty speech, paraphasias, and auditory comprehension deficits similar to fluent aphasia. Other researchers have noted the symptoms of nonfluent aphasia, with the primary deficit in expression. The variation in specific location and severity of the brain injury from person to person undoubtedly contributes to these conflicting findings.

Despite the occurrence of speech and language disorders in the TBI population, the cognitive and personality disorders of these clients are usually of more concern. These young adults and their families need time and support in accepting the limitations imposed upon them by the disorder. The person who has sustained an injury of this type is "different" in many subtle (and some not so subtle) ways and may need to develop new life goals, vocational skills, and living arrangements. Thus, speech-language pathologists who work with the TBI population may become more involved with cognitive retraining and community reentry than traditional speech and language therapy.

2. Causes. Traumatic brain injury is caused by a blow to the head so severe that brain damage results. The primary damage is due to the impact of the brain against the skull at the time of the blow, causing damage or destruction to cortical brain cells in the area. Then, secondary swelling of the injured site can put pressure on the entire brain hours or even days after the intiial injury has occurred. This pressure can cause the destruction of more cortical nerve cells. Finally, the movement of the brain within the skull may tear various nerve fibers and pathways apart from one another. Thus, the normal connections and communication between different parts of the brain may be obliterated.

3. Treatment. The individual with a traumatic brain injury frequently experiences language disorders as a result; but as in dementia, the language disorder is often just one element in a larger picture of reduced functional competence. In many cases, the language disorder occurs because of underlying cognitive deficits in areas such as attention and short-term memory (Love and Webb, 1992). Emotional and personality distur-

bances can further complicate the individual's willingness to engage and succeed in treatment.

Current treatment procedures for TBI patients stress cognitive retraining and rehabilitation over traditional language therapy (Adamovich et al., 1985; Hagen, 1984). According to Hagen (1984), the goal of treatment should be reorganization of cognitive processes rather than the relearning of language. Hagen explains that as cognitive processes are reorganized, phonological, semantic, syntactic, and verbal-reasoning abilities will improve as well.

Adamovich and colleagues suggest a three-level therapy hierarchy including arousal and alerting, operative retraining, and self-reliant functioning. The first stage, arousal and alerting, may occur in the early postcoma stages or even when the individual is still in a coma. Auditory, oral-peripheral, verbal, tactile, visual, and even *gustatory* (taste) stimuli are presented with the goal of eliciting a conscious response from the patient. As the individual becomes more alert and aware, the required responses should become longer and may involve following commands or responding verbally to questions. Since the patient is typically agitated at this stage of recovery, care must be taken to keep him or her calm and responsive, and not to trigger increasingly combative behavior (Hagen, 1984). This type of stimulation program can be carried out by occupational or physical therapists, speech-language pathologists, or nurses (Adamovich et al., 1985).

The operative retraining phase focuses on more specific activities designed to improve "attention, perception, discrimination, organization, memory, and higher-level problem solving" (Adamovich et al., 1985, 98). Programs must be specific to the individual's needs, strengths, and weaknesses. Typically, early tasks in this stage involve nonlinguistic stimuli and responses. When the client has been successful, linguistic tasks are introduced. Hagen (1984) suggests that since TBI patients are usually better with nonlinguistic cognitive abilities, these can be used to cue linguistic responses and behavioral sequences.

The last stage described by Adamovich and

colleagues, self-reliant functioning, is essentially a carryover phase, where skills worked on in the clinic or hospital are generalized to the home and community. As with any other generalization phase, there may be difficulties in achieving complete success in carryover. In this stage, individuals with traumatic brain injury must become aware of contingencies and the consequences of their actions. Judgment and appropriate response to situations are stressed.

As speech-language pathologists gain experience with the traumatic-brain-injured population, no doubt more therapy techniques and strategies will be proposed and tested. At this point, however, the speech-language pathologist working with TBI clients must take a broad perspective on communication as one of many cognitive skills, and must function in a very interdisciplinary way.

GENERAL TREATMENT PERSPECTIVES IN ADULT NEUROLOGICAL DISORDERS

Aphasia, right-hemisphere damage, dysarthria, dementia, and traumatic brain injury are most accurately regarded as *chronic,* or long-term, disorders. Although the individual may physically recover from the acute phase of a stroke or head injury, behavioral deficits of some degree are likely to last for the duration of the individual's life.

In considering the long-terms consequences of a chronic disorder, it is sometimes helpful to classify those consequences. Frey (1984) proposed the terms *impairment, disability,* and *handicap* to describe how a chronic disorder can affect an individual. According to Frey (1984)—and Yorkston et al. (1988) who adapted Frey's system for dysarthria—an *impairment* is any measurable decline in function. According to such a definition, almost all elderly individuals could be said to have impairments in hearing, speech, and cognitive functions. As we discussed at the beginning of this chapter, even normally aging individuals experience slight but measurable declines in many aspects of communication. Individuals with neu-

rological disorders can be expected to have more numerous and severe impairments.

But of what significance is an impairment? In describing how the impairment affects an individual's ability to perform various activities, we need to introduce the concept of a disability. A *disability* is a restriction, caused by an impairment, in the ability to perform a certain activity within an accepted range. For example, if a normally aging individual's impairment in short-term memory results in difficulty in comprehending conversational speech, we would say that that individual has a disability. Despite some measurable declines in function *(impairments),* most normally aging individuals probably do not experience disabilities in conversational speech. However, individuals with aphasia, dysarthria, and other neurological communication disorders usually do.

Finally, Frey (1984) and Yorkston et al. (1988) introduce the concept of a handicap. A *handicap,* according to these authors, prevents an individual from functioning independently and fulfilling his or her socially appropriate role—mother, father, grandparent, employee, and so on. Few, if any, normally aging individuals experience a handicap due to their communication abilities. However, depending on the severity of the aphasia, dysarthria, or dementia, a handicap would not be unexpected. In our example from the previous paragraph, the individual with the short-term memory impairment that results in a disability in comprehending spoken language might be considered handicapped if she is no longer able to function in her employment setting.

In planning therapy for any adult with a neurological disorder, the rehabilitation specialist must look beyond the impairment to the more functional problems the individual may be having. Does the impairment create a disability? Is the disability causing a handicap? If the impairment does not interfere with the individual's normal everyday functioning, it need not be a priority in therapy. On the other hand, a handicap or significant disability should get first priority in treatment, even if the underlying impairment cannot be eliminated. For example, an individual handicapped in his social role by a hearing impairment might try a hearing aid. A hearing aid cannot cure the underlying impairment in the auditory system, but it might help reduce the resulting handicap or disability.

Adults with neurological disorders have many impairments in speech, language, or cognitive abilities. It is important to realize that the speech-language pathologist and other rehabilitation personnel are limited in their abilities to eliminate those impairments. Some impairments lessen as the body heals; but the restoration of damaged brains remains beyond the realm of medical or behavioral science. The goal of the speech-language pathologist, occupational therapist, physical therapist, recreation specialist, and other professionals is certainly to help the client reduce her or his impairments and regain as much function as possible through drill or exercise. But, more important, these professionals help the individual manage the environment, use assistive devices, or otherwise find solutions that will lessen the disabilities and handicaps they experience.

CONSEQUENCES TO THE INDIVIDUAL

An individual who acquires a communication disorder in adulthood as a result of neurological injury or disease is usually just as shocked and disbelieving as the family. After a lifetime of simply opening one's mouth and allowing one's thoughts to flow freely, the need to grope for words and sounds can be disconcerting to say the least. Many individuals become withdrawn and depressed when they realize the extent of their disabilities. Their self-image, formed over many years of career and family achievement, may no longer fit reality. It is very difficult for most individuals with neurological disorders to accept the idea that they are no longer capable of doing some of the things that once came easily to them.

The communication disorders we have discussed in this chapter also serve to reduce an individual's independence. If communication abilities are poor, or if the individual becomes easily confused or disoriented, activities such as driving and independent travel may be impossible. Visiting friends, participating in social activities, or simply getting to therapy may be difficult. Depression over an increase in dependency can create further withdrawal and an even more dependent condition.

Swindell and Hammons (1991) found that approximately 60 percent of the aphasics in the literature they reviewed were depressed. Depression was most common six months to two years following a stroke, and it usually lasted seven to eight months. In addition, the authors found that depression was likely to recur approximately ten years poststroke.

In order to get beyond the negative psychological consequences of a neurological disorder, the individual often needs more than just personal resolve. Family and friends can help their loved one by suggesting meaningful activities, either old or new, that the individual could take satisfaction in. Hess and Bahr (1981) suggest using old skills in part-time employment, doing volunteer work, or becoming involved with community and religious activities. According to these authors, "usually the patient will not think of these activities on his own, but needs the family to support and to encourage him in these ventures" (p. 112). With a supportive family and the assistance of friends and professionals, the individual with a neurological disorder is better able to create a new life.

SUMMARY

Although normal aging brings with it some mild impairments in speech, language, and cognition, normally aging adults rarely experience communication disabilities and handicaps. A handicapping impairment in speech, language, or cognition is usually due to disease or injury to the brain or neuromotor system. Older adults are particularly susceptible to such injuries and conditions because of the accumulation of a lifetime of minor neurological insults, exposure to toxins over a life span, the use of various medications, nutritional deficiencies, and so on.

Communication disorders in adulthood include *aphasia,* a language disorder, *dysarthria,* a speech disorder, and *dementia,* a cognitive disorder. Right-hemisphere damage and traumatic brain injury may also cause communication disorders, although they are typically milder. Speech-language pathologists often play an important role in helping affected individuals regain communicative functions, both by working on specific speech and language skills and by introducing assistive devices and compensatory strategies. In addition, speech-language pathologists may diagnose and treat *dys-phagia,* or swallowing disorders, in this population.

Both the family and the individual are greatly affected by a communication disorder resulting from neurological injury or disease. Families play an important role in rehabilitation and can provide the affected member with motivation to reach out once more. The individual with the neurological disorder must often battle feelings of depression and dependency in order to restructure his life. However, with time and patience, meaningful activities can be reestablished, and, for all involved, life goes on.

R E V I E W   Q U E S T I O N S

1. How does normal aging affect communication abilities?
2. What functions (in general) have been associated with the following parts of the brain: frontal lobe, parietal lobe, temporal lobe, occipital lobe?
3. What is the location and function of the anterior language area? The posterior language area?
4. What do we mean by "subcortical structures?" What happens if these structures are damaged by stroke or injury?
5. Describe the characteristics of the three types of aphasia discussed in this chapter.
6. Describe the speech-language pathologist's treatment of the communication disorders seen in aphasic individuals. How effective is therapy?
7. What is the role of the family in rehabilitating the individual with aphasia?
8. What are the characteristics of right-hemisphere damage?

9. What is *dysarthria*? What are some common causes of dysarthria in the older adult population?
10. What is *dementia*? What are its primary causes?
11. How is dementia treated by the speech-language pathologist? What is the role of the family?
12. What are the characteristics of traumatic brain injury? What communication disorders can be seen in this condition?
13. How is traumatic brain injury treated by rehabilitation professionals?
14. Differentiate between an impairment, a disability, and a handicap. What implications do these concepts have for treatment of the adult with a neurologically based communication disorder?
15. What are the consequences to the individual of neurologically based communication disorders acquired in adulthood?

F O R   F U R T H E R   I N F O R M A T I O N

Adamovich, B., Henderson, J., and **Auerbach, S.** (1985). *Cognitive rehabilitation of closed head injured patients: A dynamic approach.* Austin, TX: Pro-Ed.

Bayles, K., and **Kasniak, A.** (1987). *Communication and cognition in normal aging and dementia.* Austin, TX: Pro-Ed.

Brookshire, R. (1992). *An introduction to neurogenic communication disorders* (4th ed.). St. Louis: Mosby Year Book.

Davis, G. (1993). *A survey of adult aphasia and related language disorders* (2nd ed.). Englewood Cliffs, NJ: Prentice-Hall.

Murdoch, B. (1990). *Acquired speech and language disorders: A neuroanatomical and functional neurological approach*. London: Chapman and Hall.

Rosenbek, J., LaPointe, L., and Wertz, R. (1989). *Aphasia: A clinical approach*. Austin, TX: Pro-Ed.

Yorkston, K., Beukelman, D., and Bell, K. (1988). *Clinical management of dysarthric speakers*. Boston, MA: College-Hill Press.

Basic Concepts in
Hearing and Audiology

Hearing is an essential part of our communication abilities. It is necessary both for the development of speech and language and in our day-to-day interactions. Without adequate hearing, a child does not have ready access to the words and sentences that are used by those around him to express ideas and concepts. Other forms of language might be taught to the child, such as a formal sign language, but few people know or use nonvocal languages on a regular basis. Unless one can hear, one cannot easily participate in the world of speech and sound in which most communication takes place.

But what do we really "hear" in this world of sound? What is *sound?* How do our ears pick it up, and how does it get from the ear to the brain? In this chapter, we will explore the nature of sound and how sounds are perceived by the auditory system. We will also examine the role of the audiologist in diagnosing hearing disorders. As we shall learn, the auditory system is extremely complex in its structure and function; and disorders can occur at many levels. It is important to understand some basic principles of sound and the hearing mechanism before disorders of this system can be understood.

THE NATURE OF SOUND

When most people think of sound, they think of a sensation that is generated by some external source and detected by the ear. Experience confirms this impression many times daily. However, if we look at sound in its most basic form, we see that it is really a series of pressure waves (Borden and Harris, 1994).

Observe the tuning fork in Figure 14-1. When a tuning fork is struck, it begins to vibrate. This means that the tines of the fork move outward to some point of maximum excursion, and then begin to move inward. This inward movement carries them past their normal *(neutral)* position to a point of maximum incursion, at which point they begin their outward journey once more. During the outward phase of their motion, the tines of the tuning fork cause air molecules around them to move outward as well and to become compressed. When the tines move inward, the air molecules become rarefied. We can see that the air molecules surrounding the tuning fork move synchronously with its vibration, creating alternating intervals of compression and rarefaction (Gelfand, 1990). When we use a sine wave to symbolize a sound wave, as seen in Figure 14-1, we are actually representing the back-and-forth movement of air molecules surrounding the vibrating body.

As the air molecules surrounding the tuning fork move back and forth in synchrony with the movements of the tines, they "bump" into air molecules adjacent to them, causing those air molecules to move in the same pattern. When these more distant air molecules begin to vibrate, they, in turn, trigger movement in the air molecules adjacent to them, even more distant from

Tuning fork

Air molecules

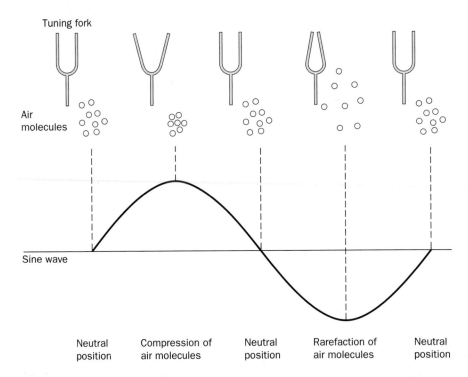

Sine wave

| Neutral position | Compression of air molecules | Neutral position | Rarefaction of air molecules | Neutral position |

FIGURE 14-1 Vibration of a tuning fork, and subsequent movement of the surrounding air molecules. These movements can be divided into cycles characterized by periods of compression and rarefaction. As the movement of air molecules around the tuning fork induces movement in more and more distant air molecules, the sound wave *travels*.

the tuning fork. In this way, waves of compression and rarefaction radiate in all directions from the original vibrating body. It is important to note that the original air molecules surrounding the tines do not travel farther and farther from the tuning fork. Rather, their motion induces motion in adjacent air molecules, just as the movement of the tuning fork induced movement in them.

Sound waves generate an actual measurable force against objects in their path. Most objects do not respond much to these forces—the pressure exerted by sound waves is small indeed. However, when these subtle pressure changes come into contact with an auditory system, particularly a human auditory system, they cause things to happen. We will explore the interaction between sound waves and the structures of the auditory system later in this chapter.

PROPERTIES OF SOUND

We have discussed some of the properties of sound with respect to voice production; let us now consider them in the context of hearing. We will concentrate here on frequency and intensity, two important properties of sound that audiologists frequently test and that affect the perception of speech.

FREQUENCY

A basic definition of *frequency* is the number of times per second that an event occurs. For example, if a tuning fork is struck, the number of times per second the tines of the tuning fork move in and out would be considered the frequency of vibration of that tuning fork. The corresponding number of compression-rarefaction cycles of air molecules per second would be the frequency of the sound wave it produced.

If there was a single compression-rarefaction cycle in one second, we would say that that sound wave had a frequency of 1 cycle per second, or 1 Hz. If there were 100 compression-rarefaction cycles in 1 second, the sound wave would have a frequency of 100 Hz. We normally perceive low-frequency sounds to be low in *pitch,* the perceptual analog of frequency. High-frequency sounds are perceived as high in pitch. The human auditory system in its prime is capable of perceiving frequencies between 20 Hz and 20,000 Hz (Borden and Harris, 1994). However, the ear is not equally sensitive to all of those frequencies. Some must be more intense for us to perceive them.

INTENSITY

Intensity refers to the amount of force generated by air molecules as they vibrate. Very forceful vibrations have high measured intensities, while weak vibratory movements have low measured intensities. Intensity in the context of the human auditory system is usually measured in units of relative pressure called *decibels,* or dB. The human ear is capable of responding to sounds as soft as 0 dB and as intense as 130 dB (Borden and Harris, 1994). It is important to note here that 0 dB does not represent the absence of sound. The dB unit is a relative scale of pressures, and 0 dB represents the pressure at which an individual with average, normal hearing can just barely detect a sound (Gelfand, 1990). Thus, some individuals with exceptional hearing may be able to perceive sounds less than 0 on the dB scale used by audiologists.

A SUMMARY OF
THE NATURE AND PROPERTIES OF SOUND

We have defined *sound* as a series of pressure waves generated when a vibrating body "hits" the air molecules surrounding it, setting them into synchronous vibration. As the air molecules move back and forth, they in turn "hit" adjacent air molecules more distant from the vibrating body. These more distant air molecules are then set into vibration themselves, causing movement in yet more distant air molecules. In this way the sound wave "travels." Two particularly important properties of sound waves are *frequency,* or the number of times per second the pressure wave repeats itself, and *intensity,* or the force with which the air molecules move. Let us now turn our attention to the receptor mechanism that responds to these subtle alterations in pressure, the human auditory system.

ANATOMY AND PHYSIOLOGY OF THE HUMAN AUDITORY SYSTEM

THE OUTER EAR AND ITS FUNCTIONS

Figure 14-2 shows a schematic of the anatomy of the ear. We can see that the structure most of us call the *ear* is actually known as the *pinna* or *auricle.* The pinna encircles a small opening that is the entrance to the auditory canal. The auditory canal terminates in a structure with which most of us are somewhat familiar—the eardrum, or *tympanic membrane.* Taken together, the pinna, auditory canal, and tympanic membrane comprise the outer ear.

The outer ear is designed to "capture" sound waves and transmit them deeper into the auditory system. In addition, the pinna and the auditory canal appear to amplify the incoming signal by 10 to 15 dB in the 2000 to 5500 Hz range due to their resonance characteristics (Martin, 1994). Finally, the pinna has the important function of helping the listener localize sound, especially for frequencies above 4000 Hz (Gelfand, 1990).

Once sound waves are captured by the pinna, they proceed through the auditory canal toward the tympanic membrane. Here, we must stop and recall that sound waves are really alternating intervals of positive and negative pressure (or compression and rarefaction of air molecules). As the

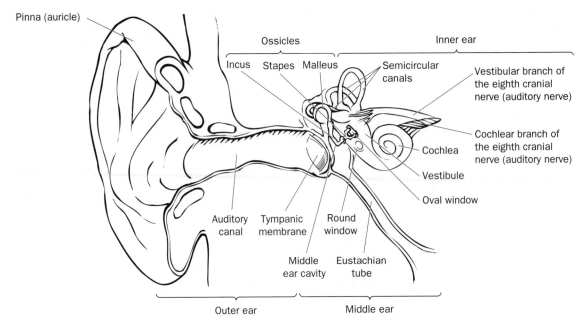

FIGURE 14-2 Anatomy of the ear.

positive-pressure phase of the sound wave pushes against the tympanic membrane, it causes the tympanic membrane to move inward. During the negative-pressure phase of the sound wave, the tympanic membrane moves back outward. As each sound wave literally "hits" the eardrum, the eardrum moves accordingly. Thus, movement is set up in the tympanic membrane that mirrors the movement of the original vibrating source. The frequency and force of the original vibrations will cause movements of a corresponding frequency and force in the eardrum—if all is well in the middle ear.

THE MIDDLE EAR AND ITS FUNCTIONS

The tympanic membrane separates the auditory canal from the middle ear cavity. The middle ear cavity, which occupies a hollow in the temporal bone of the skull, is lined with mucus membranes similar to those that line the nasal and oral cavities and respiratory tract. Indeed, the middle ear cavity can be seen as an extension of the oral cavity because the two are connected by the eustachian

tubes. The eustachian tubes originate at the back of the mouth on either side of the soft palate, and each courses upward and backward into its respective middle ear cavity. Like the middle ear cavity, the eustachian tubes are also lined with mucous membranes. Their function is to provide a passage for air into each middle ear cavity, so that equal air pressure will be maintained on both sides of the tympanic membrane.

The middle ear cavity is spanned by three tiny bones, the smallest bones in the body, known collectively as the *ossicles* (see Figure 14-2). The outermost of these—the hammer, or *malleus*—is attached to the tympanic membrane. The anvil, or *incus,* is the middle bone, and the stirrup, or *stapes* is the innermost bone. The stapes is attached to a membrane known as the *oval window,* which separates the middle ear cavity from the inner ear. Just below the oval window is a similar membrane, the round window, which also separates the middle ear cavity from the inner ear.

The middle ear, like the outer ear, functions to transmit incoming sound waves deeper into the auditory system. And like the outer ear, the middle ear does this in the medium of air. Air taken in through the nose and mouth during respiration flows up through the eustachian tube and into the middle ear cavity. Ideally, both the air in the auditory canal (on the outer side of the tympanic membrane) and the air in the middle ear cavity (on the inner side) contain equal atmospheric pressure. This is important in order for the tympanic membrane to vibrate freely. If the pressure in the middle ear cavity, for example, were lower than the pressure in the auditory canal, the eardrum would be retracted toward the side of the lower pressure. As a result, the tympanic membrane would not be able to move freely in response to the very subtle incoming pressure changes that characterize soft sounds. This phenomenon and its implications for hearing status is discussed further in Chapter 15.

Assuming equal atmospheric pressure on both sides of it, the tympanic membrane vibrates with corresponding frequency and force to the original vibrating body. As the tympanic membrane moves back and forth, the ossicles move with it. This movement of the ossicles transmits the original vibratory pattern across the middle ear cavity. Finally, the movement of the stapes against the oval window sets it, too, into vibration, still mirroring the frequency and force of the original vibrating body.

But the ossicles are more than links in a chain that transmit a sound wave. They also help modify the incoming wave so that it will better "match" the capabilities of the inner ear. Beyond the oval window lies the cochlea, a fluid-filled structure that, as we shall learn, must be set into vibration by the stapes. Because fluid is denser than air, it takes more force to set up a vibratory pattern within it. Thus, if the movements of the tympanic membrane are to be translated into movements in the cochlear fluid, the force of the tympanic membrane's vibration must be focused and amplified. This is primarily accomplished through the size difference between the tympanic membrane and the *footplate* of the stapes (the part of the stapes that contacts the oval window). Specifically, the area of the tympanic membrane is approximately seventeen times larger than the area of the footplate of the stapes. Because of this dramatic reduction in area, pressure at the stapes correspondingly increases (Bess and Humes, 1990).

It is also true, however, that when sound is very loud, the oval window can be damaged by the forceful movements of the tympanic membrane and ossicles. In such cases, particularly for high frequency and intermittent sounds, the ossicles can function to "brake" the transmission of pressure. Tiny muscles that attach to the ossicles stiffen and reduce the *amplitude* (or extent) of ossicular movement. Thus, when the vibratory pattern finally reaches the stapes and the oval window, it may be reduced enough in amplitude so that it will not damage the oval window and the delicate structures that lie beyond. Despite this protective function of the ossicles, however, noise is still an important hazard to the ear, as we shall learn in Chapter 15.

THE INNER EAR AND ITS FUNCTIONS

Deep within the temporal bone of the skull lies the inner ear. The inner ear consists of a small snail-shell-shaped spiral tube known as the *cochlea,* as well as the vestibule, semicircular canals, and related structures, and the auditory nerve (eighth cranial nerve; see Figure 14-2). The cochlea is a bony labyrinth within the temporal bone lined with several different membranes, coiled upon itself $2\frac{5}{8}$ times. Unlike the outer and middle parts of the ear, the inner ear normally contains fluid. Whereas the outer ear and middle ear transmit mechanical energy in the form of pressure variations, the inner ear transmits neural impulses in the form of electrochemical changes in nerve cells.

If we were to straighten out the cochlea, we would see that in fact, it is divided into three layers along its length, as it is in Figure 14-3. The top layer, the scala vestibuli, is just beyond the vestibule and the opening to the semicircular canals, on the inner side of the oval window. The bottom layer, the scala tympani, ends in the round window, a second membrane separating the middle ear cavity from the inner ear. Notice

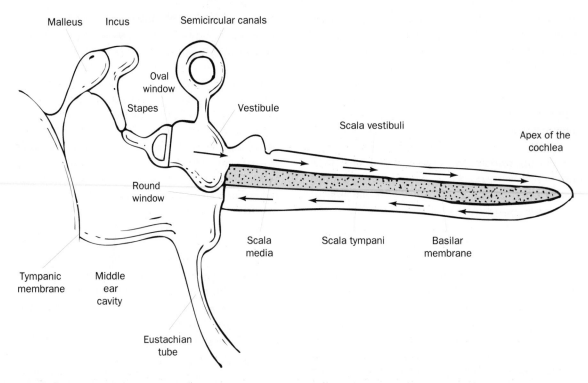

FIGURE 14-3 A schematic diagram of the cochlea showing its three layers: the scala vestibuli, scala tympani, and scala media. The cochlea is normally a coiled structure. In this schematic, however, it has been straightened so that the three layers can be clearly seen. Vibration of the stapes against the oval window sets the perilymph in the scali vestibuli and tympani into vibration.

that the scala vestibuli and the scala tympani communicate at the *apex,* or tip, of the cochlea. Both the scala vestibuli and the scala tympani are filled with a fluid called *perilymph,* similar to the cerebrospinal fluid that circulates in and around the brain and spinal cord.

The middle layer of the cochlea, the scala media, is a completely closed system filled with a fluid called *endolymph.* The top membrane separating the scala media from the scala vestibuli is Reissner's membrane. The lower division, between the scala media and the scala tympani, is the basilar membrane. The basilar membrane supports the primary organ of hearing, the organ of Corti. This extremely complex structure contains tens of thousands of delicate hair cells, divided into inner and outer groups. Both types are

embedded via various types of supporting cells in the basilar membrane.

At its base, each inner hair cell (the most important type for sound sensation) is connected to a group of nerve fibers. A series of approximately 30,000 nerve fibers ultimately exits from the cochlea to form the cochlear branch of the auditory nerve (Zemlin, 1988). This nerve carries information about sound through a variety of subcortical processing centers, and ultimately to the temporal lobe of the brain.

But how is sound transduced from the movement of the stapes and oval window into neural impulses in the hair cells and cochlear nerve? The function of the cochlea as a transducer is an extremely complex area of auditory physiology, the specifics of which are well beyond the scope of an introductory text. The following description is a simplified model of cochlear function, drawn from both theory and currently accepted research findings.

As you recall, the cochlea is fluid-filled. As the oval window moves in and out in response to the movement of the stapes, a traveling wave is set up in the perilymph, similar to waves on the ocean. We should note here that the round window serves as a "release valve" so that as the oval window moves in and out, the round window moves out and in, permitting the perilymph to ebb and flow freely without damaging fixed structures (Zemlin, 1988).

As the perilymph moves, so do the basilar membrane, endolymph, and organ of Corti. The movements of these structures against other parts of the inner ear cause a shearing motion in the hair cells. Through a mechanism not totally understood, when a hair cell is moved in this way, a nerve impulse is triggered in the nerve fibers at its base. This nerve impulse is then conducted along the cochlear branch of the auditory nerve and eventually on to the temporal lobe of the brain (Gelfand, 1990). Thus, the hair cell is the primary sensory receptor for hearing. Its movement is what eventually results in the perception of a sound.

Currently, most researchers agree that hair cells are stimulated by sounds in a frequency-specific way, depending on their location within the cochlea. As discussed previously, sound waves in the cochlea create traveling waves in the perilymph and also in the basilar membrane. These traveling waves proceed from the basal end of the cochlea (near the oval window and vestibule) to the *apex* (tip) of the cochlea. The movement, or *displacement,* of the basilar membrane increases in amplitude as the wave progresses from base to apex, until it reaches some point of maximum displacement, after which the basilar membrane drops back to its normal position. Successive traveling waves create an envelope of displacement of the basilar membrane, as shown in Figure 14-4 (Bess and Humes, 1990).

The importance of this envelope is that the location of its peak changes with the frequency of the original sound wave. Sounds of high frequency create maximum displacement near the base of the cochlea, thus stimulating hair cells in that region—near the oval window. Sounds of low frequency create maximum displacement toward the apex of the cochlea, stimulating hair cells far from the stapes and oval window (see Figure 14-4). When a particular group of hair cells at a particular location is stimulated, their movement triggers a neural impulse, which carries a message to the brain that a sound of a certain frequency has been perceived.

Of course, most sound waves are complex in nature, composed of both high and low frequencies. This means that both high- and low-frequency traveling waves will be produced in the cochlea, stimulating both basal and apical hair cells, and give rise to the perception of multiple frequencies. When we listen to music, speech, noise, or almost any other environmental sound, this is exactly what happens.

The inner ear structures we have described so far are specialized for sound sensing. However, there are additional parts of the inner ear, specifically the semicircular canals and their related structures in the vestibule, which are not specialized for hearing. Like the cochlea, these structures are also fluid-filled and lined with hair cells, although they are specialized for very different functions.

The cochlea is set up to receive sound-wave input. The traveling waves generated in the fluid in the cochlea reflect sound waves in the environment, and the hair-cell movements they cause bring the sensation of hearing. By contrast, the utriculus, sacculus, and semicircular canals are set up to receive information about the head's position in space. The hair cells in these structures move in response to changes in an individual's position. As the body moves with respect to gravity, changes in hair-cell orientation trigger nerve impulses in nerve rootlets which contribute to the vestibular branch of the auditory nerve. This nerve carries position and movement information to the sensory cortex in the parietal lobe of the

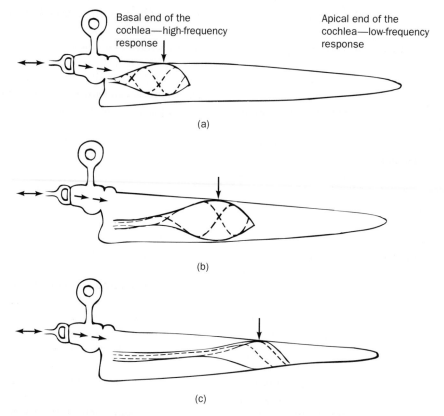

Basal end of the
cochlea—high-frequency
response

Apical end of the
cochlea—low-frequency
response

(a)

(b)

(c)

FIGURE 14-4 Schematic representation of movements of the basilar membrane, and how hair cells at various locations might be stimulated. Figure 14.4(a) shows a very high frequency sound, (b) shows a medium-frequency sound, and (c) shows a low-frequency sound and, for each, the point along the cochlea where maximum stimulation occurs. The dotted lines represent the movement of the basilar membrane at specific instants in time; the solid line represents the envelope of the displacement patterns.

brain, where those sensations are interpreted. The sense of balance is mediated by these structures, known collectively as the *vestibular system* (Zemlin, 1988).

THE FREQUENCY COMPOSITION OF SPEECH

As we discussed the function of the inner ear, we spent some time with the concept of high frequencies stimulating hair cells at the basal end of the cochlea and low frequencies stimulating hair cells at the apical end. The attentive reader may

wonder what, exactly, one needs all those frequencies for. Some might assume that the high frequencies are needed to understand women's speech while the low frequencies are needed to understand men's speech. *This assumption is not true.* As we shall learn in the following section, the frequencies required for speech perception cover a wide range and are similar regardless of whether the speaker is a man or a woman. In this section, we shall examine the frequencies produced when an individual speaks and the frequencies that must be heard if a listener is to understand the spoken word.

During a typical sample of conversational

speech, an individual of either sex is likely to produce frequencies ranging from 100 Hz to 8000 Hz. The lowest frequency component for any particular speaker is always his or her *fundamental frequency,* or the rate at which the vocal folds open and close. As we discussed in Chapter 10, this averages approximately 100 Hz for young adult men and 200 Hz for young adult women.

However, speech involves far more than a speaker's fundamental frequency. As we discussed in Chapter 10, vocal-fold vibration generates a whole spectrum of frequencies in the vocal tract. This laryngeal spectrum consists of a series of harmonics, or overtones, which are multiples of the fundamental. According to Flanagan (1958), an early researcher in this area, as many as forty harmonics of the fundamental may be present in the laryngeal spectrum. Thus, the typical speaker is actually generating frequencies (including harmonics) that extend from 100 to 200 Hz at the lower extreme to approximately 5000 to 8000 Hz at the upper extreme.

When the tongue, lips, and jaw move during speech, the laryngeal spectrum is modified so that some frequencies are amplified and others are *damped,* or reduced. This is particularly apparent when vowels are formed. Each vowel has a characteristic distribution of energy, with areas of concentration in some frequencies and an absence of energy in others. These patterns of energy can be displayed on a *spectrogram,* a visual representation of speech that shows frequency on the vertical axis, time on the horizontal axis, and energy by the darkness of the markings. Areas of energy concentration that characterize a vowel or a vowel-like consonant are known as *formants* and are symbolized as dark bars on the spectrogram.

The spectrogram in Figure 14-5 illustrates the formants of several English vowels. For the vowels "ee" and "oo," we can see formants below 1000 Hz, above 2500 Hz, and an absence of energy in the 1000 to 2500 Hz range. The vowels "eh," "ah," and "aw," by contrast, have a greater portion of their energy in the middle frequencies.

In order for a listener to discriminate one vowel from another, it is important to be able to hear each vowel's first two formants, or the first two frequency regions in which there is energy concentration. This principle was first demonstrated by the classic work of Peterson and Barney (1952). Since only two vowels ("ee" and

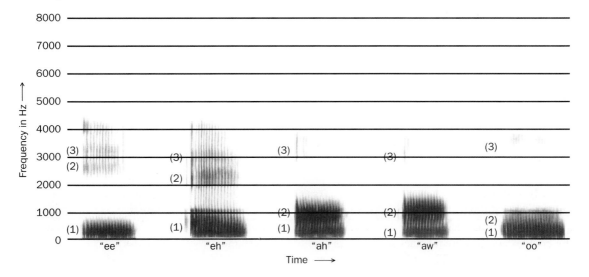

FIGURE 14-5 A spectrogram showing the frequency composition of five different English vowels. The dark bars labeled (1), (2), and (3) are the first three formants of each vowel. Each vowel has a somewhat different formant structure, which allows listeners to differentiate one vowel from another.

"eh") have a second formant above 2000 Hz, hearing up to 2000 Hz is sufficient to be able to clearly identify which vowel a speaker is producing. In fact, because of the salience of the frequency cues in the low frequencies, most vowels can be understood with frequency information up to only 1000 Hz present.

Many consonants are similar to vowels in that they, too, have a formant structure. Consonants such as "m," "n," "l," "r," "y," and "w," share this characteristic. These consonants are composed of patterns of energy concentration in some frequencies and an absence of energy in others, as determined by the shape of the vocal tract and the relative amplification and damping of the frequencies in the laryngeal spectrum. For these sounds, hearing up to approximately 2000 to 3000 Hz is necessary in order to discriminate one sound from another (Nerbonne and Schow, 1989). The spectrogram in Figure 14-6 shows the frequency components of these consonants.

In contrast, stops, fricatives, and affricates are not characterized by a formant structure. Like the phonemes we have already discussed, stops, fricatives, and affricates also contain high-frequency components; but for these sounds, the high frequencies are not simply modifications of the laryngeal spectrum. For sounds such as "s," "t," "ch," "sh," and "f," high frequencies are generated by the articulators themselves. Say the "s" sound, and listen to the hissing noise created as air rushes between your tongue tip and alveolar ridge. The noise created is completely independent of vocal-fold vibration. In fact, since it is a voiceless sound, there *is* no laryngeal spectrum present to modify. Thus, the high frequencies that characterize voiceless fricatives, affricates, and stops are generated by air turbulence as the articulators occlude or restrict the breath stream. Even for the voiced cognates of these sounds ("z," "d," "j," "zh," and "v," for example), the frequencies produced by air turbulence are most important in order to be able to distinguish one sound from another correctly.

FIGURE 14-6 A spectrogram showing the frequency components of six different English consonants. These consonants, like the vowels pictured in Figure 14.5, have a formant-like structure that aids the listener in discriminating one consonant from another. However, as produced in actual words, these consonants also are characterized by temporal (time-related) changes that are not shown in this figure.

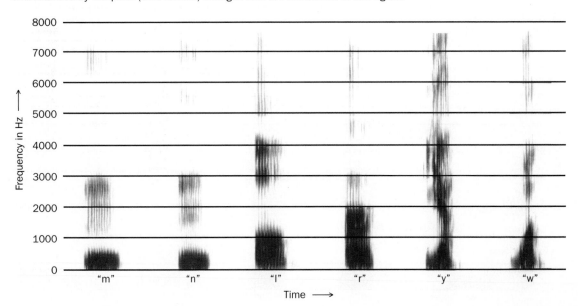

Because stops, fricatives, and affricates are formed from noise rather than from the harmonics of the laryngeal spectrum, they do not have a formant structure. Note the broad, diffuse frequency-energy patterns associated with each consonant in Figure 14-7 as compared to the more frequency specific areas of energy concentration representing the vowels in Figures 14-5 and the consonants in Figure 14-6. In order to be able to discriminate among most stops, good hearing up to 3000 Hz is necessary (Gelfand, 1990). For fricatives and affricates, even higher frequencies are necessary. To differentiate "s" from "th," for example, one must be able to hear in the frequency range of 4000 to 8000 Hz (Nerbonne and Schow, 1989). Voiceless fricatives and affricates not only contain very high frequencies but are also typically less intense than voiced sounds. As we shall see in later chapters, this combination of high frequency characteristics and reduced intensity for voiceless phonemes presents

many problems for those with hearing impairments.

Before we conclude our discussion of the frequency composition of speech and speech perception, it is important to note that frequency is not the only aspect of sound that is used in discriminating one sound from another. Some speech sounds are recognizable because of their duration, their rate of frequency change over time, or other temporal properties. Some speech sounds, such as "f" and "th," are seen rather than perceived through hearing. Most listeners do not even need to hear every sound in a word; using their knowledge of English semantics, syntax, and morphology, they can predict an entire word based on a few acoustic cues from the first phoneme or two (Craig and Kim, 1990). However, when a large enough portion of the frequency spectrum is unavailable to the listener, these other cuing systems break down, and the understanding of conversational speech may be compromised.

FIGURE 14-7 A spectrogram showing the frequency components of three voiceless fricatives, a voiceless affricate, and a voiceless stop in English. Note the relative strength of the noise components of these sounds above 2000 Hz and the weakness of noise components below 2000 Hz. Someone with poor hearing in the frequencies above 2000 Hz would have some difficulty distinguishing these sounds from one another.

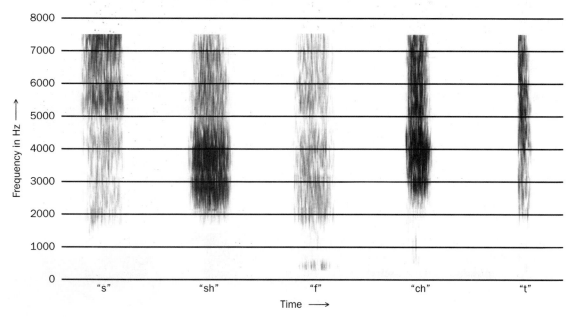

THE ASSESSMENT OF HEARING

Hearing assessment is generally undertaken because an individual is having difficulty hearing and understanding speech. In the case of a child, hearing assessment may be recommended if the child is *suspected* of having difficulty hearing speech, perhaps because of delayed speech and language development. Both adults and children may initially consult an *otolaryngologist,* a medical doctor specializing in diseases of the ear and throat, to assess the physical condition of the hearing mechanism. However, it is the role of the audiologist to determine the individual's hearing status and how it might be contributing to any communication disorder the individual is experiencing. The audiologist may also help the otolaryngologist determine the cause of the disorder and identify the location of lesions in the auditory-nervous system between the cochlea and the brain. Finally, the audiologist is charged with making recommendations for or implementing rehabilitation procedures.

In performing his or her duties in the area of assessment, the audiologist generally gives a number of audiological tests. We will review some of the testing procedures used by audiologists in the next section.

PURE-TONE THRESHOLD TESTS

1. Air-Conduction Thresholds. Most of us who had our hearing tested in our elementary school years remember headphones, little "beeps" or notes, and raising our hands in response. The sounds we heard, known as *pure tones,* are the stimuli used in pure-tone, air-conduction threshold testing.

The instrument that generates the pure tones used in pure-tone threshold testing is known as an *audiometer.* The audiometer is generally a self-contained unit including headphones for delivery of the test stimuli, a frequency-selection dial, an intensity-selection dial, and a switch that permits the audiologist to present the tone for a specified duration of time (usually one or two seconds).

A typical audiometer is pictured in Figure 14-8.

The "beeps" we remember hearing are the *pure-tone stimuli*—single-frequency, single-intensity sounds, usually at 250, 500, 1000, 2000, 4000, and 8000 Hz (Kaplan et al., 1993). Although these single-frequency pure tones do not sound like any speech or environmental sounds we are accustomed to, in fact those frequencies are important components of many of the sounds around us. The 4000-Hz tone may not sound much like an "s," but if you had poor hearing at 4000 Hz, the "s" might be indistinguishable from a "sh" or "f" to you. The pure-tone frequencies presented in a test of this type are isolated components that we would normally hear in the context of a broad spectrum of frequencies in speech, music, or noise. They do not sound familiar in and of themselves, but without them, we would not be able to recognize much of what we hear.

In doing a threshold test, the audiologist presents each frequency to the client in each ear, one frequency at a time. Initially, the stimulus tone is

FIGURE 14-8 A portable audiometer is used in pure-tone threshold testing, as well as bone-conduction testing. The headphones, right, are used for air-conduction testing, while the vibrator, left, is used for bone-conduction testing.

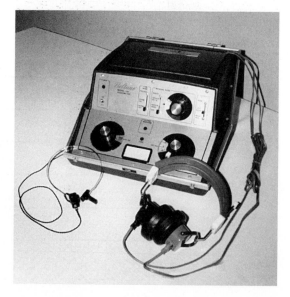

presented at a relatively loud level that the client can hear easily. However, once the client becomes familiar with the tone and the hand-raising response, the audiologist reduces the loudness until it is so soft that the client hears the tone only about half the time, or in three out of six trials. This level of loudness is known as the client's *threshold* for that frequency (Martin, 1994).

The results of a pure-tone threshold test are graphed on an audiogram, pictured in Figure 14-9. Right-ear thresholds are plotted using a red circle, while left-ear thresholds are represented by

a blue "X." The horizontal axis of the audiogram lists the frequencies that are typically tested, from the lowest on the left side of the graph (125 Hz) to the highest on the right (8000 Hz). The vertical axis of the audiogram specifies intensity level relative to the hearing level (HL) established by the American National Standards Institute (ANSI, 1989). Intensity level can be graphed from –10 dB at the top of the audiogram to 100 or 120 dB at the bottom (Kaplan et al., 1993). The lower the intensity level, the more sensitive the individual's hearing. One might consider the various intensity

FIGURE 14-9 An audiogram. Frequency is on the horizontal axis, and intensity is on the vertical axis. This figure shows an example of normal hearing as determined by a pure-tone threshold test.

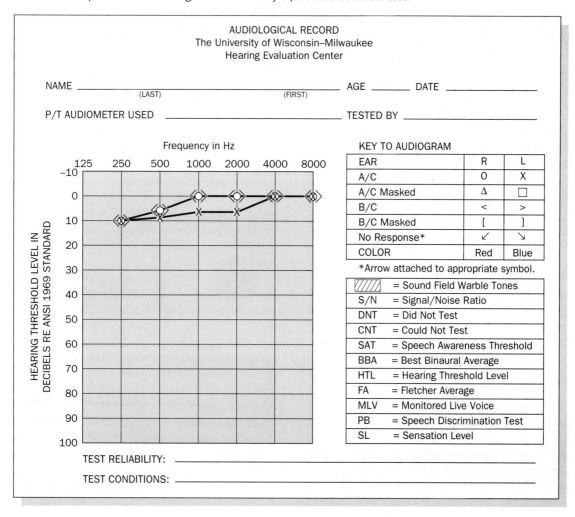

levels on the audiogram to be analogous to the numbers on the volume knob of a stereo or TV set. The higher the number, the louder the volume. An individual who needs a volume level of only 0 or 10 dB in order to just detect a tone at 1000 Hz, for example, has much better hearing than an individual who needs a volume level of 90 or 100 dB for the same task at the same frequency. If a client has normal hearing, thresholds between −10 and 15 dB should be obtained (see Figure 14-9) (Kaplan et al., 1993).

Because a pure-tone threshold test requires multiple presentations of six or seven different frequencies from (250 to 8000 Hz), first in one ear and then the other, it can be quite a lengthy procedure. This is especially true if the client is not cooperative or is unstable in terms of his or her responses. For situations where an exact description of hearing abilities is not needed, a pure-tone screening test might be more appropriate. We will discuss this procedure later on in this section.

2. Bone-Conduction Tests.

In the audiometric test we just described, pure-tone stimuli are delivered via earphones through the medium of air in the auditory canal. In a sense, then, the air-conduction pure-tone threshold procedure tests the entire auditory system (with the exception of the pinna), from the auditory canal to the temporal lobe of the brain where the sound is perceived.

There may be some instances, however, when it is desirable to test hearing starting at the inner ear, exclusive of the effects of the outer and middle parts of the ear. How is this possible, if the outer and middle ear are necessary to transmit sound waves to the inner ear?

In fact, there is another pathway for sound to reach the inner ear other than through the auditory canal, tympanic membrane, and ossicles. Although they travel best through gaseous media, sound waves can also travel through solid media. Thus sound waves can reach the cochlea through the bones and muscles of the skull and face as well as through more conventional channels. When pure tones are introduced through the bones of

the skull rather than through earphones and the auditory canal, it is possible to do bone-conduction pure-tone threshold tests.

The appropriate instrumentation for determining bone-conduction thresholds is usually available within the conventional audiometer used to assess air-conduction thresholds. Most units have a bone-conduction setting that sends the pure-tone stimuli to a small vibrator mounted on a headband instead of to the earphones. The audiologist positions the vibrator on the bony prominence behind the client's ear, known as the *mastoid process* of the temporal bone of the skull. The selected frequency is then delivered to the vibrator, which, as its name implies, vibrates against the skull. This vibrational energy is relayed through the skull directly to both cochleas, bypassing the outer and middle ears (Silman and Silverman, 1991).

Do people actually hear through bone conduction in normal conversational settings? The answer is no. The speech around us and other environmental (airborne) sounds are rarely conducted to the ear in this way. The only exception is when one hears one's own voice. In such a situation, the speaker is receiving his or her speech both through air-conduction channels and, since the source of the sound is within the speaker's body, through bone conduction as well. However, bone conduction plays almost no role in hearing the speech of others (Silman and Silverman, 1991).

The procedure for determining pure-tone thresholds via bone conduction is similar to the procedure described above for air-conduction thresholds. Testing is typically conducted at 250, 500, 1000, 2000, and 4000 Hz (Martin, 1994), in each ear separately. Bone-conduction thresholds are plotted on the same audiogram used for the air-conduction threshold results. The right ear is represented by a right-end bracket or arrow (], >), while the left ear is represented by a left-end bracket or arrow ([, <) (see Figure 14-9) (Kaplan et al., 1993).

If both air-conduction and bone-conduction pure-tone thresholds are done, much can be learned about the functioning of the client's auditory system. However, additional testing is often necessary as well, depending on the clinical situation, the age of the client, and the nature of the suspected disorder.

3. Pediatric Testing. As we will discuss in the next chapter, it is important to determine the hearing abilities of infants and young children suspected of having auditory disorders. If hearing is even moderately impaired, a child's language and phonological development can be significantly delayed. In addition, children with undiagnosed hearing disorders are at risk for a host of behavioral and academic problems as they approach their school years. Yet infants and very young children are typically incapable of following the testing protocol for conventional threshold testing.

In order to test infants and young children *behaviorally* (that is, by observing their behavioral responses to sound), audiologists have had to develop alternative procedures to those used for adults. Some of these procedures use pure tones as stimuli and thus provide a somewhat approximate pure-tone threshold. Other procedures, used on the youngest clients, involve speech. One procedure, known as *behavioral observation audiometry,* or BOA, is particularly suitable for infants (Silman and Silverman, 1991). In this procedure, stimuli (words, noise bursts, or tones) of different loudness levels are presented through loudspeakers to the infant. He or she is then observed for a response—a widening of the eyes, blink, turn of the head, or outward movement of the arms—that would indicate that the sound was heard. Because of the variability in infant response, it can be difficult to ascertain hearing sensitivity using this method.

A more sophisticated procedure for testing older babies and young children is visual reinforcement audiometry (VRA). For this procedure, the child must be capable of being conditioned through classical stimulus-response-reinforcement methods. Initially in VRA, tones are presented to the child through loudspeakers,

usually one on each side of the child, or through headphones if the child will tolerate them. As the tones are presented, a mechanical toy in or on the loudspeaker, or some other visually attractive stimulus, is automatically illuminated and activated for the child's amusement. The mechanical toy may be a monkey beating a drum set, a walking doll, a clown banging cymbals, or something similar.

After several conditioning trials, during which the toy is presented simultaneously with the tone, a test tone is presented by itself. If the child has been conditioned successfully, he or she will look toward the mechanical toy in anticipation of its movement. If this occurs, the loudness of the tone can be gradually reduced, with the expectation that if the child hears the tone, he or she will respond by looking at the toy. Each appropriate response is reinforced by activating the toy. In this way, an estimation of threshold is made. Silman and Silverman (1991) report that they have been successful using VRA on children as young as 5 months. The VRA method might also be useful for older hard-to-test populations, such as those with cognitive or developmental disorders.

Finally, play audiometry might be used when a child becomes bored or uncooperative with the hand-raising procedure that is part of conventional pure-tone threshold testing. In *play audiometry,* the child is conditioned to pick up a block or peg when she hears a sound and then to put it into a basket or pegboard (Northern and Downs, 1991). The child's responses to the test's stimuli are thus more enjoyable and age-appropriate than simple hand raising. Play audiometry can be done with pure tones presented over loudspeakers or headphones. Play audiometry is generally appropriate with preschool children. As with VRA, it can also be used effectively with those who have cognitive and developmental disorders.

Fortunately, audiologists do not have to depend on behavioral testing alone to determine the hearing status of young children. As we shall discover later in this chapter, there are several tests audiologists can administer which do not require a voluntary response. However, behavioral testing remains an important component of an evaluation of a child's auditory abilities.

PURE-TONE SCREENING TESTS (AIR-CONDUCTED)

Like pure-tone threshold tests, pure-tone screening tests involve use of an audiometer, headphones, and a similar series of frequencies. In a screening test, however, the individual's exact sensitivity is not determined. Instead, an arbitrary "normal" intensity is targeted, and all frequencies are presented at that particular level. According to ASHA guidelines (Martin, 1994), 20 dB HL (ANSI, 1989) is the preferred level. The recommended frequencies for screening are 500, 1000, 2000, and 4000 Hz.

If a client hears all of the frequencies presented at 20 dB, as indicated by a hand-raising response, she would be considered to have "passed" the screening. If she failed to respond at 20 dB to any of the frequencies presented, she would be considered to have "failed" the screening and scheduled for a rescreening. A second failure would result in a referral for the more specific threshold test, to determine the nature and degree of her hearing loss (Martin, 1994).

The advantage of a pure-tone screening test is that it can be given quickly to large numbers of children. Pure-tone screening is used routinely in public schools to identify children with potential hearing problems. The disadvantage is that this test alone is inconclusive regarding the individual's hearing status, and it may fail to identify individuals who require audiological or medical services. Patrick (1987) estimated that use of pure-tone screening by itself results in only 60 to 70 percent correct identifications. In fact, recent ASHA guidelines call for screening tests that include tympanometry (which we will discuss later) as well as the pure-tone screening procedure (Martin, 1994).

SPEECH-RECOGNITION THRESHOLD TESTS

The audiometric tests we have discussed to this point have involved detection. In such procedures, the task of the person being tested is to indicate the level at which he or she can just barely detect a signal. While pure-tone detection is important in the assessment of auditory function, it is not a frequent experience in real life. Our most important context for hearing is communication, where the stimulus is speech. A test that assesses an individual's ability to recognize or identify the speech they have heard gives us a much more functional assessment of their auditory abilities in everyday situations.

In order to assess an individual's ability to identify more meaningful stimuli, audiologists may administer a speech-recognition threshold test. In this type of test, familiar two-syllable words (e.g., *hot dog, baseball, railroad*) are presented to the client one by one, and the task of the client is to repeat them. These words are first presented at relatively high intensity levels but are gradually presented at softer and softer levels until the client can barely hear them. The *speech-recognition threshold* is defined as the lowest intensity level at which the client can correctly repeat the presented speech stimuli 50 percent of the time (ASHA, 1979).

TYMPANOMETRY

Unlike pure-tone and speech-recognition threshold tests, tympanometry does not really tell us how well an individual hears. Instead, the primary purpose of this test is to assess the status of the middle ear, in particular the movement of the tympanic membrane (Martin, 1994). In addition, this procedure does not require a behavior response from the client. Tympanic-membrane movement is elicited and measured instrumentally.

If the middle ear and eustachian tube are functioning properly, there should be equal atmospheric pressure on both sides of the tympanic membrane, and the membrane should be able to vibrate freely. However, if there is less pressure in the middle ear cavity because of eustachian-tube malfunction, the tympanic membrane will be *retracted* (pulled inward toward the middle ear cavity) slightly. Because the tympanic membrane in such a case is under pressure, it will not vibrate as well as it normally would. Alternatively, if the middle ear cavity is filled with fluid, vibration of the tympanic membrane and ossicles will also be inhibited. In such a case, sound waves would be unable to induce movement in the tympanic membrane due to the high density of the fluid behind it. Unless there is equal atmospheric pressure on the two sides of the tympanic membrane, it will not vibrate as freely as it should.

The *tympanometer* is a device that assesses the ability of the tympanic membrane to vibrate freely, or its *compliance* (Kaplan et al., 1993). This is done by inserting a probe tip into the auditory canal that makes an airtight seal against its walls. Low levels of sound are then introduced into the auditory canal through a miniature speaker *(driver)* in the probe tip. The probe tip also contains a miniature microphone to determine how much sound is being reflected outward rather than transmitted deeper into the auditory system. A compliant tympanic membrane that is vibrating freely will transmit most of the sound energy and reflect little. A noncompliant tympanic membrane that is stiff and does not vibrate freely reflects more sound.

In addition to the microphone and transmitter, a pressure valve is also built into the probe tip. The pressure valve is designed to add or remove air from the auditory canal (see Figure 14-10 for a schematic of a probe tip). This enables the audiologist to assess the eardrum's response to sound under different conditions of positive and negative pressure. The recommended term for what is being measured by tympanometry is *immittance* (Martin, 1994).

The results of this procedure are graphed automatically on a tympanogram. Unlike the audiogram, which the audiologist must fill out by hand, the tympanogram is usually directly printed out as the test is being run. Modern tympanometers can be as small as a physician's otoscope (indeed, some are built into otoscopes) and are digitally controlled. The audiologist needs only to fit the probe tip and check the adequacy of the airtight seal before initiating the instrument's analysis sequence.

Figure 14-11 shows one normal and two abnormal tympanograms. The vertical axis of each graph shows the compliance of the eardrum, with maximum compliance at the top of the axis and minimum compliance at the bottom. The horizontal axis shows pressure differences, with "0" representing equal pressure on both sides of the tympanic membrane. On the left side of the axis, note the negative numbers, indicating that

FIGURE 14-10 A schematic of a probe tip, the instrument inserted into the auditory canal during tympanometry. Tympanometry assesses acoustic immittance, or how compliant the tympanic membrane is in response to sound. The tympanic membrane's function is typically tested under several different pressure conditions.

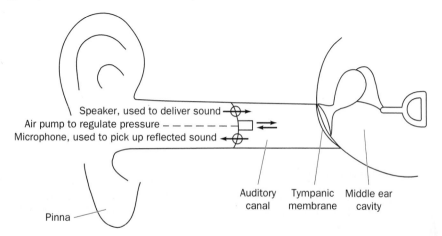

compliance is being measured when the pressure in the auditory canal is less than atmospheric pressure. On the right side of the axis, there are positive numbers, indicating that compliance is being measured when the pressure in the auditory canal is greater than atmospheric pressure.

Note that for an individual with normal middle ear function (Figure 14-11a), the eardrum is maximally compliant when the pressure is at 0—that is, when both sides of the tympanic membrane are at atmospheric pressure. When pressure in the auditory canal is increased or decreased, as depicted at either end of the graph, compliance drops sharply. The sharp upward peak in the middle of the graph is what we expect to see if the eustachian tube is functioning normally and the middle ear is clear.

In the second tympanogram, pictured in Figure 14-11b, a flat configuration can be seen. It appears that there is no point of maximum compliance, regardless of pressure condition. A tympanogram like this indicates that there is fluid in the middle ear cavity that is preventing the eardrum from moving normally. Such a result would signal the need for a referral to an otolaryngologist.

In the third tympanogram, pictured in Figure 14-11c, the peak of compliance is displaced toward the negative side of the graph. A negative peak indicates a less serious condition than that suggested by the flat tympanogram in 14-11b; however, such a result on a tympanogram would alert the audiologist to possible middle ear problems that should be referred to an otolaryngologist.

BRAINSTEM AUDITORY EVOKED RESPONSES

Brainstem auditory evoked responses (BAERs) are known by a variety of names, including brainstem auditory evoked potentials (BAEPs), brainstem evoked responses (BERs), and auditory brainstem responses (ABRs), among others. Like tympanometry, BAERs can be obtained from individuals who cannot or will not respond behaviorally. However, unlike tympanometry, which assesses function of the middle ear, the BAER procedure assesses the function of the processing centers of the auditory pathway between the cochlear nucleus and the temporal lobe of the brain.

Brainstem auditory evoked responses are very small voltage changes recorded from the surface of the scalp. They are emitted in response to sound by the cochlear branch of the auditory nerve and by other subcortical processing centers of the auditory nervous system. These evoked responses happen very quickly—between 1 and

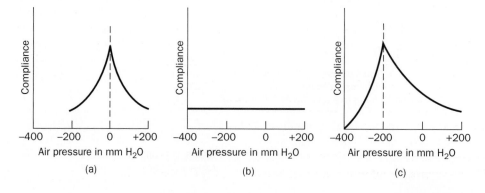

FIGURE 14-11 One normal and two abnormal tympanograms. In (a), a normal tympanogram with a peak at 0 (air pressure in mm) is seen. In (b), no point of maximum compliance is seen, indicating an abnormal condition in the middle ear. In (c), the peak of compliance is displaced toward the negative side of the graph, again indicating a problem in the function of the middle ear.

10 msec (milliseconds, or thousandths of a second)—after the onset of a sound. If the auditory nerve and other parts of the auditory nervous system are working, a very clear pattern of five peaks, or *positive potentials,* should be recorded from the scalp within this time frame. Delayed or absent peaks can indicate abnormal functioning of the auditory system and potential hearing loss (Martin, 1994).

The stimulus used to elicit BAERs is a click. However, a single click presented to the subject is not sufficient to provide a recordable BAER. Because BAERs are so low in terms of voltage, they are overpowered by other noise voltages from the body, primarily the ongoing electrical signals produced by the brain and the muscular activities of the head and eyes (Silman and Silverman, 1991). In order to separate the signal BAER from the much more powerful noise, it is necessary to present thousands of clicks and average the client's responses. The timing of the stimuli, recording of the electrical potential from the scalp, averaging of the responses, and display of the output are all controlled and implemented by computer.

Interpretation of BAERs is not a simple process. First, the click stimuli that are most frequently used are responded to by neurons in the 2000 to 4000-Hz range. Thus, even if a normal pattern of peaks in the BAER is present, it only indicates that "normal hearing is present for at least *one* frequency between 250 and 8000 Hz" (Silman and Silverman, 1991, 271; italics the author's). Hearing losses in the low and middle frequencies are not likely to be identified. Second, delayed or absent peaks could be due to numerous causes and do not necessarily mean that the individual has a hearing loss (Worthington and Peters, 1980).

Despite the limitations of the BAER procedure, it has been recommended as a means of testing the hearing of high-risk infants in order to identify potential deafness and hearing loss earlier. Although the use of BAER with the neonatal population is somewhat controversial (Murray et al., 1985), it can provide information about hear-

ing ability and neurological integrity in a population that is otherwise almost impossible to test with any degree of accuracy.

OTOACOUSTIC EMISSIONS

Otoacoustic emissions were first described by Kemp (1978), who found that he could record sounds from inside a client's auditory canal approximately 6 to 10 msec after the client had been presented with a click. Although there is some dispute regarding the origin of this sound in the auditory canal, it is now believed that the sound originates in the cochlea, from hair cells that have the specific function of amplifying incoming frequencies. The movement of these hair cells, which is intended to aid in the stimulation of nerve fibers, has the side effect of creating additional movement in the basilar membrane, which in turn causes movement in the oval window, movement in the ossicles, and movement in the tympanic membrane—in just the reverse order from normal hearing. The movement of the tympanic membrane then causes vibration of the air in the auditory canal—sound which can be recorded with a sensitive microphone. These sounds are referred to as *otoacoustic emissions,* or sounds produced by the ear.

The testing of otoacoustic emissions is not yet a staple in the audiologist's repertoire, but the clinical implications of these phenomena are currently being explored. If the hair cells themselves create otoacoustic emissions, then hair cells that are destroyed or damaged should not produce emissions. Indeed, this has been found to be the case in both animal and human subjects (Probst et al., 1991). Hair-cell damage due to *ototoxic drugs* (drugs that poison hair cells), exposure to prolonged loud noise, or *anoxia* (lack of oxygen) appears to result in altered or absent otoacoustic emissions (Glattke and Kujawa, 1991).

Possible uses of otoacoustic-emission testing could be to monitor the hearing of individuals who work in noisy environments or in those who, for medical reasons, must take ototoxic drugs. Probst et al. (1991) suggest such testing might be used to screen difficult-to-test neonatal populations, infants, and young children. Glattke and Kujawa (1991), however, point out that otoacoustic emissions testing will be limited if middle ear fluid is present, since the fluid will prevent the transmission of the emission from the cochlea, where it originates, outward toward the tympanic membrane.

In summary, this new and interesting method of measuring hearing offers promise but requires much research before it can be used routinely. Those now entering the field of audiology will need to do that research and to establish normative data and testing protocols. If this new technique can be used to detect hearing loss early, many communication and educational problems might be prevented.

SUMMARY

In this chapter, we reviewed the physical nature of sound as a series of alternating pressure waves and explored its basic properties of frequency and intensity. We also discussed the anatomy and physiology of the hearing mechanism and how speech is perceived. Speech involves a broad spectrum of frequencies, from approximately 100 to 8000 Hz. In order to clearly perceive what a speaker is saying, a listener must have good hearing in both the high- and low-frequency regions. It is important to realize that the high-frequency components of speech are crucial for the understanding of many phonemes—especially fricatives, affricates, and stops—regardless of whether the speaker is a man or a woman.

We then turned to the type of testing an audiologist might do in order to evaluate an individual's hearing. The traditional hearing test is a pure-tone air-conduction threshold test, requiring a voluntary response from the client. The bone-conduction test and the speech-recognition threshold test require a similar type of response. Pure-tone screening tests are typically used on large groups of school-aged children in order to determine quickly which of the children need further audiological or medical follow-up. Tests that do not require a voluntary response include tympanometry, brainstem auditory evoked potentials, and otoacoustic emissions. While none of these tests alone is sufficient to answer all the questions an audiologist must ask about a client's hearing abilities, together they can provide a wealth of information. We now are ready to consider some specific hearing disorders that audiologists diagnose and treat.

R E V I E W Q U E S T I O N S

1. Describe sound in terms of the movement of air molecules. What is necessary in order to generate a sound?
2. What do we mean by *frequency*? How is it measured? What is the analogous perceptual term?
3. What do we mean by *intensity*? How is it measured? What is the analogous perceptual term?
4. Draw the hearing mechanism. Include the following parts: pinna, auditory canal, tympanic membrane, middle ear cavity, ossicles, eustachian tube, cochlea, semicircular canals, auditory nerve.

5. How are the senses of balance and hearing related?
6. Describe the process of hearing, beginning with a sound and ending with the conscious recognition of the sound.
7. What frequencies are important for a person to hear in order to be able to discriminate between vowels? Most consonants? Consonants such as "f," "th," "s," "sh," and "t"?
8. Where do the high frequencies come from in speech?
9. What is an *audiogram*? What does it show?
10. What is a *threshold test*? How does it differ from a screening test?

11. How does an air-conduction test differ from a bone-conduction test?

12. How can infants and young children be tested for hearing abilities?

13. Describe the objective or nonvoluntary audiological tests we have discussed: tympanometry, brainstem auditory evoked potentials, and otoacoustic emissions.

FOR FURTHER INFORMATION

Bess, F., and **Humes, L.** (1990). *Audiology: The fundamentals.* Baltimore, MD: Williams and Wilkins.

Borden, G., and **Harris, K.** (1994). *Speech science primer: Physiology, acoustics and perception of speech* (3rd ed.). Baltimore, MD: Williams and Wilkins.

Gelfand, S. (1990). *Hearing: An introduction to psychological and physiological acoustics* (2nd ed.). New York, NY: Marcel Dekker.

Martin, F. (1994). *Introduction to audiology* (5th ed.). Englewood Cliffs, NJ: Prentice-Hall.

Hearing Impairment

As we learned in Chapter 14, hearing involves many different structures and processes within the auditory system. In order to hear normally, the outer and middle parts of the ear must be able to transmit incoming sound waves to the inner ear. The pinna must be intact, the auditory canal clear, and the tympanic membrane able to vibrate freely. The middle ear cavity must be filled with air at atmospheric pressure, supplied via a properly functioning eustachian tube. The ossicles must also be able to vibrate freely. Beyond these more accessible structures, the inner ear and auditory nervous system must be capable of transforming the mechanical energy supplied by the outer ear and middle ear into neural impulses and transmitting those impulses via a number of subcortical processing centers to the temporal lobe of the brain. Clearly, there are many points at which hearing function can be compromised.

In this chapter, we will learn about different types of hearing impairment. We will explore the causes and characteristics of various hearing losses and the consequences of such losses. Finally, we will consider the treatment options currently available for those with reduced auditory abilities.

TYPES OF HEARING LOSS

Hearing losses are generally of four types: conductive, sensorineural, mixed, and central auditory disorders. A conductive loss occurs because sound cannot be *conducted,* or transmitted, through the outer or middle part of the ear. A sensorineural loss occurs because there is a problem in the main sound-sensing organ (the *cochlea*) or because the auditory nerve is damaged and does not transmit some or all of the neural impulses produced by the cochlea. A mixed loss has both conductive and sensorineural components. Finally, a central auditory disorder involves the highest levels of the auditory nervous system and brain. Let us examine these four types of hearing loss in more detail.

CONDUCTIVE HEARING LOSS

1. Characteristics. A conductive hearing loss is a reduction in hearing sensitivity caused by an obstruction or blockage in the outer or middle ear. It is usually mild to moderate in its severity, with hearing thresholds no worse than 60 dB (Northern and Downs, 1991). In Figure 15-1, the audiograms of two individuals with different types of conductive losses are shown. Recall that an audiogram displays the results of a pure-tone air-conduction threshold test. The audiograms in Figure 15-1 also show the results of pure-tone bone-conduction threshold tests. Note that in (a), the bone-conduction thresholds are better (closer to the top of the audiogram) than all the air-conduction thresholds. This air-bone gap indicates that the source of the hearing problem is in the outer or middle ear, because the bone-conduction threshold (which tests the inner ear only) is essentially normal.

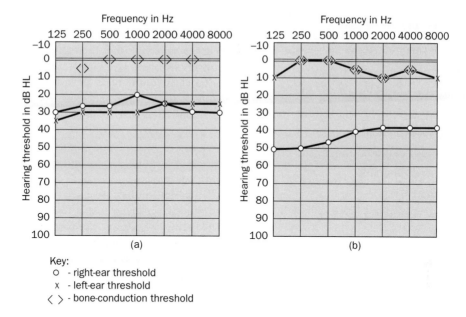

Key:
    o - right-ear threshold
    x - left-ear threshold
    ⟨ ⟩ - bone-conduction threshold

FIGURE 15-1 Audiograms showing examples of conductive hearing losses. Note that the hearing levels at the worst frequencies are not much different from the hearing levels at the best frequencies. Also note that the bone-conduction threshold is normal, indicating that the inner ear is intact. (a) shows a typical audiogram of a child with otitis media; (b) shows a typical audiogram of an older adult with otosclerosis in the right ear.

2. Causes of Conductive Hearing Loss Common conditions that cause conductive hearing impairment are listed in Table 15-1. For example, an absent or malformed pinna or an obstruction in the auditory canal (such as a dried bean or an accumulation of *cerumen,* or earwax) may cause a small degree of conductive loss. In this type of disorder, hearing sensitivity is reduced because sound waves are not being as effectively "captured" or transmitted as they would be if all structures were open and intact.

A tympanic membrane that has ruptured due to injury or the buildup of fluid in the middle ear can also cause a conductive hearing loss. The vibrations of a ruptured eardrum lack the force and focus needed to properly set the ossicles into vibration. However, we should remember that the hearing loss incurred because of a damaged tympanic membrane is not permanent. Like skin anywhere else on the body, a ruptured tympanic membrane will heal and will again vibrate appropriately. The danger of permanent hearing loss occurs primarily if the tympanic membrane ruptures repeatedly, causing significant amounts of scar tissue to form, with a consequent stiffening of the eardrum.

Probably the most frequent cause of conductive hearing loss, especially in children, is inflammation of the middle ear, or *otitis media* (Roberts et al., 1991; Northern and Downs, 1991). Grievink et al. (1993) report that over 80 percent of all children entering school have experienced one or more episodes of this disorder. Otitis media often begins with eustachian-tube malfunction: The mucosal lining of the eustachian tube swells, usually because of a cold or allergy, and occludes the tube so that air is unable to get into the middle ear cavity. As a result, the air pressure in the middle ear cavity diminishes and the tympanic membrane is *retracted,* or drawn inward. The tension placed upon the eardrum prevents it from vibrating freely, thus causing a

TABLE 15-1 Causes of Hearing Loss

I. Conductive Hearing Loss
  A. Absent or malformed pinna
  B. Obstruction in the auditory canal
  C. Ruptured tympanic membrane
  D. Scarred tympanic membrane
  E. Otitis media–middle ear dysfunction
  F. Dislocated ossicles
  G. Otosclerosis

II. Sensorineural Hearing Loss
  A. Noise exposure
  B. Presbycusis
  C. Ototoxic drugs
  D. Infections and diseases (e.g., mumps, meningitis)
  E. Anoxia
  F. Genetic disorders
  G. Maternal diseases and conditions

slight degree of hearing loss of from 15 to 25 dB (Northern and Downs, 1991).

If the eustachian tube remains obstructed, fluid eventually builds up in the air-deficient middle ear cavity. This condition is known as *otitis media with effusion* (OME), or *serous otitis media*. If enough fluid accumulates, it can exert pressure against the tympanic membrane, pushing it outward. Again, this pressure interferes with the normal *compliance* of the eardrum (its ability to vibrate freely). A mild conductive hearing loss of 25 to 30 dB may result. If the otitis media is chronic and the fluid becomes thick and gluelike, the hearing loss may be as much as 30 to 50 dB, a moderate loss (Northern and Downs, 1991). Chronic otitis media with effusion (OME) can easily become infectious if bacteria begin to proliferate in the fluid, causing pain and fever. In fact, parents are often unaware of the presence of OME in their child until infection sets in.

Otitis media is most frequent in infants and young children because their eustachian tubes are smaller, the cartilages that support them are weaker, and the tubes themselves are more horizontally situated. This increases the risk of collapse or blockage of the tubes (Paradise, 1980) and subsequent middle ear problems. As children grow older and their faces lengthen, the eustachian tube is pulled into a more vertical position and increases in strength and diameter. Thus, the incidence of otitis media can be expected to decrease with age.

In older adults, the most common cause of conductive hearing loss is otosclerosis (Martin, 1994). In otosclerosis, the part of the stapes (the last ossicle) that is attached to the oval window of the cochlea begins to develop new and spongy bone growth. As this new bone growth hardens, the stapes becomes fixed against the oval window and cannot move extensively enough to generate the necessary waves in the fluid of the cochlea. The result can be a hearing loss of as much as 50 or 60 dB for all frequencies (Wiley, 1980).

It should be noted that in all of the hearing losses described above, the primary problem is the transmission of sound waves. The bean in the auditory canal, fluid in the middle ear, or immobile stapes can all be considered obstacles to waves of alternating pressures that must reach the cochlea in order to be coded into neural impulses. If those waves are blocked, or if the structures that transmit those waves are immobile, then a broad range of frequencies usually fail to reach their destination. A conductive loss, therefore, tends to reduce sensitivity for multiple frequencies across the audiogram, and generally to a similar degree.

3. What Does the Person with a Conductive Loss Hear? The individual with a conductive loss hears sound at a much softer level than the average listener. You can easily simulate a conductive loss by placing your hands over your ears or using earplugs. If you do, you will notice that the world of sound is still around you, but it is less intense. In order for you to be able to pick out a particular sound, such as a door opening, or to understand the speech of someone who is talking at a moderate level, you need to pay much more attention than you would otherwise.

To those with a conductive hearing loss, speech and other sounds are soft in intensity but not distorted in any way. The effect is somewhat like watching a television program with the volume turned down very low. The viewer, like the person with a conductive hearing loss, needs only higher volume in order to be able to hear normally.

SENSORINEURAL HEARING LOSS

1. Characteristics. A sensorineural hearing loss is due to a disorder of the inner ear. The site of the damage is usually in specific hair cells, although if hair cells are destroyed, the nerve rootlets that attach to them frequently degenerate as well (Bess and Humes, 1990). Most patients with sensorineural loss thus have an impairment of both the sensory portion of the hearing mechanism and the neural portion.

Depending on the specific pattern of hair cell–nerve fiber damage, an individual with a sensorineural hearing loss may actually have normal hearing at several of the frequencies tested by an audiologist. However, at some point within the frequency spectrum—often, although not always, at the high end—hearing sensitivity begins to decrease, as reflected by thresholds moving toward the lower part of the audiogram. Figure 15-2 shows some examples of audiograms of individuals with sensorineural hearing losses. Note that in all cases, the bone-conduction thresholds are similar to the air-conduction thresholds for the ear with the better hearing. This means that whether the signal goes through the outer and middle ear or through bone and muscle, the thresholds are essentially the same. The absence of an air-bone gap suggests that the outer and middle ears are not contributing to the hearing loss.

2. Causes of Sensorineural Hearing Loss. Table 15-1 lists some common causes of sensorineural hearing loss. One frequent cause is

exposure to noise. As described above, the hair cells of the cochlea, particularly those near the oval window, are easily damaged by loud sounds. And unfortunately, our society is full of loud sounds, in the workplace, in recreational activities, and in the home.

In the workplace, the continuous noise of machinery or vehicles may cause permanent hearing loss. Individuals who work around airplanes, in manufacturing plants, or with heavy equipment are the most at risk. Many recreational activities also involve continuous loud noise. Rock concerts are often in a dB range that causes damage to hearing (95 to 115 dB), and both concert-goers and the musicians themselves may suffer permanent hearing impairment. Even personal music systems, such as home stereos or a Walkman® with earphones, can cause hearing loss if the individual listens at high intensity levels. Noisy recreational vehicles, like snowmobiles and speedboats, also put users at risk. Even more potentially damaging are the short-duration but very loud sounds made by gunshots. Individuals who hunt or do target shooting frequently suffer sensorineural hearing loss unless they use hearing protection. In the home, a variety of appliances, including the gasoline-powered lawnmower, ensure that even in the most secure of environments, enough noise is present to cause hearing damage.

Another cause of sensorineural hearing loss is the aging process. As individuals reach their 60s and 70s, their hearing acuity tends to diminish. Studies on the prevalence of hearing impairment show that approximately 30 percent of everyone over the age of 65 has some hearing loss. Of those over 75 years of age, nearly 35 percent are hearing-impaired (Alpiner et al., 1993). The reason for this loss of hearing is not clear. It may be due to the cumulative effects of noise exposure over a lifetime, or it may be secondary to the more generalized structural and metabolic changes that occur with age. In any case, the onset of *presbycusis* (the sensorineural hearing loss that accompanies normal aging) most often occurs in the early 70s for men and the late 70s for women (Martin, 1994). Most typically, older adults experience a high-frequency sensorineural loss, in which hear-

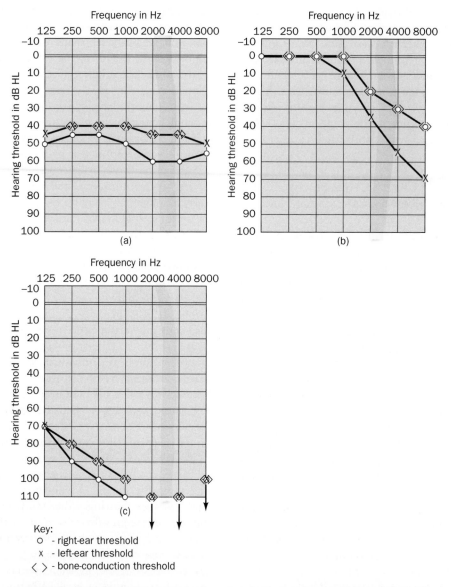

Key:
o - right-ear threshold
x - left-ear threshold
< > - bone-conduction threshold

FIGURE 15-2 Audiograms showing examples of sensorinerual hearing losses. Note that the bone-conduction threshold is similar to the air-conduction threshold in the better ear, indicating a disorder of the inner ear. (a) shows an audiogram of a child with a sensorineural hearing loss of unknown origin, (b) shows an audiogram of an older adult with a sensorineural hearing loss due to presbycusis, and (c) shows an audiogram of an individual who has become hearing impaired following a bout of the measles.

ing acuity in the highest frequencies is more impaired than it is in the lower frequencies. This results in the often paradoxical ability to hear speech without being able to understand it.

Ototoxic drugs, infections, and anoxia can also bring on sensorineural hearing loss. In the first category are drugs which, when ingested, damage or destroy hair cells. The mycin family of antibiotics falls into this classification. These drugs are sometimes necessary in order to save the life of a badly infected patient. They are generally prescribed in small amounts and with great caution, but in life-threatening situations, they may be given in quantities large enough to cause permanent damage to the hair cells of the cochlea. Besides antibiotics, some diseases and infections themselves can invade the perilymph and cause sensorineural hearing loss. Mumps and meningitis are common causes of sensorineural hearing loss in children and adults. Oxygen deprivation can have a similar effect (Bess and Humes, 1990).

Some sensorineural hearing losses have their onset prior to birth. In this category are children with genetic disorders involving malformation of the cochlea or the auditory nerve. Other sensorineural hearing losses with their onset before birth occur because of maternal infections. For example, prior to the advent of an effective vaccine, rubella was a frequent cause of hearing loss in children whose mothers contracted the disease early in their pregnancies.

Many of the factors we have mentioned—ototoxic drugs, infections, anoxia, and prenatal factors—can cause severe or profound sensorineural hearing loss in which little hearing is present except in the low frequencies (Northern and Downs, 1991). It is important to note, however, that regardless of its cause, sensorineural loss may not affect all frequencies equally. Depending on the specific hair cells or parts of the nerve involved, hearing is likely to be worse in some parts of the frequency range (typically in the highest frequencies) than it is in others.

3. Why the High Frequencies?

Why are the high frequencies so often affected in sensorineural hearing losses, especially those caused by noise exposure? To answer that question, let us consider the structure of the ear. Recall that the movement of the stapes against the oval window causes waves in the perilymph of the cochlea. When a sound is extremely loud, the pounding of the stapes against the oval window can produce sizable waves in the perilymph and violent movement in the basilar membrane.

On the basilar membrane is the organ of Corti, a structure that supports the hair cells we discussed in Chapter 14. Continuous exposure to high levels of noise can put so much physical stress on the hair cells near the oval window that they no longer function properly. Noise-exposed hair cells may fuse together, become floppy, or break off completely. Exposure to sudden bursts of noise can cause such extreme movement along the basilar membrane that it exceeds the elastic limits of the organ of Corti and the structure is actually torn apart in some places, causing hair-cell destruction (Yost, 1994). In any case, the hair cells closest to the oval window are the most vulnerable to trauma-induced damage. And those are precisely the hair cells that are necessary to hear the higher frequencies. The result is that high-frequency hearing losses are fairly common, especially in individuals (both old and young) who are frequently exposed to very loud sounds. Hearing in the low frequencies for such individuals may be relatively unscathed because the hair cells responding to low-frequency sounds are in a more protected position within the cochlea.

4. What Does the Person with a Sensorineural Hearing Loss Hear?

If the sensorineural hearing loss has a relatively flat or troughlike configuration, such as the one shown in Figure 15-2a, sound may be reduced in intensity across the frequency spectrum, as we described previously for those with conductive impairment. However, cochlear pathology or damage may result in additional difficulties for the person with sensorineural hearing disorders that are not experienced by those with conductive losses. For example, *loudness recruitment* may occur in an individual with sensorineural hearing loss. In this condition, sounds of both soft and middle-range intensities may be inaudible to the hearing-impaired individual. However, when sounds are finally made loud enough to hear, they may be at the level of discomfort. The range between audible and uncomfortable may be so reduced that it is difficult to find an intensity level at which the hearing-impaired person can listen to speech comfortably (Bess and Humes, 1990).

For those with a hearing loss that affects one part of the frequency spectrum (especially the high frequencies) more than another, additional unfortunate consequences occur (see Figure 15-2b). Recall from our discussion of the frequency composition of speech in Chapter 14 that adequate hearing sensitivity in the 2000 to 4000 Hz region is necessary for understanding many speech sounds. For some voiceless consonants, hearing between 4000 Hz and 8000 Hz is important. Thus, an individual with a high-frequency sensorineural hearing loss, such as the one pictured in Figure 15-2b, is likely to have trouble perceiving some speech sounds.

It is interesting to note that many individuals with high-frequency hearing losses are able to hear speech; they just have difficulty understanding it. A large portion of the frequencies a speaker produces are in the lower end of the spectrum, where the hearing-impaired individual has good sensitivity. However, without good acuity in the high frequencies, the ability to discriminate one consonant from another, and hence understand the word, may be reduced. For example, if a speaker said the word "Sue," the individual with a high-frequency hearing loss might hear the word at the same loudness level that a normal-hearing listener would but might perceive a "whooshing" sound followed by the vowel "oo." What did the speaker say? *Foo? Sue? Shoe? Zoo?* If the word had been embedded in a sentence, the hearing-impaired listener could use the semantic or syntactic context as a cue as to which word had been produced. In isolation, however, the word might be difficult to determine.

For the individual with a severe or profound sensorineural loss, such as the one pictured in Figure 15-2c, even very loud sounds are barely detectable. Speech, even if well amplified by a hearing aid, is difficult to understand. Such individuals are often referred to as "deaf," a condition we will investigate further in Chapter 16.

You can get an idea of what a sensorineural hearing loss sounds like by setting the graphic equalizer on your stereo so that the bass is maximally boosted and frequencies above 250 Hz are turned down completely. While this is not neces-sarily a problem in listening to music, if you try to listen to a tape of speech with this setting, you will note that it sounds more muffled and less clear than speech when the full range of frequencies is present.

MIXED LOSSES

1. Characteristics. As their name implies, mixed losses have both conductive and sensorineural components. The individual with a mixed hearing loss may have a conductive loss due to otosclerosis, for example. Otosclerosis by itself could be expected to cause an elevated threshold of approximately the same severity level across all the frequencies tested by an audiologist, as shown in Figure 15-3a. However, the same individual might also be experiencing a sensorineural loss due to presbycusis. Let us assume the sensorineural loss by itself would spare hearing in the 250 to 1000 Hz range but would cause a gradually worsening problem in the frequencies above 1000 (see Figure 15-3b). An individual who has both types of loss simultaneously would have hearing thresholds similar to those pictured in Figure 15-3c. Hearing in the lower frequencies would be impaired because of the conductive component, but hearing sensitivity in the higher frequencies would be even worse because of the sensorineural component.

2. Causes of Mixed Losses. Any combination of causes of conductive and sensorineural losses can cause a mixed loss. In adults, a common combination is otosclerosis complicated by presbycusis or a noise-induced hearing loss. Another type of mixed loss might be seen in a child who suffers from frequent bouts of otitis media. In such a case, previous infections in the middle ear cavity may have spread through the oval window to affect the cochlea, resulting in a sensorineural component to the loss as well as any current otitis-caused conductive component (Northern and Downs, 1991). Some mixed losses are genetic in nature, such as when both the middle ear structures and the inner ear are malformed, resulting in both

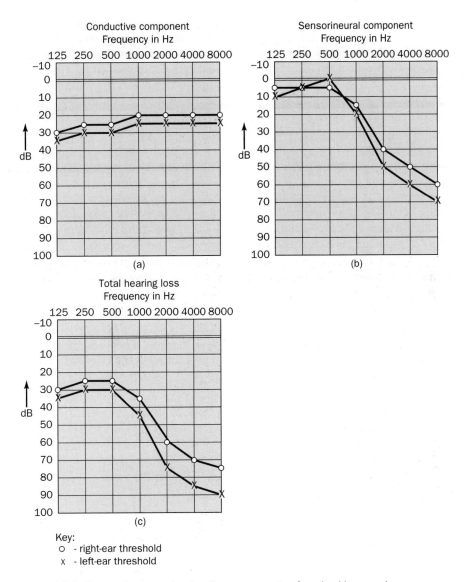

FIGURE 15-3 Two audiograms showing the components of a mixed loss, and one audiogram showing the total loss. (a) shows the conductive component, (b) shows the sensorineural component, and (c) shows the individual's actual hearing loss.

conductive and sensorineural hearing impairments. Clearly, many combinations are possible.

3. What Does the Person with a Mixed Loss Hear?
The person with a mixed loss hears speech as both soft and distorted. An increase in the loudness of the signal helps to some degree, but depending on the severity of the loss in the high frequencies, some speech sounds may be difficult to discern. Loudness recruitment may also be a problem. An individual with mixed hearing loss generally has more trouble understanding speech than does the person with conductive loss or sensorineural loss only.

CENTRAL AUDITORY DISORDERS

1. The Nature of Central Auditory Disorders.

Central auditory disorders are quite different from the hearing losses we have been discussing up to this point. Conductive, sensorineural, and mixed losses always involve decreased *acuity,* or a diminished sensitivity to sound. In conductive loss, acuity across a broad spectrum of frequencies is reduced; in sensorineural loss, acuity in some frequency regions (usually the lower) is better than acuity in others (usually the higher frequencies). However, with a central auditory disorder, acuity may be normal (Musiek, 1985). Instead, the client complains of problems such as ringing in the ears (which may also be an element of sensorineural loss), *auditory hallucinations,* or hearing things that aren't there, extreme difficulty hearing in noisy or reverberant environments, trouble following complex auditory commands, auditory inattentiveness and high distractibility, or trouble localizing sound sources (Musiek, 1985). In a child, the primary symptom may be academic difficulty, resulting in a diagnosis of auditory perceptual problems, language disorders, or learning disabilities (Martin, 1994).

Central auditory disorders are believed to be due to *lesions* (damaged areas, malformations, tumors, and the like) in the auditory nervous system's subcortical processing centers and pathways, between the cochlear nucleus and the temporal lobe of the brain (Northern and Downs, 1991; Martin, 1994) (see Figure 15-4). The cochlear nucleus is the first processing station for auditory information after the cochlear branch of the auditory nerve leaves the cochlea. Damage at this

FIGURE 15-4 A schematic representation of the auditory nervous system. Most of the fibers from the right ear go to the left side of the brain; however, some pathways do remain on the same side. Only neural connections from the right ear are shown.

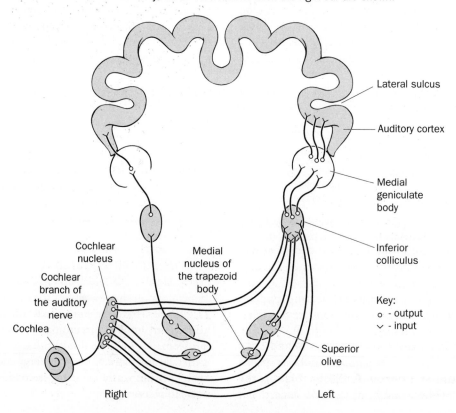

level causes sensorineural hearing loss. However, lesions above the cochlear nucleus—the medial nucleus of the trapezoid body, the superior olive, the inferior colliculus, the medial geniculate body, or any of their connecting pathways—may cause central auditory disorders.

Sometimes, auditory nervous system lesions can be diagnosed through radiographic imaging techniques such as computerized axial tomography (CT) or magnetic resonance imaging (MRI). Radiologists and neurologists are the medical specialists who perform and interpret tests of this kind. These procedures are particularly suitable for locating space-occupying lesions such as tumors along the auditory pathways. However, some lesions of the auditory nervous system may be metabolic or chemical in nature, so that function is compromised although structure appears grossly normal. Some structural changes may be too subtle to show up on CT scans or MRIs. In such cases, the audiologist's testing may provide insights into the nature of the problems and site of lesion that are not available through other testing methods (Musiek, 1985).

In order to diagnose central auditory disorders, the audiologist administers a variety of specialized tests, many of which involve distorted or competing speech signals (Martin, 1994). For example, the audiologist may look at an individual's ability to perceive words in quiet as opposed to noise, or words that have had a section of the high frequencies filtered out. The audiologist may also present two different word lists to the client, one in each ear, and observe how successfully the client can repeat each list (Musiek, 1985). The performance of the client on these and other tests can be compared to normative data or data from other subject populations with known lesions. Although many of these tests are not conclusive in and of themselves, the results of a variety of procedures taken together can help the audiologist determine the nature of the client's disorder and the probable location of the damage causing it.

2. Causes of Central Auditory Disorders.

Central auditory disorders can be caused by numerous agents. Martin mentions disease, cerebrovascular accidents, head trauma, and intracranial pressure as possible causes. Diseases of the nervous system are especially likely to affect the central auditory processes. For example, in multiple sclerosis, nerve pathways in various parts of the central nervous system become demyelinated and thus transmit nerve impulses less efficiently. If this occurs in the auditory nervous system, the transmission of auditory information can be compromised.

Cerebrovascular accidents are disruptions in the circulation of blood to the brain, caused by agents such as *atherosclerosis* (reduced diameter of the arteries due to fatty deposits), *embolisms* (blood clots that lodge in tiny blood vessels supplying the brain and auditory pathways), or a stroke. When the auditory nervous system or brain is not supplied with oxygen and nutrients, permanent damage can occur, reducing the ability of those structures to transmit and process sound.

Intracranial pressure is generally caused by tumors, although it can also be caused by swelling of the brain *(edema)* following trauma or head injury. In infants, *hydrocephalus* may cause pressure against auditory pathways and the brain. In this condition, an excessive amount of cerebrospinal fluid builds up in the brain when its usual circulatory route through the central nervous system is blocked. Pressure can damage brain and nerve cells by interfering with the flow of blood and nutrients and interrupting other metabolic processes. Some improvement in function may be seen when the source of the pressure (tumor, edema, and so on) is removed, but some degree of permanent damage is also likely to occur.

CONSEQUENCES OF HEARING IMPAIRMENT TO THE INDIVIDUAL

The effects of hearing impairment on an individual vary greatly, depending on the age of onset, the severity of the hearing impairment, and its cause. Hearing disorders with their onset in the adult years primarily affect the individual's ability to hear and understand speech in the environment. The ability to formulate language is not affected. There is some controversy regarding the degree to which speech is affected in adult-onset hearing loss, however. According to Seyfried et al. (1989), some researchers have found little loss of intelligibility when hearing impairment occurs after the age of 18. Others have found that speech tends to become slurred, imprecise, and inappropriate in loudness and inflection as the years pass.

Hearing disorders with their onset in infancy or early childhood can also cause problems for the individual in daily conversational situations. However, early-onset hearing loss affects more than day-to-day interactions. A child's ability to acquire language, a phonological system, and intelligible speech may be compromised to some degree, depending on the severity of the loss. These, in turn, can affect the educational and vocational opportunities available to the child as he matures.

As we have learned, two common causes of hearing loss are otitis media, primarily affecting young children, and presbycusis, affecting older adults. Because of the prevalence of these disorders, we will take a closer look at the consequences associated with them.

OTITIS MEDIA

For the vast majority of children who have few or infrequent episodes of otitis media, long-term consequences are not expected. Of greater concern are the children who have persistent otitis media with effusion (OME) Since this condition often exists with no overt symptoms of infection, it may not always be diagnosed. Yet a child with OME frequently has an accompanying conductive hearing loss that reduces his or her exposure to language and environmental sounds.

It has been speculated that reduced language input during the critical period of language development (birth to the age of 2 or 3) results in an increased risk for language and learning deficits in later childhood, long after the conductive hearing loss has resolved itself (Northern and Downs, 1991). Is there any evidence that children with a history of otitis media and periodic hearing loss show a higher-than-expected occurrence of language-related problems? Indeed, there have been many studies examining the link between otitis media in early childhood and the presence of later language disorders, but no unequivocal correlation has been found.

Roberts et al. (1991), in one of the most carefully controlled studies to date, found no relationship between total frequency of episodes of otitis media with effusion (OME) from birth to the age of 3 and performance on various standardized language tests involving semantics, morphology, and syntax at the age of 4½ to 6. Grievink et al. (1993) also found a lack of effect of early OME on language abilities at the age of 7. However, several other relatively well controlled studies that looked at other aspects of language did find some evidence of differences. Feagans et al. (1987) found that children with nine or more early episodes of otitis media showed more off-task behavior and distractibility and poorer ability to paraphrase a story *(narrative skills)* compared with children who had had eight or fewer episodes. Teele et al. (1990) found small but significant correlations between the number of episodes of OME and IQ score, reading and math achievement scores, and scores on some language tests. In both these studies, as in all the research in which differences were found, the relationships that were significant were weak, and the differences between OME and non-OME groups were small in magnitude.

What can we conclude, then, about the consequences of frequent episodes of OME in early childhood? When group trends are considered, the possibility of a negative effect on language development seems small, although there may be some behavioral and academic consequences for some children. Unfortunately, it is not possible at this time to predict the specific consequences, if any, for a particular child. According to Grievink et al. (1993), it may be that OME in combination with some other risk factors produces negative effects on language ability, but further research in this area is needed.

PRESBYCUSIS

As the American population ages, the consequences of hearing impairment in the elderly are raising new concern. The older individual with a hearing loss frequently feels a sense of isolation from friends and family, even before the hearing loss has been fully acknowledged. As the hearing loss and the stresses it causes become more apparent, the older adult may develop various adjustive behaviors, both positive and negative. On the positive side, some elderly individuals are able to compensate successfully for their hearing loss by becoming more attentive in listening situations. Some, either consciously or unconsciously, acquire speechreading skills.

On the negative side, the hearing-impaired individual may develop defense techniques (Maurer, 1989). These include (1) complaining and other attention-getting devices that distract the family from the hearing problem, (2) compensating for the loss by reducing activities where hearing is important, and (3) attributing poor comprehension to the fact that the speaker is "boring" or "mumbles." *Escape techniques,* according to Maurer, include withdrawal from all activities into the security of the home, daydreaming, and becoming more dependent on others. Family and friends, and the older adult himself, may wonder if such behaviors signal the onset of senility or dementia (Boone and Plante, 1993).

For the family, the untreated hearing loss of an older member may mean less contact with that individual and a growing concern for their self-sufficiency and well-being. However, untreated hearing loss in older Americans is a problem for society as well. Senior citizens are important to the volunteer efforts of many organizations. With women—the former mainstay of volunteer organizations—entering the work force in greater numbers, retired individuals are performing more and more of the unpaid work in schools, hospitals, churches, social service agencies, and even businesses across the nation. The over-65 population is a valuable resource in many communities. The premature withdrawal of such individuals from their normal activities has a negative impact on society as a whole. As the population ages, it is important to increase the number of older adults who constitute a potentially active resource group (Hollien et al., 1991). Treatment of hearing loss can contribute to that end.

TREATMENT OF HEARING IMPAIRMENT

The treatment of hearing impairment includes many components. Some hearing losses can be corrected through medical or surgical intervention, usually administered by an otolaryngologist. If a client's hearing impairment cannot be improved by medical treatment, the audiologist works with the client to select a suitable hearing aid and teaches the client how to get the most benefit from it. In addition to hearing aids, other assistive listening devices may be introduced. Those with central auditory processing disorders, who have essentially normal acuity but difficulty in interpreting and attending to speech, may receive treatment from speech-language pathologists, learning disabilities specialists, or special education personnel.

In the following sections, we examine these types of treatment in more detail. We first consider medical treatment and the kinds of problems for which it is effective; then we shift our focus to amplification and auditory training and to assistive listening devices. Finally, we look at the treatment possibilities for central auditory disorders.

MEDICAL TREATMENT

Of all the types of hearing loss, conductive impairments are the most treatable medically or surgically. Disorders of the outer ear, such as malformations of the pinna and auditory canal, can generally be corrected by reconstructive surgery. Good success has also been obtained in repairing scarred or damaged eardrums with *myringoplasty,* or surgical reconstruction of the tympanic membrane (Martin, 1994).

Otitis media is also treated medically but can be difficult to completely eradicate. Because its onset is not associated with pain or discomfort, a child can have otitis media—and a mild to moderate hearing loss—for some time with no overt symptoms. When the condition finally becomes infectious, causing pain, fever, and generalized discomfort, the usual treatment is ten to fourteen days of antibiotic therapy. Some physicians require the child to return for an ear check after the course of medication has been completed to see if the middle ear is free of fluid as well as infection. Unfortunately, the fluid is often still there. A study by Teele et al. (1980) found that two weeks after treatment, 70 percent of the children in their study continued to show middle ear effusion, even though the infection had been cured. One month after treatment, 40 percent still showed fluid in the middle ear—and, in all probability, continued hearing loss. Of course, if fluid remains in the middle ear cavity, chances are that bacteria will again begin to grow and that the child will have another infection in a few weeks.

There is considerable dispute as to how aggressively to treat persistent otitis media with effusion (Northern and Downs, 1991). According to Paradise (1980), the physician might elect to maintain the child on a *prophylactic* (preventative) dose of antibiotics. A second alternative would be myringotomy. *Myringotomy* is a surgical procedure in which a small slit is made in the tympanic membrane, through which the physician suctions out the fluid trapped in the middle ear cavity. A pressure-equalization tube (P.E. tube) is then inserted into this slit, to restore normal air flow and pressure in the middle ear cavity and to prevent additional accumulations of fluid. P.E. tubes are pictured in Figure 15-5. The tube stays in the tympanic membrane for variable time periods, ranging from a few days to years. As the tympanic membrane heals around it, the tube is usually forced out. However, if a P.E. tube remains in place beyond the point where it is needed, it may be removed by a physician.

Some physicians believe that removal of the tonsils and adenoids will help reduce the fre-

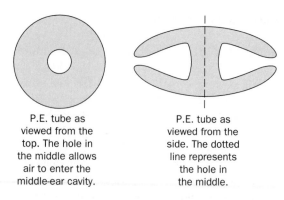

P.E. tube as viewed from the top. The hole in the middle allows air to enter the middle-ear cavity.

P.E. tube as viewed from the side. The dotted line represents the hole in the middle.

FIGURE 15-5 A typical pressure-equalization (P. E.) tube, inserted into the tympanic membrane in order to restore normal pressure to the middle ear cavity and prevent recurrences of otitis media.

quency of otitis media, although there is little evidence to support this contention (Bluestone and Klein, 1988). There are also several vaccines available for bacteria thought to cause otitis media, such as pneumococcus and hemophilus B. However, some children continue to succumb to frequent bouts of otitis media, despite the best attempts of the medical profession.

In the adult population, otosclerosis is a frequently occurring disorder that can be corrected to some degree through surgical intervention. In a procedure known as *stapedectomy,* the stapes is removed from the oval window and replaced with a synthetic prosthesis of Teflon or wire. Other procedures to correct otosclerosis exist as well, although their outcomes are more variable (Martin, 1994).

Despite the possibility for medical treatment, not all conductive hearing losses can be resolved. Otosclerosis, for example, can cause a degree of permanent hearing loss even if stapedectomy is successful. And for those with a mixed type of hearing loss, careful testing is required before surgical treatment for the conductive component is done. For example, if an older individual has a mixed hearing loss due to mild otosclerosis and severe presbycusis, surgical correction of the otosclerosis might not improve the individual's hearing significantly enough to warrant surgery.

However, in most cases, conductive hearing losses can be improved through medical or surgical intervention.

AMPLIFICATION AND AUDITORY TRAINING

Despite advances in medical and surgical treatment for hearing loss, many adults and children have hearing impairments that cannot be corrected. For example, damaged or destroyed hair cells cannot be restored or replaced. Transplant technology cannot yet provide acceptable substitutions for the cochlea, auditory nerve, or parts of the auditory nervous system. Although cochlear implants are used for the deaf, these electronic devices are experimental in nature and do not provide the kind of auditory stimuli that normal-hearing individuals perceive. In general, repair, reconstruction, and replacement of the inner ear structures remain beyond the limits of medical science.

At present, the most common device used to treat sensorineural and other medically incorrectable hearing losses is the hearing aid. Hearing aids can be purchased from a hearing-aid dealer or audiologist. Some older adults "try out" the hearing aids of friends or even purchase aids through newspaper ads or at flea markets (Garstecki, 1993). However, optimal treatment for hearing impairment should include more than the aid itself. According to Schow and Nerbonne (1989), the audiologist should provide instruction and counseling, amplification fitting, communication training, and overall coordination with other areas of intervention. These stages of treatment are described in more detail below.

1. Instruction and Counseling. Ideally, the first stage of treatment for an individual with hearing loss is instruction by an audiologist regarding the nature of the impairment and its consequences. If the client is a child, his or her parents will need instruction and counseling, both to obtain information pertaining to their child's loss and to help them deal with the emotional reaction that such a handicap often brings (Kricos, 1993).

It is also necessary for the client to develop realistic expectations for treatment outcome (Schow and Nerbonne, 1989). Unlike vision problems, which can often be corrected effectively with glasses, hearing problems are difficult to "normalize" with a hearing aid (Berger and Millin, 1989). The amplified sound that the hearing aid produces may not sound "natural" to the adult hearing-aid user. Further, background noise and loud sounds are amplified as well as speech stimuli, a feature that listeners of every age complain of (Nabelek et al., 1991). The client or parents must be aware of the limitations of treatment for hearing disorders and will hopefully be willing to engage in further training and instruction once a device is prescribed.

2. Amplification Fitting. The second stage of treatment is amplification fitting. This includes testing, recommendations, and instruction for hearing-aid use. Amplification fitting is most successfully done by an audiologist, who has broad knowledge of many brands and models of hearing aids and their characteristics as well as training in the diagnosis and management of different types of hearing loss. Once a hearing aid is selected, it is especially important for the audiologist to be sure that its settings are adjusted properly to provide satisfactory amplification (Schow and Nerbonne, 1989). For children who are too young to provide meaningful feedback, this is an especially challenging task, requiring a knowledgeable, skilled, and experienced audiologist (Bentler, 1993).

There are many different types of hearing aids currently in use. Some of these include: (1) the behind-the-ear aid, (2) the in-the-ear aid, (3) the in-the-canal aid, and (4) the programmable aid. These aids are pictured in Figure 15-6.

The behind-the-ear aid, pictured in Figure 15-6, consists of a plastic case that sits behind the ear containing the electronics of the aid and a battery; a small plastic earhook, which transmits the sound amplified by the electronic components; and a custom-fitted earmold that fits into the ear. This aid also has a volume control that the user can

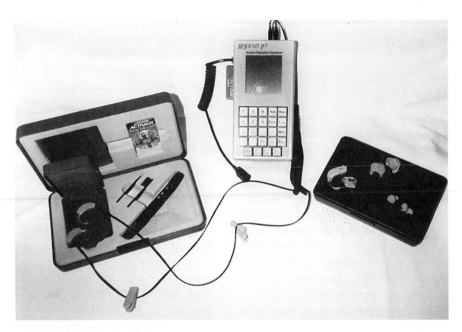

FIGURE 15-6 Types of hearing aids. From left: a programmable behind-the-ear aid, attached to an external programming device; a conventional behind-the-ear aid, two in-the-ear aids, and two in-the-canal aids.

access. The modern behind–the-ear aid can be quite powerful. This type of aid is used most frequently with children. Less than 33 percent of adults who need amplification choose this style (Sanders, 1993).

The in-the-ear and in-the-canal aids are more recently introduced styles. In 1990, in-the-ear and in-the-canal aids accounted for approximately 70 percent of all hearing-aid sales (Kirkwood, 1990). These aids, pictured in Figure 15-6, have the microphone and all amplification electronics built right into a custom-fitted earmold. The in-the-ear model has a more conventional earmold configuration, which fills the pinna. The smaller in-the-canal model fits into the external part of the auditory canal and is less visible. For both types, a small volume-control dial is provided on the body of the aid that the user can adjust. Despite their popularity, however, not everyone can wear these models. For some, the pinna or external auditory canal may be too small. More problematic in such small aids, the microphone (which takes in sound) and amplifier (which outputs amplified sound) are

very close together, causing feedback to occur if the amplification is set too high. In such cases, a behind-the-ear aid may be necessary.

Finally, a specialized type of aid, also shown in Figure 15-6, is the programmable behind-the-ear aid. In such an aid, various amplification characteristics (e.g., gain, output, frequency response curve) can be digitally programmed through use of an external computer system (Sanders, 1993). One advantage of this system is that multiple sets of amplification characteristics can be programmed into the aid and selected by the listener, as background noise and the communication environment change. However, the cost of the device is high compared to other aids, and not all those with hearing impairments can benefit from multiple amplification settings. Further, only the *selection* of the settings is digital; the actual amplification electronics are the same analog components found in conventional aids.

3. Communication Training. The third stage of treatment, following amplification fitting, is when the audiologist or speech-language pathologist begins to work on communication training with the client. For the hearing-impaired child, especially in the preschool years, communication training generally focuses on auditory training (e.g., localization, discrimination, retention, and sequencing of auditory stimuli), language development and stimulation, and speech production training (Moeller and Carney, 1993). The amount of specialized instruction the child needs in these areas will depend on the severity of his or her hearing loss. In the school years, auditory, language, and speech skills continue to be emphasized, but the development of learning and social skills are also an important part of the child's training (Laughton and Hasenstab, 1993).

For older clients, communication training typically emphasizes speechreading (sometimes called *lipreading*), improvement of listening strategies (Schow and Nerbonne, 1989), and management of the communication situation. For hearing-aid users of any age, speechreading is an important adjunct to hearing and understanding speech. In speechreading training, hearing-impaired individuals are taught to observe a speaker's lips very closely to see which sounds are being formed. Although only about 30 percent of the sounds in English are visible on the lips, important information can be gained from such observation. When these visual cues are combined with amplified auditory information, the hearing-impaired individual's comprehension is greatly enhanced (Walden et al., 1993).

Improvement of listening strategies, another aspect of communication training, can help the hearing-aid user learn to focus his or her attention more effectively and attend to important auditory cues. Because speech amplified by a hearing aid sounds distorted compared to unamplified speech, and because there tends to be more noise in the signal, direct instruction on how and what to listen for is often important (Nerbonne and Schow, 1989).

Finally, hearing-aid users can learn how to manage communication situations in order to maximize their comprehension. Managing the communication situation includes strategies such as reducing competing sounds in the environment (e.g., a blaring stereo or television set); keeping the speaker in full view so his or her lips can be seen; and asking appropriate questions when the speaker is not understood. Tye-Murray (1991) found that hearing-impaired individuals improved their comprehension significantly if they asked speakers to repeat one or two sentences, to simplify the message, to rephrase the message, or to say an important key word.

4. Overall Coordination with Other Areas of Intervention. The fourth stage of treatment involves overall coordination of the client's needs in terms of educational placement, health evaluation, and vocational consultation (Schow and Nerbonne, 1989). In an ideal situation, the audiologist would be a member of an interdisciplinary team comprised of various medical, educational, and rehabilitation personnel and would keep other team members informed about the status of the individual's hearing abilities and any changes to be expected. For children with hearing impairment, the team is usually the multidisciplinary team organized by the child's public school district to oversee the development and implementation of the child's individualized education plan (IEP), in compliance with Pub. L. No. 94-142 and 99-457. Although the specific individuals comprising the team might change slightly from year to year, a school-aged child generally receives coordinated services through the public schools from the time the hearing loss is discovered to the age of 21. For older adults with a hearing loss, the audiologist may coordinate the client's care by making appropriate referrals to physicians, psychologists, social workers, or rehabilitation counselors (Schow and Nerbonne, 1989).

ASSISTIVE LISTENING DEVICES

In the previous section on amplification and auditory training, our discussion focused on the hearing aid and how to assure maximum benefit from its use. The hearing aid is a personal device, designed to be worn by the hearing-impaired individual at all times. However, there are also amplification devices which are *situation-specific,* designed to be used by hearing-impaired individuals only in certain situations or for certain tasks.

Mechanisms of this type are known as *assistive listening devices.* This group may include warning devices, such as a louder doorbell, alarm clock, or telephone buzzer; and listening aids, such as an amplified handset for the telephone and earphone attachments for the radio and television. Long-distance listening aids for movies, church services, lectures and so on, such as FM, infrared and induction loop systems are also included under this category of assistive listening devices (Compton, 1993). The FM system includes a microphone placed near the speaker or sound source, which inputs into an FM transmitter. This wireless device transmits the sound to an FM receiver which amplifies it. The amplified sound is then directed to the listener's ear or hearing aid via a wire connection. Some of these devices are pictured in Figure 15-7.

Goodhill (1985) argues that assistive listening devices may be more important than the personal hearing aid in helping the older individual with a mild hearing loss function adequately in his or her environment. In the school setting, assistive listening devices also play an important role, even though it is assumed that the child has and uses a personal hearing aid (Flexer, 1993). This is because an assistive listening device such as an FM system amplifies the output of a microphone placed several inches from the teacher's mouth. The FM signal is thus less noisy and more easily understood than what the child hears through his or her hearing aid alone. Some would argue that the audiologist's role extends to assisting an individual select and use such devices (Palmer, 1992).

TREATMENT POSSIBILITIES FOR CENTRAL AUDITORY DISORDERS

Little information is available on the treatment of central auditory disorders. The medical-surgical

FIGURE 15-7 Assistive listening devices that may be used by those with hearing impairment. From left: the listener's part of an FM system, consisting of an FM receiver and earphones (the person talking must speak into a microphone connected to an FM transmitter); a telephone with an amplified hand set; an amplified door bell.

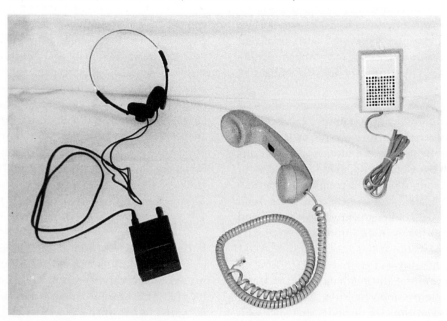

interventions and hearing aids we have discussed for conductive and sensorineural losses do not appear to be appropriate. In the school-age population, children with central auditory disorders are most likely to be seen by speech-language pathologists, learning disabilities specialists, psychologists, or special education teachers, depending on their presenting symptoms (Northern and Downs, 1991). They are less likely than adults to have identifiable lesions, diseases, or other conditions that have caused their disorder and are thus less likely than adults to be seen in a medical setting.

Watkins and Schow (1989) propose that children with "auditory-language processing problems" be seen along with children who have more severe hearing losses for work on auditory abilities and language. They advocate specific testing to determine whether the child's problem is primarily one of auditory processing or language processing and tailoring remediation programs for the individual child. Watkins and Schow appear to be making the assumption that auditory and language disorders are independent of each other to some degree; thus one can remediate one or the other or both. However, others believe there is a causative relationship between neurological dysfunction, central auditory processing disorders, and language disorders. The latter has been the subject of some dispute, since a causative relationship among those disorders has never been proven (see Northern and Downs, 1991, for a discussion of "Auditory Language Learning Dis-

orders"). It is unlikely that we will see standardized and well-accepted treatment programs for central auditory disorders until more is learned about their nature and how they interact with other neurological, cognitive, and linguistic problems.

SUMMARY

In this chapter, we looked at conductive, sensorineural, and mixed hearing losses in some detail. We also examined the concept of central auditory disorders. The consequences of hearing impairment differ, depending on the cause and degree of the loss, but can cause serious problems for both adults who lose their hearing late in life and children whose hearing impairment occurs during their language-learning years. Treatment for hearing impairment may include medical and surgical intervention, amplification and auditory training, and assistive listening devices. The specific form of treatment appropriate for central auditory disorders is somewhat more controversial but may involve speech-language pathologists, learning disabilities teachers, psychologists, or special education teachers. The need for evaluation and treatment of hearing impairment in both adults and children is an important issue in the field of communication sciences and disorders, and one in which audiologists play an important role.

R E V I E W   Q U E S T I O N S

1. What is a *conductive hearing loss*? What parts of the ear are generally affected? What are some causes of such a loss?
2. What is *otitis media*? Differentiate between serous otitis media and infectious otitis media. Draw a typical audiogram of a child with otitis media.
3. What is a *sensorineural hearing loss*? What parts of the ear are affected? What are some causes of such a loss?

4. Describe the hearing loss in the elderly population in terms of its causes, severity, frequencies involved, and prevalence.
5. Draw a normal audiogram, a 40 dB conductive loss, and a high-frequency sensorineural loss beginning just above 2000 Hz. How would you interpret each audiogram in terms of frequency and intensity?
6. What is a *mixed hearing loss*? What are three common causes of mixed losses?

7. What is meant by *central auditory disorders*? What are the symptoms? What part of the auditory system is affected?

8. Are there any long-term consequences to a child with frequent bouts of otitis media in infancy and early childhood? Explain.

9. What psychological and social consequences might an elderly person experience as the result of a hearing loss?

10. How are conductive losses typically treated? How is otitis media treated?

11. Describe the following types of hearing aid: the behind-the-ear aid, the in-the-ear aid, the in-the-canal aid, and the programmable aid.

12. Why might an individual have trouble benefiting from a hearing aid? What is the optimum sequence of treatment to get maximum benefit from a hearing aid?

13. What are assistive listening devices? How do they differ from hearing aids?

FOR FURTHER INFORMATION

Martin, F. (1994). *Introduction to audiology* (5th ed.). Englewood Cliffs, NJ: Prentice-Hall.

Northern, J., and **Downs, M.** (1991). *Hearing in children* (4th ed.). Baltimore, MD: Williams and Wilkins.

Sanders, D. (1993). *Management of hearing handicap: Infants to elderly* (3rd ed.). Englewood Cliffs, NJ: Prentice-Hall.

Silman, S., and Silverman, C. (1991). *Auditory diagnosis: Principles and applications.* San Diego, CA: Academic Press.

Deafness

I n Chapter 15, our discussion focused primarily on individuals with usable but imperfect hearing. Children with otitis media are able to hear, but the sounds around them are softer and less salient than they are to a person with normal hearing. Most older adults with a hearing loss are also able to hear, but they typically have difficulty discriminating certain speech sounds. Such persons have been referred to as "hard-of-hearing" (Vernon and Andrews, 1990). In the present chapter, we will focus on a somewhat different population. The subject of our present study will be individuals who have a hearing loss so severe that they cannot depend on hearing alone for communication. These individuals are usually referred to as "deaf," although they may also be called "severely hearing-impaired" or "profoundly hearing-impaired," depending on the degree of their hearing loss (Schow and Nerbonne, 1989). Because of the severity of their hearing disorder, this population has very different needs from the hard-of-hearing individuals we discussed earlier. In this chapter, we will look at the causes and characteristics of deafness and some of the communication and educational alternatives available for the deaf population.

TERMS AND DEFINITIONS

As in any area of communication sciences and disorders, it is important to understand the specialized way that words in the discipline are used among professionals. Any individual who experiences a hearing loss of any type is referred to as *hearing-impaired*. Hearing impairment can be classified as slight to mild (thresholds of 21 to 40 dB for children, 26 to 40 dB for adults); mild to moderate (41 to 55 dB); moderate (56 to 70 dB); severe (71 to 90 dB); or profound (over 91 dB) (Schow and Nerbonne, 1989). Those with hearing losses in the mild to moderate range are called *hard-of-hearing,* as described above. Those with bilateral hearing losses in the profound range (and sometimes the severe range as well) are considered *deaf*. Thus, *deafness* can be defined in audiological terms of hearing threshold. However, there are other ways of defining *deafness*.

Functionally, the hard-of-hearing and the deaf can be distinguished from one another by their use of the hearing modality. The *deaf*, according to this system, are those whose hearing is so limited that they must rely on visual input in order to communicate. The hard-of-hearing, on the other hand, have difficulty hearing but are still able to understand speech through the ear alone (Haynes et al., 1990). Although imprecise, this method of separating the deaf from the hard-of-hearing has implications for communication training and education.

Finally, Vernon and Andrews (1990) defined *deafness* in terms of the individual's attitude toward and use of American Sign Language (ASL) as a primary means of communication. An individual who considers himself a part of the deaf community, who uses sign language, who interacts socially with other deaf adults, and who considers himself an outsider in the hearing world may fit the definition of *deafness* even if his hearing is better than 91 dB. Conversely, an individual with a profound hearing impairment who has just acquired that condition, who still uses speech, who socializes primarily with hearing individuals, and who does not consider himself to be a part of the deaf community may not be considered "deaf" in the cultural sense. Thus, one's personal identification as deaf or hearing depends on attitudes, behavior, and culture in addition to measured hearing loss.

Of most interest to audiologists, speech-language pathologists, and special education teachers is the age of onset of a severe or profound hearing impairment, or deafness. Schow and Nerbonne (1989) label three categories of deaf individuals based on age of onset. The *prelingually deaf* are those whose hearing impairment occurred either prior to birth or prior to the completion of language development at the age of 5. This category includes those who are *congenitally deaf,* or deaf at birth, as well as those who became deaf in early childhood. The *postlingually deaf* are those whose hearing impairment was acquired after language development was complete, later than the age of 5. Finally, a third category, the *deafened,* are defined as those whose hearing impairment was acquired after completing their education, usually in the late teen years, the early twenties, or beyond. Time of onset of the hearing impairment has important implications for aural habilitation-rehabilitation, communication training, and education.

WHO ARE THE DEAF?

Information from a variety of sources indicates that in the United States, approximately 0.2 percent of the population, or two out of every one thousand individuals, is deaf (Glorig and Roberts, 1977; Schein and Delk, 1974). In 1971, this percentage included almost 2 million individuals, divided relatively evenly across the four geographic regions of the country (Schein and Delk, 1974). In the pediatric population, severe and profound bilateral sensorineural hearing loss affects approximately one child in every one thousand, or 0.1 percent of this population (Matkin, 1984). Finally, it has been estimated that 0.14 percent to 0.48 percent of all newborns have a hearing loss in the moderate to profound range (ASHA, 1989).

It is important to note that a certain segment of the deaf population is *multiply handicapped*— that is, in addition to deafness, they may also have visual impairments, cognitive disorders, neuro-motor disorders, learning disabilities, and so on. Estimates of the number of multiply handicapped deaf vary. Some researchers have reported that as little as 13 percent of the deaf population have additional handicaps, while others report up to 30 percent (Watkins and Schow, 1989). This percentage may increase as more medically fragile neonates with serious developmental problems are saved.

Unfortunately, the statistics presented above are based almost entirely on the European-American population. Information on deaf African Americans, Hispanic Americans, or Asian Americans is much more limited. In the early 1980s, it was estimated that approximately 22,000 African-American individuals were deaf and that about 18 percent of all the school-age deaf children in the United States were black (Hairston and Smith, 1983; Vernon and Andrews 1990). Maestas y Moores and Moores (1989) reported that Hispanics accounted for 9.4 percent of the deaf school-age enrollment. Because minority populations are less likely to be aware of social service and educational programs, they are less likely to seek help and so to be included in census data. Identification and culture-sensitive treatment programs for deaf individuals in minority groups is clearly an area that will need to be addressed in our increasingly diverse society.

CAUSES OF DEAFNESS

Table 16-1 lists some of the more common disorders causing deafness that might occur at various points in the life cycle. In the next section, we

TABLE 16-1 Causes of Deafness

I. Congenital deafness
   A. Genetic disorders (e.g., Waardenburg's syndrome; Down syndrome)
   B. Maternal diseases and conditions which affect the fetus (e.g., toxoplasmosis; herpes, cytomegalovirus, rubella; Rh incompatibility; diabetes; kidney disease)
II. Prelingual deafness
   A. Prematurity
   B. Perinatal anoxia
   C. Childhood diseases (e.g., meningitis)
III. Postlingual deafness
   A. Diseases and injuries
   B. Ototoxic drugs
   C. Congenital syphilis
   D. Tumors

will discuss some of these diseases and conditions in more detail.

CONGENITAL DEAFNESS

1. Genetic Disorders. As knowledge of the human genome increases, more and more cases of congenital deafness are being recognized as part of a genetic syndrome. For example, *Waardenburg's syndrome* is a well-known cause of unilateral or bilateral severe sensorineural hearing loss. Individuals with Waardenburg's syndrome typically have a white streak of hair either at the front or back hairline and widely spaced eyes that may be of two different colors (known as *heterochromia*). Their hearing loss is due to malformations of the cochlea and auditory nerve during embryonic development. These individuals generally appear normal in all other respects and are not cognitively disordered. Unless Waardenburg's syn-

drome is known to run in the family, they might not even be aware they have a genetic syndrome.

In 1978, there were over 150 genetic disorders known to cause hearing loss (Shaver and Vernon, 1978); a similar study today would undoubtedly reveal even more. Approximately 40 to 60 percent of all cases of deafness in early childhood are attributed to genetic factors (Vernon and Andrews, 1990). It is important for the audiologist to recognize that a newborn who appears to be deaf for no apparent reason may have one of these syndromes, even if the infant appears healthy and normal. ASHA recommends that all parents of such children be referred for genetic counseling (Sparks, 1984).

2. Maternal Diseases and Conditions. Health problems that affect a pregnant woman can also damage the developing child's hearing mechanism, causing congenital deafness. For example, Batshaw and Perret (1992a) cite toxoplasmosis, the herpes virus, and cytomegalovirus (CMV) as maternal infections that can cause hearing loss or deafness. Prior to the introduction of the rubella vaccine, maternal rubella was also a common cause of congenital deafness, as well as cognitive disorders and cerebral palsy. A susceptible woman who contracts this mild illness during pregnancy is at risk for producing a child with multiple handicaps (Gerkin, 1984).

In addition to diseases, maternal conditions such as diabetes and kidney trouble have been linked to congenital deafness (Vernon and Andrews, 1990). In both cases, it is not known whether the deafness is due to toxic substances in the mother's blood caused by the disorder, lack of oxygen due to vascular changes associated with the disorder, or the drugs used in treatment.

PRELINGUAL DEAFNESS

1. Prematurity. Prematurity is associated with both congenital and early prelingual deafness. A *premature infant* is one who is born at or prior to the thirty-sixth week of gestation. The causes of prematurity are many, including maternal immaturity, maternal illness, poor nutrition, drug abuse, fetal injury or malformation, or abnormalities of the placenta or amniotic sac. Premature infants are more likely to suffer respiratory distress, circulatory problems, *apnea* (the sudden cessation of breathing), stroke, and the buildup of toxins in the blood due to inadequate liver function (Batshaw and Perret, 1992a). The loss of oxygen to the brain resulting from these conditions, plus the effects of toxic substances on the maturing brain, nervous system, and organs, can result in a variety of residual handicaps for babies born too soon. The probability of multiple handicaps in this group is high (Vernon and Andrews, 1990).

2. Perinatal Anoxia.
Perinatal anoxia, a cause of prelingual deafness, refers to a condition of oxygen deprivation during birth. Perinatal anoxia can be caused by a number of factors, including premature delivery of the umbilical cord, aspiration of amniotic fluid, or an immature respiratory system, to name a few. Perinatal anoxia is most common in premature infants, but it can occur even in those at full gestational age (MacDonald et al., 1980). According to Gerkin (1984), the occurrence of deafness in children with severe perinatal anoxia is 4 percent.

3. Childhood Diseases.
Childhood diseases as a cause of prelingual (or postlingual) deafness are fortunately becoming less frequent. Prior to the advent of antibiotics, many infants were deafened as a result of severe ear infections or scarlet fever. Today, both illnesses are typically contained prior to such severe complications. Measles, mumps, and whooping cough also caused some young children to become deaf; but with immunizations against these diseases, fewer cases now occur.

Today, *meningitis* is the primary threat to the hearing of young children, accounting for from 8 to 12 percent of all cases of deafness in children (Vernon and Andrews, 1990). Meningitis is a disease of the *meninges,* the protective membranes surrounding the central nervous system. It is caused by a variety of bacteria, viruses, or fungi. As the disease advances, the infectious agent can invade the inner ear through its neural connections to the brain, resulting in severe hearing impairment or deafness. If the infection is caught early enough, it can often be treated so that no negative consequences occur. However, infants and children under the age of 3 are often unable to verbalize their symptoms—headache, sensitivity to light, stiff neck—and so the disease is often not diagnosed in time to prevent damage to the nervous system or auditory system. Vernon and Andrews (1990) report that one-third of all postmeningitic children are multiply-handicapped, with language disorders, cognitive disorders, emotional disturbances, and spasticity the most frequent associated impairments.

POSTLINGUAL DEAFNESS

1. Ototoxic Drugs.
Ototoxic drugs can cause deafness at any age, but such deafness is most likely to occur postlingually and, in fact, late in life. Several classes of drugs are known to affect the hair cells of the cochlea and the vestibular system, including aspirin, aminoglycoside antibiotics (such as neomycin, kanamycin, and streptomycin), quinine, and thalidomide (Vernon and Andrews, 1990). Small amounts of these drugs may produce temporary changes in hearing function, but large doses or prolonged treatment may cause permanent hearing loss and deafness. In nonemergency situations, physicians are able to monitor blood levels of these drugs to ensure that the threshold for ototoxicity is not exceeded. However, in cases of massive infection, where the individual's life is in danger, such a restriction may not be possible. In order to save the life of the patient, large doses of ototoxic drugs may be needed, and the patient may survive the illness with a profound hearing loss.

Ototoxic drugs are typically used to treat conditions such as rheumatoid arthritis, kidney disorders, tuberculosis, and meningitis. It is not always clear in such cases whether the patient's deafness was caused by the bacteria or virus causing the disease or the drug used to treat it. Further, individual susceptibility to the ototoxic effects of these drugs varies. Thus, the incidence of deafness attributable to ototoxic drugs, particularly in children, has not been satisfactorily established (Northern and Downs, 1991).

2. Tumors. Tumors of the auditory nerve and the auditory nervous system are rare, but they are more common in adults than in children. When they occur, they can be a cause of postlingual deafness.

IDENTIFYING THE DEAF CHILD

Children who are deafened in infancy or early childhood by illness, anoxia, or some other medical complication are often diagnosed quite promptly. Parents and physicians are likely to be alert to the possibility of hearing loss as a sequela of the disease. Changes in the child's behavior and even the child's self-report may indicate the presence of a hearing loss. However, identifying children with congenital deafness is more difficult.

In states where there are no infant hearing-impairment identification programs, the average age at which children are determined to have a hearing loss is 2½ (Gustason, 1989). Although this may seem surprisingly late, there are several reasons for such a long delay in diagnosis. If there is no obvious medical reason to suspect a hearing loss, parents who seek help from their pediatrician may be told to take a wait-and-see approach (Welsh and Slater, 1993). Referrals to an otolaryngologist and, ultimately, an audiologist may take anywhere from one to sixty months (Northern and Downs, 1991). By the time the hearing loss is confirmed and treatment is begun, the optimal period for auditory and language input may be over (Seyfried et al., 1989).

Ideally, infants with any degree of congenital hearing impairment should be diagnosed shortly after birth—certainly within the first few months of life—so that appropriate treatment can begin early and the effects of the hearing loss on speech, language, and cognitive development be mini-mized. Such a scenario would require the screening of all newborns at birth, with some reliable test or instrument that would accurately indicate the degree of loss in those with hearing impairment and confirm normal hearing in those with no disorder. This procedure is known as *universal screening.*

Until recently, universal hearing screening for all neonates had not been recommended by governmental agencies or professional groups. The best method of determining hearing status in newborns, brainstem auditory evoked responses measures (BAERs, described in Chapter 14), had been considered too costly and time-consuming for use with all infants. Further, many hospitals do not have access to the specialized equipment and trained personnel needed for such testing (Goldberg, 1993). Finally, as discussed in Chapter 14, BAERs cannot always be easily interpreted.

In place of universal screening, governmental-professional groups such as the Joint Committee on Infant Hearing (JCIH) recommended that the BAER procedure be used only on high-risk infants prior to their discharge from the hospital. High-risk factors include low birth weight, prematurity, a family history of hearing loss, congenital infection, and perinatal anoxia, among other conditions (JCIH, 1991). Because these recommendations do not have the force of law in most states, it is difficult to assess how successful the high-risk screening concept has been in identifying hearing-impaired newborns. It has been estimated, however, that consistent use of BAER testing in the high-risk population would result in the identification of 50 to 75 percent of all hearing-impaired newborns (ASHA Committee on Infant Hearing, 1989). Unfortunately, this means that the 25 to 50 percent of all hearing-impaired newborns would not be identified. Proponents of universal screening have argued that this "miss" rate is unacceptable (Goldberg, 1993).

In fact, as of this writing, universal screening is being considered much more seriously. The NIH Consensus Development Conference on Early Identification of Hearing Impairment in Infants and Young Children recently drafted a report recommending universal screening for all newborns prior to hospital discharge (Goldberg, 1993). This change in position has come about, according to Goldberg, because of the advent of otoacoustic emissions testing, or OAE (see Chapter 14).

The specific recommendations of the NIH Consensus Development Conference were that the otoacoustic-emission test (OAE) should be used initially for all newborns, with further screening using BAERs for those who fail the OAE. Such a sequence has already been legislatively mandated in Hawaii and Rhode Island. The recommendations are not without controversy, however. Goldberg (1993) quotes several researchers who have reservations about OAE testing due to the lack of data on its accuracy in identifying hearing loss in newborns. Other investigators are concerned that OAE testing at such an early age might result in too many false positives. More research is clearly needed before OAE is universally accepted among audiologists.

The issue of early identification of infants with hearing impairment is clearly an important one. The costs and benefits of universal screening will undoubtedly receive more attention as states, counties, or individual hospitals consider implementing these programs. However, identifying infants with severe and profound hearing loss is only the first step down a very long and arduous path. For once the child is identified, the question of appropriate treatment must be considered.

COMMUNICATION OPTIONS FOR THE DEAF

When a severely or profoundly hearing-impaired child is identified, the next challenge is to provide early and appropriate treatment. But what does appropriate treatment consist of? How can communication and literacy skills best be fostered in the deaf, particularly the congenitally deaf infant who has had no experience with oral language? In this section, we will explore some of the communication options and treatment methods that

have historically been used with the deaf, as well as current trends.

MANUAL COMMUNICATION

1. American Sign Language. Since the deaf, by definition, are unable to hear well enough to acquire language through auditory stimulation alone, it is not surprising that many educators of the deaf advocated the use of a language composed of hand signs and gestures for this population. The best-known of these systems is American Sign Language, or ASL.

ASL is a true language, consisting of hand signs, movements, and gestures that represent objects, actions, and ideas. In addition to its semantic component, ASL has specific hand signs to indicate plurals, tense, and other word changes *(morphology),* and rules for combining signs into longer units *(syntax).*

The historical roots of ASL go back to the early 1700s and Old French Sign Language (FSL), standardized and popularized as an educational tool by Charles Michel, abbé de l'Epée (1712–1789). Old French Sign Language was brought to the United States by Laurent Clerc, a deaf student of the l'Epée school, and Thomas Hopkins Gallaudet, an American educator of the deaf, who founded the first school for the deaf in the United States in 1817. Some varieties of sign language were already in existence among the deaf in the United States, however, and it is believed that modern American Sign Language is a mixture of these plus the system of Clerc. ASL became extremely popular in the education of the deaf in the United States and was used almost exclusively in schools for the deaf until the early 1900s (Vernon and Andrews, 1990).

ASL is considered by most deaf individuals to be their native language, and it is an important prerequisite for acceptance into the deaf community. It has the advantages of being highly visible and easy to learn for most deaf individuals. For the congenitally deaf child, language development in ASL can parallel the hearing child's language development in English. Numerous studies over the past decades indicate that the deaf children of deaf parents, who begin learning ASL at birth, perform better in terms of academic achievement than the deaf children of hearing parents who were exposed to only auditory stimulation for the first years of life (Vernon and Andrews, 1990).

On the negative side, ASL is understood by only a limited segment of the population. A deaf individual who communicates solely through ASL is unable to interact with mainstream society without an interpreter. This has implications for employment, health care, and educational and social opportunities. In addition, it is important to note that ASL is not English. Both are languages, but they are different languages, in the same way that Spanish and English are different languages. ASL semantics are unlike English semantics, of course—signs and gestures are used instead of words. However, ASL also differs from English in terms of morphology and syntax. If we were to literally translate the English sentence "Are you a good student?" into ASL, the result would be "You good learn person you," with facial expressions conveying much of the interrogative nature of the sentence. Further, in ASL there are no corresponding signs for many English function words, such as *a, the, that, is, are, am,* and so on. Thus, the child who learns ASL as a native language must learn English as a second language if he or she is to acquire literacy skills.

2. Fingerspelling. American Sign Language is a manual language not based on English. At the other end of the manual communication continuum is fingerspelling, which is completely based on English. In fingerspelling, each of the twenty-six letters of the alphabet is represented by a different hand position. Figure 16-1 shows the American manual alphabet. The deaf individual spells out words using these hand signs in the same way that he would if he were writing. Words are combined into sentences using English syntactic and morphological rules, again analogous to writing.

The advantages of fingerspelling as a means of communication for the deaf are numerous. First, the deaf individual who communicates via fingerspelling does use and learn English. Second, the hand signs are easily seen and unambiguous. Finally, it is an easy way for deaf individuals to communicate with their hearing families, friends, and coworkers. Most people can master the manual alphabet in about twenty minutes, and although it takes more time and frequent use to become a proficient communicator, fingerspelling can provide an important link between the deaf and the hearing (Vernon and Andrews, 1990).

Unfortunately, there are also many disadvantages to using fingerspelling as a primary means of communication. The biggest disadvantage is the same as the most prominent advantage: The system is based on English. For an individual who already knows English, for whom deafness was acquired in late childhood or adulthood, this method may be attractive. But for a congenitally deaf infant with no knowledge of English, this is an extremely difficult system to learn. Fingerspelling is also much slower than ASL or conversational speech. Vernon and Andrews (1990) estimate that experienced fingerspellers can produce 80 to 90 words per minute, while conversational rates are 100 to 200 words per minute. It is also very tiring to do for long periods of time.

Although fingerspelling might not be a desirable communication system by itself, it is still extremely useful as an adjunct to ASL. Deaf people often use it for proper names (last names, street names, cities, and the like), technical terms, and other words for which there is no sign. As we shall see in a moment, fingerspelling can also be combined with ASL in a more formal way, to produce more Englishlike communication systems. Thus, fingerspelling remains a useful communication alternative.

3. Signed English Systems. One might hypothesize that the advantages of a signed language could be preserved, and competence in English enhanced, if ASL semantics were combined with signs for English morphological markers, and English syntax. Indeed, this approach to

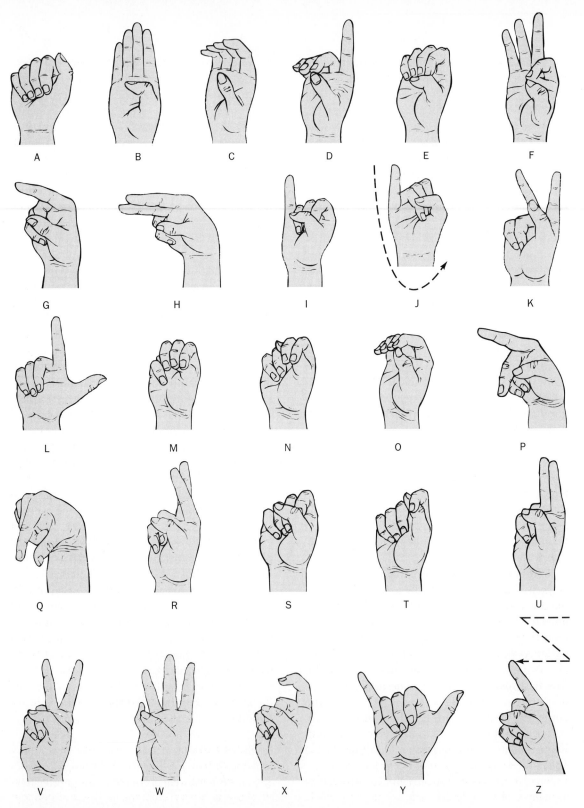

FIGURE 16-1 The American manual alphabet.

manual language does exist in the form of signed English systems (Hipskind, 1989), or manual codes of English (MCE) (Vernon and Andrews, 1990). Some examples of such systems are Seeing Essential English (SEE 1), Signing Exact English (SEE 2), Linguistics of Visual English (LOVE), and Signed English. Although these systems differ from one another in various ways, all seek to combine English grammar with the semantics of ASL where possible. In a manually coded system, the sentence "Are you a good student?" would be translated exactly, using a combination of ASL signs, fingerspelled words, such as *a,* and English word order. Unfortunately, because English and ASL are so different, many ASL signs must be modified, and some must be created, in order to conform to English rules. For example, since there is no ASL sign for *student,* the individual using SEE 1 would need to use a specially created hybrid sign.

The primary advantage of signed English systems is that they make the English language visible for the deaf child. Like the other forms of manual communication, manual codes are easy to see and unambiguous. However, these systems are not as popular as the typical normal-hearing student might imagine. First, they are considered by many linguists and educators to be slow, cumbersome, and difficult to learn. Because signed English systems require so many more movements than ASL to express the same idea, they are also more tiring for the user. Finally, signed English systems have been criticized as being merely codes and not natural languages. Critics contend that they are neither English nor ASL, that they include too many arbitrary hand positions that are difficult to form, and that they eliminate the facial expressions and eye and body movements that give ASL its expressiveness. It has been noted that deaf individuals who know these systems do not use them among themselves (Vernon and Andrews, 1990).

Signed English systems might be compared to Esperanto, a communication system invented in 1887 to serve as an international language. Esperanto was created specifically to incorporate as many words and grammatical forms as possible

that were common to many European languages. It was also intended to be easy to learn, with phonetic spellings and symbols used in the written form. Yet despite these careful plans and good intentions, how popular has Esperanto become? Do you speak it? Have you ever even heard of it? Clearly, it is difficult to launch a hybrid language that is not a natural language to any group.

4. Pidgin Sign English. As you recall from Chapter 5, *pidgin* is a type of communication that evolves when two groups of people who speak different languages come together. It is typically a simplified language, usually based on the language of the dominant group. Pidgin Sign English fits most of these criteria. It has evolved from interactions between hearing speakers of English and deaf speakers of ASL. It employs ASL signs (unlike signed English systems, where many of the ASL signs are replaced or modified) but combines these signs in the same order as words in an English sentence. Pidgin Sign English is simplified in that English morphological endings and articles, such as *a* and *the,* are eliminated. However, Pidgin Sign English retains more of the vocabulary and verb forms of ASL than of English.

Because of its similarity to ASL, Pidgin Sign English is more accepted in the deaf community than any of the more formal manual codes of English (Vernon and Andrews, 1990). It is often used in conjunction with speech by both deaf and hearing individuals during interpreting and Total Communication (to be discussed shortly) and in college teaching (Hipskind, 1989). It is also more accessible to hearing users than ASL because the word order is familiar to English speakers. It is possible that Pidgin Sign English is on its way to becoming a *creolized language* (a language derived from a pidgin but more complex) and that eventually, ASL and English will have more features in common.

5. Cued Speech. Cued speech was developed in the 1960s by R. Orvin Cornett (Cornett, 1967). Although it consists of hand gestures and symbols, it is very different in aim and concept from any of the other manual systems we have described. ASL and signed English systems provide visual analogs for letters and words and have their own systems of grammatical rules. In contrast, cued speech provides visual analogs for lip and tongue positions during speech. It includes eight hand positions for consonants and four for vowels. The speaker uses these hand signals as he or she speaks to inform the deaf listener of tongue positions and voiced-voiceless contrasts that are not visible by observing the lips and face. As such, cued speech is really a supplement to speechreading rather than an independent manual method.

At present, cued speech is recommended by some researchers and educators and criticized by others. It appears to be useful for postlingually deaf individuals who rely on lipreading, and for deaf individuals who are learning speech. However, its use for initial language learning is discouraged (Hipskind, 1989).

ORAL COMMUNICATION

Throughout history, there have been those who argued that no matter how profound the hearing impairment, the deaf individual would be best served by learning language through maximum use of whatever hearing he or she has left along with speechreading and communicating through oral speech. This combination of the use of residual hearing, speechreading, and speech is referred to as the *oral method.*

The oral method, like ASL, has its historical roots in eighteenth-century Europe. At the same time that de l'Epée of France was teaching the deaf to use signs, Samuel Heinicke (1727–1790) of Germany was advocating the use of speechreading and speech in the education of the deaf. Heinicke believed that the foundation of rational thought and all education was oral language, and thus if the deaf were to become educated, they needed to learn to communicate orally. The oral method also became popular in England. In fact, Gallaudet at first intended to study the oral approach used in England when he arrived in Europe in 1815. However, Thomas Braidwood, the head of the English school for the deaf, refused to let Gallaudet study with him. Instead, Gallaudet met with students and teachers of the French school, became impressed with their methods, and eventually brought the French system of signing to the United States.

Despite the popularity of the "manual method" (specifically ASL) in schools for the deaf in the 1800s, the oral method gained ascendancy by the turn of the century. Inventor Alexander Graham Bell was an important proponent for this change. From 1900 and into the 1960s, many schools for the deaf in the United States reversed their earlier custom and began to use oralism. In fact, in some schools, the use of sign was punished (Brill, 1984).

In the decades since the 1960s, the pendulum has swung again, and the use of an exclusively oral approach in most schools for the deaf has waned. However, the oral approach continues to be an important component in the overall treatment of the deaf. In the next section, we will consider each of the three elements of the oral method in more detail.

1. The Use of Residual Hearing. Prior to the development of electronic amplification systems, educators of the deaf advocated providing the deaf individual with sound by shouting into his or her ear, or into an *ear trumpet,* a horn-shaped device (Nerbonne and Schow, 1989). In modern times, the child would be provided with the most powerful hearing aid available, as early in life as possible, and his or her parents would be instructed in auditory stimulation techniques. Under optimal circumstances, an aural rehabilitation (AR) specialist—an audiologist, speech-language pathologist, or teacher of the deaf—would provide training for the parents so they could effectively teach the child language. This professional would also ensure that appropriate testing and amplification was secured and would arrange other rehabilitative services, such as occupational or physical therapy, if needed.

Most researchers stress the need for early amplification and auditory training if functional use of hearing for language learning is to be attained—preferably at or before the age of 1 (Clark and Watkins, 1985), but certainly before the age of 3 or 4 (Watkins and Schow, 1989). In their review of the literature, Watkins and Schow cite several studies that document the positive effects of intervention programs begun prior to the age of 3. In contrast, other authors (Boothroyd, 1982; Wedenberg, 1981) suggest that children who receive these auditory training programs after the age of 6 will probably never learn to use their hearing for understanding speech and language.

It is tempting to conclude from these studies that if amplification and auditory training are only provided early enough, all deaf children will be able to use their residual hearing for language input. However, most researchers and educators agree that this is simply not the case. Those with hearing loss in the severe range (71 to 90 dB) generally do better with amplification than those with losses in the profound range, over 91 dB. According to Norlin and Van Tassell (1980, 24), "In general, an increase in the severity of the hearing-impairment is associated with progressively greater difficulty in the capacity to extract and learn the rules of an oral language system." Vernon and Andrews (1990, 103) are more direct, stating "There are many deaf people who get no benefit from amplification and others who only hear loud noise but understand no speech." It is clear that even with amplification and early auditory training, the deaf child is limited by the sensitivity of his or her auditory mechanism, and not all deaf children can use the amplified auditory channel for language input.

2. Speechreading. Speechreading also plays an important part in the oral method. *Speechreading* or *lipreading* is a technique for understanding what a speaker is saying by interpreting the movements of his or her mouth. However, there is some dispute about whether or not a deaf individual needs formalized or analytic training in this aspect of communication. Watkins and Schow (1989) believe it is not necessary for the parent or caregiver of a deaf child to draw special attention to the mouth movements of a speaker. Their view is that "speechreading develops naturally in the hearing-impaired child as a supplement to listening; therefore, training efforts should at first be primarily directed toward establishing listening skills" (p. 327). When speechreading is taught informally in conjunction with listening training, it is known as the *synthetic approach* (Hipskind, 1989).

In the adult population, speechreading was traditionally taught using the analytic approach, in an intensive manner over a long period of time. Some programs, such as the National Technical Institute for the Deaf (NTID) continue to use this method (Vernon and Andrews, 1990). Intensive and specific training is most likely to be used when speechreading is considered the primary channel for language input. However, improved hearing-aid technology and more powerful amplification devices have shifted the focus of speechreading somewhat. Today, speechreading can often become a supplement to amplified auditory information and thus is more effective (Hipskind, 1989).

It should be noted that it is extremely difficult to read lips accurately without the contribution of auditory input. Approximately two-thirds of the forty-two phonemes of English are either not visible on the lips or are easily confused with one another (Vernon and Andrews, 1990). Further, when the speaker's face is not in full view of the listener, or when the lighting is poor, the difficulty of comprehension is increased. Those who are most successful understanding speech through speechreading are likely to be deafened adults who have had many years of normal auditory (and visual) language input. Such individuals can use their excellent knowledge of English semantics, morphology, and syntax to fill in the gaps when they are unable to see particular sounds; and even then, some information is typically lost. Those who lack good English skills have great difficulty deciphering the incomplete and ambiguous input speechreading provides. Congenitally deaf children with profound hearing loss who are completely unfamiliar with spoken English are the least likely to benefit from speechreading.

3. Speech. Intelligible speech is difficult for deaf individuals to attain, especially those who are congenitally or prelingually deaf. According to Seyfried et al. (1989), degree of hearing loss appears to have a great impact on speech proficiency, with the more severe hearing impairment associated with less intelligible speech. However, the research summarized by Seyfried and her colleagues found a tremendous range in speech proficiency among those with hearing losses in excess of 70 dB. Some of the deaf children who served as subjects in the various studies were rated as very intelligible, while others were rated as very unintelligible. It is interesting to note that in the studies reviewed by Seyfried et al., no improvement in speech intelligibility was noted beyond the age of 7.

Besides degree of hearing loss, many other factors influence speech intelligibility in deaf children. Age of onset of deafness is clearly an important consideration. Those who lose their hearing postlingually, in later childhood or adulthood, require speech therapy primarily to retain their articulatory proficiency. According to Vernon and Andrews (1990), those deafened after the age of 10 will most likely remain fully intelligible, while those deafened at the age of 4 or 5 will have partially intelligible speech. New words are likely to be mispronounced, and voice quality will become more nasal and monotonous over time. Those who are deaf congenitally or prelingually usually have a limited repertoire of intelligible words and phrases, but their spontaneous conversation is often understood only by their families, friends, and coworkers.

Early treatment is yet another factor to consider in speech intelligibility. It is well established that early amplification and auditory training typically result in superior speech (see Markides, 1983, for example). Other factors include the child's motivation, motoric capabilities, the effectiveness of the instructor, and the child's natural aptitude for speech. According to Vernon and Andrews (1990), "Just as every child who studies music cannot become a professional musician, all hearing-impaired children do not have the potential for speech."

TOTAL COMMUNICATION

Total communication is an approach to teaching the deaf based on both manual and oral communication. The deaf child instructed using the total-communication method is fitted with amplification and provided with auditory stimulation and direct or indirect speechreading training. His vocalizations are reinforced, and his speech is encouraged. Simultaneously, the child is exposed to some form of manual communication, usually Pidgin Sign English or one of the signed English systems. Thus, in total communication, both oral and manual methods are used in a combined and integrated manner. Although such *bimodal* (manual and oral) input is popular in theory, in practice there are many disputes regarding which of the manual systems should be used (Vernon, 1987).

The purpose of total communication is to give the child as many opportunities as possible to learn language. It is believed that when a combined system is used, deaf children with sufficient hearing, motivation, and aptitude will learn oral language. For those who are not able to benefit from the auditory signal, manual input is available. Watkins and Schow (1989) describe total communication as a continuum between oral and manual methods rather than a dichotomy. In all probability, the child using total communication will not depend exclusively on either oral or manual input. Instead, the child will rely on auditory stimulation and use speech to some extent in some situations and rely more on manual input in others. Each child and family, according to these authors, needs to find their own balance point between the use of oral communication and the use of manual communication.

According to Maestas y Moores and Moores (1989), this combined oral-manual form of communication has been gaining popularity in educational settings for the hearing impaired since the late 1960s. These authors report that because of the shift toward total communication, there has been a shift away from use of manual-only or oral-only approaches. For example, between 1968 and 1975, 302 education programs for the deaf changed from oral-only communication to some form of total communication (Jordan et al., 1976).

Critics of total communication point out that both the structural integrity of English and the signed system are dramatically altered when the two are attempted simultaneously. Total communication is cognitively demanding for the speaker, who must concentrate on two languages at once. It tends to be slow, and speakers often reduce the complexity of their utterances in order to communicate more quickly. Because such elements as articles and auxiliary verbs may be left out, the English input to deaf children is not perfect. However, proponents argue that the English input in total communication is far superior to anything derived from lipreading (Vernon and Andrews, 1990).

MANUAL VERSUS ORAL VERSUS TOTAL COMMUNICATION

Given the information presented above, what is the best method of communication for the deaf? Deaf individuals themselves prefer ASL because (1) it is their natural language, (2) it is easily perceived and unambiguous, and (3) it enculturates the deaf individual into the deaf community. However, as we have noted, exclusive use of ASL limits the deaf person to certain communication partners and segregates him or her from mainstream society. Pidgin Sign English and the signed English systems have some potential, but they are even less well known than ASL.

The oral method appears to be a good method of communication for some deaf individuals but not for others. For those able to use residual hearing, speechread effectively, and produce intelligible speech, oralism maximizes opportunities for integration into mainstream society with a concomitant increase in vocational and social opportunities. For the congenitally and prelingually deaf, however, the oral method may result in incomplete and ambiguous language input from which the individual is unable to profit.

The total-communication approach and the concept of a continuum between exclusive oral use and exclusive manual use appears, at first glance, to contain much promise. However, in trying to

teach a child two languages simultaneously, a parent runs the risk of teaching neither well. Total communication also places a tremendous burden on family members, who must go through the effort and expense of securing amplification and early auditory training and must simultaneously seek instruction in signing. To some parents, total communication might seem like "total commitment"—commitment to the deaf child's needs over and above all else. Clearly, the question we posed on what appropriate treatment for the deaf consists of is not an easy one to answer.

OPTIMAL TREATMENT FOR DEAF INDIVIDUALS: CURRENT VIEWS

Let us return to our goals for "appropriate treatment for the deaf": (1) to facilitate normal communicative development; (2) to develop oral communication skills; and (3) to establish standard English language skills, including reading and writing. Over the years, much research has been conducted in an attempt to determine which communication approach fulfills any one or all of these goals most effectively. As is often the case in controversial areas, there are results which support almost every conceivable point of view (Vernon and Andrews, 1990, provide an extensive listing of the literature).

At this point, a flexible total-communication approach appears to be favored by many educators to foster communication, speech, and literacy in the deaf. Early exposure to signing is considered important, particularly for profoundly deaf infants, in order to provide them with an easily learned, unambiguous communication system during the most active language-learning years. However, early amplification and auditory training are also recommended to improve speechreading and speech skills so that the child's integration into a hearing society will be facilitated (Seyfried et al., 1989). Maestas y Moores and Moores (1989) also believe that there is a growing adaptability among educators of the deaf to use both manual and oral methods to different degrees for different children and a retreat from a hard-and-fast belief in the superiority of one method over another. To be sure, there are still some programs and schools that teach only the oral method or only the manual methods (probably fewer of these, according to Maestes y Moores and Moore, 1989). However, there appears to be more willingness on the part of educators to look at the particular needs of a particular child and to adapt the communication system to that child's needs and abilities rather than the other way around.

An important element in the treatment of the deaf infant and child that we have so far neglected is the family. Although educators of the deaf may have their opinions about optimal treatment, it is really the family that makes the ultimate decision, at least in the early years. If parents cannot be convinced of the importance of learning and using sign language, or if they refuse to accept hearing aids for their child, there is little anyone can do. The aural rehabilitation (AR) specialist mentioned earlier is the primary professional to interact with and educate the parents about their child's hearing loss and to describe the communication options available. The parents' natural interaction styles, values, skills, and commitment must all be taken into account when a communication system is being decided upon (Watkins and Schow, 1989). After all, in the first few years of life, the primary burden of intervention falls upon the parents. They must be treated as full partners in any decisions that are made.

NEW TECHNOLOGIES

New devices and procedures are constantly being explored and introduced to help the deaf to process sound more effectively. One of these is the cochlear implant, which bypasses the outer and middle ear and cochlea in furnishing stimuli to the auditory nerve. Another is the vibrotactile aid, which provides a tactile analog of sound.

COCHLEAR IMPLANTS

Cochlear implants are devices that provide sound stimuli directly to the auditory nerve of the deaf person. These fairly recent additions to the field of aural rehabilitation were only approved for general use in 1984 (Berger and Millin, 1989). A cochlear implant consists of a microphone, which receives speech from the environment. From the microphone, the speech signal is fed into a signal processor, about the size of a Walkman®, which filters and amplifies the input to emphasize the fundamental frequency and first two formant regions. In the simplest and most common models, the signal is divided into twenty or more frequency-specific channels, each of which is delivered to a different location in the cochlea (Working Group on Communication Aids for the Hearing-Impaired (WGCAHI), 1991; Berger and Millin, 1989).

The processed signal is then transmitted via an external magnetic induction device worn behind the ear to an internal receiver that is implanted under the skin of the *mastoid process,* the bony prominence behind the ear. Only a thin fold of skin separates the external device from the internal receiver, so the transmission of current from one to the other is easily accomplished. Finally, a series of twenty or more microelectrodes extend from the internal receiver into the scala tympani, where they are implanted at regular intervals along the anterior portion of the cochlea. These microelectrodes directly stimulate the nerve fibers surrounding them, just as the movement of hair cells in the normal ear would. These nerve fibers ultimately communicate with the auditory nerve, which carries the sensation of sound to the brain (Working Group on Communication Aids for the Hearing-Impaired, or WGCAHI, 1991).

The cochlear implant is an extremely invasive device. The individual who undergoes this procedure risks losing any residual hearing he or she might have had, degeneration of nerve fibers in the area of the electrodes, balance disturbances, infection, and failure of the device. Originally, cochlear implants were approved for use only in postlingually deafened adults who could not benefit from conventional hearing aids. However, their use has increased to include prelingually deaf adults; and some children are now receiving implants on an experimental basis. Implants for children are extremely controversial because of the potential risks of the procedure. However, the WGCAHI reports that over 270 children received an older, single-channel implant that is no longer available, and many others have received the newer, multichannel implants described above.

How effective are cochlear implants? Both positive and negative research results have been reported. Many implanted patients appear able to differentiate environmental sounds, discriminate the voices of different individuals, and use the auditory input they receive from the device as a supplement to speechreading. In terms of speech perception unaided by visual input, some subjects are reportedly able to identify words in isolation and in the context of sentences, although many cannot (WGACHI, 1991).

In general, postlingually deafened clients who receive implants do better in word recognition and speech perception than do the prelingually deaf. (WGACHI, 1991). For congenitally deaf children, both age of implantation and practice with the device appear to be important factors. Osberger et al. (1993) reports that children who receive their implants before the age of 10 are more successful in developing intelligible speech than are those who receive their implants after the age of 10. Fryauf-Bertschy et al. (1992) found that congenitally deaf children did not appear to improve in terms of their speech perception until they had been using the cochlear implant for over twelve months. The same authors reported only limited word recognition for these children after eighteen to twenty-four months of use. Clearly, many factors must be considered in determining the prognosis for success with a cochlear implant for any given individual.

VIBROTACTILE AIDS

As we learned in Chapter 14, speech is a complex combination of frequencies. If you look at the spectrograms of the various vowels and consonants presented in Chapter 14, it is clear that different speech sounds have different characteristic patterns of frequency within the speech spectrum of 0 to 8000 Hz. Vowels, for example, are composed of *formants,* concentrated energy at specific frequencies. Fricatives, in contrast, have widely distributed energy throughout the entire spectrum. Under normal conditions, the auditory system processes the various frequency components of a particular speech sound; and the listener, quite unknowingly, synthesizes them into a recognizable phoneme.

Vibrotactile aids are based on the premise that other sensory systems are also capable of processing complex input that listeners can synthesize into recognizable elements. Specifically, vibrotactile aids present gentle vibrations to the surface of the skin in particular patterns. In the more sophisticated models, an array of tiny vibrating elements is arranged in a rectangular matrix and attached to some site on the body: the fingertip, hand, wrist, forearm, collarbone, thigh, stomach, or the pinna of the ear. Different frequencies are associated with different spatial locations within the matrix. High frequencies, for example, might cause vibrators at the top of the matrix to go into motion, while low frequencies might have a similar effect on the vibrators at the bottom of the matrix. This is not unlike the arrangement in the cochlea, where different spatial locations along the basilar membrane are stimulated by different frequencies.

Theoretically, an individual should be able to recognize one spatial pattern from another and associate different patterns with different speech sounds. As in normal speech, individual phonemes (or *vibremes* perhaps, in this case) might be combined into words and sentences that the listener would continue to recognize. One might hypothesize that it would take some time for an individual to learn to recognize tactually presented patterns and associate them with speech sounds. It might also be hypothesized that a postlingually deafened individual would have more difficulty learning to "hear" through his skin in this way than would a congenitally deaf individual, who was never familiar with conventional sound.

Research investigating the effectiveness of vibrotactile devices has been promising. Several investigators who used prelingually deaf children as subjects found an increase in spontaneous vocalizations, receptive vocabulary, and auditory language comprehension (Proctor and Goldstein, 1983; Goldstein and Proctor, 1985; Geers, 1986). For postlingually deaf adults, investigators tried to compare the word-recognition skills of individuals using vibrotactile devices to the skills of those with cochlear implants. In a review presented by WGCAHI (1991), it appeared that there was considerable overlap in the performances of the two groups. In general, the worst performances in word recognition were by the least skilled individuals using vibrotactile devices, and the best performance was by a client with a cochlear implant. However, in many cases, the word-recognition abilities of subjects with vibrotactile aids were similar to those of subjects with cochlear implants.

Osberger et al. (1993) specifically compared speech intelligibility in children with cochlear implants, vibrotactile aids, and conventional hearing aids. She and her colleagues found that the most normal-sounding speech was produced by children who received cochlear implants prior to the age of 10, and the least intelligible speech was produced by those who received either a cochlear implant or a vibrotactile device *after* the age of 10. It is interesting to note that the cochlear-implant subjects and the vibrotactile subjects were *both* about as intelligible as children who used conventional hearing aids and whose hearing thresholds were between 100 and 110 dB.

The results of the Osberger study fit in well with the tentative recommendations made by WGCAHI (1991). The members of WGCAHI concluded that individuals with hearing losses of between 25 and 90 dB would develop better auditory perception and speech intelligibility using a conventional hearing aid than using either a vibrotactile device or a cochlear implant. Conversely, those with hearing losses greater than 115 dB would probably not do well with a conventional hearing aid and should be considered candidates for either of the alternative systems. Recommendations for those with hearing losses between 90 and 115 dB are less clear-cut. Such

listeners, according to WGCAHI, might derive some benefit from conventional aids but should also be considered for alternative systems, depending on current age, age of onset of deafness, health factors, and other variables.

Research and development in alternative hearing systems is continuing at a rapid pace. Today's recommendations may be completely overturned by technological advancements tomorrow or next year. The audiologist who works with the deaf in selecting amplification and other interventions will have the challenge of keeping informed of new developments, procedures, and technologies that can give the deaf the option of becoming full members of the hearing world.

EDUCATIONAL ALTERNATIVES FOR THE DEAF

Educational options for the deaf vary widely from state to state and from school district to school district. Urban areas, with their higher concentration of population, typically serve a larger number of deaf individuals and thus tend to provide more specialized educational programs and placement alternatives. Rural areas, where there may be only one or two deaf students for hundreds of miles, are usually more restricted in the options they provide. Some of the more common types of programs for the deaf are described below.

RESIDENTIAL SCHOOLS

Historically, most deaf children have, at one time or another, attended a residential school for the deaf. Today, despite the mandate of Pub. L. No. 94-142 and the current emphasis on integrating handicapped students into the regular classroom, each state continues to have at least one school for the deaf. According to *American Annals of the Deaf* (1985), approximately 32 percent of the school-age deaf population attends a residential school. Of those, 61 percent reside at the school while the remaining 39 percent live at home and commute. Residential schools, according to

Lowenbraun (1988), continue to educate a wide range of deaf students, but they tend to enroll more children with profound hearing loss or multiple handicaps.

Residential schools for the deaf have traditionally provided a centralized source for the specialized educational needs of the deaf, comprehensive services from preschool to high school, and even outreach programs for parents of deaf babies. The residential school also provides a community of deaf peers and role models with whom the child can establish meaningful relationships and who will help the child understand and cope with deafness (Vernon and Andrews, 1990). Students generally attend classes with others of their age (unlike many integrated programs, where deaf students of widely different ages may be grouped), and a full range of extracurricular activities are available.

On the negative side, residential schools for the deaf separate the child from his family and community. Removing the child from mainstream society and educational institutions initiates a cycle of segregation that may limit future opportunities. In addition, residential schools for the deaf do not always use curricula similar to the public school curriculum for hearing children. Thus, the child in such a school may not acquire the knowledge base needed for future employment.

DAY SCHOOLS

Day schools are found in large metropolitan areas where a sufficient population of deaf children exists to justify a separate school to which they can commute on a daily basis. All children commute; no children actually live at the school. Day schools are very similar to residential schools in both their advantages and disadvantages (Lowenbraun, 1988).

DAY CLASSES

Day-class programs for the deaf are held in regular schools where the majority of the students are hearing. Deaf students are assigned to a class for the hearing-impaired as their primary academic unit; however, depending on the policies of the school or district, they may also participate in some classes and activities with the hearing students in the school. At one time, only hearing-impaired students with relatively well developed hearing and speaking abilities were considered for integration into regular classes in the host school. However, in the wake of Pub. L. No. 94-142 and the Americans with Disabilities Act, many profoundly deaf students are now being integrated as well, with the help of sign-language interpreters in their regular classes (Lowenbraun, 1988).

Day classes are potentially advantageous in that they permit deaf students to live at home and be educated in their home districts. Students in day classes are more likely than those in residential schools to be exposed to age-appropriate academic curricula, especially if they are integrated for any academic subjects. On the negative side, however, day classes may include children of widely different ages, especially if there are few deaf students in the district. There is no guarantee that the curriculum in the day class for the deaf will parallel the curriculum for hearing children. Even with an interpreter, deaf students may have difficulty keeping up in their integrated classes because of differences in language ability and learning style. And, finally, deaf children in such programs may feel themselves to be a stigmatized minority in the host school and may be unwilling or unable to participate in regular extracurricular activities.

RESOURCE ROOMS AND ITINERANT SERVICES

A fourth educational option is to assign the hearing-impaired child to a regular classroom as his or her primary academic unit and to remove the child periodically from that classroom for special instruction. A *resource room* is a room staffed by a special education teacher who typically provides individualized programs for children with many different handicaps. Students attend the resource room for specified portions of the school day, but they return to their regular classrooms at some point. *Itinerant services* is the term used for instruction provided to individuals or small groups by speech-language pathologists, audiologists, or teachers of the deaf who travel to several schools. The resource room–itinerant services option is used primarily for those with a mild to moderate hearing impairment or with deaf children functioning near grade level (Lowenbraun, 1988).

For the deaf or hard-of-hearing student who is having difficulty with grade-level academic work, this educational model has numerous pitfalls. During resource-room participation or itinerant instruction, the student is removed from his or her classroom, thereby missing whatever information is being presented at that time. The resource room or itinerant teacher rarely covers the exact material that is being missed; they are more likely to work on specific skills such as auditory training or speech. Thus, the student who participates in this type of program may gain experience in various preacademic and communication skills but may fall further and further behind in academic subjects.

POSTSECONDARY EDUCATION

Since the 1960s, there has been an increase in the number of postsecondary college and vocational programs for the deaf. The best-known liberal arts college for the deaf, Gallaudet College, was established in 1864, and it remained the sole option for postsecondary education for the deaf for one hundred years. In the 1960s, the National Technical Institute for the Deaf in Rochester, New York, was established, as well as regional vocational technical programs in St. Paul, Minnesota; Seattle, Washington; and New Orleans, Louisiana. By the early 1980s, 102 such programs existed, serving over 5000 deaf students (Maestas y Moores and Moores, 1989). About 40 percent of all deaf individuals participate in some type of postsecondary education, approximately equivalent to that reported for the total population of young adults (Armstrong and Schneidmiller, 1983).

CONSEQUENCES OF DEAFNESS TO THE INDIVIDUAL

The foregoing sections might lead the reader to believe that recent technological developments and increased communication and educational options have assured deaf individuals of appropriate identification, intervention, and assistance. Unfortunately, this is not always the case. In the words of Maestas y Moores and Moores (1989, 286):

In spite of documented improvements including the use of different communication systems, more placement options, early intervention programs, qualitative improvements in individual hearing aids, and so forth, there is no reason for sanguinity over either the current situation or projections for the near future. Large numbers of deaf adolescents still possess minimal speech, linguistic, academic and vocational skill. Progress has been incremental, with no real qualitative breakthroughs, with the possible exception of the expansion of postsecondary programs.

Because of their difficulty in communicating, deaf individuals often feel isolated from hearing society, and even from their own families. They may depend on clubs for the deaf and the deaf community for a sense of belonging and support. Communication problems also often limit their educational attainment. Despite having an IQ distribution similar to that of the hearing population, deaf high school students typically achieve reading and language skills only in the fourth- to sixth-grade range and math skills in the sixth- to seventh-grade range (Maestas y Moores and Moores, 1989). Hearing high school graduates are expected to perform at the twelfth-grade level (although certainly many do not achieve that level).

The combination of communication limitations and reduced educational attainment also serves to limit vocational choices. In the past, many deaf individuals performed unskilled labor and worked in factories, despite their intellectual capacity for higher-level employment. With many of these jobs being lost to automation and the shift away from heavy industry in the United

States, the deaf face increasing unemployment unless they can secure better educational and vocational training (Vernon and Ottinger, 1989). The Americans with Disabilities Act of 1991 may help alleviate the situation somewhat by requiring employers to provide interpreters and assistive devices for the hearing-impaired on the job. However, the deaf individual must have the educational qualifications to be hired in the first place, and achieving those qualifications will be a challenge.

CONSEQUENCES OF DEAFNESS TO THE FAMILY

To a family consisting of two deaf parents, the birth of a deaf child is neither a surprising nor a traumatic event. When only one of the parents is deaf, deafness in the child is still not usually seen as a devastating event. However, only about 3 percent of all deaf children have two deaf parents, with an additional 7 percent having one deaf parent. The remaining 90 percent of deaf children, born to hearing parents, face a more complicated family situation.

The hearing family of a deaf infant is profoundly affected by that child's hearing loss. Any time a handicapped child is born, there is a period during which the family may experience shock, denial, anger, and guilt. Although these feelings are likely to fade and reemerge only periodically over the years, it is important that the parents come to accept the irreversibility of their child's condition. Until they do, it is difficult for them to make the many decisions that must be made and that will have important future consequences. Help from various professionals must be sought, hearing aids might be purchased, and training in a variety of procedures should be obtained. The parents might decide to try a total-communication approach, which requires the entire family to learn and use sign language. Or they might aggressively pursue the more experimental forms of treatment for deafness, including a cochlear implant.

For a hearing family, the child's impairment often involves unanticipated and considerable amounts of time and money. Parents may doubt their ability to care for the child properly or to communicate with him or her, and they may withdraw as a result. According to Vernon and Ottinger (1989, 245), "many families do not communicate fluently and comfortably with their severely hearing-impaired members. Very few learn sign language or other effective communication methods. Such a lack of communication is devastating educationally, psychologically and sociologically."

Counseling is often needed to help families begin to cope with the deaf individual's needs constructively. Until recently, there were few professionals knowledgeable in the areas of both psychology and deafness and who also possessed the necessary communication skills. However, according to Vernon and Ottinger (1989), the situation is currently improving as new training and research programs are established. There continues to be a need for special services for deaf individuals and their families, but there is also an increased interest among psychologists as well as professionals in other disciplines that will help answer that need as time goes on.

SUMMARY

In this chapter, we discussed deafness from many different perspectives. Various definitions of deafness were given, as well as causes of severe and profound hearing impairment. Information about identifying deaf infants was also presented. With the advent of otoacoustic-emissions technology, universal hearing screening of all newborns may some day become a reality. Options for communication for the deaf—manual, oral, and total—were also explored at some length. The manual method, in particular, was shown to include a number of different methods that share only the common feature of using the hands instead of the speech mechanism to convey messages. The advantages and disadvantages of each method were discussed.

Treatment of the deaf continues to change as

new technologies for restoring hearing are developed. Both cochlear implants and vibrotactile aids have been introduced within the past decade, and both are still being experimented with. Finally, educational options and settings for the deaf were presented.

REVIEW QUESTIONS

1. Define *deafness* in terms of audiometry, function, and culture.
2. What is meant by *prelingual* and *postlingual deafness*? Why is the distinction between them important?
3. What are some causes of deafness?
4. How is deafness diagnosed in young children? Why has universal hearing screening recently become a popular idea?
5. What is meant by the *manual method of communication*? The *oral method*? *Total communication*?
6. Why do signed English systems lack the support given to ASL by the deaf community?
7. What are some advantages and disadvantages of ASL? Of the oral method? Of total communication?
8. When and where did the manual method originate? The oral method? Why was the manual method first used in the United States? Why did the oral method replace it?
9. What is the currently accepted optimal treatment for infants and young children with suspected deafness? What difficulties does this treatment impose on the (hearing) family?
10. What new technologies have been developed to aid the deaf in hearing-sensing speech?
11. What are the options currently for education of the deaf? What are the advantages and disadvantages of each?

FOR FURTHER INFORMATION

Moores, D. (1987). *Educating the deaf: Psychology, principles and practices* (3rd ed.). Boston, MA: Houghton Mifflin.

Schow, R., and **Nerbonne, M.** (Eds) (1989). *Introduction to aural rehabilitation* (2nd ed.). Austin, TX: Pro-Ed.

Vernon, M., and **Andrews, J.** (1990). *The Psychology of deafness*. New York, NY: Longman.

Professional Preparation and Practice

I f you have found the subject of communication sciences and disorders interesting, a career as a speech-language pathologist or audiologist may be for you. In this chapter, the educational sequence required for both professions is discussed. As mentioned in Chapter 1, the American Speech-Language-Hearing Association (ASHA) is the national professional organization that sets the education and training standards for speech-language pathologists and audiologists. We will review their requirements, in terms of course work and clinical experience, for the certificate of clinical competence.

A certified speech-language pathologist or audiologist has a wide variety of employment opportunities open to him or her. In this chapter, we will also explore a number of professional work settings and the types of clients and disorders a *clinician* (practicing speech-language pathologist or audiologist) might work with in each.

EDUCATIONAL PREPARATION IN SPEECH-LANGUAGE PATHOLOGY

The student wishing to become a speech-language pathologist needs a solid foundation in the biological and physical sciences, mathematics, and behavioral sciences at the college level. ASHA (1992b) currently requires a minimum of three semester hours in each area. These courses are usually taken in the student's freshman and sophomore years, along with the school's other general requirements in the arts and humanities.

In the junior and senior years, more specific course work in basic human communication processes is typically taken. This includes classes in such areas as anatomy and physiology of the speech and hearing mechanisms, the physics of sound, hearing science, speech science, language development, phonetics, linguistics, and developmental psychology. At this point, students are usually eligible to declare a major in communication sciences and disorders, speech and hearing sciences, speech pathology and audiology, or whatever the equivalent department at their institution is called. They may also begin some of their course work in speech disorders, language disorders, and hearing disorders.

During the undergraduate years, students are also required to observe speech-language therapy sessions. Students must accrue twenty-five clock hours of observation prior to doing any clinical *practicum* (therapy) themselves. Depending on the school the student is attending, supervised clinical practicum may begin at the end of the undergraduate career (although it is sometimes deferred until the graduate program). In their supervised practicum experience, students meet with a client weekly and are responsible for planning and carrying out therapy for that client. A clinical supervisor who is a member of the faculty or staff of the department helps the student plan therapy, observes the student's work with the client, and provides frequent feedback.

After receiving a bachelor's degree, the student must be accepted into a master's program to complete his or her academic and clinical training.

The master's degree is considered the entry-level degree for professional practice as a speech-language pathologist. At this level, specific courses in language disorders, phonological disorders, fluency disorders, voice disorders, cleft palate, adult neurological disorders, augmentative and alternative communication, and audiology, among others, are taken.

During the graduate program, the student must also engage in supervised clinical practicum. ASHA requires that graduate students in communication sciences and disorders work with adults with language disorders, children with language disorders, adults with speech disorders, children with speech disorders, and even individuals with hearing disorders. Further, the student must see clients in a minimum of three different settings. For most students, this means having some clients in the college or university clinic and doing two internships in schools, hospitals, or other agencies. A total of 350 clock hours of supervised clinical practicum is required (although after two internships, most students have more than that). Students are not paid for the therapy they do as a part of their educational program.

EDUCATIONAL PREPARATION IN AUDIOLOGY

At the undergraduate level, educational preparation in audiology is similar to what we have just discussed for speech-language pathology. College freshmen and sophomores take courses in the biological and physical sciences, mathematics, and behavioral sciences. These are followed in the junior and senior years by classes in the anatomy and physiology of the speech and hearing mechanisms, the physics of sound, hearing science, speech science, phonetics, language development, linguistics, and developmental psychology. At the end of the undergraduate program, students may take some courses in audiology.

Enrollment in a master's degree program follows completion of the undergraduate degree. At this level, students take professional course work in audiological testing, the neurophysiology of hearing, hearing-aid fitting, pediatric audiology, and aural rehabilitation, among other areas. A total of 350 clock hours in supervised clinical practicum is also part of the graduate education program in audiology. The student must have experience with the evaluation and treatment of children and adults with hearing disorders of various types and severities and the selection and use of amplification and assistive devices for both adults and children (ASHA, 1992b). A number of hours spent working with those who have speech and language disorders is also required. As in speech-language pathology, students in audiology must accrue clinical practicum hours in three different settings.

REQUIREMENTS FOR CERTIFICATION IN SPEECH-LANGUAGE PATHOLOGY OR AUDIOLOGY

In order to be awarded ASHA's certificate of clinical competence, the student must have completed a master's degree in the appropriate area (speech-language pathology or audiology) at an ASHA-accredited institution. This means that the graduate program the student attends must be approved by ASHA's Educational Standards Board. A list of accredited programs can be obtained by writing to ASHA, 10801 Rockville Pike, Rockville, MD 20852. During the master's program, the student completes all the course work required by ASHA, plus the 350 clock hours of clinical practicum in the appropriate areas at three different sites.

The second criterion for the certificate of clinical competence is obtaining a passing score on a national professional examination. The national examination in speech-language pathology and audiology, a specialty-area test of the National Teacher Examination (NTE) program, is administered three times a year by the Educational Testing Service (ASHA, 1992b) at over 400 locations throughout the United States. This test is usually taken during or at the end of the student's last semester of graduate studies. Different forms of the test are given to speech-language pathologists and audiologists, appropriate to their specialization. Registration materials may be obtained by calling 609-771-7395 or by writing to NTE Programs, Educational Testing Service, P.O. Box 6051, Princeton, NJ, 08541-6051.

Upon graduation from a master's program, students are eligible for employment as speech-language pathologists or audiologists. However, their first year of employment is considered the clinical fellowship year (CFY), and during this time, they must be periodically observed or otherwise monitored by an experienced speech-language pathologist or audiologist with the certificate of clinical competence. Thus, the third criterion for the certificate of clinical competence is completion of the clinical fellowship year.

When the student has received a master's degree at an approved institution, passed the national examination in speech-language pathology or audiology, and finished a clinical fellowship year, the certificate of clinical competence is awarded by ASHA. At that time, the individual is also eligible for full membership in ASHA. If membership in ASHA is not desired, it is possible to apply for certification without membership.

Some individuals who major in communication sciences and disorders do not choose to go on for a certificate of clinical competence. For those interested in careers as researchers in basic communication processes, a clinical background, clinical experience, and clinical certification might not be considered necessary. Such individuals usually go directly from a master's program to a doctoral (Ph.D.) program and emerge as "speech scientists" or "hearing scientists."

OTHER TYPES OF CERTIFICATION

Besides a certificate of clinical competence from ASHA, a speech-language pathologist or audiologist may need additional types of certification in order to practice their profession. If employment in the public schools is desired, credentialing through the state's board of education will be necessary. School certification affects primarily speech-language pathologists, although some school districts require audiologists to be certified in the schools as well.

Each state has its own requirements, but the equivalent of a certificate of clinical competence is an important basis of public school certification in most states. The individual seeking certification may also need to provide proof of course work in the field of education, such as in educational psychology, methods of teaching, and instruction in reading. Finally, in order to be certified in the public schools, the applicant must have completed a *school practicum experience,* or student teaching. This practicum experience for the speech-language pathologist or audiologist does not involve classroom teaching; rather, it involves the assessment and treatment of children with communication disorders in the public school setting.

In addition to school certification, the speech-language pathologist and audiologist must also consider the licensing laws in the state in which they wish to practice. Most states require that speech-language pathologists and audiologists be licensed through the state's department of professional regulation. Holders of a certificate of clinical competence from ASHA typically have little trouble getting a license in any state.

Finally, if audiologists wish to sell hearing aids, almost all states require a hearing-aid dispensing license. In order to obtain this license, the audiologist may have to take an examination prepared by the state's hearing-aid examining board. If an audiologist moves to another state, another examination may be necessary. Both audiologists who wish to sell hearing aids and *hearing-aid dispensers* (individuals who sell hearing aids but are not audiologists) take the same examination.

CHANGES ON THE HORIZON

As of this writing, some changes are being discussed regarding the educational preparation of audiologists. Some audiologists feel that the entry level degree for practice in audiology should be a professional or clinical doctorate rather than the master's degree (Ad Hoc Committee on Employment Impact of Clinical and Professional Doctoral

Degrees into the Practice of Audiology, 1994). A doctoral degree would require additional course work and clinical practicum beyond the scope of the current master's degree in audiology, although the exact duration and content of the doctoral program has not yet been decided. Holders of this degree would have the title Doctor of Audiology, or Au.D. The Au.D. would not be the same type of degree as the Doctor of Philosophy, or Ph.D., which is a research degree required for teaching at the college or university level.

The field of communication sciences and disorders is growing and advancing rapidly. As more and more diversification occurs within the field, it is likely that additional educational preparation will be necessary for those who intend to practice in specialized areas. Speech-language pathologists as well as audiologists must be prepared to keep up with these changes and to continue their education beyond the master's degree.

WORK SETTINGS FOR SPEECH-LANGUAGE PATHOLOGISTS

Speech-language pathologists are employed in many different types of work settings, treating both adults and children with a wide array of communication disorders. One of the advantages of a career in this field is the variety of professional opportunities available. Some of the more common employment sites are public schools, hospitals, residential health-care facilities, nonresidential health-care facilities, and colleges and universities.

PUBLIC SCHOOLS

The largest number of speech-language pathologists are employed in the public schools—56 percent, according to Slater (1992). However, within the public schools, many different types of jobs are possible.

The traditional role of the speech-language pathologist in the public schools is to work with children in the elementary grades (kindergarten through the sixth grade). Most speech-language pathologists serve in more than one school, although they may be assigned a particular school as home base. Language, phonological, fluency, and voice disorders are typically seen. Speech-language pathologists may work with children individually or in small groups and conduct classroom activities in consultation with the classroom teacher. Additionally, the work of the speech-language pathologist may involve children who are having difficulty learning, especially learning to read. Some of these children may have language disorders that underlie their learning disabilities. Speech-language pathologists in the elementary school setting must have an understanding of the curricula at various grade levels and be able to interact effectively with other teachers in helping children to succeed in school.

Because of new policies regarding integration of the handicapped, today's public school speech-language pathologist has the opportunity to work with children who have many different handicaps. Some school districts have speech-language pathologists who specialize in working with students with moderate and severe mental and physical disabilities. In such cases, the speech-language pathologist and an occupational or physical therapist may do therapy together with a multiply-handicapped child, in what is called *cotreatment*. Clearly, a team approach is important in such a setting, as well as the ability to cooperate with other professionals.

Most public schools in the nation now have programs for 3- to 5-year-old preschool children with speech and hearing handicaps, as required by Pub. L. No. 94-142 and 99-457. Some school speech-language pathologists work primarily with this age group. Since many of these children have additional handicaps besides communication disorders, speech-language pathologists in preschool environments must be able to work with those who have cerebral palsy, cognitive disorders, autism, and many other conditions. Professional services may include home visits, counseling parents on home programs, and cotreatment with occupational and physical therapists.

Speech-language pathologists may also work with adolescents and young adults in junior high

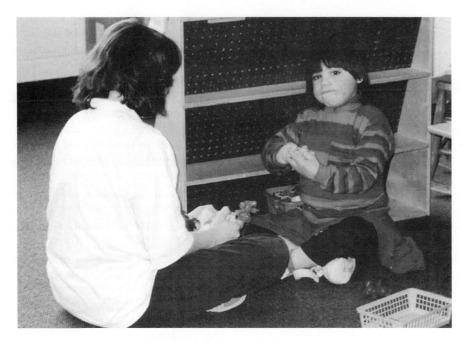

FIGURE 17-1 Speech-language pathologists in the public schools work with preschool children who have a variety of handicapping conditions.

and high school. In this population, voice and fluency disorders are often seen, as well as persistent language and phonological disorders. Students who have newly arrived in the United States, who need help sounding and interacting more like their peers, may also be on the speech-language pathologist's caseload. There are usually fewer students at this age who need speech therapy services, but those who do are more likely to have suffered negative emotional and social consequences as a result of their disorder. Thus, the speech-language pathologist in this setting needs good counseling skills.

HOSPITALS

According to Slater (1992), approximately 16 percent of all speech-language pathologists are employed in hospitals. As was the case with public schools, there are many different populations and disorders that a speech-language pathologist might work with in a hospital setting.

In the hospital setting, speech-language pathologists frequently see older adults with aphasia, as well as young and old adults with head trauma, individuals with head and neck cancer who must have parts of the speech and voice mechanism removed, and in some cases, young children with neurological disorders or cleft palate in the birth to three-year age group. Depending on the specific hospital, the speech-language pathologist may be asked to do videoendoscopic evaluations of laryngeal functioning, treat adults and children with swallowing disorders, or assess the adequacy of velar functioning in cases of hypernasality.

Some hospital speech-language pathologists may be engaged primarily in diagnosis and assessment of those who enter the hospital with speech, language, or swallowing disorders as part of their presenting symptom pattern. In an *acute-care hospital*, which serves patients in the initial or active stages of disease, the speech-language pathologist is responsible for providing information on the patient's communication functioning to other members of the medical team, so that a complete and accurate diagnosis of the patient's disease or disorder can be made. For example, the results of a comprehensive speech and language evaluation could provide important information to the medical team in determining whether the patient's disorder includes upper motor neuron involvement, lower motor neuron involvement, basal ganglia involvement, or some combination. In this role, the speech-language pathologist must be able to interact effectively with other medical specialists, such as neurologists and otolaryngologists.

In a *rehabilitation hospital,* a facility to which a patient may be discharged after a stay in an acute-care hospital, speech-language pathologists are primarily engaged in rehabilitation and therapy. Poststroke and post–head trauma patients may be seen in such a facility, as well as those who are recovering from cancer treatment. Patients in a

FIGURE 17-2 Speech-language pathologists in a hospital setting may provide diagnostic services using specialized testing procedures. (Mark Avery Photography)

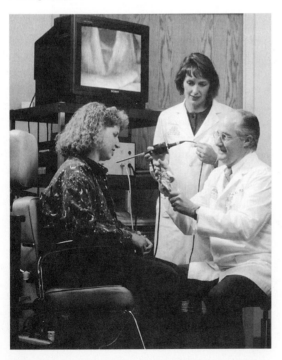

rehabilitation hospital are usually stabilized in terms of their medical condition, but they are not yet able to function optimally. In such a setting, the speech-language pathologist would attempt to improve the patient's communicative functioning prior to discharge to the home and family. It should be noted that rehabilitation hospitals are not always independent units; they are often associated with, or even part of, acute-care hospitals. This type of facility may serve outpatients as well as inpatients.

Other hospital settings in which speech-language pathologists can be found include Veterans Administration (VA) medical centers, which serve active and retired military personnel. These centers, formerly called VA hospitals, are located in almost every major city in the country. In the past, the patients seen in these hospitals were exclusively male, but with more women joining the armed forces, this is beginning to change. Speech-language pathologists in VA medical centers typically see clients with aphasia, head injury, and other neurological disorders for both diagnosis and treatment.

RESIDENTIAL HEALTH-CARE FACILITIES

Residential health care facilities include residential institutions and group homes for adults with developmental disabilities (cognitive disorders, pervasive developmental disorders, physical handicaps), and for those whose ability to function independently has been limited by head injury. Some centers provide residential care for children, although there are fewer of these than in the past, due to increased opportunities for education in the public schools for handicapped children. Despite the availability of local programs, residential schools for the deaf continue to attract some children, and these institutions typically employ speech-language pathologists. Finally, this category also includes nursing homes, and semi-independent living facilities for geriatric populations. According to Slater (1992), approximately 8 percent of speech-language pathologists work in such settings as their primary place of employment.

FIGURE 17-3 Adults with developmental disabilities may need technological assistance in order to communicate with maximum effectiveness. (Courtesy Prentke Romich)

Residential health care facilities offer some truly unique opportunities for speech-language pathologists. The residents of these centers often benefit greatly from the use of augmentative and alternative communication devices. Those with an interest in technology in the speech field will find many opportunities to experiment with such devices in providing residents with basic communication skills. In addition, a goal for many residents, especially young adults with developmental disabilities, is to move to less restrictive community environments and jobs in sheltered workshops. Very often, improved communication is a major factor in successfully completing such a transition. For older individuals, the loss of speech and language abilities that comes with injury and disease can mean loneliness and separation from family and friends. The speech-language pathologist in a residential setting plays a major role in improving the quality of life for all these individuals.

NONRESIDENTIAL HEALTH CARE FACILITIES

Nonresidential health care facilities include speech and language clinics, medical practices, doctors' offices, agencies, and private practices. Slater (1992) found that almost 10 percent of speech-language pathologists report this as their primary work setting. An example of this type of setting would be a group of ear, nose, and throat specialists (*otolaryngologists*) who work together in a medical practice and hire a speech-language pathologist to do speech and voice evaluations and therapy for their patients. Speech-language pathologists in this type of employment are clearly a part of a medical team, and they are responsible for keeping the referring physician apprised of the client's status.

A recent development in the area of nonresidential health care facilities is the growth of agencies that furnish speech, hearing, and sometimes physical and occupational therapy services through contractual arrangement. For a negotiated fee, such agencies agree to provide various rehabilitative services in private schools, nursing homes, and other institutions that do not employ their own therapists. Speech-language pathologists and other professionals who work for such agencies then travel to these locations, where they do the types of assessment and therapy specified in the contract. A speech-language pathologist in such an employment setting must be able to function independently and must be knowledgeable about a broad range of disorders.

Some speech-language pathologists set up their own offices, where they treat clients referred to them by area physicians and teachers. This is known as a *private practice*. Running such an establishment takes some knowledge of advertising, costs, taxes, accounting, and other elements of conducting a business. Large private practices may eventually turn into speech clinics, in which the owner of the practice employs several speech-language pathologists and audiologists to see clients on-site. A private practice might also evolve into an agency as described above. For example, the owner of the private practice may contract with residential facilities and otolaryngologists' offices to provide speech-language therapy services on a regular basis. For those with an entrepreneurial spirit, private practice may be a very satisfying work setting. Slater (1992) reports that about 7 percent of all speech-language pathologists are employed in private practice full-time and another 22 percent do part-time private practice work.

COLLEGES AND UNIVERSITIES

About 5 percent of speech-language pathologists report their primary work setting to be a college or university. Speech-language pathologists who are faculty members of college and university departments usually hold the Ph.D. degree. Their jobs include teaching courses to graduate and undergraduate students, doing research in their area of specialty, supervising student practicums and internships, and serving on various university committees. Some speech-language pathologists

in this setting work exclusively as clinical supervisors. These individuals typically have a master's degree and several years of experience as a practicing speech-language pathologist as prerequisites for supervision. Colleges and universities may also hire *speech scientists,* individuals who do not have clinical experience or certification.

Speech-language pathologists in this setting are expected to function as members of the university community as well as members of an educational team. The primary focus of their work is the preparation of students, rather than direct client care. A college or university setting can be a challenging one because of its conflicting demands—from clients in the department's clinic, students who need certain courses and clinical experiences at specific times, and administrators who are concerned with research productivity and budget limitations. However, this job setting can also be extremely rewarding for those who want to be on the cutting edge of new knowledge and new techniques.

WORK SETTINGS FOR AUDIOLOGISTS

Audiologists work for many of the same agencies and institutions that employ speech-language pathologists. In general, however, the audiologist has a somewhat different relationship with his or her clients than the speech-language pathologist does. In most settings, speech-language pathologists tend to see the same clients over a period of weeks or months, during which time they attempt to change their clients' communication behavior in some way. In a few settings, speech-language pathologists restrict themselves almost exclusively to diagnosis and assessment—which involves seeing different clients every day—but that is far less common.

Audiologists, on the other hand, are more commonly involved in assessment as opposed to therapy-type activities. They may see clients periodically—such as for several assessment sessions, perhaps two or three sessions for hearing-aid fitting, and, several months later, for a follow-up session—but they do not generally see their clients as frequently or work with them as intensively as do speech-language pathologists. It would be misleading to think that speech-language pathologists and audiologists do similar types of work just because they are employed in some of the same settings.

Audiologists can be found in many different types of settings, working with both adults and children with a variety of communication disorders and other handicapping conditions. Some of the more common employment sites for audiologists are nonresidential health care facilities, hospitals, public schools, and colleges and universities.

NONRESIDENTIAL HEALTH CARE FACILITIES

The most common job setting for audiologists is the nonresidential health care facility, according to Slater (1992). Approximately 45 percent of the audiologists in her survey reported that this was their primary employment site. This category includes physicians' offices, free-standing speech

and hearing clinics (those not affiliated with a hospital or university), and private practices. About 20 percent of the audiologists Slater surveyed reported that they were employed full-time in a private practice, while 37 percent reported part-time private practice work.

A typical nonresidential health care facility that might employ an audiologist is a medical practice composed of several otolaryngologists who hire such an individual to evaluate the auditory functioning of their patients. In this setting, the audiologist would see patients with a variety of otologic diseases and conditions. Assessments of hearing, middle ear function, balance, and the auditory nervous system might all be performed. Hearing-aid evaluation and fitting are also typically done, as well as counseling of patients. Knowledge of otologic diseases, plus the ability to interact with physicians and other specialists, are very important for the audiologist in this position.

An audiologist in a private practice would perform many of the same duties as the audiologist in a medical practice. However, audiologists in

FIGURE 17-4 Audiologists have an important role in providing education and counseling for their clients regarding their hearing impairment. (Mark Avery Photography)

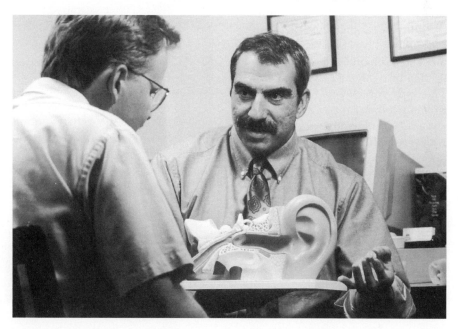

private practice often contract with hospitals, nursing homes, industries, and other settings where audiological services are desirable but where it is not possible to hire a full-time audiologist. In addition, audiologists in private practice might choose to become dispensing audiologists and sell hearing aids. The range of services provided would depend on the expertise and experience of the audiologist, the amount of capital available for the purchase of specialized equipment, and the needs of the community.

Another type of nonresidential health care facility is a regional center for the deaf and hard of hearing where individuals with severe and profound hearing loss can be fitted with appropriate amplification and receive communication training. Services may be provided to both adults and children. In this setting, the audiologist is likely to see at least some clients on a regular basis for auditory training and perhaps work in improving speech and language skills. Counseling for family members, teachers, and employers who are involved with the client are also an important part of the audiologist's job.

In the nonresidential health care facility, audiologists may have responsibilities in any or all of the following areas: the assessment of hearing, balance, and auditory nervous system function; the selection and fitting of hearing aids; the sale of hearing aids; hearing-aid checks and repairs; taking impressions and fitting individuals for custom hearing protection or swimmer's earplugs; communication training for clients with hearing impairment; counseling for those with hearing impairments; and running support groups for individuals with chronic hearing-balance disorders and their families. Since many of these health care facilities are for-profit businesses, the audiologist must also be knowledgeable about the costs of doing business, how to set fees for services provided, and related issues.

HOSPITALS

Hospitals are another common employment site for audiologists, according to Slater (1992).

Approximately 21 percent of audiologists work in hospitals. As we discussed in the context of speech-language pathology, hospitals are tremendously varied in terms of the age, type, and condition of patients they treat; clearly, jobs for audiologists can vary tremendously as well.

In research hospitals, and hospitals affiliated with universities and medical schools, the audiologist may be part of a team that provides new and experimental services to clients with hearing impairments. For example, an audiologist might work closely with a team that does cochlear implants. Team members might include otolaryngologists, speech-language pathologists, a child psychologist, a teacher of the hearing-impaired, and the child's classroom teacher. The audiologist would work with the child both before and after he receives the device. In hospitals with neonatal intensive care units, the audiologist may have an

FIGURE 17-5 Specialized tests audiologists might perform include testing the sense of balance in clients who complain of dizziness. The procedure pictured is called *posturography*. (Mark Avery Photography)

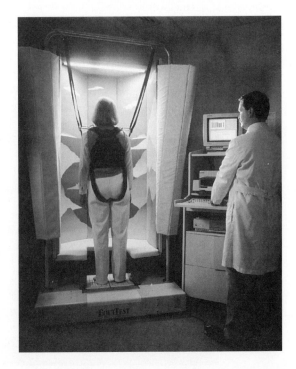

important role in screening the hearing of high-risk newborns, perhaps using emerging techniques like otoacoustic emissions.

In an acute-care hospital, the audiologist is likely to be part of a team of medical and health care professionals that sees patients in the initial or most serious stages of disease or injury for evaluation purposes. The audiologist in such a setting must develop expertise in diagnostic techniques that the average audiologist might not use routinely. In some hospitals, the audiology department sees outpatients referred by physicians in the community as well as inpatients. The ability to interact with a broad range of medical specialties is important in this setting.

Veterans' Administration medical centers are another potential work setting for audiologists. Diagnosis of hearing disorders, hearing-aid selection and fitting, and communication training are all services that are typically provided here.

PUBLIC SCHOOLS

Approximately 13 percent of audiologists are employed in the public schools, according to Slater (1992). In the school setting, the audiologist is rarely assigned to a particular school but, instead, serves several schools or even an entire school district. The audiologist for a school system usually coordinates yearly hearing screenings and provides follow-up for children who fail the hearing screening. Follow-up may include identification of children with potentially medically correctable hearing loss and children whose hearing loss appears to be interfering with communication abilities.

Once identified, the child with a hearing loss is likely to be referred to a hospital- or clinic-based audiologist for further testing and to a dispensing audiologist for hearing-aid fitting. However, after the child has been tested and fitted with an aid, the audiologist in the school provides in-service training for the classroom teachers regarding the hearing aid and monitors the child's use of the aid. In addition, the school audiologist interacts with the parents and teachers of hearing-impaired children to help educate them about the child's hearing loss and to implement measures (such as seating near the front of the class) to maximize the child's communication effectiveness.

Because children identified as hearing-impaired are eligible for special education services, the school audiologist also participates in multidisciplinary staffings during which individual educational plans are formulated. Clearly, it is important for audiologists to have a good working relationship with the teachers in their schools and to be knowledgeable about the kinds of academic challenges their students will face.

COLLEGES AND UNIVERSITIES

Like speech pathologists in colleges and universities, many audiologists in this work setting are faculty members in a department of communication sciences and disorders, speech and hearing sciences, or speech-language pathology and audiology. Faculty members typically hold Ph.D. degrees. Their responsibilities include teaching graduate and undergraduate classes, conducting research, supervising student clinical practicums, and serving on university committees. Some audiologists in colleges and universities are employed primarily as clinical supervisors. These individuals usually hold a master's degree and have at least several years of experience as practicing audiologists. In addition to audiologists, colleges and universities might also include hearing scientists on their faculties.

Not all university programs that train speech-language pathologists train audiologists as well. Certification from ASHA's Education Standards Board is given separately for programs in speech-language pathology and programs in audiology. Thus, some audiologists in college and university settings work exclusively with speech-language pathology students, who need course work and some clinical practice in hearing disorders in order to fulfill ASHA's requirements for certification.

As previously discussed, the university setting is different from most other job settings in that student training, rather than patient care, is the pri-

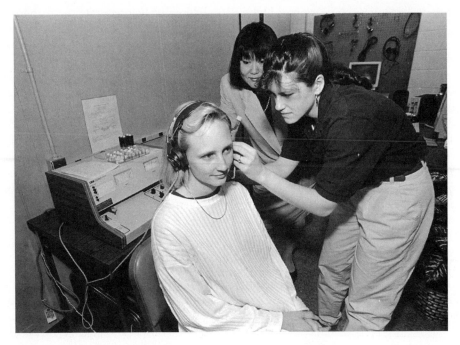

FIGURE 17-6 Audiologists in university settings teach and supervise students as they learn to use various methods and instruments to assess auditory functioning.

mary mission. The audiologist serves as an educator and mentor, and only occasionally as a clinician. For those who enjoy the teaching role, however, and who seek opportunities for independent research, colleges and universities can offer a fulfilling career.

OTHER SETTINGS

Although less common, there are a number of other settings in which audiologists can find employment. For example, Slater (1992) reports that approximately 2 percent of audiologists are employed in industry. Audiologists in industrial settings are generally hired to administer hearing conservation programs. This includes monitoring the noise levels in factories and periodically screening the hearing of workers exposed to high levels of noise. Counseling on the use of hearing protection might also be a part of the industrial audiologist's role. In addition, some audiologists are hired as researchers and consultants by com-

panies who manufacture hearing aids and audiological testing equipment.

Like speech-language pathologists, audiologists may be hired at residential health care facilities, particularly residential schools for the deaf. However, only a very small percentage, about 2 percent, have their primary employment in such settings (Slater, 1992).

EPILOGUE

One of the advantages of a career in speech-language pathology or audiology is the variety of opportunities available in terms of work settings, age groups, and special populations. Whether you enjoy working with preschoolers, school-age children, adolescents, adults, or senior citizens, as a speech-language pathologist or audiologist you can usually find a way to work with your preferred age group. And should your preference change, there is the opportunity to move into different job settings working with different age groups and disorders.

Speech-language pathologists are currently in demand in both public school and hospital settings. In the public schools, mandates to serve children of preschool age, and those with severe and profound handicaps, have resulted in an increased demand for speech-language therapy services. The financial limitations of local school districts and an effort to keep property taxes down may cause a slowing of the demand; however, as of this writing, the employment picture continues to be positive. In hospital settings, speech-language pathologists are also in demand. Many hospitals have only recently begun hiring professionals in this area, and frequently have difficulty finding qualified candidates. The broadening of the hospital speech-language pathologist's duties to include work with those with swallowing disorders and stroboscopic examination of the larynx has increased the motivation of hospitals to seek these professionals.

In the area of audiology, demographic changes in the population of the United States bode well for the future demand for such professionals. As the baby-boom generation matures into old age, a growing segment of the population will have need for hearing aids and communication training. Further, technological improvements in hearing aids will make them more and more attractive to hearing-impaired individuals who currently are unable to profit from amplification.

What will the future bring? Perhaps some insights can be gleaned from examining the past. In the years since World War II, the professions of speech-language pathology and audiology have become well established in both educational and medical settings. Despite changing economic conditions over that period of time, including both recessions and periods of growth, the demand for professionals in this field has continued to be strong. The challenge for tomorrow's speech-language pathologists and audiologists will be to maintain a high level of professional competence, so that our continued inclusion in the health care and educational systems will be justified and strengthened. With an estimated 10 percent of the population experiencing a communication disorder at some time in their lives (Boone and Plante, 1993), chances are good that the services of speech-language pathologists and audiologists will continue to be valued.

REVIEW QUESTIONS

1. What educational preparation is required for future speech-language pathologists at the undergraduate level? At the graduate level?
2. What educational preparation is required for future audiologists at the undergraduate level? At the graduate level?
3. What are the requirements for ASHA's certificate of clinical competence?
4. What are some typical work settings for speech-language pathologists?
5. What are some typical work settings for audiologists?

FOR FURTHER INFORMATION

ASHA (1992). *Membership and certification handbook.* Rockville, MD: ASHA.

ASHA (1993). *Preferred practice patterns for the professions of speech-language pathology and audiology. ASHA, Supplement No. 11, 35.*

Recent volumes of the *ASHA* journal. This journal contains articles and reports pertaining to clinical practice in speech-language pathology and audiology.

Glossary

abduct To bring apart, or open.

absence seizures Staring spells or brief lapses of consciousness that may occur from a few to hundreds of times per day. Formerly called "petit mal seizures."

acceptable stuttering A term used by Guitar and Peters (1980) to refer to noticeable but not severe dysfluency, where the speaker continues to feel comfortable despite the dysfluency.

accessory behaviors Behaviors associated with stuttering, such as eyeblinks, postponement techniques, or circumlocutions, that are not part of the individual's core dysfluencies (repetitions, prolongations, and so on).

acquired disorder A disorder that occurs after normal development has been achieved.

acquisition training A phase in the remediation of a phonological disorder during which the speech-language pathologist teaches the client how to produce the defective sound correctly.

acuity Sensitivity. For example, "auditory acuity" refers to how well a person can hear.

acute care Care rendered while a patient is in the most active or serious phase of a disease or condition, usually the earliest phase.

adaptation A behavioral term referring to the cessation of a response to a repetitious stimulus. For example, a child may respond initially to the presentation of a certain syllable over loudspeakers; but as the syllable was repeated over and over, the child's response would ultimately fade. Adaptation in stuttering refers to the ten-

dency of the stuttering response to fade as the stutterer reads and rereads the same passage.

adaptive functioning or behavior A person's ability to perform the tasks of daily living appropriate to his age, gender, and social status. Adaptive functioning includes social skills, communication, self-care, and so on.

adduct To bring together, or close.

adenoids Lymphoid tissue located at the back wall of the throat just behind the soft palate (the nasopharynx). Adenoid tissue is generally most massive in childhood and shrinks after adolescence and into adulthood.

aerodynamic Having to do with the movement of air. The "aerodynamic" aspects of vocal fold vibration are those in which moving air aids in either blowing the vocal folds apart or sucking them together.

affricate A type of speech sound produced by first making complete closure of the articulators, and then opening or releasing them to only a slight degree. Affricates thus have an abrupt onset, like a stop, but a hissing, continuant-like conclusion.

agrammatism Failure to use correct syntax and morphology during sentence formulation.

air-bone gap The difference in dB HL between a client's air-conduction thresholds and his or her bone conduction threshold. The presence of an air-bone gap suggests a conductive hearing loss.

air conduction threshold test A type of hearing test in which pure tones of various frequencies and intensities are presented to a client through earphones.

allophone   A sound that can be used interchangeably with a second sound in a particular language, with no resultant change in meaning in the word in which it is used. For example, an unreleased "p" and an aspirated "p" can be used interchangeably at the ends of words in English, with no change in the word meaning. These two different phones are thus "allophones" in English.

allophonic variant   When two sounds are allophones, one can be called the allophonic variant of the other.

alternative communication   A type of communication medium which replaces speech and speaking for an individual. Alternative communication can include manual signing; pointing to words, letters, or pictures on a communication board; or using an electronic communication device, among other systems.

alveolar ridge   The part of the hard palate in which the teeth are embedded. The alveolar ridge can be felt as a bump behind the upper incisors.

Alzheimer's disease   A degenerative organic brain syndrome that results in a progressive loss of cognitive abilities and independent functioning. It is characterized by the formation of plaques and fibrillary tangles in the brain.

American Sign Language (ASL)   A formal language based on hand positions, movements, and facial expressions instead of spoken words, primarily used by the deaf for communication.

amplification fitting   The process of selecting an appropriate hearing aid for a hearing-impaired individual.

amplitude perturbation quotient   Cycle-to-cycle variability in intensity or amplitude. Amplitude perturbation quotient is most often used as a measure of voice quality. Large amounts of cycle-to-cycle variability result in higher amplitude perturbation quotients, and, at least theoretically, correlate with a hoarse or rough-sounding voice.

amyotrophic lateral sclerosis   A degenerative disease of the motor neurons of the brain and spinal cord, which results in muscular paralysis and atrophy. It is usually fatal within three to five years of the onset of symptoms. Amyotrophic lateral sclerosis is sometimes called "Lou Gehrig's Disease."

ankyloglossia   "Tongue-tie," or a shortened lingual frenulum that attaches the tongue to the floor of the mouth and reduces its range of movement.

anomaly   Unusual characteristic.

anoxia   Lack of oxygen for breathing.

anterior   A term used in anatomical descriptions meaning "toward the belly." In a human being, *anterior* means "toward the front."

anterior language area   A part of the brain (more specifically, a part of the cerebral cortex) located in the left hemisphere in most individuals, which plays an important role in speech-sound selection and sequencing and in the motor planning and execution of speech.

aphasia   A language disorder of adulthood resulting from damage to the anterior or posterior language areas of the brain (or both). Aphasia is characterized by difficulty comprehending the speech of others, problems with word-finding, and/or difficulty formulating meaningful and grammatical sentences, despite unimpaired cognitive abilities.

aphonia   Loss of voice.

aphonic   An adjective referring to the cessation of voice production.

apnea   Cessation of breathing.

apraxia   The inability to perform skilled voluntary motor movement. Apraxia of speech refers to an inability to formulate speech sounds voluntarily with the tongue and lips, despite normal use of these structures for eating, drinking, reflexive vocalizations, and automatic speech (such as expletives).

articulation   The physical production of speech sounds using the speech production mechanism—the larynx, throat, hard and soft palates, alveolar ridge, tongue, teeth, lips, and nasal cavities.

articulation disorder   An inability to physically produce the sounds of English with the precision or speed expected for the individual's age level.

articulators   The structures used to produce speech sounds, specifically the larynx, throat or pharynx, tongue, velum or soft palate, hard palate, alveolar ridge, tongue, teeth, lips, and nasal cavities.

artificial larynx   A device used to generate sound and introduce it into the oral cavity, around which speech sound can be formed. Artificial larynges are most often used by those with a laryngectomy.

arytenoid cartilages   Two triangular-shaped cartilages that sit on top of the posterior aspect of the cricoid cartilage in the larynx. The vocal folds are attached posteriorly to the vocal processes of the arytenoid cartilages.

ASL   See *American Sign Language*.

aspiration   In the context of speech-language pathology, aspiration usually refers to the taking in of food and/or liquid into the respiratory system when the swallowing process is disordered. In the context of phonetics, it refers to a sharp release of air, causing a frication noise.

assimilation processes   A phonological concept referring to the substitution of one consonant in a word for a second consonant, so that instead of two different consonants, only one is produced in both positions. For example, the word *cat* might be produced as "tat."

asymmetric tonic neck reflex   A primitive reflex seen in normally developing children between the ages of birth and 3 months. This reflex causes a child to extend the arm and bend the knee on the side of the body toward which the head is turned.

ataxia   Difficulty with balance, gait, and/or eye-hand coordination, usually due to disorders of the cerebellum.

atherosclerosis   A condition in which deposits of cholesterol build up on the inside walls of blood vessels, narrowing their diameter and restricting circulation.

audiogram   A graphic representation of the results of a threshold test, in which the frequencies tested (usually seven or eight) are plotted on the horizontal axis, and intensity needed for a response is plotted on the vertical axis.

audiological   Refering to the study or practice of audiology.

audiologist   A professional who specializes in the evaluation and treatment of hearing impairment.

audiology   The study and treatment of hearing disorders.

audiometer   A device used to test hearing that emits specific frequencies (usually 125, 250, 500, 1000, 2000, 4000, 6000 and 8000 Hz) at user-controlled intensity levels. Most audiometers can be used for either air-conduction thresholds (via standardized ear phones and cushions) or bone conduction (via a calibrated vibrator placed on the mastoid process).

auditory   Referring to the ear or the sense of hearing.

auditory canal   Also known as the external auditory meatus; the passage from the external opening in the pinna inward to the tympanic membrane (eardrum).

auditory discrimination   The ability to hear the difference between one auditory stimulus and another. Auditory discrimination is particularly important during language learning, in which the ability to hear differences between the various speech sounds of a language is an important precursor to both receptive and expressive language development.

auditory nerve (VIIIth cranial nerve)   The nerve that arises from the cochlea (cochlear branch) and carries auditory information to higher-level neural processing centers. The auditory nerve also has a vestibular branch, which carries information about the head's position in space to higher-level processing centers.

auditory training   Specific drill and instruction designed to maximize an individual's ability to perceive and process auditory information. Auditory training is used primarily with the hearing-impaired, although it may also be used with children who have language and learning disorders due to auditory perceptual problems.

augmentative communication   Nonverbal means of supplementing spoken language. For examples, see *alternative communication*.

aural rehabilitation   The process of training individuals to use their residual hearing, usually in conjunction with amplification, for communication purposes.

auricle   The visible external part of the ear located on the side of the head.

autism   A severe pervasive developmental disorder involving disordered patterns of social interaction, communication, and activities and interests. The typical individual with autism has difficulty making eye or physical contact, relating to others, and communicating both verbally and nonverbally. In addition, the autistic individual often demands sameness in the environment, does not play with objects in a symbolic way, and is fascinated by repetitive movements.

autistic   An individual who has been diagnosed with autism is referred to as "autistic."

babbling   Strings of consonant-vowel or vowel-consonant combinations made by young children in the early phases of language development.

basal ganglia   A collection of processing centers in the brain, below the level of the cortex, that are important in the mediation of movement. The basal ganglia are often linked to the nonconscious or automatic aspects of voluntary movement.

basilar membrane   A structure within the cochlea that divides the scala media from the scala tympani. The basilar membrane supports the organ of Corti and thousands of hair cells, the primary sound-sensing organ of the auditory system.

behavioral observation audiometry   A type of hearing testing used for very young children, in which an auditory stimulus (speech, tone bursts, noise) is presented and the child's response to that sound observed.

behavioral theory (of language development)   Hypothesizes that language development

occurs because the child's early attempts at vocalizations and requests are linked to meaning by listeners and reinforced.

Bernoulli effect   A phenomenon in which air rushing through a constricting passage causes a reduction in perpendicular pressure against the sides of that passage, thus creating a partial vacuum, which draws the sides of that passage toward one another. The Bernouilli effect is hypothesized to be active during vocal fold vibration when the vocal folds are in the closing phase of their cycle.

bidialectal   Able to use two dialects, and to switch between them as the situation demands.

bilabial   Produced with two lips. Bilabial sounds in English include "p," "b," and "m."

bilateral   Involving both sides, usually of the brain or body. When used in the context of hearing, involving both ears.

Black English   A dialect of Standard American English spoken primarily by individuals of African-American heritage in segregated urban and rural areas.

Blissymbols   A coded system of printed symbols used to represent words and concepts. Blissymbols are very concrete in their depictions of objects and actions and have been used successfully with individuals with cognitive disorders.

bone-conduction threshold test   A type of hearing test in which pure tones are delivered through a vibrator attached to the client's mastoid process (the bony prominence behind the ear). The tones are made softer, then louder, then softer again in order to determine the intensity level at which the client can just respond to the tone.

bouncing   A technique used by stutterers to help them produce words and sounds that are difficult for them. Bouncing involves easy, relaxed, and voluntary repetitions of a feared sound or word, for example, *b-b-ball*.

brainstem   A part of the brain that controls many automatic functions, such as breathing and heart rate. It is located between the spinal cord and the cerebrum (cerebral hemispheres). The brainstem is not a specific structure, but rather a general designation that includes the pons, midbrain, medulla, and, according to some, the diencephalon.

brainstem auditory-evoked responses (BAER's)   Electrical responses recorded from the surface of the scalp which represent the processing of auditory information by various neurological centers in the auditory nervous system. In order to locate the response to an auditory stimulus against the background of the brain's much more powerful ongoing electrical activity, thousands of auditory stimuli (usually clicks) are presented, and the electrical activity of the brain is averaged over them.

Broca's aphasia   A language disorder of adulthood resulting from damage to the anterior language area of the brain. Broca's aphasia is characterized by relatively good auditory and reading comprehension, but difficulty selecting and sequencing specific phonemes and producing grammatical sentences.

cancellation   A technique used by stutterers to reduce the frequency of dysfluency. In cancellation, a stutterer who stutters on a particular word repeats it several times in a more relaxed manner until he can say it with a more controlled dysfluency pattern (or fluently).

carrier phrases   Phrases that are used over and over again in the course of an activity.

CAT scan (computerized axial tomography scan)   A radiographic technique in which successive X-rays of a certain structure are taken at a variety of angles and then reconstructed by computer so that soft-tissue lesions may be seen.

causality   A Piagetian construct describing a young child's realization that individuals other than himself can cause events in the environment. For example, a child demonstrates causality when he places an adult's hands on a toy that he is unable to operate.

central auditory disorders   Difficulty attending to, processing, responding to, and/or localizing sound, despite (in many cases) normal hearing acuity. Central auditory disorders are generally hypothesized to be caused by a lesion or delayed development in the auditory nervous system above the level of the cochlear nucleus.

cerebellum   Part of the brain located at the base of the cerebrum, associated with motor functions such as balance, gait, and fine motor sequencing.

cerebral cortex   Outermost part of the brain; divided into two hemispheres, and characterized by patterns of *sulci* (depressions) and *gyri* (swellings). Each area of the cortex is associated with specific sensory, motoric, or cognitive functions. The cortex directs all conscious activities of the brain.

cerebral hemispheres   See *cerebral cortex*.

cerebral palsy   A developmental neurological disorder characterized by motor impairment, due to damage to the motor areas of the brain sustained shortly before, during, or shortly after birth. The most common forms are spasticity and dyskinesia. Additional disorders, such as cognitive disorders, sensory and perceptual disturbances, seizures, communication disorders, and social/emotional problems may also be present.

cerebrovascular accident   Interruption of the blood supply to the brain, caused by either the rupture of a blood vessel or blockage of a blood vessel. Also called a "stroke."

cerumen   Waxy substance produced by cells lining the auditory canal, with the function of trapping dust and foreign particles at the entrance to the auditory system.

chronic laryngitis   See *laryngitis*.

chronological age   An individual's actual age in years and months. An individual's chronological age may be different from his or her mental age.

circumlocutions   An accessory behavior used by some stutterers in which a feared word or sound is avoided by substituting other words with similar meaning. Circumlocutions are also seen in some aphasic individuals who have word-finding difficulties: in such cases, the individual uses synonyms or descriptions to communicate the meaning of the word he cannot remember.

cleft lip   A congenital condition in which the maxillary process on one side or the other (or both) of the developing face fails to unite with the intermaxillary segment during the sixth to eighth weeks of embryonic development, resulting in an upper lip in a newborn which has a slit-like opening under one or both nostrils.

cleft palate A congenital condition in which the maxillary process on one side or the other of the developing palate fails to join with the premaxilla; or in which the maxillary processes fail to unite with each other *behind* the premaxilla; occurring between the eighth and twelfth gestational weeks. In either case, there is an interruption of the hard or soft palates, the natural division between the oral cavity and the nasal cavity.

clinician In speech-language pathology and audiology, a clinician is a practicing professional who works with individuals with communication disorders.

cochlea A snail shell-shaped structure in the inner ear which houses the organ of Corti and hair cells, the primary organs of hearing. In the cochlea, the mechanical energy of sound waves is translated into neural impulses.

cochlear implant A prosthetic device for the severely and profoundly hearing-impaired consisting of a microphone (or receiver for speech and environmental sounds), signal processor, external magnetic induction device, internal receiver, and a number of electrodes. The electrodes are implanted into the cochlea, where they furnish direct stimulation to the auditory nerve. The individual using a cochlear implant is thus able to "hear," despite bypassing the outer and middle parts of the ear and the hair cells of the cochlea.

cochlear nucleus First neural processing center for auditory information. The cochlear nucleus receives information directly from the cochlear branch of the auditory nerve, processes it, and transmits it to higher parts of the auditory nervous system.

code-switching The ability to switch from one dialect to another as the situation demands.

cognitive Related to thought and thinking ability.

cognitive disorder A delay in the development of mature thinking abilities, characterized by significantly below-average performance on a standardized IQ test and deficits in adaptive functioning (social and vocational skills, communication, self-care, and so on). Cognitive disorders are developmental in nature and, thus, have their onset prior to the age of 18 years.

communication The process by which messages are encoded, transmitted, and decoded. Communication requires only a sender, a message, and a receiver.

communication board A device used for alternative or augmentative communication. A traditional communication board consists of letters, words, or symbols printed on a folder, piece of cardboard, or actual board that a communicatively impaired individual points to in order to communicate. An electronic communication board may print out the individual's message on paper tape or produce it with a synthetic voice.

compliance In the context of audiology, compliance refers to ease of tympanic membrane movement in response to an auditory stimulus.

conductive hearing loss A hearing impairment caused by a problem in the outer or middle ear. Typically, a conductive hearing loss causes a reduction in hearing sensitivity in the range of 15-60 dB, with all frequencies being affected to approximately the same degree.

congenital Present from birth. Congenital disorders are those that a child is born with.

congenital deafness Deafness that is present from birth. Congenital deafness may be due either to genetic causes or to the effects of prenatal illnesses and injuries.

conjunctions Words that link two shorter sentences or ideas, such as *and, but,* and *although.*

constituent According to the psycholinguistic theory of Chomsky, "constituents" are the meaningful elements of a communicative event. For example, the subject of a sentence would be a constituent, the verb would be another, a prepositional phrase might be another, and so on.

constructional tasks   Tasks involving the ability to reproduce two- and three-dimensional forms, designs, or structures from a model.

contact ulcers   Irritated and granulated areas of tissue located at the posterior or back of the vocal folds. Contact ulcers are believed to be caused by vocal abuse, although gastric reflux may be a predisposing and maintaining factor.

"content" component of language   The symbols used in a particular language to represent objects, actions, ideas, and concepts. Also called "semantics."

context   The situation in which a communication takes place, including the previous knowledge and experience both the speaker and the listener bring with them to the communication situation.

contractures   A condition sometimes seen in cerebral palsy in which abnormal tension in and shortening of a muscle causes a joint to remain in a fixed position.

controlled fluency   A term used by Guitar and Peters (1980) to refer to a stutterer's ability to maintain fluent-sounding speech provided that he or she pay special attention to his or her speech patterns and to controlling fluency in addition to the content of the communication.

conversion aphonia   A psychologically based voice disorder characterized by a lack of ability to phonate; the individual can only produce a whisper. This voice disorder is due to psychological conflict or stress, not to any disease of or injury to the vocal folds themselves. Individuals with conversion aphonia are generally not aware of the true nature of their disorder.

cordectomy   A surgical procedure undertaken in cases of laryngeal cancer localized to a small area of a single vocal fold. Only the affected vocal fold is removed, while the other laryngeal structures are left intact.

correlational   Related through association. A correlation between two phenomena, such as score on an IQ test and score on a language test, simply means the two abilities are related,

not that one phenomenon causes the other. Correlation does not imply causality.

cortex   See *cerebral cortex.*

cortical   Relating to the cerebral cortex.

cortical blindness   Inability to see due to a lesion in the primary visual cortex of the brain, despite an intact visual system.

cortical deafness   Inability to hear due to a lesion in the primary auditory cortex of the brain, despite an intact auditory system.

crack cocaine   A purified form of cocaine prepared in an alkaloidal base which vaporizes at low temperatures. It is typically smoked.

creole   A creolized language; a more formal version of the earliest pidgin language that evolves when two different language groups come into contact. Creole includes many vocabulary items from the language of the dominant group, combined with phonological and grammatical systems of the nondominant group.

cricoid cartilage   The topmost ring of the trachea. The cricoid cartilage is shaped like a signet ring, with the narrow band in the front and the larger signet portion in the back. The arytenoid cartilages sit on top of the posterior aspect of the cricoid cartilage.

cued speech   A method of teaching spoken English to the deaf which involves a series of hand positions to indicate the position of the tongue in the mouth.

CV syllable   A syllable consisting of a single consonant followed by a vowel.

cycle format   A therapy technique used for children with phonological disorders proposed by Hodson and Paden (1983). A cycle format involves working on a particular phonological process, first using one set of phonemes, then another (regardless of mastery of the first) until the correct phonological rule has been learned.

damping   Reduction in intensity.

deaf   Severe or profound hearing impairment, usually involving a hearing loss of over 91 dB in the better ear. "Deaf" can also be defined as an individual who must rely on visual cues (rather than strictly auditory cues) for communication or who uses American Sign Language and identifies himself as a member of the deaf community.

decibel   A unit of sound intensity calculated using the $\log_{10}$ of the ratio between the pressure of the sound in question and a reference pressure. In audiology and auditory research, different reference sources might be used, thus the reference for the dB measure should always be specified (for example, 10 dB SPL, or 5 dB HL).

decreolization   The process by which a creole language attains the semantic, syntactic, and morphological features of the dominant language and becomes indistinguishable from it.

deep structure   A construct proposed in the psycholinguistic theory, referring to an individual's knowledge of the conceptual elements to be encoded into a message and their relationships to one another.

deinstitutionalization   The process of relocating institutionalized residents (usually cognitively and/or physically disabled) from large, public-run facilities to their own homes, state-run group homes, nursing homes, or other smaller living centers.

delayed auditory feedback (DAF)   A technique used by some clinicians to establish fluency in the early stages of a fluency-shaping program. The speaker is fitted with earphones and speaks into a microphone that feeds into an electronic device that can be adjusted for delayed output. Through the earphones, the speaker hears his own voice as he speaks, but with a 100–250 msec delay.

dementia   A cognitive disorder that causes an individual to become disoriented with respect to time and space, and to become impaired in terms of memory, social skills, communication abilities, and functional skills.

denasality   Lack of appropriate nasal resonance in the voice. Denasality is particularly apparent when the speaker is producing the sounds in English which require nasal resonance: "m," "n," and "ng."

desensitize   To make one less sensitive or fearful about a particular situation. This process is often attempted in stuttering therapy to help a stutterer overcome his fear of various speaking situations or speaking to certain people.

developmental disorder   A disorder present prior to mature function, which interferes with or prevents normal development or the acquisition of a skill.

diagnosogenic theory   A theory regarding the cause of stuttering articulated by Wendal Johnson. He hypothesized that stuttering occurs because of parental overreaction to a child's normal dysfluency, which in turn makes the child anxious about speaking and increases his dysfluency until the stuttering syndrome is developed.

dialect   A systematic variation of the standard form of a language that is spoken by a large number of people. A dialect may be based on geographical isolation, ethnic background, race, gender, social class, or age, among other factors.

diplegia   A motor disability involving the legs only or the legs more than the arms.

diplophonia   Production of two frequencies at once by the vocal folds.

disfluency   Any interruption to the smooth forward flow of speech.

distortion   A type of speech-sound production error in which the desired phoneme is produced with a minor modification that makes it inappropriate, i.e., not one of the acceptable allophonic variants of that phoneme, and usually outside the phonological system for that language.

dominant hemisphere   The hemisphere of the brain believed to be more fully developed for language and handedness; the hemisphere that is associated with temporal-sequential processing and that contains the language-processing areas. In most individuals, this is the left hemisphere.

Down syndrome   Also known as Trisomy 21. A chromosomal aberration in which the individual has three #21 chromosomes instead of two. Characteristics of Down syndrome include cognitive disorders, a broad, flat face with upward-slanting eyes and a protruding lower lip, short stature, simian palmer creases, cardiac abnormalities, and other anomalies.

drawing inferences To conclude by reasoning something that has not been directly stated.

dressing apraxia A disorder caused by damage to the right hemisphere of the brain, resulting in an inability to accurately place clothes on one's body, despite knowledge of how the clothes should be placed, and a lack of significant motoric disability.

duckbill A prosthetic device used for patients who have had the larynx removed due to cancer. The duckbill provides a connection between the trachea and esophagus, so that air from the lungs can be channeled into the trachea and serve as the power source for setting the top of the esophagus into vibration. The design of the duckbill also prevents food and liquids from being channeled from the esophagus to the trachea.

dysarthria A speech disorder caused by damage to the neuromotor system, which results in weakness, paralysis, incoordination, involuntary movements, or disturbed muscle tone in the speech musculature. Speech symptoms may include imprecise articulation, hyper- or hyponasality, voice quality disorders, and/or difficulties coordinating respiration and phonation.

dysphagia A swallowing disorder in which food and liquids are not completely channeled from the pharynx into the esophagus during swallowing and there is some leakage into the respiratory system.

dysphonic Pertaining to difficulty producing voice or phonation; poor vocal quality.

dyspnea Labored or noisy breathing; shortness of breath.

dysrhythmic phonations A type of dysfluency in which the transition from one phoneme to the next or one syllable to the next is abnormal. For example, a phoneme that is prolonged prior to the individual's saying the rest of the word would be a dysrhythmic phonation.

echolalia The tendency to repeat whatever is said to one.

edema Swelling; filled with fluid. Cerebral edema refers to a swelling of the brain. Vocal fold edema, or swollen vocal folds, is a common cause of voice quality disorders.

effusion Fluid that fills a body cavity. When discussing otitis media, effusion refers to fluid in the middle ear cavity.

ego A part of the psyche as conceptualized by Freud. The ego is hypothesized to be the thinking and reasoning aspect of one's self.

elaborated code According to Trudgill (1974), a way of using language that incorporates as many standard aspects of phonology, semantics, morphology, and syntax as the individual is capable of, so that the message can be understood by the listener independent of context; a style of speaking that relies on the formal aspects of language for communication rather than on shared experience, knowledge, and nonstandard linguistic or nonverbal devices.

embedded clause A group of words containing both a noun and a verb, which function as part of a larger sentence as the subject, predicate, or modifier. For example, in the sentence "Here's the book that I liked so much," the part of the sentence including the words "that I liked so much" is an embedded clause. It has both a noun and a verb, and thus could stand as its own sentence, but it functions as part of a larger sentence.

embolism A blood clot.

embryonic Relating to the embryo, or the developing being.

empirical A type of science where knowledge is gained from performing systematic observations, evaluating the results of those observations, and drawing conclusions.

endolymph A type of fluid that is present in the scala media of the cochlea.

endoscopy Use of a fiberoptic rigid or flexible scope to inspect the interior of the body.

epiglottis A leaf-shaped cartilage that is part of the larynx. The epiglottis is attached by its point to the thyroid cartilage and is usually acknowledged to have a role in protecting the airway during swallowing.

esophageal speech/voice An alternative type of voice production that is used by individuals who have had a laryngectomy. Esophageal speech/voice consists of taking air in to the esophagus (instead of into the trachea and lungs, as would normally occur), and "burping" it back up, setting the muscular ring at the top of the esophagus into vibration. This vibration then serves as the individual's "voice."

esophagus   A tubular structure lined with smooth muscle that connects the mouth and pharynx to the stomach; a part of the digestive system.

etiology   Cause; origin.

eustachian tube   Passageway between the middle-ear cavity and the back of the throat, which permits air to flow into the middle ear cavity. The eustachian tube normally opens and closes hundreds of times per day.

expressive language   The semantic, morphological, and syntactic structures that one is able to produce (as opposed to understand).

extensor muscles   Muscles that tend to straighten a limb when contracted. The extensor muscles of the legs allow one to stand up against gravity. There are also extensor muscles of the back and neck, which permit the head to be held upright.

eye-gaze board   A type of alternative or augmentative communication consisting of a plexiglass board, or a board with a hole in the middle. Two-sided cards (or two sets of cards) are needed for placement at each corner of the board. The handicapped individual uses his or her eyes to point toward the corner of the board with the desired picture or word. The communication partner sits opposite this individual, in order to see in which direction the eyes point.

facilitated communication   A form of communication recently introduced for autistic or physically handicapped individuals, in which a facilitator holds the arm or hand of the handicapped individual when pointing to letters, words, or pictures on a communication board. Whether the resulting messages emanate from the facilitator or the handicapped individual has been the source of considerable controversy.

false vocal folds   Two bulges of muscle and connective tissue in the larynx that protrude into the airway above the level of the true vocal folds. The false vocal folds are not normally used to produce voice; instead, they are believed to have a protective function for the respiratory system during swallowing.

fetal alcohol syndrome   A birth defect caused by maternal consumption of alcohol during pregnancy. Children with fetal alcohol syndrome may display growth retardation, small head, droopy eyelids and unusually small eyes, underdevelopment of the upper jaw, joint abnormalities, congenital heart disease, hearing loss, cognitive disorders, hyperactivity, short attention span, and other physical and developmental problems.

fetal cocaine exposure   A group of symptoms common in children exposed to cocaine in utero. Children with fetal cocaine exposure may display abnormalities in behavioral state, attention, muscle tone, and reflexes. They may also show movement disorders, learning disabilities, short attention span, and hyperactivity among other developmental disorders.

fistula   A hole or interruption in a bodily surface. A fistula may occur following surgery as scar tissue begins to form, thinning the tissues to the sides of the scar to the point that a rupture is possible.

flexor muscles   A group of muscles that cause a particular limb to bend or flex.

fluency   The smooth flow of speech, from one sound to another, one word to another, and one idea to another; lack of hesitations or repetitions when speaking.

fluent aphasia   A language disorder caused by damage to the posterior language area of the brain, characterized by difficulty with language comprehension, word finding, and appropriate sentence formulation. Individuals with fluent aphasia typically have relatively normal fluency and intonation during oral speech, but may substitute pronouns and neologisms for the contentive words of an utterance.

"form" component of language   The rules used in a particular language that govern the occurrence and sequencing of phonemes (phonology), sequencing of words in word combinations (syntax), and surface structure changes to alter slightly the meanings of words (morphology).

formant An area of energy concentration in the speech spectrum, seen on a spectrogram as a dark bar.

fragile-X syndrome A genetic/chromosomal disorder due to a weak area at the end of an individual's X chromosome, which often breaks off. Individuals with this genotype are characterized by cognitive disorders, language disorders, a prominent jaw, large ears, and mild connective tissue abnormalities.

frenulum Small slip of tissue connecting one bodily structure to another. For example, the *lingual frenulum* connects the bottom of the tongue to the floor of the mouth.

frequency The number of times an event repeats itself. In acoustics, frequency refers to the number of times per second a sound wave repeats itself. The frequency of a sound wave is measured in hertz, or cycles per second.

fricative A sound produced by forming a narrow constriction with the articulators and forcing the breath stream through it. This maneuver typically results in a high-frequency hissing sound that is characteristic of the fricative class.

frontal lobe The frontmost part of the brain bounded posteriorly by the central sulcus, separating it from the parietal lobe; and inferiorly by the lateral sulcus, separating it from the temporal lobe. The frontal lobe is associated with rational thought and intelligence and with voluntary motor movement.

frontal prominence Part of the primitive face of a developing embryo which occupies the central region of the developing head, bounded inferiorly by the stomodeum, or primitive mouth.

"function" component of language Pragmatics, or the social and interactional aspects of language use.

functional disorders In the field of communication sciences and disorders, functional disorders of speech and language are those with no identifiable cause. The only exception to this is in the area of voice, where functional disorders are those that are caused by an individual's abuse and misuse of the vocal mechanism.

fundamental frequency The number of times per second the vocal folds open and close. A typical fundamental frequency for a male voice is 100 Hz, or 100 vocal fold vibratory cycles per second. A typical fundamental frequency for a female voice is 200 Hz, or 200 vocal fold vibratory cycles per second.

gait Walking pattern.

gastric reflux Leakage of the stomach contents up into the esophagus, sometimes all the way to the level of the larynx.

generalization In behavioral terms, use of a particular response in situations outside the context in which it was taught. In speech and language therapy, generalization occurs when a client can use the target communication behavior outside the therapy room in normal conversational settings.

genetic syndrome A set of symptoms caused by an abnormality of one or more of the millions of genes that direct the formation and functioning of the organism.

geneticist A medical specialty concerned with heredity.

glide A type of speech sound formed by moving from one articulatory position to another. The acoustic transition between the two positions is what is perceived by the listener as the glide phoneme.

global aphasia A language disorder caused by damage to both the anterior language area and posterior language area in the dominant hemisphere of the brain. Global aphasia is characterized by both expressive and receptive language disorders—difficulty with comprehending spoken language, word finding, oral formulation of speech sounds, and sentence construction.

glottal Referring to the *glottis,* or the space between the vocal folds.

glottal stop A type of speech sound produced by adducting or closing the vocal folds and then suddenly releasing a burst of air.

glottis The open space between the vocal folds.

grammar A common term referring to the usage of both syntax and morphology.

gross motor abilities Activities that are performed with the large muscles of the body, such as sitting, standing, walking, throwing a ball, or riding a tricycle.

gyrus One of the convolutions, or "swellings," that make up the cerebral cortex, surrounded by *sulci,* or depressions, on either side.

habituation A behavioral term referring to the tendency of an organism to cease responding to a stimulus after a certain number of trials. Habituation can also be used to refer to the repetition of a response until it becomes natural.

hair cells In audiology, the primary sensory receptors of sound in the organ of Corti, embedded in the basilar membrane in the cochlea.

handling A term used by neurodevelopmentalists that refers to moving a cerebral palsied child through normal movement patterns (instead of the abnormal patterns they typically rely on), with the hope that with such experience, the child will be better able to attempt more normal movement patterns on their own.

hard of hearing Reduced auditory sensitivity. However, despite this reduction in sensitivity, the hard-of-hearing individual still relies to a great degree on auditory input for everyday communication.

hard palate The bony part of the separation between the oral and nasal cavities.

harmonic-to-noise ratio A measure of vocal quality in which the amount of energy in the harmonic components of a voice are compared to the amount of energy in the nonharmonic or noise components of a voice.

harmonics In acoustics, whole-number multiples of the fundamental frequency. For example, if an individual's fundamental frequency is 100 Hz, we would expect harmonics at 200 Hz, 300 Hz, 400 Hz, 500 Hz, and so on.

hearing-aid dispensers Individuals who are licensed to sell hearing aids. Some audiologists choose to become hearing aid dispensers. However, most hearing-aid dispensers have more limited training and experience with the auditory system and are not audiologists.

hearing-impaired Any individual with a reduction in auditory sensitivity. This term includes both the hard of hearing, who rely on the sense of hearing in communication, and the deaf, who rely on visual means of communication.

hemilaryngectomy A surgical procedure done to remove cancer in the laryngeal area. In a hemilaryngectomy, only one vocal fold and the surrounding structures on the same side are removed.

hemiplegia A weakness or paralysis on only one side of the body. Generally, the arm is more affected than the leg.

hemisphere Divisions of the brain, including a left half and a right half.

hemorrhagic stroke A rupture of a blood vessel in the brain.

hertz (Hz) A unit of frequency equal to one cycle per second.

heterochromia A condition in which the iris of one of an individual's eyes has a different color than the iris of the other.

heterogeneous (a.) In genetics, a term referring to the possession of one gene for one trait, and a matching gene for a different trait. For example, if an individual has one gene for blue eyes and one gene for brown eyes, that individual is said to be "heterogeneous" for eye color. In such cases, the gene that was dominant would be expressed (in the example given, the individual would have brown eyes, since brown eye color is dominant over blue). (b.) Things that are different are often called heterogeneous in the general sense.

holophrases A single word expressing a complex idea or relationship. Holophrases are often seen in the emerging language of children in the 13- to 18-month period.

hydrocephalus Accumulation of cerebrospinal fluid in the ventricles of the brain, which occurs when the ducts that transmit this fluid from one ventricle to another become blocked.

hyoid bone The only bone in the body that is not attached to another bone. The hyoid bone is a horseshoe-shaped bone at the top of the larynx, just inside the mandible or jawbone.

hypernasal Speech that is produced with an excessive amount of nasal resonance, due to an opening between the oral and nasal cavities.

id A part of the psyche conceptualized by Freud. The id is hypothesized to be the part of every individual that demands its wants and needs be fulfilled.

immittance An audiological term referring to the capability of the tympanic membrane to move freely in response to sound waves.

incidence The frequency with which a particular condition or disorder occurs over time.

infectious laryngitis See *laryngitis*.

integrated therapy A model for remediating communication disorders in the child's home or school environment in the context of ongoing activities.

intelligibility How well a speaker can be understood by the average listener.

intensity A measure of the magnitude or loudness of a sound wave; the amount of energy or force involved in the production of a sound wave.

interdisciplinary team A group of different professionals, such as a doctor, surgeon, speech-language pathologist, physical therapist, occupational therapist, and dietician, convened for the purpose of evaluating and/or planning treatment for an individual with a multifaceted disorder.

interjections A term used in the context of fluency disorders which refers to a speaker's use of filled pauses ("um" "er," "uh," and so on) that interrupt the smooth flow of speech.

intermaxillary segment In the developing embryo, the intermaxillary segment can be seen between the sixth and eighth weeks of gestation. It consists of the fused medial nasal processes, which form the middlemost portion of the upper lip and the premaxilla.

internship For the student in speech-language pathology or audiology, an internship is a clinical practicum experience at an external site (e.g., a school or hospital), which takes place toward the end of the graduate program.

intonation Upward and downward changes in a speaker's fundamental frequency during connected speech, which indicate such linguistic conventions as the end of the sentence and whether the sentence is declarative or interrogative, and which carry the emotional meaning of the message.

intracranial pressure The amount of pressure being exerted by the brain against the inside of the skull. Increases in intracranial pressure can occur if there is swelling of the brain due to head trauma, if there is a localized swelling due to the pooling of blood from a ruptured blood vessel, or if there is a blockage of the normal movement of cerebrospinal fluid through the ventricles of the brain, among other causes.

intraoral pressure The amount of air pressure built up behind an articulatory closure during speech production.

IQ Abbreviation for *intelligence quotient,* a score derived from performance on a standardized test of intelligence.

ischemic stroke A cerebrovascular accident caused by the blockage of a blood vessel or vessels that supply blood to the brain. A blood clot or embolism is often the cause of such a stroke.

itinerant Moving from place to place. An itinerant speech-language pathologist is one who serves several facilities, spending part of a day or week at each one.

jargon A type of prelinguistic language behavior most typically seen in children in the 7- to 12-month period, although it may extend to the 18- to 24-month period in some cases. Jargon is characterized by nonrepetitive strings of syllables uttered with appropriate-sounding intonation patterns. A similar phenomenon may be seen in adults with fluent aphasia.

labial Referring to the lips.

labiodental A type of articulatory closure made with the lower lip against the top teeth.

language A set of symbols that represent objects, actions, and ideas and a system of rules for generating novel combinations of these symbols. The components of language are semantics, syntax, morphology, pragmatics, and phonology.

language acquisition device (LAD) According to the psycholinguistic theory of language development, the language acquisition device is conceptualized as a uniquely human structure or neural organization that causes humans to be born with some basic knowledge of linguistic categories and allows them to learn language.

language disorder A deficit in the comprehension and/or production of the semantic, syntactic, and/or morphological forms appropriate for the chronological age of the child. A language disorder might also include delays or deficits in pragmatic skills.

laryngeal spectrum The fundamental frequency of a speaker's voice, plus the harmonics generated by vocal-fold vibration as the movements of the vocal folds cause secondary movements in the air molecules in the vocal tract.

laryngectomee A person who has had his or her larynx removed, usually because of cancer of the larynx.

laryngectomy A surgical procedure in which an individual's larynx is removed. As a result of this operation, the individual breathes through a stoma, or hole in the neck, to which the trachea is attached. The mouth and nose connect only to the esophagus and digestive tract.

laryngitis Inflammation of the vocal folds. Infectious laryngitis is due to bacterial or viral infection of the upper respiratory tract and vocal folds. Chronic laryngitis is inflammation that occurs without infection, or persists after an infection has subsided, and is usually due to vocal abuse and misuse.

laryngologist A medical doctor who specializes in treatment of diseases of the upper respiratory tract, including the throat and vocal folds.

laryngoscope A device that is used to visualize the vocal folds. A fiberoptic laryngoscope uses a fiberoptic light source that illuminates the vocal folds. Some fiberoptic laryngoscopes are inserted into the mouth (rigid endoscopes), while others are inserted through the nose (flexible fiberoptoscopes).

larynx The part of the upper respiratory tract that includes the cricoid cartilage at the top of the trachea, the arytenoid cartilages and true vocal folds, the false vocal fold, the epiglottis, and the thyroid cartilage.

lateral nasal process In a developing human embryo, the lateral nasal processes arise during the fifth and sixth gestational weeks. During this period, they enclose the nasal placodes, and form the outer rim of the nostrils.

learning disability A general term referring to an individual's difficulty with some academic subjects despite normal performance on intelligence tests. Individuals with learning disabilities usually perform at or even above age level in some cognitive areas, but do very poorly in others.

lesion Abnormality in a bodily tissue; an injury or area of pathological change.

lingua–alveolar A place of articulatory contact in which the tongue tip or blade is placed near or against the alveolar ridge to cause a constriction in the vocal tract.

linguadental A place of articulatory contact in which the tongue tip is placed near or against the top teeth to cause a constriction in the vocal tract.

linguapalatal A place of articulatory contact in which the middle portion of the tongue is placed near or against the palate to cause a constriction in the vocal tract.

linguistic Relating to language.

Linguistics of Visual English (LOVE) A manually coded system of English used by the deaf in which signs from American Sign Language are combined using English morphology and syntax.

lipreading The practice of using visual cues from a speaker's lips to understand what the speaker is saying.

lisp An error in speech-sound production. The term "lisp" is often used more specifically to describe an error is the production of "s" or "sh," especially a fronted distortion. A lateral lisp involves a lateralized distortion of fricatives.

literal paraphasia   Word error involving the substitution of incorrect phonemes from contiguous words or syllables, e.g., "cack the par" instead of "pack the car," or "veletision" instead of "television."

longitudinal study   A research study that examines the same group of subjects at several points in time, over the course of weeks, months, or years.

loudness recruitment   An audiological phenomenon in which the threshold of individuals' hearing, or the minimum intensity needed for them to hear, is very close to their pain threshold, the intensity that causes discomfort. In such a case, sounds made loud enough for the individuals to hear also cause pain.

lower motor neuron   A nerve fiber that has its origin in the brain or spinal cord, where it connects or synapses with an upper motor neuron, and that terminates in a muscle or muscle group in which it causes contraction.

lymph glands/system   A glandular system that circulates lymphatic fluid throughout the body. Lymphatic fluid contains white blood cells and eventually is returned to the venous blood supply.

malocclusion   An abnormal relationship between the maxillary arch (upper jaw) and the mandibular arch (lower jaw) when the teeth are closed. In a closed position, the teeth of the upper jaw should be aligned with the teeth of the lower jaw such that the surfaces of the upper teeth fit into the grooves of the lower teeth. Any deviation in that alignment or relationship is called a malocclusion.

mandibular arch   The lower jaw.

manner of articulation   The way in which a speech sound is made; the type and degree of constriction in the vocal tract that is needed to produce a particular sound. For example, the "stop" manner of articulation involves complete occlusion of the breath stream; while the "fricative" manner involves partial occlusion.

manual communication   A general term referring to any of several forms of communication often used by the deaf in which the transmission of the sender's message is done via the hands rather than via the speech mechanism. Some forms of manual communication are the manual alphabet, manually coded English, and American Sign Language.

manually coded English systems   A type of manual communication that uses signs instead of English words; but it combines and alters these signs according to the syntactic and morphological rules of English. New signs are added, depending on the specific system used, for morphological endings, articles, auxiliary verbs, and other grammatical devices.

maxillary process   In the developing human embryo, the maxillary processes arise from the first branchial arch (the mandibular arch) as upward growths of that structure. Between the fourth and eighth weeks of development, these structures grow toward midline, where they join with the central parts of the nose and upper lip (intermaxillary segment).

means-end behavior   A construct based on the work of Swiss psychologist Jean Piaget which describes the behavior of a child in the sensorimotor phase who is able to use one object, or a tool, in order to retrieve or act upon another object.

medial nasal process   In the developing human embryo, the medial nasal processes are ridges of tissue that form the inner part of each nostril. The medial nasal processes eventually unite to form the central division between the nostrils (the intermaxillary segment).

meninges   Protective layers of connective tissue that surround the brain and spinal cord, and within which cerebrospinal fluid circulates.

meningitis   A bacterial or viral infection of the meninges, or protective covering of the brain and spinal cord.

mental age   The age equivalent of a child's cognitive abilities. A child's mental age, or ability to think and reason, may be more advanced (or less advanced) than his or her chronological age, or actual age in years and months.

mental retardation   A term used to describe individuals whose cognitive abilities and functional skills are below expectation for their chronological age. "Mental retardation" is usually used to denote those with across-the-board developmental delays, rather than those with deficient skills in specific learning areas.

metabolic disorder   Abnormality in the way a toxic by-product of a bodily process is broken down and detoxified. For example, during the breaking down of food into constituent elements that can be absorbed at the cellular level, an important chemical reaction may fail to take place, resulting in some toxin building up in the body.

metastasize   When a cancer spreads from one organ of the body to another.

microcephaly   An abnormally small head, usually due to deficient brain growth.

minimal contrast   Two phonemes that differ according to only one feature. For example, "p" and "b" are both bilabial stops that differ only in the feature of voicing.

minimal pair   Two words that are identical except for a single phoneme. For example, *hat* and *bat* are identical except for the initial phoneme.

mixed dominance   A condition that occurs when the left hemisphere of an individual's brain is dominant for some functions, while the right hemisphere is dominant for others. In most individuals, the left hemisphere of the brain is generally dominant.

mixed hearing loss   A reduction in auditory acuity due to both conductive components (a blockage or abnormality in the outer or middle ear) and sensorineural components (an abnormality in the inner ear).

mongolism   An outdated term previously used to refer to an individual with Down Syndrome.

morphology   Surface changes to a word that result in a change in its meaning. For example, the addition of the "s" morpheme to the word *dog* results in a change of meaning from singular (one dog) to plural (many dogs).

motor cortex/area   An area of the cerebral cortex that is immediately anterior to (or in front of) the central sulcus, at the posterior-

most aspect of the frontal lobe. The motor cortex functions to activate upper motor neurons that, in turn, transmit commands to specific muscle groups in the execution of a voluntary movement.

MRI (magnetic resonance imaging)   A recently developed type of imaging technology which permits soft tissue structures deep within the body to be visualized. It is often used to determine site of lesion following stroke and other types of brain injury.

multifactorial inheritance   A type of genetic transmission in which several different genes (not just one or two of a pair) must all be present in an individual in order for a particular trait to be expressed.

multi-infarct dementia   An acquired cognitive disorder of adulthood caused by many small strokes (infarcts) that damage the intelligence centers of the brain and their connecting pathways.

mutism   The inability to speak.

myringoplasty   A surgical procedure in which a rupture or excessive scarring of the tympanic membrane is repaired through a skin graft.

myringotomy   A surgical procedure in which a small incision is made in the tympanic membrane to release the pressure caused by fluid build-up in the middle ear, and to permit the fluid to drain.

nasal   Relating to the nose or nasal cavities.

nasal placodes   Specialized areas of tissue seen on the lateral aspects of the frontal prominence of a developing embryo during the third or fourth week of gestation. The nasal placodes will eventually form the mucosal lining of the nostrils and nasal cavities.

neoglottis   A surgically created muscular structure at the top of the esophagus in laryngectomees. After surgical removal of the larynx, the surgeon sews together the remnants of the cricopharyngeus muscle, normally found at the lower border of the thyroid cartilage, around the top of the esophagus. If the laryngectomee takes air into the esophagus and contracts these muscles (the neoglottis), he can produce some voicing.

neologisms   Literally, "new words," or made-up words which do not make sense. Neologisms are often seen in the speech of those with fluent aphasia.

neurofibrillary tangles   Aggregations of microscopic filaments and tubules in the nerve cells of the brain. Neurofibrillary tangles are seen during autopsy in the brains of individuals with Alzheimer's disease. It is believed that they interfere with the brain's normal function and contribute to the symptoms seen in dementia.

neuroleptic drugs   Psychoactive drugs that relieve pain, tranquilize, or sedate an individual.

neurologist   A medical doctor who specializes in the diagnosis and treatment of disorders and diseases of the nervous system (brain, spinal cord, and nerves).

neuromotor disorder   A disorder or disease of the nervous system (brain, spinal cord, and nerves) that affects an individual's motor (movement) abilities.

neurosurgeon   A medical doctor who specializes in surgical treatment of disorders and diseases of the nervous system (brain, spinal cord, and nerves).

nondominant hemisphere   The hemisphere of the brain believed to be less important in the comprehension and production of language and in determining handedness; the hemisphere that is associated with holistic and spatial processing. In most individuals, this is the right hemisphere.

nonfluent aphasia   A language disorder due to damage to the anterior language area in the left hemisphere and characterized by slow and effortful speech, poor articulation, groping for the correct phoneme, short length of utterance, telegraphic speech, reduced grammatical complexity, reduced rate, and abnormal rhythm.

novel utterance   A combination of words that an individual puts together based on his or her knowledge of the morphological, phonological, and syntactic rules of the language, that he or she has never heard before.

object permanence   A construct based on the work of Swiss psychologist Jean Piaget that describes the behavior of a child in the sensori-motor phase who demonstrates searching behavior when a toy or food item is hidden. "Object permanence" is usually interpreted to mean that a child is aware of the existence of an object even when it is out of sight.

obturator   See *speech bulb.*

occipital lobe   The posterior-most part of the cortex, bounded anteriorly by the posterior aspects of the parietal lobe and the temporal lobe. The occipital lobe is associated with vision and visual perception.

olfactory   Relating to the sense of smell.

omission   In phonetics, an omission occurs when an individual leaves out a phoneme during the production of a word and does not replace it with anything. For example, *og* instead of *dog* is an omission.

ophthalmologist   A medical doctor who specializes in the diagnosis and treatment of disorders and diseases of the eye.

oral apraxia   Inability to perform voluntary movements with the oral musculature, despite normal muscle strength, coordination and tone, an absence of involuntary movements, and the ability to perform such movements at a vegetative level. The individual with oral apraxia is able to close and pucker the lips while eating, for example, but is unable to perform the same behavior on command.

oral cavity   The mouth.

oral method   A method of teaching communication to the deaf in which the individual is provided with a hearing aid, auditory training, and lipreading instruction, and is expected to comprehend by using his (amplified) residual hearing combined with visual cues of the speaker's message and to express himself using speech.

oral–peripheral examination   An evaluation performed by a speech-language pathologist to check for abnormalities in the client's speech production mechanism. Both structure and function are observed.

organ of Corti   A structure in the cochlea (inner ear) containing the hair cells, the main sensory organs of hearing.

organic disorder   Any speech or language disorder with a known physical cause. This includes speech and language disorders of neurological, structural, bacterial/viral, or genetic origin.

orthodontist   A dental specialist whose expertise is in the movement and repositioning of existing teeth to optimize oral function and appearance.

ossicles   A chain of three tiny bones (the malleus, incus, and stapes) that spans the middle ear cavity.

otitis media   An inflammation of the middle ear.

otoacoustic emissions   Recordable sound waves in the auditory canal produced by movements of specialized hair cells in the inner ear, which help transmit and amplify sound waves in the cochlea. A by-product of this movement is the generation of additional movement in the perilymph of the cochlea, stimulation of the oval window, induced movement of the ossicular chain and tympanic membrane, and finally, the production of sound waves in the auditory canal.

otolaryngologist   A medical doctor who specializes in diagnosis and treatment of diseases and disorders of the ears and throat. Most otolaryngologists specialize in diseases of the nose as well, and thus should technically be called "otorhinolaryngologists."

otologist   A medical doctor who specializes in diagnosis and treatment of diseases and disorders of the ear.

otorhinolaryngologist   See *otolaryngologist.*

otosclerosis   A disease of the middle ear in which the footplate of the stapes where it attaches to the oval window becomes spongy. This results in poor transmission of sound waves to the cochlea and conductive hearing loss to various degrees.

ototoxic   A substance or agent that destroys the hair cells of the cochlea, causing sensorineural hearing loss.

oval window   Membrane separating the middle-ear cavity from the cochlea. In the middle-ear cavity, the footplate of the stapes is attached to the oval window.

overgeneralization   A phenomenon seen during language development beginning between 2 and 3 years of age, in which a child applies regular plural or past tense endings to words that are irregular in English. For example, a child who says "comed" instead of "came" is overgeneralizing.

overtones   Harmonics or harmonic partials.

Pub. L. No. 94-142   Public Law 94-142, The Education for All Handicapped Children Act. Passed in 1975, it mandated an appropriate public education for all handicapped children from ages 3 to 21 years, at the public's expense, in the least restrictive environment.

Pub. L. No. 99-457   Public Law 99-457, Amendments to the Education of the Handicapped Act. This law broadened and strengthened the mandate of Pub. L. No. 94-142 by extending the services provided by schools to handicapped infants and toddlers, the 0- to 3-year-old population.

palatal collapse   A condition that may occur following surgery to repair a cleft of the hard palate. As the repaired cleft heals, it may pull the maxillary arches of the hard palate inward, so that the upper teeth close against the inner surfaces of the lower teeth.

palatal lift   A prosthodontic device composed of an anterior bridge portion that fits against the hard palate, and a posterior "tail" portion which keeps the soft palate in an elevated position. This device is typically used in cases where the palate is of normal length but is weak or paralyzed.

palatal shelves   In the developing embryo, the palatal shelves are specialized sections of the maxillary processes that grow inward and join with the premaxilla to form the hard palate between the eighth and twelfth weeks of gestation.

palatal vault   The upward arch of the hard palate just behind the alveolar ridge.

palatine processes   See *palatal shelves.*

papillomas   A wart-like growth caused by the papova virus that covers the vocal fold and interior parts of the larynx, and may obstruct the airway. Papillomas are most common in children between the ages of 6 months and 6 years.

paralysis Inability to move a limb or muscle group.

paraphasia Speech errors involving substitutions of phonemes from other words or syllables, or substitutions of an inappropriate word for the desired word. See *literal paraphasia* and *verbal paraphasia*.

paraplegia Weakness, paralysis, or spasticity affecting the legs only, with little to no involvement of the arms.

parenthetical remarks Inserted clauses that contain information not relevant to the main idea of the sentence. Remarks of this type may be considered pragmatic devices used to give listeners background information about the subject of a sentence or a sophisticated type of dysfluency.

parietal lobes The part of the cortex bounded anteriorly by the frontal lobe, posteriorly by the occipital lobe, and inferiorly by the temporal lobe. The parietal lobe is associated with conscious recognition of touch, pressure, pain, and bodily position.

Parkinson's disease A progressive neurological disorder of unknown origin which is characterized by a loss of cells in the substantia nigra (a structure related to the basal ganglia) and a reduction in the production of dopamine, a neurotransmitter. Individuals with Parkinson's disease have difficulty with voluntary movement because of rigid muscles, a slow and shuffling gait, slurred speech, weak and monotone voices, and tremor.

pedunculated Attached to a bodily structure or surface by means of a narrow stalk.

peer modelling A therapy technique recently introduced for those with pervasive developmental disorders and autism. Children with these disorders are mixed in classrooms and daycare centers with normally developing children and encouraged to interact with and imitate them.

perilymph Fluid found in the scala tympani and scala vestibuli of the cochlea.

percent jitter A specific algorithm used to calculate the amount of cycle-to-cycle variability in the frequency of an individual's voice. This cycle-to-cycle variability is typically perceived as a rough voice quality.

percent shimmer A specific algorithm used to calculate the amount of cycle-to-cycle variability the intensity in an individual's voice. This cycle-to-cycle variability is typically perceived as a rough voice quality.

perinatal Occurring at the time of birth.

peripheral nerves Nerves that have their cell bodies in the brainstem or spinal cord, and whose axons go out to specific muscles or sensory organs in the body.

perseverate The tendency to repeat an action or response that was previously correct when it is no longer appropriate.

pervasive developmental disorder (PDD) A heterogeneous group of disorders characterized by symptoms in two or more of the following areas: failure to develop normal social relationships, failure to develop communication skills, and failure to develop normal activities and interests. Autism is considered a severe form of PDD.

pharyngeal fricative A fricative sound produced by placing the back of the tongue in close proximity to the back of the pharynx or throat.

pharynx Throat.

phonation Vibration of the vocal folds; the act of producing voice.

phone Any sound that can be produced by the human speech mechanism.

phoneme Any sound produced by the human speech mechanism that denotes a change in meaning.

phonetic placement A therapy strategy used during the establishment phase of therapy for phonological disorders. The client is instructed on proper production of the sound, and correct placement of the tongue, lips, and so on are practiced.

phonological disorder A disorder involving the inability to produce specific speech sounds expected of the child's chronological age, or a failure to reach the intelligibility level expected of the child's chronological age due to speech-sound production problems. Phonological disorders may reflect a child's faulty knowledge of the phonological rules of his native language or an inability to physically produce sounds correctly due to organic or functional factors, or both.

phonological process A simplification of adult-form phonological rules. Commonly acknowledged phonological processes are syllable simplification, assimilation, and substitution processes.

phonological representation Internal knowledge of the phonological system of one's native language, even if one cannot produce all of its elements.

phonological system All the phonemes and acceptable allophonic variants that are used in a particular language.

phonology The study of speech sounds and how they function in a language, including rules for their occurrence and ordering.

phrase structure rules A concept from the psycholinguistic theory of language, referring to the basic constituent elements (such as adjective-noun or noun-verb phrases) underlying all sentences in all languages and how these elements are related.

pidgin A simplified form of language with a reduced vocabulary and grammar that evolves as a common form of communication between two different language groups.

Pidgin Sign English A form of manual language used by deaf speakers of ASL in communicating with hearing persons. It includes ASL signs, combined according to English syntactic rules.

pinna The outermost part of the ear, attached to the side of the head and composed of cartilage and other connective tissues.

pitch How high or low a sound is perceived to be in terms of musical notes; the perceptual analog of frequency.

plaques Areas of lipoid deposits observed in the brains of those with Alzheimer's disease (dementia).

polypoid degeneration A functional voice disorder characterized by swelling, edema, and excessive epithelial tissue of the vocal folds.

positioning A term used by those who work with children and adults with neuromotor disorders, especially cerebral palsy. "Positioning" refers to placement of the individual in postures (hip flexion, weight-bearing on forearms, etc.) that increase trunk and shoulder stability and facilitate voluntary movement.

posterior At the back of.

posterior language area A location within the left (dominant) hemisphere of the brain, which includes parts of the left temporal, parietal, and occipital lobes, and which appears to be important in the comprehension of both spoken and written language.

postlingual deafness Deafness that has its onset after an individual has developed speech and language.

postponements An accessory behavior of stuttering in which the individual tries to avoid stuttering on a particular sound or word by postponing its production. Common postponements include looking up at the ceiling, pretending to be lost in thought, shuffling feet, or saying "you know" or some other filler several times.

place of articulation Point of maximum constriction in the speech mechanism during the formation of a sound.

play audiometry A method of hearing testing for children of preschool age in which the child responds to the test frequencies or stimuli by making some action with a toy (such as putting a peg in a pegboard).

practicum Supervised therapy done during the speech-language pathology or audiology student's educational program.

pragmatics Rules governing the use of language in communicative situations.

prefrontal region/area The anterior-most part of the frontal lobe.

prelingual deafness Deafness that has its onset before the individual acquires speech and language.

premaxilla The anterior-most and central part of the hard palate.

premotor cortex/area Area of the brain directly in front of the motor cortex (lateral portion), toward the posterior part of the frontal lobe. The premotor cortex is associated with voluntary movement, particularly in decision making prior to movement, and in visually guided movements.

preparatory set A technique used to control stuttering that follows mastery of cancellation and pullouts. The individual mentally prepares to ease into speech in a relaxed way, especially on a word he or she anticipates having difficulty producing.

presbycusis Hearing loss that occurs as a result of aging.

pressure equalization (PE) tubes Very small tubes surgically inserted through the tympanic membrane in individuals with chronic otitis media in order to restore atmospheric pressure in the middle-ear cavity and facilitate normal opening of the eustachian tube.

prevalence The number of individuals experiencing a disorder at any one time, divided by the total population.

primitive speech acts (PSA) According to the sociolinguistic theory of language development, primitive speech acts are nonverbal communicative behaviors, such as pointing and vocalizing in order to get attention, that precede formal language development.

prognosis Expected outcome.

prosody The rhythm and melody pattern of connected speech, including fluctuations in vocal pitch, loudness, quality, and sound and syllable duration.

prosthetic device Any device designed to replace a missing or damaged bodily structure or to assist in some normal function.

prosthodontist A dentist who specializes in the creation of appliances to replace missing teeth or assist in closing off the oral cavity from the nasal cavities during speech. For example, a prosthodontist would be the professional to construct a speech bulb for a cleft palate child.

protoword A consistently used pattern of speech sounds which is associated with a particular object or person by the young child that produces it, but which does not resemble an adult word, and typically is not generalized to other situations.

psychoactive drugs Drugs that affect an individual's state of consciousness, mood, perceptions, or cognitive abilities.

psychodynamic A change in psychological state that produces a change in behavior.

psychogenic disorder A disorder caused by psychological stress or conflict, unmet emotional needs, or other imbalances between an individual's internal resources and external circumstances. The individual with a psychogenic disorder is not usually aware of its origin and believes the disorder to have a physical base.

psycholinguistic theory A comprehensive theory of language articulated by Noam Chomsky which posits that certain linguistic knowledge and abilities are inborn and that the acquisition of rules governing word order (syntax) is central to language learning.

pullouts In stuttering, *pullout* refers to a technique used by the stutterer to get out of a stuttering block and involves relaxation and voluntary repetitions or prolongations. Use of pullouts follows mastery of the cancellation technique.

pure tone In audiology, pure tones are single-frequency stimuli used in certain types of hearing tests.

pure-tone threshold In audiology, a certain type of hearing test in which pure tones are used as stimuli, and in which the individual being tested must respond to successively less and less intense tone presentations until that individual's threshold (or point at which the tone can be detected about half the time) is determined for each frequency.

quadriplegia When discussing neuromotor disorders, quadriplegia refers to involvement of all four limbs.

radiation therapy A type of treatment for cancer in which the cancerous mass is bombarded with radiation in an effort to shrink or eliminate the tumor.

radical neck dissection A type of treatment for cancer of the larynx sometimes done during laryngectomy when cancer has been detected outside the larynx in the lymph glands. In radical neck dissection, various muscles, blood vessels, glands, and nerves are removed from the left, right, or both sides of the neck.

radiologist A medical doctor who specializes in the use of X-rays and other visualization techniques in the diagnosis and treatment of various disorders.

Rebus A type of symbol system occasionally used on communication boards for very young children or individuals with cognitive disorders who cannot read.

receptive language The semantics, morphology, and syntax that an individual can comprehend.

recurrent laryngeal nerve A nerve that provides motor innervation for most of the muscles of the larynx.

reduplicative babbling Repeated strings of consonant-vowel syllables, typically produced by children in the early part of the 7- to 12-month age range.

reflex An involuntary, primitive, and stereotyped movement pattern in response to a particular stimulus. As the child gains greater control over voluntary movement, reflexes tend to drop out, although some are present throughout life.

register A particular method of voice production that remains constant over a given frequency range. Most singers acknowledge "head" and "chest" registers. Speech pathologists use the terms "vocal fry," "modal," and "falsetto" or "loft" registers.

reinforcement In behavioral terms, a reward or pleasurable consequence that follows a desired behavior, given with the expectation that such a consequence will increase the frequency of the desired behavior in the future.

relative average perturbation In terms of voice-quality measurement, one of many ways of calculating cycle-to-cycle differences in frequency between successive glottal pulses. Such a measure is believed to reflect the perception of vocal roughness or hoarseness.

repetitions A type of disfluency in which sounds, syllables, words, or phrases are involuntarily repeated.

residual errors Speech sound-production errors, typically on "s," "r," "l," or fricative sounds, that remain in an older child or adult who previously had a more serious phonological disorder.

residual hearing The limited amount of hearing seen in individuals with severe or profound hearing loss, typically in the low frequencies.

resonance Phenomenon by which vibratory movement in one body is induced in another body. In voice, "resonance" refers to the frequencies created when the vibrating vocal folds set air in the vocal tract into vibration.

resource room In current educational practice, the resource room is a service-delivery model. Children are taken from their regular classrooms for a certain portion of the day to attend the resource room, staffed by some type of special education personnel (learning disabilities teacher, speech-language pathologist) who helps the children with areas in which they are having difficulty.

restricted code When discussing dialect and dialectal differences, "restricted code" refers to a form of dialect that incorporates numerous extralinguistic variables and is not easily understood by those who do not share the same background and experiences as the speaker.

retract To pull back or inward. A "retracted" tympanic membrane is one that is forced inward toward the middle-ear cavity by a relatively higher pressure in the auditory canal, and a relatively lower pressure in the middle-ear cavity.

revisions A type of disfluency in which words or phrases are changed in form, or revised, during speech.

round window A membrane between the cochlea and the middle-ear cavity that acts as a release valve as the oval window, under the stimulation of the stapes, moves back and forth.

rubella Also known as the German measles; a mild viral infection that causes a dull red rash on the body, fever, and sometimes tiredness and body ache. The virus that causes rubella can damage the developing nervous, auditory, and visual systems of a fetus in the first trimester of pregnancy.

sacculus   A membranous sac located in the inner ear which functions to provide information about balance and the head's relationship to gravity to the central nervous system.

scala media   The middle fluid-filled duct of the cochlea, bounded above by Reissner's membrane and below by the basilar membrane, which houses the organ of Corti and the hair cells, the primary hearing receptor organs.

scala tympani   The lower fluid-filled duct of the cochlea, bounded above by the basilar membrane.

scala vestibuli   The upper fluid-filled duct of the cochlea, bounded below by Reissner's membrane, originating at the vestibule and oval window.

scanning   In augmentative communication, the automatic movement of a cursor from one letter or symbol to the next on an electronic communication board. In order to stop the cursor and make a selection, the user has only to trigger some simple switching mechanism, such as a foot or knee peddle.

screening   Cursory examination of speech, language, or hearing abilities that determines whether or not an individual's performance falls within some predefined "normal" range. Passing a screening indicates grossly normal abilities; failing a screening should be followed by more complete testing to determine the nature and extent of the problem.

secondary behaviors   In stuttering, synonymous with "accessory behaviors."

secretions   Fluids produced by the body.

Seeing Essential English (SEE 1)   A manual form of communication available to the deaf in which the signs (semantics) of American Sign Language are combined with English morphology and syntax so that exact English sentence forms are achieved.

seizure   Involuntary movements of various types that occur when abnormal neuroelectrical impulses are built up in the brain, usually in the area of a brain lesion, and are then discharged.

semantic redundancy   Information that is repeated in a sentence or message through use of words meaning the same thing, e.g., The big car was huge.

semantic/cognitive theory   A theory of language development that posits a child learns language as his knowledge of the world around him, including objects and their properties, increases and that early word combinations are based on semantic meaning rather that syntactic rules.

semantics   The meanings of words; symbol-concept relationships.

semicircular canals   Part of the inner ear located just above the vestibule, composed of three half-circle ducts filled with fluid, which function as part of the mechanism that provides information about balance and the head's relation to gravity to the central nervous system.

semitone   One-twelfth of an octave; or one musical half-step.

sensorineural hearing loss   A hearing impairment caused by damage to the inner ear. This type of loss can range from mild to profound, and can affect thresholds at various frequencies similarly or differently (in some cases, there is a pronounced loss in the high frequencies only).

sensory cortex/area   That part of the cerebral cortex directly behind the central sulcus at the anterior-most part of the parietal lobe, which is important in the conscious recognition and perception of sensations from the surface of the body and the body's position in space.

sensory integration   The combining of sensation and perception from different modalities (hearing, vision, touch, smell, taste) in order to form concepts of various types.

sensory modality   One of the sensory channels: hearing, vision, touch, smell, taste.

sign language   A general term for any linguistic system based on gestures, typically used by the deaf. Some forms of sign language are complete languages unto themselves, such as American Sign Language. Others are hybrid languages, incorporating American Sign Language signs with English morphology and syntax.

signal-to-noise ratio   The amount of signal

energy present compared to noise energy. In voice measurement, "signal–to–noise ratio" is one metric for quantifying the amount of energy in the harmonic partials of a voice compared to the amount of energy in the noise elements in a voice; thus this is purported to be a measure of voice quality.

signed English systems   Manual forms of communication available to the deaf in which the signs (semantics) of American Sign Language are combined with some aspects of English morphology and syntax. Examples of signed English systems are SEE 1, SEE 2, and LOVE.

Signing Exact English (SEE 2)   A manual form of communication available to the deaf in which the signs (semantics) of American Sign Language are combined with English morphology and syntax so that exact English sentence forms are achieved.

sine wave   In acoustics, the most basic type of sound wave, composed of only one frequency.

sociolinguistic theory   A theory of language development which posits that language learning occurs as an outgrowth of early nonverbal communication patterns and a need to communicate intentions and desires more precisely.

spasticity   A condition resulting from damage to the motor areas of the cortex and their connecting pathways (the upper motor neurons) in which an individual's ability to perform voluntary movements is limited by weakness, slowness, restricted range of movement, and excessive muscle tone.

specific language impairment   A condition in which the child appears normal in terms of nonverbal intelligence-test performance, emotional development, and physical and sensory capabilities, yet displays a delay of at least twelve months in receptive and/or expressive language acquisition.

spectrogram   A visual display of the frequency content of speech as a function of time. Frequency is typically on the vertical axis, while time is on the horizontal axis.

speech   The act of physically transmitting a message through use of the larynx, pharynx, tongue, lips, jaw, teeth, respiratory system, and so on. "Speech" includes articulation, fluency, and voice production.

speech bulb   A device used by an individual with a repaired cleft palate who continues to have insufficient palatal length for good velopharyngeal closure. The front of the device looks like a denture or retainer; from this protrudes a supporting stem-like structure and a bulb which fits into the upper part of the pharynx, between the oral and nasal cavities.

speech-language pathologist   A professional who specializes in the evaluation and treatment of speech (articulation, fluency, and voice) and language disorders.

speech-language pathology   The study and treatment of speech and language disorders.

Speech Recognition Threshold (SRT) test   A type of audiological test in which an individual listens to a list of words presented at a very soft intensity level and attempts to repeat them. The softest level at which an individual can repeat the words he hears is known as the "speech recognition threshold."

speechreading   The practice of using visual cues from a speaker's lips to understand what the speaker is saying.

spina bifida   A condition that occurs during fetal development in which the vertebrae, skin, and muscles normally overlaying the spinal cord do not form correctly, thus leaving a part of the spinal cord exposed.

spontaneous fluency   Smooth transitions between speech sounds and words in all speaking situations, which the speaker produces without paying conscious attention to the speech-production process.

Standard American English   An idealized form of American English, used in writing and public speaking, but rarely spoken spontaneously.

stapedectomy   A surgical procedure performed on individuals with otosclerosis in which the stapes is removed from the oval window and replaced with a Teflon or wire prosthesis.

stenosis   The narrowing of a bodily passageway or cavity.

stereotyped movements   Movements that are produced involuntarily or unconsciously in response to some stimulus.

stereotypic utterances   In aphasia, a normal-sounding, usually social, utterance that the aphasic individual can produce, such as "Hi, how are you?" despite difficulty with language that requires retrieval and formulation, such as describing pictures.

stimulability   In testing for phonological disorders, "stimulability" refers to the ability of the person being tested to correct their faulty sound-production pattern with auditory, visual, or tactile/kinesthetic cuing.

stomodeum   The primitive mouth seen in a developing embryo between the forebrain area and the first branchial (mandibular) arch.

stridor   Noisy breathing.

stuttering   Involuntary repetitions and prolongations of speech sounds and syllables (and sometimes words and phrases) that interrupt the smooth transition of one speech sound or syllable to another during spontaneous speech and fragment the flow of speech.

stop   In phonology, a type of speech sound made by completely occluding and then suddenly releasing the breath stream.

stroke   A cerebrovascular accident, which occurs when a blood vessel supplying blood to the brain ruptures or becomes blocked, causing parts of the brain to be deprived of oxygen and often permanently damaged.

subcortical   Below the level of the cortex (the outer surface of the brain). Structures such as the thalamus, basal ganglia, and cerebellum are all considered subcortical.

subglottic   Below the level of the glottis (the opening between the vocal folds).

subglottic pressure   Air pressure from the lungs which builds up under the vocal folds. Subglottic pressure correlates well with loudness of a voice.

submucous cleft   A failure of the muscles in the two sides of the soft palate to unite with one another during embryonic development; sometimes the posterior-most part of the bony hard palate also is not fused. However, the skin or mucosal covering is intact, and thus the cleft can not be seen upon visual inspection of the oral cavity.

substitution   A type of speech-sound production error in which one phoneme, such as "th," is used in place of the correct phoneme, such as "s."

substitution process   A phonological process in which one class of phonemes is substituted for another. For example, all fricative and affricate phonemes may be replaced by stop phonemes of similar place of articulation.

sulcus   A valley or depression in a bodily surface.

supplementary motor cortex/area   Area of the brain directly in front of the premotor cortex (medial portion), toward the posterior part of the frontal lobe. The supplementary motor cortex is associated with voluntary movement, particularly in decision making prior to movement, and in global preparation of the body through regulation of muscle tone.

superego   According to Freudian theory, the part of the psyche that absorbs social rules and mores, which it tries to impose on the demands of the id so that the individual can behave in socially acceptable ways.

syllable-structure processes   In phonology, predictable ways of simplifying syllable structure seen during early phonological development in children. Some examples of syllable structure processes are final consonant deletion, deletion of unaccented syllables, and consonant cluster reduction.

synchronous   Happening at the same time.

syntax   Rules that govern word ordering in sentences and acceptable word sequences.

Tardive Dyskinesia   A neurological disorder characterized by involuntary movements of the face, tongue, and jaw that occurs as a result of prolonged ingestion of neuroleptic drugs.

telegraphic speech   A stage of language development commonly seen between the ages of 2 and 3 years, characterized by the use of simple, imperfect sentences consisting almost entirely of nouns and verbs. Articles, adjectives, auxiliaries, and even prepositions are usually eliminated.

temporal lobe   A part of the cortex located below the frontal and parietal lobes, and anterior to the occipital lobe. The temporal lobe is associated with auditory reception and processing, as well as with long-term memory established through the temporal lobe's connections with the limbic system.

tense pauses   In stuttering, tense pauses are a type of dysfluency in which the speaker ceases voicing/speaking periodically between words despite having something to say.

teratogen   A substance that causes mutation and/or deformity to a developing fetus.

threshold   The point at which a sensation can be just barely detected. In audiology, "threshold" usually refers to the loudness level at which an individual can respond to a particular stimulus about half of the time.

thyroid cartilage   Large cartilage at the front of the neck which protects the upper part of the trachea, the swallowing mechanism, and the vocal folds.

total communication   A philosophy or educational strategy for the deaf that involves maximizing residual hearing through use of hearing aids and auditory training, training in speech production, and simultaneous use of some form of sign language (usually a pidgin sign English combined with fingerspelling) for both language input and output.

trachea   The windpipe; the passageway for air into the lungs.

tracheoesophageal speech   A method of voice production for individuals who have had the larynx removed. A small hole is created at the back of the trachea and into the esophagus, through which a valving device is inserted. This valve permits air to be channeled into the esophagus, so that voicing can be produced by the muscles at the top of the esophagus, powered by air from the respiratory system.

transcortical motor aphasia   A type of non-fluent aphasia in which the affected individual has difficulty in producing grammatical sentences and instead uses telegraphic speech.

transcortical sensory aphasia   A type of fluent aphasia in which the affected individual has severe difficulty with both comprehension and reception of language. Jargon is common; however, affected individuals can often repeat phrases normally.

transformational rules   According to the psycholinguistic theory of Noam Chomsky, transformational rules are grammatical rules that an individual uses to get from the internally structured language in which meaning is expressed to the form of language that is used by others in the individual's environment.

transient ischemic attack   A "small stroke" in which a blood vessel becomes partially or temporarily blocked.

traumatic brain injury (TBI)   An injury to the head caused by external force, as opposed to a penetrating injury such as a gunshot wound. Also called "closed head injury."

tremor   Involuntary, repetitive back-and-forth movement of some bodily structure.

true vocal folds   Two bulges of muscle and connective tissue in the larynx which protrude into the airway just below the level of the false vocal folds. They are attached anteriorly to the inside wall of the thyroid cartilage, and posteriorly to the arytenoid cartilages. The vocal folds are normally open during breathing, although they are voluntarily brought together in order to produce voice or to impound air in the thoracic cavity. In addition to voice production, the vocal folds also serve as a protective valve to keep food and liquids from going into the respiratory system.

tympanic membrane   Eardrum; a thin membrane at the end of the external auditory canal that separates the outer ear from the middle ear.

tympanogram   Graphic representation of the compliance of the tympanic membrane, under conditions of atmospheric, high and low pressure, in response to sound.

tympanometer   Instrument that presents various sound-pressure conditions into the external auditory canal to test compliance of the tympanic membrane and status of the middle-ear cavity.

tympanometry   Procedure used to assess compliance of the tympanic membrane, and, by inference, status of the middle ear.

unilateral   One side.

universal hearing screening   A procedure often argued for by audiologists and speech-language pathologists in which all newborns would be screened for hearing status directly after birth, prior to leaving the hospital.

upper motor neurons   Nerve fibers which have their origin in the motor areas of the cortex (the motor cortex, premotor cortex, or supplementary motor cortex), and which course downward into lower neurological centers. Upper motor neurons may terminate in the basal ganglia, cerebellum, brainstem, or spinal cord. In the latter two termination sites, upper motor neurons connect or synapse with lower motor neurons, which innervate specific muscles.

utriculus   A membranous sac located in the inner ear which functions to provide information about balance and the head's relationship to gravity to the central nervous system.

variegated babbling   Also called "nonreduplicative babbling." Variegated babbling occurs when the child combines a variety of different phonemes in nonrepetitive vowel, consonant-vowel, and occasionally consonant-vowel-consonant syllables. This type of babbling is typically produced by children in the later part of the 7- to 12-month age range.

velum   Soft palate.

verbal apraxia   Apraxia of speech. See *apraxia*.

verbal paraphasias   Speech errors that involve substituting an inappropriate word for a desired word, e.g., saying "I eat with a comb" instead of "I eat with a spoon."

vestibular system   The utriculus, sacculus, and semicircular canals, organs which are part of the inner ear, but furnish information to the central nervous system regarding balance and position with respect to gravity.

vestibule   A part of the inner ear just beyond the oval window, which forms the entrance to the cochlea.

vibrate   To move back-and-forth rapidly; a regularly repeating action.

vibrotactile aid   A type of "hearing" aid that transmits sound as patterns of vibratory stimulation to the skin on the hand, arm, or some other bodily surface. Usually used by those whose severe hearing impairment makes conventional hearing aids of little use.

visual   Relating to the sense of sight.

visual-field defects   Difficulty with visual awareness and comprehension of stimuli that are in some specific part of the visual field. Some individuals with lesions of the left hemisphere will have difficulty seeing objects in their right visual field.

Visual Reinforcement Audiometry   A type of audiological testing procedure used with very young children and infants. The child is conditioned to look toward a loudspeaker containing an attractive toy, which lights up when a certain auditory stimulus is sounded.

vocal abuse   Shouting, yelling, imitating power tools, and other vocal behaviors that cause overly forceful adduction of the vocal folds and potential injury to the connective tissue on the vocal fold margins.

vocal folds   See *true vocal folds*.

vocal intensity   The force with which the vocal folds come together during vibration, and the corresponding loudness with which the voiced signal is perceived.

vocal nodules   Benign vocal fold lesions that typically occur bilaterally at the junction of the anterior one-third and posterior two-thirds of the vocal folds as a result of vocal abuse and/or misuse.

vocal polyps   Benign vocal fold lesions that typically occur unilaterally at the junction of the anterior one-third and posterior two-thirds of the vocal folds as a result of trauma. They are somewhat more complex and better organized than nodules.

vocalization   Production of sound by vibration of the vocal folds.

voice   the tone produced by the vibration of the

vocal folds, plus the vocal tract resonances that are created as air molecules are also set into vibration in the supralaryngeal vocal tract.

voice disorders   Abnormal vocal pitch, loudness capability, variability, quality and/or nasality that interferes with the speaker's ability to communicate or participate in vocational or social situations.

voice prothesis   See *duckbill*.

voicing   In phonetics and phonology, whether or not vibration of the vocal folds occurs during the production of a phoneme. For example, "b" is a voiced phoneme, while "p" is unvoiced.

Waardenburg's syndrome   A genetic syndrome passed on from generation to generation through the autosomal dominant mode of transmission. Individuals with this syndrome typically have widely spaced eyes, sometimes of different colors, and may have a white lock of hair at the forehead or nape of the neck. They are also likely to have moderate to severe sensorineural hearing loss in one or both ears.

Wernicke's aphasia   A fluent aphasia characterized by moderate to severe problems with auditory comprehension and fluent-sounding speech that frequently is empty of content words, or contains many made-up words (neologisms and jargon).

References

Abel, E., and **Sokol, R.** (1987). Incidence of fetal alcohol syndrome and economic impact of FAS-related anomalies. *Drug and Alcohol Dependence, 19,* 51–70.

Adamovich, B. (1981). Language versus cognition: The speech-language pathologist's role. In R. Brookshire (Ed.), *Clinical aphasiology: Proceedings of the conference* (pp. 277–281). Minneapolis: BRK Publishers.

Adamovich, B., Henderson, J., and **Auerbach, S.** (1985). *Cognitive rehabilitation of closed head injured patients: A dynamic approach.* Austin, TX: Pro-Ed.

Ad Hoc Committee on Employment Impact of Clinical and Professional Doctoral Degrees for Entry into the Practice of Audiology (1994). *Employment impact of the doctoral degree for entry into the practice of audiology: Final activity report.* Rockville, MD: ASHA.

Air, D., Wood, A., and **Neils, J.** (1989). Considerations for organic disorders. In N. Creaghead, P. Newman, and W. Secord (Eds.), *Assessment and remediation of articulatory and phonological disorders* (2nd ed., pp. 265–301). Columbus, OH: Merrill Publishing.

Aksu, F. (1990). Nature and prognosis of seizures in patients with cerebral palsy. *Developmental Medicine and Child Neurology, 32,* 661–668.

Alexander, R. (1987). Prespeech and feeding development. In E. McDonald (Ed.), *Treating cerebral palsy: By clinicians for clinicians* (pp. 133–152). Austin, TX: Pro-Ed.

Allen, R. and **Oliver, J. M.** (1982). The effects of child maltreatment on language development. *Child Abuse and Neglect, 6,* 299–305.

Alpiner, J., Kaufman, K., and **Hanavan, P.** (1993). Overview of rehabilitative audiology. In J. Alpiner and P. McCarthy (Eds.), *Rehabilitative audiology: Children and adults* (2nd ed.; pp. 3–16).

American annals of the deaf. (1985). Directory issue, *130* (2).

American Cancer Society (1991). *Cancer facts and figures.* Atlanta, GA: American Cancer Society.

American National Standards Institute (ANSI) (1973). *American national standard psychoacoustical terminology. ANSI* S3.20-1973. New York, NY: American National Standards Institute.

American National Standards Institute (ANSI) (1989). *American national standard specification for audiometers.* ANSI S3.6-1989. New York, NY: American National Standards Institute.

American Psychiatric Association (APA) (1994). *Diagnostic and statistical manual of mental disorders* (4th ed.). Washington: Author.

American Speech-Language-Hearing Association (ASHA) (1979). Guidelines for determining the threshold level for speech. *ASHA, 21,* 353–356.

American Speech-Language-Hearing Association (ASHA) Committee on Language, Speech and Hearing Services in the Schools (1982). Definitions: Communicative disorders and variations, *ASHA, 24,* November, 949–950.

American Speech-Language-Hearing Association (ASHA) Committee on Infant Hearing (1989). Audiologic screening of newborn infants who are at risk for hearing impairment. *Asha, 31* (March), 89–92.

American Speech-Language-Hearing Association (ASHA) (1990). Knowledge and skills needed by speech-language pathologists providing services to dysphagic patients/clients. *ASHA Supplement No. 2, 32,* 7–12.

American Speech-Language-Hearing Association (ASHA) (1992a). Vocal tract visualization and imaging. *ASHA Supplement No. 7, 34,* 37–40.

American Speech-Language-Hearing Association (ASHA) (1992b). *Membership and certification handbook.* Rockville, MD: ASHA.

American Speech-Language-Hearing Association (ASHA) (1993a). Code of ethics. In: American Speech-Language-Hearing Association Council on Professional Ethics (Eds.), *Ethics: Resources for professional preparation and practice* (pp. 1.5–1.9). Rockville, MD: ASHA.

American Speech-Language-Hearing Association (ASHA) (1993b). Preferred practice patterns. In: ASHA, *Preferred practice patterns for the professions of speech-language pathology and audiology, ASHA Supplement No. 11, 35,* 3–96.

American Speech-Language-Hearing Association (ASHA) (1994). ASHA policy regarding support personnel. *ASHA, 36* (March, Suppl. 13), p. 24.

Andrews, G. (1984). The epidemiology of stuttering. In: R. Curlee and W. Perkins (Eds.), *Nature and treatment of stuttering: New directions* (pp. 335–356). Boston, MA: Allyn and Bacon.

Andrews, G., Craig, A., Feyer, A., Hoddinott, S., Howie, P., and Neilson, M. (1983). Stuttering: A review of research findings and theories circa 1982. *Journal of Speech and Hearing Disorders, 48,* 226–245.

Andrews, G., Guitar, B., and Howie, P. (1980). Meta-analysis of the effects of stuttering treatment. *Journal of Speech and Hearing Disorders, 45,* 287–307.

Andrews, M. (1986). *Voice therapy for children.* New York, NY: Longman.

Andrews, M., and Summers, A. (1991). *Voice therapy for adolescents.* San Diego, CA: Singular Publishing Group.

Aram, D. (1991). Comments on specific language impairment as a clinical category. *Language, Speech and Hearing Services in Schools, 22,* 84–87.

Aram, D., Ekelman, B., and Nation, J. (1984). Preschoolers with language disorders: Ten years later. *Journal of Speech and Hearing Research, 27,* 232–244.

Aram, D., Morris, R., and Hall, N. (1993). Clinical and research congruence in identifying children with specific language impairment. *Journal of Speech and Hearing Research, 36,* 580–591.

Armstrong, D., and Schneidmiller, K. (1983). *Hearing impaired students enrolled in U.S. higher education institutions.* Washington, DC: Gallaudet College Office of Planning.

Aronson, A. (1990). *Clinical voice disorders: An interdisciplinary approach* (3rd ed.). New York: Thieme.

Baken, R. (1987). *Clinical measurement of speech and voice.* Boston: College-Hill Press.

Barr, M. (1979). *The human nervous system* (3rd edition). Hagerstown, MD: Harper and Row.

Batshaw, M., and Perret, Y. (1992a). Hearing. In M. Batshaw and Y. Perret, (Eds.) *Children with handicaps: A medical primer* (3rd ed., pp. 321–349). Baltimore, MD: Paul H. Brookes.

Batshaw, M., and Perret, Y. (1992b). Heredity: A toss of the dice. In M. Batshaw and Y. Perret, (Eds.) *Children with handicaps: A medical primer* (3rd ed., pp. 11–22). Baltimore, MD: Paul H. Brookes.

Batshaw, M., Perret, Y., and Kurtz, L. (1992). Cerebral palsy. In M. Batshaw and Y. Perret, (Eds.) *Children with handicaps: A medical primer* (3rd ed., pp. 441–469). Baltimore, MD: Paul H. Brookes.

Batshaw, M., Perret, Y., and Reber, M. (1992). Autism. In M. Batshaw and Y. Perret (Eds.) *Children with handicaps: A medical primer* (3rd ed., pp. 407–420). Baltimore, MD: Paul H. Brookes.

Battles, D., Aldes, M., Grantham, R., Halfond, M., Harris, G., Morgenstern-Lopez, N., Smith, G., Terrell, S., Cole, L. (1983). Position paper: Social dialects. *ASHA, 25* (9), 23–24.

Bayles, K. (1982). Language and dementia producing diseases. *Communicative Disorders: A Journal for Continuing Education, 7,* 131–146.

Bayles, K., and Boone, D. (1982). The potential of language tasks for identifying senile dementia. *Journal of Speech and Hearing Disorders, 47,* 210–217.

Beckey, R. (1942). A study of certain factors related to retardation of speech. *Journal of Speech Disorders, 7,* 223–249.

Bentler, R. (1993). Amplification for the hearing-impaired child. In J. Alpiner and P. McCarthy (Eds.), *Rehabilitative audiology: Children and adults* (2nd ed.; pp. 72–105).

Berger, K., and Millin, J. (1989). Amplification/assistive devices for the hearing impaired. In R. Schow and M. Nerbonne (Eds.), *Introduction to aural rehabilitation* (2nd ed.; pp. 31–80). Austin, TX: Pro-Ed.

Bernthal, J., and Bankson, N. (1993). *Articulation and phonological disorders* (3rd ed.). Englewood Cliffs, NJ: Prentice-Hall.

Bess, F., and Humes, L. (1990). *Audiology: The fundamentals.* Baltimore: Williams and Wilkins.

Bettelheim, B. (1967). *The empty fortress: Infantile autism and the birth of the self.* New York, NY: Free Press.

Biklen, D. (1990). Communication unbound: Autism and praxis. *Harvard Educational Review, 60,* 291–315.

Biklen, D., and Schubert, A. (1991). New words: The communication of students with autism. *Remedial and Special Education, 12,* 46–57.

Bishop, D., and **Adams, C.** (1992). Comprehension problems in children with specific language impairment: Literal and inferential meaning. *Journal of Speech and Hearing Research, 35,* 119–129.

Blager, F., and **Martin, H. P.** (1976). Speech and language of abused children. In H.P. Martin (Ed). *The abused child: A multidisciplinary approach to developmental issues and training* (pp. 83–92). H. P. Martin, Ed., Cambridge, MA: Ballinger.

Bloodstein, O. (1975). Stuttering as tension and fragmentation. In J. Eisenson (Ed.), *Stuttering: A second symposium.* New York, NY: Harper and Row.

Bloodstein, O. (1987). *A handbook on stuttering.* Chicago, IL: National Easter Seal Society for Crippled Children and Adults.

Bloom, L. (1970). *Language development: Form and function of emerging grammars.* Cambridge, MA: MIT Press.

Bloom, L. (1973). *One word at a time: The use of single word utterances before syntax.* The Hauge: Mouton.

Bloom, L., and **Lahey, M.** (1978). *Language development and disorders.* New York, NY: Wiley.

Bluestone, C., and **Klein, J.** (1988). *Otitis media in infants and children.* Philadelphia, PA: W. B. Saunders.

Boberg, E. (1984). Intensive adult/teen therapy program. In W. Perkins (Ed.), *Stuttering disorders.* New York, NY: Thieme-Stratton.

Boone, D., and **McFarlane, S.** (1994). *The voice and voice therapy* (5th ed.). Englewood Cliffs, NJ: Prentice-Hall.

Boone, D., and **Plante, E.** (1993). *Human communication and its disorders* (2nd edition). Englewood Cliffs, NJ: Prentice-Hall, Inc.

Boothroyd, A. (1982). *Hearing impairments in young children.* Englewood Cliffs, NJ: Prentice-Hall.

Bordon, G., and **Harris, K.** (1994). *Speech science primer: Physiology, acoustics and perception of speech* (3rd ed.). Baltimore: Williams and Wilkins.

Bralley, R., and **Stoudt, R.** (1977). A five-year longitudinal study of development of articulation proficiency in elementary school children. *Language, Speech and Hearing Services in the Schools, 8,* 176–180.

Brantley, H., and **Clifford, E.** (1979). Cognitive, self-concept, and body-image measure of normal, cleft palate and obese adolescents. *Cleft Palate Journal, 16,* 177–182.

Brill, R. (1984). *International congresses on education of the deaf: An analytical history 1878–1980.* Washington DC: Gallaudet College Press.

Broen, P., and **Moller, K.** (1993). Early phonological development and the child with cleft palate. In K. Moller and C. Starr (Eds.), *Cleft palate: Interdisciplinary issues and treatment: For clinicians by clinicians* (pp. 219–250). Austin, TX: Pro-Ed.

Bronheim, H., Strain, J., and **Biller, H.** (1991). Psychiatric aspects of head and neck surgery. Part 1: New surgical techniques and psychiatric consequences. *General Hospital Psychiatry, 13,* 165–176.

Brookshire, R. (1992). *An introduction to neurogenic communication disorders* (4th ed.). St. Louis: Mosby Year Book.

Brown, R. (1973). *A first language, the early stages.* Cambridge, MA: Harvard University Press.

Brown, W., Jenkins, E., Kuawczum, M., Wisniewski, D., Rudelli, R., Cohen, I., Fisch, G., Wolf-Scheien, E., Miezejeski, C., and **Dobkin, C.** (1986). The fragile X syndrome. In H. Berg, K. Wisniewski, & D. Snider (Eds.). *Mental retardation: Research, education and technology transfer* (Vol. 477, pp. 129–150. New York, NY: New York Academy of Sciences.

Bzoch, K. (1989). Etiological factors related to managing cleft palate speech. In K. Bzoch (Ed.), *Communicative disorders related to cleft lip and palate* (3rd ed.; pp. 79–105). Austin, TX: Pro-Ed.

Carlson, F. (1987). Communication strategies for infants. In E. McDonald (Ed.), *Treating cerebral palsy: By clinicians for clinicians* (pp. 191–208). Austin, TX: Pro-Ed.

Cartwright, G., Cartwright, C., and **Ward, M.** (1989). *Educating special learners* (3rd edition). Belmont, CA: Wadsworth.

Case, J. (1991). *Clinical management of voice disorders* (2nd ed.). Austin, TX: Pro-Ed.

Cashdan, S. (1972). *Abnormal Psychology.* Englewood Cliffs, NJ: Prentice-Hall.

Catts, H. (1986). Speech production/phonological deficits in reading-disordered children. *Learning Disabilities, 19,* 504–508.

Catts, H., Swank, L., McIntosh, S., Stewart, L. (1989). Precursors of reading disabilities in language-impaired children. Paper presented at the annual convention of the American Speech-Language-Hearing Association, St. Louis, MO.

Chambers, J. (1983). Preface. In J. Chambers (Ed.), *Black English: Educational Equity and the Law* (pp. ix–xiv). Ann Arbor, MI: Karoma.

Charney, E. (1992). Neural tube defects: Spina bifida and myelomeningocele. In M. Batshaw and Y. Perret, (Eds.) *Children with handicaps: A medical primer* (3rd ed.; pp. 471–488). Baltimore, MD: Paul H. Brookes.

Chasnoff, I. (1990). *Drug use in pregnancy: Epidemiology and clinical impact*. Paper presented at the Spectrum of Developmental Disabilities XII, Baltimore, MD.

Cheng, L. (1987). Cross-cultural and linguistic considerations in working with Asian populations. *Asha, 29* (June), 33–38.

Chomsky, N., and **Halle, M.** (1968). *The sound pattern of English*. New York, NY: Harper and Row.

Churchill, J., Hodson, B., Jones, B., and **Novak, R.** (1985). A preliminary investigation comparing phonoloigcal systems of speech disordered clients with and without histories of recurrent otitis media. Paper presented and the annual convention of the American Speech-Language-Hearing Association, Washington DC.

Clark, T., and **Watkins, S.** (1984). *Programming for hearing impaired infants through amplification and home intervention* (4th ed.). Logan, UT: Utah State University, Project SKI-HI.

Clifford, E. (1973). Psycohological aspects of orofacial anomalies: Speculations in search of data. In R. Wertz (Ed.), *ASHA Reports #3: Orofacial anomalies: Clinical and research implications*. Washington, DC: American Speech and Hearing Association.

Colton, R. (1994). Physiology of phonation. In Benninger, M., Jacobson, B., and Johnson, A. (Eds.), *Vocal arts medicine: The care and prevention of professional voice disorders*. New York, NY: Thieme Medical Publishers.

Colton, R., and **Casper, J.** (1990). *Understanding voice problems: A physiological perspective for diagnosis and treatment*. Baltimore: Williams and Wilkins.

Colton, R., Sagerman, R., Chung, C., Young, Y., and **Reed, G.** (1978). Voice change after radiotherapy. *Radiology, 127,* 821–824.

Compton, C. (1993). Assistive technology for deaf and hard-of-hearing people. In J. Alpiner and P. McCarthy (Eds.), *Rehabilitative audiology: Children and adults* (2nd ed.; pp. 441–469).

Conlon, C. (1992). New threats to development: Alcohol, cocaine, and AIDS. In M. Batshaw and Y. Perret, (Eds.) *Children with handicaps: A medical primer* (3rd ed., pp. 111–136). Baltimore, MD: Paul H. Brookes.

Conture, E. (1990). *Stuttering* (2nd edition). Englewood Cliffs, NJ: Prentice-Hall.

Converse, J. (1963). The techniques of cleft palate surgery. In J. Irwin (Ed.), *ASHA report Number 1: Proceedings of the conference: Communicative problems in cleft palate*. Washington: American Speech and Hearing Association.

Cooper, J., and **Griffiths, P.** (1978) Treatment and prognosis. In: M. Wyke, (Ed.), *Developmental dysphasia*. London: Academic Press.

Cornett, R. (1967). Cued speech. *American Annals of the Deaf, 112,* 3–13.

Courchesne, E., Yeung-Courchesne, R., Press, G., Hesselink, J., Jernigan, T. (1988). Hypoplasia of cerebellar vermal lobules VI and VII in autism. *New England Journal of Medicine, 318,* 1349–1354.

Covington, A. (1976). Black people and Black English: Attitudes and deeducation in a biased macroculture. In D. Harrison and T. Trabasso (Eds.), *Black English: A Seminar*. Hillsdale, NJ: Lawrence Earlbaum Associates.

Craig, C., and **Kim, B.** (1990). Effects of time gating and word length on isolated word-recognitions performance. *Journal of Speech and Hearing Research, 33,* 808–815.

Craig, H., and **Evans, J.** (1993). Pragmatics and SLI: Within-group variations in discourse behaviors. *Journal of Speech and Hearing Research, 36,* 777–789.

Crais, E., and **Chapman, R.** (1987). Story recall and inferencing skills in language-learning disabled and nondisabled children. *Journal of Speech and Hearing Disorders, 52,* 50–55.

Creaghead, N. (1989). Development of phonology, articulation, and speech perception. In N. Creaghead, P. Newman and W. Secord (Eds.), *Assessment and remediation of articulatory and phonological disorders* (2nd ed.; pp. 35–68). Columbus, OH: Merrill Publishing Company.

Cronin, T. (1977). The bilateral cleft lip with cleft of the primary palate. In J. Converse (Ed.), *Reconstructive plastic surgery, Volume 4* (2nd ed.). Philadelphia, PA: W. B. Saunders.

Crothers, B., and **Paine, R.** (1959). *The natural history of cerebral palsy*. Cambridge, MA: Harvard University Press.

Damste, P. (1994). Smelling and swimming after laryngectomy. In R. Keith and F. Darley (Eds.), *Laryngectomy rehabilitation* (3rd ed.; pp. 555–559). Austin, TX: Pro-Ed.

Darley, F., Aronson, A., and **Brown, J.** (1975). *Motor speech disorders*. Philadelphia, PA: W. B. Saunders.

Davis, G. (1993). *A survey ot adult aphasia and related language disorders* (2nd ed.). Englewood Cliffs, NJ: Prentice-Hall.

Denhoff, E., and **Robinault, I.** (1960). *Cerebral palsy and related disorders*. New York, NY: McGraw-Hill.

Desai, S. (1983). Early cleft palate repair completed before the age of 16 weeks. *Plastic and Reconstructive Surgery, 36,* 300–304.

DeWeese, D., and **Saunders, W.** (1982). *Textbook of otolaryngology* (6th ed.). St. Louis, MO: Mosby.

Dore, J. (1974). A pragmatic description of early language development. *Journal of Psycholinguistic Research, 4,* 343–350.

Dorf, D., and **Curtain, J.** (1982). Early cleft palate repair and speech outcome. *Plastic and Reconstructive Surgers, 70,* 74.

Doyle, P., Danhauer, J., and **Reed, C.** (1988). Listeners' perceptions of consonants produced by espohageal and tracheoesophageal talkers. *Journal of Speech and Hearing Disorders, 53,* 400–407.

Dworkin, J. (1978). Protrusive lingual force and lingual diadochokinetic rates: A comparitive analysis between normal and lisping speakers. *Language, Speech, and Hearing Services in Schools, 9,* 8–16.

Dworkin, J., and **Culatta, R.** (1985). Tongue strength: Its relationship to tongue thrusting, open-bite, and articulatory proficiency. *Journal of Speech and Hearing Disorders, 45,* 277–282.

Edwards, M., and **Shriberg, L.** (1983). *Phonology: Applications in communicative disorders.* San Diego, CA: College Hill Press.

Elbert, M. (1985). Cognitive aspects of articulation learning. In *Children's phonology disorders: Pathways and patterns* (pp. 9–18). Rockville, MD: ASHA.

Ellis Weismer, S. (1985). Constructive comprehension abilities exhibited by language-disordered children. *Journal of Speech and Hearing Research, 28,* 175–184.

Feagans, L., Sanyal, M., Henderson, F., Collier, A., and **Appelbaum, M.** (1987). Relationship of middle ear disease in early childhood to later narrative and attention skills. *Journal of Pediatric Psychology, 12,* 581–594.

Feig, L. (1990). *Drug exposed infants and children: Service needs and policy questions* (DHHS report). Washington DC: U.S. Government Printing Office.

Fein, D. (1983). Projections of speech and hearing impairment to 2050. *ASHA, 25* (11): 31.

Felsenfeld, S., Broen, P., McGue, M. (1992). A 28-year follow-up of adults with a history of moderate phonological disorder: Linguistic and personality results. *Journal of Speech and Hearing Research, 35,* 1113–1125.

Flanagan, J. (1958). Some properties of the glottal sound source. *Journal of Speech and Hearing Research, 1,* 99–116.

Flexer, C. (1993). Management of hearing in an educational setting. In J. Alpiner and P. McCarthy (Eds.), *Rehabilitative audiology: Children and adults* (2nd ed.; pp. 176–210).

Flores, T., Wood, B., Levine, H., Koegel, L., and **Tucker, H.** (1982). Factors in successful deglutition following supraglottic larnygeal surgery. *Annals of Otology, Rhinology and Laryngology, 91,* 579–583.

Flower, R. (1994). Introduction to the professions. In: F. Minifie (Ed.), *Introduction to communication sciences and disorders* (pp. 1–41). San Diego, CA: Singular Publishing.

Flynn, P., and **Byrne, M.** (1970). Relationship between reading and selected auditory abilities of third-grade children. *Journal of Speech and Hearing Research, 13,* 731–740.

Foster, N. (1987). Age-related changes in the human nervous system. In H. Mueller and V. Geoffrey (Eds.), *Communication disorders in aging: Assessment and management* (pp. 3–35). Washington DC: Gallaudet Press.

Fox, D., Lynch, D., and **Brookshire, B.** (1978). Selected developmental factors of cleft palate children between two and thirty-three months of age. *Cleft Palate Journal, 15,* 239.

Fraser, F. (1971). Etiology of cleft lip and palate. In W. Grabb, S. Rosenstein, and K. Bzoch (Eds.), *Cleft lip and palate: Surgical, dental and speech aspects* (pp. 54–65). Boston, MA: Little, Brown.

Fraser, M. (1987). *Self-therapy for the stutterer* (6th edition; Publication #12). Memphis, TN: Speech Foundation of America.

Frey, W. (1984). Functional assessment in the '80s: A conceptual enigma, a technical challenge. In A. Halpern and M. Fuhrer (Eds.), *Functional assessment in rehabilitation.* Baltimore, MD: Paul H. Brookes.

Fryauf-Bertschy, H., Tyler, R., Kelsay, D., and **Gantz, B.** (1992). Performance over time of congenitally deaf and postlingually deafened children using a multichannel cochlear implant. *Journal of Speech and Hearing Research, 35,* 913–920.

Fukutake, T., and **Yamashita, T.** (1993). Speech rehabilitation and complications of primary tracheoesophageal puncture. *Acta Otolaryngologica Supplement, 500,* 117–120.

Garstecki, D. (1993). Rehabilitative audiologists and the hearing-impaired population: Continuing and new relationships. In J. Alpiner and P. McCarthy (Eds.), *Rehabilitative audiology: Children and adults* (2nd ed.; pp. 17–34).

Gates, G., and **Hearne, E.** (1982). Predicting esophageal speech. *Annals of Otology, Rhinology and Laryngology, 91,* 454–457.

Geers, A. (1986). Vibrotactile stimulation: A case study with a profoundly deaf child. *Journal of Rehabilitation Research and Development, 23,* 111–118.

Gelfand, S., (1990). *Hearing: An introduction to psychological and physiological acoustics* (2nd ed.). New York: Marcel Dekker.

Gelfer, M. (1987). An AER study of stop-consonant discrimination. *Perception and Psychophysics, 42,* 318–327.

Gerkin, K. (1984). The high-risk register for deafness. *Asha, 25* (March), 17–23.

Gierut, J. (1992). The conditions and course of clinically induced phonological change. *Journal of Speech and Hearing Research, 35,* 1049–1063.

Gilman, S., and **Winans, S.** (1982). *Manter and Gatz's essentials of clinical neuroanatomy and neurophysiology* (6th ed.). Philadelphia, PA: F. A. Davis.

Gilmore, S. (1994). The physical, social, occupational, and psychological concomitants of laryngectomy. In R. Keith and F. Darley (Eds.), *Laryngectomy rehabilitation* (3rd edition; pp. 396–486). Austin, TX: Pro-Ed.

Glattke, T., and **Kujawa, S.** (1991). Otoacoustic emissions. *American Journal of Audiology, 1,* 29–40.

Glorig, A., and **Roberts, J.** (1977). *Hearing levels of adults by age and sex.* (Series II, No. 11. U.S. Vital Health Statistics). Bethesda, MD: National Center for Health Statistics.

Golbus, M. (1980). Teratology for the obstetrician: Current status. *Obstetrics and Gynecology, 55,* 1–9.

Goldberg, B. (1993). Universal hearing screening of newborns: An idea whose time has come. *Asha, 35* (June/July), 63–64.

Goldstein, M., and **Proctor, A.** (1985). Tactile aids for profoundly deaf children. *Journal of the Acoustical Society of America, 77,* 258–265.

Goodhill, V. (1985). Presbycusis. In V. Goodhill (Ed.), *Ear Diseases, Deafness and Dizziness* (pp. 719–730). Hagerstown, MD: Harper and Row.

Goodstein, L. (1968). Psychosocial aspects of cleft palate. In D. Spriesterbach and D. Sherman (Eds.). *Cleft palate and communication* (pp. 201–224). New York, NY: Academic Press.

Gordon, E., Drenth, V., Jarvis, L., Johnson, J., and **Wright, V.** (1978). Neuropsychologic syndromes in stroke as predictors of outcome. *Archives of Physical Medicine and Rehabilitation, 59,* 339–403.

Gorlin, R. (1993). Development and genetic aspects of cleft lip and palate. In K. Moller and C. Starr (Eds.), *Cleft palate: Interdisciplinary issues and treatment: For clinicians by clincians* (pp. 25–48). Austin, TX: Pro-Ed.

Graber, T. (1949). Craniofacial morphology in cleft palate and cleft lip deformities. *Surgical and Gynecological Obstetrics, 88,* 359.

Graber, T. (1950). Changing philosophies in cleft palate management. *Journal of Pediatrics, 37,* 400.

Graber, T. (1954). The congenital cleft palate deformity. *Journal of the American Dental Association, 48,* 375.

Graham, J. (1983). The course of the patient from presentation to diagnosis. In: Y. Edels (Ed.), *Laryngectomy: Diagnosis to rehabilitation* (pp. 1–17). London: Croom and Helm.

Green, G. (1989). Psycho-behavioral characteristics of children with vocal nodules: WPBIC ratings. *Journal of Speech and Hearing Disorders, 54,* 306–312.

Greenlee, M. (1974). Interacting processes in the child's acquisition of stop-liquid clusters. *Papers and reports on child language development, 7,* 85–100.

Gregory, H. (1984). Prevention of stuttering: Management of early stages. In: R. Curlee and W. Perkins (Eds.), *Nature and treatment of stuttering: New directions* (pp. 335–356). Boston, MA: Allyn and Bacon.

Grievink, E., Peters, S., van Bon, W, and **Schilder, A.** (1993). The effects of early bilateral otitis media with effusion on language ability: A prospective cohort study. *Journal of Speech and Hearing Research 36,* 1004–1012.

Groher, M. (1984). *Dysphagia: Diagnosis and management.* Boston, MA: Butterworths.

Grunwell, P. (1987). *Clinical phonology* (2nd ed.). Baltimore, MD: Williams and Wilkins.

Guitar, B., and **Peters, T.** (1980). *Stuttering: An integration of contempory therapies* (Publication #16). Memphis, TN: The Speech Foundation of America.

Guskin, J. (1970). The social perception of language variation: Black and White teachers' attitudes towards speakers from different racial and social class backgrounds. Unpublished doctoral dissertation, The University of Michigan, Ann Arbor, Michigan.

Gustason, G. (1989). Early identification of hearing-impaired infants: A review of Israeli and American progress. *The Volta Review,* October/November, 291–295.

Hagen, C. (1984). Language disorders in head trauma. In A. Holland (Ed.), *Language disorders in adults: Recent advances* (pp. 245–282). San Diego, CA: College-Hill Press.

Hairston, E., and **Smith, L.** (1983). *Black and deaf in America: Are we that different?* Silver Spring, MD: T. J. Publishers.

Hall, B. (1991). Attitudes of fourth and sixth graders toward peers with mild articulation disorders. *Language, Speech and Hearing Services in Schools, 22,* 334–340.

Hall, K., and **Tomblin, B.** (1978). A follow-up study of children with articulation and language disorders. *Journal of Speech and Hearing Disorders, 43,* 227–241.

Hammill, D., Leigh, J., McNutt, G., and **Larsen, S.** (1981). A new definition of learning disabilities. *Learning Disabilities Quarterly, 4,* 336–342.

Hamre, C. (1992a). Stuttering prevention I: Primacy of identification. *Journal of Fluency Disorders, 17,* 2–23.

Hamre, C. (1992b). Stuttering prevention II: Progression. *Journal of Fluency Disorders, 17,* 63–79.

Handleman, J., Harris, S., Kristoff, B., Fuentes. F., and **Alessandri, M.** (1991). A specialized program for preschool children with autism. *Language, Speech and Hearing Services in the Schools, 22,* 107–110.

Hardy, J. (1994). Cerebral palsy. In G. Shames, E. Wiig, and W. Secord (Eds.), *Human communication disorders: An introduction* (4th ed.; pp. 562–604). New York, NY: Macmillan.

Harris, S., Handleman, J., Gordon, R., Kristoff, B., and **Fuentes, F.** (1991). Changes in cognitive and language functioning of preschool children with autism. *Journal of Autism and Developmental Disorders, 21,* 281–290.

Haynes, W., Moran, M., and **Pindzola, R.** (1990). *Communication disorders in the classroom.* Dubuque, IA: Kendall/Hunt.

Healy, A. (1990). Cerebral palsy. In J. Blackburn (Ed.), *Medical aspects of developmental disabilities in children birth to three* (2nd ed., pp. 59–66). Rockville, MD: Aspen Publishers.

Healey, E. (1991). Characteristics of children who stutter. In: E. Healy (Ed.), *Readings on research in stuttering* (pp. 51–54). New York: Longman.

Hegde, M. (1991). *Introduction to communicative disorders.* Austin, TX: Pro-Ed.

Hess, L., and **Bahr, R.** (1981). *What every family should know about strokes.* New York, NY: Appleton-Century-Crofts.

Hewitt, N. (1971). Reactions of prospective English teachers toward speakers of a nonstandard dialect. *Language and Learning, 21,* 205–212.

Hinojosa, J., and **Anderson, J.** (1991). Mothers' perceptions of home treatment programs for their preschool children with cerebral palsy. *American Journal of Occupational Therapy, 45,* 273–279.

Hipskind, N. (1989). Visual stimuli in communication. In R. Schow and M. Nerbonne (Eds.), *Introduction to aural rehabilitation* (2nd ed.; pp. 125–180). Austin, TX: Pro-Ed.

Hollien, H., Gelfer, M., and **Carlson, T.** (1991). Listening preferences for voice types as a function of age. *Journal of Communication Disorders, 24,* 157–171.

Horii, Y. (1979). Fundamental frequency perturbation observed in sustained phonation. *Journal of Speech and Hearing Research, 22,* 5–19.

Howard, J. et al. (1989). The development of young children of substance abusing parents: Insights from seven years of intervention and research. *Zero to Three, 9,* 8–12.

Howie, P. (1984). Concordance for stuttering in monozygotic and dizygotic twin pairs. *Journal of Speech and Hearing Research, 24,* 317–321.

Howie, P., Tanner, S., and **Andrews, G.** (1981). Short- and long-term outcome in an intensive treatment program for adult stutterers. *Journal of Speech and Hearing Disorders, 46,* 104–109.

Hubbard, C., and **Prins, D.** (1994). Word familiarity, syllabic stress pattern, and stuttering. *Journal of Speech and Hearing Research, 37,* 564–571.

Hyman, L. (1975). *Phonology: Theory and analysis.* New York, NY: Holt, Rinehart and Winston.

Ingram, D. (1976). *Phonological disability in children.* New York, NY: American Elsevier.

Jakobsen, R., Fant, G., and **Halle, M.** (1963). *Preliminaries to speech analysis.* Cambridge, MA: M.I.T. Press.

Jarvik, L., and **Bank, L.** (1983). Aging twins: Longitudinal psychometric data. In K. Schaie (Ed.), *Longitudinal studies of adult psychological development* (pp. 40–63). New York, NY: Guilford Press.

Jenkins, J., Sells, C., Brady, D., et al., (1982). Effects of developmental therapy on motor impaired children. *Physical and Occupational Therapy in Pediatrics, 2,* 19–28.

Jewell, G., and **Weiner, S.** (1984). *Geri.* New York, NY: Ballantine Books.

Johnson, W. (1955). A study of the onset and development of stuttering. In W. Johnson and R.

Leutenegger (Eds.), *Stuttering in children and adults*. Minneapolis, MN: University of Minnesota Press.

Johnson, W. (1959). *The onset of stuttering*. Minneapolis, MN: University of Minnesota Press.

Johnson, W. (1961). Measurement of oral reading and speaking rate and disfluency of adult male and female stutterers and nonstutterers. *Journal of Speech and Hearing Disorders, Monograph Supplement Number 7*, 1–20.

Joint Committee on Infant Hearing (JCIH) (1991). 1990 Position Statement. *ASHA* (Suppl. 5), 3–6.

Jones, K. (1988). *Smith's recognizable patterns of human malformation* (4th ed.). Philadelphia, PA: W. B. Saunders.

Jordan, I., Gustason, G., and **Rosen, R.** (1976). Current communication trends of programs for the deaf. *American Annals of the Deaf, 121*, 527–531.

Kail, R. (1994). A method for studying the generalized slowing hypothesis in children with specific language impairment. *Journal of Speech and Hearing Research, 37*, 418–421

Kaiser, A., and **Warren, S.** (1988). Pragmatics and generalization. In R. L. Schiefelbusch and L. L Lloyd (Eds.), *Language perspectives II*. Austin, TX: Pro-Ed.

Kamhi, A., (1981). Nonlinguistic symbolic and conceptual abilities of language-impaired and normally developing children. *Journal of Speech and Hearing Research, 24*, 446–453.

Kamhi, A., and **Catts, H.** (1989). Language and reading: convergences, divergences, and development. In: A. Kamhi and H. Catts (Eds.), *Reading disabilities: A developmental perspective* (pp. 1–34). Boston, MA: College-Hill Press.

Kamhi, A., Gentry, B., Mauer, D., and **Gholson, B.** (1990). Analogical learning and transfer in language-impaired children. *Journal of Speech and Hearing Disorders, 55*, 140–148.

Kanda, T., Yuge, M., Yamori, Y., et al. (1984). Early physiotherapy in the treatment of spastic diplegia. *Developmental Medicine and Child Neurology, 26*, 438–444.

Kaplan, H., Gladstone, V., and **Lloyd, L.** (1993). *Audiometric interpretation: A manual of basic audiometry* (2nd ed.). Boston, MA: Allyn and Bacon.

Kapp, K. (1979). Self-concept of the cleft lip and/or palate child. *Cleft Palate Journal, 16*, 171–176.

Kapp-Simon, K. (1986). Self-concept of primary-school-age children with cleft lip, cleft palate or both. *Cleft Palage Journal, 23*, 24.

Katz, R. (1986). Phonological deficiencies in children with reading disability: Evidence from an object naming task. *Cognition, 22*, 225–257.

Katzman, R., and **Terry, R.** (1983). Normal aging of the nervous system. In R. Katzman and R. Terry (Eds.)., *The neurology of aging* (pp. 15–50). Philadelphia, PA: F. A. Davis.

Kemp, D. (1978). Stimulated acoustic emissions from within the human auditory system. *Journal of the Acoustical Society of America, 64*, 1386–1391.

Kent, R. (1983). Facts about stuttering: Neuropsychologic perspectives. *Journal of Speech and Hearing Disorders, 48*, 249–254.

Kent, R. (1993). Normal aspects of articulation. In J. Bernthal and N. Bankson (Eds.)., *Articulation and phonological disorders* (3rd edition, pp. 1–62). Englewood Cliffs, NJ: Prentice-Hall.

Kent, R., and **Burkard, R.** (1981). Changes in the acoustic correlates of speech production. In D. Beasley and G. Davis (Eds.), *Aging: Communication processses and disorders* (pp. 42–62). New York, NY: Grune and Stratton.

Kirk, S. (1958). *Early education of the mentally retarded*. Urbana, IL: University of Illinois Press.

Kirk, S. (1965). Diagnostic, cultural and remedial factors in mental retardation. In S. Osler and R. Cooke (Eds.), *The biosocial basis of mental retardation* (pp. 129–145). Baltimore, MD: Johns Hopkins Press.

Kirk, S. (1972). *Educating exceptional children*. (2nd ed.). Boston, MA: Houghton Mifflin.

Kirkwood, D. (1990). 1990 U.S. hearing aid sales summary. *The Hearing Aid Journal, 43* (12), 7–9, 12–13.

Kleinsasser, O. (1979). *Microlaryngoscopy and endolaryngeal microsurgery: Technique and typical findings*. Baltimore, MD: University Park Press.

Koike, Y. (1967). Application of some acoustic measures for the evaluation of laryngeal dysfunction. *Journal of the Acoustical Society of America, 42*: 1209.

Kowal, S., O'Connell, D., and **Sabin, E.** (1975). Development of temporal patterning and vocal hesitations in spontaneous narritives, *Journal of Psycholinguistic Research, 4*, 195–207.

Kowalski, L., Batista, M., Santos, C., Scopel, A., Salvajoli, J., Novaes, P., and **Trippe, N.** (1993). Prognostic factors in glottic carcinoma clinical stage I and II treated by surgery or radiotherapy. *American Journal of Otolaryngology, 14*, 122–127.

Kricos, P. (1993). The counseling process: Children and parents. In J. Alpiner and P. McCarthy (Eds.),

Rehabilitative audiology: Children and adults (2nd ed.; pp. 211–233).

Ladefoged, P. (1962). *Elements of acoustic phonetics.* Chicago, IL: The University of Chicago Press.

Lahey, M. (1988). *Language disorders and language development.* New York, NY: Macmillan.

Lang, A., and **Blair, R.** (1984). Parkinson's disease in 1984: An update. *Canadian Medical Association Journal, 13,* 1031–1037.

Larson, C. (1989). Basic neurophysiology. In D. Kuehn, M. Lemme and J. Baumgartner (Eds.), *Neural bases of speech, language and hearing* (pp. 46–86). Boston, MA: College Hill.

Laughten, J., and **Hasenstab, M.** (1993). Assessment and intervention with school-age hearing-impaired children. In J. Alpiner and P. McCarthy (Eds.), *Rehabilitative audiology: Children and adults* (2nd ed.; pp. 136–175).

Lawson, W., Biller, H., and **Suen, J.** (1989). Cancer of the larynx. In E. Myers and J. Suen (Eds.), *Cancer of the head and neck* (2nd ed.). New York: Churchill Livingstone.

Leeper, H., Sills, P., and **Charles, D.** (1993). Prosthodontic management of maxillofacial and palatal defects. In K. Moller and C. Starr (Eds.). *Cleft palate: Interdisciplinary issues and treatment: For clinicians by clinicans* (pp. 145–188). Austin, TX: Pro-Ed.

Lehmann, W., and **Krebs, H.** (1991). Interdisciplinary rehabilitation of the laryngectomee. *Recent Results in Cancer Research, 121,* 442–449.

Lenneberg, E. (1967). *Biological foundations of language.* New York, NY: John Wiley and Sons.

Leonard, L. (1991). Specific language impairment as a clinical category. *Language, Speech and Hearing Services in Schools, 22,* 66–68.

Lieberman, P. (1963). Some acoustic measures of the fundamental periodicity of normal and pathological larynges. *Journal of the Acoustical Society of America, 35,* 344–353.

Linebaugh, C. (1984). Mild aphasia. In A. Holland (Ed.), *Language disorders in adults: Recent advances* (pp. 113–132). San Diego, CA: College-Hill Press.

Ling, D. (1976). *Speech and hearing impaired child: Theory and practice.* Washington, D.C.: Alexander Grahm Bell Association for the Deaf.

Locke, J. (1980). The inference of speech perception in the phonologically-disordered child. Part II: Some clinically novel procedures, their use, some findings. *Journal of Speech and Hearing Disorders, 45,* 445–468.

Loewe, F., and **Lerner, A.** (1956). *My Fair Lady* (vocal score). New York, NY: Chappell and Co. (p. 19).

Loman, B. (1967). *Conversations in a Negro American dialect.* Washington DC: Center for Applied Linguistics.

Lord, J. (1984). Cerebral palsy: A clinical approach. *Archives of Physical Medicine, 65,* 542–548.

Love, R., and **Webb, W.** (1992). *Neurology for the speech-language pathologist* (2nd ed.). Boston, MA: Butterworth-Heinemann.

Lowe, R. (1994). Phonology: An overview. In R. Lowe (Ed.), *Phonology: Assessment and intervention applications in speech pathology* (pp. 1–11). Baltimore, MD: Williams and Wilkins.

Lowenbraun, S. (1988). Hearing impaired. In Meyen, E. and Skrtic, T. (Eds.), *Exceptional children and youth* (3rd ed.; pp. 321–350). Denver, CO: Love Publishing.

Lubs, H. (1969). A marker X chromosome. *American Jouranl of Human Genetics, 21,* 231–244.

Lynch, H., and **Kimberling, W.** (1981). Genetic counseling in cleft lip and cleft palate. *Plastic and Reconstructive Surgery, 68,* 800–815.

MacDonald, H., Mulligan, J., Allen, A., and **Taylor, P.** (1980). Neonatal asphyxia I: Relationship of obstetric and neonatal complications to neonatal mortality in 38–403 consecutive deliveries. *Journal of Pediatrics, 96,* 898–902.

Maestas y Moores, J., and **Moores, D.** (1989). Educational alternatives for the hearing impaired. In R. Schow and M. Nerbonne (Eds.), *Introduction to aural rehabilitation* (2nd ed.; pp. 271–291). Austin, TX: Pro-Ed.

Maragos, N. (1994). Anatomy and physiology of the larynx. In R. Keith and F. Darley (Eds.), *Laryngectomy rehabilitation* (3rd ed.; pp. 49–55). Austin, TX: Pro-Ed.

Markides, A. (1983). *The speech of hearing-impaired children.* Oxford: Manchester University Press.

Martin, F. (1994). *Introduction to audiology* (5th ed.). Englewood Cliffs, NJ: Prentice-Hall.

Martin, R., and **Lindamood, L.** (1986). Stuttering and spontaneous recovery: Implications for the speech-language pathologist. *Language, Speech, and Hearing Services in Schools, 17,* 207–218.

Masterson, J. (1993). The performance of children with language-learning disabilities on two types of cognitive tasks. *Journal of Speech and Hearing Research, 36,* 1026–1036.

Masterson, J., Evans, L., and **Aloia, M.** (1993). Verbal analogical reasoning in children with and without language-learning disabilities. *Journal of Speech and Hearing Research, 36,* 72–82.

Mateer, C. (1989). Neural correlates of language function. In D. Kuehn, M. Lemme and J. Baumgartner (Eds.), *Neural bases of speech, language and hearing* (pp. 259–291). Boston, MA: College Hill.

Matkin, N. (1984). Early recognition and referral of hearing-impaired children. *Pediatrics in Review, 6,* 151–156.

Maurer, J. (1989). Aural rehabilitation for elderly adults. In R. Schow and M. Nerbonne (Eds.), *Introduction to aural rehabilitation* (2nd ed.; pp. 459–503). Austin, TX: Pro-Ed.

McCollum, A. (1984). Grieving over the lost dream. *Exceptional Parent, 14,* 9–12.

McCormick, L. (1990a). Child characteristics that affect learning. In L. McCormick and R. Schiefelbusch (Eds.), *Early language intervention: An introduction* (2nd ed.; pp. 144–179). Columbus, OH: Charles E. Merrill.

McCormick, L. (1990b). Developing objectives. In L. McCormick and R. Schiefelbusch (Eds.), *Early language intervention: An introduction* (2nd ed.; pp. 182–214). Columbus, OH: Charles E. Merrill.

McCormick, L. (1990c). Extracurricular roles and relationships. In L. McCormick and R. Schiefelbusch (Eds.), *Early language intervention: An introduction* (2nd ed.; pp. 262–301). Columbus, OH: Charles E. Merrill.

McCormick, L. (1990d). Terms, concepts and perspectives. In L. McCormick and R. Schiefelbusch (Eds.), *Early language intervention* (2nd ed.; pp. 4–36). Columbus, OH: Charles E. Merrill.

McCormick, L., and **Schiefelbusch, R.** (1991). *Early language intervention* (2nd ed.). Columbus, OH: Charles E. Merrill.

McDonald, E. (1987a). Cerebral palsy: Its nature, pathogenesis and management. In E. McDonald (Ed.), *Treating cerebral palsy: By clinicians for clinicians* (pp. 1–20). Austin, TX: Pro-Ed.

McDonald, E. (1987b). Speech production problems. In E. McDonald (Ed.), *Treating cerebral palsy: By clinicians for clinicians* (pp. 171–190). Austin, TX: Pro-Ed.

McDonald, E., and **Aungst, L.** (1970). Apparent impedence of sensory functions and articulatory proficiency. In J. Bosma (Ed.), *Second symposium on oral sensation and perception.* Springfield, IL: Charles C. Thomas.

McKenna, J., Fornataro-Clerici, L., McMenamin, P., and **Leonard, R.** (1991). Laryngeal cancer: Diagnosis, treatment and speech rehabilitation. *American Family Physician, 44,* 123–129.

McNutt, J. (1977). Oral sensory and motor behaviors of children with /s/ or /r/ misarticulations. *Journal of Speech and Hearing Research, 20,* 694–703.

McWilliams, B., Morris, H., and **Shelton, R.** (1990). *Cleft palate speech* (2nd ed.). Philadelphia: B. C. Decker.

McWilliams, B., and **Paradise, L.** (1973). Educational, occupational, and marital status of cleft palate adults. *Cleft Palate Journal, 10,* 223.

McWilliams, B., and **Witzel, M.** (1994). Cleft palate. In G. Shames, E. Wiig, and W. Secord (Eds.), *Human communication disorders* (pp. 438–479). New York: Merrill Publishing.

Meyers, S., and **Freeman, F.** (1985). Mother and child speech rates as a variable in stuttering and disfluency. *Journal of Speech and Hearing Research, 28,* 436–444.

Miller, E. (1977). The management of dementia: A review of some possibilities. *British Journal of Social and Clinical Psychology, 16,* 77–83.

Miller, N. (1994). *Nobody's perfect.* Baltimore, MD: Paul H. Brookes.

Moeller, Dorothy (1976). *Speech pathology and audiology: Iowa origins of a discipline.* Iowa City, IA: The University of Iowa.

Moeller, M., and **Carney, A.** (1993). Assessment and intervention with preschool hearing-impaired children. In J. Alpiner and P. McCarthy (Eds.), *Rehabilitative audiology: Children and adults* (2nd ed.; pp. 106–135).

Molfese, V., Molfese, D., and **Parsons, C.** (1983). Hemispheric processing of phonological information. In S. Segalowitz (Ed.), *Language functions and brain organization* (pp. 29–49). New York, NY: Academic Press.

Moller, K. (1993). Interdisciplinary team approach: Issues and procedures. In K. Moller and C. Starr (Eds.), *Cleft palate: Interdisciplinary issues and treatment: For clinicians by clincians* (pp. 1–24). Austin, TX: Pro-Ed.

Moore, G., and **Kester, D.** (1953). Historical notes on speech correction in the pre-association era. *Journal of Speech and Hearing Disorders, 18,* 48–53.

Mowrer, D., Wahl, P., and **Doolan, S.** (1978). Effect of lisping on audience evaluation of male speakers. *Journal of Speech and Hearing Disorders, 43,* 140–148.

Murdoch, B. (1990). *Acquired speech and language disorders: A neuroanatomical and functional neurological approach*. London: Chapman and Hall.

Murphy, C., Yeargin-Allsopp, M., Decoufle, P., and Drews, C. (1993). Prevalence of cerebral palsy among ten-year-old children in metropolitan Atlanta, 1985–1987. *Journal of Pediatrics, 123,* S13–20.

Murray, A., Javel, E., and Watson, C. (1985). Prognostic validity of auditory brainstem evoked response screening in newborn infants. *American Journal of Otolaryngology, 6,* 120–131.

Musiek, F. (1985). Application of central auditory tests: An overview. In J. Katz (Ed.), *Handbook of clinical audiology* (3rd ed., pp. 321–336). Baltimore, MD: Williams and Wilkins.

Nabelek, A., Tucker, F., and Letowski, T. (1991). Toleration of background noises: Relationship with patterns of hearing aid use by elderly persons. *Journal of Speech and Hearing Research, 34,* 679–685.

Naremore, R. (1980). Language variation in a multicultural society. In T. Hixon, L. Shriberg, and J. Saxman (Eds.), *Introduction to communication disorders* (pp. 177–216). Englewood Cliffs, NJ: Prentice-Hall.

National Joint Committee on Learning Disabilities (1991). Learning disabilities: Issues on definition. *ASHA, 33,* (Suppl. 5), 18–20.

Nelson, L. (1986). Language formulation related to disfluency and stuttering. In J. Fraser (Ed.), *Stuttering therapy: Prevention and intervention with children* (Publication #20; pp. 19–38). Memphis TN: Speech Foundation of America.

Nelson, N. (1993). Language intervention in school settings. In D. Bernstein and E. Tiegerman (Eds.), *Language and communication disorders in children* (3rd ed.; pp. 273–324). Columbus, OH: Merrill Publishing.

Nerbonne, M., and Schow, R. (1989). Auditory stimuli in communication. In R. Schow and M. Nerbonne (Eds.), *Introduction to aural rehabilitation* (2nd ed.; pp. 81–124). Austin, TX: Pro-Ed.

Newman, P., and Creaghead, N. (1989). Assessment of articulatory and phonological disorders. In N. Creaghead, P. Newman and W. Secord (Eds.), *Assessment and remediation of articulatory and phonological disorders* (2nd ed.; pp. 35–68). Columbus, OH: Merrill Publishing.

Newman, R., and Byers, R. (1982). Squamous carcinoma of the larynx in patients under the age of 35 years. *Otolaryngology Head and Neck Surgery, 90,* 431–433.

Nicolosi, L., Harryman, E., and Kresheck, J. (1989). *Terminology of communication disorders: Speech-language-hearing* (3rd ed.). Baltimore, MD: Williams and Wilkins.

Nielsen, J., Sillesen, I., Sorensen, A., and Sorensen, K. (1979). Follow-up until ages 4 to 8 of 25 unselected children with sex chromosome abnormalities compared with sibs and controls. *Birth Defects, 15,* 15–73.

Nippold, M., Erskine, B., and Freed, D. (1988). Proportional and functional analogical reasoning in normal and language-impaired children. *Journal of Speech and Hearing Disorders, 53,* 440–449.

Norlin, P., and Van Tasell, D. (1980). Linguistic skills of hearing-impaired children. *Monographs in Contemporary Audiology, 1,* 1–32.

Northern, J., and Downs, M. (1991). *Hearing in children* (4th ed.). Baltimore, MD: Williams and Wilkins.

Obler, L., and Albert, M. (1981). Language and aging: A neurobehavioral analysis. In D. Beasley and G. Davis (Eds.), *Aging: Communication processes and disorders* (pp. 107–121). New York, NY: Grune and Stratton.

Odom, S., Hoyson, M., Jamieson, B., and Strain, P. (1985). Increasing handicapped preschoolers' peer social interactions: Cross-setting and component analysis. *Journal of Applied Behavior Analysis, 18,* 3–16.

Office of Technology Assessment (OTA), U.S. Congress (1985). Selected chronic conditions, technology, and biomedical research. In U.S. Congress, Office of Technology Assessment, *Technology of Aging in America* (pp. 61–103). Washington DC: U.S. Government Printing Office.

O'Grady, R., Nishimura, D., Kohn, J., et al. (1985). Vocational predictions compared with present vocational status of 60 young adults with cerebral palsy. *Developmental Medicine and Child Neurology, 27,* 775–784.

Ogura, J., and Thawley, E. (1980). Cysts and tumors of the larynx. In M. Paparella and D. Shumrick (Eds.), *Otolaryngology, volume 3. Head and neck* (2nd ed.). Philadelphia, PA: Saunders.

O'Reilly, D., and Walentynowicz, J. (1981). Etiological factors in cerebral palsy: An historical review. *Developmental Medicine and Child Neurology, 23,* 633–642.

Osberger, M., Maso, M., and Sam, L. (1993). Speech intelligibility of children with cochlear implants, tactile aids or hearing aids. *Journal of Speech and Hearing Research, 36,* 186–203.

Osborn, J., and **Kelleher, J.** (1983). A survey of cleft lip and palate surgery taught in plastic surgery training programs. *Cleft Palate Journal, 20,* 166.

Overman, C., and **Geoffrey, V.** (1987). Alzheimer's disease and other dementias. In H. Mueller and V. Geoffrey (Eds.), *Communication disorders in aging: Assessment and management* (pp. 3–35). Washington DC: Gallaudet Press.

Owens, R. (1990). Development of communication, language and speech. In G. Shames and E. Wiig (Eds.), *Human communication disorders* (3rd ed., pp. 30–73). Columbus, OH: Merrill Publishing.

Owens, R. (1993). Mental retardation: Difference and delay. In D. Bernstein and E. Tiegerman (Eds.), *Language and communication disorders in children* (3rd ed.; pp. 366–430). Columbus, OH: Merrill Publishing.

Owens, R. (1994). Development of communication, language, and speech. In G. Shames, E. Wiig, and W. Secord (Eds.), *Human communication disorders: An introduction* (4th ed.; pp. 37–81). New York, NY: Macmillan.

Paden, E., Matthies, M., and **Novak, M.** (1989). Recovery from OME-related phonological delay following tube placement. *Journal of Speech and Hearing Disorders, 54,* 94–100.

Paden, E., Novak, M., and **Beiter, A.** (1987). Predictors of phonologic inadequacy in young children prone to otitis media. *Journal of Speech and Hearing Disorders, 52,* 232–2432.

Palmer, C. (1992). Assistive devices in the audiology practice. *American Journal of Audiology, 1,* 37–51.

Paradise, J. (1980). Otitis media in infants and children. *Pediatrics, 65,* 917–943.

Paradise, J., Bluestone, C., and **Felder, H.** (1969). The universality of otitis media of infants with cleft palate. *Pediatrics, 44,* 35.

Paradise, J., and **McWilliams, B.** (1974). Simplified feeder for infants with cleft palate. *Pediatrics, 53,* 566–568.

Parker, G. (1979). Parental characteristics in relation to depressive disorders. *British Journal of Psychiatry, 134,* 138–147.

Patrick, P. (1987). Identification audiometry. In F. Martin (Ed.), *Hearing disorders in children* (pp. 399–425). Austin, TX: Pro-Ed.

Peach, R. (1987). Language functioning. In H. Mueller and V. Geoffrey (Eds.), *Communication disorders in aging: Assessment and mamagement* (pp. 185–213). Washington DC: Gallaudet Press.

Perkins, W. (1977). *Speech pathology: An applied behavioral science.* St. Louis, MO: C. V. Mosby.

Perkins, W. (1978). *Human perspectives in speech and language disorders.* St. Louis, MO: C. V. Mosby.

Perkins, W. (1980). Disorders of speech flow. In: T. Hixon, L. Shriberg and J. Saxman (Eds.), *Introduction to communication disorders* (pp. 449–490). Englewood Cliffs, NJ: Prentice-Hall.

Perkins, W. (1984). Techniques for establishing fluency. In W. Perkins (Ed.), *Stuttering disorders.* New York, NY: Thieme-Stratton.

Perkins, W. (1992). *Stuttering prevented.* San Diego, CA: Singular Publishing Group.

Perkins, W., and **Kent, R.** (1986). *Functional anatomy of speech, language and hearing: A primer.* Boston, MA: College-Hill.

Perkins, W., Kent, R., and **Curlee, R.** (1991). A theory of neuropsycholinguistic function in stuttering. *Journal of Speech and Hearing Research, 34,* 734–752.

Pernkopf, E. (1963). *Atlas of topographic and applied human anatomy, Volume I.* Philadelphia, PA: W. B. Saunders.

Peters, T., and **Guitar, B.** (1991). *Stuttering: An integrated approach to its nature and treatment.* Baltimore, MD: Williams and Wilkins.

Peterson, G., and **Barney, H.** (1952). Control methods used in a study of the vowels. *Journal of the Acoustical Society of America, 24,* 175–184.

Piper, M., Mazer, B., Silver, K., et al. (1988). Resolution of neurological symptoms in high-risk infants during the first two years of life. *Developmental Medicine and Child Neurology, 30,* 26–35.

Plotkin, R., Wirls, C., and **Finney, B.** (1970). Developmental evaluation of the cleft infant. Presented at the Annual Meeting of the American Celft Palage Association, Portland, OR, 1970.

Poole, I. (1934). Genetic development of articulation of consonant sounds in speech. *Elementary English Review, 11,* 159–161.

Powell, T., Elbert, M., and **Dinnsen, D.** (1991). Stimulability as a factor in the phonological generalization of misarticulating preschool children. *Journal of Speech and Hearing Research, 34,* 1318–1328.

Prather, E., Hedrick, D., and **Kern, C.** (1975). Articulation development in children aged two to four years. *Journal of Speech and Hearing Disorders, 40,* 179–191.

Prins, D. (1984). Treatment of adults: Managing stuttering. In R. Curlee & W. Perkins, (Eds.), *Nature and treatment of stuttering: New directions.* San Diego, CA: College-Hill.

Prior, M., and Cummins, R. (1992). Questions about facilitated communication and autism. *Journal of Autism and Developmental Disorders, 22,* 331–338.

Probst, R., Lonsbury-Martin, B., and Martin, G. (1991). A review of otoacoustic emissions. *Journal of the Acoustical Society of America, 89,* 2027–2067.

Proctor, A., and Goldstein, M. (1983). Development of lexical comprehension in a profoundly deaf child using a wearable, vibrotactile communication aid. *Language, Speech and Hearing Services in Schools, 14,* 138–149.

Ramig, L., and Ringel, R. (1983). Effects of physiological aging on selected acoustic characteristics of voice. *Journal of Speech and Hearing Research, 26,* 22–30.

Ratokalau, N., and Robb, M. (1993). Early communication assessment and intervention: An interactive process. In D. Bernstein and E. Tiegerman (Eds.), *Language and communication disorders in children* (3rd ed.; pp. 148–184). New York, NY: Macmillan.

Reed, V. (1994). *An introduction to children with language disorders* (2nd ed.). New York, NY, Macmillan Publishing.

Richardson, J. (1983). Vocational adjustment after total laryngectomy. *Archives of Physical Medicine and Rehabilitation, 64,* 544–549.

Richman, L. (1976). Behavior and achievement of cleft palate children. *Cleft Palate Journal, 13,* 4–10.

Richman, L. (1978). The effects of facial disfigurement on teachers' perception of ability in cleft palate children. *Cleft Palate Journal, 15,* 155–160.

Richman, L. (1983). Self-reported social, speech and facial concerns and personality adjustment of adolescents with cleft lip and palate. *Cleft Palate Journal, 20,* 108–112.

Richman, L., and Eliason, M. (1993). Psychological characteristics associated with cleft palate. In K. Moller and C. Starr (Eds.), *Cleft palate: Interdisciplinary issues and treatment: For clinicians by clinicians* (pp. 357–380). Austin, TX: Pro-Ed.

Robbins, J., Fisher, H., Blom, E., and Singer, M. (1984). A comparative acoustic study of normal, esophageal and tracheoesophageal speech production. *Journal of Speech and Hearing Disorders, 49,* 202–210.

Roberts, J., Burchinal, M., Davis, B., Collier, A., and Henderson, F. (1991). Otitis media in early childhood and later language. *Journal of Speech and Hearing Research, 34,* 1158–1168.

Robertson-Tchabo, E., and Arenberg, D. (1987). Cognitive performance. In H. Mueller and V. Geoffrey (Eds.), *Communication disorders in aging: Assessment and mamagement* (pp. 72–106). Washington DC: Gallaudet Press.

Rohe, D. (1994). Loss, grief, and depression after laryngectomy. In R. Keith and F. Darley (Eds.), *Laryngectomy rehabilitation* (3rd ed.; pp. 487–514). Austin, TX: Pro-ed.

Rosenbek, J., LaPointe, L., and Wertz, R. (1989). *Aphasia: A clinical approach.* Austin, TX: Pro-Ed.

Ross, E. (1981). The aprosodias: Functional anatomic organization of the affective components of language in the right hemisphere. *Archives of Neurology, 38,* 561–569.

Ross, E., and Mesulam, M. (1979). Dominant language functions of the right hemisphere: Prosody and emotional gesturing. *Archives of Neurology, 36,* 144–148.

Ross, R. (1987). Treatment variables affecting facial growth in complete unilateral cleft lip and palate. *Cleft Palate Journal, 24,* 5.

Roth, F., and Clark, D. (1987). Symbolic play and social participation abilities of language-impaired children and normally-developing children. *Journal of Speech and Hearing Disorders, 52,* 17–29.

Ryan, B. (1974). *Programmed therapy of stuttering in children and adults.* Springfield, IL: Charles C. Thomas.

Ryan, S. (1993). *Normative data for vocal intensity.* Unpublished master' thesis, University of Wisconsin-Milwaukee, Milwaukee, WI.

Salmon, S. (1994a). Methods of air intake for esophageal speech and their associated problems. In R. Keith and F Darley (Eds.), *Laryngectomee rehabilitation* (3rd ed.; pp. 219–234). Austin, TX: Pro-Ed.

Salmon, S. (1994b). Pre- and postoperative converences with laryngectomees and their spouses. In R. Keith and F Darley (Eds.), *Laryngectomee rehabilitation* (3rd ed.; pp. 133–148). Austin, TX: Pro-Ed.

Salmon, S. (1994c). Artificial larynxes: Teaching their use. In R. Keith and F Darley (Eds.), *Laryngectomee rehabilitation* (3rd ed.; pp. 179–189). Austin, TX: Pro-Ed.

Salmon, S. (1994d). Artificial larynxes: Types and modifications. In R. Keith and F Darley (Eds.), *Laryngectomee rehabilitation* (3rd ed.; pp. 155–178). Austin, TX: Pro-Ed.

Salmon, S. (1994e). Factors that may interfere with acquiring esophageal speech. In R. Keith and F Darley (Eds.), *Laryngectomee rehabilitation* (3rd ed.; pp. 179–189). Austin, TX: Pro-Ed.

Sander, E. (1972). When are sounds learned? *Journal of Speech and Hearing Disorders, 37,* 55–63.

Sanders, D. (1993). *Management of hearing handicap: Infants to elderly.* Englewood Cliffs, NJ: Prentice-Hall.

Saunders, W. (1964). *The larynx.* Summit, NJ: Ciba.

Savich, P. (1984). Anticipatory imagery ability in normal and language-disabled children. *Journal of Speech and Hearing Research, 27,* 494–501.

Saville-Troike, M. (1986). Anthropological considerations in the study of communication. In O. Taylor (Ed.), *Nature of communication disorders in culturally and linguistically diverse populations* (pp. 47–72). San Diego, CA: College-Hill.

Sax, M. (1972). A longitudinal study of articulation change. *Language, Speech and Hearing Services in Schools, 3,* 41–48.

Schein, J., and **Delk, M.** (1974). *The deaf population of the United States.* Silver Spring, MD: National Association of the Deaf.

Schery, T. (1985). Correlates of language development in language-disordered children. *Journal of Speech and Hearing Disorders, 50,* pp. 73–83.

Schleichkorn, J. (1983). *Coping with cerebral palsy.* Austin, TX: Pro-Ed.

Schlesinger, I. (1977). The role of cognitive development and linguistic input in language acquisition, *Journal of Child Language, 4,* 153–169.

Schow, R., and **Nerbonne, M.** (1989). Overview of aural rehabilitation. In R. Schow and M. Nerbonne (Eds.), *Introduction to aural rehabilitation* (2nd ed.; pp. 3–30). Austin, TX: Pro-Ed.

Sedory, S., Hamlet, S., and **Connor, N.** (1989). Comparison of perceptual and acoustic characteristics of tracheoesophageal and excellent esophageal speech. *Journal of Speech and Hearing Disorders, 54,* 209–214.

Seyfried, D., Hutinson, J., and **Smith, L.** (1989). Language and speech of the hearing impaired. In R. Schow and M. Nerbonne (Eds.), *Introduction to aural rehabilitation* (2nd ed.; pp. 181–240). Austin, TX: Pro-Ed.

Shames, G. (1990). Disorders of fluency. In G. Shames and E. Wiig (Eds.), *Human communication disorders* (3rd ed.; pp. 306–347). Columbus, OH: Merrill Publishing.

Shames, G., and **Florance, C.** (1980). *Stutter-free speech: A goal for therapy.* Columbus, OH: Merrill Publishing.

Shapiro, B., Batshaw, M., and **Perret, Y.** (1992). Normal and abnormal development: Mental retardation. In M. Batshaw and Y. Perret (Eds.), *Chil-dren with disabilities: A medical primer* (3rd ed.; pp. 259–289). Baltimore, MD: Brookes Publishing.

Shaver, K., and **Vernon, M.** (1978). Genetics and hearing loss: An overview for professionals. *American Rehabilitation, 4*(2), 6–10.

Shipp, T., and **Hollien, H.** (1969). Perception of the aging male voice. *Journal of Speech and Hearing Research, 12,* 703–710.

Shons, A. (1993). Surgical issues and procedures. In K. Moller and C. Starr (Eds.), *Cleft palate: Interdisciplinary issues and treatment: For clinicians by clinicians* (pp. 49–78). Austin, TX: Pro-Ed.

Shprintzen, R., Siegel-Sadewitz, V., Amato, J., and **Goldberg, R.** (1985). Anomalies associated with cleft lip, cleft palate, or both. *American Journal of Medical Genetics, 20,* 585.

Shriberg, L. (1980). Developmental phonological disorders. In T. Hixon, L. Shriberg and J. Saxman (Eds.), *Introduction to communication disorders* (pp. 263–309). Englewood Cliffs, NJ: Prentice-Hall.

Shriberg, L., and **Kwiatkowski, J.** (1982). Phonological disorders I: A diagnostic classification system. *Journal of Speech and Hearing Disorder, 47,* 226–241.

Shriberg, L., and **Kwiatkowski, J.** (1988). A follow-up study of children with phonologic disorders of unknown origin. *Journal of Speech and Hearing Disorders, 53,* 144–155.

Shriberg, L., and **Smith, A.** (1983). Phonological correlates of middle-ear involvement in speech-delayed children: A methodological note. *Journal of Speech and Hearing Research, 26,* 293–297.

Silman, S., and **Silverman, C.** (1991). *Auditory diagnosis: Principles and applications.* San Diego, CA: Academic Press.

Silva, P. (1980). The prevalence, stability and significance of developmental language delay in preschool children. *Developmental Medicine and Child Neurology, 22,* 768–777.

Silverman, E. (1976). Listeners' impressions of speakers with lateral lisps. *Journal of Speech and Hearing Disorders, 41,* 547–552.

Silverman, F. (1989). *Communication for the speechless.* Englewood Cliffs, NJ: Prentice-Hall.

Silverman, F. (1992). *Stuttering and other fluency disorders.* Englewood Cliffs, NJ: Prentice-Hall.

Silverman, F., and **Paulus, P.** (1989). Peer reactions to teenagers who substitute /w/ for /r/. *Language, Speech and Hearing Services in Schools, 20,* 219–221.

Singer, M., Blom, E., and **Hamaker, R.** (1981). Further experience with voice restoration after total laryngectomy. *Annals of Otology, Rhinology and Laryngology, 90,* 498–502.

Singer, M., Blom, E., and **Hamaker, R.** (1989). Voice rehabilitation following laryngectomy. In E. Myers and J. Suen (Eds.), *Cancer of the head and neck* (2nd ed.). New York: Churchill Livingstone.

Skeels, H. (1966). *Adult status of children with contrasting early life experiences.* Monographs of the Society of Research in Child Development 31. Chicago, IL: University of Chicago Press.

Skeels, H., and **Dye, H.** (1939). A study of the effects of differential stimulation on mentally retarded children. *Proceedings and Addresses of the Sixty-Third Annual Session of the American Association on Mental Deficiency, 44* (1), 114–130.

Slater, S. (1992). 1992 Omnibus survey: Portrait of the professions. *Asha, 34,* 61–65.

Smit, A., Hand, L., Freilinger, J., Bernthal, J. and **Bird, A.** (1990). The Iowa articulation norms projects and its Nebraska replication. *Journal of Speech and Hearing Disorders, 55,* 779–798.

Smith, R., and **McWilliams, B.** (1966). Creative thinking abilities of cleft palate children. *Cleft Palate Journal, 3,* 275.

Sommers, R., Leiss, R., Delp, M., Gerber, A., Fundrella, D., Smith, R., Revucky, M., Ellis, D., and **Hanley, V.** (1967). Factors related to the effectiveness of articulation therapy for kindergarten, first, and second grade children. *Journal of Speech and Hearing Research, 10,* 428–437.

Sonies, B. (1987). Oral motor problems. In H. Mueller and V. Geoffrey (Eds.), *Communication disorders in aging: Assessment and mamagement* (pp. 185–213). Washington DC: Gallaudet Press.

Sparks, S. (1984). *Birth defects and speech-language disorders.* Boston, MA: College Hill.

Spearman, C. (1904). "General intelligence" objectively determined and measured. *American Journal of Psychology, 15,* 201–293.

Spriestersbach, D. (1973). *Psychosocial aspects of the cleft palate problem: Volume I.* Iowa City, IA: University of Iowa Press.

Stampe, D. (1969). The acquisition of phonetic representation. In R. Binnick, A. Davison, G. Greene and J. Morgan (Eds.), *Papers from the fifth regional meeting of the Chicago Linguistic Society* (pp. 433–444). Chicago, IL: Chicago Linguistic Society.

Stampe, D. (1973). *A disseration on natural phonology.* Unpublished doctoral dissertation, University of Chicago.

Stark, R., and **Tallal, P.** (1981). Selection of children with specific language deficits. *Journal of Speech and Hearing Research, 46,* 114–122.

Starkweather, C. (1987). *Fluency and stuttering.* Englewood Cliffs, NJ: Prentice-Hall.

Starkweather, C., and **Gottwald, S.** (1984). Parents' speech and children's fluency. Convention address, American Speech and Hearing Association, 1984.

Starkweather, C., Gottwald, S., and **Halfond, M.** (1990). *Stuttering prevention: A clinical method.* Englewood Cliffs, NJ: Prentice-Hall.

Starr, P., Chinsky, R., Canter, H., and **Meier, J.** (1977). Mental, motor and social behavior of infmats with cleft lip and/or cleft palate. *Cleft Palate Journal, 14,* 140.

Stemple, J. (1984). *Clincial voice pathology: Theory and management.* Columbus, OH: Charles E. Merrill.

Stockard, J., Stockard, J., and **Sharbrough, F.** (1978). Nonpathological factors influencing brainstem auditory evoked potentials. *American Journal of EEG Technology, 18,* 177–209.

Stoel-Gammon, C., and **Dunn, C.** (1985). *Normal and disordered phonology in children.* Baltimore, MD: University Park Press.

Stool, S., and **Randall, P.** (1967). Unexpected ear disease in infants with cleft palate. *Cleft Palate Journal, 4,* 99–103.

Streissguth, A., Barr, H., and **Sampson, P.** (1986). Attention, distraction and reaction time at age 7 years and prenatal alcohol exposure. *Neurobehavioral Toxicolocy and Teratology, 8,* 717–725.

Swiercinsky, D., Price, T., and **Leaf, L.** (1987). *Traumatic head injury: Cause, consequence and challenge.* Shawnee Mission, KS: The Kansas Head Injury Association.

Swindell, C., and **Hammons, J.** (1991). Post-stroke depression: Neurologic, physiologic, diagnostic, and treatment implications. *Journal of Speech and Hearing Research, 34,* 325–333.

Taylor, J. (1992). *Speech-language pathology services in the schools* (2nd ed.). Boston, MA: Allyn and Bacon.

Taylor, O. (1983). Black English: An agenda for the 1980's. In J. Chambers (Ed) *Black English: Educational equity and the law* (pp. 133–143). Ann Arbor, MI: Karoma Publishers.

Taylor, O. (1986). Historical perspectives and conceptual framework. In O. Taylor (Ed.), *Nature of communication disorders in culturally and linguistically diverse populations* (pp. 1–18). San Diego, CA: College-Hill.

Taylor, O., and **Payne, K.** (1994). Language and communication differences. In G. Shames, E. Wiig, and W. Secord (Eds.) *Human communication disorders: An introduction* (4th ed.; pp. 136–173). New York, NY: Macmillin.

Teele, D., Klein, J., Chase, C., Menyuk, P., Rosner, B., et al. (1990). Otitis media in infancy and intellectual ability, school achievement, speech, and language at age 7 years. *Journal of Infectious Diseases, 162,* 685–694.

Templin, M. (1957). Certain language skills in children, their development and interrelationships. *Institute of Child Welfare, Monograph Series, No. 26.* Minneapolis, MN: University of Minnesota Press.

Throneburg, R., Yairi, E., and **Paden, E.** (1994). Relation between phonologic difficulty and the occurrence of disfluencies in the early stage of stuttering. *Journal of Speech and Hearing Research, 37,* 504–509.

Tiegerman, E. (1993). Autism: Learning to communicate. In D. Bernstein and E. Tiegerman (Eds.), *Language and communication disorders in children* (3rd ed.; pp. 431–481). New York, NY: Macmillan.

Tompkins, C. (1991). Automatic and effortful processing of emotional intonation after right of left brain damage, *Journal of Speech and Hearing Research, 34,* 820–830.

Toohill, R. (1975). The psychosomatic aspects of children with vocal nodules. *Archives of Otolaryngology, 101,* 591–595.

Travis, L. (1931). Neurophysiological dominance. Reprinted with permission in *Journal of Speech and Hearing Disorders, 43,* 275–277. Originally appeared in L. Travis, *Speech pathology.* New York, NY: D. Appleton and Company.

Travis, L. (1971). The unspeakable feelings of people with special reference to stuttering. In: E. Travis (Ed.), *Handbook of speech pathology and audiology* (pp. 1009–1034). Englewood Cliffs, NJ: Prentice-Hall.

Travis, L. (1978). The cerebral dominance theory of stuttering: 1931–1978. *Journal of Speech and Hearing Disorders, 43,* 278–281.

Trost-Cardamone, J., and **Bernthal, J.** (1993). Articulation assessment procedures and treatment decisions. In K. Moller and C. Starr (Eds.), *Cleft palate: Interdisciplinary issues and treatment: For clinicians by clincians* (pp. 307–336). Austin, TX: Pro-Ed.

Trudgill, P. (1974). *Sociolinguistics: An introduction.* Harmondsworth, Middlesex, England: Penguin Books.

Tye-Murray, N. (1991). Repair strategy useage by hearing-impaired adults and changes following communication therapy. *Journal of Speech and Hearing Research, 34,* 921–928.

Ulvestad, R., and **Carlstrom, J.** (1993). Otologic and audiologic concerns and treatment. In K. Moller and C. Starr (Eds.), *Cleft palate: Interdisciplinary issues and treatment: For clinicians by clinicians* (pp. 189–218). Austin, TX: Pro-Ed.

U.S. Department of Health and Human Services (1982). The health consequences of smoking: Cancer, a report of the Surgeon General, (Public Health Service), Washington, DC: Government Printing Office.

Van Riper, C. (1982). *The nature of stuttering* (2nd ed.). Englewood Cliffs, NJ: Prentice-Hall.

Vaughan, C. (1982). Current concepts in otolaryngology: Diagnosis and treatment of organic voice disorders. *New England Journal of Medicine, 307:* 863–866.

Vernon, M. (1987). Controversy in sign language. *ACEHI Journal, 12,* 155–164.

Vernon, M., and **Andrews, J.** (1990). *The psychology of deafness.* New York: Longman.

Vernon, M., and **Ottinger, P.** (1989). Psychosocial aspects of hearing impairment. In R. Schow and M. Nerbonne (Eds.), *Introduction to aural rehabilitation* (2nd ed.; pp. 31–80). Austin, TX: Pro-Ed.

Walden, B., Busacco, D., and **Montegomery, A.** (1993). Benefit from visual cues in auditory-visual speech recognition by middle-aged and elderly persons. *Journal of Speech and Hearing Research, 36,* 431–436.

Wall, M., and **Myers, F.** (1984). *Clinical management of childhood stuttering.* Austin, TX: Pro-Ed.

Ward, M. (1971). *Them children.* New York, NY: Holt, Rinehart and Winston.

Wardhaugh, R. (1976). *The contexts of language.* Rowley, MA: Newberry House Publishers.

Watkins, S., and **Schow, R.** (1989). Aural rehabilitation for children. In R. Schow and M. Nerbonne (Eds.), *Introduction to aural rehabilitation* (2nd ed.; pp. 295–378). Austin, TX: Pro-Ed.

Webster, R. (1980). Evolution of a target-based behavioral therapy for stuttering. *Journal of Fluency Disorders, 5,* 303–320.

Wedenberg, E. (1981). Auditory training in historical perspective. In F. Bess et al. (Eds.), *Amplification in education* (pp. 1–25). Washington, DC: Alexander Graham Bell Association for the Deaf.

Weiner, F. (1981). Treatment of phonological disability using the method of meaningful minimal contrast: Two case studies. *Journal of Speech and Hearing Disorders, 46,* 97–103.

Weiss, C., Gordon, M., and **Lillywhite, H.** (1987). *Clinical management of articulatory and phonologic disorders* (2nd ed.). Baltimore, MD: Williams and Wilkins.

Wellman, B., Case, I., Mengert, I., and **Bradbury, D.** (1931). Speech sounds of young children. *University of Iowa Studies of Child Welfare, 5,* 1–82.

Welsh, R., and **Slater, R.** (1993). The state of infant hearing impairment identification programs. *Asha, 35* (April), 49–52.

Werker, J. (1989). Becoming a native listener. *American Scientist, 77,* 54–59.

Wertz, R. (1984). Language disorders in adults: State of the clinical art. In A. Holland (Ed.), *Language disorders in adults: Recent advances* (pp. 1–78). San Diego, CA: College-Hill.

Wertz, R., LaPointe, L., and **Rosenbek, J.** (1991). *Apraxia of speech in adults: The disorder and its management.* San Diego, CA: Singular Publishing Group.

Wexler, K., and **Mysak, E.** (1982). Disfluency characteristics of 2-, 4-, and 6-year old males. *Journal of Fluency Disorders, 7,* 37–46.

Wiig, E., and **Secord, W.** (1994). Language disabilities in school-age children and youth. In G. Shames, E. Wiig and W. Secord, (Eds.), *Human communication disorders: An introduction* (4th ed.; pp. 212–247). New York, NY: Macmillan.

Wiley, T. (1980). Hearing disorders and audiometry. In T. Hixon, L. Shriberg and J. Saxman (Eds.), *Introduction to communication disorders* (pp. 491–529). Englewood Cliffs, NJ: Prentice-Hall.

Williams, F. (1976). *Explorations of the linguistic attitudes of teachers.* Rowley, MA: Newberry House Publishers.

Williams, R., and **Wolfram, W.** (1977). *Social differences vs. disorders.* Washington D.C.: American Speech and Hearing Association.

Wilson, D. (1987). *Voice problems of children* (3rd ed.). Baltimore: Williams and Wilkins.

Wingate, M. (1964). Recovery from stuttering. *Journal of Speech and Hearing Disorders, 29,* 312–321.

Wingate, M. (1969). Sound and pattern in "artificial" fluency. *Journal of Speech and Hearing Research, 12,* 677–686.

Wingate, M. (1970). Effects on stuttering of changes in audition. *Journal of Speech and Hearing Research, 13,* 861–873.

Wingate, M. (1983). Speaking unassisted: Comments on a paper by Andrews et al. *Journal of Speech and Hearing Disorders, 48,* 255–263.

Winitz, H. (1984). Auditory considerations in articulation training. In H. Winitz (Ed.), *Treating articulation disorders: For clinicians by clinicians.* Baltimore, MD: University Park Press.

Wirls, D. (1971). Psychosocial apsects of cleft lip and palate. In W. Grabb, S. Rosenstein, and K. Bzoch (Eds.). *Cleft lip and palate* (pp. 119–129). Boston, MA: Little, Brown.

Wolf-Schein, E., Sudhalter, V., Cohen, I., Fisch, G., Hanson, D., Pfadt, A., Hagerman, R., Jenkins, E., and **Brown, T.** (1987). Speech-language and the fragile X syndrome. *ASHA, 29,* no. 7, 35–38.

Wolfram, W. (1986). Language variation in the United States. In O. Taylor (Ed.), *Nature of communication disorders in culturally and linguistically diverse populations* (pp. 1–18). San Diego, CA: College-Hill.

Working Group on Communication Aids for the Hearing Impaired (WGCAHI) (1991). Speech-perception aids for hearing-impaired people: Current status and needed research. *Journal of the Acoustical Society of America, 90,* 637–685.

Worthington, D., and **Peters, J.** (1980). Quantifiable hearing and no ABR: Paradox or error? *Ear and Hearing, 1,* 281–285.

Yairi, E. (1981). Disfluencies of normally speaking two-year old children. *Journal of Speech and Hearing Research, 24,* 490–495.

Yairi, E. (1982). Longitudinal studies of disfluency in two-year old children. *Journal of Speech and Hearing Research, 25,* 155–160.

Yairi, E. (1983). The onset of stuttering in two- and three-year old children: A preliminary report. *Journal of Speech and Hearing Disorders, 48,* 171–178.

Yairi, E., and **Ambrose, N.** (1992a). A longitudinal study of stuttering in children: A preliminary report. *Journal of Speech and Hearing Research, 35,* 755–760.

Yairi, E., and **Ambrose, N.** (1992b). Onset of stuttering in preschool children: Selected factors. *Journal of Speech and Hearing Research, 35,* 782–788.

Yairi, E., and Lewis, B. (1984). Disfluencies at the onset of stuttering. *Journal of Speech and Hearing Research, 27,* 154–159.

Yorkston, K. (1981). Treatment of right hemisphere damaged patients: A panel presentation and discussion. In R. Brookshire (Ed.), *Clinical aphasiology: Proceedings of the conference* (pp. 277–281).

Yorkston, K., Beukelman, D., and Bell, K. (1988). *Clinical management of dysarthric speakers.* Boston: College-Hill Press.

Yost, W. (1994). *Fundamentals of hearing: An introduction.* San Diego, CA: Academic Press.

Zemlin, W. (1988). *Speech and hearing science: Anatomy and physiology* (3rd ed.). Englewood Cliffs, NJ: Prentice-Hall.

Index

Page numbers in **boldface** indicate tables or illustrations.